The Myth of Disenchantment

The Myth of Disenchantment

MAGIC, MODERNITY, AND THE BIRTH OF THE HUMAN SCIENCES

Jason Ā. Josephson-Storm

The University of Chicago Press   CHICAGO & LONDON

The University of Chicago Press, Chicago 60637
The University of Chicago Press, Ltd., London
© 2017 by The University of Chicago
Published 2017
Printed in the United States of America

26 25 24 23 22 21 20 19 18 17   1 2 3 4 5

ISBN-13: 978-0-226-40322-9 (cloth)
ISBN-13: 978-0-226-40336-6 (paper)
ISBN-13: 978-0-226-40353-3 (e-book)
DOI: 10.7208/chicago/9780226403533.001.0001

The University of Chicago Press gratefully acknowledges the generous support of Williams
College toward the publication of this book.

Library of Congress Cataloging-in-Publication Data

Names: Josephson, Jason Ānanda, author.
Title: The myth of disenchantment : magic, modernity, and the birth of the human sciences /
Jason Ā. Josephson-Storm.
Description: Chicago ; London : The University of Chicago Press, 2017. | Includes
bibliographical references and index.
Identifiers: LCCN 2016049463 | ISBN 9780226403229 (cloth : alk. paper) | ISBN
9780226403366 (pbk. : alk. paper) | ISBN 9780226403533 (e-book)
Subjects: LCSH: Science and magic. | Philosophy, Modern. | Myth. | Magic—History. |
Science—Philosophy.
Classification: LCC BF1623.S35 J67 2017 | DDC 001.09/03—dc23 LC record available at
https://lccn.loc.gov/2016049463
♾ This paper meets the requirements of ANSI/NISO Z39.48-1992 (Permanence of Paper).

The absence of myth is also a myth: the coldest, the purest, the only true myth.

GEORGES BATAILLE, "L'absence du mythe," 1947

CONTENTS

This monograph was born at *Harizanmai*, "Absorption in Needles," a Tantric Buddhist tattoo parlor in Kyoto. I was at that time immersed in a book project about how contemporary Japanese history meant changes in the locus of enchantment, but in ways unanticipated by classical theorists of modernity. On a particular afternoon in March of 2011, I was getting the finishing touches applied to a set of tattoos when news came over the radio that a major earthquake had occurred just off the coast of Tohoku. The bulletin came as a shock, but earthquakes are not terribly uncommon in Japan, and so the tattooing continued as usual. At least, that is, until the video footage began to come in. At that point, tattooing was put on pause, and everyone in the parlor gathered in front of the television. The scale of the tragedy took a long time to become fully evident, and so we made small talk—having the sort of conversations that would not normally have been possible between the patrons and artists when everyone was focused on their work. I mentioned my research project, and heard animated anecdotes about protective talismans and ghostly premonitions. One of the Japanese patrons asked me, curiously, if these sorts of things didn't go on in America. Before I could answer, however, another patron (whom I took to be from Scandinavia) jumped in, assuring everyone that Japan was a unique case and more spiritual than the West. He looked to me to confirm the sentiment, which I did my best to refute. But it gave life to a worry that had been bothering me for some time—by using Japanese history to challenge the thesis that equated modernity and disenchantment, I risked reinforcing clichés about a mystical Orient. Besides, I was fully aware that many Americans and Europeans also believed in protective icons and ghostly visions. So I began to wonder if I might have been better off expanding my project's scope in a way that also reappraised the linkage between modernization and enchantment in Europe and America.

In the days that followed, I found myself changing projects. I had been planning to conduct additional archival research in Tokyo. But in the wake of the tsunami and ensuing Fukushima nuclear disaster, a prolonged stay in the Tokyo area seemed risky and the disruption to the Japanese infrastructure made travel difficult. This, combined with my sense that the project I wanted to work on was bigger than the original research I had begun, settled my decision to approach the work differently. After making sure that my Japanese friends and colleagues were safe, I relocated to Bochum, Germany, on the first of April, and there began a visiting research position at Ruhr-Universität.

Over the next six months, I delved into German materials, looking for parallel evidence of the history of enchantment. I was fortunate that Helmut Zander, a leading historian of esotericism, was both in residence and open to discussions about the material I was discovering. From these conversations with him and other European scholars, the basic outlines of this work began to take shape. For a while, I imagined a comparative project, but I realized I had enough to say about European materials alone to fill several monographs.

In the years since, the project benefited enormously from an extended intellectual dialogue with two friends at Williams College: Denise Buell and Christian Thorne. The book would not exist without their regular suggestions and perceptive insights.

Inspiration also came from discussions with Zaid Adhami, Daniel Barbu, Jeremy Bellay, Philippe Borgeaud, David Brakke, Alexandra Cuffel, Ryan Coyne, Charles Fox, Sarah Hammerschlag, Uli Harlass, Bert Harrill, Jackie Hidalgo, Alex Hsu, Jeff Israel, Doug Kiel, Adam Knobler, Volkhard Krech, James Manigault-Bryant, Levi McLaughlin, Keith McPartland, Nick Meylan, Okada Masahiko, Arie Molendijk, Dimitry Okropiridze, Bill Pees, Mark Reinhardt, Frédéric Richard, Neil Roberts, Justin Shaddock, Grant Shoffstall, Hugh Urban, Youri Volokhine, Anna Zschauer, my parents (both philosophers in their own right), and others I have alas forgotten. Thanks are also due to my students in REL 317, "Disenchantment, Modernity, and the Death of God," especially Mendy Bindell, Ranana Dine, Yasmine Nichols, and Antonia Wei Ling, who were the first critics of early chapters. Student research assistants Lauren Brantley, Aaron Hamblin, Hilary Ledwell, Jessica Plumbley, and Jasmine Thomasian also provided useful help. Thanks are due also to Chris Lovell for tutoring me in Latin, even if most of the neo-Latin sources did not make the final cut. Figures are thanks to Tatiana Tate, with suggestions by

Orion Buske. I'd also like to thank Johanna Rosenbohm for copyediting and Emily Ham for indexing. I would also like to express my gratitude to the librarians at the archives consulted (see the list below).

I have greatly benefited from feedback on written drafts by Michael Bergunder, Tom Carlson, Healan Gaston, Eleanor Goodman, Andrew Jewett, Chris Photon Johnson, Seth Josephson, Hans-Martin Krämer, John Modern, Jim Nolan, Julian Strube, Helmut Zander, my formerly anonymous reader Jeff Kripal, and my remaining anonymous reader at the University of Chicago Press; and from discussions of work in progress presented at the American Historical Association meeting in New York, Northwestern University, the University of North Carolina at Chapel Hill, Syracuse University, Williams College, Ruhr-Universität, Universität Heidelberg, and Université de Genève. I would also like to thank the participants of the Williams College workshop "Holy Spirits: Spiritualism and the Foundation of Religious Studies," where I tried out what I thought was a different project, but I now realize was this one struggling to be born.

I would also like to thank Alan Thomas and Randy Petilos at the University of Chicago Press for their guidance and help shepherding it through publication.

Although the majority of the research occurred during my 2011 sabbatical, the writing largely happened during teaching semesters while hiding out from my students and colleagues in the following Western Massachusetts cafés: Brewhaha, Dobrá Tea, Dottie's Coffee Lounge, Haymarket, Lenox Coffee, and Tunnel City Coffee. Thanks are due to these establishments for providing congenial places to bang away at my laptop.

Further archival research in England, France, Germany, and Austria was made possible by a Williams College, Class of 1945 World Fellowship grant.

I am also grateful to Williams College and Käte Hamburger Kolleg for an additional leave semester at Ruhr-Universität in Bochum, Germany, which enabled me to put the finishing touches on this book and start writing the next one.

I owe more than I can say to my new bride—Dalena Storm—who brings love and a new name to my life.

*

An earlier version of chapter 4 originally appeared as "God's Shadow: Occluded Possibilities in the Genealogy of Religion," *History of Religions* 52, no. 4 (2013): 309–39, © 2013 by The University of Chicago, all rights reserved; and a portion of chapter seven appeared as "Specters of Reason: Kantian Things and the Fragile Terrors of Philosophy," *J19: The Journal of Nineteenth-Century Americanists* 3, no. 1 (2015): 204–11, © 2015 University of Pennsylvania Press, all rights reserved. Thanks are due to both journals for permission to include the material here.

To meet the needs of academic publication, this manuscript has been significantly trimmed from its initial draft. Rough chapters on French social theory, American philosophy, Japanese accounts of Western Esotericism, and German Monist Leagues were cut as orthogonal to the main narrative. Out of a desire to minimize the scholarly apparatus, I have limited citations to the roughly one thousand most relevant sources and eliminated the stand-alone bibliography. The result, while still lengthy, is leaner and stronger, but the reader should not mistake brevity—and the occasional simplifications it requires—for lack of depth.

*

This work is dedicated to my grandmothers and to the victims of the Tohoku earthquake and other disasters, both natural and manmade.

A NOTE ON TEXTS AND TRANSLATIONS

Archives consulted (physically or digitally) Bibliothèque nationale de France; the Frazer Collection at Trinity College, University of Cambridge; the Rudolph Carnap Papers at the University of Pittsburgh Library; the University of Vienna Archive; and the Max Weber Archive at the Bayerischen Akademie der Wissenschaften.

Translations from Danish, French, German, Japanese, Latin, Polish, Spanish, and Swedish are my own unless otherwise noted, and I accept full responsibility for any errors.

INTRODUCTION

> The war against mystery and magic was for modernity the war of liberation leading to the declaration of reason's independence. . . . To win the stakes, to win all of them and to win them for good, the world had to be de-spiritualized, de-animated.
>
> ZYGMUNT BAUMAN, *Intimations of Postmodernity*, 1992

> Eusapia is within our walls. . . . Her presence communicates a kind of incoherent life to material objects, and peoples the void with phantoms.
>
> GEORGES MONTORGUEIL, *Les Parisiennes d'à présent*, 1897

Paris, 1907. Marie Curie sat in the sumptuous chambers of an apartment on the Boulevard Saint-Germain. As the lights were dimmed, the chemist joined hands with the man sitting next to her, and together they watched the psychic medium across the table begin to shake and mumble, speaking in a strange low voice, overcome by the force of a possessing spirit called "John King." Eusapia Palladino, as the psychic was called, was believed to be able to make objects move without touching them and to produce "visions of lights or luminescent points, visions of hands or limbs, sometimes in the form of black shadows, sometimes as phosphorescent."[1] Indeed, as Curie and others later recounted, in that very séance, luminous points began to appear in the darkness, as if crowning Eusapia's head in a shimmering halo. Slowly, the medium extended her hands and ran them through Marie Curie's hair, passing on a glowing luminescence. It seemed that the presence of unseen powers had been confirmed.[2]

By all rights, Marie Curie should not have been there. She was in many respects a paragon of the period's scientific establishment, a hardheaded and critical thinker who had made a number of stunning discoveries. The first woman to win a Nobel Prize, she is one of the very few people in history to win it twice (physics and chemistry). Curie's presence at a spiritualist séance is a problem because a great many theorists have argued that one of the things that most makes the modern world modern is the rejection of animism—basically, that we have eliminated ghosts, demons, and spirits from the contemporary worldview.[3] While historians of spiritualism know different, it is widely believed that modernizers like Curie had no truck with invisible forces. Most scholars, therefore, would be surprised to learn that she was conjuring ghosts or studying paranormal manifestations as part of her physics research. This book will address not only spiritualism's allure, but also why that account of modernity as despiritualization is itself a myth.

It is tempting to imagine that Curie wanted to believe in the spectral persistence of the souls of the dead because of her recent widowhood. After all, her husband, Pierre, had passed away in April 1906, and her diaries from the period frequently expressed her profound longing to communicate with him.[4] But this was not the first séance Marie Curie had attended, and indeed the Curies had engaged in psychical research together before his sudden death.

For three years, starting in 1905, some of France's most famous scientists had assembled in apartments and laboratories in Paris to study this particular Italian spirit medium—Eusapia Palladino. In addition to the Curies, others often in attendance were the celebrated physiologist Jacques-Arsène d'Arsonval, the eminent psychiatrist Gilbert Ballet, the aristocratic doctor Count Arnaud de Gramont, and three future Nobel Prize winners—the physicist Jean Baptiste Perrin, the physiologist Charles Richet, and the philosopher Henri Bergson.[5] The French were not the only ones interested in Eusapia; from 1872 until her death in 1918, her powers were tested by teams of researchers in England, Italy, Poland, Germany, Russia, and the United States.[6] The paranormal researchers who investigated Eusapia were not marginal eccentrics, but the cutting edge of the period's academic establishment.[7] Yet these researchers were exploring areas that were often marked out by their contemporaries as occult, if not downright magical.[8] They did so not as a legacy of medieval "superstitions," nor generally as a way to overturn science, but rather as a means to extend its borders.

Not everyone who met with Eusapia was a believer in the powers of the beyond; some were convinced she was a charlatan, but others came to grant that something extraordinary happened in those darkened rooms. In Paris one could find the full spectrum—from skeptics to spiritualist believers to those who preferred to explain the sessions in terms of previously unrecognized forms of energy. Bergson, for example, began with serious doubts, but ended up producing a paranormally informed philosophy and even becoming president of the British Society for Psychical Research in 1913.[9] This is perhaps less surprising for a philosopher famous for formulating *élan vital*, and one whose sister Moina Mathers (née Mina Bergson) was a cofounder of one of the period's most famous magical organizations, the Hermetic Order of the Golden Dawn (see chapter 6). But other figures whose professions were more conventionally scientific were also affected by their experiences with Eusapia.

In one of the last letters before his death (addressed to Louis Georges Gouy, April 14, 1906), Pierre Curie remarked, "We have had several more séances with the medium Eusapia Palladino (we already had sessions with her last summer). The result is that these phenomena really exist and it is no longer possible for me doubt them. It is incredible but it is so; and it is *impossible to deny it* after the sessions, which we performed under perfectly controlled conditions." He added: "In my opinion, there is here a whole domain of completely new facts and physical states of space about which we have had no conception."[10] While Marie lacked some of her husband's enthusiasm, she remarked in French in a letter to a friend on April 16, 1906, "We recently attended a few séances with Eusapia, some of which have seemed very convincing. It is a matter of the greatest interest."[11] In a Polish letter to a friend, however, she was less guarded, declaring, "Personally, I am quite willing to accept the existence of unusual powers in mediums such as Eusapia or Ms. Stanisława [Tomczyk]."[12] Even the psychologist William James—although he had not witnessed Eusapia firsthand—asserted, "That her phenomena *probably are* genuine seems to me established."[13]

The point here is not to mock William James and the Curies for their gullibility, much less to advocate on their authority that mediums really did once channel the dead. Indeed, our main business is not to discuss physics or spirits as such, but rather to provide a cultural and intellectual history of social scientists and philosophers. In so doing, I challenge one conventional notion of modernity and suggest that we should be less surprised than we usually are to find scientists of all stripes keeping company with magicians; that reason does not eliminate "superstition" but piggybacks upon it; that mechanism often produces vitalism; and that often, in a single room, we can find both séance and science. The single most familiar story in the history of science is the tale of disenchantment—of magic's exit from the henceforth law-governed world. I am here to tell you that as broad cultural history, this narrative is wrong. Attempts to suppress magic have historically failed more often than they've succeeded. It is unclear to me that science necessarily deanimates nature. In fact, I will argue à la Bruno Latour that we have never been disenchanted.[14] And for those readers who have already suspected the persistence of magic in modernity, I will trace the genealogy of the myth of disenchantment and how it came to function as a regulative ideal.

A PHILOSOPHICAL ARCHAEOLOGY OF THE
DISENCHANTMENT OF THE WORLD

Enlightenment's program was the disenchantment of the world. . . . In the authority of universal concepts, the Enlightenment detected a fear of the demons through whose effigies human beings had tried to influence nature in magic rituals. From now on, matter was finally to be controlled without the illusion of immanent powers or hidden properties.

MAX HORKHEIMER AND THEODOR ADORNO,
Dialektik der Aufklärung, 1947

While many of the old master narratives have been unraveling, it is still widely supposed that the defining feature of modernity is the departure of the supernatural. Modernization is often equated with the rise of instrumental reason, the gradual alienation of humanity from nature, and the production of a bureaucratic and technological life world stripped of mystery and wonder. Scholars often pin this narrative to Max Weber's phrase *die Entzauberung der Welt*, the disenchantment (or literally "de-magic-ing") of the world. Indeed, if there is one thing we've been taught to take for granted, it is that the contemporary, industrial, capitalist societies of Western Europe and North America have lost their magic, and that it is this absence that makes them modern. As the Canadian philosopher Charles Taylor summarized in 2011, "Everyone can agree that one of the big differences between us and our ancestors of 500 years ago is that they lived in an 'enchanted' world and we do not."[15]

Disenchantment is also a component of the standard account of secularization.[16] According to thinkers like Taylor, part of the way that religion lost its grip on the modern subject was through science eliminating the supernatural.[17] In recent years, support for the classical secularization thesis has withered in the face of religious revivals, but even the most vociferous critics of the death of God usually grant the decline of magic—at least, in Western Europe, if nowhere else. Indeed, part of relativizing secularism is often to present secularism as Protestant, which in turn is positioned as antimagical. If the postsecular resurgence of religion is tied to the limits of reason, magic and technology are still widely believed to be opposed, and only a few would claim that magic is making a comeback.

First and foremost, I want to challenge this model, to rewrite this particular account of modernity and its rupture from the premodern past. As discussed below, I am not alone in the study of modernity's enchantments, but the task takes on a special urgency because versions of the disenchantment thesis have recently found fresh purchase, anchoring new movements in philosophy and political theory. Although they do not speak with one voice, a host of thinkers—Karen Barad, Jane Bennett, William Connolly, Eduardo Kohn, Manuel Vásquez, and others—have charged modern philosophy with despiritualizing nature and rendering matter dead and inanimate.[18] In response, they aim to recover alternate animating ontologies sometimes referred to as "agential realism" or "enchanted materialism."[19] While I am sympathetic to these movements, I think that their diagnosis of the current dilemma too quickly grants, even as it inverts, the myth of Euro-American modernity and its putative relationship to rationality and nature. Simply put, these new philosophers, like the poststructuralists they seek to replace, are rebelling against a hegemon that never achieved full mastery. The enchanted ontologies and spiritualized orientations to nature they describe as missing have been available all along. In what follows, it is the both the mythic construction and contradictions of the supposedly hegemonic ontology that I want to explore.

I am particularly interested in the formation of the old-fashioned but entrenched narrative that describes the history of the modern scientific paradigm in terms of the rise of mathematical physics and the construction of an influential model of a "clockwork universe" that no longer needed spirits or a deity to drive the motor of the cosmos.[20] Leaving aside how few historical physicists actually subscribed to this austere model, what is fascinating to me is the way in which the image of a mechanical world took on its own life—especially among social theorists—and thus how it escaped the purview of the natural sciences to achieve an ambivalent status in the cultural formation of the contemporary world picture.[21] From my perspective, this particular world picture is a myth insofar as it has taken on its own narrative force and bears little relationship to the status of physics at any given moment. Yet, some version of this world picture was often presented exactly *not* as a myth, but as an ahistorical and universal "Real" against which other myths were shattered.[22] To be clear, I am not attacking the ontology of contemporary physics, but am instead interested in how a particular historical image of physics came to imprint the human sciences, and by doing so, spilled over into the master description of modernity as such, even as the physicists themselves were often pushing against that model from the inside.

In what follows, I ask: In the face of things like Curie's scientific séances, spiritualist revivals, and the modern resurgence of magical orders like the Golden Dawn, how did we get the idea that modernity meant disenchantment in the first place? I will answer this question by exploring the haunting presence of magic in the very instances when disenchantment was itself being theorized. While we know that wonder still dwells in the counterculture and it is probably a truism that scientists often hold to strange ideas outside of their specific domain of expertise, I want to investigate the least likely people—the very theorists of modernity as disenchantment—and show how they worked out their various insights inside an occult context, in a social world overflowing with spirits and magic, and how the weirdness of that world generated so much normativity. This will put us in a position to disaggregate disenchantment into inconsistent and semi-overlapping claims—regarding the loss of wonder, the de-animation of the world, the progressive rationalization of superstition, and, of course, the end of magic—which I show nevertheless share a common root.

It is important, indeed, to track the persistence of the occult across the disciplines and not just in the natural sciences—in Bruno Latour's own sociology, for instance. It is a sociological truism that those who study foreign cultures are themselves less religious, and few would imagine anthropologists to be easy believers in the magical.[23] Indeed, as contemporary anthropologist Tanya Luhrmann has noted, for much its history "a central task in sociology has been to explain how the elimination of magic was ever possible, and how it was that Western society moved into its rational mode."[24] But I will show that the human sciences (*Geisteswissenschaften*) emerged as academic disciplines in the nineteenth century alongside flourishing theosophical and spiritualist movements, and shared the latter's fascination with magical knowledge and the spirits of the dead. There is much evidence that the spiritualists read social theory and, conversely, that the social theorists were often up on their spiritualism.[25] Moreover, it was often the self-professed magicians—not the sociologists who were the first to decry despiritualization and the general loss of magic, even as they called for revivals.

Other scholars have argued that religious studies, for one, has its origins in the European empires; this is a trenchant point that may nonetheless need refining, since the canonically early figures in the discipline—Max Müller, Max Weber, Marcel Mauss—never went to India or met an Aboriginal Australian firsthand. They were, however, profoundly enmeshed in the occult milieu, and much of what they thought they knew about the non-West was mediated by European esotericism. Indeed, the very objects of their concern, their methods, and even their self-definition still bear the marks of this important early encounter with the occult. The larger project works out this occult side of the human sciences—not just the texts and thinkers who did not make it into the canon, but also those canonical figures whose esoteric preoccupations have been systematically ignored or suppressed. Instead of displacing Eurocentrism by means of explicit comparison, what follows is a work of *erasure*.

The private lives of many theorists of disenchantment seemingly run contrary to their own models; by exposing this, I aim to disrupt the old master narratives to make way for new ones.[26] By analogue to a similar move in gender studies, in part I am trying to "queer," or render strange, the hegemonic tradition.[27] Furthermore, while the social sciences are often supposed to be one of the vectors for secularization and the displacement of magic, I will show that sociology and its cousins were more likely to birth new revivals of paganism, shamanism, and even magic.[28]

It was not just the human sciences but also their accounts of modernity as disenchanted and secularized that were ironically articulated in the very period during which Britain, France, and Germany were in the midst of occult revivals. Indeed, I will argue that it was specifically in relation to this burgeoning culture of spirits and magic that European intellectuals gave birth to the *myth of a mythless society*.[29]

To clarify this seeming paradox, I need to explain what I mean by "myth." The term *myth* is often used either polemically to indicate an erroneous belief or romantically to suggest an archaic or even sacred mode of narrative discourse.[30] Although I admit to willfully evoking the polemical usage, by "myth" I mainly mean to gesture toward those repeated narrative symbols (e.g., the death of God, Achilles's heel, the naked truth) that are adopted as prefabricated tropes or metaphors and whose transposition carries unconscious meaning from one domain to another.[31] The prefabricated trope I am most interested in is "the myth of modernity" itself, by which I mean not the stories from a particular epoch, but the very fable that there was such an age as "modernity" and that it had certain features.

By way of explanation, Hans Robert Jauss has reminded us that modernity was not a historical event for which we might determine a date: 1492? 1648? 1789? 1868?[32] Modernity is first and foremost the sign of a rupture.[33] As a term and concept, it is a device for positing significant historical breaks. To speak of "the modern" means nothing so much as to talk of the current, of the putatively new: to describe a kind of novelty.[34] That the term has been used for hundreds of years might seem through sheer repetition to forfeit its claims to originality.[35]

We might know now that modernity is as much a *spatial* as temporal category, and that to call a culture modern is to ally it with newness and to consign its opposite to colonization or the scrap heap of history.[36] It is as much a project as a periodization. But the project of modernization and the period of modernity are typically entwined because modernization works by projecting an aspirational and utopian myth of modernity toward which it aspires. In this respect utopian modernity is always located elsewhere (e.g., often, colonized subjects thought of the metropole as embodying modernity; or German philosophers looked to France as the epitome of the modern while French thinkers looked to England for the same). It might seem that only the dystopian modernity is thought of as here and now. We should also remember that to call an era modern, even when criticized from a postmodern vantage, is to characterize the epoch in terms of its discontinuity with the past.

There are different ways to stage that newness. "Modernity" is regularly equated with everything from specific artistic and philosophical movements to particular historical ruptures to distinctive sociological processes, such as urbanization, industrialization, globalization, or various forms of rationalization. I will not unravel all the possible associations and nuances of the term. From among these, I aim to undermine the myth that what sets the modern world apart from the rest is that it has experienced disenchantment and a loss of myth. I am not claiming that industrialization never happened, nor am I denying that rationalization occurred in any cultural sphere; rather, I am interested in the process by which Christendom increasingly exchanged its claim to be the unique bearer of divine revelation for the assertion that it uniquely apprehended an unmediated cosmos and did so with the sparkling clarity of universal rationality. Sometimes this account of modernity has been celebratory, rejoicing in the ascent of European science and the end of superstition. But equally often, it has been a lament, bemoaning a loss of wonder and magic.

*

Another key impetus for my project is to provide a response to Horkheimer and Adorno's monumental *Dialectic of Enlightenment* and an intervention into critical theory more broadly. Insofar as critical theory represents a single interpretive community, it might appear that we are mainly united by a common literary canon and our willingness to repeat a particular story that this canon enshrines. Variants of this tale are to be found not only in *Dialectic of Enlightenment*, but also to some degree in many works of the Frankfurt School and its periphery, including: Theodor Adorno, *Negative Dialektik* (1966; *Negative Dialectics*), Erich Fromm, *Escape from Freedom* (1941), Max Horkheimer, *Eclipse of Reason* (1947), Leo Löwenthal, "Das Dämonishe" ("The Demonic," 1921), Georg Lukács, *Die Zerstörung der Vernunft* (1954; *The Destruction of Reason*), and Herbert Marcuse, *One-Dimensional Man* (1964). One can even find it with a different affective tone in many of the writings of Jürgen Habermas.[37]

Critical theory broadly addresses the following problem: What went wrong with modernity such that it produced the horrors of totalitarianism and mass destruction, and not the utopia of a classless society?[38] As expressed in the *Dialectic of Enlightenment*, the question becomes one of "why humanity, instead of entering a truly human state, is sinking into a new kind of barbarism."[39]

The Frankfurt School's answers to the broader question are essentially similar within a certain range of variations and important elaborations. To juxtapose a few: Fromm, 1941: "Freedom, though it has brought [modern man] independence and rationality, has made him isolated and, thereby, anxious and powerless," and hence he is tempted to submit to new totalitarian leaders in order to "escape from the burden of his freedom."[40] Horkheimer, 1947: "It seems that even as technical knowledge expands the horizon of man's thought and activity, his autonomy . . . appear to be reduced. Advance in technical facilities for enlightenment is accompanied by a process of dehumanization."[41] Marcuse, 1964: instead of providing "freedom from toil and domination," "Technological rationality . . . becomes the great vehicle of better domination, creating a truly totalitarian universe in which society and nature, mind and body are kept in a state of permanent mobilization for the defense of this universe."[42] The primal form of critical theory's master narrative is that autonomous reason (or freedom or science or enlightenment), once yoked to the domination of nature, turns into its opposite—namely, the domination of humanity.[43] In other words, the intellectual energies that were supposed to liberate us are now used to keep us in chains. To my taste, the version of this formulation that is most perspicacious is the pithy phrase in the *Dialectic of Enlightenment:* "Enlightenment reverts to mythology."[44]

It is easy to see the Weberian cast of this narrative and how it is linked to the de-animation of nature. Again, juxtapositions make this clear. Löwenthal, 1921: "The primitive metaphysical world picture vanishes and makes room for the enlightened clearing (*Auf-Klärung*) of a heaven now stripped of stars. . . . The world becomes disenchanted (*die Welt wird entzaubert*), the vividness of the demon's grimace turns into the abstractness of the [scientific] question."[45] Fromm, 1941: "Man had overthrown the domination of nature and made himself her master. . . . The abolition of external domination seemed to be not only a necessary but also a sufficient condition to attain the cherished goal: freedom of the individual."[46] Horkheimer, 1947: "Reason has become completely harnessed to the social process. Its operational value, its role in the domination of men and nature, has been made the sole criterion. . . . As the end result of the process, we have . . . an empty nature degraded to mere material, mere stuff to be dominated, without any other purpose than that of this very domination."[47] Habermas, 2001 "To the extent that nature is made accessible to objectivating observation and causal explanation, it is depersonalized. Nature as an object of science is no longer part of the social frame of reference."[48] Again, *Dialectic of Enlightenment*: "The disenchantment of the world means the extirpation of animism. . . . Nature, stripped of qualities, becomes the chaotic stuff of mere classification."[49]

In summary, magic and spirits had to go if the world was to be amenable to systematic and rational interpretation. By turning nature into an object to control, humanity was caught in its own trap. Beyond the domination of nature, enlightenment became the domination of humans over each other. Instead of being liberated into a new kind of autonomy, people were turned into objects, or more properly, into abstractions—mere numbers and statistics.[50] The objectification of nature had led toward the objectification of humanity, and the concentration camps and Gulag are tragic expressions of this deeper impulse.

I see myself as a disciple of critical theory, and I find *Dialectic* intensely useful and have returned to it repeatedly; yet it is effectively a late expression of an old myth. It rests on a set of basically mythical binaries (myth/enlightenment, nature/human) whose breaches it stages, but nevertheless maintains.[51] More important for our purposes, it works by granting the triumph of disenchantment and de-animation even as it traces the negative impacts of this process and its potential returns in new myth. But *this assertion of loss* relies on the assumption that reason once ruled or turned into its opposite.[52] Yet, this event never occurred. It too is a myth.

Let me put this differently. What I am saying is that not only is myth myth; not only is the opposition to myth myth; *but the recognition of the opposition to myth as myth* is itself myth. To clarify, we know that the tale of Prometheus was a myth; Adorno and others have shown us that enlightenment's claim to progress was a myth and that enlightenment's attack on mythology only bred more irrationalism in response; what is needed now is the recognition that this last claim—our enlightenment critique—has yielded myth. As a critical theorist, you can achieve high levels of reflexivity on the issue and still have your initial argument swept out from under you. If what you are doing in the mode of enlightenment critique is lamenting the disillusion of myth, then myth has not been dissolved. Your mourning reinstates the object of your grief.

Faced with this impasse, I aim to ascertain how Horkheimer and Adorno (and the legacy of thinkers they draw on) came to the idea that enlightenment was fundamentally disenchanting and thus bequeathed their left Weberianism to our generation. To do so requires a methodological epoché, a suspension of our central terms. What follows will take precisely *not* as given the meaning of magic, religion, or science. This is necessary because the key terms of our analysis had different meanings in different historical moments, and their reoccurrence obscures breaks, discontinuities, and important shifts. Moreover, concepts are partially defined differentially, and current terminology often bears the legacy of lost oppositions. Accordingly, we must pay careful attention to the construction of putative antagonisms (e.g., between myth and enlightenment).

To this discourse analysis, I will contribute another area of suspicion. Because de-animation is central to many of the accounts of disenchantment (not the least in *Dialectic*), in addition to discussing magic as understood in the historical context in question, I will also attend to instances when nature is conceptualized as populated with animating entities and/or spiritual forces. Put differently, reaching past *Dialectic of Enlightenment*, I aim to perform a philosophical archaeology of this conception of modernity, the one that identifies the modern with the Enlightenment and the end of magic, the domination of nature, and the extirpation of spirits.

REFLEXIVE RELIGIOUS STUDIES: THE ENTANGLED FORMATION OF RELIGION, SCIENCE, AND MAGIC

In general terms, this book is a case study in what I have been calling "reflexive religious studies." Contemporary sociologists such as Ulrich Beck, Anthony Giddens, and Scott Lash have begun to work out the way that sociology itself reflexively shapes society.[53] Similarly, the French sociologists Pierre Bourdieu and Loïc Wacquant articulated a "reflexive sociology" capable of studying sociology itself in sociological terms.[54] This is by far the most interesting insight to come out of these movements, and it is probably best to phrase it dynamically. Sociology suffers from a certain problem: any social knowledge it produces gets fed back into the system, which is thereby changed. This means that sociology is always describing the social field the way it was *before* sociology described it.

Beck, Giddens, and Lash point to two distinct kinds of problems. The first is in the domain of information theory. Their observation might seem to fit easily into a Weberian notion of rationalization; that is, it might initially appear that academic social science produces feedback in culture in such a way that it produces greater coherence in the social sphere that it then studies. But in fact, it also introduces a new element: the sociological study of society adds a new incalculability. It is as though the thing that information gathering cannot properly reckon with is the *effect* of information gathering on the system. Thus, it would appear to be an analogue to the observer effect in quantum mechanics and need to be factored in. In other words, a reflexive sociology becomes necessary as sociologists try to reckon with the project of gathering sociological information about and within a society that has taken on the insights of sociology.

The second problem cuts deeper, and for our purposes is more important. As Beck and Giddens are both aware, sociology contributes to the production of certain kinds of societies. They do not just mean professional bodies like the American Sociological Association. Instead, sociology as a discipline authorizes certain kinds of information gathering or surveillance (or censuses), which then produce new kinds of social locations and new kinds of collective organizations and institutions. Sociological surveys, for instance, influence their subjects producing new kinds of social identities. Reflexive sociology, therefore, is needed to be able to theorize the kind of societies sociology produces.

Sociology is not the only discipline that has this problem. Anthropologists have had to deal with the way that anthropological theory changes the peoples that they study; for example, producing new tribes and authenticating some forms of indigenous culture over others.[55] The analogue of this issue for literary theorists becomes how to interpret the vast volume of novels and poems that have been written with literary theory in mind. As Christian Thorne has observed, queer theory has gained a sufficient purchase in American education that it has now begun to shape the sexuality of undergraduates. There is thus a need for a reflexive queer theory to theorize the effect that queer theory has on constructing the interpretation of different sexual acts and identities.[56]

In what follows, I aim to extend this insight to formulate a reflexive religious studies. For some time, scholars in the field have been engaged in interogating the relationship between their own personal faiths and their object of study.[57] This has been useful, but what I am calling for in the name of reflexivity is not so much autobiographical reflections as a reflexivity addressing the discipline as such.[58] As I conceive it, reflexive religious studies would reckon with ways that the academic study of religion—in a range of disciplinary formations—is porous and tends to seep into the cultures that it purports to study. Moreover, as I have been arguing for some time now, the category "religion" is itself transformative, such that importing it as a second-order category (in scholastic, legal, and other discourses) transforms the society into which it has been introduced, effectively transforming other cultural systems into "religions." "Reflexive religious studies" would examine those societies in which the category "religion" and its entangled differentiations (e.g., the distinction between religion and the secular) have begun to function as concepts. It would trace the continuities and disruptions that this category produces in older conceptual orders and aim for precision. And it would also necessarily take into account how the disciplines of religious studies shapes and produces religions.

While to my knowledge there has never been a serious previous attempt to work out a reflexive religious studies, scholars have spent some time thinking about the way in which the higher criticism of the Bible produces different kinds of religious projects. The old fashioned version of this trope is to read the Protestant Reformation, for example, as inspired by Erasmus's humanism. To the degree that there is a version of this narrative about religious studies today, it is often to imagine that the discipline is secularizing, that the act of comparison between religions tends to relativize and therefore extinguish religious beliefs. But this is far from the whole picture. The first insight of reflexive religious studies is that the social scientific study actually reverberates in the religious field, revitalizing and even producing religions. Examples are easy to find. One does not have to look hard to see that the study of shamanism, for instance, has actually worked to produce contemporary neo-shamanic movements.[59]

*

There is another way that taking this meta-level view of the category religion will help our current inquiry. It is my contention that tracing the genealogy of the notion of a conflict between religion and science will give us clues to both the appearance and occlusion of enchantment. While I will explain disenchantment on many levels, I will argue that *one* of the mechanisms that both makes magic appealing and motivates its suppression is the reification of a putative binary opposition between religion and science, and the production of a "third term" (*superstition, magic*, and so on) that signifies repeated attempts to stage or prevent reconciliation between these opposed discursive terrains. Let me explain.

Many accounts of modernity have been undergirded by the legend of a titanic struggle between two opposing forces—religion and science—in which the latter is often declared victor. The myth that these two powers had always been in contestation was formed in the nineteenth century; and then, like many other myths we'll explore, it was projected backward in a series of dramatized confrontations.[60] Today many nonspecialists mistakenly believe that Galileo was really tortured by the Inquisition for promoting heliocentrism or that medieval Europeans thought that the world was flat before Columbus proved them wrong.[61]

Nonetheless, religious studies and science studies have now spent decades relativizing their respective objects. Scholars of religion now know that "religion" is not a universal part of human nature, but is a culturally specific category that initially took shape in Western Christendom at the end of the seventeenth century and then was radically transformed through a globalization process over the course of the long nineteenth century, producing both "world religions" and discourses around "religion" as an autonomous domain of human experience.[62] Although the issue is more controversial, philosophers of science also know that there is no single universal scientific method, and that "modern science" emerged in the long nineteenth century with a radical reformulation of European natural philosophy and expanded through globalization and the selective absorption and disintegration of local knowledge systems.[63]

By combining these two critiques, the contemporary historian Peter Harrison has delineated how religion and science emerged together in European thought through a parallel process of mutual distinction and reification.[64] In broadest of strokes, Harrison demonstrates that science and religion come into being with a common epistemic basis that if anything made possible the birth of modern science.[65] But eventually they came to be understood as separate systems with their own spheres. Hence this initial cooperation collapsed as the sciences gained part of their respective notion of coherence in contradistinction to religion as an irrational belief system, while religion became "a kind of negative image of science, and this contrast has become important for the integrity of the boundaries of science."[66] In effect, both discursive systems gained coherence through a purification process in which they came to be distinguished from each other.

Harrison's account is only part of the picture. While he describes the history of a binary opposition between religion and science, Serge Margel has emphasized an earlier dialectic between religion and superstition that gave each term its meaning; moreover, Michel de Certeau has noted that science was formulated through rhetorical opposition to superstition.[67] More recently, Wouter Hanegraaff has argued that the broader enterprise of the European academy was predicated on excluding forms of pagan knowledge it marked as superstitious, magic, or occult.[68] Both concepts of religion and science came into existence by being distinguished from "superstition," understood as the false double of religion and later as the false double of science or scientific knowledge (in both humanistic and naturalistic modes). Accordingly, instead of binaries, I see a trinary formation in which religion is negated by science, which is in turn negated by superstition or magic.

Put differently, the concept of true or orthodox "religion" was in some sense constructed by being distinguished from the false religion of "superstition" (we can hear echoes of Protestant anti-Catholicism and earlier Christian anti-paganism). Similarly, true "science" or proper scholarship was formulated in opposition to "superstition" (often understood as occult or fake science). Moreover, from both vantages, the prototypical superstitions were belief in spirits and "magic." In this respect, terms like *superstition* and *magic*, while fluid, open ended, and constantly changing, nevertheless were not completely empty signifiers because they inherited these older polemics. Superstition went from "wrong" because it was diabolical or pagan to "mistaken" because it was antiscientific.

Overlaps between "religion" and "science" were often described as "superstition" or pseudosciences.[69] Policing "superstitions" became part of the way that the categories of "religion" and "science" were formed in differentiation. Furthermore, it is worth emphasizing that the rejection of "superstition" was necessarily incomplete, and hence it was always possible to partially transform it into a site of resistance. I am fascinated by a kind of sublation or occlusion that functions by suppressing something at the same moment that another aspect of the suppressed is being reincorporated. Treating esotericism or magic as predominantly "rejected knowledge" only captures part of the picture. It explains how categories like "superstition" were produced to exclude certain beliefs or knowledges, but it doesn't explain what makes those forms of knowledge appealing in the first place. My intuition is that while this type of negation is basically disempowering, it also represents a location from which one can criticize the original position.

Approached differently, the construction of science and religion as antagonists implied a third position representing where the categories both convene and collapse. In my last book I deployed this trinary in a genealogy of the category "religion," but here I want to follow the third term. Negatively valenced, it is understood to be *superstition* and in this respect appears as the double of either religion or science. Hence, a certain cross-section of scientists trumpeted the power of their respective domain by suggesting that all of religion was a superstition. Positively valenced, the third term is *magic*, which was often supposed to take the best elements of religion and science together or to recover things suppressed by "modern" science or religion. Indeed, most of what gets classified as contemporary esotericism or occultism came into being as an attempt to repair the rupture between religion and science.[70]

Restated in broad terms, once "religion" and "science" are formulated as opposing discursive terrains, religion-science hybrids become both threatening and appealing. They are threatening because they risk destabilizing the system's points of closure and because they suggest pre-hybrid and therefore supposedly premodern systems. But also they are appealing because they promise to heal the split between the two notionally opposed terrains. Moreover, the more "magic" becomes marked as antimodern, the more it becomes potentially attractive as a site from which to criticize "modernity." Finally, for all the polemical attacks against superstition and magic, disenchanting efforts were only sporadically enforced within the disciplines, such that notions of magic and spirits keep resurfacing as redemptive possibilities.

All told, this triadic structure is not the only reason that European thinkers came up with the theory of disenchantment and put it into place as a regulative ideal (the chapters that follow will explore other entangled issues). But, as I will demonstrate, looked at from the reverse vantage point, the myth of disenchantment has two divergent effects—first, it functions as a regime of truth, embedding the paradigm of modernity in the core of the sciences and giving energy to various projects aiming to eliminate superstition; and second, it is self-refuting, giving life to the very thing it characterizes as expiring, stimulating magical revivals, paranormal research, and new attempts to spiritualize the sciences.

In sum, in the binary operation between religion and science, superstition/magic functions as the third term in a Derridean sense.[71] "Magic" is the point where the system does not close. Like all of these terms, it has a dynamic function. Its role emerges from a position as the negation of the negation; and therefore, looked at from one perspective, it is the conjunction from which the system emerges. From another perspective, magic is either an imitation of the science or an imitation of religion; the origin of the religion or the origin of science; or the excluded middle.

OVERVIEW OF THE WORK: EUROPE IS NOT EUROPE

Although the God of monotheism may have taken a few knocks—if not actually "died"—in the nineteenth-century European story of "the disenchantment of the world," the gods and other agents inhabiting practices of so-called "superstition" have never died anywhere.

DIPESH CHAKRABARTY, *Provincializing Europe*, 2000

Throughout the academy there continues to be a massive and ongoing investment in the modernization thesis, which when not taken for granted is alternately celebrated or condemned.[72] Fortunately, two small but significant groups of dissenters have rejected this grand narrative: first, a cluster of postcolonial thinkers has worked to shatter the reflexive linkage between Eurocentrism and modernization;[73] and second, a handful of historians working on Europe and America have come to emphasize contemporary enchantments therein.[74] The first group has demonstrated how the claim that disenchanted modernity was the distinctive feature of the West was used to justify colonization and violence. The second group of scholars has argued that magic is everywhere in Euro-American "modernity"—in the religious world, the secular world, popular culture, literature, the scientific academy, and so on. In what follows I build on the insights of both movements and in so doing I aim to historicize—or we might say, following Dipesh Chakrabarty, to "*provincialize*"—the myth of modernity and its various incarnations in European social theory.[75]

The first implication of taking both movements together, however, is a seeming paradox—postcolonialists have demonstrated that modernity is just another name for Europe. Meanwhile, historians have shown that European history does not really fit the classic trajectory of modernity. Accordingly, if the rejection of the supernatural is supposed to be the defining feature of both European culture and modernity, then in this respect—Europe is not Europe.

Let me approach this differently. In the first volume of *Histoire de la sexualité*, Michel Foucault set out to challenge what he called the "repressive hypothesis"; namely, the widespread belief in the twentieth century that earlier generations were sexually repressed. In doing so, Foucault expressed a set of doubts that I want to loosely adapt here to address what we might call the "myth of disenchantment," the "modernity hypothesis," or the "modernity paradigm."[76] First doubt: Is the disenchantment of the world truly an established historical pattern? Was there actually a historical rupture between the epoch of magic and the critique of disenchantment? Does modernity really define a singular breach, or is it a mythic epoch? Call this the *historical doubt*.

Once this doubt begins to take hold, it leads to new doubts whose resolution will be of interest to postcolonialists and historians of enchantment alike—if we reject the old European story of the "disenchantment of the world" (and I think there are plenty of good reasons to do so), we still have the second doubt: Why did European societies come to think of themselves as disenchanted? How did Europe come to imagine—even to the extent of taking it as the central feature of its civilization—that it did not believe in spirits, despite persistent evidence to the contrary? Why were social scientists drawn irrevocably to the very beliefs they decried as primitive superstitions? How in the face of widespread belief in spirits and magic did disenchantment come to function as a regime of truth or disciplinary norm in the human sciences? In other words, how did Europeans come to end up with a society that both re-presses magic and in which magic proliferates? When and how did the myth of disenchantment emerge? As I address these issues in what follows, the phrase *occult disavowal* will be my shorthand for the regulative function of the myth of disenchantment that results in the simultaneous private embrace and public rejection of enchantment. Call this the *critical-historical doubt.*

This in turn leads to a third and final doubt: Have the workings of domination in Euro-American societies really belonged primarily to the mode of disenchantment? Or is the critique of disenchantment part of the same power mechanism as the thing it criticizes? This is the *politico-theoretical doubt.*

To respond to these entangled issues, the work that follows is first and foremost therefore a novel history of the human sciences that, having suspended the assumption of disenchantment, shows how their disciplining processes occurred against a background of magic and religious revivals. Doing so should enable us to undercut the modernization thesis by revealing its paradoxical origins in the shared terrain between spiritualists, sorcerers, and scholars.

The argument of the book proceeds as follows:

An initial background chapter, "Enchanted (Post) Modernity," takes as its starting point present-day sociology and anthropology. It shows that today in neither Europe, nor America, nor the rest of the globe can one find the disenchanted world anticipated by the major theorists of modernity. It then uses sociological data to explore the function of enchantment today. Moreover, it unlinks traditional accounts of secularization and disenchantment to show that in many cases ghosts and spirits come to fill the space evacuated by the putative death of God. Significantly, it begins to excavate one of the logics of occult disavowal by showing how belief in one form of enchantment often comes at the cost of another, such that supernatural beliefs can actively function in the service of disenchantment.

Part 1, "God's Shadow," begins with chapter 2, "Revenge of the Magicians,"which is historical in scope. It takes as its starting point various figures— from Giordano Bruno to Isaac Newton—who have been blamed for the rise of instrumental reason and the disenchantment of nature, and it demonstrates their respective magical projects. It then recovers two moments often seen as the watershed of modernity—Francis Bacon's formulation of the scientific method and the French *philosophes'* publication of the *Encyclopédie*—to demonstrate that neither embody the disenchantment usually attributed to them. In so doing, it separates the putative "birth of science" from the death of magic, and shows that the enlightenment project was initially articulated not in terms of a conflict between religion and science or faith and reason, but as a divine science. Nevertheless, it sees in both movements the roots of occult disavowal in the myth of modernity as the end of superstition.

The third chapter, "The Myth of Absence," traces the myth that the *philosophes* and the mechanistic cosmology had eliminated the divine. It demonstrates that several key mythemes—the mythless age, the de-divination of nature, nihilism, and the death of God—had a conjoined genesis in German philosophical circles several decades before Nietzsche. Focusing on the writings of G. W. F. Hegel, Friedrich Hölderlin, Friedrich Jacobi, and Friedrich Schiller, it shows how a generation of German philosophers came to believe that they lived in a uniquely mythless epoch and then transmitted this particular lament to later generations, including our own. Turning to Jacob Burckhardt, it shows how the myth-of-the-end-of-myth was projected backward, producing the historiography of other epochs, such as the Renaissance and the Enlightenment.

Chapter 4, "The Shadow of God," highlights a crucially important dialectical movement. It shows how a putative opposition between religion and science, combined with fears of despiritualization and mourning for the death of God, motivated the rise of spiritualism and occult movements, and contributed to the birth of religious studies as a discipline. Looking at Edward Burnett Tylor, Friedrich Max Müller, Éliphas Lévi, and Helena Blavatsky, it demonstrates how scholars, spiritualists, and magicians not only moved in common social circles, but also shared an engagement with spirits, mysticism, and "Oriental" mysteries. The chapter maps out the messy intermediate terrain between two spheres that considered themselves to be different and were sometimes opposed, but nevertheless exhibited the same basic habits of thought—including a myth of lost magic.

Chapters 5, "The Decline of Magic," and 6, "The Revival of Magick," turn to the birth of the classical disenchantment narrative, noting that while it is often attributed to Max Weber, one of its earliest significant formulations is in the second edition of *The Golden Bough*, by the Scottish folklorist James Frazer. Chapter 5 argues that Frazer came late to the narrative of magical decline, and that he did so within a context of psychical research and in the face of a folkloric narrative itself about the departure of fairies and the decline of magic. It shows how Frazer formulated an influential trinary opposition between religion, magic, and science while encoding this typology within a disenchantment narrative. The following chapter turns to the infamous British magician Aleister Crowley, who overlapped with Frazer at Trinity College, Cambridge. This chapter shows that Crowley drew on the very text in which Frazer worked out disenchantment to stage his revival of modern "magick" [*sic*]. Hence, the narrative of disenchantment was self-refuting insofar as it reinvigorated the very thing it described as endangered.

In part 2, "The Horrors of Metaphysics," the seventh chapter, "The Black Tide: Mysticism, Rationality, and the German Occult Revival," shifts the focus back to the German-speaking world. It begins with Sigmund Freud's references in *The Interpretation of Dreams* to a "brilliant mystic" named Carl du Prel. It explores one of Freud's interlocutors, the German-Jewish physician Max Nordau, who theorized his own conception of degeneration alongside a broader contention that modernity led to irrationalization and mysticism. The chapter then shows how conceptions of magic and spirits haunted the German reception of Immanuel Kant and became entangled with the history of academic philosophy and psychoanalysis, and their counterpart constructions of noumena and the unconscious. It explains how Arthur Schopenhauer came to theorize the efficacy of magic and demonstrates the importance of "mysticism" as a vanishing mediator between a philosophy dedicated to exploring reason's limits, and a psychoanalysis focused on the roots of irrationality. It then explains why Freud polished Frazer's narrative of disenchantment into a developmental theory even as he began his own exploration of an occult terrain. Thus, it explores how Freud projected his own taboo desires onto the figure of the savage.

The next two chapters look to the places where the myth of the absence of myth has established its most systematic philosophical purchase: critical theory and Vienna Circle positivism. Chapter 8, "Dialectic of Darkness: The Magical Foundations of Critical Theory," focuses on the German neo-pagan poet and philosopher Ludwig Klages, who formulated much of the terminology and critique of modernity as the "domination of nature" that would later become associated with the Frankfurt School. It then looks at Klages's influence on German-Jewish philosopher and literary theorist Walter Benjamin, demonstrating that much of the terminology that seems so peculiar to Benjamin—*the aura, constellations, correspondences, angels*, and *Ur-images*—all were current in German esoteric circles while Benjamin was coming to his most important ideas.

Having shown that the Enlightenment critique has roots in an esoteric milieu, critical theory's putative enemies—the positivists—would seem to be the worst candidates for closet magicians. "The Ghosts of Metaphysics: Logical Positivism and Disenchantment," chapter 9, explores the connections between the Vienna School of positivism and the esoteric milieu. It shows how the founders of logical positivism, such as Otto Neurath, presented their philosophy as a kind of magical revival. It also demonstrates that other positivists—such as Rudolf Carnap, Hans Hahn, and Kurt Gödel—had a profound preoccupation with ghosts and the paranormal. Taken as a whole, the book demonstrates how magic, like metaphysics, also haunts the beginnings of analytic philosophy.

The final chapter, "The World of Enchantment; or, Max Weber at the End of History," focuses on Max Weber's preoccupation with "disenchantment" (*Entzauberung*) in the same period that Freud was formulating his own version of that myth. It complexifies conventional readings of disenchantment by showing how the term fit into Weber's theory of rationalization. Examining a set of Weber's letters that have only recently been made available to scholars, the chapter argues that despite Weber's reputation for being deaf to religion, "mysticism" was not wholly negative, but perhaps a positive reaction to the "iron cage" of modernity. It demonstrates that Weber came to theorize "the disenchanting of the world" (*die Entzauberung der Welt*) not out of frustration with Prussian bureaucracy, but rather in reaction to a Swiss neo-pagan commune.

To foreshadow the complexity of the argument that follows, I am not merely complicating Weber's master narrative, but also examining those historical moments or knots in which enchantment and disenchantment turn into each other, or are indistinguishable. In other words, I want to show that what appears to be a binary opposition—enchantment versus disenchantment (*Verzauberung gegen Entzauberung*)—fails to match up.

CHAPTER ONE

Enchanted (Post) Modernity

This book began as an attempt to make sense of some of the systems of belief which were current in sixteenth- and seventeenth-century England, but which no longer enjoy much recognition today. Astrology, witchcraft, magical healing, divination, ancient prophecies, ghosts and fairies, are now all rightly disdained by intelligent persons.

KEITH THOMAS, *Religion and the Decline of Magic*, 1971

The postmodern condition is nevertheless foreign to disenchantment.

JEAN-FRANÇOIS LYOTARD, *La condition postmoderne*, 1979

If you were to travel to the small town of Kotohira on the Japanese island of Shikoku, you might, after strolling past one of the country's oldest Kabuki theaters and partaking of the region's famous udon noodles, find yourself at a famous shrine, the town's central attraction for tourists and pilgrims.[1] There, on the grounds of this ancient site, you would find a dedicatory plaque sporting a very modern image, that of Japan's first cosmonaut, AKIYAMA Toyohiro, clad in a spacesuit standing next to his craft. Despite its space-age content, however, the plaque gives thanks to Konpira, the so-called god of sailors, for Akiyama's safe voyage through interplanetary space. This confluence of technology and public religiosity is by no means unique to the Konpira Shrine. Analogous examples dot the Japanese cultural landscape. As I have argued elsewhere, generally speaking, recent Japanese history meant changes in the locus of enchantment, in ways unanticipated by classical theorists of modernity.[2] In one of the most technologically and scientifically advanced nations today, one finds—in addition to old-fashioned faith healers and spirit mediums—flash drives that double as magical charms, funeral rituals for old photographs and discarded electronics, iPhone apps for automatic exorcisms or traditional fortune-telling, and Buddhist stupas dedicated to Thomas Edison and Heinrich Hertz as the "Divine Patriarchs of Electricity and Electro-Magnetic Waves."[3]

Despite the Orientalist cliché of a mystical Asia, Japan does not have a monopoly on contemporary enchantments. In study after study, scholars of the Global South have charted not only traditional but modern forms of magic,

including: Internet-based virtual Haitian Vodou; epidemics of spirit possession among Malaysian factory workers; clairvoyant Brazilian spirit surgeons;
modern witchcraft persecutions in South Africa and Indonesia; Vietnamese
divinities that are appeased with cans of Coke and Pepsi; aerosol sprays to
evoke the protection of Santísima Muerte in Mexico; gun-toting spirit mediums in Uganda; an Indian guru supposedly capable of magical materializations, faith healing, and even bringing people back from the dead; and a
notorious pair of demonically possessed underpants in Ghana.[4] It would seem
that Latin America, Africa, and indeed most of Asia are inhabited by sorcerers
and alive with spirits.

While lingering enchantments used to be taken as a rationale for the backwardness of non-European others, today they are often regarded as evidence
that the disenchantment model is an uncomfortable fit outside the land of its
birth. Hence contemporary scholars like Denis Byrne explicitly reject "the
common assumption that post-Reformation disenchantment encompasses the
non-European world."[5] While I agree with Byrne's sentiment as far as it goes,
in this short chapter I want to challenge the idea that disenchantment is the
order of the day even in the so-called heartland of modernity.

WEIRD AMERICA

There is a constant war between the messengers of God and ghosts and demons, danc-
ers and drinkers, and, for all anyone knows, between God's messengers and God himself—no one has ever seen him, but then no one has ever seen a cuckoo either. . . . Here
is a mystical body of the republic, a kind of public secret: a declaration of what sort of
wishes and fears lie behind any public act, a declaration of a weird but clearly recognizable America.

GREIL MARCUS, *The Old, Weird America*, 2011

It is hard not to be skeptical of claims to disenchantment as I write these words
in a café adorned with flyers advertising "crystal healing," "energy balancing,"
"chakra yoga," and "tarot" readings.[6] Undeniably, what Catherine Albanese
and Courtney Bender refer to as American "metaphysical religion" would
seem to be on display in coffee shops, co-ops, and bookstores throughout
the country.[7] Moreover, in Europe and America, films, novels, and television
series continue to overflow with magic, providing symbolic resources—what
Christopher Partridge and Jeffrey Kripal refer to as "occulture"—that are often
recouped by this religious counterculture (e.g., rituals appearing first in *Buffy
the Vampire Slayer* are adopted by contemporary Wiccan covens).[8] It would

seem that many of the stories we tell ourselves in the modern West are about superheroes and magicians, ghosts and monsters, and that these creatures often spill over into other parts of the culture. As Kripal observes in regard to the seeming ubiquity of such cultural materials: "The paranormal is our secret in plain sight."[9]

Even setting aside the abundance of explicitly fictional forms of enchantment, studies of American reading habits similarly suggest that "New Age" print culture has "expanded exponentially in the past thirty years" with "nonfiction books" about magic, guardian angels, and near-death experiences appearing in the upper echelons of Amazon's best-seller lists.[10] Moreover, the last ten years have seen a proliferation of "reality" television series that claim to report evidence for ghosts, psychics, extraterrestrials, monsters, curses, and even miracles.[11] In both the United Kingdom and the United States, it is also easy to turn on the television and encounter the prognostications of celebrity psychic mediums.[12] It might seem that contemporary audiences are at least willing to flirt with the existence of spirits and the supernatural.

A variety of sociological evidence would seem to support this intuition. In 2005, Gallup conducted a telephone survey with 1,002 American adults asking them if they believed in things like ESP, ghosts, telepathy, and witches (see figure 1). Not only did a surprising number of the American respondents reportedly believe in each of these (e.g., almost a third believe in ghosts), but also other polling firms, while not covering identical beliefs, have produced similar numbers.[13] For a recent example, a YouGov 2015 survey of 1,171 Americans showed that 48 percent of those sampled agreed with the claim "Some people can possess one or more types of psychic ability (e.g., precognition, telepathy, etc.)," while 43 percent agreed with the statement "Ghosts exist."[14] Even slight differences in the wording produce different responses, but taken together it appears the majority of Americans are at least open to the idea of ghosts and psychic powers, while a not-insignificant number believe in necromancy.

Remarkably, if one takes a closer look at the Gallup 2005 polling data, it shows something even more interesting: belief in different forms of the "paranormal" (see note for terminology) are not confined to a single subculture.[15] For example, believers in telepathy and witchcraft are likely only semi-overlapping sets because, as the survey indicated, 73 percent of those responding believe in at least one of the poll's ten paranormal categories (see figure 2).[16] Although it might sound shocking, this percentage is nearly identical to earlier iterations of the Gallup poll from 2001 and 1990.[17] The implications of these statistics are worth underscoring because, if this data is accurate, it means that *only approximately a quarter of Americans are not believers in the paranormal.* We

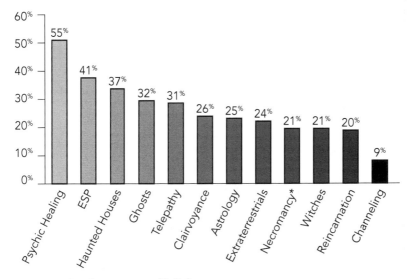

FIGURE 1. American paranormal beliefs, 2005

For the label "necromancy," the prompt was "that people can communicate mentally with some-one who has died." For "psychic healing," the prompt was "psychic or spiritual healing or the power of the human mind to heal the body." David Moore, "Three in Four Americans Believe in Paranormal," Gallup News Service, June 16, 2005; and Linda Lyons, "Paranormal Beliefs Come (Super)Naturally to Some," Gallup News Service, November 1, 2005.

live in a land of wonders in which most people are believers and skeptics are the clear minority.

It might be tempting to discount these polls as mere journalistic sensational-ism, but sociologists have found similar results. In 2005 and 2007, sociologists at Baylor University conducted a fairly robust set of phone interviews (sample size of 3,369) from across the United States. Their main focus was a complete picture of American religious beliefs, but a similar pattern emerges (see figure 3).[18] Again we see evidence that about half of the American population believes in ghosts, while a clear majority believes in demonic possession. This latter claim accords with the fieldwork of the American sociologist Michael Cuneo, who in 2001 suggested that belief in demonic possession was not only wide-spread, but also on the increase such that "exorcism is more readily available today in the United States than perhaps ever before."[19] Moreover, in a section of the 2007 survey not depicted in figure 3, 55 percent of those polled claimed they had personally experienced being "protected from harm by a guardian angel."[20] In sum, the picture painted by the Baylor study is one of an America enthusiastically engaged with angels, demons, and other invisible spirits.[21]

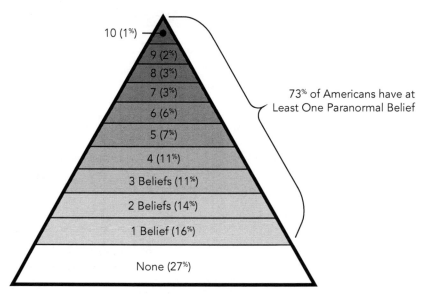

FIGURE 2. Percentage of Americans with multiple paranormal beliefs, 2005

They include in the paranormal: ESP, haunted houses, ghosts, telepathy, clairvoyance, astrology, communication with the dead, witches, reincarnation, and channeling. Moore, "Three in Four Americans Believe in Paranormal"; Lyons, "Paranormal Beliefs Come (Super)Naturally to Some."

Sociologists Christopher D. Bader, F. Carson Mencken, and Joseph O. O. Baker published an analysis of relevant portions of the Baylor data in *Paranormal America* (2010), which they combined with fieldwork interviewing self-described psychics and Bigfoot hunters. Bader, Mencken, and Baker ultimately summarize their findings in strong terms:

> *The paranormal is normal* . . . . Statistically, those who report a paranormal belief are not the oddballs; it is those who have no beliefs that are in the significant minority. Exactly which paranormal beliefs a person finds convincing varies, but whether it is UFOs and ghosts or astrology and telekinesis, most of us believe more than one. If we further consider strong beliefs in active supernatural entities and intense religious experiences the numbers are even larger.[22]

In sum, Bader, Mencken, and Baker also estimate that more than two-thirds of Americans believe in the paranormal.[23]

Demographic trends can also be extracted from the data as specific paranormal beliefs can be identified with different populations. For example, African American women were the most likely to believe in ghosts and the possibility of communication with the dead, while Caucasians were more likely to believe that they have been abducted by extraterrestrials.[24] But believing in at least one form of the paranormal is not confined to a particular counterculture and is evidently the norm throughout the country.

Nor has it vanished with compulsory mass education. While there is a connection between education and specific paranormal beliefs, there is little correlation between level of education and having paranormal beliefs as such. For instance, Bader, Mencken, and Baker conclude that college graduates are less likely to believe in UFOs but more likely to believe in psychics.[25] Other surveys targeting the issue specifically have also suggested that "higher education fuels [a] stronger belief in ghosts." At the very least, college seniors are more likely to be open to the possibility of ghosts and psychical powers than their less educated peers.[26] A related point worth underscoring is that sociological evidence suggests that self-identified magicians and witches are generally

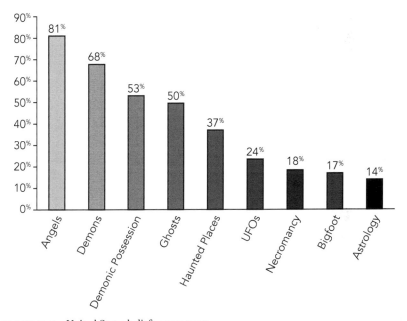

F I G U R E 3 . United States beliefs, 2005, 2007

Baylor University, *The Baylor Religion Survey, Wave 1* (Waco, TX: Baylor Institute for Studies of Religion, 2005) and *The Baylor Religion Survey, Wave 2* (Waco, TX: Baylor Institute for Studies of Religion, 2007). 2005 data unless marked. Combining "absolutely exist" and "probably exist" as well as "strongly agree" and "agree."

better educated than average and more likely to hold a college degree.[27] Hence, it would be a mistake to assume that education necessarily leads toward disenchantment.

An important corollary of these surveys more broadly is that paranormal belief can be found on both sides of the political aisle, albeit in different typical forms. This is significant because in the popular culture, the occult is often associated with reactionary right-wing politics, especially fascism (e.g., the occult Nazis in Steven Spielberg's *Raiders of the Lost Ark*). This argument has a scholarly pedigree in sources such as Theodor Adorno, "Theses against Occultism" (*Thesen gegen den Okkultismus*), the German context for which will be explored in chapters 8 and 9.[28] In contrast, one can also find the reverse association between "New Age hippies" and left-wing politics. Yet, one of the most straightforward implications of the wide diffusion of paranormal belief is that there is no particular political affiliation that is more "irrational" or more magical than the other (at least, according to this axis).

History bears this out insofar as one can find enchantment across the political spectrum (e.g., both pro- and anticolonialist Theosophists). But this evidence does not neutralize political readings of magic. Specific beliefs do correlate with demographic backgrounds and ideological commitments.[29] Different paranormal beliefs have elective affinities with different political movements. One could go some length to explore the progressive political coordinates of, say, spiritualism in nineteenth-century America.[30] But we should resist too quickly assuming a clear political bifurcation between believers in magic and skeptics.

On a related note, as the Cameroonian philosopher Achille Mbembe reminds us, belief in witchcraft is often taken as paradigmatic of cultural backwardness and is sometimes supposed to be the very thing that makes Africa, for example, difficult to modernize.[31] But the historian Owen Davies has demonstrated that despite the common claim that Salem was the last great witchcraft persecution in this country, "we now know of more people killed as witches in America after 1692 than before it," with extrajudicial murders of suspected witches continuing at least until the 1950s.[32] Although Davies does not explicitly draw this conclusion, he provides a lot of evidence that it was the rise of Wicca that began to shift the discourse around witches post-1954. Additionally, the commercialization of Halloween combined with the popular *Bewitched* television series popularized a more harmless image of the witch.[33] But, in the same period, some Evangelical communities have if anything amplified their so-called war against witches.[34] Indeed, even today, Pat Robertson, the controversial chairman of the Christian Broadcasting Network, cautions his viewers against the dangers of witches and their curses on a seemingly regular basis.[35] All told, it should not be surprising that surveys suggest that more than a quarter of Americans believe in witches.[36]

There has been some excellent scholarship on the decline of belief in miracles over the course of European history.[37] Indeed, the loss of faith in divinely inspired wonders is often taken to be a hallmark of the grand trajectory of disenchantment. But as useful as historians have been for recovering the context and politics of natural philosophy, as a broad trajectory, notions of a post-miraculous age run into trouble in the face of contemporary sociological evidence. For instance, a large survey of more than 35,000 Americans conducted by the Pew Research Forum in 2007 reported that 79 percent of those polled believed that "miracles still occur today as in ancient times."[38] Less than a fifth of all those surveys rejected the existence of contemporary miracles as a whole. It is worth remarking that some of those who reject the idea that miracles occur today must include a significant number of Protestants committed to the cessation of miraculous gifts at the end of the apostolic age (discussed in chapters 2 and 5). So one might imagine that many of those denying the currency of contemporary divine wonders are doing so on religious grounds. At the very least, it would seem that many Americans still live in "worlds of wonder."[39]

By looking at Bader, Mencken, and Baker's American demographic information in greater depth, it is striking that the groups least likely to believe in the paranormal generally define themselves in religious and not secular terms. For instance, Evangelical Christians are particularly skeptical about the "paranormal."[40] But rather than stripping the world of animating forces, Evangelicals are more likely to believe that ghosts, aliens, and psychic powers are caused by demons or witches. It is hard to read this as a straightforward sign of disenchantment.

This is an important clue to the mechanisms of occult disavowal, as Evangelicals are not alone in exchanging one sort of enchantment for another. Instead of a single amorphous New Age, different metaphysical communities are often dismissive of one another. Self-identified magical practitioners often discount spiritualists as frauds and vice versa; while psychics are often anti-ritualists, suggesting that mental powers explain what people think of as magic. Taken together, this indicates that supernatural beliefs often destabilize one another. By way of shorthand, I will refer to this pattern as "an interchange of enchantments," as a gesture toward the way that supernatural beliefs can actively function in the service of disenchantment.

Finally, although social science predictions should be taken with a grain of salt, Bader, Mencken, and Baker—extrapolating survey trend lines combined with predicted demographic shifts—suggest that by 2050 it is likely there will be a further "14 percent increase in the mean number of reported paranormal beliefs in the United States."[41] If they are right, instead of further disenchantment, America will get more magic in the coming decades.

HAUNTED EUROPE

God is out but spirits and ghosts are filling the vacuum.

ROAR FOTLAND, quoted in "Norway Has a New Passion: Ghost Hunting,"
New York Times, 2015

That Europe is more secular than America is often taken as a given, and it might stand to reason that the United States is more enchanted. Indeed, it might seem plausible that the American children of the dissenters have forged an extraordinary nation of crystal salesmen and PTA witches. At the very least, given that the intensity of organized religion in the United States seems to be an outlier from global norms, some Americans might suspect that magical beliefs are more widespread in our country than others. But here too survey evidence seems to contradict this conclusion.

European survey data shows where various accounts of disenchantment and secularization appear to come apart at the seams. The United States and the United Kingdom seem quite different according to measures like church attendance and reported belief in God. Church attendance appears to be quite disparate (roughly 40 percent of people in the United Stated report to being regular churchgoers, compared to less than 15 percent in the United Kingdom[42]). In a widely publicized 2011 Gallup survey of 1,018 Americans adults, 92 percent responded yes when asked, "Do you believe in God?" This figure is not much changed from the 96 percent of Americans who said yes to the same question in Gallup's initial 1944 study, although, to be fair, when given the chance to express doubt, the 2011 numbers are less robust.[43] By comparison, a parallel Eurobarometer study from 2010 showed that only 37 percent of Britons said that the statement "You believe there is a God" came closest to their personal belief.[44]

Despite radically different percentages of people who believe in God, however, Americans and Britons have similar paranormal beliefs. For example, a pair of Ipsos MORI polls in 2007 (1,005 subjects) and 2008 (1,070) showed that belief in ghosts, guardian angels, and telepathy was comparably widespread in Great Britain and Northern Ireland, with 12 percent of those surveyed even agreeing that "certain magical words, or spells, can have real effect" and 19

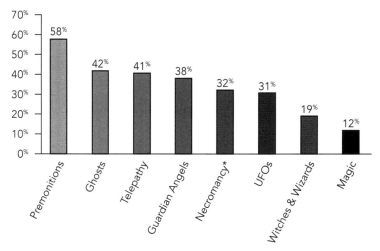

F I G U R E   4 . British beliefs, 2007, 2008
"Necromancy" is my shorthand for "possible to receive communications from the dead." Ben Schott, "Schott's Almanac Survey on Beliefs," Ipsos MORI, October 31, 2007, accessed October 19, 2015, https://www.ipsos-mori.com/Assets/Docs/Archive/Polls/schottsalmanac2.pdf; and "BBC Survey on Trust Issues," Ipsos MORI, January 22, 2008. I have used the most recent poll in the chart.

percent believing in the existence of "witches and wizards" (see figure 4). Even more important for comparative purposes, in a 2005 Gallup telephone survey, 1,010 British subjects were polled using the same questions as the American sample above, thus controlling for variance in wording. In brief, it showed that analogous proportions of both groups believed in ghosts, haunted houses, and astrology, while Britons were a little more skeptical of the existence of witches and a little more likely to believe in the possibility of communication with the dead (see figure 5).[45] In sum, it would seem that despite being in some sense less godly, Britain seems to be no less haunted.

This is worth highlighting because it suggests that increasing atheism is not necessarily correlated to a decline in enchantment. Although I would hesitate to put it in such sensational terms, the British *Daily Mail* tabloid was not so far off in 2014 when it asserted: "[Are Brits] more likely to believe in the supernatural than God? [The number] of people who think they have a sixth sense is higher than those who regularly attend church," citing belief in the supernatural at 55 percent, against 49 percent belief in God.[46] This sounds like a complete contradiction, but it is our first indication of a phenomenon that will become apparent in later chapters; namely, that the death of God

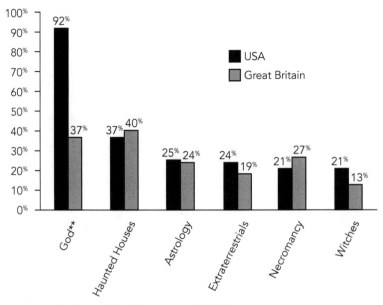

F I G U R E 5 . American and British paranormal beliefs, 2005, 2010, 2011

See Lyons, "Paranormal Beliefs Come (Super)Naturally to Some." Belief in "God" has been taken from TNS Opinion and Social, "Biotechnology Report," *Eurobarometer* 73, no. 1 (2010): 204; and Frank Newport, "More Than 9 in 10 Americans Continue to Believe in God," Gallup News Service, June 3, 2011, discussed above.

does not necessitate the death of magic, and if anything, secularization seems to amplify enchantment.

Although reliable polling data on such subjects is sparse for other parts of Europe, the evidence suggests that despite significant regional variations, paranormal belief is widespread across Europe.[47] A 2000 German telephone survey of 1,500 people conducted by the Institut für Grenzgebiete der Psychologie und Psychohygiene in Freiburg examining both beliefs and experiences showed a widespread engagement with the paranormal in contemporary Germany and concluded that a surprising 73 percent of German interviewees were willing to tell an interviewer that they had personally experienced the paranormal.[48] Moreover, a French survey also conducted in 2000 with the same sample size demonstrated somewhat greater degrees of skepticism in general, with only 21 percent stating that they believe in spells and sorcery (*les envoûtements, la sorcellerie*) and only 13 percent in ghosts (*les fantômes, les revenants*), but with a majority (54 percent) believing in "magnetic healing" (*les guérisons par magnétiseur*).[49] A Russian survey (2006, sample size of 1,600) showed that *a majority of Russians* (53 percent) believe that "magic rituals (*magicheskikh ritualov*, магических ритуалов; e.g., love spells, the evil eye, curses) can be used to influence the lives of others" with 24 percent undecided, while 44 percent (with 36 percent undecided) believe in either "angels, demons or spirits."[50] Indeed, scholars have described a significant "occult revival" in post-Soviet Russia, with one study from 1998 observing that "no less than 39 percent of all non-fiction publications in the humanities" concerned occult topics.[51] Yet, despite widespread paranormal beliefs, popular attitudes toward the divine differ remarkably across Europe. Although this comes from about ten years later than the paranormal surveys, according to a 2010 Ipsos MORI poll, the percentage of those that "definitely believe in God" in Germany was 27 percent (sample size 1,003 respondents), France at 19 percent (sample size 1,004), and Russia 56 percent (sample size 524).[52]

Some interpretations of Weberian disenchantment describe not the death of magic, but instead a vanishing sense of mystery and a greater confidence that everything has a scientific explanation (I'll provide my own reading of Weber's notion in detail in chapter 10). But this common interpretation of Weber's model too runs into trouble when met with contemporary sociological data. American conservatives increasing distrust of science is a well-known phenomenon of recent decades.[53] Moreover, in a 2013 survey of 2,036 Britons, by the think tank Theos suggested that a striking 77 percent believe that "there are things in life that we simply cannot explain through science or any other means."[54] While there has not yet been an analogous survey of American belief, it would seem that at least some sense of mystery remains with us.

In summary, there are many different ways of formulating the secularization thesis, which is, after all, not our main topic; but at the very least, the sociological data would seem to run directly counter the account of the "decline of magic" put forward by Keith Thomas in 1971. As quoted in the section epigraph, he set out to solve the problem of why magical beliefs "no longer enjoy much recognition today." While still an incredibly valuable study, it would seem that Thomas was wrong, in that forty-five years later one can find strong evidence of belief in nearly his exact list of "astrology, witchcraft, magical healing, divination, ancient prophecies, ghosts and fairies" (see figure 1).[55] Thomas's categories are still with us.

To be clear, I am not arguing that belief in phenomena such as ghosts has remained unchanged throughout modern European history; there have clearly been significant shifts in the term's meaning as a conception of "spirit" has globalized and to that extent absorbed other conceptions of the supernatural.

As will be discussed, there have even been serious attempts to eliminate belief in spirits, and certainly spirits have periodically fluctuated in popularity.[56] One could argue that their construal as a "belief" is itself a privatization of the uncanny. Nor am I denying that the shift in terminology from *supernatural* (or even *superstition*) to *paranormal* may represent a naturalization or partial secularization of the category in question. But those qualifications aside, my main point is that beliefs of this sort have clearly not suffered an irrevocable and precipitous falling-off. Anthropologists have argued that acceptance of some form of the paranormal—and especially belief in spirits—is the contemporary *global norm* rather than the exception.[57] So at the very least, if magic has been in decline since the sixteenth century, it does not seem to have declined much.

CONCLUSION: NEW AGE (POST) MODERNISTS?

New Age post-modernists share a preference for the emotional, the irrational, the mystical, and the magical. . . . They focus on all that modern science cannot explain, and so, for example, they offer guides to ghostly abodes and arrange visits to haunted houses. . . . The supernatural and the occult are popular, too. . . . Paganism and pantheism return as post-modern religions.

PAULINE ROSENAU, *Post-Modernism and the Social Sciences*, 1992

If one looks at America and Europe through the eyes of an outsider—with the same sort of gaze often leveled at non-Europeans—it seems hard to assert that we live in a straightforwardly disenchanted world. The equivalent forms of evidence anthropologists have been bringing back from the far reaches of the globe regarding indigenous belief in spirits, witchcraft, folktales, and popular depictions of the supernatural can be found in the West. Moreover, as I have been arguing, evidence for this sort of belief is not merely anecdotal but seems to be borne out on an empirical level. Roughly an amazing three-quarters of Americans hold at least one supernatural belief. Sure, we have plenty of skeptics, and one might hazard the guess that more of them are housed in the academy than elsewhere; still, evidence suggests that higher education merely opens one up to some paranormal beliefs rather than others. In most respects it would appear these skeptics are in the minority.

I have also been working to pry apart the notion that belief in God and belief in magic are coterminous. While there may be good reasons to reject the secularization thesis, if secularization happened anywhere, it is often thought to have occurred in Western Europe or the former Soviet Union. That these places are no less magical than postsecular America at least should begin to challenge the facile equation between secularization and disenchantment.

But there is another possible explanation for contemporary enchantments that I want to interrogate here—namely, that current belief in the supernatural represents an anomalous return of the repressed. According to some thinkers, modernity is over; but this argument can preserve the old-fashioned modernization thesis by granting modernity's myth even while suggesting we have moved beyond it. Maybe modernity and its grand narratives have died and thus returned us to an age of superstition and enchantment. According to the set of argumentation and periodization that loosely gets clustered under the name of "postmodernism," perhaps postmodernism has meant the return of irrationality. It is this argument that I want to interrogate in the following few pages.

One does not have to look hard to find versions of this claim. For instance, Ernest Gellner has argued:

> Max Weber thought that rational industrial production brought with it the cold 'disenchanted' vision of the world. . . . A really advanced industrial society does not any longer require cold rationality from its consumers; at most, it may demand it of its producers. But as it gets more advanced . . . more consumers, fewer producers; less time at work, more at leisure. And in consumption, all tends towards easy and facility of manipulation rather than rigor and coldness . . . one of the advantages of the affluent society, of the further advance in the equalisation of conditions, is that re-enchantment itself is now mass-produced, standardised, and rationalised.[58]

Gellner imagined that something about our current economic order has produced a new kind of culture industry, designed to commodify and mass-produce a new form of magic. In this he was basically following Adorno, who had contended already in 1951 that "by its regression to magic under late capitalism, thought is assimilated to late capitalist forms."[59] Similarly, the contemporary sociologist George Ritzer has argued that the current iteration of globalization has produced "cathedrals of consumption" (like Disneyland and megamalls) in order to "enchant" consumers into making even more purchases.[60] Both theorists see contemporary late-stage capitalism itself as a return of enchantment. I think there is some truth in their analysis of the powers of capitalism. Moreover, in the chapters that follow, I will argue that secularization enchants. In that sense, the death of God feeds into the revitali-

zation of magic. But I would resist the implicit assumption that the early capitalist (or precapitalist) world was any less bewitched.

At the moment, I want to focus on a different version of this argument.
This is one that sees our current moment as unusual precisely because of
a return of magic. As popularly presented, this is less about capitalism than
a question of the rise of "cults" or a resonance between postmodernity and
magical thinking. As Geoffrey Nelson has argued, "The period following the
Second World War has seen an unprecedented burst of religious creativity of
a world scale. . . . Cults and new religions have sprouted in profusion, old religions such as witchcraft and the occult movements have acquired new life, and
missionaries from Asia have successfully introduced varieties of Hinduism,
Buddhism and Islam into the West. . . . The wave of new religious movements
may be seen as one aspect of a rising tide of spirituality that is producing a re-
enchantment of the world."[61] Although his periodization is slightly different,
Christopher Partridge has also suggested that a New Age re-enchantment has
emerged on the other side of the disenchantment of modernity.[62] Nelson and
Partridge are far from alone—a number of scholars have suggested the mid-
twentieth century as a significant turning point in Euro-American religion
that may have reversed the secularization or disenchantment trajectories of
earlier modernity.[63] Indeed, it is often a standard account of Euro-American
religious history to emphasize the 1960s as either a time of "religious crisis" or
"spiritual awakening." In either case, the rise of the New Age, Asian religions,
neo-paganism, and the religious counterculture in general usually play part
in that story.[64]

Some scholars have run postmodernism and the New Age together, seeing
them as sharing a rejection of "the Enlightenment" and its values. As quoted
in the section epigraph, Pauline Rosenau has argued for a correlation between
New Age religions, occult beliefs, and the rise of postmodernism.[65] Zygmunt
Bauman also maintains that postmodernity "brings 're-enchantment' of the
world after the protracted and earnest, though in the end inconclusive, modern
struggle to dis-enchant it."[66] David Lyon has also argued: "One of the most
palpable similarities between postmodernity and the New Age is that both are
responses to—or even expressions of—a crisis of modernity. Enlightenment
Reason, that glorifies objectivity and abhors ambivalence is doubted and attacked in both."[67] I will demonstrate that postmodernity too is a mythical epoch, which relies on a notion of modernity I aim to discredit. But it is common
to hear that our current period has seen a crisis of reason and a resurgence of
enchantment, or that magic reappears as the spirit of "the Enlightenment"
fades.

While I would not discount the cultural shifts of the last half century, I see them as an expression of a longer trajectory. Indeed, if the 1960s and 1970s saw the rise of the New Age, the 1990s the mainstreaming of the paranormal, and the 2000s a series of well-publicized religious revivals, one could also look to the nineteenth century and associate it with a host of equally significant moments: the 1840s with the birth of spiritualism, the 1850s with its globalization, the 1870s with birth of theosophy (see chapter 4), the 1890s with a host of the fin-de-siècle occult movement, and so on, into the twentieth century. Indeed, it is easy to show how debates over the reality of spirits and the supernatural have preoccupied Euro-American thinkers over the *longue durée*. As Jeffrey Kripal has remarked, "We could easily go on for dozens, for *hundreds*, of pages demonstrating how these questions [about the paranormal] lay at the very center of Western intellectual and cultural life."[68] If we take the postmodernists at their word and see our current epoch as bewitched, I will follow Kripal's request to demonstrate that even at its high point, "modernity" was itself enchanted.

* Part I *

God's Shadow

When will all these shadows of God no longer darken us? When will we have completely de-defied nature?

NIETZSCHE, *Die fröhliche Wissenschaft*, 1882

CHAPTER TWO

Revenge of the Magicians

Do not trust those who analyze magic. They are usually magicians in search of revenge.

BRUNO LATOUR, *Les microbes, guerre et paix*, 1984*

With the contemporary reappraisal of enlightenment—led by Max Horkheimer and Theodor Adorno—the main debate among some theorists is about who is most to blame for the disenchantment of nature. It is as though if we could identify the one person responsible for modernity's intellectual wrong turn, thinking could be put back on a firmer course. A number of candidates have been proposed: Was it Giordano Bruno, who expelled humanity "from the Closed World to the Infinite Universe"?[1] Was it René Descartes, whose bifurcation of mind and matter relegated the physical world to mere extension (Lt. *res extensa*)?[2] Was it Isaac Newton whose mathematical physics centrally contributed to the mechanization of the world picture?[3] Was it Francis Bacon, whose construction of the scientific method equated knowledge with the domination of the natural world?[4] According to some accounts, they are all equally culpable for dethroning humanity from the center of the cosmos, conquering nature, despiritualizing matter, or eliminating magic.[5]

At the outset, I want to address a central problem with these narratives of modernity and their respective scapegoats/heroes: all the disenchanters above to some extent saw themselves as magicians. This is important because it shows that enchantment and disenchantment can be brought together in a paradoxical unity, if unstably or dialectically so. To illustrate, let me retread the aforementioned list.

---

* The epigraph for this chapter was also quoted as an epigraph in Randall Styers, *Making Magic: Religion, Magic, and Science in the Modern World* (New York: Oxford University Press, 2004), 3.

At this point, we know from the historians of science that magic and science keep bleeding into each other. The paradigmatic case is Giordano Bruno, who has been so convincingly classified as a magus that one could forget that for many centuries he counted as a hero of science. Given the popularity of *Giordano Bruno and the Hermetic Tradition* (1964) by Frances Yates, it may be hard to imagine the Dominican monk as anything but a magician.[6] But it is worth remembering that Bruno used to occupy pride of place in many scientific disenchantment narratives. For example, Alexandre Koyré in *From the Closed World to the Infinite Universe* (1957) and to a lesser extent Arthur Lovejoy in *The Great Chain of Being* (1936) both credit Bruno with the ideas the older historiography had extended to Copernicus—namely, destabilizing the geocentric solar system and exiling humankind into an infinite cosmos.[7] Prior to Yates, over a century of scholarship had treated Bruno as the scientific martyr par excellence, a reading that persists in some popular histories.[8]

Today more of Bruno's works are available, including his *De magia* (On magic), and now we know he was fascinated with magic and that his aim was not despiritualizing astronomy, but elaborating an infinite and richly animated cosmos full of spirits and demons.[9] Insofar as Bruno was a martyr, it is now hard to see him as a scientific one. The important point is that nearly all the equivalent major figures in the early history of science—from Roger Bacon to Johannes Kepler—have been made magical in more or less Bruno's fashion.[10]

René Descartes's wide reading in Kabbalistic and magical texts is a well-established part of his biography—as is his interest in Rosicrucianism—to which he dedicated his early writings.[11] In the autobiographical section of *Discourse on Method* (*Discours de la méthode*, 1637), Descartes recounted that as a young man he had thought that he was capable of distinguishing between true knowledge and that of magicians and alchemists, with the clear implication that as an adult he had become less capable of maintaining this distinction.[12] While most scholars place Descartes's obsession with magic in his youth, anyone coming to his writings without presuppositions is going to notice the importance of occult themes—from magical spells, illusions, prophetic dreams, to demons (*malin génie*). Descartes is also known to have believed in the prophetic power of visions to foretell death or danger.[13] Even more telling, he claimed that his philosophical system was rooted in a lost divine science, discovered by the ancients but long suppressed.[14] In effect, the Cartesian method—the very method that is now often thought to be the birth of modern philosophy—was supposed to be the popularization of a previously secret occult tradition. On balance, however, Descartes can be seen as primarily an advocate of disenchantment insofar as he repeatedly asserted that his theological science could disclose the mechanistic workings of even the most occult of phenomena.

Isaac Newton is a clearer case. For a long time scholars have known that he had an obsession with alchemy and the philosophers stone, and that he dedicated much of his life to searching for hidden codes in the Bible.[15] As contemporary historian Charles Webster argues, "Newton in particular saw himself as a magus figure intervening between God and His creation."[16] It is not hard to find evidence for this claim, and in Newton's unpublished papers one can find an extensive collection of magical and Kabbalistic texts and his own translations of alchemical writings. Even during his lifetime, Leibniz and others charged Newton with importing "occult qualities" into Cartesian mechanism and in effect enlivening nature with hidden forces—like gravity—and mysterious action at a distance.[17] Strikingly, the father of modern physics even took a stab at authoring his own prophecy about the end of the world, which he also saw as predicted by his model of the cosmos.[18] Indeed, Newtonian physics was not the stripped-down mechanism he is associated with, but a dynamical cosmos inclined toward apocalypse and dissolution, which required active intervention by God and angels. In sum, it is hard to imagine Newton as a disenchanter insofar as he explicitly rejected the very clockwork universe he is often said to have discovered in favor of an animated world.[19] As John Maynard Keynes famously put it: "Newton was not the first of the age of reason. He was the last of the magicians."[20] But Newton was not in fact the last of his kind.

Francis Bacon and his connection to magic will be treated momentarily; but despite the fact that it was once held that few oppositions were more fundamental than that between science and magic, historians of science have been providing counterevidence for a long time now, as in study after study, individual scientists' and philosophers' alchemical experiments, magical pre-occupations, mystic visions, or grandiose sense of prophetic mission have been trotted out to dramatic effect. In sum, historians have shown that for generations of scientists—from Robert Boyle to Robert Oppenheimer—scientific and magical worlds were often intertwined.[21] At bare minimum, we should know by now that the alchemist and the chemist are often two sides of the same figure, and we should no longer be surprised to discover scientists who aim at producing enchantment and wonder.

I introduced this list of figures to make the basic point that if the magical preoccupations of the establishment have been outside the canon of Western thought (or we might say, outside the text of "modernity"), this is not because the "rationalist" tradition has excluded magicians. Rather, it is because later scholars have consistently occluded this aspect of their patriarchs' individual projects. Biographers from Whiggish historians to postmodernists alike have often suppressed these esoteric undercurrents in order to bury those things that did not fit the received narrative. That the heroes of the "age of reason" were magicians, alchemists, and mystics is an embarrassment to proponents and critics of modernity alike.

Read together, these studies of the occult preoccupations of the establishment also suggest a new problem: If the philosophical elite were regularly drawn to magic and spirits, why have these attitudes vanished from the historiography? Why is magic seemingly both ubiquitous and repressed? This chapter begins to address these questions by looking for the early roots of occult disavowal.

The first part of the chapter focuses on Francis Bacon—perhaps the most famous putative disenchanter—to show how knowledge and magic, enchantment and disenchantment were entangled in his work. In Bacon's writings one can find a telling transformation of the meaning of *superstition* that in retrospect will begin to seem epochal. The second part of the chapter addresses the famous *Encyclopédie*, often described as the culmination of "the French Enlightenment." It shows how the existence of God and the promise of knowledge were mutually constituted in the work and further exposes its own intermingling of magic and disenchantment.

FRANCIS BACON AND THE SCIENCE OF MAGIC

> For the Persian magic, which was the secret literature of their kings, was an application of the contemplations and observations of nature.
>
> FRANCIS BACON, "A Brief Discourse of the Happy Union of the Kingdoms," 1603

Francis Bacon (1561–1626)—often described as "the father of modern science" and the ur-progenitor of "the Enlightenment"—is the single figure most frequently accused of providing a rationale for the domination of nature and hence the disenchantment of the world. At first pass, the charges certainly seem plausible, since even scholars who have never read his work firsthand often associate Francis Bacon with the saying "Knowledge is power" and equate his experimental method with torturing nature.[22] As Ernst Cassirer put it: "Bacon sits as a judge over reality, questioning it as one examines the accused. Not infrequently he says that one must resort to force to obtain the answer desired, that nature must be 'put to the rack.'"[23] In *Dialectic of Enlightenment*, Horkheimer and Adorno begin with Bacon as the key figure in their diagnosis of enlightenment and its failings, arguing that:

> Bacon well understood the scientific temper which was to come after him. The "happy match" between human understanding and the nature of things that he envisaged is a patriarchal one: the mind, conquering superstition, is to rule over *disenchanted nature*. Knowledge, which is power, knows no limits, either in its enslavement of creation or in its deference to worldly masters.[24]

For the Frankfurt School, Francis Bacon exemplified all that was wrong with science and instrumental rationality. Later scholars have often been unable to resist putting Michel Foucault and Bacon in dialogue, often in such a way as to suggest that Foucault's analysis of knowledge-power (*le savoir-pouvoir*) is basically a repudiation or inversion of a Baconian knowledge-as-power ideology that set European thought down dangerous paths.[25] Two influential accounts of the despiritualization of nature, William Leiss's *Domination of Nature* (1972), and Carolyn Merchant's *The Death of Nature* (1980), also lay their charges at Bacon's feet—a verdict that has been echoed by more recent scholars.[26] It might be tempting, therefore, to see Francis Bacon as the single most important architect of disenchantment.

Nevertheless, we now know that Francis Bacon saw himself as an alchemist with a prophetic mission to recover the lost knowledge of Adam in order to prepare man for an immanent apocalypse.[27] In his writings, Bacon drew centrally on occult texts in the formation of his intellectual project, and he took as given various aspects of the magic described by avowed magicians such as Cornelius Agrippa, as can be seen in Bacon's description of sympathies or correspondences, the importance of judicial astronomy, and even the power of the evil eye, not to mention his attempt to induce the transmutation of metals.[28] It is thus easy to establish Bacon's undertaking in the continuity of esotericism.

Faced with these contradictory readings, Francis Bacon might seem to epitomize the paradox of a magician of disenchantment. In what follows, I explore Bacon's conception of magic and to expose the seeds of the logics of occult disavowal. This in turn should give us a sense of where enchantment and disenchantment turn into each other.

*

Francis Bacon was so complementary to magic that nearly all his biographers have been forced to address the issue, although they normally frame it as part of a transition from superstition to science. Paolo Rossi, *Francesco Bacone: Dalla magia alla scienza* (Francis Bacon: From magic to science, 1957) is celebrated for showcasing the primacy of Bacon's alchemical interests, but suggests that trajectory with its very title. This characterization is partially right insofar as Bacon did attempt to purge superstition and the diabolical, but I will argue that his aim was neither modern science nor disenchantment, but purified magic.[29]

Critically, Bacon described his famous experimental method—considered by some to be the foundation of modern science—explicitly in terms of *magic*. As he put it in *De Dignitate et Augmentis Scientiarum* (The dignity and advancement of learning, 1623): "Magic aims to recall natural philosophy from a miscellany of speculation to a greatness of works," which was exactly what he was trying to do with his own project.[30] Bacon further defined magic "as the science which applies the knowledge of hidden forms to the production of wonderful operations; and by uniting (as they say) actives with passives displays the wonderful works of nature."[31] Magic was a pragmatic, or instrumentalist, form of natural philosophy of exactly the sort Bacon saw as missing from scholasticism.

Bacon did not just want to enchant natural philosophy; he also aimed to improve magic. As he argued in *De augmentis*, "I must here stipulate that magic, which has long been used in a bad sense, be again restored to its ancient and honorable meaning. For among the Persians magic was taken for a sublime wisdom, and the knowledge of the universal harmony of things (Lt. *scientia consensuum rerum universalium*)."[32] Bacon thought the crucial problems with magic were its tendancy toward secrecy and its presumption of the hubris of individual genius. Magic could not make real progress because magicians resisted collaboration and cloaked their insights in obscure jargon. Accordingly Bacon worked not to eliminate magic, but to "restore it"—opening up magic; stripping away secrecy, falsehoods, and obscurantism; and subjecting it to public scrutiny. In total, what we now call Baconian science was intended to be public *anti-esoteric* or *anti-occult* magic. To see him as a straightforward disenchanter is flat-out wrong, as Bacon wanted more people to have magic, not fewer.

*

By the same token, Bacon's epistemology has been popularly misunderstood. He never said "Knowledge is power,"—at least, not in the sense that everyone from Cassirer to Adorno understands him to have used the phrase.[33] The Latin expression *scientia potestas est* does occur in *Sacred Meditations* (*Meditationes Sacrae*, 1597), but it is in the middle of a discussion of various heresies.[34] In context, Bacon is navigating a position between those who think that God is the author of evil and those who think that God is powerless. When the expression appears it is a reference to *divine* power and knowledge.[35] The phrase is excerpted from a larger clause that means something different. Indeed, the full phrase *nam et ipsa scientia potestas est* was translated the following year by either Bacon or one of his contemporaries into English as "for knowledge it selfe [*sic*] is a power whereby He [God] knoweth."[36] Our modern version of the slogan should therefore not be "Knowledge is power" but "*God's power is knowledge*." This theological statement is not a praise of instrumental rationality, but an expression of divine potency and by implication human finitude.

Bacon's conception of knowledge was predicated on human fallibility, made worse by a universe he described as a vast dark labyrinth, full of blind alleys, hidden passages, and intricate convolutions.[37] Further obscuring things was the postlapsarian condition of the human mind, which was imperfect and at best a distorting mirror of an already deceptive world.[38] Adorno and company would seem to have gotten Bacon's "happy match" between mind and world exactly wrong. Instead, Bacon argued that because the human mind was profoundly defective and the world fundamentally enigmatic, the best a person could hope for was a fragmentary form of knowledge, and even then, this was only possible by means of faith in God.

This is important because excavating the Christian (and in particular, Protestant) mission behind Bacon's scientific magic is key to understanding the roots of occult disavowal. The thing that made magic unpalatable to many of Bacon's contemporaries was its association with "superstition" and hence both Catholicism and the devil. To explain this bundle of concepts, we have to retrieve the history of the term superstition.

For much of European history, the presumed opposite of religion (Lt. *religio*) was superstition (Lt. *superstitio*).[39] For example, in *Summa Theologica* (1265–74), Thomas Aquinas opposed religion to superstition, which he understood as the practice of offering "divine worship either to whom it ought not, or in a manner it ought not."[40] For Aquinas, religion as true worship gains coherence as a category only by excluding false modes of worship (superstitions). The definition of both is built into the structure of their opposition.

By the sixteenth century, "superstition" referred primarily to misdirected worship and the powers that the devil granted unscrupulous people. By way of example, in *Reprouación* [*sic*] *de las supersticiones y hechizerías* [*sic*] (1530),

Pedro Ciruelo, a member of the Spanish Inquisition, argued: "All types of superstitions (*supersticiones*) come from evil spirits. . . . The devil has discovered and taught men all superstitions."[41] Although the archetypal superstition was diabolically inspired pagan idolatry, in the context of the famous European persecution of witches launched in the fifteenth century, "witchcraft" was itself a superstition—not because it did not work, but because witches were confused about the source of their power.

In the hands of the Protestant reformers, "superstitious" was often deployed as a near synonym to "Catholic."[42] But by using this language, Protestant theologians were not disenchanting Catholicism—if anything, they were linking the Papacy to paganism and witchcraft. Indeed, Luther titled one of his later works "Against the Papacy at Rome, Founded by the Devil" (*Wider das Papsttum zu Rom, vom Teufel gestiftet*, 1545).[43] Lest the reader think this is mere metaphor, one might note that in his commentary on Galatians (1535), Luther states explicitly, "For it is undeniable that the devil lives, yes, rules, in all the world. Therefore witchcraft and sorcery are works of the devil, by which he not only injures people but sometimes, with God's permission, destroys them."[44] He also charged his theological opponents with being literally inspired by the devil.[45] Statements of this sort were not confined to Luther but can be seen in the language of many of the reformers.[46] Hence, one of the principal rhetorical innovations of the period was the transposition of demonological discourse about witches and heretics onto the Roman Church itself. In a nutshell, one might describe the Protestant Reformation (contra-Weber) as producing a super-enchantment of Europe by making the Catholic Church seem both pagan and magical.[47]

In Bacon's writings, he too used "superstition" as a code for Catholics and pagans, and also to indicate the doppelgänger of religion.[48] As he put it in *Essayes or Counsels, Civill and Morall* (1625), "Superstition, without a veil is a deformed thing; for as it addeth deformity to an ape to be so like a man, so the similitude of superstition to religion makes it all the more deformed."[49] Thus paraphrased, religion and superstition resemble each other so much that it is uncanny. In this Bacon is following a long history of accepted usage. But he also used *superstition* in an unusual way: to describe a kind of epistemological idolatry. In the early uncompleted sketch for his natural philosophy, *Valerius Terminus* (ca. 1603), he cautioned against "the inherent and profound errors and superstitions in the nature of the mind, and of the four sorts of Idols or false appearances that offer themselves to the understanding in the inquisition of knowledge."[50]

Bacon also discussed mental idols (of the tribe, cave, marketplace, and theater) in one of the most famous sections of *Novum Organum* (The new organon, 1620), where he uses the scriptural language of idolatry to talk about general errors of thought.[51] With a host of theological predecessors, Bacon argued that natural philosophy, like the Puritans, smashes idols; however, Bacon had not fully replaced the older meaning of idolatry and indeed elsewhere evoked the worship of Neptune as an example of an "Idol of the Tribe."[52] Hence, iconoclasm was working in both theological and philosophical registers and in so doing fortified Bacon's Christian mission as well as his philosophical enterprise.

Strikingly, Bacon's use of the term *superstition* involves a similar doubling of registers. Superstitions are not just types of false worship for Bacon, but they are also a type of intellectual error involving mistakes about causality.[53] Yet, the exemplars of this definition continue to be the same sort of paganism or idolatry that were the focus of older usage of the term. It is telling that Bacon explicitly stated that superstitions resemble the faulty thinking of the pagan Greeks who could not recognize a natural explanation of thunder because they were convinced that the lightning appeared at the summons of the gods.[54] Although Bacon may not have been the first to do so, the important thing is that he makes "superstition" the direct opposite and obstacle of not only *religion*, but also natural philosophy, stating: "Nor should we fail to mention that in every age natural philosophy has had a troublesome and difficult adversary, namely superstition."[55] While it would be an anachronism to presume a hard division between theology and natural philosophy, I want to emphasize that Bacon was using "superstition" in a distinctive way.

This is key because a launching point for the current project is the observation that a crucial moment in the eighteenth century is an incomplete shift in the oppositional structure of a religion-superstition binary to a science-superstition binary. In Bacon's day, an attack on "superstition" was part of an attempt to de-demonize, or we might say "Protestantize," magic. Later, when Bacon was retroactively transformed into the natural philosopher, and then scientist par excellence, the opposition between religion and superstition was ultimately transposed into an opposition between science and superstition. But again, obstacles to science and obstacles to faith were one and the same. Scientists inherited the theologians' list of superstitions, and indeed, both groups often attacked the same paradigmatic superstitions, such as astrology, magic, and spirits.

While Bacon was describing superstition as a kind of false belief, he was not trying to banish it completely. He concluded his description of superstition in the essay cited above by noting: "There is a superstition in avoiding superstition. . . . The good [should] be not taken away with the bad."[56] In *Novum Organum*, Bacon is even more explicit:

> Lastly, matters of *superstition* and *magic* (in the common acceptation of the word) must not be entirely omitted. For although such things lie buried deep beneath a mass of falsehood and fable, yet they should be looked into a little; for it may be that in some of them some natural operation lies at the bottom; as in fascination, strengthening of the imagination, sympathy of things at a distance, transmission of impressions from spirit to spirit no less than from body to body, and the like.[57]

Bacon was appropriating the conceptual structures that had previously been understood as "magic," and purifying them in order to enchant what would become science. In other words, the enterprise of Bacon's distinctive version of natural philosophy is grounded in an anti-superstitious magic, or we might say, rational magic.

Bacon is following a long line of European magicians who worked to excise the demonic from magic in order to make magic less heretical. The most important of these was probably Heinrich Cornelius Agrippa von Nettesheim, whose *De occulta philosophia libri tres* (Three books of occult philosophy, 1533) set the gold standard for spellbooks, even as Agrippa criticized the superstitions of demonic magic. To be sure, his motivating assumption was that demons were real and dangerous. From Bacon's reputation you might think that the difference between the two men is that Bacon did not believe in animating spirits. But this would be wrong.

The enterprise Bacon sought to conjure into being was not cold mechanism, but an approach appropriate to a vibrant and spiritually energized nature. Indeed, he described a world completely enlivened by spirits with their own appetites.[58] The Baconian project was not an attempt to strip the world of animating forces. In sum, Bacon cannot be the intentional author of the despiritualization of nature.

The further problem is that while many of the quotes attributed to Bacon are false attributions, in one respect his critics are right, because he discussed subduing nature and putting "her" in bonds.[59] The references are infrequent and it is always possible to argue that they do not represent his mature thought, but they are there.[60] I am not interested in debating which moralizing tone (praise or blame) to extend to Bacon's work. I don't think being a magician is necessarily redemptive, just as I don't think being a disenchanter necessarily makes one a hero. The key point is that the critics of Bacon who see him as despiritualizing and torturing nature cannot be right about both. Nature can only be tortured if it is alive. Bacon cannot be a disenchanting mechanist and at the same time engage in vexing a vibrant nature.

THE *PHILOSOPHES* AND THE SCIENCE OF GOOD AND EVIL SPIRITS

For some years, the spirit of philosophy, while rejecting devout theologizing, has not opposed otherworldly knowledge.

MARIE-DANIEL BOURRÉE DE CORBERON, *Journal*, 1776

Superstition is more offensive to God than atheism.

DENIS DIDEROT, *Pensées philosophiques*, 1746

In 1751, Denis Diderot and Jean le Rond d'Alembert commenced the publication of their great work, the *Encyclopédie; ou, Dictionnaire raisonné des sciences, des arts et des métiers*, whose aim was the linking together of all human knowledge.[61] In their first volume, Diderot and d'Alembert provided the reader with their vision of the division of the world, which they represented in the form of a great systematic taxonomy, or grand tree, of knowledge (*Système Figuré des Connaissances Humaines*). Significant for our purposes is the location of religion in this system. While Diderot and d'Alembert were inspired by the map of human learning articulated by Francis Bacon, the *philosophes* radically altered the place of "religion" in their conceptual hierarchy.[62] For Bacon, religion was located in an autonomous sphere of revelation; the *philosophes*, by contrast, located religion within the realm of reason more generally and philosophy more specifically.[63] This structure places the study of religion in the domain of philosophical or scientific inquiry and outside of ecclesiastic authority, but it still constitutes itself around an idea of the divine.

More specifically, the *Système Figuré* imagines the study of religion as the focus of a "Divine Science" or "Science of God" (*Science de Dieu*). Despite the later infamy accorded to "godless" *philosophes*, their system actually includes an important role for comparative theology. Furthermore, for all their attacks on priests, according to the *philosophes*, the Supreme Being is a philosophically demonstrable truth. A rational religion, such as the Cult of the Supreme Being (*Culte de l'Être suprême*), is therefore implied by the whole project.[64] This is worth underscoring because, as will be shown in the next chapter, the *philosophes* quickly garnered a false reputation not for deism (which would be fair), but for virulent atheism, which has proved hard to shake.

Crucially, the *Système Figuré* further subdivides the Science of God into two asymmetrical branches: Natural and Revealed Theology (*Théologie Naturelle et Révélée*), on the one hand, and the Science of Good and Evil Spirits (*Science des Esprits Bien et Malfaisans*) on the other. Lest we think by "spirits" Diderot and company meant something like psychology, know that this last entry is further split into "divination" and "black magic" (*Magie Noire*).[65] For comparison, this means that magic occupies a position roughly comparable to "geology" in its scale and importance in the chart that defines the project of the *philosophes*. There is no indication that magic is any less real or legitimate.

This poses a problem for theorists who believe that Diderot and company lived in age that was already disenchanted. For instance, it is often assumed that the *philosophes* lived after the end of the witch trials in Europe.[66] But even this latter claim is mistaken; witches were legally executed in Western Europe as late as 1782.[67] Even in France, a priest named Bertrand Guillaudot was burned as a witch by the government of Dijon in 1742, and his confession led toward the arrest and trial of twenty-nine accomplices. Although most of these were let off with fines, four were executed in 1745.[68] This was only five years before Diderot published the first prospectus for the *Encyclopédie* (1750). Regardless of its legal status, belief in magic and witchcraft was still widespread in France and would remain so long after Diderot was gone.[69] Hence, the appearance of magic in the prospectus to the *Encyclopédie* might suggest that rather than working toward disenchantment, the *philosophes* were promoting their own magical project.

Before I get carried away, however, you should know that in the very moment that the Science of Spirits is being generated, it is occluded. When one reads the actual entries in the *Encyclopédie*, the Science of Spirits is interpreted not as a way to better understand God, but as a rotten branch of the tree of knowledge.[70] It has become a dead end, not worth studying, a superstition. Thus, while the Science of Spirits might appear to be a legitimate domain of knowledge, it is instead classified as an irrational approach to a subject that is viewed as essentially rational.[71]

In this section I want to explain the appearance and disappearance of the Science of Spirits in the *Encyclopédie*, taking us a step closer to undoing the myth of "the Enlightenment" and exposing a further wrinkle in the history of the logics of occult disavowal. To foreshadow, in addition to inheriting Francis Bacon's taxonomy of the disciplines, the *philosophes* also drew on his discourse against superstition. The further complexity is that in doing so they also produced a counterposition from which they too could be attacked.

*

The first thing to note is that *superstition* is a key term not only in the *Ency-clopédie* but also for the whole enlightenment movement, for what it believed it was overcoming. After all, as cited above, Diderot attacked superstition; Voltaire too argued that "superstition sets the world on fire; philosophy puts out the flames."[72] Similar sentiments were echoed by other *philosophes*, such as Jean Castilhon, who dedicated a whole book to the subject (*Essay sur les er-reurs et les superstitions*, 1765).[73] Even Immanuel Kant in *Kritik der Urteilskraft* (1790; *Critique of the Power of Judgment*) would state explicitly: "Liberation from superstition (*Aberglauben*) is called enlightenment."[74] This is important because insofar as Adorno and Horkheimer's *Dialectic of Enlightenment* is meant to capture the project of the *philosophes* (and this is debatable), it would seem that the dialectic offered by Diderot and company was not enlightenment versus myth, but enlightenment versus superstition.

The focus of the campaign against "superstition" can be seen in the *En-cyclopédie* entry on the subject written by Louis de Jaucourt, which states: "Superstition is a certain kind of enchantment or magical power, that fear exercises on our soul; unhappy daughter of the imagination, it assaults the imagination with specters, dreams, and visions, it is [superstition], that ac-cording to [Francis] Bacon, has forged idols for the vulgar, invisible spirits, fortunate and unfortunate days, irresistible bonds of love and hate."[75] The reference to Francis Bacon establishes his place in the *philosophes'* genealogy of "superstition." Furthermore, as with Bacon, superstition functions first and foremost as a category of intellectual error and overabundant imagination. Yet, as the quote above illustrates, the *Encyclopédie*'s main examples of superstition might just as well have come from the period's theologians.[76] It would seem the main superstition the *philosophes* opposed was belief in the demonic.[77] This is because, like Bacon, they had inherited a theological conception of "super-stition" understood primarily in terms of paganism, idolatry, and magic. Vol-taire said as much in his philosophical dictionary: "Superstition [was] born in Paganism."[78] Indeed, contemporary scholar Wouter Hanegraaff has argued that "the basic error the Enlightenment ideologues tried to remove from Chris-tian culture *was* paganism," which they merely redefined from worshiping demonic spirits to believing that such things exist.[79]

I think this argument is mostly right, but it does not fully explain why the "Science of Good and Evil Spirits" appeared in the first place. Our first clue is the disproportionately long *Encyclopédie* entry by Diderot on a group called the *théosophes* (theosophists) who are associated with the problematic spiritual science.[80] For the nonspecialist, "theosophists" might suggest the Theosophical Society founded in New York in 1875 (discussed in chapter 4). But Diderot has in mind earlier Christian *théosophes*. He lists Paracelsus, Valentin Weigel, Robert Fludd, Jakob Böhme, Jan Baptista van Helmont, and Pierre Poiret.[81] For our purposes, the two important members of this list are Paracelsus and Böhme.

The Swiss-German physician Paracelsus (Philippus Aureolus Theophrastus Bombastus von Hohenheim, 1493–1541) is mostly remembered for his contributions to alchemy. His project was rooted in a direct assault on the Greek Galenic model of the humors that was central to European medical thought in the period. Paracelsus aimed to banish this "pagan" medicine and replace it with a practical Christian natural philosophy, based on recovering signs that God had hidden in the natural world.[82] Moreover, Paracelsus described nature as vibrantly alive with hidden spirits, and part of his call for revitalizing medicine was that it needed to recover lost magic.[83] The historian Charles Webster has argued that the first major conflict of the scientific revolution was between Paracelsus and Galen, not Copernicus and Ptolemy.[84] Leaving aside the usefulness of the scientific revolution as a periodization, if one were to grant Paracelsus pride of place, it would invert many of the established narratives about that scientific revolution, because we would have to make Christianization and enchantment central to that epoch.

For Diderot, Paracelsus is the principal *théosophe*, but the next most significant theosophist was probably the Lutheran mystic Jakob Böhme (also written Boehme, ca. 1575–1624).[85] Böhme, a self-educated shoemaker from the German-speaking town of Görlitz, claimed to have received a mystical vision around 1600 in which God showed him the key to all creation.[86] In his subsequent writings, Böhme elaborated on a Paracelsian idea of divine signatures and attempted to discover a hidden revelation, albeit one that was more theological than chemical. Significantly, Böhme distinguished a positive and divine "magic" (*Magia*) from a negative "sorcery" (*Zauber*).[87] He also rooted this divine magic in the power of the will, combined with imagination to work literal wonders.[88] This is relevant because Böhme de-ritualized magic and gave magical power roots in something very like faith. Böhme is important for our purposes because his theology came to be known—perhaps in spite of his intentions—as "theosophy," which later thinkers would present as a mystical, but nevertheless Christian, alternative to various forms of religious orthodoxy.[89]

In the *Encyclopédie*, Diderot described the *théosophes* in general terms as anti-*philosophes*, who detest philosophy and the "empire of reason" and who are dedicated to imagination instead of rationality, contending: "[The théosophes] corrupted Theology, obscured Philosophy and took advantage of their chemical knowledge. . . . There are still some théosophes among us . . . who have taken a violent dislike to Philosophy and to Philosophes and who would succeed in extinguishing among us the spirit of discovery and of research and plunging us again into barbarism."[90] Diderot went on to argue that these mystics pursue the manipulation of the world through magic and search for the "hidden" principles of God and Nature; interesting enough, the same principles pursued by *philosophes*, but through the wrong mode of "false" mystical union rather than rational speculation.[91] Diderot was effectively not only rejecting the magical manipulation of spirits, but also discarding *unio mystica*, or the inward looking experience of God, as a false path. The possibility of a world that is itself fundamentally outside of rational comprehension is a threat to the whole philosophical enterprise. We can see why the *théosophes* might have been unappealing to the *philosophes*.

For all his critique of theosophy as such, the *Encyclopédie* suggests a markedly different attitude toward Paracelsus, and this attitude points toward a similar ambiguity in the whole project. In the "theosophy" article, Diderot for the most part spared Paracelsus from criticism and focused his attack Böhme and the others.[92] But this is not all. Diderot also wrote positively about Paracelsus in other places in the work. For example, in a strange footnote to his entry on "The Academy of Architecture," Diderot remarked: "Paracelsus said that he had studied in neither Paris, nor Rome, nor in Toulouse, or in any academy. That he had no other university but that of Nature in which God displays his wisdom, his power and his glory, in such a way that they can be sensed by those who study them. It is to Nature, he added, that I owe my being, and what truth there is in my writings."[93] This digression basically praising Paracelsus might seem out of place, but it is not the only entry that demonstrates a familiarity with alchemical or magical sources, nor are those sources always treated with derision.[94] For instance, in the *Encyclopédie* entry on "Chemistry" (*Chymie ou Chimie*), Diderot's friend Gabriel François Venel explicitly called for a "New Paracelsus."[95]

Crucially, as noted above, "magic" appears as a science in the figural system of the *philosophes*; moreover, the anonymous entry on "Magic (*Magie*)" is not completely dismissive, dividing its subject into three subtypes: divine, supernatural, and natural magic.[96] Divine magic is described as a kind of spiritual or charismatic gift bestowed on saints and prophets by God.[97] This entry does not deny the existence of miracles, but suggests a possible cessation of such gifts in the current—perhaps post-apostolic—age, thereby evoking the Protestant debates about the cessation of the charismata.[98]

Supernatural magic is rejected as false basically because it relies on belief in the illusory power of demons.[99] In effect, this is a legacy of an older theology of disenchantment that suggests that only God and not the devil can work miracles.[100] But it is also consistent with the changing legal conception of witchcraft in the period. In the early eighteenth century, many Western European law codes redefined witchcraft as an issue of pretense, fraud, or deception rather than blasphemy or dangerous *maleficia* (as it had been primary understood), but like the changing notions of witches' "superstition," this did not necessarily mean that the law completely denied that witches had powers.[101] Rather, it meant that witches' powers (as those of the devil in general) were increasingly understood as diabolical illusions and only later as delusional.[102] Moreover, the new laws meant that European states could still imprison witches (even if they were less likely to execute them). For instance, the British government continued to enforce the 1735 Witchcraft Act into the twentieth century. After predicting the sinking of a British ship in World War II, the psychic medium Helen Duncan was imprisoned as a witch according to this act in 1944.[103] Let that register for a second.

By pinning supernatural magic to illusory demons, the author of the *Encyclopédie* entry was straddling the line between granting demons deceptive powers and dismissing their existence (even if likely leaning toward the latter). By contrast, "natural magic" is described as the "exhaustive study of nature, the wonderful secrets discovered there in," and praised for "the inestimable benefits which this study has brought to all of humanity in almost all the arts and sciences."[104] This entry seemingly suggests that natural magic was itself a source of the *philosophes'* whole project. Nor was this an isolated reference: a closer look and one can see that "natural magic" appears elsewhere in the *Encyclopédie* in a positive light.[105] This is a problem because in many accounts, natural magic was supposed to be long gone by the eighteenth century.

Since natural magic often used chemicals and crucibles, it has been mistaken for natural philosophy or science by another name, but while some of the *Encyclopédie* entries may suggest this, the *philosophes* did not own the expression "natural magic." Indeed, historians have long characterized the period of the *Encyclopédie* in terms of a shift in reading habits and the proliferation of a cheap literary format known as the *Bibliothèque bleue* (called such because they were originally bound in blue paper).[106] Many of these blue books were spellbooks that described natural magic, and thus give a sense of its meaning.

The contemporary British historian Owen Davies has estimated that in the eighteenth century, tens of thousands of cheap magical grimoires were in public circulation, and the most infamous of these was *Secrets merveilleux de la magie naturelle et cabalistique du Petit Albert* (Marvelous secrets of natural magic and the Kabbalah of Lesser Albert).[107] The Lesser Albert would be hard to mistake for a scientific work. It includes love charms and instructions for making protective talismans. Its most famous recipe describes how to amputate the hand of a hanged criminal and use it to cast a spell of invisibility.[108] This was the most popular work of "natural magic" in the era of the *philosophes*.

To be clear, I am not suggesting that Diderot and the *philosophes* were cutting off the hands of criminals and secretly casting hexes; nor am I saying that the *Encyclopédie* is a spellbook. I am arguing instead that it draws on and repurposes a positively valenced natural magic even as it works to suppress it. Tellingly, Diderot associates "natural magic" with the *théosophes* and in condemning them, attempts to banish the Hermeticism that set the stage for enlightenment. Thus we see how the concept of "natural magic" was a double-edged sword. On one hand, it could suggest that magic is merely a misunderstood natural phenomena, but on the other, it could mean that nature is inherently magical.[109] "Natural magic" is hardly alone in this respect. We will encounter enough terms that function both to disenchant and enchant in different registers that I'd like to use "bimodal concept" as shorthand for these in the future.

To recap, as the taxonomy of the *Encyclopédie* suggests, the *philosophes'* project more broadly imagines its own antithesis, which it understands as a kind of mystical science of spirits.[110] In other places, the movement draws on aspects of this very same science, even positing problems that only spirits seem to solve.[111] This should not be a total surprise, because the *Encyclopédie* represents a diverse group of thinkers. It is no secret that some encyclopedists were Freemasons, alchemists, and even magicians.[112]

I am mostly interested in the *Encyclopédie* on its own rather than in a particular thinker, but if one had to pick a disenchanter from out of a lineup of encyclopedists, Diderot might seem to fit the charge, as he is known as "the first of the atheists."[113] Nevertheless, Diderot mentioned studying with a committed alchemist in his youth, and some scholars have seen in his project a semi-concealed Paracelsian cosmology, made more credible by his frequent positive references to Paracelsus.[114] Diderot's writings also demonstrate that he had read the texts of magicians.[115] Moreover, in his philosophical writings, Diderot argued against dead mechanism in favor of a vitalist reading of nature.[116] This is worth emphasizing because if Diderot exiled God, it was in order to enchant nature with powers previously reserved for the divine.[117]

While the *philosophes* sought to amplify the light of reason to banish superstitions, their movement was being mythologized, and not always flatteringly so. Diderot's lifetime already saw active counterprograms and new anti-*philosophes* declaring themselves. Opponents often framed the *philosophes* in terms of mechanism and anti-Catholicism, arguing that Diderot and company were secretly working to spread Protestantism—or even worse, libertinism—and unbelief.[118] But this was not the only narrative on offer.

The former Jesuit Augustin Barruel saw darkness behind the philosophy of light, and in his widely read *Mémoires pour servir à l'histoire du jacobinisme* (1798; *Memoirs Illustrating the History of Jacobinism*), Barruel described a vast conspiracy of philosophers, Freemasons, and occultists aiming to hurl Europe into chaos and anarchy. This was precisely a pagan and enchanted enlightenment, albeit one no less anti-Christian.[119] This was not as farfetched as it seems; many occult thinkers of the period saw themselves as allies of the *philosophes*, and they often argued against the deployment of *evil* spirits, even as they sought to expand human knowledge via an engagement with angels or neutral elemental powers.[120] And while the narrative of an occult enlightenment did not find much traction, as we'll see in the next chapter, it was the charge that the hubris of the age was a conspiracy to kill God that later produced haunting echoes.

CONCLUSION: THE MYTH OF ENLIGHTENMENT

An attentive reader will notice that I have largely avoided a certain phrase—namely, "the Enlightenment." There is a method to my circumlocutions. If like some scholars you imagine a myth is alive only so long as it is being re-elaborated and retold, then it would seem that one of today's most vivacious myths is about a lost age called "the Enlightenment," often pinned to the eighteenth century and characterized as the dawn of modernity. In the last ten years, thousands of books and articles both academic and popular have been published on the subject.[121] But this is a newer phenomenon than one might think. While the late nineteenth-century roots of the Enlightenment as a periodization in German philosophical circles will be discussed in the next chapter, "the Enlightenment" mainly came to occupy a place in the shared memory of the Anglophone world in the 1950s, and began flourishing only in the 1980s as the conflicting critiques and defenses of the Enlightenment and its presumed project proliferated.[122] One can see a similar pattern in France.[123] The Enlightenment leaped into view as a period largely by way of translation or transposition from German scholarship and a struggle over the meaning of the Weimar Republic, and intensified after the Second World War.[124] In sum, the Enlightenment as a self-conscious period and entity is an anachronism.[125]

Similarly, despite a whole crowd of scholars who see themselves as defending the Enlightenment from "postmodern" critique, when we look to those works that are supposed to have originated the critique, it turns out they were mostly talking about something else. Michel Foucault largely used a different periodization in his works. *Folie et Déraison: Histoire de la folie à l'âge classique* (Madness and unreason: History of madness in the classical age, 1961), for example, divides its temporality between an age of reason and a classical age, neither of which fit our sense of the Enlightenment as an epoch.[126] What is more, *Dialectic of Enlightenment* describes "Enlightenment" as a project not a period and it is hard not to read it alongside the Nazis' Reichsministerium für Volksaufklärung und Propaganda (Reich Ministry for Popular Enlightenment and Propaganda). To the extent that Horkheimer and Adorno's critique of enlightenment is focused on historical figures, it seems that Francis Bacon is an important early representative, but they describe a process stretching back into the dawn of historical time and reaching its culmination in positivism. Indeed, some scholars have suggested that all along, the Frankfurt School really had in mind the legacy of the scientific revolution.[127]

Before moving on, I want to briefly historicize this latter periodization. The "scientific revolution" was not a master historiographical epoch before it was popularized by Alexandre Koyré in *Études galiléennes* (1939).[128] The various thinkers who have been retroactively associated with the scientific revolution did not generally think of themselves as pursuing a common undertaking; nor was there a common conception of "science," much less an epochal discovery of a unitary "scientific method." The term *science* entered English and French in the twelfth century as a synonym for "knowledge," but it took an Aristotelian notion of logically demonstrable and certain truth based on reasoning from first principles.[129] It was the opposite of empirical experimentation, which was basically regarded as a probabilistic and dependent on the senses and hence uncertain. But Newton and company did sometimes deploy "science" to give natural philosophy the prestige previously associated with logical certainties.

As Sydney Ross has observed, there was a long period (roughly 1800–1850) when the words *philosophy* and *science* were functionally regarded as synonyms.[130] Over the course of this period, however, physics and chemistry gained increasing prestige for their capacity to be transformed into easily demonstrable technological achievements. Ultimately, in English and French the meaning and status of *philosophy* and *science* basically switched. Physics, rather than philosophy, was seen as the paragon of certain knowledge (despite its roots in probabilistic experimentation), and the human sciences emerged as older humanistic disciplines fractured or attempted to refashion themselves with the natural sciences as a model.

It is worth noting that *Wissenschaft*—what would become the main term for "science" in the German-speaking world—initially had a different trajectory. According to lexicographic sources, like Johann Christoph Adelung's *Grammatisch-kritisches Wörterbuch der hochdeutschen Mundart* (Grammatically critical dictionary of the High German dialect, 1808), during the eighteenth century, *Wissenschaft* referred to "the circumstance in which one knows something or has knowledge or a report of it," but under the influence of the period's philosophical debates, this sense of *Wissenschaft* was displaced by a meaning of the term as referring to "objective truths," such that "there are accordingly as many *Wissenschaften* as there are [ways in which] general truths, or truths of one kind, are examined as grounded in one another."[131] In sum, at the end of the eighteenth century, *Wissenschaften* was generally used in the plural, and instead of a single scientific method, it pointed toward a plurality of truths.

Over the course of the nineteenth century, *Wissenschaft* came to function as a reference to any form of systematic knowledge or academic discipline, even as its meaning came to be shaped by its use as a translation term for the French and English "science." Nevertheless, for a long time, *Wissenschaft* continued to be modeled primarily on philology as the prototypical science.[132] This had the effect of reducing the separation between the natural sciences and the humanities we find in the American academy—the later German bifurcation between *Geisteswissenschaften* (human sciences) and *Naturwissenschaften* (natural sciences) popularized by Wilhelm Dilthey being less strict. But even philology, with its rigorous method of historical-critical textual analysis, could just as easily be positioned in opposition to religion and the authority of revealed texts.[133] Moreover, the language of *Wissenschaft* also more closely tended to ally philosophy with science—a result being that philosophy's gradual separation from theology would come to suggest a problem for "religion."

Over the course of the nineteenth century, English, French, and German academics would come to establish scientific unity via a putative opposition between "science," now fully identified with reason, and "religion," increasingly associated with faith or perspectival belief. These shifts in turn increasingly amplified the authority of a unitary conception of "science" as the source of civilizational progress.[134] If today the term *science* has come to stand for both truth and the crystalized essence of all that is modern, in what follows I will trace the various others against which "science" (or enlightenment) was historically constituted.

*

While the next chapter will excavate the seeds of the myth of the Enlightenment in nineteenth-century German philosophy, here I have worked to reconstruct some figures often associated with "the Enlightenment" and the "scientific revolution" as much as possible in their own context. In so doing, I have made several broad points.

Many of the thinkers we associate with the disenchantment of nature— from Giordano Bruno to Francis Bacon—were themselves magicians. We keep reminding ourselves of this fact because we have internalized a false myth of modernity that makes this a surprise. These magicians of disenchantment point us to the limit of the categories. While classical narratives of modernity can explain magicians in terms of atavistic resistance, they cannot account for magicians who themselves worked to produce disenchantment on one hand and magic on the other. This demonstrates that science and magic could be brought together even if unstably, producing at least temporarily natural magic and supernatural science. Abandoning these oppositions should put us into a position to undo some of the myth of modernity.

Additionally, when we return to the thinkers associated with enlightenment, they do not fit the received narrative, as they have a messy relationship to religion, to spirits, and to esotericism itself. Meanwhile, enlightenment rationalism and scientific empiricism were entangled with theological speculation. This is far from the nineteenth century's myth of a religion-science binary. In this sense, "the Enlightenment" turns out to have challenged the secularization that is attributed to it.

Importantly, following Francis Bacon and the *philosophes'* campaign against superstition, the conceptions of philosophy and then science would come to inherit a Christian (or even Protestant anti-Catholic) polemic predicated on excluding features of an imagined "paganism," which were labeled with terms such as *superstition, magic,* and *myth.*[135] Simply put, the terms *magic* and *superstition* formerly referred to an arbitrary collection of beliefs and practices understood to be diabolical, dangerous, and pagan and only later came to indicate those that were primarily supposed to be ineffective, primitive, or savage. The phrase *the occult* came to function as a repository for the contrasting category to modernity. Not that all were persuaded. Indeed, it might seem there was no real historical rupture between the epoch of magic and the critique of disenchantment.

Another implication of what I have said above is that the very logic that suppressed such things as theosophy and magic made them appealing. It gave these categories a certain allure (as locations for the critique of modernity or enlightenment, or as ways to suture the fissure between religion and science); but it also made their suppression key to pretensions of scientific status. The *philosophes* had conjured their own enemies into being. More important, the putative opposition between magic and science was inherently unstable, and having romanticized both science and religion, one can find repeated attempts to restage their reconciliation. In the era of science, occult sciences proliferated and yet were rarely able to fully shake the aura of an imagined paganism.[136]

To foreshadow my larger argument in the chapters that follow, the human sciences came into being with the shared presumption that "modernity" represented a historical and cultural rupture decisively demarcating contemporary Europe from both its past and its non-European other. Although the human sciences were born alongside interest in the occult and spiritualism, the disavowal of "superstition" became crucial to the formulations of the human sciences that have all tended to take as given—at least, at the moment of their birth—the idea of newness inherent in the modern rupture. In that sense, modernity has functioned as a master paradigm, or episteme.

As we shall see, the founders of the human sciences all tended to take as given the idea that there was something distinctive and original in "modern" European thought and culture, even as they treated the specifics of European history as the blueprint for universal history that all cultures were supposed to follow. Moreover, they inherited the bias that this distinctiveness was to be found in the dismissal of magic, myth, and spirits. There were necessarily vested interests, both colonial and disciplinary, in maintaining this claim to uniqueness. But European culture was not as different in this respect from Africa and Asia as they wanted to believe. They were wrong. Modernity was a false paradigm. It was itself a myth.

CHAPTER THREE

The Myth of Absence

We must have a new mythology, but this mythology must be placed in the services of ideas; it must become a mythology of reason.

Das älteste Systemprogramm des deutschen Idealismus, 1796/97

Modern poetry's inferiority to classical poetry can be summed up in the words: *we have no mythology* .... The new mythology must be formed from the deepest depth of the spirit. It must be the most artificial of all artworks.

FRIEDRICH SCHLEGEL, *Rede über die Mythologie*, 1800

In 1913, the German-Jewish philosopher Franz Rosenzweig made a startling discovery among a collection of papers acquired that year by the Prussian Royal Library in Berlin. He found a strange and fragmentary manifesto written in G. W. F. Hegel's handwriting in about 1796 but, as Rosenzweig went on to argue, expressing sentiments that would have been completely alien to Hegel's thought in that period.[1] Even today, scholars dispute whether the ideas in the fragment should be attributed to Hegel or his comrades F. W. J. Schelling or Friedrich Hölderlin, yet "Das älteste Systemprogramm des deutschen Idealismus" (The oldest systematic program of German Idealism), as Rosenzweig titled it, is generally regarded a momentous landmark in German philosophy.[2] What is important for our purposes is that it suggested a cultural absence or vacuum that could be remedied only by creating a "new mythology," and it was not the only work in the period to make such a demand.

One of the most striking features of German philosophy from the eighteenth and early nineteenth centuries is a passion for mythology. In point of fact, Germany shared this fascination with other parts of Europe.[3] But it is in the writings of German thinkers such as Johann Herder, the Jena Romantics, the Brothers Grimm, Richard Wagner, Friedrich Nietzsche, and later Martin Heidegger that one can find this sentiment elevated to a "longing for myth."[4] While the turn toward myth was largely a retrieval project aimed at "Oriental," Greek, or antique Germanic source material, not all of this impulse was nostalgic.

Starting in the late eighteenth century, a number of German philosophers—from the author of *Systemprogramm* to the Schlegel brothers to Schelling—lobbied for the construction of a new mythology.[5] In *System des transzendentalen Idealismus* (System of transcendental Idealism, 1800), Schelling suggested: "In mythology there was a medium [for science in poetry], before the occurrence of a breach that now seems beyond repair. But how a new mythology could come into being, which is not the [conscious] invention of an individual poet, but of a new generation represented, as it were, in a single poet—this is a problem whose solution can be sought only in the future destinies of the world, and in the unfolding of history."[6]

At first pass, it is hard not to be puzzled at these appeals for a new mythology. They might seem destined to disappoint. While a mythology was believed to give cultures their coherence, in German, as in English, to call something a "myth" (*Mythos*) was already to suggest at least embellishment, if not outright falsehood. A consciously formulated myth would seem to be a paradox. In order to construct a mythology, it might appear you cannot think of it as such. Indeed, scholars who have addressed this subject generally assume that this attempted *mythopoesis* was a complete failure. And almost no one would suggest that this longing for myth had a far-reaching impact, except insofar as it contributed to the contours of German nationalism.[7]

Here is where the consensus is exactly wrong. In the very act of calling for a new myth, German thinkers had actually come up with one. And as I'll argue, it had legs. To be sure, these philosophers were not the myth's sole authors, but they succeeded in giving form to more widely held sentiments. What later scholars have typically missed is that the real myth was not in their proposed solutions: it was not Orientalized reconstructions of Aryan mythology nor Teutonic revivals. Its core was the very idea that, as Schlegel stated, "we have no mythology."

In nutshell, the myth born from this philosophical conjuncture was an anti-myth, a myth that described itself in terms of longing, absence, and mythlessness. Its paradox is that only by being a myth that there was no myth could its status as myth go unnoticed and hence not be demystified. It was a myth in search of myth. Insofar as this myth is still our myth—or at least an animating narrative across many sectors of modern society—their project worked. Let me explain why.

*

There is a narrative that scholars have repeated so often that it can sound like a fable. Although applied to different time periods, from the birth of Greek philosophy to the Renaissance to the scientific revolution to the Enlightenment, its outline is nearly always the same: that at a particular moment the darkness of superstition, myth, or religion began to give way to modern light, exchanging traditional unreason for technology and rationality.[8] When told in a soaring tone, this is a tale of triumph; and when recounted in a different and descending emotional register, it can sound like the inauguration of our tragic alienation from an idealized past. To be clear, the absent myth has two significant components—that we have lost myth and that we need myth—and the celebratory version of this narrative omits the latter theme. But notwithstanding variations in tenor and cast of actors, it is basically the same story, which has been imposed on a range of epochs.

Sometimes—especially in a certain older genre of anthropological theorizing—the turning point is said to have occurred in the movement between vague lost eras or mentalities, such as the supposed shift from mythology to rationality, from metaphysics to positivism, or from the age of magic to the age of science. When presented as grand phase transitions, these old-fashioned social scientific models inadvertently disclose their own "mythic" progenitors in sources, such as Hesiod's five ages (Golden, Silver, Bronze, Heroic, Iron). To be clear, I am not arguing against periodization as such, but rather concerned with the reuse of grand historical story lines. Even when articulated with a greater degree of specificity, it is striking that many different historical ruptures—from the Protestant Reformation to the age of Enlightenment—have all been told according to the same basic narrative blueprint.

It could almost go without saying that these were not the self-narratives of the periods in question; not only were they less likely to be self-conscious of themselves as epochal, but insofar as there were new movements in these eras, they were often presented as returns—for example, the Italian recovery of Plato or the Evangelical emphasis on primitive Christianity. So why do scholars keep recycling the same basic plot to talk about these disparate events?

I argue in this chapter that there is a reason we keep telling essentially the same story about the dawn of rationality. It is not a narrative that originated independently in five different historical periods; rather, it largely came from one. It was formulated mostly in German in the nineteenth century and was then transposed backward into different historical epochs and geographical locations. In effect, it was an interpretation gone in search of something to interpret; or we might say, it was a myth on a quest for an event on which to project its own genesis. The pages that follow will trace some of the seeds of this myth-of-the-end-of-myth.

Tellingly, the absent myth had influential mythemes whose very language points toward their largely poetic character. You likely know one of them as "the death of God," another as "the end of the age of myth"; still another we might call "the eclipse of the gods" or "the de-deification of the world." These motifs are neither identical nor fully distinct, and while today they are associated foremost with different strains of existentialism or postmodernism, they share an origin, and it was much earlier than is often supposed. They have been prolifically retold because they have instigated different responses—a myriad of attempts to replace divine death with religious revivals, occult and artistic movements, and further philosophical gestures. Moreover, like other myths, they are basically narrative tropes that can be extended to different historical instances.

These mythemes have also come down to us in abbreviated form. As I will show, they were originally formulated not in linear teleological terms, but as a spiral, whose final act we have generally overlooked.

*

The previous chapter showed that the thinkers usually associated with "the Enlightenment" and the "scientific revolution" were far from disenchanting materialists. This chapter will trace the *idea* that the *philosophes* and the new scientific mechanism dispelled the divine. It begins from the following observation: many of the most portable formulations of generalized secularization and disenchantment were all articulated in a narrow period of history within a small circle of German philosophers and poets. This is the community and moment that gave us nihilism, the death of God, the end of myth, and the de-spiritualization of the world as characterizations of an age. Moreover, it was the following generation of German thinkers that not only embraced this terminology, but also engaged in some of the first explicit philosophical theorization about "alienation" and "secularization."

The first part of the chapter charts the historical context of late eighteenth-century Germany, locating the origins of what have become disparate tropes in the political context of the period and in a debate within German philosophy about rationality, Spinoza, and the specter of nihilism. The second part of the chapter focuses on the roots of the formulation that will concern us most; namely, "the disenchantment of the world." While that phrase owes its particular place in our cannon to the writings of Max Weber, it is widely asserted that Weber's inspiration was Friedrich Schiller (although this turns out to be only partially correct). This section of the chapter will trace Schiller's particular version of universal history and his famous formulation of the eclipse of the gods (1788). It explains how these themes resonated in the world of early German Romanticism and shows how they did so against a backdrop of interest in theosophy, magic, and spirits. The final section of the chapter returns to the myth of mythless modernity and shows how it moved from philosophy to history in German-speaking circles in the 1860s to 1870s, where it gave shape to the notions of both the Renaissance and the Enlightenment as historical periodizations.

NIHILISM, REVOLUTION, AND THE DEATH OF GOD: F. H. JACOBI AND G. W. F. HEGEL

Nothing frightens man so much, nothing darkens his mind to such a degree, as when God disappears from nature . . . when purpose, wisdom and goodness no longer seem to reign in nature, but only a blind necessity or dumb chance.

FRIEDRICH JACOBI, "Fliegende Blätter," *Minerva*, 1817

Near the end of the nineteenth century, Friedrich Nietzsche memorably described his epoch in apocalyptic terms, stating in 1882: "The greatest recent event—that 'God is dead'; that the belief in the Christian God has become unbelievable—is already starting to cast its first shadow over Europe."[9] Elsewhere in the same text, Nietzsche puts these oft-quoted words in the mouth of a madman: "God is dead! God remains dead! And we have killed him! . . . The holiest and the mightiest thing the world has ever possessed has bled to death under our knives: who will wipe this blood from us? . . . What then are these churches now if not the tombs and sepulchers of God?"[10] Nietzsche is conjuring a divine specter, whose haunting shadow marks the signs of God's absent presence extending over the whole of modernity.

This famous phrase—"God is dead"—might seem to be Nietzsche's single most significant contribution to philosophy, and indeed, it is often characterized as such.[11] But despite what is popularly believed, Nietzsche did not coin this expression. The phrase appears in German much earlier. One can find it in a well-known seventeenth-century hymn, "Ein trauriger Grabgesang" (A mournful dirge, 1641/42) by the Lutheran pastor and poet Johann von Rist, which contains the lines:

God Himself lies dead,
He died on the cross,
And thereby from [His] love for us,
Heaven was won.[12]

This hymn evokes the theology of substitutionary atonement with the generally Protestant tendency to emphasize Christ's sacrifice in terms of forensic
(or penal) substitution—put in plain language, God died for our sins. In these
theological terms, the death of God evokes not the departure of Christianity,
but the divine self-sacrifice that opened the gates to salvation.

The question becomes, how did we get a sociological shorthand for secularization from a theological dirge? The pages that follow will explain. Our
first clue is that not only was Nietzsche a latecomer to this particular phrase,
he was not even the first philosopher to utter it. Our second clue is that the
"death of God" dates not from the end of the nineteenth century, but from
its beginning; and it shares an origin with characterizations of nihilism and
mythlessness.

*

In 1796, the German novelist Jean Paul (Johann Paul Friedrich Richter) published a graphic depiction of a dream in which Christ testifies to God's absence before an ensemble of ghosts, as follows:

> All the dead exclaimed—"Christ, is there no God?" And [Christ] answered
> "There is none!" . . . Christ continued—"I traversed worlds. I ascended into
> suns, and flew along the Milky Way through the wastes of the heavens; but
> there is no God! I descended as far as Being throws its shadow, and gazed
> down into the abyss, and cried aloud—'Father, where art thou?' but I heard
> nothing but the eternal storm which no one rules. . . . And when I looked up
> to the immeasurable world for the Divine Eye, it stared back at me with an
> empty, bottomless socket, and Eternity lay brooding upon chaos . . . Cry on, ye
> discords! Cleave the shadows with your cries; for [God] is not!"[13]

The passage juxtaposes a divine absence with a series of ghostly presences in
ways that anticipates Nietzsche's funerary oration on divine death. But it does
not actually use the pithy phrase "God is dead." For that we have to look to
elsewhere.

In 1831, Hegel gave a series of lectures on the philosophy of religion at the University of Berlin. In one lecture, more than fifty years before Nietzsche's *Die fröhliche Wissenschaft* (1882; *The Gay Science*), Hegel had already stated: "*God died, God is dead*—this is the most dreadful thought, that everything eternal and true does not exist."[14] This was hardly the first occasion he had made a similar pronouncement. Already in *Glauben und Wissen* (1802; *Faith and Knowledge*), Hegel had observed: "The unending grief—that previously existed only historically in culture (*Bildung*) and as an emotional feeling—is where modern religion is based, as it [too] feels that *God Himself is dead.*"[15] Indeed, nearly all Hegel's major works contain some reference to the grief inspired by perceptions of divine death, and variations on the death of God appear as a regular phrase.[16]

Hegel was not alone in poetic laments of this sort. If his 1802 writings were the first appearance of the death of God as philosophy (although perhaps foreshadowed by Richter in 1796), and the birth of "the end of myth" came either from the *Systemprogramm* (1796/97) or Friedrich Schlegel's *Rede über die Mythologie* (Speech on mythology, 1800), then these mythemes nearly coincide.[17] To foreshadow the other themes of interest here, the "eclipse of the gods" is first discussed by Friedrich Schiller in 1788, and "nihilism" (*Nihilismus*) enters philosophical usage in the same period, appearing independently in 1787 and 1799. What was it about this generation of German intellectuals that caused them to produce these influential mythemes? The following will first describe a significant debate in early German philosophical circles about pantheism and nihilism, and go on to deal with the political changes in the period that proved such fertile ground for a critique of enlightenment.

The Pantheism Controversy

Perhaps we will live to see the day when a dispute will arise over the corpse of Spinoza like that between the archangel and Satan over the corpse of Moses.

FRIEDRICH JACOBI, Letter to Moses Mendelssohn, April 26, 1785

The Pantheism Controversy (*Pantheismusstreit*) started in 1783 as a minor fight between two philosophers, Moses Mendelssohn and Friedrich Jacobi, about their recently deceased colleague Gotthold Lessing.[18] Jacobi claimed that in a private conversation shortly before his death Lessing had confessed: "The orthodox concepts of the Deity are not for me; I cannot stomach them. *Hen kai pan!* I know nothing else."[19] This enigmatic Greek phrase, *Hen kai pan* ('Ev καὶ Πᾶν, the One-in-All), made Jacobi think that Lessing was a follower of Spinoza. Why this phrase was a shibboleth among Spinozists is a matter of some dispute.[20] But the following day, Lessing ostensibly confirmed to Jacobi that "there is no other philosophy than the philosophy of Spinoza."[21]

Lessing's confession might sound trivial today, but the debate quickly expanded to include almost all the major German philosophers of the period and sparked successor arguments such as the atheism and materialism controversies.[22] To understand why this issue came to call into question the fate of reason and even belief in God, you need to know what Spinoza evoked in the period.

Contemporary scholar Jonathan Israel has argued that covert Spinozism was the key factor in the "radical enlightenment," giving inspiration to both its secularizing impulse and republican spirit.[23] Given that Spinoza's *Tractatus Theologico-Politicus* (1670; *Theological-Political Treatise*) was read alongside works such as *Traité des trois imposteurs* (ca. 1777; *The Treatise of the Three Imposters*, which basically accused Moses, Jesus, and Mohammad of charlatanism), one can see why an allegiance to Spinoza might therefore have suggested a commitment to upending the established forms of church and state.[24] But it would anachronistic to describe the alarm at Spinoza as resistance to secularism.

Spinoza was portrayed as a heretic, whose philosophy was both polytheistic and atheistic. These contradictory readings flow from different interpretations of Spinoza's slogan *"Deus sive Natura,"* another bimodal concept that could be understood as either divinizing nature or naturalizing God. For a pagan interpretation of the phrase, the German philologist Johann Wachter described a Cabbalist Spinoza deifying (*Vergötterte*) the world and filling it with gods.[25] But the French philosopher Pierre Bayle's reading of Spinoza qua atheism was more influential. For Bayle, not only was Spinoza an atheist, but "Spinozism is only a particular method of explaining a doctrine, which prevails in the [East] Indies."[26] It is striking to see the compulsive need to further Orientalize Spinoza, a figure whose very Jewishness rendered him already "Oriental" in the eyes of many Europeans. But this should be seen alongside Bayle's claim that the core of Asian religion was the contention that "there is nothing to seek, nor anything to pin one's hopes on, except the nothingness and the void that is the first principle of all things."[27] Recast, Buddhists worshipped nothingness and the void. Bayle saw Spinoza as one representative of this vast system of nothing-ism or "atheism" centered in the "Orient." This idea of atheism will take some further explaining.

The term *atheism* (Fr. *athéisme*) had entered modern European languages by way of French only in the mid-sixteenth century as a rehabilitation of the Greek ἄθεος (*átheos*, godless or impious), but initially it was used to refer to any kind of intellectual, moral, or behavioral "ungodliness," from idolatry to deism to homosexuality.[28] As *atheism* gradually stabilized to mean a denial of God, it was primarily understood as a matter of the heart, not the mind.[29] This conception was given scriptural grounding, particularly in Psalm 14:1, "The fool hath said in his heart, There is no God" (KJV). Atheism was not an intellectual position so much as an emotional impulse rooted in a willful denial of divine punishment for one's sins.

Prior to Bayle's day, belief in God was thought to be an inborn trait and the existence of God such an obvious fact that atheism could only be asserted through a kind of bad faith or self-deception motivated by carnal passions. The sane human conscience would not allow God to be denied completely, and it was widely believed that libertine atheists must be either mad or profoundly racked with guilt.[30] To be sure, theologians argued against intellectual positions they saw as atheistic, but terminating a position in atheism was what supposedly rendered that line of thought absurd. It was believed that no one could rationally deny the existence of God because it was such a manifest and inescapable truth.

Although by the eighteenth century some cracks had begun to appear in this consensus, the *philosophes* generally assumed that the pursuit of reason and commonsense empiricism both led toward God. More concretely, Cartesian mechanism and Newtonian physics were both theological projects, and their influential interpreters Nicolas Malebranche and Samuel Clarke, if anything, more strongly emphasized God's omnipotence.[31] Some French intellectuals did believe in the absconding god of deism, and rejected organized religion as an unnecessary intermediary between humanity and the Book of Creation. But for most French *philosophes* and even more easily for their German Protestant cousins, rationality left God and morality intact.

It was this basic contention that Jacobi challenged in the Pantheism Controversy.[32] Moreover, he did so at a moment when the very concept of enlightenment was being formulated. This is important because even after the Pantheism Controversy was forgotten, many of its debates were basically transposed onto accounts of "the Enlightenment." Indeed, if we wanted to reconstruct the seeds of the genealogy of the myth of the Enlightenment, we might look to the beginning of the 1780s, when the term *Aufklärung* (enlightenment) came to take on a new meaning in German academic circles to describe something that was happening in France.[33] The conversation about enlightenment was instigated in part by a footnote that appeared in an essay in the *Berlinische Monatsschrift* in 1783. In the midst of condemning civil wedding ceremonies, the German theologian Johann Friedrich Zöllner asked a fateful semi-rhetorical question: "What is enlightenment (*Aufklärung*)?" and thus launched a controversy about the term's meaning and importance.[34] Kant's response is well known today, but Kant's essay was hardly representative and it was largely ignored until the late nineteenth century.[35] Zöllner's prompt solicited varied explanations of "enlightenment" over the ensuing decade, covering everything from popular moral instruction to emotional awakening. Indeed reactions were so diverse that by 1790, an anonymous contributor to the *Deutsche Monatsschrift* complained that *Aufklärung* had no particular meaning and represented nothing more than a free-for-all of idiosyncratic definitions.[36]

As an intervention in this debate about the meaning of enlightenment, the Pantheism Controversy had lasting implications. In the first case, the charge that a well-respected enlightener like Lessing had come under the sway of Spinoza was troubling because it amplified fears of philosophical crypto-Spinozists who were only outwardly pious. But most important, Jacobi argued that Lessing's pantheism was not merely a personal predilection, but an inevitable outcome of Lessing's allegiance to enlightenment. Put differently, while the *philosophes* thought they could embrace both reason and deism, Jacobi suggested that their whole project inevitably terminated in pantheism and hence fatalism and atheism. Accordingly, as Frederick Beiser and Hermann Timm have argued, the Pantheism Controversy disrupted the assumption that one could work from reason to God.[37] It suggested that instead of an identification between God and logos, reason was fundamentally anti-theological.

To make sense of this, we have to recognize that Jacobi understood Spinoza primarily as the foremost systematic advocate of the principle of sufficient reason: that nothing happens without a reason or cause—a position that the scholastics characterized as *Ex nihilo nihil fit* (Nothing comes from nothing).[38] At first glance, this principle might suggest merely that the world is rational and nothing happens without a reason. But Jacobi understood the principle of sufficient reason in terms of *proximate* or *mechanical* causation, stating: "We conceive of a thing if we can derive it from its proximate causes, or if we can grasp its immediate conditions in a series what we grasp or derive in this manner gives us a mechanical connection."[39] This was a problem for Jacobi because if every event happened due to an earlier determinate cause, there was no longer any room for freedom (and hence no room for ethics) or miracles (hence no room for God). That is, for Jacobi, if natural philosophy is right and everything has a proximate cause, then the universe is deterministic, and we are nothing but clockwork automatons imprisoned in a mechanical cosmos.

Jacobi put the term *nihilism* (*Nihilismus*) into common philosophical usage to describe this philosophy of *Ex nihilo nihil fit.*[40] To interpolate, nihilism
was synonymous with a species of naturalistic rationalism that reduced everything to mechanical causation, evacuating the world of God and meaning.[41]
But Jacobi had one more trick up his sleeve, because in his first use of the term
nihilism in print (*Jacobi an Fichte*, 1799), he attacked not just materialism, but
also Johann Gottlieb Fichte's idealism.[42] Jacobi's argument was that Fichte
had reduced everything to consciousness and subjectivity. Furthermore having
abandoned Kant's thing-in-itself, Fichte had left no room for God or meaning external to consciousness. If all was human ego, nothing was God. Taken
together, Jacobi argued that these normally opposite philosophical positions
of empiricism, rationalism, and idealism all necessarily terminated in nihilism
because they all presumed reason could wholly apprehend the world.[43]

The Pantheism and successor controversies inspired heated discussions
across the German philosophical world, and eventually Jacobi succeeded in
making "nihilism" the philosophical problem par excellence. Nihilism had
come to mean more than emotional atheism, but rather robust materialism or
even robust idealism that reduced the world to either human subjects or sheer
mechanical causation. Indeed, in Jacobi's eyes, nihilism was the natural crys-
tallization point for philosophy and was unavoidable as long as one venerated
the power of reason. If one could not reason one's way out of reason, then it
seemed philosophy would be forced to devour itself from within. But instead
of causing his peers to reaffirm their faith in God and religion, Jacobi's critique
had produced unintended consequences.

First and foremost, Jacobi had introduced new doubts into the heart of
philosophy. Generations of European intellectuals had effectively taken for
granted that they had Christian or at the very least deistic conversation part-
ners. Bayle and company's reevaluation of China had produced the possibility
of nontheistic interlocutors, but almost nobody thought they were writing philosophy for an Asian audience. Had they done so, it would have been with the
assumption that they were writing to inferiors. To be sure, there had been a few
outspoken atheists before Jacobi charged Lessing and then Fichte with atheism (especially in the circle around Baron d'Holbach), but the general assumption was that they were few in number and easy to refute. Yet, following Jacobi,
it seemed to many that atheism could not be rationally disproven because
an ethical and philosophical nihilism emerged from the use of reason itself.
Granting this position seemingly placed Jacobi's contemporaries between the
devil and the deep blue sea: either reject reason and enlightenment, or champion atheism and immorality.

One potential way out was to embrace Kant's critical philosophy, which supposedly located faith and reason in their respective domains.[44] But an alternate possibility was a positively valenced pantheism. Jacobi had inadvertently popularized the very position he attacked. In the midst of these debates, Johann Herder published *Gott: Einige Gespräche über Spinozas System* (God: Some discussions of Spinoza's system, 1787), which rebutted the charge that Spinoza was a mechanist and insisted that Spinoza's God was a mind animating the universe with forces.[45] Jacobi had made too good of a case that pantheism was the natural outcome of philosophy. Thus, in Germany at least, a whole crop of philosophers—including Goethe, Hegel, Heinrich Heine, Herder, Hölderlin, Novalis, Schelling, Schiller, and Schlegel—began to explore Spinoza or pantheism, and the expression *Hen kai pan* often appeared as a common motto among them.[46]

For our purposes, the most important thing about the pantheism dispute is that it led to early references to the death of God, and to an increasing sensitivity to the dangers of a mythless or nihilistic age. It was not physics that produced the nihilistic clockwork universe, but philosophy. As noted above, Jacobi himself had made reference to God's disappearance from nature in favor of a world ruled by blind chance. Many of the figures discussed in this chapter—including Hegel, Hölderlin, Jean Paul, Schelling, Schiller, and Schlegel—all were directly influenced by Jacobi or the Pantheism Controversy.[47] Hence, it came to be seen as an earth-shattering episode in the memory of German philosophy.[48] Indeed, political events if anything soon amplified its impact.

*

By way of context, the French Revolution if anything seemed to justify Jacobi's fears, as enlightenment came to evoke less rational Protestantism or enlightened absolutism than regicide. Furthermore, the effects of the French Revolution quickly spilled over into the German political sphere. Readers not overly familiar with the details of German history need to know at least the following thumbnail sketch. When the Revolution happened in France, the Holy Roman Empire was already fragmented into hundreds of small, largely autonomous principalities, bishoprics, and semi-independent city-states. From 1792 until Napoleon's final defeat at Waterloo in 1815, the German states were often at war with France, and for extended periods some states were effectively little more than French vassals. The conflict caused the slow collapse of the Holy Roman Empire, and it finally fell into dissolution in 1806. Along the way, the various German states began devouring each other, a process that the contemporary

German historiography refers to as mediatization (*Mediatisierung*).[49] This was a massive shift. By some counts Germany had about 1,800 distinct political units in 1789, but by 1815 the German Confederation had only 39 members (and by 1871 German was united).[50]

Here is the important point: one of the key features of this historical moment was a literal secularization as German states appropriated property previously belonging to the church. Versions of this happened first in French-occupied territories; but after 1802 it became policy all over the Empire, and the process continued even after the Empire collapsed. Many Catholic universities were suspended, thousands of monasteries were disbanded, and the ecclesiastical territories previously governed by bishops were given over to secular states.[51] Thus when the German philosophers and poets who witnessed these shifts began writing about the death of God, they were making grand themes out of the specifics of their local history.

*

Hegel and Richter were not the only ones to describe divine death. References to the death of God also occur in Heinrich Heine (1835), Bruno Bauer (1841), and Max Stirner (1844), all significantly before Nietzsche put pen to paper.[52] Stirner's version even evokes Nietzsche's famous deicide while blaming it on enlightenment: "When in our days they brought to a victorious finish the work of enlightenment, the vanquishing of God: they did not notice that man has murdered God in order to become now 'sole God on high.'"[53] Taken together, these scattered references to the death of God are still not sociological descriptions of secularization, nor are they sober reflections on de-Christianization; rather, they are modern jeremiads or laments. They indicate more a presence of grief than an absence of religion. Although Heidegger would later imagine a moment in which the Deity is so far gone that even God's departure goes unremarked, the God described here is retreating but pursued.[54]

Strikingly, it was among Hegelians of the 1830s and 1840s that we find the death of God shifting from the terrain of poetical abstraction into some of the earliest theorization about "alienation" (*Entfremdung*) and "secularization" (*Säkularisierung, Verweltlichung*) as general patterns of history.[55] This is less of a surprise when we remember that Marx and Feuerbach were working out their respective theories of alienation in the *Economic and Philosophic Manuscripts of 1844* and *Das Wesen des Christentums* (1841; *The Essence of Christianity*). Moreover, there is good evidence that the first deployment of *secularization* to describe an epochal process of de-Christianization is in the writings of the Christian theosophist and right-Hegelian Richard Rothe, *Die Anfänge der Christlichen Kirche und ihrer Verfassung* (The beginning of the Christian church and its constitution, 1837).[56] The theme of theosophical disenchantment (in a different sense) is discussed in the next chapter. Later, these *Vormärz* writings would seem prophetic in the face of the new political-religious fault lines that emerged in Western Europe following the revolutions of 1848; and even though the Anglophone world largely avoided the impact of those revolutions, the publication of Charles Darwin's *On the Origin of Species* (1859) would come to evoke similar concerns. Still, it is worth underscoring that Rothe and company extrapolated recent German political history into macro-historical trends in ways that continue to be influential today.

Furthermore, the death of God was felt outside the churches as philosophers began to search for secure nontheological foundations for epistemology, morality, and mathematics, while inheriting standards of certainty, ethics, and rational harmony that preserved earlier Christian presuppositions. Restated, divine absence was not merely a problem for orthodox faith, but undergirded academic disciplines that devoted ages to trying to recover lost certainties. If this was secularization, it came at the expense of many endeavors we usually regard as secular. Still, as this section has shown, a small fight between German philosophers catalyzed by the French Revolution was transformed into a poetic characterization of modernity and the nihilism that lurked at its core. But this was not the only fallout from the rejection of mechanism.

In the same period and among the same circle of thinkers, one can find reference to the de-divination of the world and the end of myth. Indeed, from another vantage, it was less the rise of pantheism or the death of the Christian deity that was a problem, but instead a new alienation from a cosmos of dead matter. The following section explores the genesis of that insight.

THE ECLIPSE OF THE GODS: FRIEDRICH SCHILLER

The old world began to decline. . . . The gods vanished with their retinue—Nature stood alone and lifeless. Dry Number and rigid Measure bound her with iron chains.

NOVALIS, *Hymnen an die Nacht*, 1800

Less than a year before his untimely death from tuberculosis at the young age of twenty-eight, the German poet and philosopher Novalis (Friedrich Leopold, Baron von Hardenberg) published his most famous work, *Hymnen an die Nacht* (1800; *Hymns to the Night*). As evidenced in the quote above, these hymns—instead of merely bewailing de-Christianization—mourn de-Paganization. In so doing, they evoke a lost vibrant nature, abandoned by the gods. As Novalis continued: "No longer was the Light the abode of the Gods, and the heavenly token of their presence—they drew over themselves the veil of the Night. The Night became the mighty womb of revelations—into it the Gods went back—and fell asleep."[57]

The gods have left the world and retreated into darkness and slumber. This quasi-pagan lament was not unique, and many of Novalis's contemporaries gave vent to a similar longing. Nor was Novalis merely a poet; his incomplete philosophical writings suggest that he was searching for a solution to a crisis that would have been readily intelligible to many of his fellows.[58] Novalis's proposed solution is considered below, but our primary concern is his diagnosis of calamity in the vanishing (*Verschwinden*) or eclipse of the gods.

The death of the gods seems like only a subtle modification of the more famous "death of God" discussed above, merely the addition of an *s*. It is not surprising that scholars often conflate the two. But while they share a historical origin, I want to show here where the tropes diverged and how dying gods serve as a prototype for the disenchantment myth. To trace the wellspring of this theme, we will turn to Novalis's teacher at the University of Jena, the German philosopher and playwright Friedrich Schiller (1759–1805). The pages that follow are structured around one of his poems, "The Gods of Greece" ("Die Götter Griechenlands," 1788, revised 1800).

Written in 1788, during the height of the pantheism controversy and on the eve of the French Revolution, "The Gods of Greece" is more than merely a lyrical evocation of antiquity or contemporary events. Accordingly, in what follows I read it in three keys: first as universal history, then as theosophy, and finally focusing in on the theme of disenchantment. It might seem strange to give that much weight to a single poem, but many of the thinkers crucial to the history of the disenchantment narrative from Hegel to Frazer to Max Weber to Sigmund Freud to Ludwig Klages, all made reference to "The Gods of Greece" and usually in the context of despiritualization. It is hard to exaggerate the impact that this poem had on future characterizations of modernity, and it is in Schiller's writings more broadly that the eclipse of the gods took its classic shape.

*

"The Gods of Greece" is a long, hundred-line poem. Here is my translation of the key lines from the 1788 version without attempting to preserve rhyme or meter (1800 variation indicated in notes), numbered for later reference:

1. When the poetic art's picturesque shroud[59]
   still delightfully enveloped the truth!
2. The fullness of life flowed through creation,
   and, they felt what will never be felt again.
3. Pressed to Nature's loving bosom,
   they acknowledged her higher nobility.
4. For initiated eyes everything pointed to
   the traces of a god.
5. Where now as our wise men claim, only
   a soulless ball of fire revolves,
6. Then Helios guided his golden chariot
   in silent majesty.

.   .   .   .

7. To enhance One above all,
   the world of gods had to perish.

.   .   .   .

8. Unconscious of the pleasures that she bestows,
   never impressed by her own perfection,
9. Never aware of the forces that guide her,
   never enriched by my own gratefulness,[60]
10. Numb to her artist's glory,
    like the pendulum's dead stroke,
11. Godless Nature,
    slavishly serves the law of gravity!

.   .   .   .

12. When the gods were still human,
    humans were more divine.[61]

*

The first thing you need to know about "The Gods of Greece" is that it is only superficially about Greek culture. To understand why, we have to pierce the veil of German philhellenism. A widely studied aspect of German culture in

Schiller's day was a movement in German classicism (often credited to Johann Joachim Winckelmann), that directed its attention toward Greece rather than Rome. Since at least Eliza Butler's pioneering *The Tyranny of Greece over Germany* (1935), historians have characterized late eighteenth-century Germany in terms of its reverence for Greek culture, a theme that has been explored in multiple monographs.[62] While this is a valuable line of research, there are two crucial points that are easy to overlook amidst the welter of details: first, Germans were far from the only Europeans to romanticize classical Greece in the period; and second, Greece broadly functioned in this discourse as the epitome of primitive naturalism.

In the broadest of strokes, Greece, having been colonized by Rome and then the Ottomans, represented for many Europeans not Athenian urbanity or philosophical sophistication, but an idyllic past that was identified with a lost naturalness. Accordingly, a host of influential European thinkers described the Greeks of antiquity in terms that suggested Rousseau's noble savage.[63] Winckelmann praised both the aesthetics and primitiveness of Greek culture by, for example, comparing Homer's heroes to "swift-footed [American] Indians" (*schnelle Indianer*).[64] In effect, the Greeks were positioned where nineteenth-century anthropology would situate Native American or African "savages" as historical relics, but instead of denigrating the Greeks as backward, the German classicists were celebrating their primitiveness.[65] Moreover, from 1770 to 1832 Greeks were attempting to rebel from the Ottoman Empire, and while not all European classicists supported Greek independence, when they did so, philhellenism functioned as a species of postcolonial critique.[66] Insofar as Germans saw themselves as inheritors of Greek civilization, this was an idealized internal or ancestral primitivism.

We can see this in Schiller's writings. In *Über naive und sentimentalische Dichtung* (On naïve and sentimental poetry, 1795) an influential work of aesthetic theory, Schiller suggest that ancient Greek culture was both close to nature and represented the childhood of humanity.[67] This is our first clue that "The Gods of Greece" is about more than a particular civilization; rather, it explores the primordial condition of humanity, the point of maximal naturalness. It is only about Greece inasmuch as Greece signifies the de-alienated human condition.

Although full of classical allusions, the structuring principle behind "The Gods of Greece" was an interest in universal history that would find formal presentation in Schiller's lectures at Jena the following year.[68] The poem's broader philosophical context is the birth of history itself. In less hyperbolic terms, it is no secret that European conceptions of time underwent epical shifts in the eighteenth and nineteenth centuries. One might think of the gradual displacement of the biblical six-thousand-year chronology in favor of the "dark abyss of time" conditioned by vast geological ages, or the standardization of international timekeeping alongside Greenwich mean time and the marine chronometer. Most important for our current purposes was the novel reflection on the meaning of history itself, often described in terms of "philosophy of history" or "universal history."[69] Under these last headings, philosophers and historians engaged in a concerted effort to discover the universal natural laws that governed the evolution of human history and society.[70] This rise of new universalizing metanarratives served as the precondition for any kind of grand narrative of progress or disenchantment.

"The Gods of Greece" is thus primarily a statement about both the dawn of humanity and the grand architectonics of history. Concretely, "The Gods of Greece" suggests three historical epochs—a golden age of myth (verses 1–6), the advent of Christianity (verse 7), and the rise of natural philosophy (verses 8–11)—not unlike the four ages of the world Schiller described elsewhere.[71] The crucial feature of primitive humanity is not a Hobbesian war-of-all-against-all or the barbarism of "savage superstition," but a unity with nature (see verses 1–4).[72] As Schiller recounted in *Über naive und sentimentalische Dichtung*, "As long as we were mere children of nature, we were happy and complete; we have become free and lost both."[73] Moreover, in the same work Schiller provides a typology of poetry, including the elegy (*Elegie*), a kind of poem rooted in the sadness evoked by lost nature and the passing of a golden age.[74] "The Gods of Greece" portrays the arc of history as an elegy of estrangement from the natural world.

The first transition between ages occurs when monotheism banishes the pagan deities (see verse 7). Another of Schiller's poems, "Die vier Weltalter" (1802; "The Four Ages of the World"), suggests something similar with these lines: "The age of divine fantasy / has vanished (*verschwunden*), never to return. / The gods have fallen from heaven's throne / and the Virgin's Son has been born."[75] There were plenty of historical precedents for this. Famously, Plutarch in *On the Eclipse of the Oracles* (ca. 100 CE) had recorded the expression "The great Pan is dead" as part of a larger attempt to explain the decline of oracles.[76] Late antique and medieval Christian authors had described Greco-Roman gods as demons that could be exorcized, and in that sense killed by Christ and his apostles.[77] But Schiller's elegiac tone is important. Instead of celebrating the Christian triumph over paganism or reveling in the technological mastery of the environment, it would seem that Christianity is itself the cause of estrangement from nature. In the place of the death of God, we have Christ as executioner.

We see a similar sentiment in Novalis, who also described Christianity as having killed pagan deities:

> Where there are no gods, ghosts reign, and the actual period of origin of Euro-pean ghosts, which also almost completely explains their shape, is the period of transition from the doctrine of the Greek gods (*griechischen Götterlehre*) to Christianity.[78]

For Novalis, the vestigial dead gods of paganism are literally haunting Europe. Together, these are our first clues that in the hands of Christian, or even post-Christian, thinkers to announce the death of a "pagan" deity has a different theological force from announcing the death of God as such. Indeed, Schiller's contemporaries saw "The Gods of Greece" as being unequivocally anti-Christian.[79] But in most respects, this was an unfair charge.

*

Schiller's personal faith is still a subject of scholarly debate.[80] It is tempting, however, to see Schiller's religious views as expressed in the Christian Kabbal-istic conception of divine emanation that appeared in his *Theosophy of Julius* ("Theosophie des Julius" in *Philosophisch Briefe*, 1786).[81] As the title indi-cates, the theosophy that Diderot and others had worked to expunge contin-ued to have an appeal, and Schiller was far from alone in turning to theosophy as either antidote or complement to reason.

Contemporary scholars such as Ernst Benz have noted that there was a revival of theosophy in German philosophical circles following the pantheism controversy.[82] Decades earlier, the Pietist theologian Friedrich Christoph Oet-inger (1702–82) had already begun to recoup Jakob Böhme in Germany as a way to oppose the rationalism of Leibniz and Christian Wolff.[83] Accordingly, after the enlightenment project began to sour, various German philosophers actively turned to Böhme and other theosophists as potential sources of specif-ically German thought. It should therefore come as no surprise that one finds references to Böhme or theosophy in not just Schiller and Novalis, but also Hegel and Schelling.[84] Moreover, Schlegel even hinted that Böhme's theoso-phy was one route to a Christian Spinozism.[85]

To return to Schiller's *Theosophy*, he remarked, "Nature is an infinitely divided God.["86] He then elucidated his version of theosophy with an optical analogy that could almost have come from Jewish Kabbalistic tradition as articulated in the *Zohar*: just as the prism scatters a single ray of white light into a spectrum of colored bands, so too God's essence is refracted into the play of substances that animate the natural world. Both humanity and nature are thus expressions of divine radiance. As he went on to describe it:

> Everything in and outside of me is only the Hieroglyph of a Power, which is similar to me. The laws of nature are the ciphers, which the [Divine] Thinker assembles to make itself understandable to other rational beings—they are the alphabet, by means of which all spirits confer with the Perfected Spirit and with themselves."[87]

It would seem that like Böhme, Schiller imagined the world as populated by a multiplicity of minds or spirits, which are nothing less than God's path to self-knowledge via creation. It is unclear how much this theology survived into his later periods.[88]

If one reads "The Gods of Greece" in light of Schiller's *Theosophy*, the gods it refers to are divine signatures (see esp. verse 4). From this vantage, the poem describes three stages: seeing the divine in the world (1–4); only being able to see the divine as outside the world (7); to finally perhaps not being able to see the divine at all. In theosophical terms, this would be nothing less than the fall of humanity, which is crucially the self-alienation of God.

Nevertheless, Schiller described "The Gods of Greece" differently in a 1788 Christmas letter about the poem to the writer, lawyer, and Freemason Christian Gottfried Körner, stating: "The general rule here is that the artist and especially the poet never portrays the real, but only the idealized or the artistically mediated truth of the object. . . . The God that I put in the shadows in 'The Gods of Greece' is not the God of the philosophers, nor the benevolent dream of the masses, but rather a freak produced by running together flawed and distorted conceptions. The Greek gods I depicted in this light are merely the lovely characteristics of Greek mythology condensed into one conception."[89] It appears that the gods were less actual entities than artistic conceptions—or more specifically in his technical vocabulary, they were what he referred to as aesthetic semblances (*Schein*).[90] References to "gods" were how the ancient poets depicted an enchanted nature.

That said, the gods were not *mere* fictions. Schiller may have been first and foremost an "aesthetic pagan," but it is worth underscoring that aesthetics was the core issue of his grand philosophical project.[91] There is not space here to fully work out Schiller's aesthetic theory, but in sum he was attempting to suture morality to aesthetics by making art the means of joining sensibility with the harmony of reason.[92] Put in starker terms, Schiller saw in aesthetics the possibility of reuniting mind and world. Thus, the theosophical and aesthetic readings are not incompatible because Greek "gods" could be both aesthetic semblances and divine signatures pointing toward the true divinity or nature beyond them. At the very least, it seems unlikely that Schiller's poem was intended to attack the Christian deity.

*

The real resentment in "The Gods of Greece" was directed against a natural philosophy that reduced the vibrant world of the primitive humanity into dead mechanism. As one can see from verses 5 through 6 and 8 through 11, this attitude has stripped the soul from the sun god, transforming him into merely a hunk of celestial matter, and has even rendered the whole of nature into nothing but a clockwork pendulum. Accordingly, the thrust of the piece is not an assault on Christianity, but rather a critique of mechanism. We might hear echoes of Jacobi's contention that the exploration of proximate causation leads toward determinism and nihilism. But despite some later readings of Schiller's project, he was not antiscientific, nor was Schiller straightforwardly against enlightenment.

Schiller had studied medicine at the Karlsschule in Stuttgart, and his early medical writings—such as *Philosophie der Physiologie* (The philosophy of physiology, 1779)—emphasized the dynamic interaction between the heterogeneous substances of body-mind. So while it would be a mistake to suppose that Schiller was a classical holist, he clearly had sympathies with various forms of medical vitalism and was committed to the refutation of reductionist biological mechanism.[93] Restated, Schiller's hostility to mechanism was not an advocacy for faith or a repudiation of reason. Rather, he wanted to reject a clockwork cosmos in favor of a living world.

We can see this project in "The Gods of Greece," which expresses hostility toward the mechanical philosophy physics associated with Descartes and Christiaan Huygens and to a lesser extent Newton.[94] It was far from the only text of Schiller's that gave vent to similar criticisms.[95] For Schiller, mechanism is fundamentally alienating; it silences nature, instead of compelling it to speak. Where once humanity celebrated the wonders and beauty of the natural world, we are now numb to its majesty, and have reduced it to mere instrument. This was not a new claim, but "The Gods of Greece" crystallizes in poetic form sentiments that had long paralleled the rise of mechanism and hence gave expression to alternate ontologies that had long been in the works. Indeed, we can see versions of this critique of the mechanization of the world picture down to our present day. Crucially, Schiller identified this loss with the departure of animating spirits, or at the least with the vanishing of the gods. As he put it in a fragment preserved in his literary remains: "Everything divine is vanishing from the world and the old gods are making room for humanity."[96]

The image from "The Gods of Greece" that epitomized its elegy for the modern world, that of "Godless nature," would recur in the writings of Freud and others. Lacking any theosophical subtext (or Schiller's positive project, discussed below), the poem was read as a characterization of the disparity between a lost premodern mentality and the contemporary alienated individual: as if in some ancient epoch we saw the world alive with gods, and we now see it as drained of both divinity and *meaning*. The original German phrase *Die entgötterte Natur* also communicates nuances that are difficult to translate into English, above all the verbal quality of *entgöttert*: not just "godless" or "Godless," but "de-god-ed" or "de-deified," stripped of a former divinity. Read in the context of the poem, however, there is a certain ambiguity about the beginning of de-deification. Did it set in when Christ displaced the "world of gods"? Or did it appear when scientists transformed the sun into a " soulless" (*Seelenlos*) ball of fire? Likely Schiller imagined both as phases, but it is worth looking at what the two readings entail.

In the first case, the interesting thing is that it is not a modernization narrative. If Christianity caused the alienation from nature, then de-deification set in long before Galileo and Newton. Moreover, it prevents Christianity from posing as an alternative to disenchantment, since religion is at the heart of the thing. In the latter case, estrangement is rooted in the more familiar rise of philosophical reason, but Schiller's philosophical vitalism already hints that he imagined a way to reunite what had been cast asunder.

*

"The Gods of Greece" was almost instantly controversial, inspiring essays and response poems that variously condemned or defended the work.[97] Schiller's poems were ultimately enshrined in the German literary canon, providing inspiration for later generations. Although Schiller was not the only critic of mechanism, the image of the eclipse of the gods found many resonances in nineteenth-century Europe. One can find fugitive or vanishing gods evoked by period thinkers across the political spectrum and long after Hellenism was exchanged for other nationalist narratives. The trope occurs over the next few decades in works in German by Hegel (1795–1830), Novalis (1800), Friedrich Hölderlin (1800), Heinrich Heine (1827), Ludwig Feuerbach (1846), and Louise Dittmar (1848); in Danish by Adam Oehlenschläger (1808–9); and in English by Bryan Procter (1823) and Elizabeth Barrett Browning (1844).[98] It would also be picked up by many of the thinkers discussed in the following chapters.

Taken together, these early responses suggested a lost animist or pagan past in which humanity was in harmony with nature, and they often share an attempt to pinpoint the moment that this bond was shattered. For some it was the rise of mechanism, but for others it was Christianity that had dispelled old gods. But they generally granted the sentiment of the elegy as though pantheism had been humankind's spurned inheritance.

In Hegel's writings, the god eclipse appeared in both poetry and philosophy. In 1796, Hegel wrote a poem, "Eleusis," inspired by Schiller. The relevant lines are:

But your halls are silent, O Goddess!
The Circle of the Gods has flown back to Olympus,
Fleeing from the consecrated altars,
And the defiled human grave![99]

Hegel is not famous as a poet (perhaps for good reason), but these lines indicate how important Schiller and the death of the gods were for Hegel's early thinking.[100] Elsewhere, in fragments dating from roughly the same period, Hegel remarked that Christianity had "emptied Valhalla, felled the sacred groves, [and] extirpated the national imagery as a shameful superstition."[101] Indeed, it is probably fair to say that the entire project of Hegel's philosophy was to join the divisions between humanity and nature, man and God, reason and myth, which are encapsulated in the mythemes we have been discussing.[102]

In *Vorlesungen über die Philosophie der Geschichte* (delivered 1822–30; *Lectures on the Philosophy of History*) Hegel goes to the greatest lengths to formulate his own version of disenchantment. In these lectures, Hegel's main argument is that disenchantment—or more precisely, de-divination (*Entgötterung*)—really starts with Judaism. For Hegel, antique Judaism is where *Geist* (spirit-mind) first comes into self-consciousness, but in so doing, it already begins to see itself as the fundamental root of existence and therefore as distinct from the sensible world. God and the spiritual world are seen as distinct from the natural world. Further, the more God is exalted, the more "nature is conceived as having the ground of its existence in another."[103] Every emphasis on divine power and unity makes God more otherworldly. The natural world becomes the domain of understanding. "Men are regarded as individuals, not as incarnations of God; sun as sun, mountains as mountains— not as possessing Geist and will."[104] The result of this is that nature becomes accessible to a kind of positivism or scientism. The thinking of nature is now accessible in terms of *Verstand* (literally "understanding," but Hegel used it as a technical term for the particular kind of thinking faculty that transforms sense data into empirical knowledge). For Hegel, the ancient Israelites, because they are only just beginning the process of empirical knowledge, are not very good scientists. Their *Verstand* has not yet resulted in any gains; as Hegel put it, "nature is *entgöttert*, but not yet understood."[105] Here we have Hegel arguing for a version of disenchantment or de-divination as the core innovation of Judaic monotheism. Later in life Max Weber would express a similar position.

The main reason I introduce Hegel's philosophy of history here is to make the basic point that the departure of the gods is not just a lyric convention or an occultist article of faith, but it is also a serious argumentative framework, first in philosophy and then in various scholarly disciplines, as I will demonstrate at some length in the chapters that follow.

THE ROMANTIC SPIRAL: FRIEDRICH HÖLDERLIN

Every development, including yours, advances in a spiral—leaving nothing behind, re- turning to the same point on an upper curl.

HUGO VON HOFMANNSTHAL, "Letter to Richard Strauß," 1912

As a poem, "The Gods of Greece" is a melancholy elegy for a lost golden age. Schiller's 1789 lectures on universal history, however, are more hopeful. He describes early human history in idealistic terms, but then argues that "from a Paradise of ignorance and slavery, [humanity] should work its way upward, even if it also takes a thousand years, to ascend to a Paradise of knowledge and freedom."[106] For Schiller, paradise lost could not only be regained, but perhaps even improved. This idea of progress as return in a greater synthesis was not unique to Schiller. It is an example of what M. H. Abrams calls the "Romantic Spiral," the historiographical structure that fuses narratives of historical de- cline and progress to suggest that the goal of history is a return of the past in a higher key.[107] While I'm not interested in wading into fraught debates about the meaning of "Romanticism," I think Abrams's pattern holds insofar as many of the figures we have been discussing deployed narratives of despiritualization and even the death of God with a conception of a higher-order return.[108]

By contrast, today the myth of disenchantment is usually evoked to characterize a loss, or the supremacy of one culture over another, but it is rarely described as being necessary for re-enchantment in a higher mode. We rarely hear claims like: *We had to be free of nature so that we could give nature freedom*; or *magic had to be eliminated so that we could make it real*; or *God had to die in the church so that God could be reborn in the world*. But these are the sorts of narrative tropes implied by early uses of the proto-disenchantment myths.

Later chapters will pinpoint the moment the narrative became truncated, but for further insight into the Romantic Spiral, we can look to the German poet Friedrich Hölderlin (1770–1843), the college friend of Schelling and Hegel. The Romantic Spiral is often evident in Hölderlin's work, but nowhere more clearly than in a 1795 text known as *"Die Vorrede zur vorletzten Hyperion-Fassung"* (The Preface to the Penultimate Version of [the Novel] Hyperion), which states:

> The blessed unity, Being (in the only sense of that word) is lost to us, and we had to lose it if we were to gain it again by striving and struggle. We tear ourselves loose from the peaceful Εν και παν [*Hen kai pan*, One-in-All] of the world, in order to restore it through ourselves. We have fallen away from nature, and what was once one, as we can believe, is now in conflict with itself, and each side alternates between mastery and servitude. Often for us, it is as though the world were *everything* and we *nothing*, but often it is as though we were *everything* and the world *nothing* . . . . To end the eternal conflict between our self and the world, to restore the peace of all peace, to bring us back into unity with nature so as to form one unending whole—that is the goal of all our striving, whether we understand it or not.[109]

Hölderlin is describing a historical progression that will be familiar to any Hegelian. It is history in three stages—primal unity, an extended alienation, and then a higher unity—which subsumed the previous opposition between humanity and nature. It would seem this essay describes what Hegel would later make famous as the dialectical progression of thought from early abstraction, through its own negation, and on to a new position that sublates the old opposition. In that sense, the Absolute *Geist* passes through alienation from itself as nature to an eventual return in a higher state. In a thumbnail of Hegel's version of this grand trajectory, however, this is not the return of nature, but actually something more like the technologic rationalization of the world.

In *Über die ästhetische Erziehung des Menschen* (On the aesthetic education of man, 1794), Schiller also discusses a three-stage historical cycle, beginning with the physical domination of nature over humans, human emancipation, and finally a new state of coexistence between reason and nature.[110] As he argued, we have to dominate nature so that we can escape its tyranny, but the future goal is a return of a new harmony that no longer requires this oppositional struggle.

Varieties of this broader philosophy of history were widespread among the nineteenth-century German philosophers, who often saw reconciliation with nature as the goal of their project and understood it in terms of a higher synthesis. As Schelling put it, "All philosophizing consists in recalling the condition in which we were at one with nature."[111] This is evidence that it is glib to characterize German "Romanticism" as a species of traditionalism or conservatism. Rather than being reactionaries, these philosophers were looking for a form of progress that could embrace a higher synthesis. Indeed, Hölderlin advocated a Jacobin politics that would have made any radical enlightener proud.

The key issue for many of these thinkers was not how to get back to a nostalgic past, but how to produce the union of opposites or reconcile humanity and nature, subject and object. Schiller and his fellows had different versions of what this was going to take, but even the later thinkers he inspired were attempting to identify the reconciliation or synthesis of the contradictory terms. As Oehlenschläger stated: once Christianity killed the gods, "the Holy Cross must become one with Thor's Mighty Hammer!"[112]

Novalis's attempted solution to disenchantment was novel insofar as he called for a return of a higher-order magic, which he called "magical idealism" (*Magischer Idealismus*).[113] Although he died before he could fully articulate his system, tantalizing clues can be found in various fragments such as: "Nature is a petrified magical city"; "The physical magus knows how to enliven Nature, to use it at will, as with his body"; and "In the age of magic, the body obeys the soul, or the spirit world."[114] Because Novalis uses the term *magic*, he is therefore addressing alienation from nature as a kind of disenchantment, not merely de-paganization, or the end of myth. Although his magic includes simultaneously artistic, scientific, and philosophical goals, at the very least it would seem that it is the key to enlivening petrified nature.

To return to Hölderlin, his poem "Bread and Wine" ("Brod und Wein," 1800), inspired by Schiller's "Gods of Greece," fuses Dionysus and Christ, as expressed in their shared symbolism of bread and wine. Like Schiller's work, it begins with the Greek world to describe the despiritualization of nature. But it completes the Romantic Spiral latent in Schiller's version to suggest both the gods' departure and their eventual return. This is summarized in the line "Therefore, we also help to remember the Celestial Ones [*Himmlischen*], those who were once with us, / and who will return when the time is right."[115] The whole poem mixes longing for "fugitive gods" (*entflohenen Götter*) with messianic expectations. It would seem that for Hölderlin, the gods needed to die in Greece so that they could be reborn in modern Germany. As will be shown in chapter 10, this return of the gods would find expression in the twentieth century in a literary circle around the German poet Stefan George, which in turn was central to the later revival of Hölderlin and his work.

To summarize in slightly anachronistic terms, in the hands of early theorists, disenchantment had to happen in order for a higher enchantment to appear at a later date. But if today the prediction of despiritualization sounds prescient and the return far-fetched, the reverse was striking in the period. This is because, as the next chapter will show, just half a century after Schiller decried the de-animation of nature, a full-blown spiritualist revival was in full swing—and indeed, many thought the cosmos was animated by spirits of the dead.

A MYTH IN SEARCH OF HISTORY: JACOB BURCKHARDT

The Italians were the first modern people of Europe who gave themselves boldly to speculations on freedom and necessity. . . . Their belief in God began to waver.

JACOB BURCKHARDT, *Die Kultur der Renaissance in Italien*, 1860

It is a commonplace of critical theory that narratives about the past are really the present in disguise. But the sheer level of repetition in our versions of disparate ages might leave one wondering what contemporaneous moment was projected backward to become our most common story of the past. The issue is how the characterization of an epochal rupture between myth and logos, or between reason and superstition, gained purchase in the historical narratives that are often repeated unthinkingly by nonspecialists today. Restated, how did the myth-of-the-end-of-myth take hold as a narrative about a specific historical period?

There is not space here to give this issue full treatment, but one place we can see this "myth of absence" transforming itself into historiography is in the work of Nietzsche's friend, the Swiss historian Jacob Burckhardt (1818–97). Burckhardt is interesting for our purposes for three reasons: first, it is easy to demonstrate the influence of Schiller and company on his work; second, Burckhardt searched for the moments when myth fell into decay and modernity was born; and third, he was the central figure in producing the Renaissance as a historical period. Indeed, Burckhardt's ambivalent construction of that historical epoch served as a prototype for later narratives of the rupture of modernity that have been hung on a host of different periods.

In a set of lectures Burckhardt gave on Greek history, which were published after his death as *Griechische Kulturgeschichte* (A cultural history of Greece, 4 vols., 1898–1902), Burckhardt referred to Schiller and specifically to "The Gods of Greece," while elsewhere he mentioned Jacobi, Hegel, Herder, and Schelling.[116] More important, Burckhardt also looked for the rejection of mythology, which he saw as having begun in the fifth century BCE and the time of the "sophists." As he argued, "Philosophy is essentially as always dedicated to the destruction of myth," and when combined with a new sense of irreverence toward the gods, it accelerates the "decay of mythical understanding."[117] In sum, the rise of philosophy in classical Greece was the end of mythology.

Ancient Greece was not the birth of modernity for Burckhardt. Instead, he turned to a different periodization that he would make his own. If Burckhardt is remembered today, it is for his role in the formation of the Italian Renaissance as a periodization with *Die Kultur der Renaissance in Italien* (1860; *The Civilization of the Renaissance in Italy*), which remains in print.

Burckhardt did not coin the term *Renaissance*. We owe this word to the French historian Jules Michelet, whose work also fits the chapter's broader theme—Michelet was a reader of Schiller, who described "the death of the gods," remarking that with the death of Pan "the old universal god of nature was no more. . . . The gods of old had come to an end."[118] But Michelet instantly complicated this god eclipse because he argued that the exile from pagan nature in Christian Europe led to the rebellion that was European witchcraft (a movement that he romanticized in *La sorcière* [The witch, 1863]). It is worth noting that despite the temporal proximity of the last Swiss juridical execution of a witch (1782), the early nineteenth century was the period in which European historians began to theorize a definitive rupture between the persecution of witches and their own epoch.[119] Indeed, it is tempting to see the whole disenchantment narrative in European thought as an attempt to universalize this particular cultural shift. Nonetheless, Michelet is significant here because he coined the term *Renaissance* in *Histoire de France au xvie siècle* (1855). Unlike our current usage of the term, for Michelet the Renaissance was essentially French, largely scientific in nature, and spanned a long period from the age of exploration to its later fulfillment in the French Revolution.[120]

Regardless, Burckhardt is more important to our larger argument because he defined *Renaissance* in terms of the time period and geography that nonspecialists know today, and it was Burckhardt who portrayed the Renaissance as a movement that drew together art, philosophy, and politics. Crucially, he did not just set the stage for a historical period, but also made the case that the Renaissance was the birth of the "modern man." Furthermore, this was a figure toward which Burckhardt felt a distinct apprehension. In the most famous passage in the text, Burckhardt expressed his ambivalence toward the Renaissance and all that it had wrought, characterizing the "development of the Italian into modern man," as follows: "In the Middle Ages both sides of human consciousness . . . lay dreaming or half awake beneath a common veil. The veil was woven of faith, illusion, and childish prepossession, through which the world and history were seen clad in strange hues. . . . It is in Italy that this veil first melted into air; an *objective* treatment and consideration of the State and of all the things of this world became possible. . . . Man became a spiritual *individual*, and recognized himself as such."[121]

For Burckhardt, the modern individual, having been liberated from the "veil," or myth of Christian faith, was born into a host of contradictions, tormented by a raging battle between rationality and selfishness.[122] As he also remarked, "When once the veil of illusion was torn asunder, when once the dread of nature and the slavery to books and tradition were overcome, countless problems lay before them for solution."[123] In other words, Burckhardt was describing an epochal rupture in which myth, superstition, and tradition were lost, but also one in which the newfound freedom of reason results in a profound alienation, atomization, and conflict.[124]

This should sound familiar, as it is narrative that has been told with weight toward either the positive or the negative about a range of epochs. Accordingly, in his construction of the Renaissance, we can see Burckhardt begin to chart a narrative that later scholars would essentially pin on different periods from Socratic philosophy to the Enlightenment to modernity to the condition of postmodernity. In a way, "modernity" postdated Burckhardt insofar as Baudelaire coined the term *modernity* (Fr. *modernité*) in 1863, and it took decades before *modernity* was transformed to mean an all-consuming epoch and given the kinds of weight that Burckhardt had already given to the "modern man" of the Renaissance.

Strikingly, however, we can see Burckhardt's influence on the historian and philosopher Wilhelm Windelband, who in 1878 first tried to popularize the idea of "*Die Aufklärung*" (the Enlightenment) as a periodization; he did so in a volume that addressed Burckhardt's version of the Renaissance.[125] Furthermore, Heidegger and Wilhelm Nestle—two of the most significant thinkers who articulate the claim that Socratic philosophy represented an epochal break from primordial past—were both readers of Burckhardt.[126] Later, another reader of Burckardt, Alexandre Koyré, would popularize the "scientific revolution" as a periodization in part to steal the Renaissance's thunder.[127] Max Weber and his version of disenchantment are discussed in chapter 10, but before moving on, I want to underscore the observation that Weber read Burckhardt, and he did so before writing *The Protestant Ethic*.[128] It was that last work that essentially shifted the birth of modern rationality from the Italian Renaissance to the Protestant Reformation.

Burckhardt's portrayal of the Renaissance as a complete period was a prototype for a host of later narrative tropes we now associate with not just the Renaissance, but also classical Greece, the Enlightenment, the Protestant Reformation, and, of course, other vaguer descriptions of the birth of modernity. To exaggerate slightly, we might say that Burckardt was one of the authors of modernity as a literary device.

To be completely clear, I am not arguing that Burckhardt singlehandedly produced the idea of a historical rupture and the alienation of man from nature or the womb of myth. Rather, I see him as one of a generation of thinkers crucial in transforming the more abstract mode of quasi-pessimistic universal history suggested by Schiller and company into a concrete historiography. Indeed, Burckhardt was at the vanguard of projecting the myth of disenchantment into the past and providing it with a genesis and pedigree.

CONCLUSION: THE MYTH OF THE MODERN LOSS OF MYTH

> Now mythless man stands there, surrounded by every past there has ever been, eternally hungry, scraping and digging in a search for roots, even if he has to dig for them in the most distant antiquities. The enormous historical need of dissatisfied modern culture, the accumulation of countless other cultures, the consuming desire for knowledge— what does all this point to, if not to the loss of myth?
>
> NIETZSCHE, *Die Geburt der Tragödie*, 1886

With such a long chapter, I will keep the conclusion mercifully short. I would like the reader to keep in mind the following ideas as we move forward. The *philosophes* were *not* in fact godless apostles of a stringently mechanical and de-animated nature, nor did they initiate a war of science against religion. The Pantheism Controversy was one key moment—maybe *the* key moment—when some Europeans convinced themselves that enlightenment rationality had initiated a treacherous slide toward the death of God and the de-animation of the world. From that point forward, it seemed to some that nihilism or atheism lurked in the heart of philosophy. When natural philosophy was cannibalized by the new notion of "science," it also came to seem that scientific progress pointed away from the divine.

It was Schiller who produced one of this discourse's most portable formulations. In "The Gods of Greece," the arc of history showed not just de-Christianization, but a broader loss of the gods and the end of a harmony with a living nature. Nevertheless, nostalgia, or neo-traditionalism, was not the only response to this kind of grief. Looking at Schiller alongside Hölderlin, we can see one specific feature of early nineteenth-century disenchantment narratives that has since gone missing; namely, the return in a higher state. Hence, disenchantment already included re-enchantment. It would be the work of later thinkers to make a modern rupture seem inevitable and to transform the spiral of disenchantment into an arrow with teleological inevitability.

Lastly, Burckhardt asked the historian's question: When did the modern age begin? His answer was that the "modern man" was born in the Renaissance, and while others would transpose this periodization into other epochs, the disenchantment narrative had found its coroner.

CHAPTER FOUR

The Shadow of God

God is dead; but given the way people are, there may still for millennia be caves in which
they show his shadow.—And we—we must still defeat his shadow as well.

NIETZSCHe, *Die fröhliche Wissenschaft*, 1882

There is already a standard narrative in place about the birth of religious studies as an academic discipline. It is generally imagined by scholars as emerging
from the encounter between the trajectory of Enlightenment rationalism and
non-European culture. The rise of higher criticism led to the reappraisal of the
Christian Bible as a historical document, while simultaneously European travelers were presented with an unanticipated diversity abroad, which challenged
their long-standing assumptions about the autonomy of Christian revelation.
To make sense of these diverse cultures, Europeans extended to them the essentially Protestant category of "religion." Comparative religion is represented
as a self-conscious reaction to theology from which it differentiates itself in
the same moment that it is relying on a Protestant conception of religion itself.
It is often regarded as secularizing and Protestant in the same breath. This is
not seen as a contradiction, since both Protestant and non-Protestant scholars
have tended to interpret modernity as an essentially Protestant project. For
some Protestant thinkers, this secularizing Protestantism could represent a
kind of triumph, while for the others the Protestant character of modernity
often represents its failings. Religious studies, in this account, is thus one engine of Protestant disenchantment.[1]

In this chapter, I challenge this conception of religious studies as a disenchanting discipline and shift the classical account of the field's origins and
preoccupations. While emphasizing different nations and thinkers, historians
of the discipline have generally pegged the start of religious studies to the
mid-nineteenth century and described it as predicated on the formation of an
academic discipline independent from theology.[2] By contrast, another set of

scholars have emphasized comparative religion as a central component of "the Enlightenment" itself, emerging from the rise of toleration and the liberation of European rationalism from religious orthodoxy.[3] A few scholars have stressed that the roots of the field go further back into antiquity or the age of European exploration.[4] Regardless of their chronology, these accounts generally stage religious studies over and against Christian orthodoxy, whether they celebrate or condemn the field's rationalist Protestant character.[5]

In what follows, I invert much of this narrative and show religious studies as emerging from a very different milieu and in a very different context, demonstrating the shared history of religious studies, spiritualism, and theosophy. I place my re-narration of disciplinary formation along with a minority account that has emphasized the influence of esotericism on specific scholars' work (especially Mircea Eliade and the Eranos Circle).[6] But the modes that they generally present as exceptions, I show here to be the ordinary functioning of the discipline. As an antidote to the dominant narrative, I show that the discipline emerged in relation to enlightenment critique and was connected to a vibrant tradition very different from mainstream Protestantism, namely esotericism. The doppelgänger of religious studies turns out not to be philology but theosophy.

SPIRITS OF A VANISHING GOD

"When future times write the history of our century . . . they will tell our grandchildren that the conviction of the pervasive conformity to scientific laws penetrated all levels of the people for the first time in our century," observed the German sociologist Georg Simmel in *Etwas vom Spiritismus* (Note about spiritualism, 1892), adding a caveat: "We, who are still in the midst of these things, still notice all sorts of counter-movements and side-currents. . . . Alongside that progress of natural science and the increased insight into the strict regularity and comprehensibility of all events, we find the belief in the *spirits of deceased people* who have either returned to earth or have always been with us, and are able to communicate with us as to this and the next world through the mediation of persons with special gifts."[7]

Simmel knew that the nineteenth century would be remembered as a period of the rise of scientific authority. Indeed, in both German and Anglophone spheres, the notion of a conflict between "religion" and "science" had taken hold, to religion's detriment.[8] Despite the period's vibrant religious revival movements, in the eyes of many, organized religion was in danger, wounded from its battle with science, assailed by critical reason and nihilistic skepticism, and in the eyes of some, in the process of vanishing. While most Europeans in the nineteenth century did not in any sense suppose that God was dead, they did remark on a lingering sense of divine absence.[9]

Simmel, however, was sensitive enough to the epoch's countermovements to observe that those who lived through it also experienced its culture as vibrantly animated by ghosts. He went on to note that "thousands of people from all of the civilized countries in Europe and America adhere to spiritualism, that hundreds of books are published on it—in 1870 over one hundred thousand spiritualist books were sold in the United States of America."[10] If anything, Simmel was understating the case. A recent crop of historians have shown that spiritualism was a major transnational movement in the nineteenth century and into the twentieth, perhaps peaking with as many as two and a half million members in the United States and Great Britain, and affecting everything from women's rights movements to literature to psychoanalysis.[11]

The following section presents the first major dialectical movement under consideration here. It shows how fears of despiritualization and laments about the death of God contributed to the rise of spiritualism, occult movements, and new religions. It is perhaps not surprising that the *philosophes'* attempt to banish mystical "sciences" failed as much as it succeeded. Indeed, the same epoch that saw the birth of the human sciences also saw an intense fascination with ghosts and the widespread popularity of the Theosophical Society and other forms of "public" esotericism. Against these shifts, the figure of the ghost or spirit came to play a distinctive role in the writings of seminal theorists of the nineteenth century (Hegel, Marx, and Spencer).

Beliefs about the possibility of contact with dead spirits were not new in the nineteenth century; there were plenty of earlier precedents in the works Emanuel Swedenborg and others. In the mid-nineteenth century, however, there was a resurgence of interest in the possibility of communicating with the dead. In part this was inspired by the popularity of the Fox sisters (1848–88), but also by changing ideas of the nature of biological life.[12] This interest had its origins in a new attitude toward the departed that no longer fit ghosts into the neat place provided by ecclesiastical authorities.[13] Spirits therefore emerged as a new possibility in the secular West not as atavistic survival, but as a product of the nineteenth century, which was then projected back into the past in various forms (such as gothic novels). In this way, ghosts represent the present haunting the past.

"Modernity" was haunted in other ways as well. Just as the nineteenth century produced new ghosts, it also gave birth to new mysticisms. Faced with an evaporating God and world full of spirits, some turned toward the alternate mode of knowing rejected by Diderot and the *philosophes*. In this context, the term *théosophie* resurfaced to describe different attempts to overcome the perceived failings of modernity. While "the Enlightenment" is often accused of radical anthropocentrism, it was anthropocentric mysticism that imagined itself to be enlightenment's antidote. Despite its earlier meaning as a form of Christian esotericism, Helena Blavatsky and her followers started using the term *Theosophy* to describe their Westernized appropriation of "Oriental" thought (discussed below), but they were not alone in using the term, which continued to evoke alternate forms of knowledge.[14] Beyond theosophy, there was a broader occult or esoteric undercurrent that relied on many of the tropes that Diderot had rejected. Common to these various groups and individuals was frequently a drive to recover a divine science, often combined with the new wave of spirit phenomena.

The nineteenth-century surge of interest in spirits gave birth to a range of spiritualist and occult groups. These movements can be interpreted as a kind of internal critique and supplement to "modernity," legible especially in relationship to contemporary practices and debates about imperialism, as well as scientific and religious authority. They evoked the absent uncanny *Unheimlich* supposedly suppressed by contemporary skepticism, which they claimed could be rediscovered through a recovery of the *Heimlich* (secret, concealed, hidden).

For these movements, the existence of spirits had two contrasting but sometimes complementary functions. First, they provided a kind of necro-vitalist critique of the limits of science by presenting a world paradoxically and vibrantly alive with the souls of the dead. While one persistent counter-enlightenment impulse had been formulated as an epistemological critique (think Nietzsche), another form taken by those who rejected enlightenment was as a challenge to the perceived completeness of materialism and the universal dominion of science in the face of spirits.[15] Spirit phenomena were sometimes imagined as outside the realm of causation and accordingly as evidence of miracles, which seemingly provided an exit from the deterministic nihilism that Jacobi had criticized.[16]

Second, and more important, the spiritualist séance functioned as a religious laboratory that appeared capable of providing an empirical route for the modernization of religion. These movements embodied dissatisfaction with the perceived consequences of enlightenment while benefiting from many of its basic assumptions. Their practitioners often called them "occult sciences." It was believed by many spiritualists that the rupture between religion and science (or faith and reason) could be repaired through these spirit-based demonstrations of the powers of the soul. Instead of "empires of reason," they worked to establish a rational "science of spirits."[17]

*

Religious studies arose precisely in a cultural context where spirits and the occult were lively objects of inquiry even as the fledgling discipline defined itself in contrast to spiritualism and theosophy. The conventional historiography would view these movements as completely separate. It turns out they are not so easy to tell apart. In this chapter, I want to map out the messy intermediate terrain between two spheres that consider themselves different but nevertheless exhibit the same basic habits of thought.

Scratch the surface and we quickly find a preoccupation with spiritualism among foundational scholars of religious studies. William James, Marcel Mauss, and Andrew Lang all took seriously the possible reality of spiritualist phenomena. Spiritualism is also addressed, if ultimately criticized, in the work of Émile Durkheim, Rudolf Otto, and Bronislaw Malinowski, among others.[18] In each case, these thinkers appropriated certain aspects of the contemporary spiritualist undercurrent while simultaneously distancing themselves from active spiritualism. Nowhere is this clearer than in the writings of the English anthropologist E. B. Tylor. A closer look at Tylor's work illuminates the depth of his preoccupation with managing the significance of spirits and the claims of spiritualists.

THE HAUNTED ANTHROPOLOGIST:
E. B. TYLOR

> The world is again swarming with intelligent and powerful disembodied spiritual beings, whose direct action on thought and matter is again confidently asserted as in those times and countries where physical science had not as yet so far succeeded in extruding these spirits and their influences from the system of nature . . . As of old, men live now habitual intercourse with the spirits of the dead.
>
> E. B. TYLOR, *Primitive Culture*, vol. 1, 1871

Edward Burnett Tylor (1832–1917), considered one of the founders of the anthropological study of religion, is most famous for promoting the concept of animism as the foundation of "primitive" religion. Tylor's minimalist definition of religion, that religion is belief in "spiritual beings," continues to be influential today.[19] Against his contemporaries—who compared the thinking of "savages" to madness—Tylor advanced the notion that a kind of natural religion is everywhere established rationally. The Tylorian savage, like a primitive *philosophe*, engages in an essentially empiricist study of the world around him or her, positing explanations for his or her experiences according to the kinds of forces he or she understands. The primitive's experiences with death and dreams give birth to an idea of spirits or ghosts, which are then believed to pervade the natural world, serving as the foundation for primitive religion. This is almost the same definition of religion described by the spiritualists themselves, who also believed that spirits were and should be the foundation for religion.

Tylor argued that over time the rude animism of the savage is ultimately replaced by polytheism; and then, finally, the most rational system of all—monotheism—emerges. Again, in Tylor's evolutionary teleology, we arrive at a Voltaire-esque rational Supreme Being as the ultimate fruit of human cognition, and a rational religion that looks like Tylor's minimalistic Quaker faith.[20] Although never explicitly stated as such, cultural progress means the gradual elimination of paganism.

Tylor also explained why humans, despite our inherent empiricism and rationality, are not all believers in a rational Supreme Being. To do so, he invokes the concepts of superstition and survivals. Tylor argued that in direct contrast to a positive and progressive religion, humans also retain certain holdovers from previous cultural forms.[21] According to a false etymology originally proposed by Cicero, Tylor calls these survivals, or remnants, "superstitions." These false "superstitions," which ought to vanish through successive stages in human cultural evolution, obscure or occlude the essentially rational nature of religion. Indeed, in a move reminiscent of the *philosophes'* project, Tylor argues that the goal of ethnography is precisely "to expose the remains of crude old culture which have passed into harmful *superstition*, and to mark these out for destruction."[22]

"Magic" and the "occult sciences"—two terms Tylor treats as synonymous—represent the most dangerous form of superstition.[23] In his account, magic belongs to "the lower races" and the "lowest known stages of civilization," and the racialization is clear insofar as he means it to be the providence of Africans, Aborigines, and Native Americans.[24] Magic resembles science in its style of reasoning but is based in a basically backward way of thinking or a confusion that mistakes an analogy or a symbol for the thing it represents.[25] Magic is based in a savage semiotics, which fails to appreciate the civilized realization of the meaninglessness of the relationship between the sign and the thing. Tylor gave the example of a West African "Obi-man" who makes a packet of grave dust and bones in order to kill an enemy, thereby mistaking symbolic killing with real death.[26] Moreover, in these primitive societies, Tylor argued, the sorcerer is also the priest and implicitly the primitive scientist.[27] It would seem magic is at the intersection between religion and science, and hence is the paradigmatic superstition.

By positioning magic as a type of superstitious thinking associated with the lowest primitive, Tylor suggested that it would fade with the coming of modern civilization.[28] This is an early kernel of a disenchantment narrative. But Tylor was forced to complicate it because he was aware that many of his contemporaries embraced the occult sciences and spiritualism, and that magic, far from vanishing, seemed to be flourishing.[29]

This realization puts pressure on his embrace of linear evolution. If the definitional feature of superstition is its archaism, newfangled superstitions would appear to be a fundamental contradiction. Indeed, the very distinction between modern and primitive culture central to his whole project would seem to be in danger of collapse. Moderns might turn out to be no less magical animists than his putative savages.

Tylor's response was to produce a new category of "active revival" to describe a "passive superstition" that resurfaces in strength.[30] Magic—and witchcraft in particular—serves as a paradigmatic case of this return of the repressed, representing the nightmarish reappearance of the archaic in the modern.[31] Thus, Tylor spent a good number of pages effectively telling his readers to resist magic at all cost, but while doing so acknowledged that the revival of magic is tied to the popularity of spiritualism.[32]

The spiritualism of his day, therefore, occupies an important position in Tylor's system. Insofar as religion is essentially belief in spiritual beings and insofar as spiritualism seems to be the "animism" Tylor posited at the origin of religion, spiritualism is both the quintessential religion and the quintessential superstition. This is all the more striking, because as Robert Segal observes, for Tylor, primitive spiritualism was materialist in that "primitives" did not have a concept of immateriality.[33] Accordingly, spirits were part of the physical world. For Tylor, the problem with modern religion is that it has shifted religion into an immaterial or ethical realm. But nineteenth-century spiritualism, as a science of spirits with material impact (and hence explainable according to quasi-mechanistic models such as animal magnetism), would therefore seem to be a return to a pre-dematerialized religion. It would then appear to be the ideal form of a revival, and Tylor treated it as such, arguing "modern spiritualism" is "a direct revival from the regions of savage philosophy and peasant folklore."[34] But in order to make spiritualism into a proper archaic return, Tylor had to obscure spiritualism's position and history as a reaction to enlightenment itself. He had to dismiss its contemporary origins and instead insist that it is a holdover from an ancient and savage past, and he did so repeatedly in *Primitive Culture*.[35] Of course, he was not alone in this. Many spiritualists validated their project by similarly imagining continuity between contemporary spiritualism and earlier epochs in human history.

Perhaps more surprising is own Tylor's attendance at séances. According to notes unpublished during his lifetime, in November 1872, Tylor went to a series of spiritualist events, attempting to ascertain the truth of the phenomena.[36] He ultimately concluded that there "may be a psychic force" involved, but remained skeptical of the existence of spirits as independent entities. Tylor seems to have believed in the possibility of a kind of vitalism, even as he rejected spiritualism itself as a superstitious survival. His conclusions were never published, but Tylor's attendance at séances was no secret.[37] Yet Tylor failed to take the next step and recognize that he was one of his own primitives—or at least, that Victorians were the real animists.

His intellectual heir, Andrew Lang, however, used evidence from spiritualism to argue that primitive animism was not pure self-deception, but instead represented insights into the spiritual world and the powers of the human mind. Primitive protoscience was right about some things. By bridging to the indigenous, Lang was identifying a latent aspect of Tylor's own program and explicitly deployed it as a critique of materialism.[38] What this also tells us is that for a brief moment, there was space for modern animism or a secular science of spirits inside Tylor's own anthropology, even if this possibility was ultimately foreclosed.

THE MAGICIAN AND THE PHILOLOGIST: ÉLIPHAS LÉVI AND MAX MÜLLER

Behind the veil of all the hieratic and mystical allegories of ancient doctrines, behind the darkness and strange ordeals of all initiations, under the seal of all sacred writings, in the ruins of Nineveh or Thebes, on the crumbling stones of old temples and on the blackened visage of the Assyrian or Egyptian sphinx, in the monstrous or marvelous paintings which interpret to the faithful of India the inspired pages of the Vedas, in the cryptic emblems of our old books on alchemy, in the ceremonies practiced at reception by all secret societies, there are found indications of a doctrine which is everywhere the same and everywhere carefully concealed.

ÉLIPHAS LÉVI, *Dogme et rituel de la haute magie*, 1854

A critique of enlightenment is explicit in the writings of other scholars from the period, here illustrated by two thinkers in the study of religion: Friedrich

Max Müller, the canonical founder of the discipline of the scientific study of religion; and Éliphas Lévi, absent from our field's historiography but famous in his period as a professed magician and for popularizing the term *occultism* (*occultisme*).[39] To be clear from the outset, I am not suggesting that we want to recoup Lévi as a central thinker in the field of religious studies, but I believe juxtaposing both figures is productive.

Éliphas Lévi (1810–1875) was born in Paris as Alphonse-Louis Constant, the son of a shoemaker. Constant attended seminary in preparation for entering the Catholic priesthood, but departed prior to ordination.[40] In the 1840s, he was very active in Christian socialist circles.[41] Constant got in trouble with the authorities for authoring *La Bible de la liberté* (The Bible of freedom, 1841), an ecstatic work of creative theology that described a pantheist divinity and called for a quasi-feminist, mystical socialism. The work already touched on themes that would continue to be important to his later explicitly occult works—particularly, a positively valenced Lucifer and a gesture toward an enchanted India.[42] *La Bible de la liberté* was confiscated on publication, and Constant was charged with promoting blasphemy and subversion. Ultimately found guilty, he was sentenced to the prison of Sainte-Pélagie in Paris. While in Sainte-Pélagie, Constant came across the writings of Emanuel Swedenborg, with their elaborate cosmology of the afterlife.[43] Starting in the 1850s, Constant reinvented himself under the Hebraic name Éliphas Lévi and began writing books about magic and the occult sciences. By the time he died, Lévi had become one of the most famous "magicians" in Europe. He also actively used the word *théosophie* in a positive sense in his work, although he preferred the term he coined and popularized *occultism* to describe his own efforts.[44]

Throughout his writings on magic, Lévi set out to invert the program of enlightenment. He started from the presupposition that magic—the original science of the magi—has been largely lost or has fallen into disrepute, concealed under allegories whose true meaning has been mislaid. Remarkably for writings later recognized as the mid-nineteenth century's most important works of magic, Lévi often began his writings by testifying to magic's contemporary absence. He mainly argued that wise initiates originally guarded magic as a divine science, but it was suppressed by the fearful masses and fell into superstition and half-remembered allegory.[45] This is not a version of disenchantment a scholar would recognize, but it is important to note that the precondition for a project rooted in the recovery of magic is the assumption that magic has gone missing.

Ironically, in his retrieval of enchantments, Lévi deployed a definition of superstition that would have appealed to Tylor, writing: "Superstitions are religious forms surviving the loss of ideas. Some truth no longer known or a truth which has changed its aspect is the origin and explanation of all of them. Their name, from the Latin *superstes*, signifies that which survives; they are the dead remnants of old knowledge or opinion."[46] While for Tylor the role of superstitions as survivals is precisely the reason they need to be banished, Lévi took this in the opposite direction, arguing that superstitions represent lost knowledge that needs to be rediscovered. As he elaborated, "that forgotten science of Magic, still lives undivided in hieroglyphical signs and, to some extent, in the living traditions or *superstitions* which it has left outwardly untouched."[47] Accordingly, Lévi sought to "recover" lost wisdom, as intentionally occluded knowledge that can be unveiled (*dévoilé*) by the true magical initiate.[48] This unveiling process works through a programmatic comparison of religions and mythologies, viewing all religions as expressions of a perennial or occult philosophy (*philosophia perennis*, *philosophia occulta*), glossed as "transcendental magic."

Strikingly, Lévi positioned *magic* (also described as "occult science" or "transcendental science") as the mediating term between philosophy/science and religion, stating that magic "reconciles perfectly and incontestably those two terms, so opposed on the first view—faith and reason, science and belief."[49] Instead of an antagonism between religion and magic, Lévi described an opposition between a disenchanting materialism and a spiritual vision of the cosmos. Unlike later anti-Christian occultists, Lévi situated his occult science and Catholicism as natural allies.[50] Magic, in this account, is less an alternative to the established churches than an attempt to reinforce religion in the face of modern skepticism. Moreover, religious studies—at least, in Lévi's hands (and, as we'll see later, in Müller's)—is an explicit denial of secularism.

Despite his emphasis on God and his commitment to a version of Catholicism, some of Lévi's notoriety came from his intentional deployment of satanic imagery, which he justified by stating, "The Devil is God as understood by the wicked."[51] On the one hand, Lévi denied the reality of the devil as an active agent of evil. On the other, he suggested that what seems diabolical is revealed to be the true essence of the divine when penetrated by the gaze of the magical initiate.[52]

*

The text that made Lévi's reputation, *Dogme et rituel de la haute magie* (Doctrine and ritual of high magic, published initially as pamphlets in 1854 and then in two volumes, 1855–56), is basically a work of comparative magic. While there had been previous attempts to discover Egyptian mysteries or "Oriental" spirituality, Lévi was one of the first major thinkers to make the comparative analysis of "world religions" in general the proper business of a magician—basically adapting Hermeticism to the age of comparative theology—a program that would be picked up in Theosophical circles.[53]

Initially, Lévi described his project as a reaction to a previous generation of scholarship that had attempted to expose the world's mythologies as a product of primitive miscomprehension of the natural world.[54] He rejected this smug reductionism because it seemingly dismissed all religion as nothing more than primitive superstition. In contrast, Lévi deployed terminology evocative of Christian Neoplatonism and Paracelsian semiotics, arguing that the divine "Logos" has been revealed to all peoples, and that "analogy is the key of all secrets of Nature."[55] Different mythologies therefore encode veiled insights into both nature and the mind of God (which for Lévi are linked). Accordingly, he proposed an esoteric science rooted in investigating the parallels in mythological source material to discover new truths both divine and scientific.

Each volume of *Dogme et rituel* is divided into twenty-two chapters. Although never explicitly stated, the rationale behind this structure can be found in the tarot. For readers unfamiliar with it, the tarot is a stylized deck of playing cards divided into four suits and twenty-two trumps known as major arcana. Although today associated with fortune-telling, when it first appeared in fourteenth-century Europe, the tarot was understood merely as a card game. In 1781, Antoine Court de Gébelin argued that the tarot had originated in Egypt as an encoded form of the Book of Thoth. As such, he suggested, it was actually an occult instrument.[56] Building on Court de Gébelin's claims, Lévi seems to have furthered the transformation of the tarot into a central piece of occult paraphernalia.[57]

Each chapter of *Dogme et rituel* corresponds to one of the major arcana of the tarot. The cards thus provide a key for unlocking a symbolic level to the text. This formal structure distinguishes the work from conventional academic scholarship, but it also illustrates Lévi's emphasis on polysemy and the power of analogy. Lévi claimed that when the tarot cards are arranged in order, it reveals itself to be a narrative work encoded by the Egyptian prophet Hermes Trismegistus, which itself is the key to unlocking other symbolic systems.[58] Moreover, each of the major arcana is connected to a Hebrew letter, such that through combination and recombination in the right sequence, the cards can be made to reveal Kabbalistic truths about the emanations of God.[59] In part, anticipating Carl Jung, Lévi regarded the tarot as a set of archetypes that represent cross-cultural mythic universals. But more important, Lévi saw the tarot as "the universal key to the initiations of the Logos" and the true bible of the magi hidden in plain sight.[60] The tarot's polysemy traces fundamental connections that allow us to decode God's revelation to different religions. While this kind of claim would be out of the reach of a contemporary scholar of religion, we will see its resonance with Müller's own theological commitments shortly.

*

In a later work, *La clef des grands mystères* (The key to great mysteries, 1861), Lévi employed his Hermetic hermeneutics to get at what he considered to be the essence of religion—namely, humankind's engagement with the "mysterious," or with all that lies beyond human knowledge.[61] He maintained: "Mystery is the abyss, which ceaselessly attracts our unquiet curiosity by the terror of its depth."[62] Müller and Herbert Spencer would later grapple with this idea that religion is directed toward the unknown or unknowable.[63] For Lévi, however, this mystery originates in the inability of human beings to grasp "the infinite," which he asserted is by definition incomprehensible.[64]

Religion will never vanish in the face of science because human language is fundamentally limited and one can "never find in the language of the finite the complete expression of the infinite."[65] Accordingly, human reason "may twist and coil its spirals ever-ascending" toward the absolute, but it will never eliminate its own foundations, which lie beyond its bounds.[66] In order to represent the incomprehensible we must resort to symbolic language, which is in itself necessarily paradoxical.[67] Symbolic language directed toward the unknown appears contradictory because it aims at using limited terms to suggest the infinite. Science can only be expressed in finite language, so other means, such as the comparative method, are needed to unlock the symbolic power of infinity.

Given his Christian theological commitments and neo-Catholic background, it should be no surprise that for Lévi, the ultimate symbol is the paradox of the Trinity and that God is the supreme mystery.[68] Moreover, Lévi argues that the symbols that represent humanity reaching toward the infinite are also the divine (or infinite) God revealing himself to humanity.[69] This longing for the infinite comes not from human nature but from God, and represents the bond between human and divine.[70] In sum, the myths of different religions are metaphorical love letters exchanged between God and humankind.

*

In a provocative later book, *The Science of Spirits* (*La science des esprits*, 1865), Lévi tried to recover the divine science abandoned by the *philosophes*. He strove to rehabilitate both magic and divination as approaches to the divine. But in recovering the science of the spirits, Lévi also distanced himself from contemporary spiritualism. Fundamentally his intervention was metaphysical, or we might say, ontological—Lévi believed the spiritualists were wrong about what sort of *stuff* spirits were made of. By way of explanation, in comparison to contemporary thinkers like Jane Bennett who imagine a "vital materialism," Lévi argued for a magnetic vitalism or occult pneumatology that grounded his reenchantment efforts.[71]

Lévi charted his alternative to materialism in detail—referring at various points in his writings to "the great magnetic agent" (*le grand agent magnétique*), "the world soul" (*l'âme du monde*), or most frequently to "astral light" (*la lumière astrale*).[72] Behind the mechanistic world of dead matter, Lévi described the universe as bursting with life and even mind, arguing that "there is no void in nature; all is peopled. There is no true death in nature; all is alive."[73] Flows of magnetic energy, or basically pure life, infuse all living things, bringing them into connection with one another and illuminating all corners of the world. Although it is invisible to our waking eyes, this hidden side of the world can be seen by the eye of the soul or the imagination, which allows us to perceive the infusion of the world with "astral light."[74]

The human mind also imprints this astral world with its own dreams or mental images, which live on long after the originator has died. Hence, one can see with the eye of the soul impressions of the imaginations of people from ages past, appearing like visions, phantasms, spirits, or demons in the astral light.[75] The rituals of different religions are designed to evoke the imagination and transform the astral light.

The science of spirits (and Lévi's occult project more generally) presented itself as a way to use the imagination and will to manipulate these astral forces. This is his break from spiritualism—because in order for the science of spirits to work, the spiritualist would have to recognize that spirits are not truly possessed of autonomous agency, but merely impressions left on the astral plane. Moreover, at its root, this astral light is a radiance originating from the mind of God (think the *fiat lux* of Genesis 1:3). To discover this light is therefore a return to the divine. Accordingly, Lévi directed an invective against all forms of spiritual mediumship that do not partake in the true "communion" with infinite being, or in other words, God.[76] The true science of spirits is revealed to be a kind of esoteric Christianity. Surprisingly, an esoteric Christianity will be revealed as the hidden core of Müller's comparative project as well.

In sum, Lévi's project demonstrates that comparative religion was the basic business of a magician (or at least, of this magician). It shows that the study of world mythology could be rooted in an attempt to enchant Europe rather than disenchant the globe. It is also hints at the kind of theological commitments engendered by the search for a hidden unity behind the world's religions. It suggests too that the study of religion can appear not just as an emergence from Protestant theology, but also as a kind of Catholic mysticism or Christian esotericism.[77]

The Philologist

[After the death of the body,] what remains is only the eternal One, the eternal Self (*ewige Selbst*), that lives in us all without beginning and without end, and in which each individual has his true being in which he lives and moves. Each temporal Ego is just one of the million incarnations (*Erscheinungen*) of this eternal Self. . . . The Self is the bond that binds together all souls, the red thread that runs through all being. . . . The Self that runs through the whole world, through all hearts, is the same for all men; it is the same for the highest and the lowest, it is the same for Creator and created; it is the "Âtman" of the Veda, the oldest and truest word for God.

MAX MÜLLER, "Das Pferdebürla," *Deutsche Rundschau*, 1896

Friedrich Max Müller (1823-1900), born in Dessau, studied philology in Leipzig, Berlin, and Paris, before moving to England, where he was appointed Taylorian Professor of Modern European Languages at Oxford in 1854 (the year before Lévi published his magical manifesto). Today Müller is probably most famous for overseeing the publication of *Sacred Books of the East* and for arguing that mythology is a "disease of language." His importance to the field of religious studies is clear in the historiography, and he is generally portrayed as a rationalist figure, fundamental to the secularizing trend of the discipline.[78] He might seem to be a bad candidate for a critique of enlightenment, yet in many ways his project approximated that of the magician.

Like Lévi, Müller's main work on comparative theology is an attempt to arrive at a common philosophy located behind the diversity of the world's mythological systems. Recognizing that previous scholars had rejected as superstitions much that did not fit into their worldview, Müller attempted to recover the lost wisdom of the East as a way to supplement something missing from the contemporary European world.[79] In this respect, Müller can be seen as benefiting from the legacy of the German Romantics, especially Friedrich Schiller, whose influence Müller readily admitted.[80] Müller was not as programmatic as Lévi in recovering the magic missing from the West. Instead he believed that while each religion had its own grains of truth, one must separate these truths from the chaff of "superstition." Müller saw the essence of religion as a transcendent reach for an "infinite" *beyond rationality*. In that, Lévi would have been in agreement.

In his construction of an academic "science of religion," Müller worked to fulfill an enlightenment-inspired mission to produce a rational and empirical field of study. He worked to exclude the academic theology of his day, and the legacy of its absence can be seen in the whole field. In its methodology, the science of religion seems at first pass to also rule out the possibility of the divine. But like the occult sciences, Müller's new field also aimed to occupy the intersection of religion and science.

Müller's project, indeed, reveals its esoteric Christian substructure in a series of Gifford lectures he gave late in his life, later published as *Theosophy; or, Psychological Religion*.[81] These lectures have been largely overlooked perhaps because they do not fit the image of Müller as arch-secularist or impartial scholar. As a result, Müller's esotericism has been suppressed by omission from the normative accounts of the formation of the discipline.

Emphasizing these lectures allows us to see a very different side to Max Müller. Indeed, while Müller is often presented as a fairly conventional Lutheran, his contemporaries knew differently.[82] As recollected by the translator and educator Thomas McCormack in his obituary for Müller:

> As to his personal belief, which is not easy to grasp in its precise details in his works, we may say generally that Professor Max Müller was a Vedantist. He was a believer in the Brahman doctrine of the *âtman*, or soul-in-itself, the monad soul; he believed in a "thinker of thoughts," a "doer of deeds," a Self within the person, which was the carrier of his personality, and a Self without, which was the carrier of the world, "God, the highest Self"; and these two Selves are ultimately the same Self: *Tat tvam asi*, That art thou, as the Brahman said.[83]

Although I will argue that Müller was less a Hindu than a kind of Christian mystic, foregrounding this version of Müller allows us to see an aspect of his thought that provided a hidden unity to even his earlier writings in religious studies. The lectures Müller delivered at the University of Glasgow in 1892 offer the ideal entry point.

Having already given Gifford lectures in preceding years on "Natural Religion," "Physical Religion," and "Anthropological Religion," Müller dedicated his final lectures to the topic of "Theosophy." In Müller's own estimation, these lectures are the "key" to the whole series of Gifford talks, representing the final culmination of both physical and anthropological religion and therefore the essence of his approach to comparative religion.[84]

Müller began the set of lectures by charting his vision for the study of comparative religion, describing the importance of the burgeoning discipline and the techniques at its disposal. This form of scholarship is described as philological and based on the comparison of textual religions, but the conventional reading of Müller would have trouble accounting for the theological register of his language and its evocation of a kind of *prisca theologia*, or ur-theology, behind the religions of the world.[85] Müller wrote:

> We learn that that no human soul was ever quite forgotten, and that there are no clouds of superstition through which the rays of eternal truth cannot pierce. Such moments are the best rewards to the student of the religions of the world—*they are the moments of true revelation, revealing the fact that God has not forsaken any of his children.*[86]

The metaphor here is one of superstitions as dark clouds periodically pierced by the light of divine truth. The role of the scholar of religion is to engage in a search for fragments of God's revelation, which illuminate the sacred texts of different religions. Rather than being a secularizing enterprise, Müller's *Religionswissenschaft* provides proof of a kind of theological monism despite apparent religious pluralism.[87] The parallels to Lévi's project are plain: like the magician, Müller's vision for the study of religion suggested the Hermeticist notion of *prisca theologia*—namely, that a diversity of "paganisms" all point toward an original and universal divine truth.

Müller's most famous phrase, "He who knows one [religion], knows none," now appears less as a call for scholastic breadth than a religious mission itself.[88] Indeed, elsewhere he referred to prophecies of Hermes Trismegistus and then added the gloss "Every religion, even the most imperfect and degraded, has something that ought to be sacred for us, for there is in all religions a secret yearning after the true, though unknown God."[89] In sum, Müller seems to position comparative religion as a form of classical Christian Hermeticism.[90]

Müller, like Lévi, charted an explicitly Christian project, albeit one informed by his engagement with Hinduism—which emerges from his assumption that while all religions have some truth, they do not have it in equal measure. Hence Müller could argue that comparative religion proves Christianity to be "infinitely superior to all other religions," and it should have nothing to fear from the newfound discipline. This should not come as a surprise because while other religions seem to have semi-occluded the divine light, the very meaning of religion is so interwoven with Christian theology that it would appear Christianity alone has access to the full plenitude of divine revelation.[91]

Müller's account of the discipline concludes with a description of three registers, or types, of natural religion, each of which is focused on the perception of the infinite in a different mode, and again showing clear parallels to Lévi.[92] First Müller describes "Physical Religion," which is directed toward the belief in the invisible as the power behind the visible. Its determinate characteristic is the "discovery of the Infinite in nature," which Müller describes as essentially an evolutionary progression, beginning with the belief in the gods of nature and culminating in the recognition of an infinite monotheistic divinity.[93] He contrasts this "Physical Religion" with "Anthropological Religion," which he describes as founded on the "discovery of the Infinite in man."[94] By this Müller means to describe how various peoples have come to their belief in the immortality of the soul.[95] In essence, these two forms of religion chart the apprehension of the infinite in nature and in humankind.

Having discussed these forms of religion in previous lecture series, Müller dedicated his 1892 lectures to demonstrating how these two infinities relate to each other. He did so by describing a third type of religion, "real religion," as emerging from the combination of physical and anthropological religion. "Real religion" arises from the realization that these two orders of infinity— God and the immortal soul—are commensurate.[96] That is, instead of two infinities there is but one; or in other words, it is the identification of the human soul with the divine.[97] Müller floated various possibilities for christening this third form of religion. In the running are the terms *theosophic*, *psychic*, or *mystic*. Each has its problems: "*Theosophic* conveys the idea of speculations on the hidden nature of God; *Psychic* reminds us of trances, visions, and ghosts; *Mystic* leaves the impression of something vague, nebulous, and secret."[98] His solution is to call this highest and most advanced form of religion "Psychological Religion" or "Theosophy," which he defined as "all attempts at discovering the true relation between the soul and God."[99] While the reader might be tempted to overlook the normative claim built into this statement, Müller went on to describe this theosophy in positivist terms as the "knowledge of the unity of the Divine and the Human."[100]

As is clear, Müller is attempting to appropriate the term *theosophy* for his own project of comparative theology.[101] In adopting this term to describe the study of religion, Müller knew that he was picking a fight with the Theosophical Society. The conflict was not as farfetched as it might at first appear, since, as discussed below, the Theosophical Society presented an institutional alternative to Müller's own discipline of religious studies. Moreover, when one explores Müller's book in detail, the distinction between these two projects turn out to be even harder to maintain.

As becomes increasingly clear over the course of these lectures, Müller is not describing Theosophical religion in dispassionate or anthropological terms. Instead he is arguing for the Theosophical discovery of the relationship between human and God as a true insight into the structure of creation, and simultaneously the evolutionarily highest point of religion. As he will argue, true religion's ultimate form can be encapsulated in the Hindu identification of Brahman and Atman, which anticipates Theosophy's purest expression in the writings of Christian mystics with their *unio mystica*.[102] He will later produce the gloss "Theosophy or Mystic Christianity" to describe the essence of this higher form of religion.[103]

Müller focused attention on the Hindu Veda in a way that evokes the position occupied by the tarot as the heart of Lévi's system.[104] In his lectures, Müller explained that the Veda is the beginning of Indian Theosophy, a form of religion that only takes its "fullest realization" in the Vedānta.[105] As a significant instance of "natural revelation," it should not surprise the reader that the Veda is a key—if not the central—text for Müller's project. He also characterized it in terms redolent with esoteric imagery: the Veda is described as a work of "seven seals," each of which must be unlocked by the serious scholar.[106]

In the following lecture, Müller expanded on this esoteric metaphor, describing the Veda's unveiling: "Unless we learn to understand this metaphorical or hieroglyphic language of the ancient world, we shall look upon the Upanishads and on most of the Sacred Books of the East as mere childish twaddle; but if we can see through the veil, we shall discover behind it not (indeed, as many imagine) profound mysteries or esoteric wisdom, but at all events intelligent and intelligible efforts in an honest search after truth."[107] Here Müller evoked in relationship to Indian sacred texts imagery of "hieroglyphics" and "veils" similar to those used by Lévi almost forty years earlier. The difference is that for Müller, behind the mask of these ancient texts one finds not "esoteric wisdom," but what is basically rational—or at the very least, philosophical—conceptions. That said, Müller was also ultimately committed to proving that these very same works express a kind of universal mysticism. He described this mysticism as rational because, he argued, "The true relation of the two souls, the human soul and the divine, is, or ought to be, as clear as the most perfect logical syllogism."[108]

In what might sound like circular reasoning, the truth behind the *Sacred Books of the East* turns out to be rational because its ultimate claims about the relationship between humans and God are true. Still, it is a truth attested to by magicians and mystics. Put differently, Müller is treating Vedānta Hinduism as both mystical and rational, but objecting to those who would read it as backward nonsense. Because he has attributed to it his own insights about the relationship between divinity and the soul, Müller's own rational mysticism is therefore presented as Vedānta Hinduism stripped of its mysteries (one might think of Müller's confession of faith cited above).

*

For Müller there are three moments where Theosophical Religion came into fully into being: Vedānta Hinduism, Greek Neoplatonism, and Christian mysticism.[109] Each of these represents the flourishing of Aryan thought taken to its ultimate fulfillment.[110] It is Christianity that has greater "theosophic wealth" than the others, but its aims turn out to be shared.[111] All aspire to a mystical recognition that the individual soul is part of God's soul. This is a claim Müller earlier described as the identification of Brahman and Atman, but now he recasts it in Christian terms.[112] As Müller elaborated, "The principal object of the Christian religion has been to make the world comprehend the oneness of the objective Deity—call it Jehovah . . . with the subjective Deity—call it self, or mind, or soul, or reason or Logos."[113] By echoing so-called Gnostic conceptions of the divine, this claim would have been rejected by a number of Christian theologians. Müller compensated in the pages that follow by arguing that mysticism the real heart of Christianity.

To do so, Müller focused on the Neoplatonic Christian theological concept of the "logos," which he argued is both the essence of Christianity and the best description of the relationship between God and man.[114] He argued that "logos" originally meant the "word" understood as "thought embodied in sound."[115] It therefore described a fundamental truth: "Word and thought, as I hope to have proved in my *Science of Thought*, are inseparable."[116] In both *Science of Thought* and *Science of Language*, Müller argued for the identity of speech and thought, or what we might call reason and language. The implication is that there are no concepts without language, no meaningless words; and moreover, that each word represents a separate concept.[117] Furthermore, building on arguments made originally by both Leibniz and Locke, Müller argued that concepts function at the broad level to denote general ideas, understood at the level of the species (or category) rather than the individual exemplar.[118] This was an argument Müller made repeatedly.

In his lectures on "Theosophy," however, Müller disclosed the Neoplatonist metaphysics he omitted elsewhere, remarkably revealing that his philosophy of language is indebted to a Neoplatonist concept of forms: "We must use our words as we have defined them, and species means an idea, or an εἶδος (*eîdos*); that is, an eternal thought of a rational Being. Such a thought must vary in every individual manifestation of it, but it can never change. Unless we admit the eternal existence of these ideas in a rational Mind or in the Primal Cause of all things, we cannot account for our seeing them realised in nature, discovered by human reason, and named by human language."[119] Paraphrased, meaning exists in the mind of God. According to Müller, this is both what was meant by the Greek concept of the logos and is the claim proved by his own philological research. While it was perhaps predictable that Lévi was a mystical Neoplatonist, coming from Müller's position in the historiography, it is more surprising.

Lest we take this "Primal Cause" language to be merely a metaphor, the lecture then takes a seeming swerve as Müller staged this Neoplatonic concept of εἶδος in relationship to a biological concept of species. He was interested in ratcheting the theology up rather than down, stating: "The idea that the world was thought and uttered or willed by God, so far from being a cobweb of abstruse philosophy, is one of the most natural and most accurate, nay most true conceptions of the creation of the world, and, let me add at once, of the true origin of species."[120] Müller had Darwin in his sights. Such a stark claim would be out of place in contemporary religious studies, but Müller was unashamedly placing his theological commitments on the table. As he made explicit, God's reason does the work behind evolution, and there is a fundamentally unbridgeable gap between humans possessed of divine Logos and animals.[121] Regardless of what developed in nature, human intelligence is not evolved. It is clear that Müller's main target is not the religious believer, but the skeptical scientist. Hence he argued: "It is of no use for Physical Science to shut its ears against such speculations [about the forms in the divine Mind] or to call them metaphysical dreams."[122] In sum, the Platonic forms are no mere allegory.

Having represented logos in Christian Neoplatonist terms, Müller was able to cast his own philological research as Christian theology:

> I am glad to see that my critics have ceased at last to call my *Science of Thought* a linguistic paradox, and begin to see that what I contended for in that book was known long ago, and that no one ever doubted it. The *Logos*, the Word, as the thought of God, as the whole body of divine or eternal ideas, which

Plato had prophesied, which Aristotle had criticised in vain, which the Neo Platonists re-established, is a truth that forms, or ought to form the foundation of all philosophy.[123]

The logos turns out to be the heart of both Christianity and Müller's own project. This is not all. As he argued, "The Logos, therefore, the thought of God, was the bond that united heaven and earth, and through it God could be addressed once more as the Father, in a truer sense than He had ever been before."[124] The logos is nothing less than the Word in the mind of God functioning as the bridge between man and the divine.

For Müller, oneness with God is not merely a feature of Christianity, but is the goal strived for by all religions, or at the very least, all theosophical religions.[125] In a solar metaphor he continued throughout his final lecture, Müller described the human soul as the light of the Godhead and the goal of religion to recognize this light and embrace the human union with the divine. Theosophical religion, aka mystical Christianity, is the ultimate expression of these aims because it achieves the divine union toward which all religion is directed.[126]

Amazingly, Müller argued, one can achieve the realization of this truth through the labors of a historian of religion. Indeed it turns out that this recognition of the oneness of the divine and human souls asserted by philosophers and mystics is also the goal of comparative theology. As Müller concluded:

> In this, my last course, it has been my chief endeavor to show how [physical and anthropological religion] always strive to meet and do meet in the end in what has been called Theosophy or Psychological Religion, helping us to the perception of the essential unity of the soul with God. Both this striving to meet and the final union have found, I think, their most perfect expression in Christianity . . . as what Master Eckhart called the surrender of our will to the Will of God. . . . And if the true meaning of religion is the highest purpose of religion, you will see how after a toilsome journey the historian of religion arrives in the end at the same summit which the philosopher of religion has chosen from the first as his own.[127]

We might say the same of the philologist and the magician. Strains of Neoplatonism and Hermeticism can be seen in both. Both Lévi and Müller also had as their end goal a kind of Christian mysticism or theosophy, which they read into Eastern and Western religion alike. They both thought that the juxtaposition of different mythologies would cause them to open up and reveal God's truths.

They differed, however, as to the means for unlocking this revelation—the tarot versus Indo-European philology. Moreover, while they both postulated a hidden core behind all religions, the infinite truths of *Deus absconditus*, for Müller, the essence of the divine was reason; while for Lévi, it was ultimately beyond the grasp of rationality. Nevertheless, both saw the study of religion as a means to approach the infinite.

THEOSOPHICAL DISENCHANTMENT: HELENA BLAVATSKY

Studies on India are of interest to a wider and wider audience, and "theosophy" has almost been made fashionable among us by the adepts of a certain brand of Western occultism. . . . Theosophical ideas become an extremely important and precious framework that was missing from the regular nomenclature of India, for classifying certain ideas that otherwise could not be put under the heading either of "religion" or of "philosophy."

FERDINAND DE SAUSSURE, "La théosophie brahmanique," 1907

This section emerges from a simple insight with important implications—religious studies had a historical doppelgänger, a parallel movement, that drew from nearly the same social sphere, shared many intellectual objectives and political coordinates, and for a time was more successful in recruiting members and placing different religions in dialogue.[128] Approached without presuppositions you might imagine that the relevant discipline is comparative theology or some kind of lost comparative philosophy, but as the section heading suggests, the movement I have in mind is theosophy—and in particular, the Theosophical Society founded in 1875. Moreover, not only does theosophy share its name with Müller's term for the core of *Religionswissenschaft*, but many scholars of religion were also members of the Theosophical Society. Indeed, the closer one looks, it appears that theosophy had a certain allure as the esoteric side of the discipline of religious studies. The further problem is that theosophy was both dedicated to magic and promoted a disenchantment myth, such that having read the account of theosophical disenchantment, it is going to be even harder to identify disenchantment as a merely scholarly trope.

The Theosophical Society was a large movement peaking in 1928 at about 45,000 official adherents and more than a thousand lodges in over forty countries, not counting a number of influential offshoots.[129] It was also crucial to the Euro-American adoption of yoga and Buddhism, and was the dominant source of many features of globalized metaphysical religion, from auras to spiritual evolution to the idea of ascended masters.[130] A particular Theosophist—Alice Bailey—is often regarded as the main source of the very expression "New Age."[131]

Crucially, the Theosophical Society explicitly claimed to occupy the mediating position between religion and science. This was the location Max Müller had imagined for the "science of religion," but it was also the position Éliphas Lévi had accorded to "magic." Both were influences on the founder of the movement—Helena Blavatsky's first major work, *Isis Unveiled* (1877), which, while primarily modeled on Lévi's writings, drew from Müller's project and the Indian texts that he helped make available.[132] The ease with which Blavatsky merged religious studies and magic goes some distance in demonstrating their fundamental similarities. Moreover, insofar as religious studies is a science whose theological presuppositions we have been working to flush to the surface, the Theosophical Society appears as a religious movement whose scientific impact also needs to be exposed. The further surprise is that while Müller's claim to scientific status came by way of philology, theosophists also had a lasting impact on linguistics.

*

Perhaps the most important esoteric theorist of the late nineteenth century, Helena Petrovna Blavatsky (1831–91), was born to an aristocratic-military family in the Russian city of Yekaterinoslav (today Dnipropetrovsk, Ukraine). In 1849, shortly before her eighteenth birthday, Helena married a provincial official more than thirty years her senior. The marriage was disastrous, and within three months, Helena Blavatsky had left her husband to travel across the globe. The actual extent of her voyages is unknown, but she would later claim to have visited Egypt, India, America, and even Tibet, allegedly studying with various spiritual masters en route.[133] In 1873 Blavatsky arrived in New York, where she developed a reputation as a spiritualist medium and occult journalist. In 1875 she joined the American lawyer and Civil War veteran Colonel Henry Olcott in founding the Theosophical Society. Initially dedicated to psychical and occult research, the group evolved to focus on cross-cultural comparison.[134] The most significant development in the Theosophical Society's history occurred in 1878, when Blavatsky and Olcott relocated to India. Although the founders themselves returned to Europe in 1884, they left in place important transnational connections.

*

Blavatsky promoted an influential version of the myth of disenchantment. This is already evident in "The Science of Magic" (1875), in which she intervened in a debate between spiritualists about the existence of magic. Blavatsky argued that commanding spirits is itself a magical science and that "magic exists and has existed ever since prehistoric ages."[135] She then described the history of magic in antiquity and emphasized its brief flourishing in various Neoplatonic and alchemical circles. But then, Blavatsky argued, magic was persecuted by the Christian church, and it "finally died out in Europe" when confronted with "the frozen-hearted skepticism [of] its native country,"[136] or we might say, suffered a deathblow at the hands of enlightenment thought.

This sounds like an account of the decline of magic we might get in a dozen different sources. European modernity, and especially scientific skepticism, has meant the departure of enchantment.[137] This was a set of claims that Blavatsky amplified elsewhere, portraying the nineteenth century in terms of a "death-grapple" between science and theology, which resulted in the rise of a particularly pernicious form of materialism (like Müller, she was especially opposed to Darwinian evolution).[138] But Blavatsky was neither a herald of progress nor a melancholy sociologist. Instead, she embraced an Orientalist cliché about the lost wisdom of a timeless Asia, arguing that "in India, magic has never died out, and blossoms there as well as ever."[139]

In *Isis Unveiled* Blavatsky also came up with an alternate explanation for why magic was particularly scarce in modern Western Europe: "Magic being what it is, the most difficult of all sciences to learn experimentally—its acquisition is practically beyond the reach of the majority of white-skinned people," to which she added that because of their "sense of superiority over those whom the English term so contemptuously 'niggers,' the white European would hardly submit himself to the practical tuition of either Kopt, Brahman, or Lama."[140] To paraphrase, magic is innately difficult for white people to learn, and European prejudice makes it harder. Blavatsky was embracing what is now described as the racist stereotype of the "magical negro," but she was also identifying her project with the minoritized position.[141]

One of Blavatsky's innovations was her embrace of a particular philosophy of history that took seriously a vast chronology. In a different part of the work, Blavatsky projected back an extended temporality of prehistory, arguing that magic was the spiritual science of ancient sages, whose powers had not yet been achieved by modern science.[142] She also described history as broadly cyclical, arguing that civilizations rise, reach their height, and then collapse into barbarism.[143] The divine science of the ancients was largely lost in one such collapse. Nevertheless, she anticipated an eventual recovery of all that had been lost: "Physical science has reached the limits of its exploration; theology sees the spring of its inspiration dry. Unless we mistake the signs, the day is approaching when the world will see proofs that only ancient religions were in harmony with nature, and ancient science embraced all that can be known. . . . Who knows the possibility of the future? An *era of disenchantment* and rebuilding will soon begin—nay, has already begun. The cycle has run its course, a new one is about to begin."[144]

Blavatsky used the term *disenchantment* to describe not the death of magic, but her perception of an affect resulting from the failures of both science and theology. Moreover, Blavatsky and Tylor would have agreed about modern magic as a recovery of primitive science, the difference being that for Tylor, primitive science was generally incorrect, while for Blavatsky, the ancients had true wisdom. Finally, like Müller, Blavatsky argued that to know one religion requires that one know them all. In her account, different religions have preserved rays of light due to their shared origin in the primordial theosophy (religion/magic/science), which is their common ancestor.[145]

In Blavatsky's hands, theosophy was partially a quasi-academic retrieval and philological interpretation of Asian texts; but she also claimed privileged access to inner teachings that had been preserved by a secretive group of "Ascended Masters" still living in Asia. While this might sound farfetched, the grounding assumption of the early Theosophical Society was precisely this claim: the perennial philosophy had vanished in Europe, only to be preserved by the "mahatmas," or Great Brotherhood of India and Tibet. In some respects, this was comparable to Müller and company's turn toward India as a source for lost wisdom. An important difference, however, is that instead of spending their time in European libraries painstakingly translating ancient texts, the Theosophists went to South Asia in search of Gurus and further revelations.

*

In her influential magnum opus *The Secret Doctrine* (1888), Blavatsky posited a developmental history of languages, describing an evolution from monosyllabic to agglutinative to inflected languages that evoked the linguistic theories of her day (except for the fact that she pinned one of these language phases onto Atlantis).[146] Her aim was a reconstruction of the ancestor of Sanskrit, or what scholars today would call Proto-Indo-European.[147] In many respects Blavatsky was following academic linguistics of her period, but she was also attempting to reconstruct the original perennial philosophy (which she identified with magic and esoteric wisdom). It is worth emphasizing that trying to use a comparative method to recover a primordial revelation was something theosophists and many scholars of religion shared.

The influence between theosophy and linguistics was not unidirectional. Theosophy also had a broader impact on linguistic theory. It is no accident that the only thing Ferdinand de Saussure actually completed for publication during the long period he was giving his famous "Course in General Linguistics" (1906–11) was a review article about Brahmanical theosophy (cited in the epigraph above). Saussure was far from a theosophist. But he was likely drawn to the work because he had just spent five years attending the séances of a psychical medium who claimed to have visions of a past life in India. Hence it seems likely Saussure undertook a reading in Indian philosophical and "theosophical" literature to reassure himself that the medium was making it all up.[148]

Much later, one of linguistics' signal contributions to the human sciences is the controversial notion of linguistic relativity, or the "Sapir-Whorf hypothesis"—usually understood to mean that language determines thought. Debates around linguistic relativity often focus on *Language, Mind, and Reality* (1941) by Benjamin Lee Whorf. That the essay was initially published in the *Theosophist* journal rarely accords more than a passing mention.[149] But Whorf was a practicing Theosophist, and if you reread that essay with that knowledge in mind, the theosophical connections are impossible to ignore. Not only did he describe "Mantra Yoga" as "the next great step" of "Western consciousness" and cite theosophical authors to make his argument, but he also testified to the theosophical origin of his ideas: "It is known, or something like it is known, to the philosophies of India and to modern Theosophy."[150] In these respects, linguistic relativity might seem to be a theosophical position.

*

The main point of this brief section has been to touch on some of the many parallels between religious studies and the Theosophical Society. Before concluding, I want to show how much the two movements overlapped. The French philologist Émile Burnouf (cousin to Eugène Burnouf)—in his own day famous as a Sanskritist and author of *La science des religions* (1876)—publically lent his authority as a Buddhologist to the Theosophical claims to be authentic interpreters of the original Buddhism.[151] Nor was he the last. Walter Evans-Wentz, the American anthropologist and scholar of Buddhism, a lifelong theosophist, embedded theosophical concepts in his famous version of *The Tibetan Book of the Dead* (1927), which remains in print.[152] The Japanese scholar D. T. SUZUKI (SUZUKI Daisetsu Teitarō), founder of the academic study of Zen Buddhism, had joined the Theosophical Society in Tokyo in 1920, and later testified to the authenticity of Blavatsky's teachings.[153] This does not exhaust the list, and beyond famous and committed members, there were many more scholars who took the Theosophists seriously enough to engage with their writings.[154]

More broadly, the Theosophical Society mediated transcultural exchanges between Europe and Asia; connected scientists and magicians, scholars, and native practitioners; and delivered public access to the "secrets" of esotericism.[155] Even after the Theosophical Society began waning in 1929,[156] it embedded its idiosyncratic concepts in a range of domains. Indeed, scholars of religion are still grappling with the legacy and unconscious influence of Theosophical terminology.[157]

CONCLUSION: SPECTERS OF THE TRANSCENDENT

Here you see the transcendent character of the Self maintained, even after it has become incarnate, just as we hold that God is present in all things, but also transcends them.

MAX MÜLLER, *Three Lectures on the Vedânta Philosophy*, 1904

The main aim of this chapter has been to locate Max Müller and E. B. Tylor in the spiritualist and Theosophical milieu of their period and to explore habits of thought scholars shared with occultists like Éliphas Lévi and Helena Blavatsky. I have also introduced a theme that will be important over the course of this book—namely, that the loss of magic was a common trope among self-professed magicians. If these points are granted, the broad goal of this chapter has been met; but as a religious studies scholar myself, I want to use this conclusion not only to deepen those points, but also to explore the implications of this alternative cultural context for the origins of the discipline.

There is a shadow over the discipline of religious studies. The *Encyclopédie*'s early definitions of religion have God in them and seek to explain the diversity of world religions according to a causal agency originating in that divinity. After all, the entry on "religion" in the *Encyclopédie* begins, "The foundation of all religion is that there is a God who has dealings with his creatures and who requires them to worship him."[158] But a monotheistic deity has become increasingly displaced by terms like *the sacred* or *the transcendent*.[159]

On the one hand, this shift signals the recognition that not all the traditions conventionally grouped under the category "religion" worship a monotheistic divinity. On the other hand, this recent transformation in the meaning of religion suggests both a secularization and radical broadening of the definition. The changing language marks a critical difference. This shift in meaning seems to represent the vanishing of God, and words like *transcendent, infinite,* or *sacred* are attempts to cover for an absence, to describe a shadow. Yet the very category of "religion" was formulated around a Christian concept of God. In talking and writing about religion, it is often mistakenly assumed that religions have a common hidden essence that marks them as "religious." In excluding God from its explanatory apparatus, "religion" remains as a category structured around a hole or fissure. In other words, we find ourselves in a discipline organized around a core that no longer exists and we cannot in good conscience reconstruct. Moreover, this constitutive absence menaces the very task of discipline formation and the forms of circumscription it presumes. The language of haunting is particularly appropriate here, as it evokes a ghostly presence that is simultaneously the sign of a fundamental absence.

In the study of religion, terms like *the transcendent* are supposed to be more cosmopolitan or universal, structuring the definition of religion. Thus, defining the field around these terms instead of *God* was supposed to be more inclusive. For the most part, this vocabulary does not work for other cultures; and it does not accurately describe assumed commonalities. The new terminology is nearly just as Christian as that which it has replaced. Indeed; this language—imported in many ways from mysticism—is easily transformed into a suppressed Christian triumphalism; or the claim, as William Blake put it, that "all religions are one." If God is dead, God is still haunting the study of religion; and "the transcendent" is a divine shadow. This chapter has worked to reveal some of the early processes by which versions of mysticism fostered the substitution of the transcendent for God.

Moreover, this absent or abstract God is precisely the deity of the *philosophes* approached by different means. Whether framed phenomenologically or through an interpretation of cultural symbols, insofar as the academic study of religion takes God or the transcendent as its organizing principle, the field functions as a modern mysticism, striving for a hidden center. Mircea Eliade was less exceptional than he has been presented. These mystical undercurrents are also in tension with the discipline's self-presentation as a secular science, understood as the rational study of an irrational subject. Thus, bringing this occult underground to the surface has generally met with resistance. Even as religious studies has attempted to purge mysticism in its public disciplining process, a specter remains and refuses to vanish. As portions of religious studies have become increasingly specialized, the transcendent shadow has resurfaced in other disciplines in the so-called "turn to religion in postmodern thought."[160]

Jeffrey Kripal, Steven Wasserstrom, and Hans Thomas Hakl have explored the mystical side of twentieth-century religious studies, but mysticism goes further back, to the "origins"—whatever those are—of the discipline. Indeed, what Kripal advocates as "academic gnosticism" or "comparative mysticism" has long been a common thread in the discipline's history.[161] While not every scholar is a mystic, the very terms that have defined the field, that have structured the profession, pull in this direction. The contrary reaction has often been to close down dialogue by arguing that those things marked as "religions" have no common essence, and thus to risk balkanizing the discipline.[162] It should not be surprising, then, that many of the most influential members of the field have turned to mystical language in their attempts to produce grand syntheses. When following this latter route, religious studies might seem as but the crest of the modern esoteric wave.

Scholars of nineteenth-century religion have increasingly come to recognize that spiritualism was one of the most important transnational movements of the era.[163] This was also the period that religious studies was born, and it is now a matter of revising our narrative of the history of religious studies in the face of this insight. The cultural setting of the disciplinary formation of religious studies has been misread. It was neither antireligious skepticism nor mainstream Protestantism, neither secular disenchantment nor liberal theology. Instead, it appears as though occultists, spiritualists, and many scholars of religion were fellow travelers, or at least, inhabitants of the same conceptual universe.

I would like to reconstruct some of this milieu in concrete historical terms. As fellow Oxford professors, it should be no surprise that E. B. Tylor and Max Müller knew each other and corresponded regularly.[164] The surprise is that, as I have shown, despite their different politics and positions in the historiography, Müller and Éliphas Lévi were not far apart intellectually. Socially they were not that far apart either, as both were acquaintances of the English novelist and politician Edward Bulwer-Lytton.[165] Further, members of the Theosophical movement equally appropriated the work of Lévi and Müller into their project.[166] Blavatsky's cofounder of the Theosophical Society, Henry Olcott, connects all four figures.

In fact, Olcott even corresponded with Müller. In one letter remaining from this exchange (sent to Olcott on June 10, 1893), Müller betrays both his conflicts with the Theosophical Society and the similarity of their ultimate aims. In response to the Theosophists, Müller denies the very existence of an esoteric Buddhism, arguing "Buddhism is the very opposite of esoteric. . . . There was much more of that esoteric teaching in Brahmanism."[167] Here he seems to be privileging his appropriation of Hindu materials over the Theosophists' use of Buddhism. It is perhaps even more telling that Müller argues against the Theosophists' "mahatmas," suggesting that even if they were real, no "living Pandit" knows more than what is contained in the text. It becomes clear that what is at stake for Müller is the value of European philology versus native informants, contacted spiritually or in the flesh (and in that, he might as well be attacking anthropology as theosophy). Nevertheless, both Müller and the Theosophical Society viewed Indian materials as crucial for the "enrichment" of European religion.[168]

Although he never met Lévi in person, Olcott made it his business in 1884 to track down Lévi's two remaining pupils for discussions of their departed master.[169] Furthermore, in a diary entry from October 1888, Olcott recounted that not only had he met with Müller—who welcomed him as a fellow Orientalist—but also that Müller had introduced him to Tylor. Olcott noted that despite his warm reception, he and Müller agreed to disagree about the existence of the hidden masters and other issues.[170]

Despite Müller's rejection of the Theosophical Society, his work continued to speak to members of the movement. P. D. Ouspensky, a Russian former Theosophist and follower of the Greco-Armenian thaumaturge G. I. Gurdjieff, was inspired by Müller's lectures on theosophy in the formulation of his own mystical system. In the text that announced that project as *Tertium Organum*, we return full circle, because like the French *philosophes*, Ouspensky was inspired by Francis Bacon (particularly Bacon's *Novum Organum*) to produce what Ouspensky saw as a continuation of Bacon's grand synthesis of philosophical and mystical knowledge. To do so, Ouspensky believed he was activating the mystical aspect of Müller's theosophy and partaking in his quest for the infinite behind all religions.[171] *Tertium Organum* implies an alternate genealogy of the study of religion, rooted not merely in "the Enlightenment" or in Hume's rationalism, but also in Romantic recovery and magic.

It might be tempting to equate accounts of disenchantment with the embrace of secularization or a theoretical commitment to cultural evolution. But this is an assumption that gets harder to sustain when confronted by Lévi's and Blavatsky's discussions of the European loss of magic as part of broad narratives of the alienation of divine revelation. It would seem that both magicians and sociologists have had reason to describe an atomized and alienated

Western modernity. It would also seem that even in occult circles, where testifying to spirits and enchantments was a regular experience, theorists found reasons to describe magic as marginalized. All this should make us more suspicious of the function of the myth of disenchantment, as it often occurs alongside attempts to reinstate missing wonders.

This has implications not only for the field of religious studies but also for narratives about secularism and disenchantment. Living as we do in the perceived shadow of an absent God, models of secularization have been pressed to explain the current so-called religious revival, manifesting as it does now in the face of scientific modernity.[172] Insofar as the discipline of religious studies is both a fulfillment and a counterreaction to "modernity," it has, therefore, a parallel function to those other revivals. Common to both is a kind of occlusion that functions by suppressing something at the same moment that another aspect of the suppressed is being reincorporated.

Despite the way in which religious studies represents a recovery of the *théosophes*, it has repeatedly distanced itself from the science of spirits.[173] A secular study of the science of spirits remains excluded even as a semi-occluded occult pervades the underground of the field. This rejection of spirits represents the victory of a kind of quasi-materialist ontology that has clearly delimited and disciplined the realm of the possible. Moreover, religious studies is still haunted by the legacy of the *philosophes* in its rejection of "superstition." Particularly striking from this vantage point is the production of a superstition-religion binary. In defining *religion* in terms of monolithic essences (*transcendent, sacred*, etc.), the discipline has historically produced a "remainder" of things that do not count as religion and are therefore outside our realm of inquiry. Much of what was rejected was labeled as superstition and relegated to the fields of folklore or anthropology (as will be discussed in the next chapter). Although some of this has begun to shift, the exclusions built into this structure gave shape to the formation of religion as category both academically and legally, and continue to determine the field's trajectory. While the word *superstition* has vanished from our conversation within the discipline, the things once occluded under its name remain blocked from view.

CHAPTER FIVE

The Decline of Magic:
J. G. Frazer

As religion grows, magic declines into a black art.

JAMES FRAZER, *The Golden Bough* (third edition), 1906

They thought that she was not Bridget Cleary at all, but a witch.

JAMES FRAZER, *The Golden Bough* (third edition), 1913

In March of 1895, the Irish newspaper *Nationalist & Tipperary Advertiser* ran an article titled "Mysterious Disappearance of a Young Woman: The Land of the Banshee and the Fairy." It reported that a local Clonmel woman had vanished under strange circumstances:

> Her friends who were present assert that she had been taken away on a white horse before their eyes, and that she told them when leaving, that on Sunday night they would meet her at a fort on Kylenagranagh hill, where they could, if they had the courage, rescue her. Accordingly, they assembled at the appointed time and place to fight the fairies, but, needless to say, no white horse appeared.[1]

In the weeks that followed, the fate of the twenty-six-year-old seamstress Bridget Cleary would make international headlines. As reported by the *Nationalist* and other papers, her husband, Michael, and other family members had originally claimed that Bridget had been spirited away by the fairies. When her badly burned body was found a few days later, Michael Cleary asserted that the corpse was not his wife, but either a witch or a nonhuman changeling that had taken her place; the real Bridget, he said, would soon appear.[2]

As the case came to trial in the following months, it became a lightning-rod issue for those supporting and opposing Ireland's right to Home Rule. Did the Irish really believe in fairies and magic? If so, did this disqualify them from self-governance? Or was Michael Cleary's reference to fairies merely an attempt to justify the murder of an unfaithful spouse?[3] Thus the issue basically became whether Ireland was still enchanted, and whether or not that was normal, and these questions were frequently addressed by the recently founded discipline of folklore studies (British Folklore Society, established 1878).[4] Mainly, self-appointed experts asserted that "superstitions" such as belief in ghosts, magic, and fairies were common to most if not all peoples.[5] Moreover, scholars generally granted that these "superstitions" had always persisted and were in no danger of vanishing in the face of modernity. Accordingly, the verdict of judge and jury in the Cleary case was that rural Ireland had never been truly disenchanted—that belief in "magic" and "fairies" endured and was the primary motive for Bridget's murder.

Bridget Cleary was far from the only public case of "superstition" in the last decades of the Victorian period. The English politician John Morley, observing what he saw as a rise of religious enthusiasm in 1873, argued that "our age of science is also the age of deepening superstition and reviving sacerdotalism."[6] By the same token, while looking back on the late Victorian epoch, the British journalist George Holbrook Jackson characterized the period in terms of a "revival of mysticism."[7]

Indeed, while in the eyes of many the nineteenth century was increasingly godless, Victorian scholars were in a position to know different. In the latter part of the century, folklorists could point to a range of evidence that suggested anything but disenchantment. Along with the previously discussed rise of spiritualism and Theosophy, this evidence included a boom in the number of Anglican priests; the birth of the Salvation Army (1865); the popular attention given to apparitions of the Virgin Mary reputed in France at Lourdes (1858), Pontmain (1871), and Pellevoisin (1876) and Germany at Marpingen (1876); and in the United States, the appearance and then suppression of the Ghost Dance revival in 1890.[8]

Hence, it is all the more striking that the 1890s brought out a classical version of the disenchantment thesis, and from the pen of someone not just embedded in the field of folklore studies, but intimately aware of the Cleary case and contemporary evidence of magical survivals. I speak of the Scottish folklorist and classicist James George Frazer (1854–1941), who both reacted viscerally to the "Witch Burning of Clonmel," as it was known, and authored the most significant early formulation of the disenchantment narrative in terms of the death of magic. While many sociologists understand the term *disenchantment* to refer to the classical theory that cultures evolve through successive stages from magic to religion to science, this claim is not formulated as such in Max Weber's writings, but does appear in those terms in Frazer's works.[9] The common usage of *disenchantment* therefore to describe this three-phase cultural evolution is a conflation of those two theorists and misses Frazer's historical priority and influence.

Part of the work of this chapter will be to locate Frazer's role in the genesis of the disenchantment narrative. Despite his immense influence in the early twentieth century, Frazer's star has been on the wane for quite some time. His masterwork, *The Golden Bough*, is mentioned in the historiography but today rarely gets cited approvingly. To the degree that there is an established line about Frazer, scholars characterize him as an "undertaker" of religion or an arch-secularist, and this is not meant as a compliment.[10] So while Frazer lingers in undergraduate textbooks, unlike the profusion of Weberians and the occasional committed Freudians, there are few, if any, "Frazerites" remaining in the academy.[11] He has also largely vanished from the pedigree of philosophers of disenchantment, and when scholars have reconstructed the history of the narrative, they tend to begin with Weber or even Descartes.[12] This is a striking omission because Frazer was a large influence on subsequent theorists from Freud and Weber to the Frankfurt School and the Vienna Circle.

Tracing Frazer's version of the evolution of human thought should help us understand the roots of the disenchantment narrative as it appears today, long after *The Golden Bough* has been discredited. While disenchantment has come to be a driving *sociological* narrative, its early form as the project of a *folklorist* has concrete implications. This is because despite what I've just written, there is a certain belatedness to Frazer's formulation. Reading the history of British folklore studies with an eye to the end of magic does indeed produce a number of precedents for Frazer's famous formulation. But the shock is that disenchantment appears not primarily in the theory of the master folklorists, but within the folktales themselves that often located fairies, magic, and miracles in a bygone age. In fact, the departure of fairy enchantments was one of the first motifs that the nascent discipline discovered. Although these tales were not his only source, Frazer seems to have been allowing his theory to be imprinted by folkloric conceptions—not, as we may have thought, the other way around. And though Frazer is famous for his repudiation of magic, I show that he had an unsettled relationship to magic, such that his work could lead to easy recuperation by European magicians.

In the pages that follow, I begin by locating Frazer's project in the larger context of Victorian folklore, and show that his vacillations were not peculiar to him but endemic in the early days of the discipline.

THE CULTURAL RUINS OF PAGANISM

It is commonly imagined that superstition avoids great cities, and locates itself amid woods and streams in the depths of the country. A slight acquaintance with the inhabitants of London must speedily dissipate this idea. On the outskirts of our prodigious city, where the sheen of the gas-lamps mingles with the light of the glow-worm in the fields, beliefs as ancient as the world still prevail in unimpaired force. The Lamia of antiquity, that roamed about moonlit shores, and through the dark recesses of forests, to entrap and devour stray children, has found her way to the environs of London.

JAMES AUGUSTUS ST. JOHN, *The Education of the People*, 1859

Since the early 1970s, anthropologists have formulated a now standard autocritique of their discipline, succinctly summarized as the claim that "theories of anthropology represent nothing more than types of imperialist ideology."[13] The essence of this observation is not only that anthropology emerged from the asymmetrical power relations between Europe and conquered peoples, but also that anthropologists facilitated the practical enterprise of managing empires. Furthermore, anthropologists reinforced the inequalities that existed between European elites and the rest of the world, by objectifying indigenous peoples under the ahistorical categories of the "primitive" and "the savage without history" as part of the process of legitimating European expansion and civilizing missions.[14] All of this critique is applicable. Yet, for all the scholarship on the history of anthropology, the history of folklore studies has received remarkable little attention, perhaps because it remains a comparatively marginal field in the contemporary Angolophone academy.[15]

This gap in the scholarship is important for three reasons: first, folklore studies had an outsized influence on the other social sciences of the period; second, its politics were a mess, but they do not map well onto the standard critique of anthropology; and finally, to the degree to which folklorists were invested in the notion of cultural survivals, they often argued that the central feature of modernity was not the departure of the supernatural, but its uncanny persistence in the face of modernization. Therefore it becomes important to locate Frazer, a classicist turned folklorist, in this milieu.

*

Superficially, folklore studies might seem to resemble anthropology insofar as it produced a comparable ahistorical other. By way of illustration, in the 1884 essay "The Method of Folklore," Andrew Lang famously summarized the field as follows: "The student of folklore is thus led to examine the usages, myths and ideas of savages, which are still retained in rude enough shape, by the European peasantry."[16] To be a folklorist was therefore to study the superstitions of "savages" as preserved in the world of the European peasant. If British anthropology was about objectifying foreign "primitives," folklore seems to have been preoccupied with the savages within the home islands, even as folklorists like Lang (and Frazer) gestured at the importance of studying both. In this sense, folklore studies inhabited a position we might today associate with sociology: as a kind of internal anthropology of the modern West.

To trace what was specific to the historical trajectory of British folklore, we need to know right off that its conception of the "folk" emerged across a set of domestic, rather than extra-national, screens of difference. It can be viewed as developing from the long process of internal turmoil, consolidation, and cultural differentiation of the United Kingdom, which during the Victorian period was experienced as an internal English empire imposed variously on the Welsh, Scottish, and Irish nations. By the 1850s, the conception of humanity as classified into distinct "races" was also coming into vogue. These factors combined to produce racializing discourses that differentiated supposedly superior "white" Britons, referred to as "Teutons" or "Anglo-Saxons," against the supposedly inferior race of "Celts," while simultaneously further stigmatizing other minority "races."[17] Folklore as a field started from the assumption that all these minority groups possessed distinct cultures and thus folkloric traditions. Moreover, coming into the nineteenth century, British identity was partially routed through the Protestantisms of the official Anglican Church and the Scottish Kirk. While Protestant dissenters were largely invisible to folklorists, the field also focused on Catholic, Jewish, and "pagan" customs and their purported survival in local communities. In effect, the only people who truly lacked folklore were urban, educated English Protestants.

British folklore studies, accordingly, coalesced around a particular set of tensions regarding its basic subject, "folklore." On one hand, some folklorists described the project as rooted in uncovering and exposing those superstitions that were an obstacle to modernization. In that sense, they were actually working to demolish their own subject matter and extend the reach of "civilization" deeper into the British world and later its colonies.[18]

On the other hand, many folklorists often worked to preserve local cultures and traditions in danger of being lost by "modernization." Representatives of internal minorities were overrepresented in the early history of folklore studies, which had important members who were Jewish (Moses Gaster, Joseph Jacobs), Scottish (Lang, Frazer), Welsh (John Rhŷs), and Irish (Douglas Hyde,

Thomas Keightley, Ella Young); and they often figured prominently in various political campaigns to encourage the devolution of Great Britain's internal empire. Indeed, Douglas Hyde's trajectory from folklorist and cofounder of the Gaelic League to first president of Ireland is extreme but emblematic of one of the political impulses that animated the discipline.[19] Because of the era's facile equation between the civilizing and the Anglicizing process, we could see folklore studies as either analyzing those groups who need to be assimilated or as reinforcing those cultural resources that might resist Anglicizing. It thus could be seen as either a consolidation of empire or resistance to imperialism and modernization.

Given that for much of anthropology's early history, its practitioners were external to the populations that they observed, even when anthropologists spoke out on behalf of non-European peoples, it is hard not to imagine the kind of *Dances with Wolves* version of anticolonialism, which portrays a white savior figure as crucial to the protection of indigenous cultures. Early folklorists from internal minorities seem therefore to be in a different camp because they were able to speak not just *for* the Irish, say, but *as* Irish. Still, they were not the whole of the conversation. Within the community of early folklorists, one might find procolonialists and anticolonialists; some were attempting to consolidate enlightenment, while others seemingly worked to undermine it.

*

Early folkloristics' fundamental orientation presupposed a persistence of the primitive within the modern. Despite the field's deep political fault lines, folklorists were largely united in the notion of "superstitions" as cultural survivals. It was largely taken as given that folktales, myths, and rituals were "antiquities" representing remnants of prehistoric cultural systems.[20] The supposition that folkways were ubiquitous in even civilized cultures tended to undercut the notion that cultures represented complete evolutionary stages. Again, the comparison to anthropology is useful because while early anthropologists often saw non-European "savages" as living museum relics preserving complete stages of cultural evolution,[21] the folklorists were invested in seeing "primitives" within European culture, and thus they were inclined to see cultural evolution as incomplete; this meant that folklorists often insisted on the persistence of superstition and belief in magic.

A version of the disenchantment of the world—or at least, the idea that modernization or urbanization would abolish superstition—was a known narrative, but folklorists often presented it as the nonscholarly or naïve view.

As this section's epigraph illustrates, scholars argued that even in urban and modern London, "beliefs as ancient as the world still prevail in unimpaired force." The average Joe might imagine that all superstitions would vanish with the coming of progress, but the folklorist knew different and was even more likely to stage the counterargument: that modernity was still haunted.[22]

By way of another example, in *Primitive Manners and Customs* (1879), the English folklorist and archeologist James Farrer reminded his readers that Victorian Britons lived amidst the cultural (and physical) ruins of the Roman world, and he went on to describe "the mass of purely pagan ideas, which varnished over by Christianity, but barely hidden by it, grow in rank profusion in our very midst and exercise a living hold."[23] Embracing an analogue as old as the discipline, Farrer argued for a vision of folklore studies as a kind of cultural archeology capable of recovering pagan structures beneath their contemporary Christian veneer. The assumption of the whole enterprise is that such cultural relics still exist, and in such a state that they can be analyzed.

In part because British folklorists were initially more restricted than anthropologists in their geographic focus, they often imagined that within Britain, they saw evidence of a specific pre-Christian religion, associated with the mysterious "Druids" and preserved in fragmentary form in local folkways, standing stones, and peasant superstitions.[24] In effect, they often supposed that tales of goblins and fairies were vestigial remnants of half-remembered pagan gods.[25] Accordingly, in addition to its spadework in excavating national essences and local cultures, folklore studies was almost from the get-go preoccupied with reconstructing the cultural ruins of a pagan past.

Insofar as folklore studies cohered around "superstition" as a master category, the field presumed an ability to perceive continuities across cultural epochs. Indeed, folkloristics was able to make a case for itself only to the degree that superstitions remained, and remained relevant. They also provided empirical evidence to bolster this claim. In the Germany, Britain, and France of 1879, Farrer reminded his readers, enchantment still lingered with superstitions around specific days, and belief in magic charms, wise-women, and even witchcraft. By way of example, he provided statistical evidence indicating the persistence of superstitions around unlucky Fridays in France and observed that

> many a German that lay dead on the carnage fields of the late [Franco-Prussian, 1870–71] war was found to have carried his word-charm as his safest shield against sword or bullet. Most English villages still have their wise men or women whose powers range, like those of the shamans in savage tribes, from

ruling the planets to curing rheumatics or detecting thieves; and witchcraft still has its believers, occasionally its victims, as of yore.[26]

For all the folklorists' talk of evolution, evidence like this suggested to many that peasant life remained fundamentally unchanged from that of pre-Christian Europe and hence would have pushed against any narrative of disenchantment as a universal or uniform trajectory. Initially, at least, James Frazer agreed with this assumption.

THE GOLDEN BOUGH BEFORE DISENCHANTMENT

The primitive Aryan, in all that regards his mental fibre and texture, is not extinct. He is amongst us to this day. The great intellectual and moral forces which have revolutionised the educated world have scarcely affected the peasant.

JAMES FRAZER, *The Golden Bough* (first edition), 1890

Frazer is today famous as a cultural evolutionist and for describing the transition from magic to religion. It is often said that this argument appears in his most well-known work, *The Golden Bough*. In fact, these claims do not make an appearance in the first edition in 1890. In this edition, Frazer blurs rather than distinguishes magic and religion, and he largely overlooks grand narratives of cultural evolution. Instead, his main argument is that little has changed in the religious-magical landscape of Europe.

The main aim of the first edition of *The Golden Bough* was to reconstruct the whole edifice of primitive "Aryan" religion, which, like other folklorists, Frazer saw expressed in the seasonal rituals of the European peasant.[27] In this project, Frazer had a number of interlocutors, including Max Müller. Frazer, however, dismissed Müller's analysis of the Veda and philological reconstruction of primitive religion on the basis of myths, and went straight to the Italian peasant. In this, Frazer followed the standard model in folklore studies by simultaneously romanticizing and denigrating the rural population of Europe. In the first edition of the work, he betrayed some ambivalence about superstition, making it simultaneously valuable as the remnant of the ancient Aryan religion, and yet also a sign of the primitive savagery in the heart of modern Europe.

The narrative of the work is far from the teleological progression of epochs for which Frazer would later be famous. While he described an evolving transformation of elite thought, he imagined that the mentality of rural Europe had remained largely unchanged from time immemorial. In other words, before he

ever formulated a narrative of disenchantment, Frazer emphasized timeless-
ness, albeit with some exceptions.[28] This was, of course, in keeping with the
disciplinary assumptions of early Victorian folklore studies.

It is worth emphasizing the distinctions Frazer did *not* make in the first
edition, but which became crucial to later editions. He initially described
contemporary European peasants as practicing religion mostly for the sake
of this-worldly magical effects.[29] In this the peasant preserves the character
of "primitive religion," whose rites, Frazer argued, are "magical rather than
propitiatory."[30] Magic is not opposed to religion, nor is it prior to it, in the first
edition's account; instead it is merely one type of religious ritual. This would
not have been a controversial claim; there were many precedents for the assertion that magic was a lower type of religion.[31] Furthermore, Frazer maintained
that primitive religion is "superstitious," and hence generally amalgamated
rather than differentiated the categories of religion, magic, and superstition.[32]

The main thrust of *The Golden Bough* is that Christ, especially as figured in
the passion narrative, is just the latest incarnation of a primitive Aryan god or
King of the Wood. Christianity (or at least, Catholicism), is really paganism in
Semitic guise.[33] Frazer concluded the first edition of *The Golden Bough*: "The
result, then, of our inquiry is to make it probable that, down to the time of the
Roman Empire and the beginning of our era, the primitive worship of the
Aryans was maintained nearly in its original form in the sacred grove at Nemi,
as in the oak woods of Gaul, of Prussia, and of Scandinavia; and that the King
of the Wood lived and died as an incarnation of the supreme Aryan god, whose
life was in the mistletoe or Golden Bough."[34] As Frazer has argued over the
course of the text, it was a King of the Wood who dies and is reborn as a sign of
the agricultural cycle and toward whom Aryans had historically directed rites
in order to assure the fertility of the womb and field. Frazer cued his readers to
the identification between Aryan paganism and Catholicism in the final paragraph of the first edition, which conjures the sound of Catholic church bells,
ringing out the *angelus* and echoing through the groves of modern Nemi, and
concludes with the sentence: *"Le roi est mort, vive le roi!"*[35]

Frazer began his scholarly career as a classicist and the first edition is an
attempt to show that contemporary Europe has preserved classical paganism
more than it wants to admit. As we know from a query letter Frazer wrote to
his publisher George Macmillan in 1889, one of the aims of the work was to
demonstrate the continuities between Aryan paganism and Christianity.[36] Basically, Frazer wanted his reader to think of Christian faith or at least Christian
praxis as superstitious and atavistic. Here the characterizations of Frazer as an
undertaker of religion are fair. But the work would undergo significant shifts

in later editions that would make its aims and basic arguments quite different. Instead of continuities, it would come to emphasize evolutionary progressions.

*

If the main claim of the first edition of *The Golden Bough* is that very little has changed from the primitive Aryan cult to the modern Catholic Church, why and when does Frazer move on to a disenchantment narrative? Using Frazer's letters, we can date the shift with some degree of precision. Its first appearance is in a letter Frazer sent to the Australian anthropologist Walter Baldwin Spencer on November 28, 1898, as part of a longer correspondence between the two about how to interpret the "totemism" of the Australian aborigines. In this context, Frazer wrote:

> I am coming more and more to the conclusion that if we define religion as the propitiation of natural and supernatural powers, and magic as the coercion of them, magic has everywhere preceded religion. It is only when men find by experience that they cannot compel the higher powers to comply with their wishes, that they condescend to entreat them. In time, after long ages, they begin to realise that entreaty is also vain, and then they try compulsion again, but this time the compulsion is applied within narrower limits and in a different way from the old magical method. In short religion is replaced by science. The order of evolution, then, of human thought and practice is magic—religion—science. We in this generation live in a transition epoch between religion and science, an epoch which will last of course for many generations to come. It is for those who care for progress to aid the final triumph of science as much as they can in their day.[37]

In this letter Frazer had arrived at his famous master narrative: the cultural evolution of humankind and the progression from magic to religion to science. Frazer's sketch here nicely matches the popular summary of the myth of disenchantment. I explore this narrative and its implications in greater detail in the next section, but it is worth underscoring that Frazer's initial rhetorical purpose is especially clear in this passage: he takes for granted the opposition between religion and science and seems to be suggesting that he can use the disenchantment narrative to facilitate the death of religion. In other words, the myth of disenchantment is itself supposed to be secularizing.

If this letter represents the *terminus ante quem* by which the disenchantment narrative had been formulated, it does not take us very far in teasing

out the details of what inspired Frazer.[38] There is some disagreement about
this in the small world of Frazer studies. Peter Baker has argued it emerged
from Frazer's falling-out with Andrew Lang; Robert Ackerman has shown
that Frazer remained friends with Lang until much later and has argued that
the new schema emerged organically from Frazer's reading of ethnographies
of Australian Aborigines; finally, Robert Fraser (no relation to James Frazer)
emphasizes the publication in 1896 of *An Introduction to the History of Religion* by Frank Byron Jevons.[39] Of these, the last suggestion has the most merit,
insofar as Frazer seems to have imported some of his distinction between
religion and magic from Jevons, but Jevons explicitly rejected reading them
chronologically.[40]

Instead, Frazer's turn to disenchantment is more closely mirrored in *Die
Religion des Veda* (The religion of the Veda, 1894), an otherwise overlooked
work by the German philologist Hermann Oldenberg, which argued that in
pre-Vedic India there was widespread popular belief in the efficacy of magical
arts (*Zauberkunst*) directed toward compelling spirits and nature demons;
and as demons became gods, magic evolved into religion.[41] The work largely
confines its conclusions to the Indian case, but it utilizes the basic evolutionary
schema that Frazer would make famous. From a catalog of Frazer's library in
1907, we know that he possessed a nearly complete collection of Oldenberg's
writings.[42] Frazer refers to *Die Religion des Veda* in the notes to a translation
he did in 1897.[43] More conclusively, there is a brief reference to Oldenberg in
the preface to the second edition of *The Golden Bough*.[44]

Taken together, I think Frazer's turn toward disenchantment was in some
sense intellectually overdetermined.[45] But there was another place Frazer
could have found disenchantment, and in a form that parallels some of its
later iterations. Following the Bridget Cleary case in 1894, Frazer as well as his
peers in folklore studies returned to the issue of fairy belief. In that context,
Frazer could not help but noticing a central motif: the departure of the fairies,
which represented one primary site within the field for theorizing about the
transformations of modernity and the departure of magic.

THE DEPARTURE OF THE FAIRIES

The boy and his sister stood gazing in utter dismay and astonishment, as rider after
rider, each one more uncouth and dwarfish than the one that had preceded it, passed the
cottage, and disappeared among the brushwood, which at that period covered the hill,
until at length the entire rout [*sic*], except the last rider, who lingered a few yards behind
the others, had gone by. "What are ye, little mannie? and where are ye going?" inquired

the boy, his curiosity getting the better of his fears and his prudence. "Not of the race of Adam," said the creature, turning for a moment in his saddle: "the People of Peace shall never more be seen in Scotland."

HUGH MILLER, *The Old Red Sandstone*, 1841

Civilization has crept in upon all fairy strongholds and disenchanted the many fair scenes in which they were wont to hold their courts. . . . The light of science has shone upon every green mound and dispossessed it of its fairy inhabitants.

ROBERT FERGUSSON, *Rambling Sketches in the Far North*, 1883

From almost the beginning of its history, British folklore studies was preoccupied with a class of beings known as the "fairy," and indeed, the terms *folktale* and *fairy tale* were regularly treated as near synonyms.[46] Had folklore studies originated in a different cultural milieu, it would likely have found a different representative classification. But when thinkers from the British Isles turned their attention toward regional cultures, their informants often described fabulous creatures, magical objects, and unusual features of the physical landscape in terms of the "fay" or "fairy." Indeed, the term *fairy* (also written *faerie*, *fae*, *fay*, *faye*) was not just a particular class of magical beings but first and foremost a general reference to the unusual, fated, bewitched, or enchanted.[47] Early folktales are full of references to fairy mounds, fairy rings, fairy animals, fairy enchantments, and, of course, the strange doings of fairies more generally. Hence, folklore studies from the beginning would seem to have been an exploration of magic and enchantment.

"Fairy" also quickly became a master classification for a type of being, which partially subsumed a range of different local creatures (e.g., goblins, pixies, lutin) under one heading. If at the word *fairy* you are imagining a small winged pixie, then you should know at the outset that Tinker Bell came later and that folklorists usually had something much more sinister in mind.[48] With substantial regional variations, the general belief about fairies characterized them as shadowy or invisible creatures of uncertain size, adept at inflicting illness, causing accidents and deaths, blighting crops, and abducting children and sometimes adults. They were even thought to be capable of assuming human form.[49] It was not that fairies were necessarily thought to be evil, but that they were mischievous and adept at harming those who gave them offense. Significantly, fairies were also often located in the past or described as in the process of vanishing. Hence, fairy tales themselves often provided an embryonic version of the myth of disenchantment.

By way of explanation, as folklorists began sifting through the material of oral culture, they took a mess of local histories, story variations, ballads, and anecdotes, and classified them according to repeated themes (later formalized in motifs and tale types as Aarne–Thompson [AT] classification). Some of these necessarily had to do with fairies. It was observed, for example, that in many tales, a fairy offers to aid someone who is willing to marry her (in the later AT classification, motif F302.3.2.1).

Crucially for our purposes, one of the oldest and most widespread motifs was *the departure of the fairies* (motif F388), which we might gloss as the claim that while there used to be fairies everywhere, they have since, aside from a few fugitives, left our world.[50] As has been noted by several contemporary scholars, "The very idea of the fairies' departure and of the fading of the fairy faith may be seen as an integral part of the fairy lore complex."[51] For a concrete example of this motif, glance at the section epigraph, describing the fairies' exodus from Scotland as recounted to the Scottish folklorist Hugh Miller.[52]

The fairies' farewell is an old trope. An early version appears in Geoffrey Chaucer, *The Tale of the Wyf of Bathe* (ca. 1380–1400), which includes the lines:

In th'olde dayes of the Kyng Arthour,
Of which that Britons speken greet honour,
All was this land fulfild of fayerye.
The elf-queene, with hir joly compaignye,
Daunced ful ofte in many a grene mede.
This was the olde opinion, as I rede;
I speke of manye hundred yeres ago.
But now kan no man se none elves mo.[53]

To paraphrase in modern English: in King Arthur's day, the land was full of fairy enchantment, and the elf queen and her companions danced in many green meadows, but by the fourteenth century, nobody could see the elves anymore. By describing the loss of magic and the withdrawal of animating beings, the departure of the fairies could be seen as a kind of embryo for the myth of disenchantment in folkloric form. At the same time, its appearance in about 1380 means that the departure was first articulated significantly earlier than most scholars would see or even date the onset of modernization or rationalization. Although we'll look at later attempts to explain their departure, it is worth noting that this trope suggests that magic was over—banished—long before the printing press, the Protestant Reformation, the "scientific revolution," or the urbanization of England.

Chaucer's pronouncement might seem prophetic, but for the fact that the fairies would continue to be described in regions that they had supposedly abandoned, down to the present day.[54] Britons would not only talk of fairies for the next six hundred years, but they would also repeatedly describe different variations on the departure of the fairies. Indeed, it would be hard to overstate the frequency of this trope, which was expressed in hundreds of iterations in recorded oral tales, novels, and poems, such as works by Edward Bulwer-Lytton, Charlotte Brontë, Robert Graves, Rudyard Kipling, and William Butler Yeats.[55]

*

Significantly, some iterations of this motif included theorizing about the reasons behind the fairies' withdrawal from the world. In effect, storytellers were preserving folk theories of disenchantment. A few examples by way of illustration:

Already in the 1680s, John Aubrey suggested in *Remaines of Gentilisme*, "the divine art of Printing and Gunpowder have frightened away Robin-goodfellow and the Fayries."[56] This might sound as though Aubrey is describing rationalization and disenchantment, but Aubrey was a believer in supernatural apparitions, and elsewhere he recounted anecdotes of fairy abductions in a way that suggested that he thought them to be veridical.[57] So the fairies being "frightened away" are likely what he understood to be real beings going into hiding.

In 1810, the English engraver Robert Hartley Cromek asserted that the "Fareweel [*sic*] o' the Fairies" was a well-attested event of about 1790, during which thousands of fairies were witnessed entering into a hill, bidding humankind goodbye, and then vanishing.[58] By way of explanation, Cromek recounted the Scottish adage "Whare the scythe cuts and the sock rives / Hae done wi' fairies an bee-bykes" (in my modern paraphrase: plowing and mowing eradicated both fairies and bees' nests), which he explained thus: "The land once ripped by the plowshare, or the sward once passed over by the scythe proclaimed the banishment of the Fairies from holding residence there forever after. The quick progress of Lowland agriculture will completely overthrow their empire; none now are seen, save solitary and dejected fugitives, ruminating among the ruins of their fallen kingdom!"[59] While scholars would later theorize that urbanization or broader changes in rural life were engines of disenchantment, these early examples might seem to have more to do with the older strain of folklore, which suggested that fairies could not stand the presence of iron and that they were averse to plows disrupting fairy rings.[60]

*

One of the most common explanations for the departure of the fairy described them as having been expelled by the arrival of Protestantism. As one Scottish informant put it in 1838, "The Methodist preachers are driving away all the trows and bogues and fairies."[61] This might sound like a consequence of the Protestant attacks on superstition, but other versions of the motif describe the conflict literally. For example, in 1591, the English bishop Richard Corbet penned a poetic adieu to the elves, which included the lines:

By which wee note the faries
Were of the old profession,
Theyre songs were *Ave Maryes*,
Theyre daunces were procession;
But now, alas! they all are dead,
Or gone beyond the seas . . .[62]

By "old profession," the bishop does not mean that the fairies were prostitutes, but that they were Roman Catholics (hence the Ave Marias). Tellingly, this was also the period in which Catholics and Protestants had begun arguing over *the cessation of miracles* (the notion that divine miracles had ended some time after the apostolic age). While not all Protestant denominations agred that miracles had ended, Catholics were routinely attacked for believing in false miracles and other supperstitions.[63] So by 1591, one can already see versions of the narrative that suggest an antagonism between the Protestant confessions and enchantment. But the surprise of Corbet's poem is that instead of fading paganism, it is the fairies themselves who are leaving, like Catholic refugees fleeing to France.

Nor were these isolated anecdotes. Throughout the nineteenth century, folklorists recorded accounts that suggested both that preachers had expelled the fairies and that the fairies were real beings who had gone into exile.[64] Indeed, as late as 1909, the Anglo-Scottish noblewoman and occultist Lady Archibald Campbell suggested that "the tyranny of the Calvinist fanatic in Scotland" and the Christian persecution of witchcraft had dimmed people's psychical perception of the hidden folk. Moreover, she suspected that "the inroad of restless civilization" had "disenchanted many a faery centre." But she also claimed to have experienced firsthand encounters with fairies in out-of-the-way places.[65]

In sum, various iterations of the fairies' disappearance often encoded both nostalgia and speculation about exactly why magic or animating spirits might have been inclined to vanish. Frazer may have heard versions of this motif during his childhood in Scotland, but it is indisputable that he was struck by the Bridget Cleary case, citing the incident repeatedly in various publications, including later editions of *The Golden Bough*.[66] He was interested in fairy tales more broadly, and when he turned his hand to fiction, he put fairies in his work.[67] We know too that as part of his process of getting further enmeshed in the academic world of folklore studies, Frazer read many works that themselves contained the departure of the fairies.[68] Moreover, in my research at the Frazer archives at Trinity College, Cambridge, I found a collection of newspaper clippings Frazer made from 1888 to 1899 that demonstrate that he was closely following contemporary folk customs. Strikingly, in 1893, just as he was coming to theorize disenchantment, he excerpted and marked with an X an article from the *Scotsman* that included an account of the fairy farewell.[69] None of these versions of the fairy farewell were identical with Frazer's theory, but they do suggest a certain backdrop against which that thesis was formulated.

THE DREAMS OF MAGIC

The dreams of magic may one day be the waking realities of science.

JAMES FRAZER, *The Golden Bough* (second edition), 1900

When the second edition of *The Golden Bough* was issued in 1900, it came with a new subheading: *A Study in Magic and Religion*—the appearance of the new term *magic* demonstrating its importance to the work's revised structure. Though built around the skeleton of the previous edition, *The Golden Bough* was now animated by a new master narrative, what we might call a canonical version of the disenchantment thesis; namely, history as an evolutionary progression from magic through religion and on to science.[70] Not only was this historical sequence influential, but also the distinctions between the terms it rested on—*magic, religion*, and *science*—would have a lasting impact on subsequent scholarship.

There is a standard scholarly reading of *The Golden Bough* that sees the work as rooted in a secularization thesis, a naïve "faith in progress," or an Enlightenment impulse.[71] But Frazer continued to link magic and science together, and often in a manner that suggested their shared opposition to religion. This does little to disturb Frazer's reputation as anti-Christian thinker, but begins to put pressure on the received view of his attitude toward enchantment. Moreover, later editions of *The Golden Bough*, if anything, hint at a more favorable attitude toward magic. The second striking aspect of the text, which has very rarely been commented on, is that science was not the terminus of Frazer's version of the evolution of thought. As the following will explore, Frazer conceptualized a fourth position beyond science, and he also demonstrated serious misgivings about the scientific enterprise. All of this becomes hard to square with his image as a classical enlightener or proponent of unidirectional cultural evolution.

At first pass, Frazer's three phases are evocative of Auguste Comte's three conditions or stages. Comte had described the law of human progress in "three different theoretical stages: the theological or fictional stage; the metaphysical or abstract stage; finally, the scientific or positive stage."[72] I discuss Comte's project in greater detail elsewhere.[73] But a significant difference between the two models is that Frazer sees magic, rather than some form of religion, at the beginning of history. This point is worth emphasizing because it was necessary for the whole myth of disenchantment to take shape. It might not sound innovative today, but distinguishing religion from magic and locating magic at the origin of culture was a novel claim. Indeed, what Frazer in the first edition called a form of primitive religion, in the second becomes magic.[74] As Frazer explained, "Just as on the material side of human culture there has everywhere been an Age of Stone, so on the intellectual side there has everywhere been an Age of Magic."[75] What were the stakes of presenting cultural history in terms of Stone Age magic?

At the core, Frazer intended to counter two widely held views of "savage" religion. First, the ghost theory of religion—found in the work of Tylor, Herbert Spencer, and even Hume—that claims human culture was originally animistic, either in terms of spirits or ghosts.[76] In this conception, primitives saw a world alive with spirits. The second and older theory—common to much of hermeticism and reinvigorated by Andrew Lang (especially in *The Making of Religion*, 1898), and to a lesser degree Max Müller—described earliest humanity as worshipping a High God or practicing an original monotheism, which only later decayed into polytheism and magic.[77] This camp tended to suggest a primordial divine revelation from which humankind later strayed. Regardless, both of these schemas depicted religious primitives believing in spirits or gods.

The debate about primitive religion was particularly active in the period in which Frazer was revising *The Golden Bough*, but remarkably, when he chose to intervene, it was not to come to the aid of either camp. Instead, he rejected the idea that early humanity might have been under the sway of religion. It is easy to suspect that Frazer, himself of an atheistic or agnostic temperament, was necessarily opposed to the idea of primitive revelation, but also hesitant to accept the idea that religious beliefs of any sort were primitive and thus a fundamental aspect of human nature.

In his attempt to refute the idea of primordial religions, Frazer turned to a set of ethnographies that supposedly described the most "savage" of all living peoples: the indigenous inhabitants of Australia. By way of context, the latter half of the nineteenth century was a crucial period in the European colonization of Australia. Colonial settlers gradually forced the indigenous peoples out of the fertile farmlands on the coast, and this—combined with the Australian gold rushes of midcentury and increased immigration more generally— pushed European colonization into the less fertile Northern Territory. Often having been exiled from their historical lands and driven to the point of subsistence, the Australian "aborigine" became a significant object of scholarly study as emblematic of the primitive.[78] Freud, Durkheim, and other European thinkers of the period would use these reports of Australian tribes to theorize primitive mentality or the most basic form of society.[79]

Frazer's innovation was to take seriously a common theme in many of these accounts—that indigenous Australian tribes were supposedly so backward that they lacked religion altogether.[80] For example, as George Angas argued in *Savage Life and Scenes in Australia and New Zealand* (1847), the indigenous inhabitants "have no religious observances whatever. They acknowledge no Supreme Being, worship no idols, and believe only in the existence of a spirit whom they consider as the author of ill and regard with superstitious dread."[81] Frazer read and cited this account, as well as numerous others that made similar claims.[82] The widely accepted, if imperialist, notion that religion was nonexistent among the indigenous peoples of Australia allowed Frazer to make the argument that religion was not truly a universal aspect of human nature.[83] In this Frazer transformed colonial ideology into the foundations of his theoretical enterprise.

Frazer was presented with a choice as to how to characterize the most primitive form of human thought. The "savages'" lack of religion was often read in two ways: they were said to possess either "superstition" or "witchcraft" (although often the two categories were blurred). If Frazer had described the basic trajectory of human history in terms of the progression from superstition to knowledge or science, he would not have been saying anything new. This was a popular theme in Victorian Britain.[84] But instead Frazer chose "magic" as his master category, relegating "superstition" to a secondary position. As he argued: "Now in regard to the question of the respective priority of magic or religion in the evolution of thought, it is very important to observe that among these rude savages, while magic is universally practised, religion in the sense of a propitiation or conciliation of the higher powers seems to be nearly unknown. Roughly speaking all men in Australia are magicians, but not one is a priest."[85] Frazer's choice of "magic" here expresses an ambiguity that superstition lacked, allowing later thinkers with a Rousseauean bent to advocate on his authority for magic as the most natural state. This is not too far from some of the arguments Frazer himself would make.

Having shown that aboriginal peoples lack religion, Frazer then went on to argue that magic is a cultural universal, stating: "Magic remains everywhere and at all times substantially alike in its principles and practice."[86] While today it is common (especially outside the field of religious studies) to insist on the universality of religion, whether understood cognitively or culturally, the universality of magic is rarely discussed and even more rarely asserted. Even in Frazer's own period, where others had seen the ubiquity of natural religion, he has identified instead a kind of primordial natural magic.

Frazer rejected the idea of truly primitive religion. But, intriguingly, he shared a common conception of religion as rooted in belief in superior powers. As Frazer stated: "By religion then, I understand a propitiation or conciliation of powers superior to man which are believed to direct and control the course of nature and of human life. In this sense it will readily be perceived that religion is opposed in principle both to magic and to science."[87] The conflict between religion and science has been projected backward into human prehistory. The "superior powers" here are basically invisible agents or spirits. While today most people would assume that propitiating invisible powers has no place in science, they might balk at the same claim extended to magic. Instead of retreating from this position, however, Frazer repeatedly amplified it in the text, writings, for example, "Wherever sympathetic magic occurs in its pure unadulterated form, it assumes that in nature one event follows another necessarily and invariably *without the intervention of any spiritual or personal agency*."[88]

Here one might imagine the typical Victorian reader spitting out their tea. Even a Victorian with no knowledge of Hermetic magic, who had never cracked open a grimoire, would have associated magic with demons or spirits. To argue the case that magic preceded all religion, Frazer had to make his primitives basically materialists or savage scientists, and so had to assert that spirits and magic do not naturally go together. He seems to have built on what used to be called "natural magic" as opposed to "demonic magic." But the occult of his day was rooted in spirits and had come to be more so alongside the rise of spiritualism. The contemporary European magical tradition thus looks to be the very anathema of Frazer's carefully crafted typology.

Frazer was necessarily aware of this difficulty, but discounted it by suggesting that when magic deals with invisible agents, "it treats them exactly in the same fashion as it treats inanimate agents."[89] Basically, the magician systematically compels, rather than implores, demons as if manipulating impersonal forces. It is unclear how the popular idea of witchcraft as devil worship would fit this conception of magic. But in general, Frazer interpreted spirit magic not as a failure of his schema, but as a "confusion" on the part of his informants who were themselves blending religion and magic. Frazer quoted R. H. Codrington's *The Melanesians* to claim that among this group of East Indian islanders, magic is widespread, and that "almost every man of consideration knows how to approach some ghost or spirit, and has some secret of occult practices."[90] But Frazer glossed this: "The same confusion of magic and religion has survived among peoples that have risen to higher levels of culture."[91] When magic is involved with spirits or ghosts, it is not unalloyed magic, but worse, a magic-religion hybrid.

What did Frazer imagine pure magic looked like?

*

In brief, unadulterated magic looks like science. Frazer suggested that magic's "fundamental conception is identical with that of modern science."[92] Both magic and science are rooted in natural laws and the desire to understand and command the universe. They also both oppose religion. The main difference between the two turns out to be efficacy. As Frazer put it, "All magic is necessarily false and barren; for were it ever to become true and fruitful, it would no longer be magic but science."[93] Basically, we can hear the position that Kurt Vonnegut would later make famous as "Science is magic that *works*."[94] Frazer elaborated on the parallel thus: "In both [magic and science] the succession of events is perfectly regular and certain, being determined by immutable laws, the operation of which can be foreseen and calculated precisely; the elements of caprice, of chance, and of accident are banished from the course of nature. Both of them open up a seemingly boundless vista of possibilities to him who knows the causes of things and can touch the secret springs that set in motion the vast and intricate mechanism of the world."[95] Although perhaps Frazer's prose had gotten away from him, the implications of this passage are worth exploring. By his day, thinkers like Tylor had already argued that "savages" had a kind of proto- or pseudoscience.[96] The assumption was that attempting to explain the natural world led primitives to construct elaborate spiritual cosmologies. But Frazer was pushing the parallels between magic and science further than he has generally been given credit for doing. Like science, magic is based in calculation and repetition and presumes the regularity of nature and natural laws. Basically, magic is against supernatural miracles. Frazer also argues that magic is not traditionalist, but future-looking.[97]

To be fair, Frazer frequently criticized magic's failings. He characterized "sympathetic magic" as rooted in the perception of false connections or analogues, often as a kind of savage idolatry or savage semiotics that mistakes the symbol for the object it refers to.[98] Later, Frazer would characterize magic as belief in action at distance and "savage telepathy."[99] But basically, magic is a folk science rooted in the way that the mind *naturally perceives the world*—just not the way the scientist builds on these common intuitions (amplifying some, subverting others) to create his or her system.[100] In sum, science is the perfection of magic.

Despite the general evolutionary trajectory for which Frazer is famous, he also described occasions when the archaic mode of magic was reawakened. Frazer treated the first of these in positive terms. As he argued, after the age of magic had passed into the age of religion, magic was banished as superstition. Yet magic then reappered "from the obscurity and discredit into which it had fallen," to give birth to science.[101] His example is alchemy returning to become chemistry. The first thing to notice about this is that it flies in the face of Frazer's grand narrative of disenchantment. According to the standard interpretation of Frazer, magic is supposed to be gradually eclipsed (or at the very least, relegated to the masses) over the course of cultural evolution. Its return to make way for science, as a therefore positive form of liberation, complicates the picture.

This reveals that the core of Frazer's philosophy of history is that religion was a momentary aberration in the grand trajectory of human thought. Science is a reversion to the commonsensical mentality of our distant ancestors. Which is to say, religion had extinguished a despiritualized magic, which then, paradoxically, returned as science. Here Frazer does not sound like a stereotypical enlightener; instead, one might hear hints of the Romantic Spiral, as the initial term returns in a higher-order synthesis.

The complication is that in *The Golden Bough*, the second return of magic—or to put it properly, Frazer's prophetic announcement of a *possible* return of magic—is described ominously: "We seem to move on a thin crust which may at any moment be rent by the subterranean forces slumbering below. From time to time a hollow murmur underground or a sudden spirt of flame into the air tells of what is going on beneath our feet. Now and then the polite world is startled by a paragraph in a newspaper which tells how in Scotland an image has been found stuck full of pins for the purpose of killing an obnoxious laird or minister, how a woman has been slowly roasted to death as a witch in Ireland. . . ."[102] Frazer had portrayed primitive magic nostalgically, but this passage suggests a hell slumbering below the "polite world" of upper-crust European society, ready to burst forth from below. The class dimension of this fear is all too clear, with its language of the subterranean, or we might say subaltern, threatening polite society. Another way to interpret this passage in context is that perhaps for Frazer, when magic returns in the elite world (high magic or science), it is a good thing; but when it resurges in the masses, it is dangerous. Thus, magic evokes the fear that within European society there is a slumbering kernel of savagery, ready to explode in violence, terrifying rites, and occult murders.

Again, passages like this seemingly go against the universality of his evolutionary progression. Instead of an inevitable advancement from religion to science, Frazer worried that the world might slip back into a new Age of Magic. Given that for Frazer magic and science are doubles, the return of magic to combat science—and in that sense, to oppose itself—is deeply troubling. Thus Frazer was horrified by modern magic. In advocating his work as an antidote to this possible shift, we can see disenchantment as a political project, perhaps directed against popular or uneducated belief in magic. We might be tempted to imagine this project in terms of British imperialism or scientific subjugation, but that reading belies Frazer's skepticism of scientific materialism.[103] He was less of an arch-rationalist than the traditional reading of his oeuvre would suggest, as he argued: "We must remember that at bottom the generalisations of science or, in common parlance, the laws of nature are merely hypotheses devised to explain that ever-shifting phantasmagoria of thought. . . . In the last analysis magic, religion, and science are nothing but theories of thought; and as science has supplanted its predecessors, so it may hereafter be itself superseded by some more perfect hypothesis, perhaps by some totally different way of looking at the phenomena—of registering the shadows on the screen."[104] The criticisms of empirical "phantasmagoria" could evidence a skepticism toward materialism or scientific completeness. More important, of the oft-repeated thumbnail sketch of Frazer's schema as the movement from magic to religion to science, it is rarely remarked that he postulated a fourth position: there is something beyond science. But what did Frazer have in mind?

The reference to "shadows on the screen" is a clue. The evocation of the

Platonic allegory of the cave is telling and is also no accident, given that Frazer started his academic career as a scholar of Plato.[105] Hints of Neoplatonism also appear in other of Frazer's published works; for example, in the short essay "Beyond the Shadows" (1895): "Communion with those higher powers, whatever they are, which existed before man began to be, and which will exist when the whole human race, as we are daily reminded by the cataclysms and convulsions of Nature, shall be swept out of existence for ever. It strengthens in us the blind conviction, or the trembling hope, that somewhere, beyond these earthly shadows, there is a world of light eternal, where the obstinate questionings of the mind will be answered and the heart find rest."[106] Although Frazer is often portrayed by contemporary scholars as reveling in the death of magic and the end of religion, Frazer's actual vision was far from utopian. In these passages, he sounds like a mystical Neoplatonist or Hermeticist, alienated from the materiality of substance.

In summary, Frazer came to an evolutionary argument late. And if he wavered between attacking and praising magic, that makes the evolutionism harder to decipher. While in my view Frazer's anti-Christian bonafides are nearly beyond dispute, it is precisely the unsettled nature of his relationship to magic that contributed both to the uneasiness of his reception in sociological circles and to his quick recuperation by European pagan thinkers. Restated, the project of de-Christianization could be seen as either secularizing or paganizing, and Frazer seems at times to waver between the two options.

THE LOST THEORY: DESPIRITUALIZING THE UNIVERSE

> Every great advance in knowledge has extended the sphere of order and correspondingly restricted the sphere of apparent disorder in the world.
>
> JAMES FRAZER, *The Golden Bough* (third edition), 1911

If one looks only at *The Golden Bough*, even the later editions, it would seem easy to refute Frazer's grand trajectory. His conception of magic without spirits feels implausible and is hard to square with historical uses of the term. His notion of the religionless primitive seems conveniently close to British colonial ideology. And his idea of universal phases of thought sounds farfetched— all the more so when the supposed transitions between magic, religion, and science are complicated by the various returns of the repressed. There are many reasons why Frazer has so few contemporary followers.

Still, I'm a sucker for underdogs, and so I feel compelled to note that there is an overlooked account of disenchantment in Frazer's later works that, while not without its own flaws, is far more intriguing than what has come before. To see it, we need to examine one of Frazer's less studied publications, *The Worship of Nature* (1926). As cited above, *The Golden Bough* had already suggested that chaos and knowledge are opposed, to which Frazer added the observation that "a fuller knowledge would everywhere reduce the seeming chaos to cosmos."[107] At root for Frazer, the process of disenchantment is one of transforming apparent disorder into order, or we might say, reducing complexity or transforming it into meaning.

Frazer expanded this claim in *The Worship of Nature*, arguing that there is a basic human inclination to search for "the Real" or for explanatory depth beyond the "phantasmagoria of this sensible world."[108] This is necessarily a simplifying process, as we want there to be unifying order behind the confusion of sensory data. That humans postulate a coherence to the world (such as causation) that we must take as a given before we have an experience of the world as such is a realization that would have appealed to Hume. To put it in terms Fichte and other neo-Kantians would have found familiar, Frazer thought that we cannot help but posit that there is a thing-in-itself behind the phenomena, even when we have no reason to do. This is Frazer's "Real."

Frazer argued that this underlying structure of ultimate reality can be conceived in either materialistic or spiritualistic terms.[109] The first, common to the scientific project, imagines that ultimate reality is "dead, unconscious, inhuman." The second, common to philosophical idealists and religionists of all stripes, imagines that mind (whether divine or human) is the fundament of experience; the core of reality is "living, conscious, and more or less analogous to human feeling and intelligence."[110]

Regardless of whichever ultimate principle one adopts, the tendency toward simplification continues.[111] In materialist terms, for example, one initially imagines that individual clouds, rocks, and trees are essentially different things, but which can all be placed in specific taxonomies (say cumulus, igneous, pinaceae) and then represented as different combinations of the same physical elements. This is already an attempt to work out a simple system behind a welter of different entities. There is a trend toward a further simplification that reduces these fundamental types down to a single kind of substance, or to the movement of atoms and so on. If this has been the trajectory of modernity in the sciences, Frazer noted that it is also the course of the spiritual world:

This process of despiritualizing the universe, if I may be allowed to coin the phrase, has been a very slow and gradual one, lasting for ages. After men had peopled with a multitude of individual spirits every rock and hill . . . they began, in virtue of what we may call the economy of thought, to limit the number of the spiritual beings of whom their imagination at first had been so prodigal. . . . To put it otherwise, the innumerable multitude of spirits or demons was generalized and reduced to a comparatively small number of deities; animism was replaced by polytheism. The world was now believed to be governed by a pantheon of gods and goddesses, each with his or her individual character, powers, and functions, in virtue of which they were entrusted with the control of particular departments of nature or of human life.[112]

Although this goes against his earlier conception of prehistoric spirit-free magic, here Frazer is arguing that in the primitive world, the essence of any given cloud or tree was a particular spirit. But over time, the human need for simplification has then led to the reduction of the plurality of local spirits to a limited pantheon of gods. The spirits of the grove become say, Apollo, who had other sacred sites throughout the Greco-Roman world. As one might guess, this trend ultimately leads toward monotheism or henotheism; a diversity of gods were increasingly assimilated to one another until they were all seen as emanating from one deity. Frazer wrote that "as the materialistic hypothesis has reduced the multitudinous forms of matter to one substance, hydrogen, so the spiritualistic hypothesis has reduced the multitude of spirits to one God."[113] This trajectory might seem to lead to an implicit monism (perhaps qua Spinoza) in a synthesis that reduces mind and matter into modes of a common substance or results of a single distant cause.

For Frazer, however, this process does not stop with the construction of the Christian Deus out of the multifarious *deos* of the Roman world. The deity has become increasingly relieved "of his multifarious duties as the immediate agent of every event in the natural world."[114] Having become increasing abstract or rationalized, God was gradually relegated to a "higher sphere in the supernatural world, as the [mere] creator or architect of the universe."[115] We are meant to imagine the Christian Trinity (or personal God) giving way to a deist non-Trinitarianism, whose central feature is that God set the world in motion and then vanished. Here we have a *deus absconditus* as the intersection of the simplifying tendencies of materialist and religious search for the Real. If God is not precisely dead, God seems to have been rendered functionally inert.[116]

The modern world is therefore characterized by what Frazer called the "despiritualizing of the universe." If this sounds like Max Weber's "disenchantment of the world," it is no accident. As the distant inspiration for both can likely be found in the *"entgötterte Natur"* of Schiller's "Gods of Greece," which Frazer explicitly cited here as inpsiration.[117] While Weber's accounts of disenchantment will be described in greater detail in chapter 10, it is important to note here that for Frazer, despiritualization is the result of an almost inevitable evolution of human thought, rooted in our basic need to explain complexity. Frazer also argued that it is rooted in the perceived loss of mystery. It is also not the result of science eliminating religion or even magic, but the combined trajectories of religion and science alike.

It might be tempting to stop here and imagine Frazer reveling in the possibility of a grand unified theory of everything that reduces the cosmos to a single principle. But that would ignore the thread of skepticism in his work. As he noted, "The apparent simplifications of science are probably illusory, concealing inner complexities which the progress of knowledge will later reveal."[118] Indeed, Frazer lamented the move toward simplification.

Taken to both registers, Frazer expressed a profound ambivalence about both scientific materialism and monotheism (or at least the deistic despiritualization). Regardless of the implications of this statement for the spiritual realm, Frazer was pretty clear in stating that while psychologically tempting, he did not believe science would be able to embrace simplification indefinitely: "For we may suspect that the finality, which seems to crown the vast generalizations of science, is after all only illusory, and that the tempting unity and simplicity which they offer to the weary mind are not the goal but only halting-places in the unending march."[119] Recast, the vast simplifications of science are but illusions that may someday be supplanted by a return to complexity. Perhaps we might consider this to be the fourth epoch or a return of enchantment.

CONCLUSION: A DEVIL'S ADVOCATE

Without posing as the Devil's Advocate or appearing before you in a blue flame and sulphureous fumes, I do profess to make out what the charitable might call a plausible plea for a very dubious client.

JAMES FRAZER, *Devil's Advocate: A Plea for Superstition*, 1927

It is tempting to imagine the narrative of disenchantment developing from the collective trauma of the Great War. It would be as if the death of nearly a generation on the battlefields had broken the spell of old nations and shattered the illusions of a world rich with magical meanings. As Charles Edward Montague put it in *Disenchantment* (1922), "They have seen trenches full of gassed men, and the queue of their friends at the brothel-door in Bethune. At the heart of the magical rose was seated an earwig."[120] If theorists of religion and veterans like Montague had written apace, it would be easy to imagine a widespread loss of belief in magic caused by postwar nihilism. This is not merely a thought experiment, but might be an appealing argument if one mistakenly believed that Weber's version of disenchantment was popularized in *The Protestant Ethic* (1920).[121] If one were to read this as the parturition of disenchantment, it would seem to appear not just as the affective product of a broken Europe, but alongside the birth of radio and the rise of Ford's assembly line, as though the triumph of the electric light over the gas lamp meant the demise of spirits and the end of belief in witchcraft.

Scholars of religious studies should already know different. Insofar as Frazer's work holds on in some vestigial form in the field, we know that he described his progressive evolution of thought much earlier. But now that I have pinpointed disenchantment to the 1890s, this produces more problems, not fewer. Because while Frazer was putting pen to paper in 1897, the *New York Times* was reporting that theosophy and spiritualism were on the rise, and moreover that spiritualists in America and Europe already exceeded eight million followers, with no sign of slowing down.[122] Meanwhile, in 1894 psychical research and séances came directly into Frazer's world when his friend and fellow folklorist Andrew Lang publically called for a rapprochement between paranormal research and folklore, asking Frazer and his peers to take seriously the possibility of ghosts and psychical powers.[123] It was also the period in which the Cleary case was making international headlines.

The disenchantment thesis has always been a source of controversy and even puzzlement. The process it names is putatively inexorable, which leaves observers scrambling to explain all manner of still-enchanted belief and behavior. This is also where religious studies can provide insights unavailable to a present-day sociologist. The twentieth century was teeming with magic, mysticism, and unreason, and one might be tempted to lament that Weber was not in a position to know better. What do we say, then, when we realize that the disenchantment thesis had its origins not in sociology but in folklore? And not in the twentieth century but the nineteenth?

The discipline of folklore was invested in showing the persistence of magical thinking even in the face of industrialization and urbanization. It had long tracked tales of the departure of the fairies (motif F388) and the cessation of miracles (motif F900.3). It knew many a just-so story explained the end of the age of myth or the twilight of the gods. It also should have known that many tales begin from the premise that once upon a time, "magic was once a mighty force in the world, but not anymore," only to build its narrative by staging some version of magic's return.[124] So if anyone, folklorists should have been in a position to uncover the myth of disenchantment.

Frazer did the reverse and that had lasting implications. He affirmed something that Tylor had suggested only tentatively—namely, the distinction between religion and magic. Crucially, Frazer located not superstition or religion, but magic at the dawn of history. This was tantamount to the assertion that magic was primeval. Occultists and fellow travelers had long spoken of magic at the start of history. But a key difference between these accounts is that for Lévi and company, the primordial was closer to the origins of the world and therefore closer to God, while for Frazer it was archaic and therefore less developed.

Knowing Frazer's role helps recover the full oddness of the disenchantment thesis. Frazer described both magic and religion as in decline, destined to vanish in the age of science. This narrative itself was supposed to be disenchanting and even secularizing. Frazer intended *The Golden Bough* to both challenge institutional Christianity and prevent the return of magic from below. There are signs that Frazer himself imagined a future epoch beyond science that would pierce the false veil of empirical phenomena. But the real irony is that the death of magic was announced in a volume that testified on every page to magic's survival.

Freud and Weber would read Frazer, and out of his work they would fashion streamlined versions of the disenchantment thesis, stripped of its engagement with "survivals" and "reinventions." But Aleister Crowley and company would read the same author—and even the same text—and from it, stage the revival of modern magic.

CHAPTER SIX

The Revival of Magick:
Aleister Crowley

One has only to enter the magick path to find on all sides and in the most unexpected quarters, men and women whose whole life is secretly devoted to the attainment of the Royal and Sacerdotal Art. Already Magick is once more a World-Power . . . The is the Mother of the New Æon.

ALEISTER CROWLEY, "The Revival of Magick," 1917

During the summer of 1916, England's most infamous magician undertook a mystical retreat in a cabin on the shores of Lake Pasquaney, New Hampshire. His diaries suggest that he was preoccupied by vivid dreams of strange scriptures, orgies and murders, horrifying skeletons, and imagery of dying lions.[1] Having fled the Great War that ravaged Europe and accelerated the decline of his once-significant wealth, Aleister Crowley—referred to in the popular press as "the Wickedest Man in the World" and by his followers as "the Great Beast"—felt depressed and powerless.[2] Privately, he confessed to his friend and fellow occultist George Cecil Jones that he feared an end to civilization and dreaded the possibility that the mysteries of their magical order, the A∴A∴, might be lost in the depredations of war.[3] Perhaps he was also troubled by the fate of his former lover and ex-disciple, the Anglo-Jewish poet and seer Victor Neuburg, who had recently joined the British army.[4] Regardless, Crowley maintained that the world was on the cusp of a new cosmic aeon and that he personally was destined to be the Magus (or Messiah) of the age to come. Yet despite periods of intense and restless energy, he felt that something was preventing him from assuming the full duties of this new role, and he worried it might require a complete transformation on his part, or even his death.[5]

On July 12, Crowley wrote in his diary that he hoped "that some supreme violation of all the laws of my being would break my karma, or dissolve the spell that seems to bind me."[6] Five days later, on July 17, at about 2 a.m., he began the great ceremony that would allow him to completely assume the "curse" of the Magus.[7] He looked for inspiration from one work he had at hand, the multivolume third edition of Frazer's *The Golden Bough* (1906–15), and from it crafted a magical rite that would add to his infamy.[8]

It is worth emphasizing that in his moment of crisis, the twentieth century's most famous magus looked not to the writings of famous seers or sorcerers like Nostradamus or John Dee, but to a scholarly study on comparative religion. Indeed, *The Golden Bough* had long inspired Crowley's grander attempts to revive magic. It may strike some readers as outlandish that anyone was seriously practicing magic in the first world at the dawn of the twentieth century; it might seem bizarre to others that an avowed magician was reading academic scholarship. I am interested in a more fundamental enigma; namely, that Crowley was using the foundational text in the theory of disenchantment as a spellbook.

To recap, while the idea that modernity meant the death of magic is most associated with Max Weber, it was James Frazer who originally made the argument that "as religion grows, magic declines" and further contended that the modern age of science would be the end of both. Strikingly, Frazer laid out this argument in the very text that Crowley used to craft his ritual.

At the very moment when scholars began elaborating versions of the disenchantment myth and entrenching the claim that modernity meant the departure of the supernatural, Crowley's project to reverse the decline of magic seems to have worked. By this I mean not that Crowley performed some specific miracle, but that he ultimately succeeded in sparking a popular magical revival. Crowley's concept of magic, along with its debt to Frazer, can still be seen in the Ordo Templi Orientis, the Church of Satan, Wicca, the Chaos Magic movement, and a number of diverse neo-pagan organizations.

Crowley's repurposing of disenchantment gives rise to a problem: we have become wary of broad-brush sociological explanations for disenchantment. Urbanism, industrialization, the spread of public education, the rise of institutionalized reason—none of these simply killed off enchantment. As we know from international case studies, magic can coexist with factories, cities, and schools. But if anything seems likely to dispense with enchantment, it would be *the discourse of disenchantment*, which after all has the character of a death certificate or coroner's report. The seeming contradiction we have to make sense of here is the enchanting effects of disenchantment itself.

Historians in the Foucauldian vein have it worse, because we have come to expect that a discourse can constitute the very object it purports to describe. Perhaps the most famous example of this pattern is "female hysteria," whose widespread symptoms—nervousness, sexual desire, heaviness in the abdomen—seemingly vanished as soon as the medical establishment decided that the condition no longer existed.[9] The very notion of hysteria was apparently contagious. Scholars' known narratives can be self-fulfilling, producing what Karl Popper has referred to as the "Oedipus effect": "the influence of the prediction upon the predicted event"[10] (e.g., the prophecy that Oedipus would kill his father directly led to the estrangement that culminated the famous patricide; or the prediction that war between two countries is inevitable can ultimately make war a reality). A sociological prophecy that is self-fulfilling is no longer a surprise.

These theoretical models are what make the case of enchantment especially fascinating. As the following shows, Crowley made extensive references to Frazer in his letters and poems, plays, short stories, and novels, as well as in his magical writings, including spellbooks and ceremonies. Remarkably, Crowley even embedded a reference to Frazer in a letter he claimed was authored by his "Hidden Masters," thus implying that the secret gurus of magical wisdom were up on their readings of Victorian folklore. Although *The Golden Bough* was not the only book Crowley cited in his quest to revive magic, Frazer cast a long shadow over Crowley and gave shape to various iterations of his project. Crowley was also not alone in drawing on the seminal text of disenchantment to produce modern magic. Frazer's magical followers were legion. Hence we have the reverse of Foucault's pattern: the narrative of disenchantment appears to be at least partially self-refuting, by reinvigorating the very magic it said was endangered.

While Crowley's importance to the history of modern magic is widely recognized, he has been the subject of surprisingly little scholarly research. References to Crowley do appear in surveys of "Western esotericism," and there are articles on his project.[11] But the main scholarly monographs largely dedicated to Crowley can be counted on one hand: Marco Pasi, *Aleister Crowley e la tentazione della politica* (1999), Hugh Urban, *Magia Sexualis* (2006), Richard Kaczynski, *Perdurabo: The Life of Aleister Crowley* (2010), and *Aleister Crowley and Western Esotericism* (2012), edited by Henrik Bogdan and Martin Starr.[12] This chapter will explore Crowley's appropriation of Frazer and the role of *The Golden Bough* in the history of European occultism more broadly. This in turn should permit us to see how in a kind of *enantiodromia*, the theory of disenchantment was capable of becoming its opposite.

THE GREAT BEAST: A BIOGRAPHICAL SKETCH

Before I touched my teens, I was already aware that I was THE BEAST whose number
is 666. I did not understand in the least what that implied; it was a passionately ecstatic
sense of identity.

ALEISTER CROWLEY, *Magick in Theory and Practice*, 1929

An inveterate showman, Aleister Crowley actively cultivated controversy and
cloaked himself in consciously manufactured myths.[13] Born Edward Alexander Crowley on October 12, 1875, in Warwickshire, England, Aleister was
an heir to a family fortune that included a profitable brewing business, a set
of alehouses, and significant railroad investments.[14] While the family had historically been Quakers, Aleister's parents had embraced an ultraconservative
subset of the Evangelical movement known as the Plymouth Brethren. His father's death from cancer when Aleister was eleven contributed to an increasing
estrangement from his mother, who had turned even more deeply religious and
started referring to Aleister as "the Beast."[15]

After a youth spent rebelling at various boarding schools, in 1895, Aleister
matriculated at Trinity College, Cambridge. While there is no evidence that
Aleister attended any of Frazer's lectures, he certainly knew about Frazer and
later would make much of the fact that they were at Trinity at the same time.[16]
It was here that Aleister both took on the adult version of his name (from the
Gaelic for Alexander) and began his study of comparative religion and philosophy.[17]

Throughout his twenties, Crowley largely passed the time engaged in the
hobbies of the British upper class of his era. He traveled widely and inter-
nationally, played competitive chess, had erotic encounters with women and
men, did some significant mountain climbing and big-game hunting, and generally lived *la vie de haute bohème*. He also continued literary pursuits, publishing, for example, a pseudonymous collection of queer poetry, *White Stains*, in
1898. Crowley was often inspired by his interest in comparative religion and
magic, but if he had died at twenty-nine like his idol Percy Bysshe Shelley,
Crowley too would probably have been remembered largely as a poet.[18]

Two events interrupted Crowley's artistic trajectory and came to define the
course of his later life. The first of these was his encounter with the Hermetic
Order of the Golden Dawn.[19] The Golden Dawn had been founded in 1887,
when the English coroner and Theosophist William Wynn Westcott claimed
that he had discovered a set of ancient texts describing a lost Rosicrucian

society. Conveniently, these archaic writings contained the name and Stuttgart address of a certain Fräulein Sprengel, and Westcott soon claimed to be in contact with her by post. Even more conveniently, the elderly German lady allegedly passed away in 1890, shortly after initiating Westcott and his cofounders, S. L. MacGregor Mathers and William Robert Woodman, into the order. Although organized like a Masonic lodge, the Golden Dawn emphasized the practice of magic, including alchemy, spirit communication, and astrology.[20] The Golden Dawn expanded quickly, its membership coming to include influential persons, such as the Swiss artist Moina Mathers born Mina Bergson (sister of the philosopher Henri Bergson), the Irish feminist activist Maud Gonne, the author of weird tales Arthur Machen, the painter Isabelle de Steiger, the scholar and popularizer of magic A. E. Waite, and its most famous member, the Irish poet W. B. Yeats, who eventually had a magical and artistic rivalry with Crowley. Crowley joined the Golden Dawn in 1898, and although he was probably drawn to the group as much for its artistic connections as its occult teachings, it left a lasting imprint on his version of the magical path.

Another event, however, looms largest in Aleister Crowley's autobiography.[21] In March 1904, Aleister was on an extended honeymoon with his new wife, Rose Crowley (née Kelly), in Cairo. On the evening of March 16, he was entertaining her with a minor invocation when Rose entered a trance and started repeating, "They are waiting for you."[22] The couple swiftly identified the "they" as the Egyptian deity Horus. A few days later, on March 20, Crowley attempted a further ritual, during which Rose channeled what they considered to be a higher being that identified itself as Aiwass. "Aiwass" told them that "the Equinox of the Gods had come" and Crowley was needed to receive a new revelation.[23]

On April 8, Crowley sat down to prepare to receive a revelation in what he claims was an attitude of skepticism, when he was surprised by a disembodied voice speaking over his left shoulder. As he described it years later in *The Equinox of the Gods* (1936):

> The voice was of deep timbre, musical and expressive, its tones solemn, voluptuous, tender, fierce or aught else as suited the moods of the message. . . . I had a strong impression that the speaker was actually in the corner where he seemed to be, in a body of "fine matter," transparent as a veil of gauze, or a cloud of incense-smoke. He seemed to be a tall, dark man in his thirties, well-knit, active and strong, with the face of a savage king, and eyes veiled lest their gaze should destroy what they saw.[24]

Later Crowley would vacillate about whether Aiwass was best understood as an Egyptian god, an elemental, a guardian angel, or merely the astral projection of a human representative of the Secret Chiefs of the Great White Brotherhood. Nevertheless, over the span of three days, Aiwass disclosed to Crowley a scripture, *Liber AL vel Legis* or *The Book of the Law*. Its main theme was that Crowley was the messiah of a new aeon.[25] The organizing term for this revelation was the Greek word for "will" (θέλημα, *thelema*) and its central commandment was "Do what thou wilt shall be the whole of the law." Ultimately, Crowley published *The Book of the Law* with a series of commentaries and began to grow movements around them, including the A∴A∴ and the Abbey of Thelema.[26]

While Crowley would maintain throughout his life that Aiwass was something outside himself and that *The Book of the Law* was an authentic revelation, it has not escaped scholarly notice that it had distinct precedents.[27] For example, François Rabelais had famously described a quasi-utopian *Abbaye de Thélème* with the motto *Faictz* [sic] *ce que vouldras* (Do what you will). Crowley's "do what thou wilt," however, was not a pure libertinism, because he did not view the will as simply an account of volition but as the divine *Logos*, or Word of God.[28] The will was to be understood as one's true place in the divine cosmos *and* as the most fundamental impulse of one's being. Thus, the main aim of his movement was a calling to discover one's true will.

Previously Crowley had briefly been interested in Buddhism, but now changed course to renew his commitment to magic, as he stated in a letter to his brother-in-law, Gerald Kelly: "I say today to hell with Christianity, rationalism, Buddhism, all the lumber of the centuries. I bring you a positive and primaeval fact, magic by name; and with this I will build me a new Heaven and a new Earth. I want none of your faint approval or faint dispraise; I want blasphemy, murder, rape, revolution, anything, bad or good, but strong."[29] In the years that followed the *Liber AL vel Legis*, magic and Thelema came increasingly to define Crowley's identity and focus.[30] While he did not abandon poetry and fiction, Crowley also published explicitly magical works (discussed below).

Crowley's reputation as a magician grew. In part this was because he deliberately courted controversy. Crowley gained more international notoriety when the British author W. Somerset Maugham modeled the villain of his popular novel *The Magician* (1908) on Crowley. He became even more infamous after a series of legal struggles with S. L. Macgregor Mathers over the legacy of the Golden Dawn (1909–10) and high-profile libel lawsuits (1911, 1934).[31] Meanwhile, Crowley's scandalous reputation was amplified by his publication of sexually explicit poetry and fiction describing recreational drug use (e.g., *The Diary of a Drug Fiend*, 1923). By the time he died from myocardial degeneration in 1947, Crowley had become infamous across the globe.[32]

Crowley had a significant impact on the history of modern magic. He founded the A.·.A.·., succeeded Theodor Reuß (discussed in chapter 10) as leader of the Ordo Templi Orientis, and even launched a halfhearted attempt to takeover the Theosophical Society. Crowley also participated in the British Society for Psychical Research and their tests of various spirit mediums.[33] He also exerted a significant influence on the following generation of magical societies and new religions. Some—like Gerald Gardner, the founder of Wicca; Jack Parsons, the rocket scientist and leader of the American branch of the Ordo Templi Orientis; and the influential occult revivalist Israel Regardie— were Crowley's students.[34] Others, like Scientology founder L. Ron Hubbard, and Church of Satan founder Anton LaVey, read Crowley but did not know him personally.[35] Moreover, Crowley was a key figure in the Euro-American construction of Tantra and the esoteric appropriation of Eastern traditions more broadly.[36] Likewise, a fascination with Crowley lives on in international popular culture.[37]

THE GOD-EATER AND *THE GOLDEN BOUGH*

> Thus under the Golden Bough in the moonlight was the host uplifted, and the Shepherd, and the Hangman, and the Sorceress broke the bread of Necromancy, and drank deep of the wine of witchcraft.
>
> ALEISTER CROWLEY, "Temple of Solomon the King," 1909

When we started the chapter, "the Great Beast" was alone in the darkness of the New Hampshire woods with *The Golden Bough* near at hand, planning to perform a miracle. In hyperbolic terms, we might say that Crowley was attempting to immanentize the eschaton, or end the world. The ritual he chose was not intended to do this all at once, but was to empower him to carry out this mission. At the very least, Crowley imagined that he might accelerate the expiration of the aeon and assume his mantle as the age's Magus.

Comparing his private diary and a magical text that described the relevant spell (Crowley, *Liber LXX*), it is easy to reconstruct his activities and their timing.[38] At about two in the morning, Crowley hunted in the darkness until he had captured a frog and then trapped it in a chest. At dawn, he removed the frog and shortly thereafter baptized it with the name "Jesus of Nazareth." Crowley then spent the day in meditation and worship. As night again fell, he placed the frog on trial, accusing it as follows:

Jesus of Nazareth, how thou art taken in my snare. All my life long thou hast plagued me and affronted me. . . . Now, at last, I have thee; the Slave-God is in the power of the Lord of Freedom. Thine hour is come; as I blot thee out from this earth, so surely shall the eclipse pass; and the Light, Life, Love and Liberty be once more the Law of Earth. Give thou place to me, O, Jesus; thine aeon is passed; the Age of Horus is arisen by the Magick of the Master the Beast that is Man.[39]

Having condemned it to death in Jesus's place, Crowley then crucified and killed the frog. Symbolically he seemed to be taking out his frustrations on the whole of the Christian age and willing it to pass. Crowley cooked the frog's legs and ate them, ritually ingesting Christ's power. He then burned the remainder of the animal's body in order to consume the rest of the aeon. While this might sound like a particularly sadistic version of French cooking, given his overarching project, Crowley's magical aims were fairly straightforward. As he later described it in *The Confessions of Aleister Crowley: An Autohagiography*: "In order to erect the temple of the New Aeon, it appeared necessary to make a thorough clearance of the rubbish of its ruined predecessors. I therefore planned and executed a Magical Operation to banish the 'Dying God.'"[40]

If expelling the dying God was Crowley's aim and magical ritual his method, this section will be an attempt to make sense of what *The Golden Bough* was doing in the hands of a magician. It is all the more important because this rite was not the beginning of Crowley's engagement with Frazer but the result of a lifelong encounter. Tracing out the history of Crowley's engagement with *The Golden Bough* will demonstrate more concretely how he drew on comparative religion and Frazer in particular to formulate his own project of enchantment. All told, it will show how and where the academic discipline of religious studies passes over into magic.

*

In July 1903, Crowley wrote a dramatic work, *The God-Eater*, described as a "play in which the Origin of Religion, as conceived by Spencer or Frazer, is dramatically shown forth."[41] To summarize its narrative: the protagonist, having read too much scholarship in comparative religion, decides to perform a pseudo-Egyptian ritual intended to deify his dearly beloved sister. With his sister's consent, he ritually murders her, and in an ecstatic state feasts on her corpse, thereby becoming the God-Eater of the play's title. The audience learns that the ritual was a success, and the woman's mummified corpse will ultimately be worshipped as a goddess.[42]

I have never asked my undergraduates to write plays based on their coursework, and Crowley's effort demonstrates some of the trouble with such a prompt. The play imagines that new gods are born from the conjunction of primordial murder/cannibalism and the passion of altered states of consciousness. The first rite of a new faith is a sacrifice or totemic meal in which the victim is partially devoured in order to become the new deity. Communion therefore would be the ritual repetition of this ancient act of violence.

As theory, *The God-Eater* anticipates an emphasis on a traumatic kernel at the origins of religion so important to Sigmund Freud and Georges Bataille (discussed in later chapters). But as Crowley acknowledged in his autobiography, his main inspiration was Frazer's *The Golden Bough*, which, after all, had a section on "Killing the God."[43] Crowley's vision of religious studies more broadly can be found in a heavy-handed set of lines from the play in which the protagonist lays out his motivation:

The vastness of heavens and the earth
Created the idea of God.
So Levi once
Sarcastic in apostasy; *à rebours.*
So Müller, mythopoeic in his mood
Of the unmasking mythopoeia. Now
Profounder science, Spencer's amplitude,
Allen's too shallow erudition, Frazer's
Research, find men have made—since men made aught—Their Gods, and slain,
and eaten. Surface! I,
Criosda of the Mist, see truth in all
Rather than truth in one . . .
So men who made their gods
Did make in very deed: so I will make
In uttermost truth a new god, since the old
Are dead, or drunk with wine.[44]

This passage from Crowley's juvenilia captures two important themes. First, it constructs a genealogy for the study of religion that starts with Éliphas Lévi, includes Max Müller, Herbert Spencer, Grant Allen, and concludes with Frazer. That Éliphas is the Lévi being referred to here is clear from his importance to Crowley. Crowley lists Frazer and Lévi's works together in his curriculum for the A.˙.A.˙., translated Lévi writings, and even claimed to be Lévi's reincarnation (despite a small problem with birth and death dates).[45] That Crowley's list of scholars includes the French occultist further demonstrates the entanglement of academic and esoteric worlds I have been charting over the course of this book.

Second, this passage is important because it locates both the study of religion and esotericism in the vacuum produced by the death of God. In effect, this monologue anticipates part of Crowley's future project: the creation of a new god, replete with pseudo-Egyptian trappings, intended to reinvigorate humankind after the passing of Christianity. Although the idea that religious studies would inspire cannibalism is rather overwrought, the discipline surely has a direct effect on the phenomena that is purports to study. Its pursuit of a common essence behind all religions made it useful for figures like Crowley, who drew eclectically from different traditions to formulate their own idiosyncratic faiths.

One can see, for example, how a faithful reader of Müller's scholarship and *Sacred Books of the East* would be led toward a theosophical version of universal mysticism. Crowley was one such reader.[46] His post-Cairo writings make this point explicit: "Religious folk have buried this fact under mountains of dogma; but the study of comparative religion has made it clear. One has merely to print parallel passages from the mystics of all ages and religions to see that they were talking of the same thing."[47] The reference to comparative religion is serving here to legitimate Crowley's version of perennial mysticism—namely, that a common religious experience lies at the root of different religions. As Crowley continued, "The real strength of every religion lies, consequently, in its mystics."[48] Though religious leaders may use mysticism for inspiration, they have to translate it into their own terminology and dogma. Crowley also argued that this mystical experience, while profoundly spiritual, can also be physiologically triggered.

If this suggests William James's *The Varieties of Religious Experience*— which also argued for the universality of mysticism and speculated about psychological parallels—that is no accident. Crowley was also an avid reader of James. In his autobiography, Crowley explicitly referred to James as the inspiration for both his turn toward yoga and his attempt to connect magic to mysticism.[49] In his magical writings, however, Crowley emphasized a mystical evocation and *union with a specific deity* appropriate to a particular operation of magic.[50] The religious impulse behind mysticism may be the same, but in

Crowley's version, there seem to be almost as many different gods as there are possible spells.[51]

Crowley also turned to Frazer when he wanted to formalize his own comparative project. Inspired by the Golden Dawn's table of correspondences, Crowley's *Liber 777* (1909) was "an attempt to systematise alike the data of mysticism and the results of comparative religion."[52] Its organizing principle was explicitly Kabbalistic, and it was even rooted in the *yosher* schema of the *sephirot*. But what had been a mode for reading Jewish (and then Christian) scripture in terms of correspondences and divine emanations, Crowley expanded to include non-European mythology. For example, Crowley asserted an identity between the number 1, the Hebrew כֶּתֶר (Kether), the crown of God, the Egyptian deity Ptah, Scandinavian Wotan, the Greek Zeus, the Chinese Shangdi上帝, and the perfume of ambergris.[53] This meant that Zeus, Ptah, and Shangdi were all emanations of the same aspect of God, which could be evoked by rites using ambergris.

Crowley was following a pattern exemplified by Lévi and Blavatsky (although with plenty of Hermetic precedents), who had similarly investigated diverse religions, looking for symbolic equivalences.[54] But he was also building on the work of scholars of religion, whose own basic operation meant looking for cross-cultural religious patterns. Crowley saw this method epitomized in *The Golden Bough*.[55] Frazer's functional equivalences between primitive myths became evidence for the true identity of different deities and symbols. If you'll remember, Frazer had characterized "sympathetic magic" in terms of taking false resemblances or analogues to be real connections. In effect, Crowley was reading Frazer's own comparative method for its own system of associations, or more properly, as a work of sympathetic magic in its own right. Restated, in Crowley's hands, comparative religion was a way of researching new magical symbols and uncovering different aspects of the Godhead.

*

Though Crowley discovered Frazer before his Egyptian experience, *The Golden Bough* only increased in importance as Crowley systematized his prophetic mission in *The Book of the Law*. He made this clear from the outset, saying, "I know now from the experience of others that *The Book of the Law* is veritably a Golden Bough."[56] But to understand Frazer's true influence on Crowley's larger theoretical schema, we have to untangle Crowley's eschatology—a curious mix of the premillennialism of his original Plymouth Brethren faith, Johann Bachofen's primordial matriarchy, Nietzsche's criticism of Christianity, and the periodization of Frazer's later editions of *The Golden Bough*.[57]

From Crowley's upbringing among the Plymouth Brethren, he drew the idea that history was divided into different dispensations or ages in which humankind faced different tasks.[58] Like some of their evangelical cousins in America, the Brethren believed that according to the Book of Revelation, the penultimate age was supposed to be the Rapture, when good Christians would be taken up into heaven, followed by a great tribulation during which the forces of Christ and Antichrist would do battle. In Crowley's esoteric reading of Revelation, however, the Antichrist—or "Great Beast 666"—was not evil, but a prophetic figure who received a new dispensation, destined to end the Christian age and usher in a new millennia.

Crowley's characterization of the various ages of humankind was also grounded in his period's anthropological theory, if recast in Egyptian terminology. From the Swiss scholar Johann Bachofen's *Das Mutterrecht* (1861), Crowley had taken the idea that the oldest aeon was the age of the mother, a primordial matriarchy.[59] As Crowley put it in "Liber Legis: The Comment" (1912):

> The Hierarchy of the Egyptians gives us this genealogy: Isis, Osiris, Horus.
>
> Now the "pagan" period is that of Isis; a pastoral, natural period of simple magic. Next with Buddha, Christ, and others there came in the Equinox of Osiris; when sorrow and death are the principal objects of man's thought, and his magical formula is that of sacrifice.
>
> Now, with Mohammed perhaps as its forerunner, comes in the Equinox of Horus, the young child who rises strong and conquering (with his twin Harpocrates) to avenge Osiris, and bring on the age of strength and splendour.
>
> His formula is not yet fully understood.
>
> Following him will arise the Equinox of Ma, the Goddess of Justice.[60]

In the age of Isis, civilization was pastoral, polyamorous, and ruled by women and the Goddess. This age was followed by that of Osiris, when the dying God displaced the world of the mothers with a patriarchy rooted in sacrifice, restrictive morality, and rituals rooted in the cycle of death and resurrection. Christianity was only one iteration of the dispensation of that age, which Crowley associated with patriarchy.[61] From Nietzsche, whom he described as "one of our prophets," Crowley seems to have taken the idea that Christianity was a "slave morality" built on the repression of basic human needs and impulses.[62]

Following the age of Osiris, Crowley placed the tribulation of the age of

Horus, in which the old rules would be reversed in a popular liberation of humankind. The patriarchy would be overturned and a new aeon of individuality would take hold. Instead of dominance by a particular gender, each person would come to embody both sexes.[63] This new aeon would begin with war and conflict, during which Crowley claimed he had been personally called to destroy the old morality and introduce a new antinomianism. After this period of conflict, the world would enter a long aeon of Maat, associated with justice and peace.[64]

As noted at the start of this chapter, Crowley drew on Frazer in his identification of the "Dying God" as a combination of Osiris, Attis, Adonis, and Christ. In so doing, Crowley was activating the anti-Christian impulse found Frazer's text, but with a twist. Frazer's argument that Christianity rested on archaic fertility rituals was an attempt to discredit Christian exceptionalism and therefore imply that Christianity could be relegated to the dustbin of history. But Crowley read *The Golden Bough* to intimate an esoteric pagan ritual system at the core of Christianity. Instead of the classical Hermetic search for a concealed monotheism behind a plurality of "heathen" faiths, Crowley cited Frazer to assert that Christianity concealed a pagan fertility rite whose essence could be recovered through magical means. In effect, Crowley's neo-pagan Christology was rooted in *The Golden Bough*.[65] Moreover, Crowley repurposed Frazer's detailed descriptions of the classical age into modern neo-pagan rites.

As contemporary scholar Henrik Bogdan has observed, Crowley also drew on Frazer in his later commentaries on *The Book of the Law*. In Crowley's later explanation of the lines "Abrogate are all rituals, all ordeals, all words and signs," Crowley wrote:

This verse declares that the old formula of Magick—the Osiris-Adonis-Jesus-Marsyus-Dionysus-Attis-et cetera formula of the Dying God—is no longer efficacious. It rested on the ignorant belief that the Sun died every day, and every year, and that its resurrection was a miracle. The Formula of the New Aeon recognizes Horus, the Child crowned and conquering, as God. We are all members of the Body of God . . . If you are "walking in darkness," do not try to make the sun rise by self-sacrifice, but wait in confidence for the dawn, and enjoy the pleasures of the night meanwhile.[66]

Crowley was suggesting that the old myth structure of Christianity as rooted in the false miracle of the sun's death and rebirth no longer works in a post-Copernican age.[67] We can also see Crowley exploiting Frazer's version of the disenchantment narrative to explain the progression of dispensations. The progression of aeons maps easily onto Frazer's periodization: the age of Isis was the period of ancient magic, Osiris that of religion; and we are now at the cusp of the age of Horus, nothing less than the dawn of scientific modernity. Even Frazer's fourth, or postmodern, stage seems to have its equivalent in Crowely's final aeon of Maat. Nevertheless, this periodization provided as much a challenge for Crowley as it did for Frazer around exactly the same issue—the status of modern magic. After all, if magic was a holdover from a primitive age, then how did a contemporary magus like Crowley fit into the scheme?

Crowley argued that "magic" needs to be reformed into "magick." To explain the thinking behind this idiosyncratic spelling shift, you should know that Crowley adopted the spelling *magick* in order to distinguish his own reinvigorated and ostensibly scientific project from stage magic and various forms of trickery.[68] We might see this in terms of a Frazerian periodization read ontologically rather than culturally: the magic of previous aeons is no longer effective. Spells from the age of Isis, say, no longer work today. Although Crowley declined to explain why, he made it clear that in the age of Horus, one must have a scientific magick. This, the old magic has to be dispelled so that modern magic can be revived.[69]

The will be explored in greater detail in the next section, but by way of foreshadowing, Crowley mobilized a set of equivalences between magic and science he found in Frazer's work. We can find these expressed in Crowley's *Magick in Theory and Practice* (1929), which tellingly begins with two lengthy epigraphs from *The Golden Bough*. The first of these includes Frazer's statement that magic's "fundamental conception is identical with that of modern science; underlying the whole system is a faith, implicit but real and firm, in the order and uniformity of nature."[70] By quoting these lines, Crowley was underscoring Frazer's claim that the return of magic in opposition to religion could be positive (say, as alchemy). Crowley also embraced Frazer's assertion of the fundamental similarity between the mentalities of the magician and the scientist. He disregarded, however, Frazer's fear of resurgent superstition as a retreat from science back into the myths of unreason. Instead, for Crowley, magic takes on new importance, emancipating the world from repressive, moralizing religion.

This is because while Crowley described his own project as the utopian intersection of all three discursive spheres—magic, science, and (pagan) religion—he was often antagonistic toward Christianity and other established religions. Indeed, Crowley often positioned magic and science as allies against religion (treated as a euphemism for Christianity). As Crowley put it in the set of letters which were posthumously published as *Magick without Tears* (1954): "There is the sense in which Frazer (and I) often use the word [religion]: as in opposition to 'science' or 'Magic.' Here the point is that religious people attribute phenomena to the will of some postulated Being or Beings, placable [*sic*] and moveable by virtue of sacrifice, devotion, or appeal. Against such, the scientific or magical mind believes in the Laws of Nature, asserts 'If A, then B'—if you do so-and-so, the result will be so-and-so, aloof from arbitrary interference."[71] Crowley seems to have inherited Frazer's opposition of religion on the one side, and science and magic on the other, even as he himself elsewhere worked to bridge these oppositions. Moreover, he picked up on Frazer's equation of the mentality of savages and scientists and transformed that into a scholarly justification for magic. But this is not the extent of his borrowing from Frazer. More can be seen in Crowley's second Frazer epigraph in *Magick in Theory and Practice*, drawn from the third edition of *The Golden Bough*, reading in full:

So far, therefore, *as the public profession of magic has been one of the roads by which men have passed to supreme power, it has contributed to emancipate mankind from the thraldom of tradition and to elevate them into a larger, freer life, with a broader outlook on the world. This is no small service rendered to humanity.* And when we remember further that in another direction magic has paved the way for science, we are forced to admit that if the black art has done much evil, it has also been the source of much good; that if it is the child of error, *it has yet been the mother of freedom and truth.*[72]

The emphasis above is Crowley's , and it is striking that he has managed to cull the nostalgia from Frazer's prose and marshal it for the sake of reinvigorating modern magic. In the original, this paragraph was part of a larger section about magic as an early stage of human cultural evolution; however, Crowley reads it as exposing Frazer's own sympathies toward magic. Crowley delighted in the suggestion that magic did and could continue to give birth to freedom and truth.

*

The magical side of Frazer is even clearer in Crowley's attempt to transform *The Golden Bough* into a spellbook. In so doing, Crowley built on Frazer's logic of magic. Frazer had explained sympathetic magic in terms of two principles: *contagion*, the idea that once a link was created between two things the magician continued to act as though that link was still in effect, and *homeopathy* (or *mimesis*), the idea that like effects like.[73] In *Magick in Theory and Practice*, Crowley grounded his theory of magical consecration in Frazer's model.[74] This is significant because Wouter Hanegraaff has accurately criticized Frazer, demonstrating how badly Frazer's model of sympathetic magic maps onto actual magic traditions and how poorly it approximates the historical European conceptions of divine correspondences.[75] It might seem that Frazer got magic wrong.

The irony is that Crowley nevertheless used Frazer's model as the foundation of his own magical enterprise. Crowley prefaced a section on the magical link with this statement: "It is a strange circumstance that no Magical writer has hitherto treated the immensely important subject of the Magical Link. It might almost be called the Missing Link. It has apparently always been taken for granted, only lay writers on Magick like Dr. J. G. Frazer have accorded the subject its full importance."[76] Crowley next inverted Frazer's reading of the magical link, asserting the reality of these conceptual linkages as the foundation of a kind of magic that works. They are no longer, as Frazer had argued, arbitrary, superstitious associations of the savage mind. Elsewhere, Crowley summarized it thus: "It is described at no length whatever by Frazer in his book on sympathetic magic. For that most learned doctor, *vir praeclarus et optimus*, omits the single essential of his subject. It is not enough to pretend that your wax image is the person you want to bewitch; you must make a real connexion. That is the whole art of magic, to be able to do that; and it is the one point that Frazer omits."[77]

To transform Frazer's anthropology into a magical working, Crowley went to Éliphas Lévi's conception of the astral light, which he describes as the operative force behind magick.[78] Nevertheless, Crowley faulted Lévi for not fully explaining the operations of the magical link. In effect, Crowley brought both thinkers together, suggesting that Frazer's description of sympathetic magic is indeed how one learns to harness the astral light to do one's will. In Crowley's example, a magician hoping to "evoke the spirits of the storm" and call down a tempest must identify those atmospheric or stormlike aspects of herself, unite her will and the storm (presumably via the astral light), and then learn to evoke them in connection with a physical talisman that must either effect precipitation or symbolically represent it.[79] Although Crowley provided a complex typology of magical linkages in each case, they operate basically according to Frazer's conception of sympathetic magic, informed by Lévi's ontology.[80]

Magick in Theory and Practice was not the only place that Crowley drew Lévi and Frazer together. In Crowley's final major project, *The Book of Thoth* (1945), he aimed to work out a new tarot deck pregnant with his magical symbols. This meant both a new set of images for the cards—which were done in collaboration with the artist Frieda Harris—and a guide to their interpretation. As one might guess from its title, Crowley understood the tarot in Lévi's terms as a kind of Egyptian Hermetic Bible. But Crowley also drew on Frazer (and others) to produce cross-cultural associations for each of its figures. Each of the major arcana was intended to be not just representative of the European or Egyptian magical tradition, but a repository for the symbols of the full pleroma of all religions. Accordingly, Crowley used *The Golden Bough* as a resource for cross-cultural parallels and linkages.[81] His new tarot was intended to be the embodiment of "comparative religion."[82] In brief, Crowley's last work was an attempt to provide the religious studies of his day with a magical pack of cards.

DISENCHANTED MAGIC

In the course of this Training, [a student of magick] will learn to explore the Hidden Mysteries of Nature, and to develop new senses and faculties in himself, whereby he may communicate with, and control, Beings and Forces pertaining to orders of existence which have been hitherto inaccessible to profane research, and available only to that unscientific and empirical MAGICK (of tradition) which I came to destroy in order that I might fulfill.

ALEISTER CROWLEY, *Magick in Theory and Practice*, 1929

The previous section has shown Crowley's substantial debt to Frazer and religious studies more broadly. I have been aiming to illustrate how Crowley transformed an anthropological account of magic into spells, how he activated a latent perennial mysticism inherent in comparative religion, how he appropriated Frazer's ambivalence into what amounted to a scholarly endorsement of magic, and how he tried to fuse Lévi's, Müller's, and Frazer's works into a system of correspondences and even a magical tool for divination. Furthermore, we have seen how Frazer's claims about the pagan core of Christianity lent themselves to a neo-pagan rereading of the Christian tradition, and we have seen how Crowley transformed Frazer's succession of epochs into a prophetic eschatology. But there has been a hanging issue that still needs to be confronted head on. What did Crowley do with the myth of disenchantment itself? Put another way, what did Crowley do with Frazer's contention that magic is an atavistic survival, mortally wounded in its confrontation with religion and destined to vanish with the rise of science? How did a magician address the contention that magic was in decline?

Crowley's response is significant not just because of his influence on later occultists, but also because it has implications for the scholarly reappraisal of disenchantment. Many historians still portray magic in terms of survival or the occult's supposed "resistance to change."[83] But this position has recently come under fire.

In an important 2003 article, "How Magic Survived the Disenchantment of the World," Wouter Hanegraaff argues that the world had indeed been disenchanted insofar as there was social pressure toward a "culturally established ideology according to which instrumental causality amounts to a worldview capable in principle of rationally explaining all aspects of reality."[84] To simplify slightly, Hanegraaff described the history of European thought in Weberian terms as the ascendance of a kind of instrumental reason that denies the innate human sense of affective identity with the world ("'real' symbolism") in favor of the contention that the world could be fully apprehended in terms of efficient, material causation. In the face of disenchantment, Hanegraaff argues, magic has managed to survive but was largely able to do by being redefined in terms of a separate magical world where the ordinary rules of science do not apply.[85]

I think Hanegraaff is right insofar as he suggests that references by both scholars and practitioners to an unchanging or atavistic occult tradition are misleading. Magic is constantly being redefined. But I think Hanegraaff overstates the consistency of scientific ontologies and understates the diversity of responses to the rise of scientific authority by magicians and philosophers alike. In particular, as Egil Asprem has observed, Crowley's turn *toward* rather than away from science does not accord well with Hanegraaff's model.[86] Asprem is correct that Crowley's magic is not a straightforward rebellion from science, but even Asprem's otherwise excellent essay tends to underemphasize Crowley's capacity to martial skeptical themes in philosophy and, in particular, Crowley's attempt to interweave both disenchantment and re-enchantment. As Crowley argued in the passage quoted in the section epigraph, magick had to destroy magic in order to be revived. Restated, enchantment could only come from disenchantment.

*

A key point of disagreement between James Frazer and Aleister Crowley was as to the overall trajectory of magic in modernity. As one might expect, Crowley did not think that the age of magic was over. More precisely, he thought that the superstitious magic of antiquity needed to be replaced by "magick" appropriate to a new dispensation. As evidenced in the quote above, this new form of magick would surpass "profane research" (aka modern science), but it would be fueled by the destruction of older forms of magic.

Crowley charted an alternative account of the history of magick in a four-part series of articles published in the *International* in 1917 (August–November), titled "The Revival of Magick." His basic argument begins with the historic suppression of magic by the medieval Christian Church, forcing it underground.[87] This is significant because Crowley granted the claim that religion—or at least, Christianity—had seen magic as a rival that needed to be abolished.[88] Religion had indeed come to supplant magic, as Frazer suggested. He also acknowledged that established religion has been challenged by the rise of science.[89] But otherwise Crowley parted ways with Frazer and the canonical account of disenchantment.

Crowley argued that with the arrival of "metaphysics," magic experienced a revival, which he clarified thus: "Assuming that irrefutable form of idealism which contents itself with the demonstration that, knowledge being a function of the mind . . . the universe as we know it is equivalent to the contents of that mind; and assuming also that the mind contains a power able to control thought; then there is no absurdity in asserting that the mind may be master of matter."[90] Paraphrased, the opening for magick was made by philosophers like George Berkeley and worked out in the forms of philosophical idealism that described the world as the product of mental activity. Crowley's reading of idealism is unusual, to be sure, but his main claim is that once we realize that the world is in some sense the product of minds, we can no longer think of it in either Christian terms or merely as a universe of dead matter.

One might imagine that Kant would be a pivotal figure in this historical trajectory (hold on to this point, as we will discuss Kantian enchantments in the next chapter). Elsewhere, Crowley would say as much: "Those laws which we call laws of nature . . . as Kant has shown, are really no more than the laws of our own minds. The universe is a phenomenon of love under will, a mystic and poetic creation, and the intellect only stands to it as mere scansion does to poetry."[91] Although a far from orthodox reading of Kant (and more like those of S. P. Langley), Crowley attributes to Kant the realization that natural laws are merely human generalizations. While philosophical skeptics might take this to mean that the universe is fundamentally unpredictable, in Crowley's view this becomes evidence for recentering the human—or at least, consciousness—at the heart of the cosmos.

Magic, however, is not merely idealism. In Crowley's account, philosophy was merely a preparatory step on the way toward a genuine revival. It took Éliphas Lévi and Bulwer-Lytton to properly restore magic.[92] Lévi spearheaded the revival of magic by recovering the half-lost traditions of ancient magicians and translating them into modern terms. This is re-enchantment as intellectual history (rather than sociology), but Crowley gave particular weight to Lévi's role in publishing popular and accessible writings on the subject.

After Lévi's pioneering work, Crowley imagined there was a flourishing and renewal of magic.[93] Outside of France, he claimed, the Theosophical Society and the Hermetic Order of the Golden Dawn—which he saw as the disciplinary formation of magical studies—picked up Lévi's project, elaborating his science of magic. The foundation of these research institutions for the discovery of magic and the publication of magical materials and books were, in Crowley's estimation, the key to the revival of magick. Unsurprisingly, Crowley portrayed his own work of purifying magick as the culmination of this trajectory, with the result that "there is hardly a country in the world which has not dozens of members hard at work at magick."[94] I would not go so far as to endorse Crowley's model, but I want to elaborate its implications for his attempt to solve the problem of magic in the face of the rise of scientific authority.

Frazer and a host of others had imagined science as a scourge of superstition and magic. One reaction to this possible line of critique was to reject rationality or criticize science itself (see, for instance, the Munich Cosmic Circle, discussed in chapter 8). But that was not the angle Crowley took. If anything, he both granted the power of science—admittedly, while expressing the quasi-Kantian skepticism evidenced above—and sought to describe magick's compatibility with science. But we might wonder, what did harmonizing modern sciences and magick look like?

*

Hints of Crowley's solution appeared already in the first issue of the *Equinox*, the sporadically published journal that Crowley launched as the official organ of the A∴ A∴ in March 1909. From the outset, it announced its goal as "Scientific Illuminism," with the motto "The Method of Science—The Aim of Religion" emblazoned on its cover. It is worth underscoring that Crowley basically described magick as the reconciliation of science and religion.

The series opened with an editorial by Crowley clarifying his version of scientific magic as rooted in the empirical observation of repeatable experiments.[95] Mainly, this meant that aspiring magicians would share annotated diaries recording the effects and procedures of their magical practices. This was basically Francis Bacon's model for the formation of the scientific method. Similarly, Crowley argued that this approach would strip the mystery and miracle from magic while simultaneously granting its systematic practitioners access to new powers—in effect, magic's transformation into magick.

The first issue of the *Equinox* showcased a concrete example of this sort of investigation in an article by Crowley titled "Liber Exercitiorum" (Book of exercises). It provided a set of specific, and supposedly repeatable, techniques (including, e.g., "Physical Clairvoyance," which would be developed by shuffling a deck of tarot cards and then attempting to name a card without looking at its face).[96] The article promised that through training and meditative practice, one could gradually improve on chance. To Crowley this was not an amusing party trick, but the foundation for learning how to practice divination.

More significantly, *Liber Exercitiorum* is an example of Crowley's broader attempt to disenchant magic by turning into magick. This did not mean the stripping away of magical efficacy or action at a distance, nor was this a complete embrace of scientific naturalism (Crowley did imagine astral worlds and mysterious powers).[97] Rather, this was an attempt to expel the jargon and dogma from magic and to base it in empirical observation. In effect, Crowley was positivizing magic. Auguste Comte would have been proud.

To make sense of this project, we have to recognize Crowley's conception of magick, which he defined as "the Science and Art of causing Change to occur in conformity with Will."[98] Crowley added that "ANY required change may be effected by the application of the proper kind and degree of Force in the proper manner, through the proper medium to the proper object."[99] Crowley was forging a generously broad definition of magick as praxis or techne. His example is a chemist's attempt to produce chloride of gold, which is premised on the conjunction of proper materials. For Crowley, the core commonality between magic and science is that both are grounded in goal-driven activity. Crowley also explained his definition of science as follows:

Science enables us to take advantage of the continuity of Nature by the empirical application of certain principles whose interplay involves different orders of idea connected with each other in a way beyond our present comprehension.

(*Illustration*: We are able to light cities by rule-of-thumb methods. We do not know what consciousness is, or how it is connected with muscular action; what electricity is or how it is connected with the machines that generate it; and our methods depend on calculations involving mathematical ideas which have no correspondence in the Universe as we know it.) *For instance "irratio-nal," "unreal" and "infinite" expressions.*[100]

This passage is pure Crowley, but Frazer too had described magic and science as predicated on belief in the continuity of nature (hence the importance of repeatability). Crowley wanted to stress that the basic operations of science are rooted in mysterious phenomena. Fundamentally, he thought scientists are instrumentalists: they keep track of what works to produce certain effects, but work around black-box concepts even as they formulate scientific theories. For example, all the human sciences, from sociology to psychology, take for granted human decision-making, but do so without having worked out a fully formed theory of consciousness. This means that scientific truths are only perspectival or partial; as he put it, "Magick recognizes frankly (1) that truth is relative, subjective, and apparent."[101]

Crowley's skepticism was an attempt to dispel any perceived opposition between science as knowledge and magic as superstition. As he argued: "Man is ignorant of the nature of his own being and powers. Even his idea of his limitations is based on experience of the past, and every step in his progress extends his empire. . . . The question of Magick is a question of discovering and employing hitherto unknown forces in nature."[102] Magick is about discovering forces, and here Crowley probably had in mind psychical powers, unknown or ignored by science. He argued elsewhere, once again evoking Frazer, that "what is magic today is science tomorrow."[103] He clarified this in *Magick without Tears*:

> Magick investigates the laws of Nature with the idea of making use of them. It only differs from "profane" science by always keeping ahead of it. As Frazer has shown, Magick is science in the tentative stage; but it may be, and often is, more than this. It is science which, for one reason or another, cannot be declared to the profane.[104]

In the place of Frazer's idea of magic as primitive protoscience (or modern magic as atavistic survival), Crowley made magick the cutting edge.[105] Unlike many other magicians who aspired to recover lost occult arts, Crowley's magick was future oriented even as it purified older magical practices. Magick willfully rejects scientific presuppositions about human capabilities and pushes past previously assumed limits. From Crowley's perspective, it is mainstream scientists who tend to be too cautious to delve into truly novel areas. Magicians are the real pioneers capable of taking real intellectual risks. Magick is not threatened by modernity, but rather required. Science needs magic in order to push the boundaries of the possible.[106]

CONCLUSION: FROM *THE GOLDEN BOUGH* TO THE GOLDEN DAWN

> The reader is earnestly recommended to study this Ritual again and again . . . for herein are highly important and significant formulae of mystical aspiration and practical magic. In it is exemplified the technical "Dying God" formula about which in *The Golden Bough* Frazer has written so eloquently.
>
> ISRAEL REGARDIE, *The Golden Dawn: A Complete Course in Ceremonial Magic*, 1937

To emphasize the importance of Frazer to Crowley one last time, after the 1914 ritual that has been the chapter's leitmotif, Crowley wrote a set of short stories inspired by *The Golden Bough*. Although published independently in Crowley's lifetime, shortly before his death, Crowley collected these stories and requested that they be issued under the heading *Golden Twigs*.[107] In fictionalizing the world of *The Golden Bough*, Crowley presented his readers with pre-Christian "pagan" perspectives and protagonists, including the priest of Nemi and the oracle of the Corycian Cave. Crowley also included tales set in the contemporary period focused on the discovery of various magical artifacts from Frazer's archaic world. These allowed Crowley to depict modern pagan revivals and the return of magic. Together this collection of eight tales demonstrates how widely Crowley read in *The Golden Bough* and how inspirational he found it.[108]

What I have attempted to do in this chapter is to show how effortlessly Crowley was able to combine Frazer's folklore studies with William James's pragmatic mysticism and Müller's sacred books, and make them the basis for his own magical and religious projects. He was able to do so in part because the works themselves shared habits of thought that were common to the esoteric movements of the period. A perennial mysticism appeared just below the surface in James's and Müller's writings, while Frazer had (perhaps inadvertently) placed magic on a level with science. The most important thing this shows is that religious studies has had ramifications and influences on the religious field, and it was far from disenchanting. If anything, it contributed to the birth of new religious movements and re-enchantment projects.

This chapter has also been making a broader point about the paradoxes of disenchantment discourse. Frazer's very notion of a primitive epoch of "magic" (rather than superstition) was easy to romanticize. Moreover, the language of withdrawal carried with it a sense of bereavement. One of the issues with many dialectical accounts of the dis-/re-enchantment of the world is that they presume that magic had to be lost in order for someone to petition for its return. Instead, Crowley demonstrates that the myth of disenchantment alone was sufficient. He was a magician who spent his life surrounded by fellow occultists, but who nevertheless aspired to bring magic back. Crowley was not alone in this respect—many magicians claimed to recover lost magic. The fascinating thing is that Crowley's route to the revival of magic was through its disenchantment. To do so, he attempted to martial the symbolic resources and methods of science. His was both a recovery of older magical traditions and a positivist magick aimed at the future (and indeed, later we'll see how the Vienna School of positivists might have been envious).

Crowley had allies in the academy, and some of these are easy to guess. Jessie Weston, Margaret Alice Murray, and Gerald Gardner were inspired by *The Golden Bough* in their various attempts to recreate mystery cults of the Holy Grail or pagan witchcraft.[109] Others are harder to anticipate. In the middle decades of the twentieth century, we find scholars in Europe sifting through the world's non-Christian tales and myths in order to discover their universal and hidden forms—forms that, once reconstructed, could serve as preemptively de-civilizing alternatives to the various European rationalisms and positivisms. Here I am not speaking of thoroughgoing magicians or even excoriating the founders of religious studies, but alluding instead to the ancestors of post-structuralism, such as Claude Lévi-Strauss and Georges Bataille. Indeed, if you root your project through Nietzsche and the paganizing aspects of his work, or if you ally with an anticolonial defense of "Oriental" or indigenous peoples, it can be surprising how easily occult motifs worm their way into your discourse.

Frazer's progeny were many: Crowley was his wicked son, the structuralists his cousins. When Crowley's disciple Israel Regardie began a revival of *The Golden Dawn* in the United States, he too enshrined Frazer's text in the most widely read publications of the magical Order. Thus, *The Golden Bough* became a scripture for the Golden Dawn.[110]

* Part II *

The Horrors of Metaphysics

Every phenomenon of nature, profoundly analyzed, draws us into the impenetrable darkness of metaphysics.

CARL DU PREL, *Die Philosophie der Mystik*, 1885

In his horror of metaphysics, the founder of positivism excluded from his science everything really universal and cosmic.

JEAN-MARIE GUYAU, *Irréligion de l'avenir*, 1886

CHAPTER SEVEN

The Black Tide:
Mysticism, Rationality, and the German Occult Revival

Freud said to me, "My dear Jung, promise me never to abandon the sexual theory. That is the most essential thing of all. You see, we must make a dogma of it, an unshakable bulwark." . . . In some astonishment I asked him, "A bulwark against what?" To which he replied, "Against the black tide of mud"—and here he hesitated for a moment, then added—"of occultism."

C. G. JUNG, Erinnerungen, Träume, Gedanken, 1963

A meticulous reader of Sigmund Freud's *Die Traumdeutung* (*The Interpretation of Dreams*) will note a subtle metamorphosis already at work in the fourth edition of that famous text (1914). The most obvious change from previous editions is the inclusion of two essays by Freud's younger colleague Otto Rank relating the analysis of dreams to myth and poetry. Though by the eighth edition, these essays would be expunged, they show Freud and Rank extending psychoanalysis to an analysis of artistic and mythological symbolism.[1]

But there are other changes in the work that are more important for our purposes. These modifications are subtle—a paragraph here, a footnote there—and are relatively modest compared to the mutations of subsequent editions. For those attentive to the return of the repressed, the most significant change in the 1914 edition is the appearance of six footnotes all referencing the same thinker, the otherwise obscure German philosopher Carl du Prel. This may sound trivial, but their appearance is significant. One clue as to their meaning is the first of these notes, where Freud remarked:

That brilliant mystic du Prel—one of the few authors for whose neglect in earlier editions of this book I would like to express my regret—suggests that the gateway to metaphysics, so far as [ordinary] men are concerned, is not wakefulness, but dreams.[2]

Who was this "brilliant mystic (*geistreiche Mystiker*)"? A later note increases the stakes; there, Freud cited passages from du Prel, *Die Philosophie der Mystik* (1885; *The Philosophy of Mysticism*), including this line: "It is a truth that cannot be emphasized strongly enough that consciousness and the soul/mind (*Seele*) are not coextensive."[3] To which Freud commented, "I am pleased to be able to point to an author who has drawn from the study of dreams the same conclusion [as myself] about the relationship between conscious and unconscious activity."[4]

This is important because *Die Traumdeutung* is the first monograph in which Freud articulated his theory of "the unconscious" (*Das Unbewußte*) and this very word had appeared as a term of analysis in du Prel, *Die Philosophie der Mystik* fifteen-years before Freud.[5] In this footnote, Freud might seem to be attributing to du Prel nothing less than the discovery of the unconscious—or more precisely, the discovery that consciousness is only the surface of a submerged and larger unconscious mind that expresses itself in dreams. Although Freud clearly drew from many sources in formulating his signature theories, at the very least it begins to look as if Freud owed something significant to the insights of a "mystic."[6]

Taken together, these footnotes suggest a securely established Freud finally admitting to some of the inspirations for his most influential theories. There is more evidence for this interpretation. This was the same edition in which Freud also acknowledged the importance of Eduard von Hartmann; scholars have already spent some time demonstrating the influence of Hartmann on Freudian psychoanalysis and many of its master terms.[7] While this might put pressure on arbitrary preconceptions of Freud's originality, it does not seem particularly unsettling to know Freud read Hartmann. Despite Hartmann's references to the Vedic wisdom and the theosophy of Jakob Böhme, Hartmann is remembered as respectable philosopher. Du Prel is categorically different; beyond just Freud's reference to him as a "mystic," there is also the fact that today scholars remember Du Prel as a spiritualist and psychical researcher who wrote about magic and the occult.[8] Freud's footnotes might seem tantamount to a confession of serious interest in mysticism, spiritualism, or even magic.

Crucially, these changes to *Die Traumdeutung* were made after Freud discovered Frazer's *Golden Bough*; indeed, they appeared just after Freud had written the 1913 essay "*Animismus, Magie und Allmacht der Gedanken*" ("Animism, Magic and the Omnipotence of Thought"), which articulates his version of the disenchantment myth and argues that myth and magic are products of the primitive mind. It is remarkable not just that Freud read an occultist, but that he admitted to doing so after having argued that magical thinking was degenerative or retrogressive. One might therefore expect Freud to have abandoned mysticism, but he and du Prel shared more than the classical narrative would admit. Indeed, I will explore how Freud ultimately projected his own taboo beliefs onto the figure of the "savage."

Freud is important in our attempt to pinpoint the genesis of the regulative function of the myth of disenchantment. If you have been keeping score, many of the figures discussed thus far—from Francis Bacon to Friedrich Schiller to Max Müller—made little effort to conceal their interest in magic, theosophy, or the occult. To be sure, they often tried to distinguish their projects from diabolic or superstitious forms of the same, but they were generally open about them.[9] If we have since forgotten their enchantments, the amnesia came later. Thus, the question becomes: When did scholars begin to suppress their occult interests?

My intuition is that they did so much later and more sporadically then is conventionally supposed and that much of the cleanup has been retroactive. Freud is fascinating for our purposes because he hesitated between both revelation and concealment, making some of his occult interests public and confining others to his personal life. Freud also embraced both a disenchantment narrative and belief in many of the things he described as endangered. Crucially, Freud's letters can be used to reconstruct his reasoning about the matter, and we can learn much about the mechanisms of occult repression from the master theorist of repression himself.

The second purpose of this chapter is to put pressure on a common reading of Weberian disenchantment—namely, the idea that a central feature of modernity is increasing epistemic confidence. Basically, disenchantment means a vanishing sense of mystery and a greater faith in the human capacity to use instrumental reason to master the world. The problem is that in addition to certain post-Kantian movements amplifying various forms of skepticism, enchantment found a home in the heart of philosophy itself, and then philosophy transmitted this magic to a scientific discipline: psychoanalysis.

The relationship between du Prel and Freud demonstrates the importance of "mysticism" as a vanishing mediator between two conceptual edifices: a philosophy haunted by the simultaneous power and limits of reason, and its double, a psychoanalysis drawn to explore the roots of irrationality. What lurked beyond reason's limits? Was it divine consciousness or madness? Could philosophy explain magic? And what was the fate of mysticism in modernity?

Could mysticism bridge religion and philosophy/science? I will first showcase an (equally suspect) alternative to the disenchantment myth, one that saw modernity as a decline into degeneration, mysticism, and the occult. The chapter then pursues the German occult revival in the most unlikely of places, the history of post-Kantian philosophical thought. I show that it was this haunted philosophy that bequeathed its ghosts to Freudian psychoanalysis.

DEGENERATION AND MYSTICISM: MAX NORDAU

The old Northern faith contained the fearsome doctrine of the twilight of the gods (*Göt-terdämmerung*). In our days there have arisen in more highly developed minds vague fears of a twilight of the masses (*Völkerdämmerung*), in which all suns and all stars are gradually waning, and humankind with all its institutions and creations is perishing in the midst of a dying world. . . . Ghost stories are very popular. . . . So are esoteric novels, in which the author hints that he could say a deal about magic, Kabbalah, fakirism, astrology, and other white and black arts.

MAX NORDAU, *Entartung*, 1892

Thus far, I may have given the sense that the disenchantment myth was universally embraced. At the very least, I may have inadvertently produced the impression that those who did not equate modernization with alienation were mostly celebrating the wonders of progress. But here I want to introduce an alternate model, one that described modernity not as the death of magic or the despiritualization of nature, but as the rise of mysticism and the occult. Its proponent, the influential German-speaking Jewish physician and social critic Max Nordau (1849–1923), was an early interlocutor with Freud. In this section, I will set out Nordau's thesis, which he referred to as *Entartung* (degeneration, or literally "retardation"), and show how it provided a model against which other thinkers staged alternatives.[10]

Nordau did not invent the idea of degeneration; it had distant precedents in the biblical accounts of the Fall of Man and the Tower of Babel. But even acceptance of Darwin's theory of evolution would not wholly dispel the argument that species or individuals might regress to an earlier stage in the evolutionary progression. As a theory of culture, the degeneration thesis came into vogue in the later part of the nineteenth century, finding expression in everything from novels to philosophical and scientific works.[11] Nordau was central to its currency. In the widely read 1892 *Entartung*, Nordau argued,

"We stand now in the midst of a severe mental epidemic; of a sort of black death of degeneration and hysteria" in which the progress of civilization was in peril of being reversed.[12]

Crucially, Nordau started from the basic features of modernity granted by sociologists today, including urbanization, industrialization, societal differentiation, and the advancement of science; but instead of portraying these as part of a grand process of rationalization, he argued that modernity is in danger of producing a psychologically sick underclass. Although pitched in apocalyptic language, Nordau's model is not far from the Mike Judge's film *Idiocracy* (2006), which depicts a twenty-fifth-century world populated by insane and gullible morons. While Nordau was cautionary rather than completely pessimistic, he agonized about a future in which humanity descends into stupidity, moral degeneration, and madness. To coin a term, this is modernization as *ir*rationalization.

*

Nordau tellingly described mysticism as a symptom or "a cardinal mark of degeneration."[13] In his assessment, modernity was threatened by a rising tide of mysticism (*Mysticismus*), which he defined as following: "A state of mind in which the subject imagines that he perceives or divines unknown and inexplicable relations amongst phenomena, discerns in things hints at mysteries, and regards them as symbols, by which a dark power seeks to unveil, or at least to indicate, all sorts of marvels that he endeavors to guess, though generally in vain."[14] Nordau's definition of mysticism is significant because it suggests that modernity will produce more mysterious symbols, more religion, and more magic, even if only in a retarded or atavistic sense. So in place of disenchantment, Nordau foresaw a re-enchantment, which he portrayed in terms of a socially stratified hierarchy where "degenerate" masses increasingly would take refuge in magic and mysticism.[15] The modern world, therefore, is in the process of becoming more symbolically rich (if in a delusional way) rather than less.

Nordau's linking of degeneration to spiritualism was also explicit. He argued, however, that spiritualism is special, not merely a superstition, but an insane modern superstition, emerging from mysticism and derangement. He seemed to take particular horror at the idea that it might make inroads into the world of "literary men" and described psychical research as a further, ominous sign of deterioration. Nordau described spiritualism as widespread in Great

Britain and Germany, but he argued the real problem was elsewhere: "France is about to become the promised land of believers in ghosts."[16]

France was particularly worrying for Nordau because of spiritualism's rapprochement with medicine, and particularly with the hypnosis formulated by Freud's teacher, Jean-Martin Charcot (1825–93). Nordau stated his rebuttal in direct terms, arguing that in the hands of hypnotists, "possession, witch spells, second sight, healing by imposition of hands, prophecy, [and] mental communication at the remotest distance without the intervention of words have received a new interpretation and have been recognized as possible."[17] Nordau dismissed hypnotism at the outset and argued that it is the contamination of medicine by mysticism. Basically, it is degenerate medicine that lends credibility to superstitions. What is striking here is that Nordau was both condemning what would become the foundations of the discipline of psychoanalysis, and arguing that set the stage for further magic and mysticism.

For Nordau, mysticism was a harbinger of social collapse, should Europe not awaken to the signs of its own decay. At least insofar as we (more than a hundred years later) do not generally fear psychoanalysis or a flood of mysticism, we might find it easy to look at Nordau today and laugh. His contention that evolution could be reversed by urbanization is hard to take seriously, and may even seem to be racializing the working class. In one significant respect, though, Nordau was right—not in his idea of degeneration, but in his simpler observation that Western Europe was in the midst of an occult revival. The previous chapters have shown that in late nineteenth-century England, full-blown spiritualist movements and occult revivals were in place; it comes as no surprise that the German-speaking world was tracing a similar pattern. This is a subject about which scholars have already had much to say.[18] But as I will show, these revivals found a home in two unlikely places: philosophy and psychoanalysis.

KANT AS NECROMANCER:
CARL DU PREL AND ARTHUR SCHOPENHAUER

Kant's philosophy is not only an absurdity, but a wickedness and a horror; the pious and peaceful sage of Konigsberg passes for a sort of Necromancer and Blackartist in Metaphysics; his doctrine is a region of boundless baleful gloom, too cunningly broken here and there by splendours of unholy fire; spectres and tempting demons people it.

THOMAS CARLYLE, "The State of German Literature," 1827

The initiate has already accustomed the untutored understanding, which clings to the outer sense, to higher concepts of an abstract character. He is now able to see spirit forms, stripped of their corporeal shell, in the half-light with which the dim torch of metaphysics reveals the realm of shades. Let us now, therefore, having completed our difficult preparation, embark on our perilous journey.

IMMANUEL KANT, *Träume eines Geistersehers*, 1766

Träume eines Geistersehers, erläutert durch Träume der Metaphysik (Dreams of a spirit seer, illustrated by dreams of metaphysics, 1766) is an oddity in Immanuel Kant's oeuvre, and has often been an embarrassment for scholars. For readers accustomed to the dry prose of Kant's more famous works, the tone of the text will seem downright strange, vacillating between hints at occult knowledge (as above), abstract philosophical reflections, and occasional outbursts of sarcasm. As far as I know, it also includes Kant's only attempt at a flatulence joke: *"If a hypochondriacal wind should rage in the guts, what matters is the direction it takes: if downwards, then the result is a f[art]; if upwards, an apparition or a heavenly inspiration."*[19] Try that one out the next time someone you know claims to be divinely inspired.

But its playful tone is not the only thing unusual about *Dreams of a Spirit Seer*; its subject matter has also disconcerted many of Kant's acolytes. The work is a sustained discussion of ghosts and of the Swedish mystic Emanuel Swedenborg (1688–1772). Swedenborg had come to Kant's attention because of his celebrated clairvoyant visions and spirit communications. Today, scholars argue about whether the text demonstrates a Swedenborgian influence on Kant, or whether the whole thing is essentially an elaborate joke at the mystic's expense.[20] In this section, I would like to gesture at the centrality of spirits and magic to post-Kantian philosophy, and expose the roots of a tension between reason's overwhelming power and fragility, which may still be hauntingly familiar today.

Philosophy has long been haunted by spirits.[21] More than any other figure, Kant came to define nineteenth-century conceptions of rationality; but the enchantments of his legacy have been underappreciated. In *Dreams of a Spirit Seer*, Kant distanced himself from Swedenborg without fully foreclosing the possibility of spirits. Instead, perhaps revealingly, he defined spirits as immaterial beings possessed of reason (*Vernunft*).[22] This might be restated to say that ghosts are pure reason. Kant then went on to suggest that immaterial spirits were fundamentally beyond the limits of human understanding. Given that *Dreams of a Spirit Seer* just precedes Kant's critical turn, one cannot help but notice the parallels between its spirits and his *Critique of Pure Reason* (*Kritik der reinen Vernunft*, 1781).

For the uninitiated, the *Critique of Pure Reason* was an attempt to counter a quasi-Humean skepticism by surveying the grounds of possible experience. To do so, Kant conceded a version of the Humean appearance-essence breach and granted that we bring pure forms of sense experience or intuition (*reine Anschauung*, e.g., space, time) to our empirical world before they are properly earned. In fact, we only experience appearances, not the thing-in-itself (*Ding-an-Sich*). Reason then has a powerful and necessary function; but beyond its limits lies "a vast and stormy ocean" of the unknowable.[23] This ocean outside possible experience and conceivable human knowledge is where Kant would locate God.[24] Except for this gesture toward negative theology, Kant largely aimed to evacuate the region of positive content, but once he had defined a transcendent realm, others could not resist populating it. While Kant wanted to leave room for a rational faith, an inadvertent consequence of his philosophy was to further alienate philosophy from a newly mysterious hidden world.

Kant also had a lasting impact on conceptions of the unconscious mind. René Descartes, having defined the mind in terms of self-awareness, seemingly excluded the possibility of unconscious mental processes.[25] By contrast, in *Anthropologie in pragmatischer Hinsicht* (1798; *Anthropology from a Pragmatic Point of View*), Kant reflected on "the [mental] representations that we have without being conscious of them," arguing that we have indirect representations of things on the edge of our perceptions (e.g., recognizing a person when they are barely visible).[26] Kant referred to these indirect perceptions as *dunkel* (dark or obscure) mental representations. He also argued that the majority of thought is made up of this dark content and that "only a few places on the vast map of our mind are illuminated" with clear and distinct representations.[27] This was only a minor part of Kant's larger exploration of the limits of reason, but the imagery of a vast dark map of the mind suggested a vast internal region.[28]

In the nineteenth century, philosophy would make itself over in Kant's image, sanctifying both his emphasis on the powers of reason and his intuitions about the importance of reason's limits. Thus his famous distinction between the phenomenal world of experiences and the noumenal world of the thing-in-itself would serve as the central line across which much of philosophy would stage its battles. Later theorists would also use this bifurcation (and a related Kantian formulation of the distinction between faith and reason) to enshrine religion and science in separate domains or nonoverlapping magisteria. But the thing-in-itself would continue to haunt a range of disciplines, serving as a kind of Kantian monster that lurked outside the realms of reason and preyed on those who have strayed too far. We will touch on some of these beasts and their role in the uncanny legacy of post-Kantian thought.[29]

*

While some philosophers rejected Kant's *Ding-an-Sich*, they often found it difficult to escape his other ghosts. Nowhere is this clearer than in Hegel. In the logic section of *Enzyklopädie der philosophischen Wissenschaften im Grundrisse* (often called the Encyclopaedia-Logic, 1817), Hegel even described his own project in terms of "mysticism."

To explain Hegel's mysticism, you should know that despite how *dialectics* is commonly used, it was not Hegel's preferred term for his philosophy. Dialectics is just the second of three stages of thought—namely, the negative moment (Adorno's negative dialectics is redundant). The final stage for Hegel is often what he referred to as "speculation," which describes how one cognizes the unity of distinct terms. Tellingly, Hegel remarked that "speculative truth"—that is, his philosophy—"means very much the same as what used to be called *mysticism*."[30] That is, he thought that philosophy rigorously pursued should reach the same paradoxical endpoints that the old mysticism achieved via chin-stroking, top-of-the-mountain shortcuts: *The man is the woman, the woman is the man. Life is death, and death is life.* A rational philosophy will disclose "what lies beyond the compass of understanding" because *der Verstand* is just one rather limited power of the mind.[31] Hegel seemed to be suggesting that his philosophy is nothing less than the vindication of mysticism by redoing it in fully argued, entirely nonmystical terms.[32]

But if Hegel was identifying his philosophy with a disenchanted mysticism, it fell to others to use Kant to theorize magic.

*

Arthur Schopenhauer articulated his own theory of magic in *On the Will in Nature* (*Über den Willen in der Natur*, 1836). In a chapter titled "Animalischer Magnetismus und Magie" (Animal magnetism and magic), Schopenhauer referred to animal magnetism as "practical metaphysics," arguing that its effects are real, and that they "empirically confirm the possibility of a magical, as opposed to a physical effect, a possibility which the previous century had so peremptorily discarded because it did not want to give credence to any other effect than the physical, brought about in accord with the comprehensible causal nexus."[33] According to Schopenhauer, *magic is real* and efficacious. While ordinary events happen inside the categories of space, time, and ordinary causation, magic is no less genuine, operating according to what he called a "metaphysical nexus."[34] In effect, magic represents trans-spatial causation because it happened at the level of the *Ding-an-Sich*.

In Schopenhauer's scheme, not only was "white magic" real, there was actually reason to believe that black magic (*maleficium*) was also a description of actual phenomena.[35] In effect, Schopenhauer was granting a basic distinction common to much of European esotericism, which was a subject he knew well, judging from the copious citations from magical texts that filled out his chapter. But the philosopher did not grant the whole of, say, Agrippa's *Occult Philosophy*; he was suspicious of both the reality of demons and the necessity of ritual.

Schopenhauer argued instead that the essence of magic was the will, and that it was the human will that allowed one to effect magical transformations.[36] In this he seems to be anticipating Crowley (who did read Schopenhauer). Schopenhauer had long seen the exploration of the will as the fundamental contribution of his philosophy. In his masterwork, *The World as Will and Representation* (*Die Welt als Wille und Vorstellung*, 1818), he had interpreted Kant's critical philosophy to argue that we can only know the surface nature of phenomena, not their internal nature; to which Schopenhauer observed that there is an exception to this limitation, since the human body is presented to us in two ways. First, we experience it phenomenologically, as a kind of object of sensorial experience that is necessarily conditioned by the categories of space and time. But it also appears to us on the inside. In other words, we know what it is like to be a *Ding-an-Sich* because we have a body. Schopenhauer called this inward being at the root of all things the "will," and he argued that our apprehension of it is both outside the categories of space and time and unconscious. Hence, by arguing that magic also originated from the will, Schopenhauer was actually enchanting the noumena and basically suggesting his whole philosophical system had magical powers.

Further, instead of imagining that magic would vanish with the advancement of philosophy, Schopenhauer declared that his generation was witnessing the dawn of a new age of "magic" initiated by "by the transformation of philosophy brought about by Kant." As Schopenhauer elaborated: "In order to ridicule all occult sympathy or even magical effect out of hand, one must find the world highly, indeed absolutely, intelligible. But this can be done only if the world is looked into with an extremely superficial gaze that allows no notion of the fact that we are awash in a sea of riddles and mysteries and that we neither know nor understand either things or ourselves immediately and thoroughly."[37] Paraphrased, it was a skeptical reading of Kant that had made way for the return of magic. Accordingly, Schopenhauer saw the task of philosophy (as the queen of metaphysics) to be making use of the practical metaphysics of magic. But it fell to du Prel to expand the enchantments of Schopenhauer's project.

*

Kant haunts the work of Freud's "brilliant mystic," the German aristocrat, philosopher, and occultist Baron Carl du Prel (1839–99).[38] Following a career as a Bavarian army officer, du Prel completed a doctoral thesis in philosophy at the University of Tübingen, titled *Oneirokritikon: Der Traum vom Standpunkt des Transzendentalen Idealismus* (Oneiro-critique: The dream from the standpoint of transcendental idealism, 1868). But he built his scholarly reputation in the 1874 *Der Kampf ums Dasein am Himmel: Die Darwinsche Formel nachgewiesen in der Mechanik der Sternenwelt* (The struggle for existence in the heavens: The Darwinian model demonstrated in the mechanics of the cosmos). *Der Kampf ums Dasein am Himmel* was a passionate defense of Darwinism that attempted to relate it to the formation of consciousness, and even the universe.[39]

In the years that followed, du Prel's writings took a spiritualist and indeed a "mystical" turn. He worked to square the experiences of psychic mediums and German mystics with a version of transcendental idealism rooted in Kant. His version of Kant was conditioned by his readings of Arthur Schopenhauer, Johann Gottlieb Fichte, and Eduard von Hartmann. In the work Freud cited, *Die Philosophie der Mystik* (1885), du Prel waded into a nineteenth-century controversy about the meaning of the "mysticism."

Although it might be tempting to imagine a continuous tradition of German mysticism stretching from Meister Eckhart to Ludwig Wittgenstein, Eckhart had not been much read following his condemnation by the Inquisition in 1328.[40] It was the Catholic theologian Franz von Baader (1765–1841), an acquaintance of Hegel, Schelling, and Jacobi, who recovered Eckhart from near obscurity and placed him alongside Böhme and others to suggest a mystical tradition, which Baader contrasted with what he saw as the destructive rationalism of enlightenment.[41] In effect, mysticism was constructed to be a third term reconnecting humanity and God, or philosophy and nature.

Nineteenth-century conceptions of mysticism (*Mystizismus* or *Mystik*), however, were roughly split between two semi-overlapping semantic spheres. Mysticism either meant belief in mysterious spiritual powers and the efficacy of secret rituals, often epitomized by the initiates of the Greek Eleusinian Mysteries (basically, mysticism as occult magic); or it referred to a belief in truths attained through direct union with God by means of self-surrender. Accordingly, thinkers like du Prel and William James were crucial to the process of redefining mysticism as a universal aspect of human experience.[42]

Die Philosophie der Mystik also used evidence from psychical research to argue for the existence of a spiritual transcendental subject of extraordinary depths. As du Prel put it:

> If consciousness in even our highest ecstasies does not exhaust our whole being, leaving behind an immeasurable background of the Unconscious, which can furnish new divisions, then certainly man appears as a being of groundless depth, reaching with his individual roots into the metaphysical region. . . . Man [is] a double being, with one foot on the earth, the other in the realm of spirits.[43]

Our day-to-day subjectivity is only the partial manifestation of a soul (or pure ego) that really exists in the unconscious. Moreover, he argued that "individuality extends its roots down into the thing-in-itself (*Ding-an-Sich*)"[44] But rather than being a unfathomable remainder, du Prel thought that the Kantian thing-in-itself made itself available to us in mesmeric and somnambulistic states. In other words, we truly transcend space and time in dreams.

Du Prel also wanted to make the study of paranormal phenomena the main business of philosophy; in 1886, he became one of the founding members of the Münchener psychologische Gesellschaft (Munich Psychological Society), which was modeled on the British Society for Psychical Research. The results of du Prel's research, combined with his ongoing philosophical musings, ushered in a fruitful era of writing that included the publication of both 1893 *Der Spiritismus* (Spiritualism) and the two-volume *Die Entdeckung der Seele durch die Geheimwissenschaften* (The discovery of the soul through the occult sciences, 1894–95). Shortly before his death in 1899, du Prel published the final two-volume *Die Magie als Naturwissenschaft* (Magic as natural science), in which he used evidence from magic to articulate a skepticism about conventional accounts of causation. At the same time, he argued in *Die Magie* that magic is only an unknown natural science, waiting for the proper systematization.

To counter the charge that Kant and the occult make poor bedfellows, du

Prel published the first edition of Kant's *Vorlesungen über Psychologie* (Lectures on psychology), aiming to show that Kant had formulated his philosophy on the insights of Swedenborg. In so doing, du Prel hoped to prove that his own mysticism was orthodox Kantianism. It worked insofar as du Prel was read—albeit often critically—by influential thinkers like William James. Indeed, there was also an extended series of public debates between du Prel and Eduard von Hartmann over a range of issues.[45] Moreover, other philosophers and theologians like Karl Joel and Otto Pfleiderer followed du Prel in discussing the union of mysticism and philosophical thought.[46] Meanwhile, an entire generation of spiritualists was more than happy to follow du Prel in populating the noumenal with ghosts.[47] But this does not tell us what Freud was doing reading du Prel, even on the sly. To make sense of that, we need to return to the history of psychoanalysis and to locate Freud in the period's occult milieu.

HIDDEN DEPTHS:
SIGMUND FREUD

Mysticism, occultism—what is meant by these words? . . . Occultism asserts that there are in fact "more things in heaven and earth than are dreamt of in our philosophy." Well, we need not feel bound by the narrow-mindedness of academic philosophy.

SIGMUND FREUD, *Neue Folge der Vorlesungen zur Einführung in die Psychoanalyse*, 1933

If there is one received truism in the popular account of the history of psychoanalysis, it is that the falling-out between Sigmund Freud and his disciple Carl Gustav Jung centered on their differences regarding religion and the occult. Although some scholars know different, in what was for a time a foundational myth of psychoanalysis, Jung played the role of either a deeply spiritual person or a credulous mystic (depending on one's vantage point); regardless, Freud is usually cast as a skeptic.[48]

By way of illustration: the David Cronenberg film *A Dangerous Method* (2011) focuses on the triadic relationship between Jung, Freud, and their Austrian colleague (and Jung's lover) Sabina Spielrein. The film, based on John Kerr's nonfictional *A Most Dangerous Method* (1993), repeatedly depicts Jung and Freud's spiritual differences. In particular, in a dramatic scene set in Freud's office, Freud (played by Viggo Mortensen) cautions Jung (Michael Fassbender) that it is "dangerous to stray into any kind of mysticism," warning him against "wallow[ing] in the black mud of superstition," when a sudden noise, a loud crack, startles both men. Jung immediately remarks that he had a presentiment of the noise and that it was an example of a paranormal *"catalytic exteriorisation phenomenon."* Freud scoffs. But Jung predicts that the event will occur again. Freud has just resumed his monologue when a second crash temporarily stuns him into silence. Jung looks self-assured, and the viewer is meant to feel that he has been vindicated in his occult pursuits. But the scene concludes with Freud saying, "We can't afford to wander into these speculative areas, telepathy, singing bookcases, fairies at the bottom of the garden. It won't do!" Throughout the film, Freud is generally depicted as a smug skeptic while Jung is portrayed as spiritually inclined.

This view of Freud and Jung's relationship is not without precedent, not least of which is Jung's autobiography *Erinnerungen Träume Gedanken* (1962; *Memories, Dreams, Reflections*), which is likely the ultimate source of the film's account of the protagonists' spiritual conflicts.[49] As evidenced in this chapter's epigraph, Jung repeatedly described his conflict with Freud as originating in Freud's condemnation of *"schwarzen Schlammflut des Okkultismus"* (the black tide of occultism).[50] But as Jung explained, "What Freud seemed to mean by 'occultism' was virtually everything that philosophy and religion, including the rising contemporary science of parapsychology, had learned about the psyche."[51] Even the paranormal anecdote depicted in the film has a precedent in Jung's account: in 1909, an uncanny and repeated noise described as a *"katalytisches Exteriorisationsphänomen"* ironically disrupted Freud's expression of doubts about the paranormal.[52] The main differences between Jung's account and that of the film is that Freud's dialogue is not in the text.

The publication record supports Jung's self-presentation as a spiritual seeker. Jung had a childhood encounter with spiritualism that culminated in his 1902 dissertation, which was a case study of a spirit medium. Later publications such as *Seelenprobleme der gegenwart* (1933; *Modern Man in Search of a Soul*), *Psychologie und Alchemie* (1944; *Psychology and Alchemy*), and *Mysterium Coniunctionis* (1956) reiterate his mystical religiosity; and his personal account of spiritual visions is recorded in *Memories, Dreams, Reflections* and the posthumously published *The Red Book: Liber Novus* (2009). Taken as a whole, Jung's work leaves little doubt as to his engagement with magic, alchemy, spiritualism, mysticism, and theosophy. Even the main conceptual innovations of Jungian or analytic psychology—the collective unconscious, synchronicity, anima and animus—all can be seen as products of a cross-fertilization of psychology and esotericism.[53] Accordingly, it is not hard to place Jung among the magicians.

*

A number of scholars have described Freud's general skepticism and unbelief. As the historian Peter Gay puts it, "Freud's unbelief stands out sharply. . . . It is certain . . . that if Freud had been a [religious] believer . . . he would not have developed psychoanalysis."[54] With significantly more nuance, Jean-Luc Nancy describes the importance of Freud's "belief without belief" and later remarks: "Science's value for Freud is as a defense against religious illusion."[55] While Harold Bloom argues for the importance of Freud's Jewishness, he nevertheless portrays Freud's project as a kind of immanent or internal critique of Judaism projected onto a larger canvas.[56] Not all scholars read Freud as antireligious, but Freud is often classed as one of the "three masters of suspicion" alongside Marx and Nietzsche.[57]

If this consensus were right, Freud might seem to be the least likely person to dabble with the occult, mysticism, or the paranormal. But the popular image of Freud gets it wrong—it imagines a greater distance between Freud and Jung than was actually the case. Before I get to Freud's occultism, I want to discuss his skepticism.

At first pass, Freud's oeuvre supports the reading of him as a skeptic. Already in *Zur Psychopathologie des Alltagslebens* (first edition, 1904; *The Psychopathology of Everyday Life*), Freud discussed what he saw as the common psychological impulse to make meaning out of coincidences and to believe in "superstitions" like prophetic dreams. It is in the midst of this analysis of "superstition" that Freud tentatively outlined what would become his grand theory of religion. Freud wrote that "a large portion of the mythological conception of the world which reaches far into the most modern religions *is nothing but psychology projected into the outer world.*"[58] As he explained, religious symbols are the projection of internal conflicts and insecurities, based in early attempts to "explain the outer world in an anthropomorphic sense."[59] Having internalized a distinction between religion and science, Freud argued that religion is essentially superstition, embedded in infantile fantasy and anthropological fallacy. This is a critique Freud repeated, and if anything amplified, elsewhere.[60]

Crucially, Freud also adopted the myth of disenchantment. In the essay "Animismus, Magie und Allmacht der Gedanken" (Animism, magic, and the omnipotence of thought, collected in *Totem und Tabu*, 1913), Freud begins to digest his reading of Tylor and Frazer to theorize a relationship between magic and religion. Freud, however, differentiated between magic and sorcery, arguing that "sorcery (*Zauberei*), then, is essentially the art of influencing spirits by treating them in the same way as one would treat men in like circumstances. . . . Magic (*Magie*), on the other hand, is something different:

fundamentally, it disregards spirits and makes use of special procedures and not of everyday psychological methods. . . . Magic can be applied as well in cases where, as it seems to us, the process of spiritualizing Nature has not yet been carried out."[61] Basically, sorcery is based on spirits that it evokes by communicating with them as one would a person, while magic treats everything as a tool or symbol to be manipulated, such that while it can compel spirits, it does so in an instrumentalist manner.

Freud also provided a definition of magic (intended to cover sorcery as well) as the belief that that "relations which hold between the ideas of things are assumed to hold equally between the things themselves."[62] This should now be a familiar version of magic as savage semiotics rooted in the confusion between representations and the things they represent. Hence one mistakenly believes that stabbing an image, say, has the capacity to harm the person it depicts. Just as the association of ideas is unrestrained spatially, so too magic functions at a distance. It is invested in what Freud called "the omnipotence of thought." It therefore assumes that communication at a distance is also possible. As Freud put it, "Telepathy is taken for granted." By way of a methodological parenthetical, it is worth noting that Freud here classed "telepathy" as an occult superstition.[63] Keep that in mind for later.

Significantly, in this essay Freud described the by-now familiar account of cultural evolution as both disenchantment and secularization, arguing that civilizations move through "an animistic phase followed by a religious phase and this in turn by a scientific one."[64] Here we can see Freud running Tylor and Frazer's models together. Freud argued that "animism" is the first major phase of human thought, but he denied that it is properly speaking religious and went on to associate it with myth and magic.[65] Freud's additional contribution to the conversation is that he mapped this progression onto the development of the individual, associating animism with infancy, religion with the object-choice stage of childhood, and science with maturity.[66] This is roughly a cultural version of Ernst Haeckel's claim that ontogeny recapitulates phylogeny, with science representing individual/cultural maturity while magic represents childhood/primitivism.[67] In sum, mature scientific civilization should outgrow childish magic.

Freud also included a case study of a "neurotic" with magical delusions, thus associating magic with a trifecta of Victorian derision—primitives, children, and the insane. This text *might* suggest a disenchanted Freud arguing that those benighted individuals who engage in magical thinking are psychologically juvenile, whereas the psychoanalyst is truly mature and hence mythless. To be fair to the subtlety in Freud's analysis, he noted that we all have some temptation to indulge in magical thinking; he also argued that religion might have a useful role in restraining violent instincts.

The Future of an Illusion (*Die Zukunft einer Illusion*, 1927) is perhaps even more pessimistic. This often-misread work uses *illusion* as a technical term to describe a belief that is not necessarily false, but deeply aspirational in character.[68] If a "delusion" is holding to an incorrect belief (like insisting that 1 + 1 = 7), then an "illusion" is something that might happen but about which we have no guarantee (like this book will eventually win a major book award). The "American dream," the idea that success should be possible for everyone, would be an example of an "illusion" in this sense.

Religion is also such an illusion for Freud, as it is connected to wish fulfillment and future aspirations, whether messianic or based in the afterlife. Freud argued that religion is effectively a vestigial trait, left over from humankind's early development, and one we may need to outgrow. As he noted: "If this view is right, it is to be supposed that a turning-away from religion is bound to occur with the fatal inevitability of a process of growth, and that we find ourselves at this very juncture."[69] Although he cautioned of the instability that might result should the religious restrictions on immorality be lifted, we might say that *The Future of an Illusion* is based in Freud's own "illusion," or deeply felt wish, that humankind would awaken and reject at least the false illusions of religion. To be sure, this was a wish whose aspirational character he acknowledged with a great degree of self-reflectiveness.[70] Nevertheless, Freud has moved from disenchantment as an objective model to disenchantment (or at least secularization) as a therapeutic agenda; he has moved from observer to advocate.

After reading *The Future of an Illusion*, the French Nobel laureate and avowed mystic Romain Rolland contacted Freud, asking him to address the idea that a perennial mystical experience was the common foundation of the world's religions.[71] This was topical because, as noted above, the concept of "mysticism" and mystical experience had been a subject of debate in psychology and philosophical circles. In *Unbehagen in der Kultur* (1930; *Civilization and Its Discontents*), Freud responded, dismissing Rolland's mystical "oceanic feeling" as a "restoration of limitless narcissism."[72] Moreover, Freud rejected the claim that a mystical experience could be the real foundation of religion, and then seemingly closed the door on mysticism all together.

Freud's sense of the stakes of belief in the occult are clear in this excerpt from *Neue Folge der Vorlesungen zur Einführung in die Psychoanalyse* (1933; *New Introductory Lectures on Psycho-Analysis*):

If we accept the truth of what, according to the occultists' information, still occurs today, we must also believe in the authenticity of the reports which have come down to us from ancient times. And we must then reflect that the tradition and sacred books of all peoples are brimful of similar marvelous tales. . . . That being so, it will be hard for us to avoid a suspicion that . . . one of the secret motives of the occultist movement is to come to the help of religion, threatened as it is by the advance of scientific thought. And with the discovery of this motive our distrust must increase and our disinclination to embark on the examination of these supposedly occult phenomena.[73]

Here it would seem the "black tide of occultism" is nothing less than a religious foray into the conflict between religion and science, the ghost of religion in the modern era, the last gasp of dying faiths clinging to illusions: that our world reflects the human mind; that the association between ideas parallels the associations between things; that wish fulfillment is possible; that the soul is immortal; that religious metaphysics is more than mere collective psychopathology. Here Freud *might* be understood as claiming that we are at the edge of a slippery slope. If too much credence is given to any occult contentions, we might regress to the animist infancy of humankind rather than scientifically liberate ourselves from religion.

From this angle, psychoanalysis looks like the ultimate antireligion or antispiritualism, or perhaps as a secular embodiment of a post-religious form. The parallels between the Catholic confessional and the psychiatric session have been widely remarked on (not least by Freud himself), and it is telling that he often described the unconscious in terms of the devil and psychoanalysis as a kind of exorcism.[74] But more important, we can also see the psychoanalyst as the inversion of the fortune-teller. You describe your dreams, your coincidences, your (psychological) demons to the analyst, who, instead of telling you what they all mean, informs you that they are vestiges of childhood traumas, that all these things are not in the world, but so to speak, "all in your head." Freud would then *seem* to be the ultimate disenchanter.

*

But there is something I have omitted from the above narrative. Indeed, there is something suppressed within our recent memory of the history of psychoanalysis. Or more properly, there is something that has the status of an open secret, often buried in euphemistic references to Freud's "open-mindedness." To recover it, we have only to go back to Freud's account of the encounter with Jung in 1909, depicted in Jung's autobiography and Cronenberg's film alike. If we look at a letter Freud wrote to Jung on April 16, 1909, discussing the paranormal incident a different image begins to emerge. Freud remarked:

> I don't deny that your stories and your experiment made a deep impression on me. I decided to continue my observations after you left. . . . At first I was inclined to accept this as proof [of the paranormal]. . . . My credulity, or at least my willingness to believe, vanished with the magic (*Zauber*) of your personal presence; once again, for some inward reasons that I can't put my finger on, it strikes me as quite unlikely that such a phenomena should exist; I confront the despiritualized (*entgeisterte*) furniture as the poet confronted de-deified (*entgötterte*) Nature after the gods of Greece had passed away.[75]

In this letter, Freud is initially open to the possibility of poltergeist activity. Then when he finds himself doubting, Freud apologizes for his failure to believe in spirits by way of a reference to our repeated Schiller poem "Die Götter Griechenlands." By referencing Schiller, Freud is identifying his outlook with the disenchanted or de-deified nature in the poem.

This alone is not a grand shift in the narrative, but this was not the end of the letter. Freud went on to describe the "specifically Jewish nature of my mysticism."[76] He explained that he had always been sensitive toward seeing patterns of numbers as significant and for a long time had been harboring a suspicion of his eventual death at the age of sixty-one or sixty-two for numerological reasons. Freud concluded, however, with a self-deprecating remark that implied that he understood Jung's occult obsession, even if he did not share it fully.

This letter is only part of the story. Freud's friend and biographer Ernest Jones—himself much more skeptical than Freud—wrote about his mentor's engagement with the occult, noting that at various points Freud was prone to the very magical thinking he generally dismissed in his scholarly publications.[77] In personal conversation Freud was also more than willing to venture into occult territory, as Jones recounted:

> In the years before the Great War, I had several talks with Freud on occultism and kindred topics. He was fond, especially after midnight, of regaling me with strange or uncanny experiences with patients, characteristically about misfortunes or deaths supervening many years after a wish or prediction. He had a particular relish for such stories and was evident impressed by their more mysterious aspects. When I would protest at some of the taller stories

Freud was wont to reply with his favorite quotation: "There are more things in heaven and earth then are dreamed of in your philosophy." . . . When they were concerned with clairvoyant visions of episodes at a distance, or visitations from departed spirits, I ventured to reprove him for his inclination to accept occult beliefs on flimsy evidence. His reply was: "I don't like it at all myself, *but there is some truth in it.*[78]

If Jones is taken at his word, Freud could be found recounting various anecdotes about ghosts and visions, clairvoyance and precognition. Among close friends, Freud could share his fascination with the occult, suggesting that it contained some "truth." This is pretty far from the clichéd image of Freud as narrow-minded scientist.

But this is just the tip of the iceberg, as Freud's engagement with spiritualism was deep and long lasting.[79] A few months after the poltergeist incident in 1909, Freud and another of his colleagues, the Hungarian psychoanalyst Sándor Ferenczi, could be found in Vienna consulting with a psychic medium—an encounter that left Freud impressed, although not completely convinced.[80] According to the minutes of the Vienna Psychoanalytic Society, the following year, Freud held a discussion about spiritualism with the society.[81] Ferenczi even brought a psychic medium to a meeting, and the Psychoanalytic Society spent the session attempting to verify the medium's telepathic powers.[82] Although the experiment was a failure, their paranormal research continued.

In 1911, Freud joined the British Society for Psychical Research.[83] That same year, Freud attended another set of more successful séances with Ferenczi. Afterward Freud sent Jung a letter about them dated June 15, 1911:

> *In matters of occultism I have grown humble* since the great lessons Ferenczi's experiences gave me. I promise to believe anything that can be made to look reasonable. . . . My hubris has been shattered. I should be glad to know that you are in harmony with [Ferenczi], when one of you decides to take the dangerous step into publication.[84]

Freud had sent a similar letter to Ferenczi in the same period: "Jung writes that we must also conquer occultism and requests permission to undertake a campaign in the realm of mysticism. . . . You should at least proceed in harmony with each other; these are dangerous expeditions, and I can't go along there."[85] Again, while not volunteering himself, Freud seemed to be far from dissuading his colleagues from their occult pursuits. He mainly wanted them to work together. The proposed collaboration never happened, however. When relations between Jung and Freud fell apart, Ferenczi took Freud's side, and Jung went ahead with his version of the occult research project. Nevertheless, Ferenczi and Freud continued their investigations of spiritualism; and remarkably, Freud even took a turn as spirit medium himself.[86]

Although Freud was convinced that many of the spirit mediums he encountered were frauds, he still came to believe that there was some truth in the phenomena. After an extensive period of research, Freud believed that he had found evidence for telepathy. As Freud recounted in a letter to another colleague, Karl Abraham, on July 9, 1925, he had been conducting telepathy experiments with Ferenczi and his daughter Anna, and was convinced that she had "telepathic sensitivity."[87] A further group of letters exchanged between Freud and his close friend the Austrian psychoanalyst Otto Rank discussed the possibility of clairvoyant dreams (Freud for, Rank against).[88] Indeed, in a July 24, 1921, letter to the British psychical researcher Hereward Carrington, Freud admitted that if he had it all to do over again, he might choose the investigation of "occult psychic phenomena" instead of psychology.[89]

*

Freud also wrote extensively about the occult, although many of these writings were unpublished during his lifetime. He first began to explore these themes in "Eine erfüllte Traumahnung" (A fulfilled dream premonition, 1899), dated just six days after the publication of the first edition of *The Interpretation of Dreams*, but not published until 1941. In this fragment, Freud toyed with the idea of prophetic dreams before dismissing them with a naturalistic explanation.[90] If anything, Freud got less skeptical over time.[91]

In 1920, at a meeting of the inner core of the International Psycho-Analytic Association in the Harz Mountains, Freud gave a talk addressing the question "If we had to accept the phenomena summarized under the term 'telepathy,' how would it influence the theory and practice of psychoanalysis?"[92] Under Jones's encouragement, when it came time to write up the talk, Freud toned down his commitment to the paranormal.[93] The material from this talk appears in two publications, "Traum und Telepathie" (Dreams and telepathy, 1922), which appeared in Freud's lifetime, and then more directly in "Psychoanalyse und Telepaphie" (Psychoanalysis and telepathy, published in 1941, after Freud's death). In the latter work, Freud tentatively put forth the notion of thought transference as the core mechanism behind other occult phenomena, noting: "Perhaps the problem of thought transference may seem very trivial to you in comparison with the great magical world of the occult. But consider what a momentous step beyond what we have hitherto believed would be involved in this hypothesis alone."[94] In so doing, he was arguing that perhaps thought transference should be taken seriously, as it might be preferable to other magical phenomena that seemingly denied mechanistic causation. But Freud grew bolder still.

Freud's changing views are illustrated in the 1924 edition of *The Psychopathology of Everyday Life*. While in earlier editions he had described telepathy as a superstition, in the new addition he added the lines: "I must however confess that in the last few years I have had a few remarkable experiences which might easily have been explained on the hypothesis of telepathic thought-transference."[95] This edit largely passed without controversy, but in 1925, Freud issued *Einige Nachträge zum Ganzen der Traumdeutung* (*Some Additional Notes on Dream-Interpretation as a Whole*), which included a whole section on "The Occult Significance of Dreams." In this section, Freud provisionally concluded that "telepathy really exists and that it provides the kernel of truth in many other [occult] hypotheses that would otherwise be incredible."[96]

This statement attracted the attention of the English press, and Jones wrote a circulated letter to Freud bemoaning the encouragement Freud was giving to "the mystics" and expressing concern about the potential impact this would have on the psychoanalytic movement more broadly.[97] Freud responded in another public letter to his inner circle:

> Our friend Jones seems to me to be too unhappy about the sensation that my conversion to telepathy has made in the English periodicals. He will recollect how near to such a conversion I came in the communication I had the occasion to make during our Harz travels. Considerations of external policy since that time held me back long enough, but finally one must show one's colors.[98]

This was not the answer Jones sought, and it sparked a conversation on the stakes of occultism."

*

The discussion between Freud and Jones is important because it gives us a window on why thinkers like Freud would want to suppress their occult beliefs. In a follow-up letter, Jones argued that part of the issue was the different cultural contexts, telling Freud, "You are lucky to live in a country where 'Christian Science' together with all forms of so-called 'psychical research' mingled with hocus-pocus and palmistry to do not prevail as they do here."[99]

Despite the formula that presents 1920s Germany as more occult, Jones's argument is the opposite: that the Anglophone world has many different hybrid religious-occult-sciences (namely, Christian Science and disreputable forms of psychical research). Hence, he feared psychoanalysis would be seen as another of these pseudosciences.

This echoes something Freud himself put in writing in several places. In his letter to Carrington mentioned above, Freud described "skeptical materialistic prejudices" as the bane of occult study, and emphasized the importance of "demarcating psychoanalysis" from "this yet unexplored sphere of knowledge."[100] Similarly, in "Psychoanalysis and Telepathy," Freud argued that there was a "reciprocal sympathy" between psychoanalysis and the occult, because "they have both experienced the same contemptuous and arrogant treatment by official science. To this day psycho-analysis is regarded as savouring of mysticism, and its unconscious is looked upon as one of the things between heaven and earth which philosophy refuses to dream of."[101] In the allusion to Shakespeare, Freud was repeating a line he would elsewhere use to characterize occultism and mysticism (see the section epigraph), but this time including psychoanalysis and the unconscious. I want to underscore the connections because it repeats a theme I have been emphasizing in this chapter: that mysticism doubles psychoanalysis, and some European intellectuals in the period thought that the unconscious is mysterious.

Freud's main argument here, however, is that orthodox science has a justified tendency to dismiss out of hand anything that seems to be a repudiation of the scientific worldview. Elsewhere Freud would criticize the scientific prejudice that rocks could not possibly fall from the sky, which impeded the discovery of meteorites.[102] Implicit in Freud's discussion is that official science sees itself as an heir to a paradigm of empiricism and some variety of mechanistic reductionism. Basically, to be a science is to embrace a materialist worldview that a priori rejects the possibility of nonphysical causation. It would seem that aspiring sciences like psychoanalysis could not embrace ghosts (or nonphysical forms of telepathy) without coming into conflict with this image of what the scientific worldview was presumed to entail.

For Freud, orthodox science also rests on an assumption about the fundamental rationality of the human mind—presumably, the ability to collate evidence, formulate reasonable conclusions and argue for them, and so on. But psychoanalysis is the science of the irrational. As such, Freud would seem to want to have it both ways: on the one hand, benefiting from the prestige and methodology of science; but on the other hand, functioning as an internal critique of the science and the limits of rationality. According to this latter move,

Freud describes psychoanalysis as an antiauthoritarian project opposed to the negative prejudices of orthodox science. This is clear in a striking paragraph in "Psychoanalysis and Telepathy":

> Nor . . . has psycho-analysis any interest in going out of its way to defend that authority, for it itself stands in opposition to everything that is conventionally restricted, well-established and generally accepted. Not for the first time would it be offering its help to the obscure but indestructible surmises of the common people against the obscurantism of educated opinion. *Alliance and co-operation between analysts and occultists might thus appear both plausible and promising.*[103]

Here Freud is celebrating psychoanalysis as revolutionary or critical theory, directed at challenging the intellectual status quo. Moreover, he suggested that this is a quality that his emerging discipline shares with occultism. Crowley would have agreed with the sentiment of magic as vanguard to science. But one can imagine why even Freud's tentative suggestion of an "alliance" between analysts and occultists might have been upsetting to Jones, who was particularly anxious to defend the reputation of psychoanalysis.

To return to the debate between Freud and Jones, in the letter mentioned above, Jones reminded his mentor that "psycho-analysis is Freud" and that his personal beliefs were treated as characteristic of the whole movement. Therefore, if Freud were open about his occult beliefs, people would think that psychoanalysis logically led toward the occult. Jones concluded his letter with a plea that whatever Freud believed about telepathy, he should confine it to his personal life, just like his politics.[104] This seems to have been persuasive.

In a reply letter dated March 11, 1926, Freud reaffirmed his conviction that telepathy was a real phenomena but concluded that he had not considered the way it would impact public opinion of psychoanalysis. Freud suggested that "when anyone adduces my fall into sin, just answer him calmly that conversion to *telepathy is my private affair like my Jewishness* . . . and that the theme of telepathy is in essence alien to psychoanalysis."[105] Freud is also deploying a bifurcation between a private religion and a public science, and here the occult (or at least telepathy) is functioning as a kind of secret or internal religion of psychoanalysis. Although Freud did not agree to keep his belief in telepathy completely private, Jones had succeeded in dissuading Freud from making fully public his occult interests. Regardless, until the end of his life, Freud continued to believe in the "fact" of telepathy; he asserted that belief at various points in his letters, even if he was generally more cautious in published writings.[106]

This did not stop Freud from dedicating one lecture of the *New Introductory Lectures on Psycho-Analysis* (1932) to the topic of "Traum und Okkultismus" (Dream and occultism). In this lecture, Freud speculated that telepathy might have been the original, archaic method of communication between humans.[107] It is also worth noting that in this essay, Freud barely distinguished occultism and mysticism, suggesting that they both represent challenges to narrow versions of the scientific worldview. Strikingly, Freud described a change in his view of the occult, remarking:

> When they first came into my range of vision more than ten years ago, I too felt a dread of a threat against our scientific *Weltanschauung*, which, I feared, was bound to give place to spiritualism or mysticism if portions of occultism were proved true. To-day I think otherwise. In my opinion it shows no great confidence in science if one does not think it capable of assimilating and working over whatever may perhaps turn out to be true in the assertions of occultists.[108]

Although less optimistic than the grand occult-psychiatric alliance proposed in "Psychoanalysis and Telepathy," it is hard to see Freud as an anti-occultist. Instead he seems open to assimilating aspects of the occult into the conceptual terrain of psychoanalysis. Moreover, he was granting that there is something in the occult terrain that may "turn out to be true." Hence it evokes his private remarks to Jones.

All told, Freud had a much more ambivalent relationship to the "black tide" of occultism than is generally believed to be the case. To be clear, it seems unlikely Freud ever came to believe in spirits, but he took on other beliefs that he himself suggested were occult in nature. Strikingly, between 1913 and 1914—the very period of Freud's first writings on disenchantment in *Totem und Tabu* (and his first public acknowledgement of any connection to du Prel)—Freud was immersed in spiritualist experiments with Ferenczi. Indeed, the very magical thinking and "telepathy" that Freud attributed to the childhood of humanity was something that he seemingly shared. How, then, are we to make sense of Freud's projection of his own taboo beliefs onto the figure of the savage?

*

In keeping with the chapter, I'd like to imagine a psychoanalytic theory of the regulative function of the myth of disenchantment or the logic of occult disavowal (not to be confused with Freud's *Verleugnung*). To do so, I'd like to think with (or more accurately, against) the grain of Freud's theory of animism for what it can tell us about Freud and his peers, not for what his theory says about its putative "primitive" subjects.

In the broadest of brushstrokes in *Totem und Tabu*, Freud described primitive religion in terms of two intertwined mechanisms—basically, introjection and projection. Using childhood development as his starting point, Freud argues that when an instinct or desire is "met by an *external* prohibition," then usually "the prohibition does not succeed in *abolishing*" the desire. Instead the desire and the prohibition are both internalized.[109] The desire is repressed into the unconscious. The prohibition is internalized by means of what later psychoanalysts would call "introjection" (expanding on Ferenczi's *Introjektion*), which for our purposes is when a subject internalizes an attitude from another subject while misplacing attribution as to the attitude's source.[110] This could result in a neurotic or unstable psychological constellation (a love-hate ambivalence) that perpetuates an internal "conflict between the prohibition and the instinct," which instead of being resolved is displaced onto substitute objects.[111]

Freud also claimed that the "emotional life of primitive peoples" is particularly fraught and is full of psychological ambivalence.[112] This results in a "defensive procedure" that Freud called "projection," in which the subject attributes or transfers his or her own conflicted feelings onto another.[113] This broader psychological process is for Freud the mechanism by which "animism" populates the world with spirits (transforming, say, a resentment toward the dead into the idea that the departed has become a resentful spirit).[114] Although it is easy to overlook, a key piece of this process is that both desires and prohibitions can be projected onto external entities.[115]

To provide an example of what Freud has in mind: Encountering a parental prohibition against masturbation, a teenager might introject the notion that masturbation is wrong and thus feel bad about masturbating, while forgetting the original source of the prohibition. Then the teen might project the masturbatory desire onto the devil ("It is the devil that wants me or makes me masturbate") while also projecting the prohibition onto God ("The voice in my head that is telling me not to masturbate is God," or "God will punish me if I masturbate"). This is not the sum total of Freud's explanation of animism, which for Freud is centered on the "omnipotence of thought"; but it is the feature that will be useful in our explanation of Freud's own occult psychology.

It is now possible to hazard a guess about what on a psychological level motivated Freud's abiding interest in the occult. In the 1909 letter to Jung mentioned earlier, Freud described superstitious fear of his own death as the source of his "Jewish mysticism."[116] We can see why Freud might have been drawn toward du Prel's notion of the eternal mystical unconscious.

Jones observed that Freud had an intense preoccupation with death and even "repeated attacks of what [Freud] called *Todesangst* (dread of death)." Moreover, Jones also suspected that Freud's preoccupation with his own mortality led him toward "occultism."[117] Moreover, Jones recounted instances in which Freud feared or hoped that his thoughts would have an impact on the world.[118] One can find Freud therefore exhibiting deep ambivalence toward the very "omnipotence of thought" he had connected to primitive magic and animism.

Furthermore, as discussed above, Freud believed that the modern scientific worldview prohibited belief in the occult. In a telling remark in *Totem and Taboo*, Freud stated: "The scientific view of the universe no longer affords any room for human omnipotence [as understood by animists]; men have acknowledged their smallness and submitted resignedly to death and to the other necessities of nature."[119] But Freud would be the first to admit that he had an intense fear of death and insignificance, and here it seems that the contrasting category to this mortal impotence is the animist's omnipotence.

To conclude our adventures with a psychoanalytic reading, if Freud had introjected the scientific prohibition against the occult while simultaneously repressing the instinct or desire that occultism evoked, then his own theory might suggest a projection of these impulses onto others. The twist is that in Freud's humanistic imagination, it is "official science" that functions as "the other who does not let me believe," while it is the so-called primitive that is given the belief that has become taboo for Freud.

*

Freud's interest in the occult persists as an open secret, known but rarely remarked upon these days.[120] In part, this is a recent phenomena that has appeared because Freud has fewer defenders than he once had. By and large, clinical psychology has now spent several decades refashioning itself and repudiating Freud.[121] A talking cure seems out of place in an era of diagnostic manuals and increasing pharmaceutical interventions. For this group, Freud's interest in telepathy would be no problem since it has already rejected his legacy, but for the fact that psychology and paranormal investigation have long had uncomfortable resonances. Generations of psychologists, from William James down to the present day, have been tempted to imagine a kind of "omnipotence of thought," or at the very least, a mind with hidden capabilities.[122]

While parapsychology has been relegated to the margins, it has not vanished, and arguments for psi powers have appeared in well-respected psychology journals as recently as 2011.[123]

Freud's main hold these days is in the humanities. But those of us who teach his work are often relating less his particular theoretical constructions than his critical Hermeneutics. It matters little from this perspective whether, say, the Oedipal complex is scientifically verifiable. But precisely because Freud is equated with "suspicion," his dalliance with "superstition" might seem more of a difficulty. Yet, as I have argued, this is a false opposition rooted in our own highly skewed conception of rationality and the worldview it entails.

CONCLUSION: THE COSMIC NIGHT

> The more the world is emptied of an objective meaning and the more it becomes thoroughly absorbed by our own categories and thus becomes our world, then the more we find meaning eradicated from the world; and the more we find ourselves immersed in something like a *cosmic night*—to express it in a modern way. The demystification (*Entmagisierung*) or disenchantment of the world—to use an expression borrowed from Max Weber—is identical with a consciousness of being barred out, of a darkness in which we all move.
>
> THEODOR ADORNO, *Kants Kritik der reinen Vernunft*, 1959

Narrating together the history of post-Kantian philosophy and psychoanalysis and their respective entanglements with the German occult revival has allowed us to see the way that all parties were animated by tantalizing possibilities of unseen depths. While mystics narrated the "dark night of the soul," specters of shadowy noumena plagued both philosophy and psychoanalysis. Indeed, what Freud's reading of Carl du Prel suggests is an equation between the thing-in-itself and the psychological unconscious that we might instead associate with Jacques Lacan or Slavoj Žižek. That Freud already had this intuition is also hinted at in discussions that Freud had with Ludwig Binswanger, who gave this remark in 1910: "[Freud] thought just as Kant postulated the thing-in-itself behind the phenomenal world, so he himself postulated the unconscious behind the conscious[ness] that is accessible to our experience, but that can never be directly experienced."[124] Taken together, we can see that what haunts psychoanalysis is the ghost of idealist metaphysics. This is not all they had in common.

Through the nineteenth century, post-Kantian philosophers and psychoanalysts shared concerns about reason's limits. Both camps also often hinted at an ambivalence taken so far that it becomes an antinomy: reason was seen as terrible both for being too weak and too strong. Accordingly, it was both desired and feared. From one vantage point, reason itself was thought to contain the potential for monstrosity. Indeed, one might see these monsters of reason embodied in the leviathans of commerce, the titans of industry, the manacles of the asylum, or the disciplining processes of bio-politics. It is easy to fear a reason that has given itself over the rationalization or justification of unconscious desires. Even more tellingly, reason often appeared to menace the last vestiges of faith.

From the opposite perspective, however, it would appear as though there were dangers lurking outside the boundaries of reason, sabotaging the closure of its categories and signaling its vulnerabilities, like the (probably hyperbolic) map legends that marked out terra incognita with the phrase "Here be dragons." The more the limits of reason came into view, the more it seemed that reason could be overwhelmed by something arising from hidden depths. For some, this was a holy terror: God and mystical communion met at the dark heart of things beyond the categories of space and time. For others, lurking below reason was merely the monstrous instinct of a savage mind.

Freud, the master of repression, has given us both a developmental account of disenchantment and clues as to the mechanism of occult disavowal, suggesting how introjecting an image of scientific reductionism produces a semi-scientific superego, and encourages the projection of beliefs onto others. Philosophers ascribe their hidden self to primitives while projecting occult prohibitions onto a similarly imaginary scientific hegemon to justify conformity or rebellion.

*

In more specific terms, I have been gesturing at the dark side of the history of post-Kantian thought. Kant attempted to preserve philosophy from skepticism and to restore metaphysics to its role as the queen of the sciences. But a significant number of post-Kantian philosophers have dedicated their lives to arguing that philosophy is finished, impossible, or unnecessary.[125] A long list of thinkers have given expression to this self-alienation of philosophy—from Kant's "frenemy" J. G. Hamann to Ludwig Wittgenstein, from the logical positivists to the American pragmatists, Jacques Derrida to Richard Rorty. One might become convinced that at heart, philosophy has long been an antidote to itself—a fitting trajectory for a discipline whose mythic progenitor Socrates was himself an antiphilosopher. To be fair, many of the human sciences have been plagued by similar antagonisms toward their central objects. Nevertheless, attempts to ground philosophy have been both dynamic and terrifyingly self-refuting.

In sum, it was easy to invest the Kantian system with haunting specters and occult powers, as though the sage of Königsberg were a necromancer. The source of the mysticism Nordau feared was not to be found in urban degeneration, but threatened to appear in philosophy itself. Indeed, if one takes a Weberian approach to enchantment and identifies magic with a sense of mystery, one cannot help but notice that much of post-Kantian philosophy, by inadvertently extending the shores of the unknown, produced more enchantments then it dispelled. Philosophy itself was involuntarily underwriting the occult revival.

In some ways, I have been following Theodor Adorno's dialectical and Weberian reading of Kant's system. As quoted above, Adorno argued that the more that philosophers come to see the phenomenal world as being structured by subjectivity, the more it becomes disenchanted, while simultaneously the noumenal world becomes the repository for the mysteries from which we are barred.[126] It is as though we are in exile from value and meaning, trapped in a cosmic night of the soul. Increased rationality amplifies the alienation we feel toward a world that now comes to stand over and against us, and yet is also the subject of longing.

But what this reading of Kantian philosophy misses is that Freud's project suggested further fissures in the most basic level of our consciousness. Drawing on thinkers like du Prel and Schopenhauer, Freud, like Kant, had perpetuated an alienating split, but he had located it within human subjectively. Unlike the noumena—which often function as mere remainders or unreachable depths—the unconscious sent forth signs and troubling symbols. It showed evidence that it controls the more sober intellect. The mind's core is potentially irrational and capable of using rationality to justify its own appetitive desires. Reason risks being subverted from both within and without.

For all his brilliance, Kant produced a curious and inadvertent doubling of worlds, where a mysterious realm of alien things shadows the phenomenal realm. Freud exposed the neuroses at the heart of the Kantian system and internalized its anxieties into the core of modern subjectivity. What had reassured Schopenhauer about our connection to a timeless will was for Freud a troubling darkness, which like a black tide threatened to overwhelm the conscious mind. Unless, that is, one could erect some bulwark against it—or alternately master the darkness.

CHAPTER EIGHT

Dialectic of Darkness: The Magical Foundations of Critical Theory

Philosophical dialectic springs from the impulse to overcome conceptual thinking.

LUDWIG KLAGES, *Rhythmen und Runen*, 1944

Continental philosophy's main role in the American academy is to serve as the home for certain kinds of skepticism, particularly those directed toward stable conceptions of knowledge and meaning. Nonspecialists use the words *deconstruction* and *critical theory* to evoke critical insight, cynical wisdom, or the speaking of truth to power. Meanwhile, those of us who teach or write on poststructuralism, postmodernism, or critical theory often do so in reference to linguistic or antifoundationalist skepticism, critiques of modernity and reason, or the "Romantic counter-Enlightenment."

In what follows, I aim to upend the commonly received view. I locate the origins of much of critical theory in the occult milieu of fin-de-siècle France and Germany, where an alternative to modernity arose that presented itself first and foremost in reference to spiritualism, paganism, Hermeticism, mysticism, and magic. Focusing on the controversial German poet and neo-pagan mystic Ludwig Klages and what he referred to as "magical philosophy" (*magische philosophie*), I will explore Klages's influence on key critical theorists and in particular the German-Jewish philosopher Walter Benjamin.

At the outset, I want to make it clear that I am not trying to rehabilitate Klages as a thinker, nor am I trying to condemn critical theory by recovering its associations with European esotericism. Instead, I aim to retrieve a version of critical theory that was not primarily a critique of knowledge, but rather a vehicle to deliver esoteric wisdom. Along the way I expose the metaphysical underpinnings of poststructuralist antimetaphysics, unearth the buried ontologies of the antifoundationalists, and recoup hints of a vanished utopia that lies only half-submerged in this most dystopian of contemporary philosophical terrains.

> The Cosmic Circle: There was no natural community that connected the three eccentrics—the blond Viking, the tanned Roman, and the dark Oriental—it was more an alliance of three individual wizards (*Einzelzauberer*) for the collective purpose of conjuring up the [powers] of Life.
>
> FRIEDRICH WOLTERS, *Stefan George und Die Blätter für die Kunst*, 1930

The collection of Munich-based poets, mystics, and neo-pagans known as the Cosmic Circle (*Kosmikerkreis, Kosmische Runde*, or *Kosmiker*) had many similarities to other fin-de-siècle esoteric groups: they were originally led by a charismatic medium who saw spirits; they performed arcane rituals and engaged in psychical research; they celebrated a mother goddess and the pagan past; they wrote poetry and visionary tracts; they criticized their contemporary world as sick with materialism; and they read and debated with other occult thinkers.[1] One feature that made the movement distinctive—but not unique—in the late nineteenth-century occult milieu was that they shared an intense reverence for Friedrich Nietzsche, whom they described as one of the great "pagan martyrs: whose soul fought and died for the ardor of Life."[2] But the crucial thing about the Kosmikers is that they followed Nietzsche by authoring an influential antiphilosophical philosophy. This occult philosophy will be the main subject of the chapter, but first I will describe the particularities of their occultism.

The Cosmic Circle began to coalesce in 1893 when Ludwig Klages moved to Munich to work on a dissertation in chemistry. There, he encountered the visionary and mystic Alfred Schuler. They were soon joined by the neo-pagan German-Jewish poet and translator Karl Wolfskehl, who introduced the others to Johann Bachofen's *Das Mutterrecht* with its depiction of primordial matriarchy (a text whose influence on Aleister Crowley has already been examined).[3] Schuler and Klages will be discussed in detail momentarily, but in brief, Wolfskehl was initially attempting to articulate a non-monotheistic form of Judaism that could resist the rationalization process of modernity.[4] Klages, Schuler, and Wolfskehl formed the core of the Cosmic Circle (they are the trio of wizards referred to in racialized terms by Friedrich Wolters above); but its periphery included the mystic and writer Ludwig Derleth and the famous German poet, mystic, and prophet Stefan George (discussed in chapter 10).[5] Ultimately, a personality conflict between George and Klages, combined with Wolfskehl's increasing alienation from the group in the face of rising anti-Semitism, resulted in its disintegration in 1904.[6]

Many of the Cosmic Circle's particular features came from the influence of the group's leader, Alfred Schuler (1865–1923). Born in Mainz, Schuler had moved to Munich, where he intended to study archeology before deciding that his mystical insights were more real than anything that could be discovered in dry academic writings.[7] Schuler claimed that he was the reincarnation of a pre-Christian Roman leader and that he received clairvoyant visions and direct communications from pagan gods.[8] Although Schuler published little during his lifetime, he became infamous for ecstatic lectures he gave about his revelations. In the most influential of these, *Vom Wesen der ewigen Stadt* (On the essence of the eternal city, originally 1917), Schuler shared not only his idiosyncratic understanding of paganism, but also his insights into an eternal realm of the dead (*Totenreich*) beyond the veil of ordinary space and time.[9] This was Schuler's twist on a claim common to Swedenborg and later spiritualists that there is a timeless spirit world parallel to our own.

Like other spiritualists, Schuler had his own necro-vitalism. When he peered within, he claimed to be aware of a mystical force of throbbing pure life and light.[10] When this "telesmatic" force is connected with the general and maternal "cosmic radiance," it results in the erotic explosion of an inner glow, or what he called the *Blutleuchte* (literally "blood-light").[11] Later Klages described this blood-light poetically as "a continuously deepening shudder, a dark strangeness, which throbs and ferments in hidden places. A wild woeful shout mixed with the crashing of storms. . . . In it the mysteries of the maternal cosmos are revealed."[12] As this quote illustrates, the blood-light and telesma energy was part of an effort to recover the lost power of maternal, pagan antiquity.

The Kosmikers' neo-paganism was also partially a gesture toward sexual revolution. Schuler and George were both homosexuals, and they rejected the Christian sexual morality of their day. While not all the members of the Cosmic Circle were queer, they shared a common enemy in monogamy and the period's restrictive gender norms.[13] They often embraced the figure of the divine Androgyne as a countermodel to the traditional male and female binary.[14] Hence, as a way to sacralize a new sexuality, Schuler and company promoted an eroticized pansexual paganism.[15]

The Kosmikers saw themselves as re-enchanters, but we can be more specific about their philosophy of magic. After spending several years with the group, Countess Franziska zu Reventlow wrote *Herrn Dames Aufzeichnungen*

(Notes of Mr. Lady, 1913), a thinly fictionalized novel describing her experiences. Crucially for our purposes, she summarized the core of their project as follows:

> They claim to have discovered secrets of immeasurable importance and thereby have gone so far as to achieve mastery of certain inner powers. Hence sooner or later they will be in a position to work magic (*zaubern*). . . . They explained it to me like this: one succeeds by means of a mystical procedure—I believe by absolute self-absorption in the primordial cosmic principle (*kosmische Urprinzip*). . . . When this is successful, one's essence is completely permeated by the primordial cosmic substance, which is in itself all-powerful. Then one is made just as powerful, and those who are all-powerful can work magic (*zaubern*).[16]

This passage illustrates a key point. The Kosmikers claimed access to extraordinary powers, and they explained their magic by reference to a particular vibrant ontology. Indeed, as Reventlow also noted, they saw the "cosmic" as the primordial life force or organizing principle behind being.[17] Accordingly, cosmic magic was a communion with the lively principle in matter. New materialists should take note because put in a contemporary idiom, the Kosmikers are firstly granting nonhuman agency, or "thing-power"; and secondly, suggesting that union with this agency is the basis for magic.[18] A host of current thinkers would grant the first, but, while a non-magical vitalism is certainly possible, it might be trickier to exclude the second because such an account of agency seems tailor made for enchantment. Indeed, one might get the sense that the Kosmikers were working backward, adopting a particular ontology in order to justify or explain the reality of sorcery. This is even clearer in the more expansive form elaborated by the movement's primary theoretician, Ludwig Klages.

*

Ludwig Klages was born into a "carefully constrained middle-class world" in Hannover in 1872.[19] Already as a young man, Klages had dreams and visions of the "dark abysses of past eons," but he initially ignored these interests to take a more conventional path.[20] In 1893, he came to Munich to write a dissertation on the synthesis of menthone (completed in 1901). But he also met Schuler, who reawakened his youthful interest in poetry and esotericism. Soon Klages left chemistry behind—first for graphology and then philosophy. During the

First World War, Klages was a pacifist and immigrated to Switzerland, where he wrote most of his important works. In 1932, he was awarded the Goethe Medal for Art and Science by German President Hindenburg. Although Klages was not without supporters among the Nazis, in 1936, he was publically criticized by Nazi ideologues like Alfred Rosenberg, and the Gestapo dissolved his Leipzig research institute.[21] Klages remained largely based in Switzerland until his death in 1956.

What is important for our purposes is that Klages attempted to render the Cosmic project into philosophy; basically, he sought to define magic in a way that—while it might not work in a philosophy department today—was thought through and fully argued. This is how he summarized it in *Rhythmen und Runen* (Rhythms and runes, 1944): "Magic is the practice of our philosophy and our philosophy is the theory of magic. . . . Magical philosophy (*magische philosophie*) works with images and symbols, and its method is the method of analogy. The most important terms it uses are: *element, substance, principle, demon, cosmos, microcosm, macrocosm, essence, image, primal image, vortex, tangle*, and *fire*. Its final formulas are spells that have magical power."[22] What did this magical philosophy look like? The following section will explicate.

MAGICAL PHILOSOPHY AND DISENCHANTMENT: LUDWIG KLAGES

The philosophy of the academy is mechanistic theory, and their practice is mechanical. Magical philosophy rejects the [Aristotelian] law of identity [in favor of flux]; hence it denies unity, objects, duration, recurrence, and mathematics; it denies concepts and causality, because causality is the functional parallel to the logical correlation.

LUDWIG KLAGES, *Rhythmen und Runen*, 1944

The best way to introduce Ludwig Klages's magical philosophy is to paint a recognizable pastiche figure so we have something to compare it to. If we threw everything we teach in American "continental philosophy" or "theory" courses into a blender, what would it look like? Put differently, I think if one were to assemble a Franco-Frankfurt-Frankenstein's monster out of oft-taught fragments from German critical theory, French poststructuralism, a dash of feminism, and more than a hint of Heidegger, it might have the following qualities.

Despite writing philosophy, our monster would be resolutely antiphilosophy and especially antimetaphysics.[23] It would position itself as a critic of modernity, instrumental rationality, and enlightenment.[24] It would challenge the value of the binary opposition between civilized and primitive.[25] Our monster would argue that the myth of "progress" is rooted in "the domination of nature";[26] that science and technology are nothing less than an abuse of the natural world, an attempt to render it lifeless in order to extract energy that can be exploited to further human goals.[27]

It would accuse us of holding on to an absurd faith in technology while nature has lost its mystery, becoming "disenchanted" and "reified."[28] In compensation for our alienation from the natural world, it would suggest, we have seen the rise of a meaningless cult of reason that despite its criticisms of fantasy and myth, has replaced the old myths with new cults.[29] Our monster would characterize this process in terms of the privileging of the logos and instrumental or calculable reason, for which it would coin the term "*logocentrism.*"[30]

The Franco-Frankfurt-Frankenstein's monster would also observe that this same process of rationalization has been connected to the rise of the patriarchy.[31] That logocentrism has been rooted in the domination of men over women and the suppression of feminine ways of knowing and being.[32] That modern heteronormative sexuality is fragmented into artificially rigid heterosexual norms and embodies a distorted form of the universality of human love and desire.[33] It would argue that the contemporary world is fundamentally opposed to the natural flows of desire.[34] To round out the picture, our monster would be harshly critical of Hegel's *Geist* and would draw on Nietzsche as its progenitor, while at the same time distancing its project from Nietzsche's "will to power."[35] To these claims, it would add a criticism of the globalization of the modes of American capitalism (or we might say today, neoliberalism) and draw our attention to the violence of colonization.[36] Ultimately, in opposition to logocentrism, the monster would remind us of the importance of the body.[37] It would emphasize the primacy of writing, and call for a renewal of our connection to a vitalized nature and the unleashing of the productive force of an orgasmic or unbounded desire.[38]

The monster I've just described might sound like I am patching together Derrida's criticisms of logocentrism, Adorno and Horkheimer's account of enlightenment, alongside Heidegger's interrogation of technology and rejection of philosophy, Deleuze and Guattari's celebration of productive desire, and Hélène Cixous's challenge to the patriarchy and call for feminine embodiment, and perhaps even echoes of deep ecology or Jane Bennett's new vitalism, among a dozen other fashionable philosophers. It is easy to imagine teaching this pastiche at a contemporary American college, but we would be unlikely to take it too seriously. The project just sounds excessively derivative.

*

But I misled you when I claimed to be presenting a mixture of other thinkers. The problem is that just such a monster once walked. As you may have guessed, I've just surreptitiously summarized the writings of Ludwig Klages. The footnotes above locate the claims in his collected works. Take a moment to reread those paragraphs, because if they reflect some version of what you have been writing or teaching, you have in some sense been doing "magical philosophy."

It should also be emphasized that Klages's most important writings date from the 1910s and '20s and thus preceded Horkheimer's leadership of the Frankfurt School (1930),[39] Heidegger's "Question on Technology" (1954), and necessarily the birth of poststructuralism. The likeness between Klages and critical theory is unlikely to be a complete coincidence. To tip my hand a little: Adorno, Benjamin, Cassirer, Habermas, Heidegger, Horkheimer, Löwith, and Lukács;[40] and even so-called post-structuralist thinkers Agamben, Bataille, Foucault, Guattari, Lacan, and de Man all read and cited Klages's work.[41] So why haven't more people heard of Klages? He is found in many footnotes and is frequently referenced in works on Walter Benjamin or in the context of German irrationalism,[42] or *Lebensphilosophie*, but Klages's major monographs have never been translated into English, and he is rarely studied on his own terms.[43]

*

The heart of magical philosophy's uncanny resemblance to critical theory can be found in the critique of modernity Klages inherited from the occult milieu and subsequently elaborated. Already Alfred Schuler had described the rise of Judeo-Christian rationality producing alienation from the sacred maternal cosmos.[44] Like some other neo-pagans, Schuler believed that Christianity and "exoteric science" had expelled the gods and severed the connection to the natural world.[45] Moreover, he described modernity as characterized by various forms of estrangement from both the world and one's fellows, as though a positive *Gemeinschaft* had been sacrificed to a dehumanizing *Gesellschaft*.[46] Succinctly put, the Kosmikers, like many similar groups, characterized modernization in terms of disenchantment even as they proposed to supply the missing magic.

The core of Klages's philosophical work was an attempt to diagnose the causes and consequences of this "disenchantment." Tellingly, in his critique of modernity, Klages occasionally deployed the very terminology Max Weber would make famous—not just "*Entzauberung*," but later even the expression "the disenchantment of the world" (*die Entzauberung der Welt*).[47] Weber and his relationship to Klages will be discussed in chapter 10, but note now that for Klages, this meant not a sober sociological theory but an ontological estrangement from nature and magic.

Klages's project appears in embryonic form in his first major philosophical work, *Mensch und Erde* (Man and earth), originally a lecture for Free German Youth Day in 1913 and later expanded for publication.[48] Klages opened by interrogating what he saw as the central ideology of his age: the celebration of "progress" (*Fortschritt*).[49] While older civilizations often had a collective project that they were working toward, Klages thought his contemporaries merely embraced progress for its own sake.[50] No longer in aid of any particular objective, technological advancement and cultural change had run wild and have come to mean largely the ability to remake the natural landscape, to slaughter animals, and to strip away local culture.[51] For this reason Klages argued that the rhetoric of "progress" is really just the public face of the domination of nature and the exploitation of indigenous peoples. The heart of progress is the lust for power.[52]

Instead of the positivistic celebration of scientific advancement and enlightenment, Klages provided a counternarrative—that of rationalization as tragedy and alienation from Mother Earth. In his version of this narrative, the ancients knew the earth to be a "living being" and that "forest and spring, boulder and grotto were filled with sacred life; from the summits of their lofty mountains blew the storm-winds of the gods."[53] Primitive humans were in harmony with nature, which they sought to safeguard by means of rituals and prohibitions.[54] But then Christianity suppressed the old gods and stripped nature of animating forces. Modern Europeans, he went on to argue, see the earth instead as nothing but "an unfeeling lump of 'dead matter.'"[55] Thus there is nothing to stop them from plundering and polluting until all that remains is desolation.[56]

At first pass, this might remind you of Schiller; and indeed, Klages even quoted from "The Gods of Greece" at a key moment in the speech.[57] Klages's narrative is like Schiller's account, with the neo-pagan and ecological elements thrust to the fore and the criticisms of Christianity amplified. Klages argued that it is only Christendom that gave birth to the "ruthless expansive-impulse (*Erweiterungsdrang*) to enslave non-Christian races" and that "capitalism, along with its pioneer, science, is in actuality the fulfillment of Christianity."[58] Christianity had not only killed the gods and exploited nature, but it had also given the world slavery, imperialism, science, and capitalism.[59] In sum, as a committed neo-pagan philosopher, Klages had no problem identifying Christianity as the ultimate source of alienation, but this was a position he would later nuance.

The striking feature of Klages's project is that already in 1913, he had begun to formulate an account of phenomenological alienation. Modernity meant not just environmental exploitation, but also a new way of thinking. Klages argued,

> He who imagines enriching himself—when he stomps earth's blossoms into dust—is man as the bearer of calculating reason (*rechenverständigen*) and the will to appropriation, and the gods whom [modern man] has shorn from the tree of the life are the ever changing souls of the phenomenal world, from which he has separated himself.[60]

This poetic passage would be easy to mistake for a pagan account of the loss of divinities. But Klages elaborated the theme further in his most important project, "Geist und Seele" (Mind and soul, 1916 expanded into three volumes as *Der Geist als Widersacher der Seele*, The mind as enemy of the soul, 1929–32; hereafter *GWS*).

The best entrée into *GWS* is to see it as an inversion of the Hegelian dialectic. As any student of philosophy will remember, Hegel's main thesis was that world history is nothing less than the self-actualization of the absolute Spirit (*Geist*). We might vulgarize Hegel's narrative by describing it as an account of the dialectical history of the mind articulating itself via matter, during which the whole of the world would gradually be made to accord with reason. Hence one could read Hegel's philosophy as the master narrative for the ideology of progress that underwrote modern technological advancement and imperialism alike.

The surprise is that in *GWS*, Klages largely grants Hegel's description of world history, of *Geist* working itself out in the world, as mind has increasingly asserted dominance over matter, forcing it to submit to reason. As Klages put it, "The [grand] trajectory of 'world history' is in fact what Hegel suggested, the self-actualization of the absolute Geist, but in a destructive counterposition to life and with the foreseeable result of its extermination."[61] Klages reversed the Hegelian dialectic to make the narrative a travesty instead of a triumph. He saw the en-minding of the world in terms of the destruction of the natural environment, the expansion of colonialism, the disintegration of life, and the alienation from Being itself.[62] If for Hegel the *Geist* was in some sense God, for Klages it is the Demiurge (or devil) that has shattered the harmony of existence.

To make sense of this, I need to place Klages's critique of *Geist* in his own

ontology. As he observed, the ongoing philosophical debates of his era generally presumed a Cartesian split between mind and body even as philosophers
worked to resolve this dualism by granting one term or the other primacy
or collapsing the two into one bimodal substance. For Klages, these debates
overlooked both (1) the part of the mind that escapes conscious understanding
(aka the unconscious), and (2) more important, the animating principle behind
living and even nonliving things. Neither the unconscious nor this animating
force fit well into the categories of body or mind. Hence Klages attempted
to sidestep contemporary debates by reviving the classical triad: body, *Geist*
(hereafter translated "mind"), and *Seele* (soul).

The key thing about Klages's trinary is that the *Seele* is the foundation, and
both body and mind emerge from the more fundamental basis of the soul. The
soul for Klages is not the individual spirit or personality; nor is it some kind
of eternally present shadow person. Rather, it is the fundamental force of life
itself. I want to head off at the outset the most widespread misunderstanding
of his project. It is often asserted in passing that Klages was a vitalist.[63] But in
GWS, Klages attacked "vitalists," and he did so because either he thinks that
they covertly see mind as a conscious organizing principle behind all matter, or
because they see life force only in humans, animals, and plants.[64] By contrast,
Klages's "soul" is not just a feature of living beings. For him, a fundamental
level of the soul (*Die Elementarseelen*) is behind the whole of the sensible cosmos; it is rooted in the ever-proliferating, ever-changing foundation of nature
itself.[65] The whole cosmos is en-souled.

That we do not feel at one with the cosmos is evidence that we have become estranged from Being. Klages identified the source of this ontological
alienation as resulting from an in-break of *Geist* that appears like a "wedge"
inserted between body and soul, such that it has begun to "de-soul the body
and disembody the soul, and in this way finally to deaden all life."[66] Before
Geist, beings were at harmony with Being. Humans did not see themselves as
separate from the natural world. We had no need to dominate or dematerialize
the world with thought.

One can see Klages's basic paganism peeking out here because he claims
that prehistorical humanity was matriarchal. Women ruled the timeless world.
Before the imbalance of *Geist*, natural humans saw nature and the cycle of
life and death as a Great Mother Goddess (*Die Magna Mater*). That is to say,
the ancients worshipped the Earth Mother.[67] While based in an essentialized
gender binary that contemporary feminism would reject, Klages was progressive for his day insofar as he was privileging the power of the feminine. The

rise of the logos or *Geist* was therefore first and foremost a displacement of this older way of looking at the world, a kind of matricide against primordial women rulers and the earth.[68] By objectifying and abstracting Mother Nature, humanity made her exploitation and violation inevitable.

Klages argued that at its basic level, "actuality" (*Wirklichkeit*) is constantly unfolding vibrancy, a stuttering, shifting chaos of activity. This is a kind of process ontology that we might associate today with thinkers like Alfred North Whitehead or Gilles Deleuze, but Klages's reference is to Heraclitus, arguing: "Heraclitus discovered actuality, which he described with the famous phrase: *Panta Rhei*. Everything is flux. The flux itself is the very essence of the world; or, in other words, the world is events without a substrate."[69] At its most fundamental, actuality is continual flux and change. It should not be a surprise that even today European practitioners often ground their understanding of magic in similar ontologies. As Tanya Luhrmann generalized from her ethnography of magicians in 1980s London: "The idea of magic emerges naturally from a philosophy of a world in interacting flux. . . . One could forge a magical theory solely from that account of flux."[70]

As illustrated in the section epigraph, Klages too understood flux as the foundation of a philosophy of magic, but it was also the core of his phenomenological account of reification. As he contended: "The thought cosmos is a mechanical confusion of things; the living cosmos, on the other hand, to which our languages can only allude, cannot be conceptually grasped, for it only reveals itself in the instantaneous flash of its here and now appearance."[71] Klages maintained that we are all animists at heart. His evidence is the ability of poetry to capture the particularity of a specific moment: the sudden curl of a woman's lips just before she breaks into a full smile, the dappled light of one particular May afternoon, or the ferocious beauty of an oncoming storm. As Klages would argue, these flashes of beauty are outside our rational mind and the closest we come to experiencing bare life. For that reason they are pleasurable and necessarily erotic.

The *Geist*, however, needs to render the world comprehensible, which means that it must abstract from the world. As Klages put it elsewhere, "The will to rational truth is the will to deactualize the world."[72] Accordingly, Klages described the transformation from a phenomenological "world of images" (*Bilderwelt*), which is the flicker of raw experiences into its fundamental opposite, a "world of objects" (*Dingwelt*), rooted in false abstractions (*Phantoms*). The world of images is mysterious and dreamlike, full of surprises, but the *Geist* renders the world lifeless and comprehensible, a taxidermy butterfly.

In his words: "Whatever is touched by the ray of *Geist* is instantly changed into a mere thing, a quantifiable object that is afterward connected to other objects only 'mechanically.'"[73] This is Klages's version of something Marxists have long critiqued—namely, the process of reification, which, after all, literally means "thing-ification."[74]

To summarize, Klages argued that the thinking subject tends to objectify sense experience. The human mind creates static mental objects from the unfolding diversity of actuality. This is an exploitive process that transforms the living vibrant chaos of being into a world of tools or things, apprehended instrumentally and rendered functionally inanimate. We do not see the flourishing and individual character of a particular tree in a particular instant of space and time; we see a specimen of the genus *Quercus*, or we see a club with which we can beat our donkey into submission. Rather than being free to experience the world, we internalize the abyss of abstraction that requires that we make comprehensible objects from our sense experience. This might strike the reader as evocative of Adorno or Heidegger, but the difference is that Klages is explicit about the ontology that undergirds the critique of reification.

Finally, it is worth emphasizing that Klages's master narrative in *GWS* is that a progressively hyper-potentiated mind (*Geist*) or quantifying reason became yoked to the domination of nature, leading to the domination of humanity, and which unchecked could lead to the potential annihilation of all life on earth.[75]

If Klages's narrative reminds you of *Dialectic of Enlightenment* with *Aufklärung* standing in for *Geist*, it is no accident, as the work cites Klages's *GWS* in the footnotes.[76] Tellingly, Horkheimer and Adorno admit that

> Klages [and company] recognized the nameless stupidity which is the result of progress. But they drew the wrong conclusion. . . . The rejection of mechanization became an embellishment of industrial mass culture, which cannot do without the noble gesture. Against their will, artists reworked the lost image of the unity of body and mind for the advertising industry.[77]

In other words, Klages and his fellows understood the problem with enlightenment, but their solution was wrong. As Horkheimer and Adorno added, "The body cannot be turned back into the envelope of the soul."[78]

For Adorno in particular, the problem was that the rejection of disenchantment has been commercialized, leading to everything from homeopathy to astrology.[79] It would seem that Klages and the occultists were right to identify disenchantment as a problem, but their attempt to resupply the missing magic was doomed to failure insofar as it was trapped within the horizon of capitalism. Succinctly put, while the Frankfurt School was suspicious of magical revivals, they inherited Klages's apocalypticism.[80]

*

It is not just the Frankfurt School's critical theory that shows Klages's fingerprints. Almost from the beginning of his philosophical turn, Klages had begun to search for a dystopian term to characterize all that was wrong with hyperintellection. Although he briefly tried out *anthropocentric* (*anthropozentrische*) by about 1900 he had begun to settle on *logocentric* (*logozentrischen*) later rendered "logocentrism" (*Logozentrismus*).[81] Here we can see Klages working out the jargon that Derrida will make famous about half a century later.[82]

In the late article "Über Wahrheit und Wirklichkeit" (On truth and actuality, 1931), Klages specified the meaning of *logocentric* with greater precision. In a key passage, he argued that philosophy can be parsed into a rivalry between idealists and materialist, but "both parties—the idealists intentionally and the materialists unintentionally—endorse belief in the creative or formative power of the (human) mind. Therefore, we name this camp of the majority the logocentric school. In contrast, we call the minority camp the biocentric school."[83] The term *logocentrism* in its original formulation, therefore, is a way to connect two supposedly oppositional camps of philosophy (idealism and materialism).

Klages's main point is that idealists believe that reality is fundamentally mental, but even their materialist rivals argue that the human mind can accurately apprehend the world. Both groups grant that the universe rationally intelligible.[84] Moreover, both schools work to formulate criteria of generalized truths by means of an abstraction from the phenomena of raw sense experience. Accordingly, they are both expressions of what he would characterize elsewhere as "the cult of reason," which Klages saw as a dangerous faith in the power of rationality to master the world.[85] The core error of logocentrism is the assumption that there is nothing truly mysterious or incomprehensible and hence that the human mind can apprehend or dominate nature. We might say that logocentrism is the thought mode of disenchantment.

The Vanished Utopia of Cosmic Eros

If Klages's work often resembles a kind of poststructuralism or critical theory before its time, there is also much that would strike a contemporary theorist as strange—and I'm not just referring to the magic. Klages's critique of logocentrism was not a pure decentering; he had a utopian term: *biocentrism.*[86] The appearance of the utopian is part of what makes Klages's project so different from poststructuralism and the like. Derrida famously attacked logocentrism, but he (perhaps admirably) refused to offer a positive alternative. To be sure, Derrida valorized various modes such as deconstruction, dissemination, and the free play of sign, but generally he resisted the allure of utopia.

Klages's position in the genealogy of *logocentrism* helps to explain one of contemporary poststructuralism's most disconcerting features. It is easy to see that on sheer linguistic grounds, *logocentrism* has built into its basic formulation the implication of a double, an alternate center. Klages called his alternative "biocentrism," which he understood as a philosophy of life as opposed to mind. But how might one take life into one's philosophy without slipping into the world of logos and abstraction?

Part of Klages's answer is that unlike the caricature that represents him as completely against all thought, his aimed at balance. His response to the war between mind and life was *not* the death of mind. Instead, he described what he called "the vivification of the mind" (*Verlebendigung des Geistes*).[87] This was an attempt to discover a greater harmony between mind and life-body/soul. It is basically a kind of unlearning that allows a person to resist the reification of concepts and discover the living world around him or her. It is also rooted in an interpretation of phenomena as fundamentally meaningful, and what he saw as the recovery of a primitive mentality. Biocentrism's function, therefore, would be a retreat from the dissecting and classifying mentality of logocentrism and an implicit reversal of the meaninglessness of modern existence.

To be sure, Klages did not have consistent faith in utopia. Sometimes he expressed the fear that humanity had already crossed the point of no return and that it was only a matter of time before we too became extinct.[88] As he prophesized in *Mensch und Erde*, "We are in the age of the downfall of the soul" and "No teaching can return us to that which has once been lost."[89] But this did not stop him from trying.

Klages's utopian impulse appears in *Vom Kosmogonischen Eros* (On the Cosmogonic Eros, 1922), the work that goes the farthest to suggest his answer to disenchantment. Indeed, this is the text that includes Weber's patented phrase, *die Entzauberung der Welt*, as Klages put it:

The disenchantment of the world rests on the eradication of difference. Human instincts are blessed by Eros to the extent that they participate in the cosmic

Eros; and cosmic Eros is always: Eros of the difference [of the Other]. Hence, whoever seeks to negate difference is characterized by a possessiveness that is deadly to Eros, to the glowing aura of the world, and, ultimately, to actuality itself. But this is the mystery and blissful knowledge of the mystics: the holy image is revealed only from afar, although it merges with the mystic. He alone sees "the sun shining at midnight."[90]

At first pass it would seem that mystical union is the way to escape the iron cage of modernity—something we will also see in Weber. But the rest of this passage, with its reference to eros and the midnight sun, will take some explaining.

The first thing you need to know is that "the Cosmogonic Eros" is not merely self-preservation or sexual desire; nor is it merely a species of Platonic love or Christian charity.[91] The Cosmogonic Eros is the original, prehistoric consciousness of humankind, the way of relating to nature before the tyranny of *Geist*.[92] It represents a lost way of looking at the world outside the reach of logocentrism, a way of relating to things that takes nature as alive. Klages also thought it is phenomenologically grounded in moments of union or sympathetic resonance with the Other that could be described as flashes of connection that suspend conceptual thinking. Klages also seemed to have in mind something like an experience of the Kantian sublime. Unlike the negatively valenced in-break of the mind, this is a positively valenced in-break of the soul or life. Klages seems to be playing implicitly on the near homophony of the German *lieben* (loving) and *leben* (living); as one might guess, his fundamental model is something like a mystical union with the cosmos.[93] The root experience of Cosmogonic Eros is "ecstasy."[94]

According to Klages, this is also what Greek mystics meant by the state of being "Entheos" (ἔνθεος) by a god or demon.[95] What is it, Klages asked, that sets us beside ourselves? What is it that inhabits the mystic and the medium? Klages's answer, with palpable echoes of Nietzsche, is that these are all cases of ecstasy, what he called the "cosmic rush" (*Der kosmische Rausch*). It is in these moments that Klages thought we really and truly become more than ourselves.

Klages divided the cosmic rush into three forms. In his account, these are the heroic, the magic (*magische*), and the erotic.[96] The heroic-tragic form of ecstasy is associated with the epoch poetry of "the age of heroes." Its most striking feature is that the death of the personal ego occurs with the warrior's resolve to die, leading to a beautiful tragic impulse through which the warrior plunges consciously into oblivion.[97] He described the magic type of ecstasy as follows: "In the magical form, ecstasy manifests its nature in a doubled relationship to the nocturnal firmament and to the realm of the dead. Its historical high point was reached in the Median 'Magism' and in the ancient Egyptian funerary cult, and perhaps its strongest conceptual expression is to be found in Chaldean astrology."[98] We will return to this magical ecstasy momentarily, but for the moment, the most important thing to note is that it is a kind of primordial spiritualism connected to the dead and the night sky. Moreover, like the heroic, magic is associated with death and darkness.

Unlike the others, the erotic is fully an expression of life. It is therefore the superior form of ecstasy, and the only truly cosmic one. In Klages's vocabulary, the erotic is not just sex, but is also a part of pregnancy and birth. It manifests itself in the creative inspiration through which poets give birth to new forms. Erotic ecstasy, though, is fundamentally Dionysian, appearing in orgies, dancing, and nighttime revelries.[99]

If we wonder where Klages personally fell on the path to ecstasy, the answer is easy to find. Elsewhere in his literary remains, he confessed: "There are three archetypical perspectives (*Bilderwerdung*): the erotic, the heroic, and the magical. In the world of images these types are manifest as: the beloved, the hero, and the wizard. My own path was magical (to a chaotic extreme); it was the Gorgon and the horror of universal night. Even though I tried to approach Eros through love."[100] Klages would have preferred to be a lover, but he was cursed to be a magician.

In *Vom Kosmogonischen Eros* Klages argued for something that sounds like the kenosis of Christian mysticism, declaring that to achieve each of these forms of ecstasy, one needs to embrace a kind of self-surrender or passivity. But for Klages, this is a hollowing-out not for God, but for the primordial play of images or gods that represent the actuality of the cosmos. Now we have returned to the paragraph cited at the top of the section: mystical union is a way of collapsing the ego and uniting with the cosmos and in so doing healing ontological alienation. This was something Klages described in slightly different terms in *Mensch und Erde*: "Estranged from the planetary currents, modern man sees only childish superstition. He forgets that interpreting apparitions was a way of scattering blooms around the tree of an inner life, which shelters a deeper knowledge than all of science: *the knowledge of the world-weaving power of all-embracing love*. Only when this love has been renewed in humanity will the wounds inflicted by the matricidal spirit be healed."[101] So in effect, Klages's solution to Weber's *Entzauberung* is a mystical orgy of matriarchal love intended to magically bring us back into communion with Mother Nature.

I do not find this particularly convincing, but it should have been appealing to the same generation of intellectuals in the 1960s and 1970s who gave us post-structuralism and its cousins. Why wasn't it? Why don't we read Klages today?

Klages was likely excluded from the canon for several reasons. Conservative thinkers are unlikely to have been sympathetic to his pacifism, his embrace of sexual fluidity, his feminism, or his anti-Christianity, and progressives were probably thrown by his traditionalism and his attacks on progress and science; but it is probably mainly Klages's explicit anti-Semitism that prevented his canonization.

Already in his Munich days, Klages and the Kosmikers had expressed something akin to anti-Semitism. But they tended to divorce the word *Jewish* from race and described it instead as a kind of attitude.[102] This looks like the kind of anti-Judaism of a Nietzsche or Voltaire, where the real target is often Christianity. Further, many of Klages's most significant friends (Theodor Lessing, Wolfskehl, and Menyhért Palágyi) were Jews, but racists often defend themselves with tokenized friendships. Tragically, in Klages's work of the figure of the Jew—in particular, the American Jew—came to appear as the personification of all that is wrong with *Geist/Logos*. We can easily imagine the anti-Semitic tropes in play: the Jew is rootless, calculating, inauthentic, disconnected from life, moralizing, and capitalistic. Increasingly, Klages also described "the Jew" as the enemy of life.[103] Appallingly, Klages did not tone down this language as the Nazi rise to power threatened the lives of real Jews; if anything, he ramped up his anti-Semitism.[104] As an American Jew who lost extended family in the Shoah, I personally find this the most disgusting and odious part of Klages's oeuvre. Scholars who try to ignore this are making a grave error.

Having said that, one might be inclined to think of Klages as just another Nazi, but it is important to note that he was a pacifist and feminist opposed to their militarized or fascist state. And sadly, if we were going to exclude philosophers because of anti-Semitism or other forms of racism, we would have to reject both analytic (Gottlob Frege) and continental (Martin Heidegger, Paul de Man) philosophy and probably even Kant. Hence, we are left with a Klages who made some fascinating contributions, but whose project we would have to be very careful about embracing wholesale.

In summary, Klages was omitted from the canon, but it cannot have been because of his interest in enchantment. Indeed, if we use Klages as a starting point and go back to those thinkers—both German and French—whom we did enshrine in American critical theory, we find magic there too. The following section will demonstrate.

THE ESOTERIC CONSTELLATIONS OF CRITICAL THEORY:
WALTER BENJAMIN

The perceptual world (*Merkwelt*) of modern man seems to contain much less magical correspondences than the world of the ancients or even that of primitives. The only question is: Is this a case of the mimetic faculty withering away? Or is it an example of a transformation that has occurred within it? Some aspect of astrology could indicate, albeit indirectly, the direction of the transformation. As researchers of ancient traditions, we must take into account the possibility that manifest arrangements with the character of mimetic objects once existed where we are no longer capable of suspecting it today.

WALTER BENJAMIN, "Die Lehre vom Ähnlichen," 1933

Walter Benjamin, having fled Paris ahead of the German invasion, died tragically and largely unknown at the French-Spanish border in 1940.[105] Fortunately, before leaving Paris, Benjamin entrusted some of his most important unfinished writings to Georges Bataille who hid them in the library where he worked. In the decades since his death, Benjamin's impact has grown astronomically. His writings are widely cited, especially in the context of literary theory, continental philosophy, and art history. It is only a slight exaggeration to say that Benjamin's fingerprints can be seen on the analytical edifice of postmodernity, from critical theory to deconstruction.

Despite Benjamin's significance, there is a real debate about how to interpret his oeuvre and especially the tension between theological and communist registers. Some scholars have imagined Benjamin to be a Marxist in metaphorical garb; others suggest that Jewish theology is the core and historical materialism only its external trappings; while a third camp argues that Benjamin's attempt to reconcile both impulses was ambivalent or contradictory from the beginning and doomed to failure.[106] Terry Eagleton epitomizes this latter mode when he suggests, "There is no way in which the apocalyptic aspects of Benjamin's historical imagination may be neatly harmonized with his Marxism."[107] To these we might add a fourth and increasingly popular "dialectical" camp, which attempts to reconcile Benjamin's Judaism and his Marxism often by either emphasizing his embrace of contradictions or by contextualize it in leftwing Jewish thought in the period.[108] While I'm most sympathetic toward the dialectical reading, I think it still misses the main tension Benjamin was trying to solve and the precedents he had for this solution.

A key to reconciling these apparent contradictions is to see Benjamin's work in the context of European esotericism. Indeed, much of the vocabulary that seems so peculiar to Benjamin—*the aura, angels, constellations, corre-*

spondences, and even *primal images*—all had a place in contemporary German esoteric circles.[109] Moreover, Benjamin, like Klages, described his project in terms of magic. Accordingly, while he was far from the only critical theorist interested in magic, Benjamin's canonization has smuggled an occult vocabulary into the writings of those who would never admit to reading a grimoire. In sum, Benjamin is partially responsible for what makes critical theory in all its varieties a little bit magical today.

In the following pages, I will locate Benjamin in the esoteric milieu of the period, and then focus on how specific esoteric concepts appear in his project.

*

Benjamin's engagement with alchemy, mysticism, and the occult is striking even on a cursory read, but it is often explained by reference to "Jewish mysticism" and the Kabbalah.[110] This has the inadvertent effect of racializing or ghettoizing his project, as though his magic and his Judaism were coterminous. But Benjamin grew up in an assimilated family, and scholars have argued that his knowledge of the Jewish tradition—both exoteric and esoteric—was heavily influenced by Christian mystical literature.[111] While that might be overstating it, at the very least Benjamin's knowledge of the Kabbalah came first from Gentile esoteric circles. He was introduced to Jewish mysticism by the Swiss esotericist Max Pulver, who recommended the writings of Christian theosophists Franz von Baader and Baader's student Franz Joseph Molitor.[112] Benjamin's main source for the Kabbalah was Molitor's *Philosophie der Geschichte oder über die Tradition* (Philosophy of history or the tradition, 1824–53).[113] Far from a work of dry academic scholarship, this was an explicitly esoteric text that claimed to unlock the hidden meaning of the Torah by means of Christian theosophy. At the very least, while Benjamin became increasingly attentive to his Jewish heritage (and even more so alongside rising anti-Semitism), he had a deep and abiding fascination with the full spectrum of European esotericism.

*

Not only did Walter Benjamin read Ludwig Klages and meet him in person, Benjamin moved to Munich intending to study with Klages, and they kept up a lifelong correspondence.[114] Benjamin described Klages's *Der Geist als Widersacher der Seele* as "a great philosophical work," and he sparred with Klages's other students to stake out an interpretation of Klages's project.[115]

Indeed, Benjamin wrote so much about Klages that there is hardly a volume of Benjamin's collected works lacking a reference to Klages or his writings.[116]

Strikingly, Benjamin wanted to write even more about Klages, but Adorno and Horkheimer dissuaded him.[117] Yet, in the very December 5, 1934, letter in which Adorno does so, Adorno admitted that Klages's "doctrine of 'phantoms' in the section 'The Actuality of Images' from his *Der Geist als Widersacher der Seele*' lies closest of all, relatively speaking, to our own concerns."[118] The anxiety of influence seems clear and tellingly Adorno even tried to keep the letters Benjamin and Klages exchanged out of Benjamin's collected works.[119]

Benjamin's relationship to Klages is no secret and usually gets a passing mention in biographical accounts. But generally, when the subject is given sustained attention, it has been contextualized with reference to Benjamin's interest in thinkers on the right such as Carl Schmitt and Leo Strauss.[120] There are exceptions: in a 1992 article, Georg Stauth and Bryan S. Turner gesture at the importance of Klages for the history of critical theory and call for more work to be done on the subject.[121] But other Anglophone scholars have dismissed the whole idea of Klages's influence on critical theory as misguided, and in the intervening twenty years there has been little follow-up.[122] Moreover, as valuable as this scholarship has been, it tends to misconstrue the context by underestimating Benjamin's larger engagement with esotericism. Indeed, Klages was not the only member of the occult milieu that Benjamin socialized with.

Benjamin spent a good deal of time with other Kosmikers. He befriended Felix Noeggerath, a peripheral member of the circle, whom Benjamin described as a "universal genius."[123] Noeggerath in turn introduced Benjamin to Wolfskehl, and the two also became friends. Benjamin even wrote a dedication to Wolfskehl for his sixtieth birthday.[124] In his letters to Scholem, Benjamin mentions tracking down and reading fragments of Schuler's work.[125] Finally, Benjamin admitted that his distinctive prose style was inspired by Stefan George's *Denkbild* (thought images), which he greatly admired; and indeed, the influence of George on Benjamin's work was sufficiently pronounced that Adorno had to mention (and apologize for it) in the introduction to Benjamin's correspondence.[126]

Even beyond this particular group, Benjamin had a number of other friends in Western esoteric circles. The most obvious is Gershom Scholem, today famous as the founder of the historical study of Jewish mysticism. That Scholem was embedded in an esoteric milieu is uncontroversial. Steven Wasserstrom has explored Scholem's position at the heart of the Eranos Circle, which was connected to a kind of perennial mysticism.[127] Plus, Scholem was quite open about reading widely in occult literature and referred to thinkers including Franz Joseph Molitor, Aleister Crowley, Éliphas Lévi, and Arthur Edward Waite (albeit often critically) in his writings.[128]

Benjamin also socialized with a group of Jewish intellectuals he referred to as the "sorcerer Jews (*Zauberjuden*)." Formed around the eccentric German-Jewish physician and scholar of comparative religion Oskar Goldberg, the sorcerer Jews shared the aim of producing a desecularized or enchanted Judaism.[129] In *Die Wirklichkeit der Hebräer* (The reality of the Hebrews, 1925), Goldberg interpreted the Torah as evidence for the reality of gods, which, while inferior to the true God of Israel, were nevertheless real beings or powers that functioned as the biological centers of various peoples.[130] Benjamin found Goldberg's "aura" repellent, but he did not have the same response to other members of the group.[131] He struck up a friendship with Goldberg's disciple, the religious philosopher Erich Unger, who had set out to render his master's work into philosophical form.[132]

For our purposes the most important member of this circle was a thinker at its periphery, the Jewish-German intellectual Erich Gutkind, who became Benjamin's friend and Hebrew teacher, and who often hosted Benjamin and his wife whenever the couple would visit Berlin.[133] Beyond discussing his friendship with Benjamin, there is little scholarship on Gutkind except for a brief reference in Scholem's *On Jews and Judaism in Crisis*, which describes Gutkind's project as a dead end, "doomed to failure."[134] But Gutkind is a fascinating figure in his own right, and his trajectory from acclaimed New Age messiah to unknown adjunct professor is reminiscent of a Philip Roth novel. More important, Gutkind's writings anticipated Benjamin's later fusion of messianism, mysticism, and communism.

Before encountering Goldberg, Gutkind had already developed a reputation in New Age circles based on the popularity of his first major work, *Siderische Geburt: Seraphische Wanderung vom Tode der Welt zur Taufe der Tat* (Sidereal birth: Seraphic wanderings from the death of the world to the baptism of the act, 1910), the first in a series of attempts to reconcile communist utopia with a kind of mystic Gnosticism. Written with an apocalyptic intensity, *Siderische Geburt* describes European civilization in a state of crisis, remote from a God exiled by the simultaneous rise of private property and the materialism of contemporary science.[135] Modernity has fallen into an "abyss of matter and death" from which it cannot escape, and "we can no longer be satisfied by the [modern] world picture, but *only the end of the world*."[136]

Siderische Geburt describes its goal in terms of the pleroma of Christian

Gnosticism.[137] Following Jakob Böhme and parts of the Jewish (Lurianic) Kabbalistic tradition, the work describes a *creatio ex deo*—a world formed inside God and made from divine materials.[138] Matter in this schema is a kind of de-god-ed God. Fragments or sparks of divine holiness are scattered throughout the world, waiting to be discovered and reassembled. The future pleroma of world communion is therefore the re-creation of God himself. The rejection of private property would result in liberation from the mechanical world of matter and a celestial rebirth from the ashes of the old order.

Before the Second World War, Gutkind was on his way to becoming the prophet or messiah of a left-wing New Age movement. Indeed, the Serbian mystic Dimitrije Mitrinović celebrated *Siderische Geburt* in the pages of the *New Age* (June 23 and July 21, 1921), describing the book as "seraphic scripture" of "world importance" and comparing Gutkind to Saint Paul.[139] Mitrinović also helped organize a movement or brotherhood (*Blutband*) around Gutkind that drew together such luminaries as Martin Buber, Theodor Däubler, Wassily Kandinsky, Gustav Landauer, and Florens Christian Rang.[140] But when Hitler came to power, Gutkind fled from Germany to the United States. The new country was hostile to his particular brand of New Age teachings as well. It was all Gutkind could do to find work as an adjunct professor, and the one-time prophet died in relative anonymity.[141]

Critical Magic

Walter Benjamin did not just run in occult circles; although it would be a mistake to reduce the creativity of Benjamin's thought to any unitary influence, his own project can be seen in relation to these interests. Not only did Gutkind anticipate Benjamin's fusion of messianism and Marxism, but also it is easy to trace the terminology most closely associated with Benjamin to the esoteric milieu. To be sure, Benjamin was no straightforward importer of esotericism, but rather his writings suggest a sophisticated secularization or repurposing of occult themes, and my hunch is that he was drawn to these themes precisely because of his larger concern with the persistence of myth in modernity. Although there is not space to address the issue in full, here I will briefly outline the traces of esotericism legible in the texture of Benjamin's thought. This will also make it possible to say with some degree of precision where Benjamin borrowed from Klages and where he broke from him.

Constellations and correspondences. Scholars readily admit that Adorno's concept of the "constellation" (*Konstellation*) came from Benjamin.[142] The central model for a constellation might seem to be an artistic collage or assemblage, perhaps inspired by Brechtian theater or Marxist "exhibition."[143] A little knowledge of German makes it easier to maintain this impression because today German uses two different terms to translate the English constellation: *Konstellation*, which evokes a more neutral arrangement, and *Sternbild* (literally "star picture"), which evokes astrology. Hence one might assume that with *Konstellation*, Benjamin meant the former rather than the latter, but that would be a mistake. Benjamin connected astrology with *Konstellations*, and he used the formulation *Konstellationen der Sterne* when he did so.[144] Indeed, Benjamin conceptualized *constellation* alongside both astrology and the idea of correspondences so crucial to esotericism.

Benjamin basically said as much in a fragment from 1933, posthumously titled "Lehre vom Ähnlichen" ("Doctrine of the Similar"). Benjamin noted that the perception of similarities or correspondences is often the foundation for "occult knowledge," and he described this ability to perceive similarities as a "mimetic faculty" (*mimetisches Vermögen*).[145] As quoted in the lines from this fragment that I translated in the section epigraph, Benjamin argued that "the perceptual world (*Merkwelt*) of modern man seems to contain much less magical correspondences than the world of the ancients." Here we have Benjamin beginning to formulate a disenchantment narrative, but instead, it takes an odd swerve: "If, this reading from stars, entrails, and coincidences was reading as such for primitive humanity, and if there were mediating forms to the newer kind of reading, such as runes, it would be easy to assume that the mimetic faculty which was earlier the source of clairvoyance, quite gradually over the course of thousands of years found its way into language and writing."[146] Our ability to perceive correspondences has shifted from the stars to texts, but our mimetic faculty has not vanished.

Critical theorists will be struck by the reference here to "mimesis," the utopian term in the *Dialectic of Enlightenment*, but which Benjamin identifies as the psychical foundation for clairvoyance and astrology. Nor was clairvoyance mere metaphor, because as well as we can reconstruct, Benjamin was an active believer in telepathy and other psychical powers (and like Klages, he saw graphology as key to unlocking these).[147] But it is also telling that in another fragment from roughly the same period "Zur Astrologie" (On astrology, likely 1932), Benjamin imagined writing "a prolegomenon to every rational astrology" that would allow modern thinkers to unlock their mimetic faculties and see similarities where they might otherwise be missed.[148] Accordingly, there seems to be a clear connection between Benjamin's occult astrology and his notion of the constellation as way of revealing hidden correspondences.

The aura. Those who have read only Benjamin's most famous essay *Das Kunstwerk im Zeitalter seiner technischen Reproduzierbarkeit* (1936; *The Work of Art in the Age of Mechanical Reproduction*) might think that the aura is a purely aesthetic category. But in *Über Haschisch* (1927–34; *On Hashish*), Benjamin explicitly contrasts his version of the "aura" with that of "theosophists," "spiritualists" and "vulgar mystics."[149] While this shows that Benjamin was conversant with occult ideas of the aura, it also demonstrates his attempt to repurpose the term toward a new meaning, whose key point of difference from the occult aura is that it appears in not just people but also objects. But this is not the sum of it.

Even scholars who otherwise take otherwise no notice of Klages tend to suggest that "Benjamin's theory of 'aura' was taken directly from Klages."[150] This is close: the aura is not really a Klages master category—it occurs in the writings of other members of the Cosmic Circle. It was Schuler who first began to describe the decay of the aura, although arguing that it vanished not with the modernity but with the decline of Rome. As Schuler put it, *"Es ist die Aura, die schwindet"*—"it is the aura that is vanishing."[151] Moreover, in terms of his inspiration, Benjamin himself referred to an article by Wolfskehl, "Lebensluft" (Breath of life, 1929), which also repurposed the aura.[152] Moreover, Wolfskehl's essay anticipated a further theme of Benjamin's aura; namely, that it encompasses both people and objects. So it would seem Benjamin acquired the concept of the aura from occultists/Kosmikers and transformed it into a term of aesthetic theory.

Dialectical images. The concept of the dialectical image did not come directly from the broader esoteric milieu, but Benjamin saw it explicitly in relationship to Klages. Examining Benjamin's discussion of the dialectical image is thus the clearest way to show where they differed. As Benjamin explained in the essay "Johann Jakob Bachofen" (1934–35):

> With Klages, these theories emerged from the esoteric realm to claim a place in philosophy. . . . By giving substance to the mythical elements of life, by snatching them from the oblivion in which they are sunk, says Klages, the philosopher gains access to "primal images" [*Urbilder*].[153]

As Benjamin went on to note, one of Klages's central contributions to philosophy is this the idea of the primal image.[154] The primal image was connected to Klages's claim that the material world of flux is apprehended only through flashes of intermediate experience or dreams, which are amenable to allegorical reading, and in turn handed down as expressions of the souls of the past.[155] Accordingly, Klages's influence can be seen in one of Benjamin's most distinctive philosophical concepts, the "dialectical image" (*dialektischen Bilder*).

While many Benjamin scholars agree that the dialectical image is the methodological heart of Benjamin's *Arcades Project*, they differ widely regarding both the expression's meaning and Benjamin's primary inspiration.[156] In part, they have missed the meaning of Benjamin's cryptic remarks in that text, that the "dialectical image is an image that emerges suddenly, in a flash. What has been is to be held fast as an image flashing up in the now of its recognizability."[157] This already connects Benjamin's dialectic image to Klages's primal image. Adorno also acknowledged as much in the December 5, 1934, letter cited above where Adorno requested Benjamin make a further "distinction between [Klages'] archaic and [Benjamin's own] dialectical images."[158]

Insofar as these images are the core of *The Arcades Project*, it seems to be Klages with a sharp difference—a difference that can be pinpointed in Benjamin's review of *Johann Jacob Bachofen und das Natursymbol*: "This enterprise is all the more productive since it simultaneously attempts to grapple with Klages and his doomed attempt to reject the existing 'technical,' 'mechanized' state of the modern world. In his discussion, he does not evade the challenge represented by the philosophical—or rather, theological—center from which Klages directs his prophecy of doom with a force that forever puts the efforts of other critics of our culture in the shade, including those produced by the George circle."[159] Paraphrased, the key problem with Klages was his resolutely Luddite rejection of the technological world of modernity. As is well known, Benjamin was fascinated by the dreamlike quality of manmade artifacts. He was critical of the archaism of Klages's doctrine of the images and Klages's accompanying traditionalism. Benjamin was also far from a proto-ecologist; if anything, he felt a "dread of nature."[160] Thus, he was quite willing to criticize modernity, but did not believe in idealizing an archaic past. Benjamin would seem to be Klages without the disenchantment thesis; in other words, with sensitivity to the way that everyday modern objects, like archaic symbols, are equally the embodiment of the dream consciousness of myth.[161]

The cosmic rush. In *Einbahnstraße* (One-way street, 1928), Benjamin came the closest in his published writings to declaring himself a Kosmiker in the same breath that he made his departures from the majority of that movement known. As he began the relevant section: "If one had to expound the teachings of antiquity with utmost brevity while standing on one leg, as did Hillel that of the Jews, it could only be in this sentence: '*They alone shall possess the earth who live from the powers of the cosmos.'"*[162] He further clarified, "The ancients' intercourse with the cosmos had been different: the ecstatic trance [*Rausch*]. . . . This means, however, that man can be in ecstatic contact with the cosmos only communally. It is the dangerous error of modern men to regard this experience as unimportant and avoidable."[163] Between the *Rausch* of the encounter with the cosmos, the idea of communal ecstasy, and modern alienation from an archaic past, this quote might as well be Klages. In this passage, Benjamin also recounted one inversion of the modern progress narrative that should be familiar: "Technology betrayed man and turned the bridal bed into a bloodbath. The mastery of nature (so the imperialists teach) is the purpose of all technology."[164]

At first pass, Benjamin would seem to have inherited Klages's critique of technology as the domination of nature, but Benjamin disagreed with the idealized nature this critique implied. Benjamin was no tree hugger: he argued that what has been lost was not an experience of some kind of pristine or precivilization nature, but a kind of collectivity. Importantly, Benjamin associated this collectivity with the proletariat, not a group of pagan mystics.[165] Thus, we might see the flashes of cosmic energy not in bonfire celebrations in the woods, but in the Russian revolution of 1917.

Magic. In a 1916 letter to his boyhood friend Herbert Belmore (née Blumenthal, 1893–1978), Benjamin sketched out his vision of authentic criticism as follows:

> True criticism does not attack its object: it is like a chemical substance that attacks another only in the sense that, decomposing it, it exposes its inner nature, but does not destroy it. The chemical substance that attacks *spiritual* things in this way (diathetically) is the light. . . . Criticism of spiritual things is to distinguish between the genuine and the nongenuine. . . . The particular *critical magic* (*kritische Magie*) then appears, so that the counterfeit substance comes into contact with the light; it disintegrates.[166]

True criticism does not destroy so much as dissolve its object, exposing its inner nature and bringing it to life. As Benjamin elaborated in *Goethes Wahlverwandtschaften* (Goethe's *Elective Affinities*, 1922), "Criticism seeks the veracity (*Wahrheitsgehalt*) of a work of art."[167] Criticism is like a solvent that dissolves away impurities to expose the pure form of a substance. More properly, criticism is a refining or distilling apparatus, like an alchemist's alembic, which separates the true and the false. Having separated the genuine from the artificial, one exercises a "critical magic" to bring the counterfeit to light and cause it to disintegrate, while enlivening the purer aspects.

Benjamin fully intended the alchemical imagery:

> If one wants a parable, the growing work can be seen as a burning funeral pyre, before which stands the commentator as the chemist, the critic as the alchemist. Whereas for the chemist the wood and ash alone are the objects of analysis, for the alchemist only the flame preserves an enigma: that of life. Hence the critic asks after the truth, whose living flame continues to burn over the weighty driftwood (*Scheitern*) of the past and the light ashes of that which was experienced.[168]

A critical theorist is like an alchemist who burns a work to reveal the living truth it embodies. Although functioning primarily at the level of metaphor, Benjamin was modeling the work of critical theory on that of the esotericists.

In "Der Surrealismus" (Surrealism, 1929), Benjamin provides his most succinct description of his relationship to the occult milieu:

> Any serious exploration of occult, surrealistic, phantasmagoric gifts and phenomena presupposes a dialectical intertwinement. . . . We penetrate the mystery only to the degree that we recognize it in the everyday world, by virtue of dialectical optic that perceives the everyday as impenetrable, the impenetrable as everyday. The most passionate investigation of telepathic phenomena, for example, will not teach us half as much about reading (which is an eminently telepathic process) as the profane illumination of reading will teach us about telepathic phenomena.[169]

As evidenced in this passage, Benjamin advocated a serious exploration of the mysterious and occult via their embodiment in the everyday. This is not a rejection of occult exploration (much less a rejection of telepathy). Indeed, Benjamin was claiming the reverse, that the best way to understand telepathy is not in the psychical laboratory, but in its written expression. We can still understand the phantasmagoric, but not in the moments of the miraculous: we should explore these phenomena "dialectically," through the interrogation of everyday objects. For Benjamin, the problem with many occultists is that they mystify the wrong things.

We should now be in a position to make sense of the essay in which Benjamin is most critical of the occult, "Erleuchtung durch Dunkelmänner" (Light from obscurantists, 1932), which is nominally a review of "Die Geheimwissenschaften im Lichte unserer Zeit" (The occult sciences in the light of our age) by the Austrian journalist Hans Liebstöckl. In this essay, Benjamin was highly critical of the commercialization of the occult sciences, which he described as benefiting from the decline in general education. The problem with these sciences is that they claim to provide shortcuts to happiness and hidden knowledge without the penetrating study that would unlock the truth.[170] In effect, these penny occult works and the posturing of anthroposophists only serve to cheapen or even disenchant the supernatural. By contrast, Benjamin wanted to unlock the hidden magic or dream images of the everyday.[171] By decoding the meaning of works of art, toys, or arcades, the critical theorist is engaging in a kind of re-enchantment, or at the very least, revivification. Benjamin was suggesting that the most mundane figures, the reader and the loiterer, have hidden essences that can be revealed by the tools of critical theory.

The final observation I want to make in this section is that Benjamin's version of critical theory meant he was engaged in a very similar academic enterprise to the one that I am employing in this book. Throughout his writings Benjamin explicitly uncovered the esoteric entanglements of many of the figures he studied.[172] We might see his magical critical theory in terms of its attempt to mystify or complicate its subjects by unmasking their dialectical contradictions and their unconscious or hidden ideological commitments. Accordingly, the everyday contains profound secrets every bit as illuminating as that of the ecstatic.

In summary, Benjamin was more than merely the vector for Klages, Goldberg, and Gutkind; he also transformed the counter-enlightenment critique worked out by magicians into the proper business of a philosopher. Critical theory in Benjamin's legacy would therefore function as kind of re-enchantment or magic; or at the very least, as quoted above, would permit a "serious exploration of occult, surrealistic, phantasmagoric gifts and phenomena" as a path toward "profane illumination."

CONCLUSION: THE MAGIC OF THEORY

In 1936, a small group of French artists, literary theorists, and students formed a secret society centered on "a ceremony of initiation, rites, and the acceptance of a changed way of life destined to separate adepts . . . from a world that would henceforth be considered as profane."[173] They performed clandestine rituals in the Place de la Concorde (where Louis XVI had been beheaded) and traveled covertly to forest groves in pursuit of "the chthonic character of mythical reality."[174] Although we know almost nothing of the details of their rituals, the heart of their project was a voluntary human sacrifice intended to recapitulate the death of God and king alike. A sacred murder was to be the spark that would begin the "destruction of the world that exists" and would open eyes "to the world that will be."[175] They hoped that the violent transgression of ritual decapitation would give birth to a new mythology appropriate to an era associated with divine death and misplaced political sovereignty. Yet, despite having a willing victim, an executioner was lacking and the sacrifice was never performed.[176]

When I tell you that the name of this secret society was Acéphale, or the Headless, scholars of French social theory will instantly recognize their leader as Georges Bataille (1897–1962), who is known for his obsession with the image of a headless man.[177] Today Bataille is mainly regarded as the kooky uncle of French theory: scandalous for authoring erotic novels and equally provocative works on violence, the sacred, and political economy; and recognized as a decisive influence on a generation of theorists including, Baudrillard, Barthes, Blanchot, Derrida, Foucault, Kristeva, and Lyotard.[178]

Scholars know that Bataille embraced mysticism, and it is common knowledge that he was fascinated by Hermetic and occult texts, and profoundly interested in at least the symbolic power of magic.[179] He also read and cited Ludwig Klages.[180] For our purposes, it is particularly telling that in the journal intended to be the public face of the Acéphale secret society, Bataille praised Klages and noted in passing that the term *acéphale* had first appeared in a French review of Klages's work.[181] Hence, while Klages's influence on Bataille is comparatively minor, his "Headless" at least partially symbolized Klages's attack on *Geist* and logocentrism, evoking reason decapitated in order to open up a cosmic eros of beauty and terror.

I mention Bataille not primarily to give another example of Klages's influence, but to suggest that the esoteric keeps appearing in thinkers we have canonized in critical theory.

*

Critical theory's self-image is of vigilance and hyper-intellection. If you are routing it through Kant, Hegel, and Marx, you can make that boast. If you stick with Marx, then you can even call yourself materialist. If you put European mysticism at the center, however, then all those claims become suspect. Noting Klages's similarity to American versions of "continental philosophy" upends the conventional view of both critical theory and poststructuralism, not only because multiple theorist in the tradition read Klages, but also because in some respects Klages was repeating things common to other esotericists.

Indeed, except for the addition of Nietzsche, many of Klages's ideas had direct precedents in the occult milieu of the period. Although, as I demonstrated above, a suprising number of the new cannon of theorists—from Adorno to Lacan—read Klages, it is not that I think every poststructuralist or critical theorist was dominantly inspired by Klages either directly or by way of Benjamin or Bataille. Nor do I think they were all a bunch of closeted magicians. Rather, I see important engagements with occult themes and thinkers by multiple theorists in our tradition.

Perhaps later I'll write a whole book on the subject, but there are plenty of examples: Ferdinand de Saussure's attendance at spiritualist séances and writing about theosophy in the very moment he was giving his famous lectures.[182] Gilles Deleuze's first publication, which was the introduction to a work of occult magic.[183] Giorgio Agamben's interest in Paracelsus as a solution to the semiotic rupture.[184] Peter Sloterdijk's investment in Osho as a spiritual and philosophical precursor.[185] Roy Bhaskar's debt to theosophy.[186] Luce Irigaray's interest in yoga and mysticism.[187] Even Derrida expressed an interest in telepathy and attempted to ally the *pharmakeus* (magician), writing, and magic against speech and logos.[188] Not to mention thinkers like Michel de Certeau and Ernst Bloch, whose connections to mysticism are well known. I could go on.

Given the ongoing ruptures in and rewritings of structuralism, people are sifting through the rubble. If you think structuralism was mostly about linguistic skepticism, you are likely to push Benjamin and Bataille to the margins. Homing in on Klages has allowed us to begin to retrieve a version of critical theory or poststructuralism that was not first and foremost a critique of knowledge, but rather a vehicle for esoteric wisdom. With a few exceptions, poststructuralist skepticism turns out not to be a complete rejection of knowledge, but rather an attempt to work out knowledge's occult or hidden side. The recovery of continental philosophy's own secrets in no way diminishes its value, but should go some distance in recuperating its cultural context.

Klages allows us to see that beneath the critique of stable meanings, there was a buried ontology—that of a Heracletean kind of flux, which was supposed to be a positively valenced life itself. This allows us to see a critique of reification that is not primarily Marxist. We must destroy the totality of language not primarily to silence speech, but to revivify our world—in other words, to re-enchant it. We can see that the critique of logocentrism has a reverse side, a buried utopian term that was a kind of biocentrism. The critique of patriarchy and the centralized state also suggested a matriarchal community, which however much it resembled a hippie commune, was for a brief moment a possibility before being crushed by world wars. It would seem that at least fleetingly, critical theory bore the signs of a utopia.

*

This has also furthered our efforts to provide a genealogy of *Dialectic of Enlightenment*. All told, it would appear that critical theory's proximate other was the occult, with the esoteric and key thinkers of the period sharing both a critique of modernity and a vocabulary. The persistence of esotericism in Walter Benjamin's writings helps make sense of Adorno's repeated criticisms of magic and astrology and his efforts to get Benjamin to distance himself from Ludwig Klages—although, as we have seen, even Adorno and Horkheimer were willing to admit that they found something compelling in Klages's critique of enlightenment. Indeed, Adorno frequently engaged with Klages and other esotericists, albeit often critically.[189] Accordingly, Adorno's immanent critique of enchantment poses a problem for the self-understanding of critical theory today.

As noted above, critical theory is one of the central places in the academy for a left-Weberian critique of modernity. We look to critical theorists to be reminded that disenchantment has meant the domination of nature, the dehumanization of humanity, the end of wonder, and the destruction of myth. But having read Klages, we can see that important aspects of this line of critique originated in the fin-de-siècle occult milieu. So on these grounds, all the various left-Weberian attempts to overcome instrumental rationality or the iron cage by way of re-enchantment might now seem suspect.

But if the main thing we have learned from critical theory—and the *Dialectic of Enlightenment* in particular—is that disenchantment has negative consequences, then we are presented with a further problem. It would seem that in his rejection of occultism, Adorno has placed himself on the side of the disenchanters. He attacks both magic and the loss of magic. He might seem therefore to be amplifying the very disenchantment he has so strongly criticized. A further complexity, as I'll show in the next chapter, is that from this vantage, it looks as though the Frankfurt School's archnemesis, the Vienna Positivists, here seem to play the role of magicians.

CHAPTER NINE

The Ghosts of Metaphysics: Logical Positivism and Disenchantment

It has fallen to many to exorcise Metaphysics from Philosophy, but it has been left for the Logical Positivists, as they are sometimes called, to behave as if they had succeeded.

MAX BLACK, introduction to *The Unity of Science*, by Rudolph Carnap, 1934

To begin with the finale, the Vienna Circle ended with a philosophical murder. On Monday, June 22, 1936, an unemployed Austrian academic, Johann Nelböck ambushed his former thesis advisor, Professor Moritz Schlick, outside his office and shot him fatally in the heart.[1] Both men were philosophers. Schlick—known to many as the father of logical positivism—was the author of multiple influential works on the philosophy of science, epistemology, and ethics.[2] Nelböck had written a thesis in philosophy, and he attempted to justify his atrocity in philosophical terms.[3] Although admitting his personal grievances with Schlick, who he felt had prevented him from getting a job, Nelböck also maintained that the murder could be seen in terms of opposed world-views (*Weltanschauungen*) between religious faith and atheistic positivism. The murderer was basically arguing that he had become unhinged because Schlick's positivist assault on metaphysics had stripped life of its meaning.[4]

While today no one is seriously calling for a violent purge, "positivism" is often characterized as "the hegemonic epistemology in scientific discourse," and it is criticized for believing that "subjectivity is an obstacle to knowledge" or for espousing a misguided "faith in reason."[5] Accordingly, positivists might seem to be ideal missionaries for the myth of disenchantment. In this chapter I will show why this account of the logical positivists is wrong.

I start by sketching the critique of positivism in our current academic moment and touching on the attack on positivism in the writings of the Frankfurt School. Then I explore the self-image of the Vienna Circle of logical positivism. It will turn out that some of the critique is well directed: the logical positivists did position themselves as the inheritors of "the Enlightenment" and as the apex of a trajectory of disenchantment. Later sections of the chapter complicate this picture by showing how many positivists expressed an abiding interest in the paranormal and described their project in terms of magic.

The previous chapter may have left the reader with the sense that critical theory was the only philosophical movement entangled with esoteric knowledge. But, as I argue, positivism also looks like the emergence of a counter-tradition or counterculture, working out its own criticisms of modernity, formulating new utopias, and radical ontotheologies. The irony is that exposing these allegiances reveals magic precisely in those philosophers who are often described as the hegemonic enemies of enchantment.

PHILOSOPHICAL TECHNOCRACY: THEODOR ADORNO AND MAX HORKHEIMER

Our prognosis regarding the associated lapse from enlightenment into positivism . . . has been overwhelmingly confirmed.

MAX HORKHEIMER AND THEODOR ADORNO,
Dialektik der Aufklärung (new edition), 1969

In many academic circles, the word *positivism* functions as an invective.[6] Beyond the memory of a specific philosophical movement, a broadly construed "positivist paradigm" has been charged with fetishizing facts, uncritically eliding text with reality, enacting patriarchal sexism and imperialism, and worse.[7] In many critiques it is unclear whether the intended targets are any self-identified positivists, such as the followers of Auguste Comte or Ernst Mach; quantitative scientific thinking as such; or more likely, a general scholarly mentality. Historians accuse "positivism" of being unhistorical; economists fault it for being uncritical; ethicists reproach positivists for attempting to exile values; and English professors reprimand positivists for having an excessively limited view of meaning.[8]

Even when a specific philosophical camp is fixed squarely in view, logical positivism still often appears as a hegemonic nemesis. One common way to stage the continental divide is in terms of an opposition between Anglo-Austrian logical positivism (Vienna Circle) and the German antipositivisms of Heidegger or the Frankfurt School.[9] As Jean-François Lyotard has described it: "Carnap on the one hand and Heidegger on the other cut Western philosophy in two."[10] Sometimes "postmodernism" is supposed to be nothing more than a rejection of positivism.[11] Indeed, both French and German philosophers of all kinds—from phenomenologists to existentialists to poststructuralists—often define their rupture with analytic philosophy by reference to a critique of positivism.[12]

Those of us trained in continental philosophy may find it surprising to learn that there is a deeply entrenched critique of positivism in analytic philosophy as well. Analytic philosophers do emphasize logical positivism's historical importance.[13] But as Robert Scharff has summarized it: "As hard as it is nowadays to get agreement on what analytic philosophers could still possibly have in common, at least it seems safe to say that there is something they are universally against, namely, positivism."[14] Contemporary analytic philosophy is also often taken to originate in a criticism of logical positivism. While citing a different cast of critics (say, Hilary Putnam and W. V. O. Quine instead of Lyotard and Heidegger), the analytic critique is similar insofar as the positivists are often accused of a flawed repudiation of metaphysics based on a simplistic conception of science.

From these criticisms it would be easy to think that some form of positivism is both universally dominant and universally reviled. I will touch on this discursive structure in the chapter's conclusion. But in this section, I want to gesture toward the roots of a particular critique of positivism that has been so widely repeated it has become unthinking—namely, that the positivists represented the Enlightenment gone bad and scientism trying to devour philosophy, and that they tragically de-politicized theory by making a supreme value out of value neutrality. This line of critique is important because it serves as one of the central foci for the disenchantment narrative.

One important source for this image of positivism is the critique found in the Frankfurt School, particularly in the writings of Max Horkheimer and Theodor Adorno. In the previous chapter I located the Frankfurt School in the occult milieu—and indeed, I've been shadowboxing with *Dialectic of Enlightenment* throughout (often explicitly but sometimes only implicitly)—and the next few pages will gesture at Horkheimer and Adorno's confrontation with positivism.

*

Both Adorno and Horkheimer frequently criticized positivism, sometimes addressing a general attitude but often attacking the Vienna Circle directly. This culminated in the well-known positivism dispute (*Positivismusstreit*) in German sociological circles in the 1960s, but that conflict was only the last act of a long-running disagreement.[15] Horkheimer had already contrasted positivism and enlightenment in his 1927 lectures on the history of modern philosophy.[16] He even rebuked positivist social philosophy in his 1931 inaugural address to the Institute for Social Research, suggesting that the Frankfurt School needed to embody a different form of social theory.[17] To be sure, Horkheimer did not yet have the Vienna Circle in view and was criticizing broader philosophical trends.

In "The Latest Attack on Metaphysics" ("Der neueste Angriff auf die Metaphysik," 1937), Horkheimer began focusing his critique on the philosophy of the Vienna Circle, calling out thinkers who will be discussed below (Rudolf Carnap, Hans Hahn, and Otto Neurath). Horkheimer's main line of argument is that there is an opposition between the worldview of science and that of metaphysics that leads toward a split between two main philosophical camps: science-oriented positivists trying to expunge metaphysics, and antiscientific metaphysicians clinging to "romantic spiritualism" and life philosophy (*Lebensphilosophie*). While identifying problems with this new metaphysics, the brunt of the essay counterattacks the positivist critique of metaphysics. In brief, the positivists are accused of confusing "calculating thought with reason as such," and Horkheimer rejected the equation of knowledge with the logical analysis of sense data.[18] Insofar as critical theory is supposed to be a third alternative to both positivism and new metaphysics, it might seem that one of its central purposes is to confound positivists.[19]

This was a mandate that Adorno accepted. One can find criticisms of the positivists throughout his philosophical oeuvre.[20] In *Eingriffe: Neun kritische Modelle* (1968; *Critical Models*), Adorno asserted: "Especially in the Anglo-Saxon countries logical positivism, originally inaugurated by the Vienna Circle, has gained ground to the point of becoming a virtual monopoly."[21] Adorno argued elsewhere that "Positivism is the puritanism of knowledge," by which he meant that it aims to force knowledge to submit to set of norms about its own limitations.[22]

As contemporary scholar Michael LeMahieu has observed, one of the idiosyncrasies of Adorno's assault on positivism was his interpretation of Ludwig Wittgenstein as an arch-positivist.[23] For instance, in *Drei Studien zu Hegel* (1963; *Hegel: Three Studies*), Adorno describes "Wittgenstein's maxim, *Whereof one cannot speak, thereof one must be silent*," as the moment "in which the extreme of positivism spills over into the gesture of reverent authoritarian authenticity."[24] Although today Wittgenstein is not typically thought of as a positivist (especially after *Philosophical Investigations*, 1953), Adorno's assertion in *Negative Dialektik* (1966; *Negative Dialectics*) that the aim of philosophy is "to counter Wittgenstein by uttering the unutterable" makes sense in light of Adorno's reading of Wittgenstein as a positivist.[25] Thus the "negative" in negative dialectics is partially a repudiation of the "positive" of the positivist.[26]

The Frankfurt School's most thoroughgoing offensive against positivism is in Horkheimer's *The Eclipse of Reason* (1947). His argument, in a nutshell, is that modern thought has undergone a process of "formalization" or "subjectivization," by which Horkheimer meant that an older conception of reason as having both subjective and objective components has become dominated by "subjective reason," defined as "the ability to calculate probabilities and thereby to co-ordinate the right means with a given end."[27] This instrumental form of rationality (to give the left-Weberian term) has exiled objective reason from the world, resulting in "an empty nature degraded to mere material, mere stuff to be dominated, without any other purpose than that of this very domination."[28] Basically, value rationality has been displaced in favor of dehumanizing instrumental rationality.

Although Horkheimer did not exclusively blame the positivists, he described them as epitomizing this process in modern philosophy. As he summarized, positivism "is as fallacious as other glorifications of technology. Economic technocracy expects everything from the emancipation of the material means of production. . . . *Positivism is philosophical technocracy*."[29] Restated, positivism has a naïve faith in scientific progress and its potential to transform the world. It has lost the power to politicize philosophy for productive change and merely apes technological advancement. As Horkheimer put it elsewhere: "[Positivism] removed thought from philosophy and reduced the latter to the technique of organizing, by reproduction and abridgment, the matters of fact given in the world of sense. In positivism reason sustains itself through self-liquidation."[30] Positivism is therefore reason devouring itself and has become unable to prevent a "relapse into mythology."[31] Here we have the bare bones of the attack on positivism that will be articulated more fully in *Dialectic of Enlightenment*, which was written in the same period.

Even a cursory reading of *Dialectic of the Enlightenment* exposes "positivism" as the work's main dystopian term, representing enlightenment gone wrong. As Horkheimer and Adorno argued "Enlightenment is mythical fear radicalized. The pure immanence of positivism, its ultimate product."[32] They added later that "for positivism, which has assumed the judicial office of enlightened reason, to speculate about intelligible worlds is no longer merely forbidden but senseless prattle."[33] Enlightenment crystalized in positivism, where thought became nothing more than clarifying the grammar of logical language, and everything else was bracketed out as meaningless and metaphysical: "For the Enlightenment, anything which cannot be resolved into numbers, and ultimately into one, is illusion; modern positivism consigns it to poetry. . . . All gods and qualities must be destroyed."[34] All told, Horkheimer and Adorno charged the positivists with radicalizing demythologization so far that enlightenment has been crippled. By instrumentalizing reason, the positivists have turned nature into something to be mastered, and have opened the gateway to the violent return of the repressed.[35] Thus, the positivists might appear to be the epitome of disenchantment—*disenchantment personified*.

This was not merely the view of the Frankfurt School. Something similar could be found on the other side of the political spectrum. Heidegger, in the draft of his lecture course *Einführung in die Metaphysik* (delivered 1935; *Introduction to Metaphysics*), argued:

> [In Carnap's writings] the last consequences of a mode of thinking which began with Descartes are brought to a conclusion: a mode of thinking according to which truth is no longer disclosedness of what is and thus accommodation and grounding of Dasein in the disclosing being, but truth is rather diverted into *certainty*—to the mere securing of thought, and in fact the securing of mathematical thought against all that is not thinkable by it. The conception of truth as the securing of thought led to the definitive de-divination of the world (*Entgötterung der Welt*).[36]

Here Heidegger is laying the de-divination of the world at Carnap's feet. In the pages that follow, we'll see where this image of the positivists holds and where it turns out to be mere caricature.

REVOLUTIONARY ANTIMETAPHYSICS: POSITIVIST DISENCHANTMENT AND RE-ENCHANTMENT; RUDOLF CARNAP AND OTTO NEURATH

> Most philosophers did not even suspect the revolutionary importance of modern logic.
>
> RUDOLPH CARNAP, *Der logische Aufbau der Welt* (second edition), 1967

> Above all, the fight against metaphysics and theology means the destruction of bourgeois ideology.
>
> OTTO NEURATH, *Empirische Soziologie*, 1931

The Vienna Circle announced itself to the world in a manifesto titled "Wissenschaftliche Weltauffassung: Der Wiener Kreis" (The scientific conception of the world: The Vienna Circle), presented to Moritz Schlick in 1929. Schlick did not fully agree with the manifesto, however, which had been written by the political economist Otto Neurath (1882–1945), with input from the philosopher Rudolf Carnap (1891–1970) and the mathematician Hans Hahn (1879–1934).[37] Though Schlick found much he liked in the text, he disagreed with some of its argument and philosophical tone.[38] Even its title was not of Schlick's devising, and it was his student Herbert Feigl who took credit for promoting the movement as "Logical Positivism."[39]

Instead of tracing out the evolving positions of the fourteen members of the Vienna Circle, I focus on the primary authors of the manifesto: Neurath, Carnap, and later in the chapter, Hahn. This was a group Carnap referred to as "the left wing of the Vienna Circle," which he contrasted with the more conservative wing associated with Schlick and Friedrich Waismann.[40] How left wing was this portion of the Vienna Circle? The first lesson to those who taught that logical positivism was a bland philosophy directed at "just the facts" is that the core of the Vienna Circle had a politics. They were socialists or Marxists, and at various times, actively revolutionary. If we focus on these three and their initial shared philosophical, cultural, and political project, a different picture of the Vienna Circle emerges. In general, I want to bring the positivists "home" to Continental Europe and show that they were less different from the Frankfurt School than they have generally been portrayed.

There are three elements of the common critique of the logical positivists that are basically accurate: the Vienna Circle did align itself with enlightenment, it was trying to refashion philosophy in scientific terms, and it did dedicate itself to the elimination of metaphysics. Each of these critiques, however, needs to be qualified.

First, the Vienna Circle manifesto contained repeated invocations of the "Spirit of Enlightenment" (*Geist der Aufklärung*); and Carnap and Neurath had their own project—the *International Encyclopedia of Unified Science*—that they described as a successor to Diderot and d'Alembert's *Encyclopédie*.[41] Their conception of enlightenment, however, does not fit the caricatured opposition between modernism and postmodernism. This is because the Vienna Circle identified enlightenment with not just the *philosophes*, but also tellingly with Marx and Nietzsche.[42] This was enlightenment as politics and radical critique.

Second, the Vienna Circle did claim to embody the "scientific world-conception" and saw logical analysis as way to unify the sciences. As they imagined it, philosophy's primary task would be both to understand what worked about the special sciences and to formalize a mathematically informed logic that would give new rigor to all forms of empirical inquiry. But Neurath had a more sophisticated conception of science than his critics usually give him credit for. He famously described the starting point of the sciences as: "We are like sailors who have to rebuild their ship on the open sea, without ever being able to dismantle it in drydock."[43] Indeed, as his writings make clear, Neurath—far from espousing a scientific status quo—imagined a humbler science that he saw as antifoundationalist, potentially fallible, relativistic, and historical conditioned.[44] Moreover, as we'll see, it was a politicized and revolutionary science.

Third, and most important, the logical positivists are often criticized for attempting to banish metaphysics. In this they are guilty as charged. Arguments against metaphysics occur throughout the Vienna Circle's philosophical texts, and they are given succinct formulation in Carnap's article "Überwindung der Metaphysik durch Logische Analyse der Sprache" (The overcoming of metaphysics through logical analysis of language, 1931), which explicitly called for the "radical elimination of metaphysics."[45] Tracing Carnaps's argument will help clarify what the positivists intended with this gesture.

The essay is rooted in a verificationist theory of meaning often attributed to early Wittgenstein. According to this view, in order for a philosophical proposition to have meaning, it has to be subject to logical or potential empirical verification. So the proposition, "2 + 2 = 7" is a meaningful statement even if false because it has a logical meaning. Similarly, the proposition "I have a raven skull in my closet" is either true or false and hence meaningful, insofar as it is possible to open the closet and identify the aforementioned skull.

Metaphysical propositions are meaningless on this account because either they rely on grammatically malformed statements or on concepts that are beyond possible verification. As an example of the first issue, the statement "7 is red" rests on a category error—a number cannot have a color—so the statement is neither true nor false and therefore meaningless.[46] For an example of the second-type of meaningless statement, Carnap quoted from Heidegger's "What Is Metaphysics?" and focused on a passage that end with the phrase "The Nothing itself nothings" (*Das Nichts selbst nichtet*). Carnap contended that on grammatical grounds, this statement makes no sense. "Nothing" cannot function as a substantive noun, nor does "nothing" make sense here as a verb; moreover, the whole thing is both empirically and logically unverifiable. We would not be able to recognize nothing nothing-ing if it landed on our shoe. Therefore, the whole statement is meaningless.[47]

Carnap was not just holding up Heidegger for ridicule. He argued that most of the key terms in Western philosophy—from Descartes's *cogito* to Kant's *Ding-an-Sich*—are meaningless because they are unverifiable metaphysical concepts. Carnap knew that these were fighting words, and he anticipated being questioned about why so many people have historically spent so much time writing metaphysics.[48] His answer was that "metaphysics originated from *mythology*" as a kind of emotive expression of one's relationship to the world and that—like poetry and other aesthetic pursuits—metaphysics is an expression of a general attitude toward life (*Lebenseinstellung, Lebensgefühl*), not a serious description of facts.[49] Hence, the appeal of Plato or Heidegger is mostly aesthetic, like a good piece of music.[50] But then, Carnap concluded that most "metaphysicians are musicians without musical ability."[51] In effect, he wanted metaphysicians to either write poetry or retire, but regardless, to stop pretending they do philosophy. He imagined that the exorcism of metaphysics would then purge philosophy of its meaningless propositions and terms.

This assault on metaphysics is part of what gives "positivism" its name. The attempt to expunge metaphysics was indirectly modeled on Auguste Comte. Comte's "law of three stages" describes the movement of thought from theology to metaphysics to the scientific or positive. As a name for a philosophical movement, "positivism" therefore embodies the progressive demystification of the world, implying the elimination of both religion and abstraction. But there is a certain paradox in the basic formulation of "positivist philosophy" because in Comte's original system, the term *metaphysics* was itself synonymous with *philosophy*. Hence his positivism meant not only the death of God, but also a death of philosophy. Philosophy as such was an intermediate stage to be replaced by science. Accordingly, a positivist philosophy would appear to be a contradiction in terms, or perhaps an antiphilosophy.

To the degree that the Vienna Circle came to their positivism in the wake of thinkers like Frazer, Freud, and Max Weber, it might also suggest a commitment to the end of magic. Logical positivism's founding figures did plot history in terms suggestive of a disenchantment narrative. Otto Neurath described the transition "from magic to unified science," while Herbert Feigl gestured at "the history of thought from magic to science."[52] Moreover, when the Vienna Circle emphasized the urgency of their philosophical mission, they sometimes played on a different meaning of the word *metaphysics*.

One of the flyers that promoted the movement in 1929 included the following: "To All Friends of the scientific World-Conception! We live in a critical spiritual (*geistigen*) situation! Metaphysical and theological thought is taking hold in certain groups; astrology, anthroposophy, and similar movements are spreading."[53] As this illustrates, "metaphysics" was often identified with astrology and anthroposophy—in other words, as magic or occultism. Indeed, the *Metaphysische Rundschau* (Metaphysical review) was one of the more popular German occult magazines in Carnap's day.[54] When the Vienna Circle referred to the recent rise of "metaphysical thought" in their manifesto and other writings, they partially evoked also the widespread occult revival of the period as the enemy of their own movement.[55] In that, they *seemed* interested in exorcizing magic from the culture at large, not just philosophy, and the logical positivists *seem* to be the worst candidates for being any sort of magicians. I problematize positivist disenchantment bellow.

The related charge is that the logical positivists' crusade against metaphysics was essentially a secularization project.[56] There is also justification for this view. The positivists generally assumed that religion and science were in binary opposition, and they often took the side of science against religion. Carnap, for example, lists "God" as an example of a potentially meaningless metaphysical concept.[57] Neurath also frequently equated "theologians" and "metaphysicians" in his writings. But the attack on metaphysics was not merely an attempt to banish God's shadow. It had a politics that contemporary commentators generally seem to overlook.

*

Because Carnap tried to de-emphasize his previous political commitments after relocating to the United States, it is easy to forget that his significant early positivist writings took place in a political context. While the least political of the left wing of the Vienna Circle, Carnap became actively political after World War I and as a youth saw himself as a socialist with Marxist allegiances.[58] Indeed, in a diary entry from 1932, Carnap enthused about a Marxist reading of "Überwindung der Metaphysik."[59] It was partially on political grounds that Carnap fled the Nazis in 1935 and came to America.[60] Still, Carnap was rarely public with his political views and seems to have worked to obscure the political implications of his own writing. Later in life, however, Carnap remarked to a friend: "If you want to find out what my political views were in the twenties and thirties, read Otto Neurath's books and articles of that time; his views were also mine."[61] That is what we will do. Indeed, it was Neurath—Carnap's collaborator in forming the Vienna Circle—who took Carnap's politics to the next level.

To explain Neurath's political theory, we also have to look back to the end of the First World War. In 1918, as the war turned decisively against Germany, the Jewish socialist politician Kurt Eisner mobilized antiwar protestors and then members of the army against the government, and in so doing managed to effectively force the abdication of King Ludwig III of Bavaria.[62] Ultimately, under Eisner's leadership, the Bavarian Soviet Republic (Bayerische Räterepublik) was declared a free state.

Otto Neurath had a doctorate in economic history and had received his habilitation in 1917. The son of the Jewish economist Wilhelm Neurath, Otto had begun to follow broadly in his father's footsteps after several intellectual detours. After teaching at Neue Wiener Handelsakademie (the New Vienna School of Business) and directing the Deutschen Kriegswirtschaftsmuseum (the German War Economy Museum), Otto Neurath was awarded a lectureship at the University of Heidelberg.[63] But in 1919, given a chance to pitch his economic ideas to an actual socialist government, Neurath traveled to a still-turbulent Munich to meet with Eisner and his political party. Eisner was tragically assassinated less than a month later by Anton Graf von Arco auf Valley, a self-loathing, right-wing anti-Semite who had been rejected from the occult Thule Society.[64] Nevertheless, that March, Neurath was appointed president of the Central Planning Office by Eisner's successor.[65]

Over the three months following Eisner's assassination, the Bavarian Soviet Republic went through three different governments and a number of internal clashes. In the end, German troops were sent into Munich and deposed the Soviet government after a brief conflict. The free state was abolished, and its leaders arrested or executed. Neurath was charged with treason and sentenced to eighteen months of confinement. (Interestingly, Max Weber appeared as a character witness for Neurath.) Once Neurath had served a brief period of imprisonment, the sentence was commuted to exile, and he was banned from Germany until 1926.[66] Though Neurath was able to return to his home in Vienna, his professorial career in Germany was over.

In the years that followed, Neurath continued his connection to Socialist movements, becoming general secretary of the socialist Forschungsinstitut für Gemeinwirtschaft (Research Institute for Social Economy).[67] Later, he would establish a museum project in relationship to Red Vienna in order to bring philosophy to the working class. Ironically, given the tenor of later critiques, Neurath was a key figure in the left-wing politics of his era. Positivists have often been criticized for being apolitical, but Neurath, at least, put his politics into practice in a way unmatched by any of the major thinkers in the Frankfurt School.

Antimetaphysics as Ideology Critique

Neurath made explicit the political motivations for the revolt against metaphysics in *Lebensgestaltung und Klassenkampf* (Lifestyle and class struggle,

1928). As a whole, the monograph is largely an attempt to emphasize that "Scientific attitude and solidarity go together."[68] Neurath's main argument is that science is a natural complement to the lifestyle of the proletariat; members of the working class are naturally grounded in a commonsense scientific outlook because they are interested in concrete and practical matters like working conditions, safety, access to safe food, and clean drinking water. In a similar fashion, he argued, they are also unencumbered by the intellectual traditions that govern the life of the bourgeois class.[69]

Crucially, Neurath argued that "it is precisely the proletariat that is the bearer of science without metaphysics."[70] This is not science as elite technocratic project, but commonsense, practical thought. In Neurath's hands, the broader aim of positivism was to liberate the working classes, and establish common cause among engineers, scientists, and union leaders. As he put it elsewhere, logical positivists "want to show people that what physicists and astronomers do is only on a grand scale what Charles and Jane are doing every day in the garden and the kitchen."[71] The Vienna Circle manifesto strikes a similar note when it remarks that "we have to fashion intellectual tools for everyday life, for the daily life of the scholar but also for the daily life of all those who in some way join in working at the conscious re-shaping of life."[72]

Neurath argued that it was the ruling classes' vested interest in maintaining the status quo that keeps metaphysics alive. Though members of these classes are often not themselves especially religious or patriotic, he suggested, the bourgeois promotes religious values and nationalisms as a way to keep the workers in line.[73] As he elaborated:

> Many men are religious so long as they feel themselves helplessly at the mercy of unknown social forces. . . . The stubborn fighter in the class struggle makes the ruling social order responsible for all this, the order which he sees protected above all by those groups that cultivate religiosity and belief in God or metaphysics.[74]

This passage begins with a fairly conventional Marxist critique of religion, but it ends with a reference to metaphysics. This is because Neurath thinks that one of the ways that the masses are suppressed is by use of metaphysical concepts and rhetoric (e.g., appeals to patriotism, the holy, or Being-as-such). Religious and "metaphysical" ideas impede the consolidation of an international working-class movement, because they become ways to fracture the movement—pitting, say, Turkish and German workers or Muslims and

Christians against each other instead of helping them find common ground in their shared humanity and labor conditions.[75] Class ideologues promote metaphysical ideas because it keeps the workers divided and the ruling class in power.

Class revolution, it would seem, requires overthrowing both theology and metaphysics. His antimetaphysics is Marxist, and Neurath said as much: "The cultivation of scientific, unmetaphysical thought, its application above all to social occurrences, is quite Marxist."[76] The critique of metaphysics therefore functions crucially as a critique of ideology. This is clear in the passage cited in the section epigraph, in which Neurath says, "Above all, the fight against metaphysics and theology means the destruction of bourgeois ideology."[77]

Nor were Neurath and Carnap alone in their socialist-informed antimetaphysics. Hans Hahn—the third coauthor of the Vienna Circle's manifesto— was also an outspoken socialist. While Hahn's specialty was mathematics, when his attention turned to philosophy, he also attempted to align the revolt against metaphysics with a class revolution. This is most explicit in *Überflüssige Wesenheiten, Occams Rasiermesser* (Superfluous entities, Occam's razor, 1930), which if anything suggests merciless disenchantment. In this work, Hahn granted the poetic beauty of a god-filled world, remarking:

> It may be that the world was very beautiful when a god or demon could be scented on every path; it may be that it was a very poetic time when all sorts of higher beings had to be constantly kept in a reasonably good mood by prayer and sacrifice, and all sorts of evil spirits had to be kept in check by magic spells.[78]

But Hahn expresses little public sympathy for this kind of poetic fancy (his private life will be discussed in the next section). In this essay, he turns the principle of Occam's Razor (do not multiply entities more than is necessary) into a political weapon, arguing that it can be used to separate practical this-worldly philosophies from impractical metaphysical ideologies. He argues:

> [It is] no accident that the land that saw the beheading of a king also witnessed the execution of metaphysics. For all those other-worldly entities of metaphysics—Plato's ideas, the Eleatics' One, Aristotle's pure form and first mover, the gods and demons of the religions, and the kings and princes of the earth—all share a common fate, and when the emperor falls the duke must follow suit.[79]

This looks like a kind of Jacobin impulse: Occam's Razor as the guillotine of the revolution. In Hahn's conceit, the logical positivist insurrection against metaphysics is intended to ax political and metaphysical tyranny, killing kings as well as gods.

In sum, the positivist emphasis on empiricism, verification, and the sciences was often aimed at undercutting bourgeois ideology, disabling the rhetoric of nationalism, and providing a common forum for the proletariat. Rather than wilting at the appearance of fascism, the Vienna Circle also condemned not only totalitarianism, but also totalitarian ideology. Neurath made this explicit in a later essay: "Logical Empiricism is fighting 'metaphysical idealism' along the whole line. It is just this set of phantasmagoria, allowing terrible means to lofty ends, which very often reduces the preparedness of people to object to the mercilessness of totalitarianism. Think of Plato's Republic, for example, where the Nazis found fine arguments for persecution."[80] Thus, it would seem that the inheritors of the totalitarian Enlightenment (in Adorno and Horkheimer's terms) were themselves working against totalitarianism. As Neurath emphasized, their project was "anti-totalitarian through and through," although this may represent a bit of overcompensation.[81]

All told, the political philosophy of the left wing of the Vienna Circle actually overlapped significantly with the Frankfurt School, and as such, it would not have been farfetched to imagine a Frankfurt-Vienna alliance against fascism and traditional philosophy. As contemporary scholar Hans-Joachim Dahms has demonstrated in *Positivismusstreit* (The positivism dispute, 1994), in 1936, Neurath actively sought out the Frankfurt School and tried to get the positivists and the critical theorists to join forces.[82] The Frankfurt School initially considered the idea. But ultimately, Horkheimer rejected Neurath's overtures and instead in 1937 wrote the scathing critique of positivism discussed above. Neurath attempted to make amends, but Horkheimer refused to print his rebuttal in the Frankfurt School's journal. Although this was not the final exchange between the two movements, it effectively foreclosed the possibility of real collaboration.

Nevertheless, having a handle on the Vienna Circle's politics will allow us to make sense of how and why positivists described their project in terms of magic and allied themselves with sorcerers. In fact, it was precisely because of Neurath's desire to forge an alliance between the "man in the street" and the "scientific expert" that he turned the narrative of disenchantment on its head.[83]

Positivist Magic

Gnosticism was not only characterized by realistic ideas pertaining to astrology and magic but was also full of ideas dealing with angel-like "emanations."

OTTO NEURATH, "Unified Science as Encyclopedic Integration," 1938

A particular passage in the Vienna Circle's manifesto will stand out to a reader attentive to the terminology of enchantment:

> The representatives of the scientific world-conception resolutely stand on the ground of simple human experience. They confidently approach the task of removing the metaphysical and theological debris of millennia. Or, as some have it: *returning, after a metaphysical interlude, to a unified picture of this world* free from theology, which had, in a sense, *been the basis of magical beliefs (Zauberglauben) in early times.*[84]

While the emphasis is mine, the passage is equating the scientific world-conception and magical beliefs, and locating both at the dawn of humanity. Given that "the scientific world-conception" was shorthand for the logical positivists' project, the manifesto suggestively allies magic and positivism against theology and metaphysics.

If this were the only place the Vienna Circle made such a gesture, it would be easy to ignore. But positivists often made versions of this argument. We see it, for example, in notes held by the Carnap archive in which Carnap contrasts metaphysics and magic, suggesting that that magic, while false, is cognitive, and so fundamental that even an animal might exhibit magical thinking.[85] Although the importance of magic was occasionally emphasized by Carnap and other members of the movement (e.g., Richard von Mises), the identification of magic as ordinary thinking was central to Neurath's project.[86]

This is a claim Neurath repeated in many places, but it is elaborated in a commentary on the Vienna Circle manifesto titled *Wege der wissenschaftlichen Weltauffassung* (Ways of the scientific world conception, 1930):

> Following Comte, many people think of the transformation of human thinking like this: it starts with a religious-theological period, followed by a metaphysical-philosophical period, until this is replaced by a scientific-positivist one. But there are reasons for a different notion of historical change, and this is relevant from the educational and psychological point of view. If basic elements of the scientific world-conception were already present in the springtime of

humanity (*Frühzeit des Menschen*), then we have a greater chance of being able to revitalize them.[87]

Neurath's reference to Auguste Comte's three stages (theology to philosophy to science) are not a surprise. But it comes with a significant modification: Neurath located positivist thought itself at the primal stage. His is implying that deep down, people are commonsensically scientific. Neurath's rationale for doing so is explicit: if the scientific world conception is inherent to primitive humanity, then it should be easier to revive. By making this connection, he was rejecting the notion that positivism is the alienation of human thought (reason), and suggesting instead that it is natural, or at least cognitively fundamental.

As can be seen above, Neurath had a vested interest in positioning positivism in "the springtime" of humanity. But he could have identified this proto-science with different cultural phenomena; for example, he could have suggested that religion (or mythology) had a rational core, or just directly referred to primitive science. Instead, as we know from the manifesto, he identified magic with primordial human thought, which is basically Frazer's position as well. This is no accident, as when Neurath continued, he described the early age when "religion [was] accompanied by a powerful magic (*Magie*) (see Frazer and others)," when "sorcerers (*Zauberer*) with their practices exerted immense influence."[88] Given the Marxist politics discussed above, this suggests that in order to embrace magic against metaphysics, Neurath was making common cause with the proletariat and the "primitive."

Though accompanied by religion, the springtime of humanity was the age of magic. It was the sorcerers who, like skilled technocrats, provided practical guidance for humanity until their place was usurped by the Godhead, with the priest as intermediary.[89] Although this essay locates magic and religion alongside each other, in *Empirische Soziologie: Der wissenschaftliche Gehalt der Geschichte und Nationalökonomie* (1931; *Empirical Sociology: The Scientific Content of History and National Economy*), Neurath reasserted that the original mode of thought is a magical mentality:

> Man of the magical form of life has no special mode of thinking (Lévy-Bruhl), we are of his flesh and blood (Frazer). In particular, pre-animistic magic, probably the oldest, is akin to our behavior. But animistic magic too is like modern behavior, directed toward finite, earthly ends. Of course the men of magical times expected more than we do from words and other evocative measures of a fairly simple kind, whereas we tend to expect effects to be carried out by complicated machines or by specifically set-up organisms.[90]

Restated, we share our basic cognitive processes with the humanity of the magical age. Neurath speculated—following Frazer—that pre-animistic magic is the oldest stage of human thought, but hedges his bets by suggesting that even animistic magic resembles modern thinking. When we moderns want something, we still try to command it into being; but unlike ancient humanity, who used magical phrases, we do it by getting machines or other living beings to do it for us. This is as though ordering a beer from the bartender were equivalent to asking a spirit to make it rain.

Returning to the *Wege* essay, Neurath dwelled on the relationship between magical and scientific thought in greater detail:

> Magic may seem alien to us at first glance; still, in a certain respect, it is closer to modern physics or biology than theological thinking. In general, the magician works finite changes, determined by tradition, which can be perceived and therefore checked by everybody. . . . In this respect *the modern physicist is close to the magician.*[91]

Again we can hear echoes of Frazer: magic is basically primitive science. But as a type of science, Neurath continued, "magic has to do with the finite, the empirical, just as the modern engineer or physician does. The magician is judged according to his effectiveness. If his sorcery is bad, his prophecies wrong, he is dismissed or even killed."[92] Hence the magician is basically a scientific empiricist (logical empiricism was the alternate name of the Vienna Circle) whose credibility relies on accurate prediction and the ability to effect changes in the world. Magic in this account is not irrational, but "one often deliberately presents magical action as being stranger than it is. If we formulate the recorded magical statements more precisely, we certainly encounter strange contents but also familiar relations: a definite observable event is seen as a condition for another."[93] To put this in blunt terms, magic is not weird. Neurath wanted his reader to recognize that magic is instrumentalist in the same way as modern technology. It works not via the miraculous or the supernatural, but by discovering underlying regularities.

Neurath provided a range of examples to illustrate the extent to which "the magical way of thinking is related to that of the modern scientific world-conception."[94] In many ways, he argues, magicians anticipate the conclusions of modern scientists, although often on faulty theoretical grounds:

> From the fact that we reject hypotheses and general statements of the magical views—assuming they are formulated—it does not follow at all that the con-

clusions that can be drawn from them are incorrect and that they can always be checked by crude experience. . . . Frequently it is the case that an individual magical statement, which can be acknowledged by modern science, was founded on a doctrine that we have to reject.[95]

Magicians often had accurate ideas about cause and effect, but failed to put them into a proper systematic framework. For example, the magician may have been right that touching corpses makes people sick, but they attributed the cause to evil spirits rather than bacteria. Moreover, there are some correlations that the magician got right, but which matter science is only beginning to understand or explain.[96]

Neurath was at pains to argue against the assumption that technology and magic are antithetical, referring to the conceptualized difference as largely a prejudice: "If an old woman casts spells on warts, we call it superstition; when university professors do the same thing, we speak of suggestion therapy and science."[97] Neurath wanted to remind the reader that it is a mistake to judge the superstitious nature of magic based on contemporary conceptions of science. As he argued in *Empirische Soziologie*, "What we regard as useless, we mostly call 'magic,' and what we approve we call 'science.'"[98] It might seem that the distinction between magic and science is mostly polemical.

Having run magic and science together, Neurath was compelled to articulate their differences, arguing that magic is just a less orderly form of empirical research, or the science minus the system.[99] Hence, as he argued, magical theories are especially elastic and in that sense harder to discredit.[100] He went on to suggest that this prevents disenchantment: "Usually [magic] never vanishes completely. Thus even today we still meet magic everywhere in our own cultural area. Often it goes directly into technology and science, without passing first through theology."[101] Perhaps contra Weber, whom Neurath knew and whose work he read, disenchantment is fundamentally incomplete. Magic lingers on to be potentially recouped by science and technology. Here we can see Neurath nearly extracting from Frazer what is actually Crowley's position, that magic and science are two sides of the same habit of thought, and that magic is the vanguard of science.

Neurath argued that the really alien thought mode is not magic, but the metaphysical or theological. His narrative, though, is of a theology that devours itself: "the conscious reasoning of Christian theology" had destroyed empirical magic, but in doing so it was also "reducing the power of priests."[102] His argument resembles a Weberian account of rationalization insofar as it is Protestantism that completes the rejection of magic, as theology's destruction "came to completion in Protestantism." But Neurath believed when Christianity in turn declined, enchantment came out of hiding: "The decrease of church power and the simultaneous advance of scientific empiricism" have brought back magic. Thus, he gave a re-enchanted account of the modern worldview:

> Thus it is perhaps understandable that at the beginning of modern times . . . witchcraft plays a larger role than before: the earthly causality of old magic re-emerges. . . . The revitalized sense for earthly things reveals itself to some extent in science, in connection with technology and rationalized action, as well as in sorcery.[103]

For Neurath, instead of science as the culmination of disenchanting Protestant thought, modernity is the return of sorcery. In effect, magic must reappear in order to challenge theology and empty metaphysics. Occult revivals and scientific revolutions would seem to come together.

In sum, Neurath was positioning positivism and its unified science as a return, and in that sense as a completion or fulfillment of primitive magic. As he put it elsewhere: "*Unified science is the substitute for magic* which also once encompassed the whole of life."[104] As seen in the section of the manifesto cited above, positivism is a recovery—or we might say, a higher-order synthesis—of magic. The rest of the chapter shows what other enchantments were appearing along with the positivist project. In so doing, it demonstrates that magic was more than a metaphor, and that far from being dedicated to de-animating the world, the Vienna Circle often explored the possibility of ghosts and haunting spirits.

POSITIVISTS IN PARANORMAL VIENNA: RUDOLF CARNAP AND HANS HAHN

> Many friends of [Hans Hahn's] and admirers of his intellect found this [paranormal] interest of his very odd and wondered how the topic of parapsychology could even be broached in a group as strictly scientific in its orientation as the Vienna Circle.
>
> KARL MENGER, introduction to *Empiricism, Logic, and Mathematics*, by Hans Hahn, 1980

Once upon a time, an eleven-year-old girl accompanied by an older cousin set out on foot through a large forest headed toward their grandmother's house in the town of Buhai (today in Pădureni, Romania). At some point along the route, Eleonora Zugun—for that was the girl's name—looked down and saw a small coin wrapped in a handkerchief.[105] Her cousin cautioned her that it was "devil's money" and told her to leave it alone. She ignored him and took the coin to buy sweets in town. When they arrived at her grandmother's house, Eleonora refused to share with anyone, eating the sweets against her cousin's protests. In the ensuing argument, the two made enough noise to disturb their grandmother's slumber.

The old woman was alleged to be 105 years old, and though blind, she had a reputation in the family—indeed, the whole village—for being a witch. She was not the kind of person anyone wanted to make angry. On being woken by the children fighting over the devil's sweets, the old lady was enraged. She cursed Eleonora, telling her that as she had eaten candies paid for with the devil's coin, the devil was now inside her.

In the days that followed, Eleonora became the center of a series of unusual events. Witnesses reported that they saw objects shudder and levitate in the girl's presence. Soon, Eleonora developed a bad reputation in the village; as the locals would later tell a visiting researcher, "The grandmother could not die because some evil spirits would not permit her, and thus she had sent for the child, in order, by means of witchcraft, to transfer them to her."[106] Presently Eleonora herself became convinced that she was suffering from demonic possession.

Eleonora's father and a group of concerned villagers took her to the house of an old priest. No sooner had they arrived than an iron vessel exploded into pieces. Jugs cracked, heavy objects began to shift around, and the windows suddenly shattered. The priest attempted an exorcism, but the phenomena continued. Fearing Eleonora was still cursed, her family deposited her at the monastery and convent of Gorovei (Mănăstirea Gorovei) in Talpa. Even there, she seemed to be at the mercy of invisible powers that smashed and moved things. The monks became frightened and wanted to expel Eleonora, but were prevented from doing so by the prior of the monastery.

This was no fairy tale, and it was at this point that Eleonora's story enters the historical record. Kubi Klein, a reporter for the Jewish German-language newspaper *Czernowitzer Allgemeine Zeitung*, came across Eleonora and published his account of her case on April 18, 1925, under the title "*Das verhexte Dorf*" (The bewitched village).[107] News about the cursed girl spread through the region. Soon journalists and paranormal investigators were all clamoring to study Eleonora in greater detail. Fearing the impact of this attention, her family committed to her to a mental asylum, where she was kept in isolation.

Fortunately, Eleanora came to the attention of the international parapsychology community, and she was rescued from the asylum and brought to

Vienna. There she met the famous mathematician and founding member of the Vienna Circle, Hans Hahn. Hahn was also part of an elite team of paranormal researchers that tested Eleanora's psychical powers, and he later testified to their authenticity.[108]

By way of biographical background, Hans Hahn was born in 1879 in Vienna. His father, Ludwig, a Jewish convert to Catholicism, was one of the highest-ranking governmental officials in the Austro-Hungarian Empire.[109] Hans completed a doctorate in mathematics at the University of Vienna in 1902. Hahn's published papers covered a range of issues in mathematics and philosophy, from set theory to philosophy of science, but he is today largely remembered for the Hahn–Banach theorem in functional analysis and for being the dissertation advisor to Kurt Gödel (whom we will encounter again below).[110] He was also one of the core members of the Vienna Circle and a significant influence on its basic orientation.[111] Indeed, along with Carnap and Neurath, Hahn was the third coauthor of the Vienna Circle manifesto.

As a socialist, positivist mathematician, Hans Hahn might seem to be the most unlikely of psychical investigators, let alone one who would ultimately argue for the reality of some paranormal phenomena. The rest of this section will explain what Hahn was doing investigating demonic possession and poltergeist activities, particularly given that this was not an exception, but a significant hobby that Hahn shared with other positivists.

*

In the nineteenth century, the Austro-Hungarian Empire was not without its mesmerists, magicians, spiritualists, and psychical researchers, but there was little in the way of formal paranormal investigation societies.[112] That is, until 1919, in the early days of the Austrian Republic, when the brothers Willi (1903–71) and Rudi (1908–57) Schneider developed a reputation in the small Austrian town of Braunau am Inn, where they impressed visitors with physical manifestations such as levitating, emitting a glowing fog, and moving objects from a distance.[113] The Schneiders ultimately attracted the attention of a noted psychical researcher, Baron Albert von Schrenck-Notzing (1862–1929). Schrenck-Notzing was trained as a medical doctor and had begun a career as a neurologist before encountering Carl du Prel (discussed in chapter seven) and shifting his attentions to psychical research.

Schrenck-Notzing brought the Schneider brothers to Munich for testing, and in 1921 and 1922 the brothers demonstrated their powers for a range of international visitors and occult investigators, including Ludwig Klages, Alfred Schuler, and the British ghost hunter Harry Price.[114] One of the most famous participants in these experiments was the novelist Thomas Mann, who published a short monograph testifying to the reality of Willi's telekinetic phenomena, while suggesting that the spirit was a product of the medium's unconscious.[115]

Against this backdrop, Rudi Schneider was invited to Vienna to demonstrate his powers in a series of high-profile séances. A pair of physicists— Stefan Meyer, director of the Institute for Radium Research, and his assistant Karl Przibram—attended several of these sessions in early 1924. Likely they were drawn there because of speculation at the time that telekinesis might be produced by some hitherto undiscovered form of radiation. According to Meyer and Przibram's later account, they witnessed Rudi levitating objects into the air, but became convinced that it was the result of some kind of trickery. They concluded that Rudi must have been somehow slipping his hands or his feet out of the restraints and then surreptitiously moving things about.

Unable to catch Rudi in the act of cheating, Meyer and Przibram decided to see if they could produce similar effects. They invited a group of their colleagues to Meyer's apartment for a spiritualist séance where Przibram played the role of the medium. Meyer and Przibram claimed they were able to fool the audience and convincingly reproduce all the levitations and other materializations made famous by the Schneider brothers. They concluded that Rudi was a fake and gave interviews to Viennese newspapers attesting to that effect.[116]

Not everyone was convinced. Karl Menger (1902–85), Hans Hahn's graduate student and one of the younger members of the Vienna Circle, later recounted that a number of those in attendance were not fooled into thinking physicists had psychical powers so much as amused that "the tall Professor Przibram" had under cover of darkness "managed to cover himself with a bed sheet and to climb on a chair."[117] As amusing as this might have been, to Menger's peers it seemed to be far from a convincing reproduction of a spiritualist séance, much less proof that Rudi Schneider was a fraud. Moreover, on scientific grounds, even if Meyer and Przibram had been able to replicate the visual effects of levitation, it far from disproved the counterhypothesis that psychical powers were real. Indeed, a number of Viennese scientists concluded instead that paranormal phenomena needed real research, not silly pranks.

Ultimately, the controversy around the Schneider brothers led toward the formation of a paranormal investigation society drawn from the upper ranks of the Austrian scientific establishment. This group included the Nobel Prize-winning physiologist Julius Wagner-Jauregg; the pioneering theoretical physicist and professor at the University of Vienna Hans Thirring; and two influential positivists, Moritz Schlick and Hans Hahn.[118] As Menger recalled, they were "not convinced that any of the phenomena produced by the mediums were genuine; but they were even less sure that all of them were not. They believed, rather, that some parapsychological claims might well be justified."[119]

In 1927, Thirring and Hahn joined forces with two members of the peerage—the parapsychologist and astrologer Zoë, Countess Wassilko von Serecki, and the psychoanalyst Alfred, Baron von Winterstein—and together they formed the nucleus around which the Austrian Society for Psychical Research (Österreichische Gesellschaft für Psychische Forschung, ASPR) was constituted. Thirring was its first president. Although it eventually came to include more researchers and paranormal aficionados from across Austria, the ASPR did not merely rubber-stamp spirit mediums, but mixed exposing frauds with discoveries that they thought provided evidence for real paranormal phenomena.[120] In a letter Thirring wrote to Max Eissler in 1964 (currently in the archives of the University of Vienna), Thirring provided both an account of the impetus for the society's formation and a list of its founders, noting that Hans Hahn was a core member of the executive board.[121]

The investigation of Eleonora Zugun was one of their first cases, and when she was brought to Vienna, Eleonora was housed with Countess Wassilko.[122] The paranormal phenomena persisted, and worse, Eleonora began to experience a new symptom, the appearance of spontaneous abrasions on her skin resembling scratches or bite marks. Eleonora claimed that these were caused by an invisible devil (*Dracu*) that also communicated with her via automatic writing.[123]

Wassilko thought the culprit was likely Eleonora's unconscious and not the devil, but she exhaustively documented her experiences with the girl and became convinced that real paranormal phenomena were taking place. Wassilko suggested, for example, that the movement of objects was a kind of telekinesis, produced by what appeared to a "hole in the world," which she proposed might indicate that Eleonora was somehow causing objects to pass in and out of "hyperspace."[124] As farfetched as this might sound, the countess was thorough in her investigations; she brought Eleonora to be examined in clinical settings in Austria, Germany, and England by a range of authorities. Eleonora went on to become a famous medium (a silent film of her from 1927 can even be seen on YouTube today[125]). Wassilko published her colleagues' observations of the poltergeist alongside her own; in turn, Hahn went on the record to confirm the countess's observations.[126] This was not the last case they would take on together.

*

Given that paranormal research crossed over into the social sphere of the Vienna Circle, it should come as no surprise that several positivists were involved in psychical research, and the subject makes a frequent appearance in their lectures and published writings. The next few pages will provide some more examples of how this issue informed their thinking.

While Moritz Schlick never wrote about his involvement in psychical research, Hans Hahn made little secret of his interest in the paranormal. Indeed, according to his former students, Hahn often brought the subject up in lectures and argued that "in many cases one is dealing with a *genuine* phenomenon *of some kind*."[127] Hahn was also intrigued by the possibility that extrasensory perception (ESP) might be a real phenomena.[128] He continued to take part in séances and even encouraged his graduate students to participate in paranormal research with him.[129] Karl Menger recounted one occasion on which Hahn asked him to report on a séance he was unable to attend: the investigation of a female medium from Graz (perhaps Frieda Weissl). Although the details of the session are not relevant to our current concerns, Menger recounted her ability to produce a strange, inexplicable knocking and noted that his failure to explain it made him uncomfortable.[130]

Another positivist who was interested in the paranormal was Schlick's student, the junior Vienna Circle member Herbert Feigl, who today is remembered for his contributions to the analysis of probability and to the mind-body problem. In "Physicalism, Unity of Science and the Foundations of Psychology" (1963), Feigl articulated his version of verification theory, and in it he tellingly used the example of someone who claimed "telepathic or clairvoyant intuition of distant events which are inaccessible to him through the normal channels of sense perception."[131] As Feigl argued, we would be inclined to take a clairvoyant's statements as validated only if they were confirmed via normal perceptual channels.

This might seem like an incidental example except for the fact that the paranormal crops up later in the same essay, when Feigl acknowledged:

> I am inclined to think that the scientific attitude should be very different (and perhaps will be very different in the near future) with respect to the phenomena of parapsychology. If it were fully established that the phenomena of extrasensory perception, i.e., clairvoyance and telepathy, and perhaps even precognition and psychokinesis, do not result from experimental or statistical errors . . .

then our conception of the basic laws of nature may well have to be revised at least in some essential aspects.[132]

This paragraph gives us a clue as to why the positivists might have been particularly interested in the paranormal. It was not just to catch frauds, but rather came from the realization that if even one parapsychological case were to be proved real, it would force a revision of the scientific understanding of the laws of nature. Here we might be reminded of the William James, who justified his own psychical research by remarking: "If you wish to upset the law that all crows are black, you mustn't seek to show that no crows are; it is enough if you prove one single crow to be white."[133]

The Austrian-Jewish mathematician Richard von Mises was an additional member of the Vienna Circle with a connection to the paranormal. Von Mises frequently referred to paranormal phenomena in his writings, and justified his interest by noting: "I do not want to defend the occult sciences; I am, however, convinced that further unbiased investigation of these phenomena by collection and evaluation of old and new evidence, in the usual scientific manner, will lead us sooner or later to the discovery of new and important relations of which we have as yet no knowledge."[134] As this quote illustrates, von Mises, who after fleeing the Nazis became a professor of mathematics at Harvard, used his position to advocate on behalf of further research into the occult sciences. Similarly, in 1949, von Mises also addressed the American Association for the Advancement of Science on the subject of extrasensory perception, about whose existence he was cautiously optimistic, but believed required more rigorous research.[135]

One of Hahn's graduate students developed a significant affinity for paranormal research: Kurt Gödel, the Austrian mathematician and logician, who is famous today for the incompleteness theorem that bears his name. Gödel did not attend all the meetings of the Vienna Circle, but he was listed in the manifesto as one of its members. As a baptized Lutheran who still identified as a theist, Gödel was a bit of an outlier in the group.[136] Nevertheless, he shared an interest in the occult. According to his friend Georg Kreisel, ghosts and demons fascinated Gödel, and his notebooks were full of research into demonology.[137] Another friend, Oskar Morgenstern, recorded in his diary in 1940 his own surprise at Gödel's belief in "ghosts."[138] Moreover, by the time of his death, Gödel's personal library was filled with books on theosophy, spiritualism, and similar subjects.[139] Although I was not able to access the Gödel archives, contemporary scholar John Dawson states that Gödel once wrote a letter to his mother suggesting that the problem with the occult was to "disentangle genuine phenomena" from the fraudulent.[140] Dawson also asserts that Gödel's letters reference his belief in precognition and telepathy.[141] Finally, Dawson claims to have found Gödel's record of his attendance at a spiritualist séance among his papers.[142]

In sum, we can at least add Gödel to our list of positivists interested in the paranormal alongside Hahn, Schlick, von Mises, and Feigl. The last major positivist I want to connect to psychical research is Carnap himself.

*

There is a phase of Carnap's life generally omitted from shorthand biographies of the philosopher—namely, his participation in a quasi-pagan branch of the German Youth Movement (*Jugendbewegung*).[143] In general, the Youth Movement—a distant cousin of the American Boy Scouts—was a bourgeois back-to-nature movement associated with folk festivals and hiking. Carnap's particular branch of the Youth Movement was a group called the Sera Circle (*Serakreis*), led by the publisher Eugen Diederichs. Although today the publishing company Diederichs founded is an imprint of Random House, at the time it was an important outlet for works about German mysticism and Eastern religions. Diederichs was also an avid devotee of Nietzsche, and he saw the Youth Movement producing a new culture for the Nietzschean Übermensch.[144] Under Diederichs's leadership, the Sera Circle engaged in pagan celebrations that included traditional costumes, dancing, leaping over bonfires, and ritual hymns.[145]

Participating in this movement was a formative experience for Carnap. In an early draft of his autobiography, Carnap wrote about the Sera Circle; although he ultimately decided to expunge it from the text, it is still available at the Carnap archive. In the excised pages, Carnap remarked: "The spirit that lived in this movement, which was like a religion without dogmas, remained a precious inheritance."[146] It seems Carnap situated his personal spirituality in the Sera Circle's poetic neo-paganism, and as he elaborated, "I often felt as perhaps a man might feel who has lived in a strongly religious inspired community and then suddenly finds himself isolated in the Diaspora and feels himself not strong enough to convert the heathen."[147] Although famous as an atheist, Carnap nevertheless held to a kind of secularized paganism of his youth to such an extent that he felt it marked him out like a member of a diasporic faith.

Perhaps it was this background that initially drew Carnap to the occult and then the paranormal. In a May 11, 1926, entry in Carnap's unpublished diary, he mentioned discussing "occultism" with Thirring and Hahn.[148] In his intellectual autobiography, Carnap remarked that this interest in the paranormal was one of the things that set him and Hahn apart from Neurath, who (as discussed above) described positivism in terms of magic. As Carnap remembered:

> [Neurath] reproached Hahn because he was not only theoretically interested, as I was, in parapsychological investigations, but took active part in séances. . . . Neurath pointed out that such séances served chiefly to strengthen supernaturalism and thereby to weaken political progress. We in turn defended the right to examine objectively and scientifically all processes or alleged processes without regard for the question of whether other people use or misuse the results.[149]

This was not the only person who had issues with Carnap's investigation of the paranormal. According to another of Schlick's graduate students, Heinrich Neider, it was Carnap's interest in the paranormal that caused his falling-out with the world-famous Austrian philosopher Ludwig Wittgenstein. As Neider remembered: "Wittgenstein and Carnap had just engaged in a very lively discussion, and Carnap stepped out to make some tea. When Carnap returned he found Wittgenstein stomping about visibly angry, saying: 'Why do you have this rubbish?' Carnap: 'That is the Schrenck-Notzing.' Wittgenstein: 'This is the kind of book you have in your library? Do you think I would associate with a person who has such books in his library?' He departed quickly and was never seen [around those parts] again."[150] We also have Carnap's version of events from his autobiography:

> Another time we touched the topic of parapsychology, and [Wittgenstein] expressed himself strongly against it. The alleged messages produced in spiritualistic séances, he said, were extremely trivial and silly. I agreed with this, but I remarked that nevertheless the question of the existence and explanation of the alleged parapsychological phenomena was an important scientific problem. He was shocked that any reasonable man could have any interest in such rubbish.[151]

This basically accords with Neider's account, but for Carnap the rejection went both ways. There was something about Wittgenstein that bothered him.

Earlier, when we were reading Wittgenstein's book in the Circle, I had erroneously believed that his attitude toward metaphysics was similar to ours. I had not paid sufficient attention to the statements in his book about the mystical, because his feelings and thoughts in this area were too divergent from mine.[152]

It would appear that Wittgenstein dismissed Carnap as a spiritualist while Carnap rejected Wittgenstein for being a mystic. This is another example of the interchange of enchantments I have already discussed, in which one paranormal belief comes at the expense of others.

For the record, Carnap was not the only one who saw Wittgenstein as a mystic. Bertrand Russell remarked in a 1919 letter that Wittgenstein "has penetrated deep into mystical ways of thought."[153] Russell also described Wittgenstein as a mystic in the obituary he wrote for his former pupil roughly thirty-years later.[154] But this should come as no surprise, as in the *Tractatus Logico-philosophicus*, Wittgenstein frequently referred to the mystical, remarking, for example, that "there are, indeed, things that cannot be put into words. They *make themselves manifest*. They are what is mystical."[155]

The falling-out between Carnap and Wittgenstein is emblematic of many of the conflicts we have seen throughout the book, as each fails to respect the other's interest in the esoteric. This curious doubling in many ways parallels the relationship between the Vienna Circle and the Frankfurt School, whose antagonisms might appear to be proximate animosity rather than distant antagonism. On simple demographic grounds, most members of both the Frankfurt School and the Vienna Circle were left-leaning, German-speaking Jews.[156] Hence what later generations have been brought up thinking was an epochal conflict between diametrically opposed positivism and critical theory looks more like one of the left's endless internal conflicts.

Although the positivist dispute in German sociology is often remembered as a clash between the Frankfurt School and Vienna positivism (with Popper standing in the for the positivists), Ralf Dahrendorf has observed that nobody in this debate would admit to being positivists; indeed, both sides claimed to be overcoming positivism. This led Dahrendorf to suggest that positivism was a spectral "third-man" that all sides attacked in absentia.[157] Anthony Giddens goes a step further, describing the debate as being "like Hamlet without a prince."[158] This would seem to suggest a haunting by a specter of positivist hegemony that never existed or perhaps was rendered hegemonic only through sheer absence.

CONCLUSION: THE MAGIC OF DISENCHANTMENT

I now believe that it would be right to begin my book with remarks about metaphysics as a kind of magic (*Magie*). But in doing this I must not make a case for magic, nor may I make fun of it. The depth of magic should be preserved. Indeed, here the elimination of magic has itself the character of magic.

LUDWIG WITTGENSTEIN, "Bemerkungen über Frazers *Golden Bough*," 1931

In this chapter, I have been arguing against the popular criticisms of the logical positivists, repeated today by both sides of the continental philosophical divide. It turns out that the positivist project is more complicated than many of us would have thought. One can find in the left wing of the Vienna Circle Marxist-inflected political theory, ideological critique, phenomenology, and even ethics.[159] Likewise, one can find an openness to the possibility of spirits and magical knowledge that is hard to square with the way the group has been traditionally portrayed.

This chapter has also been aiming to demonstrate what Wittgenstein observed in his private notes on Frazer's *Golden Bough*, that "the elimination of magic has itself the character of magic."[160] To put this insight into my own terms, disenchantment taken to its extreme is hard to distinguish from enchantment. Neurath attempted to suggest that magic and positivism share a common core, while Carnap and Hahn took spirits and the paranormal seriously enough to investigate them—perhaps working to dispel them, but perhaps being spellbound all the same. At the very least, this all complicates the placement of positivism and mechanism on one side of a divide, and contemporary vitalism or neo-Spinozism on the other.

In sum, the Vienna Circle of positivists, despite their subsequent reputation, were profoundly entranced by the paranormal. To be clear, I am not arguing that this interest was irrational. Instead, I have been trying to put pressure on the presumed boundaries between rational and irrational, science and magic. Moreover, one could also argue that "psychical research" is itself disenchanting, but I tend to see it as a bimodal concept like the *philosophes'* notion of natural magic: both disenchanting and enchanting in different registers. The positivists certainly did both. As I have shown, some logical positivists had a political commitment to magic. Let this sink in for a second, because positivists are not generally supposed to have much of a political project, much less magic. All told, the positivists' project might seem to be crystalized disenchantment, but they were haunted by magic and the ghosts of the very metaphysics they were working to exclude.

CHAPTER TEN

The World of Enchantment;
or, Max Weber at the End of History

> While numberless societies, associations, orders, groups, etc., have been founded
> during the last thirty years in all parts of the civilized world, all following some line of
> occult study, yet there is but ONE ancient organization of genuine Mystics. . . . The
> Hermetic Brotherhood of Light. It is a Modern School of Magic.
>
> THEODOR REUSS, *Ordo Templi Orientis Constitution*, revised edition, 1917

In August 1917, Theosophists, Freemasons, mystics, and magicians from all
over Europe made their way to the Monte Verità commune in Ascona, Switzerland, the headquarters of the Hermetic Brotherhood of Light (also known
as the Ordo Templi Orientis).[1] They had been summoned by the order's
leader, the Anglo-German opera singer turned sex magician Theodor Reuß
(1855–1923), who had organized a ten-day antinationalist occult congress of
like-minded fellow travelers—one that aimed to heal the ravages of war by
reaffirming a spiritual community that knew no national distinctions.[2] This
well-attended conference included lectures on theosophy and magic, Masonic
rituals, performance art, readings of Aleister Crowley's mystical poetry, and
even a Gnostic mass.[3]

Max Weber (1864–1920) might seem to have lived in a totally different
world. After all, the pioneering sociologist is famous for his pronouncement:
"The fate of our times is characterized by rationalization and intellectualization and, above all, by the *'disenchantment of the world.'*"[4] That Weber uttered
this statement on November 7, 1917, less than three months after the occult
congress, might imply a deep fissure between academic and magical milieus.

Weber, however, was no stranger to Monte Verità. He knew Ascona well.
Indeed, he likely came to his famous concept of disenchantment while vaca-
tioning at the neo-pagan commune and after socializing with some of Reuß's
fellow occultists. Weber was at the apex of many of the trends discussed thus
far in the monograph; he socialized with Kosmikers and was drawn to Christian mysticism. Hence, the contemporary mytheme of alienation from magic—

"the disenchantment of the world"—was likely born of an excess of enchantment, not of its absence. The business of this chapter is to make sense of this connection.

*

Weber is generally recognized as one of the master theorists of modernity. Even so, there are remarkably diverse interpretations of the central problematic of his project. Was Weber primarily a sober-minded comparative sociologist aiming to put the human sciences on a sounder footing?[5] Was he first and foremost a pragmatic political theorist trying to solve the problems of democracy and liberalism in modernizing Germany?[6] Or was he principally a historian of capitalism, mapping its affective registers and social resonances?[7] Was he basically an apologist for nationalism and empire?[8] Or was he a quasi-outsider intellectual in the model of Nietzsche, Kafka, or Foucault, focused on diagnosing the disorders of Western modernity?[9] Was Weber predominantly a Protestant thinker grappling with the implications of modernization for his faith?[10] Or was he an abstract philosopher of history, aiming to discover the meaning of rationality and rationalization?[11] This list is not exhaustive, and given the multiplicity of readings, it might seem that Weber's unfinished and often fragmentary corpus is a Rorschach test designed to reflect the reader's own presuppositions.

In this chapter, I wade into the thorny world of Weberian scholarship to make a pair of targeted interventions. First, I problematize popular misreadings of Weber, and locate "the disenchantment of the world" in the multiple forms of rationality that make up his implicit system. Having complicated the picture of magic and its relationship to his broader theory of rationalization, the open question then involves both the history of disenchantment and the inevitability of its trajectory. Did Weber envision himself as standing at the end of history? Did he see re-enchantment as a possibility?

The second part of the chapter will answer these questions by exploring how Weber came to the myth of disenchantment in the middle of an occult revival and what it means that he did so. It will also attempt to make sense of his complex, and perhaps ambivalent, relationship to mysticism.

THE DISENCHANTMENT OF THE WORLD

The complete disenchantment of the world has only been carried out to its full conclusion [in Puritanism]. But that did not mean freedom from what we are today accustomed to call "superstition." Witch trials also flourished in New England. . . . [The Puritans] came to believe all magic to be diabolical.

MAX WEBER, *Die Wirtschaftsethik der Weltreligionen*, 1916

Magic, for example, has been just as systematically "rationalized" as physics.

MAX WEBER, *Der Sinn der "Wertfreiheit,"* 1917

If you come to the "disenchantment of the world" with the presuppositions of most contemporary theorists, the quotes above are going to bother you. The problem is that for many nonspecialists, disenchantment is understood either as a poetical synonym for secularization or modern rationalization; even most Weber scholars take the phrase at face value (*Die Entzauberung der Welt* means literally "the de-magic-ing of the world") and assume that a disenchanted world has absolutely no magic in it. The quotes above begin to put pressure on these views, because it would seem that disenchantment culminates not in the end of religion, but rather *within* Protestantism (even if it will later come to capture religion in turn). Disenchantment also persists alongside belief in magic. Witchcraft has been condemned but not eliminated. Moreover, those used to seeing rationality and enchantment as opposites will have trouble reckoning with how magic can itself be rationalized.

The pages that follow will aim to clarify misunderstandings by rereading Weberian disenchantment in the context of his notions of magic and rationalization. But first there is another minor confusion I must address. Both specialists and nonspecialists often assert that the expression "the disenchantment of the world" came to Weber from Friedrich Schiller.[12] Weber did indeed read Schiller.[13] Weber also refers to a "godless mechanism of the world" (*entgotteten Mechanismus der Welt*), which is likely an allusion to Schiller's "de-deified nature."[14] Thus, one can see Weber as a broad inheritor of Schiller's original lament. But *"Die Entzauberung der Welt"* is not one of Schiller's phrases. Neither was Weber the first to use the phrase. It first occurs in 1837 in the writings of the neo-Kantian philosopher Jakob Friedrich Fries. Fries suggestively uses *Entzauberung dieser Welt* (disenchantment of this world) in a discussion of Balthasar Bekker, *De Betoverde Weereld* (The bewitched world, 1691). Bekker's title is rendered in German as *Bezauberte Welt* (literally "enchanted world"), and Fries uses disenchantment to describe Bekker's repudiation of ghosts and witches.[15] But while the influence of neo-Kantian thought on Weber is well known, there is no evidence that he read this particular work.[16] Hence, while Weber was the lineage of the Schiller's notion of de-divination, Weber's disenchantment is doing a different kind of work.

*

Disenchantment is often mistakenly identified with rationalization as a whole. Nonetheless, Weber's writings suggest that while disenchantment and rationalization are related, they are not in fact identical.[17] Our first step is to clarify their relationship. The root of the problem is that for Weber, rationalization was a multifaceted process: he once remarked that he aspired to "bring out the complexity (*Vielseitigkeit*) of the only superficially simple concept of the 'rational.'"[18] Weber was particularly interested in disaggregating rationality and exploring the quite different modes of thought and action that go under that broad heading. Accordingly, he described multiple types of rationality, operating in diverse value spheres, according to different cultural logics and over the course of multiple historical phases. Although he left some intimations of what he had in mind, he died before he could complete the work of systematically relating these components together.

Later scholars have proposed radically divergent readings of Weber's system of rationalization, suggesting everything from sixteen versions of rationality to arguing that Weber essentially thought rationalization could mean anything.[19] For our purposes, I adapt the schema put forward by Stephan Kalberg, which, while incomplete, has the advantage that it convincingly extrapolates Weber's typology of social action into a plausible larger system of rationality.[20] Kalberg divides Weber's conception of social action into four ideal types of rationality and two ideal types of irrationality.[21] I will largely adapt Kalberg's broad reconstruction, but not his terminology (see note 23). I parse Weber's notion of social orientations into instrumental, value, theoretical, and formalized rationality, versus habitual and affectual irrationality.

Weber defined *instrumental rationality* (*Zweckrationalität*) in the following: "Action is instrumentally rational (*zweckrational*) when the end, the means, and the secondary results are all rationally taken into account and weighed."[22] Although not identical with current rational choice theory, this is basically practical ends-means rationality. Weber's second type of rational orientation is what he referred to as *value rationality* (*Wertrationalität*), or rationality vis-à-vis a particular value or conviction. He stated that the example "of pure value-rational orientation would be the actions of persons who, regardless of possible cost to themselves, act to put into practice their convictions."[23] This is the kind of rational orientation we might associate with religious or political convictions.

Theoretical rationality (generally referred to as "intellectual rationality" or "intellectualization") describes a type of rationality directed toward "increasing theoretical mastery of reality by means of increasingly precise and abstract concepts."[24] Theoretical rationality is rooted in a "natural rationalistic need to conceive of the world as a meaningful cosmos."[25] Accordingly, Weber described this type of rationality as originating within religion.[26] The core of the difference between theoretical and instrumental rationality is that theoretical rationality is rooted in an intellectualization process that aims toward increasing abstraction, while instrumental rationality is based in pragmatic decision-making.

Weber also described the institutionalization of various forms of rationality and their incarnation in courts, markets, and other bureaucratic organizations. Although Weber did not have a master category for institutional rationality as such, we will employ *formalized rationality* to refer to this general type, which he suggested shared a common attempt to determine action based on previous procedures and precedents.[27] In his discussion of law courts and economic markets, Weber specified two subtypes of institutionalized rationality (or originally rationally oriented actions): *formal* (*formale*) and *substantive* (*materiale*) rationality.[28] Formal rationality is a "quantitative calculation" in terms of profit, which when institutionalized leads toward greater uniformity and exchangeability. Substantive rationality is an institutionalized incentive toward a particular value criteria, and in that respect it is an institutionalized form of value rationality.[29] One might think of substantive rationality as the codification of norms that have taken on a logic of their own.

In general, Weber associated formalized rationality with the empty formalism of ritual (perhaps echoing older anti-Catholic or anti-Jewish rhetoric), but he also connects it to the calculating thinking of modern bureaucracies and markets. Basically, a bureaucrat acts not according to what is morally right or pragmatically good, but according to the rulebook or the norm of the institution. Modern economic markets are similar in Weber's account because they are based on formalized procures and, as within big bureaucracies, the individual is insignificant.

Weber argued that forms of rationality can come into conflict. A particular course of action might be irrational on instrumentalist grounds, but might be perfectly rational from the perspective of an actor's value orientation. For example, it might make sense to lie down in front of a military tank based on your convictions, even if it might cost you your life.

Alongside these types of rationality, Weber also referred to two different forms of irrationally directed actions. He described *habitual irrationality* as when an "almost automatic reaction to habitual stimuli guide[s] behavior in a course which has been repeatedly followed," and he noted it slides over into various forms of rationality to the degree that it becomes self-reflexive.[30] Moreover, formalized rationality comes closest to habitual irrationality the less reflexive it becomes. Finally, Weber mentioned in passing a second type of *affectual* (*affektuell*) *irrationality* that refers to emotional reactions that are not themselves rooted in a conscious or rational decision.[31] Here he is deploying an old opposition between emotion and reason that we might dispute today.

Additionally, Weber's writings suggest some undergirding notions about rationalization in general. He described the rationalization of six different value spheres—religious, economic, political, aesthetic, erotic, intellectual—in terms of their coming increasingly into accord with their own particular ultimate values, means, and ends.[32] As a general pattern, rationalization has led toward value spheres becoming increasingly autonomous and therefore fragmented. He also suggested that different disciplines, professions, and so on can be rationalized according to their own internal logics.[33] Further, Weber's use of rationalization suggested that it is in general a trend toward standardization, consistency, and decreased complexity (or decreased entropy).[34] Moreover, Weber implied that all forms of rationality tend to absorb irrationality, in that respect liquidating habit, tradition, and emotion into rationalized (or we might say, repressed) norms of behavior.

Finally, Weber sometimes described the rationalization of whole cultures, famously asking: "Why did not the scientific, the artistic, the political, or the economic development [in China] enter upon that path of rationalization which is peculiar to the Occident?"[35] We'll discuss the specifically Occidental-modern trajectory of rationalization below, but our primary question becomes, how do magic and disenchantment fit into this schema?

*

For a variety of reasons, specialists and nonspecialists alike have had difficulty getting a handle on Weber's conception of disenchantment. Part of the issue is that they have often taken as given an anachronistic opposition between rationality and magic. Although there are some exceptions, as recently as 2014, even leading Weber scholars like Peter Ghosh could argue that

> for Weber, by contrast, the defining feature of "magic" (if such a thing existed at all) was that it formed a conceptual antithesis to rational conduct. . . . We-

ber had no developed idea of magic as such, except as the miscellany of non-rational behaviour.[36]

This is far from the only thinker who has treated Weber's conception of magic in these terms. Much of the discourse around the disenchantment of the world assumes an opposition between rationalization and magic. Even Stephen Kalberg, whose typology of Weberian rationality has set the gold standard, has suggested that Weber saw severing "the bonds of primitive magic" as key to the growth of instrumental rationality.[37]

Nevertheless, the contemporary German sociologist Stefan Breuer has demonstrated that magic was not a major category for Weber until late in his intellectual career.[38] References to magic in the first edition of the *Protestant Ethic* (1904/05) are scant, and it is not until Weber turned his attention to researching Asian religions shortly before the First World War that he became seriously interested in theorizing enchantment. Moreover, as Johannes Winckelmann has observed, Weber began using "disenchantment" as an interpretive category for the first time in 1913.[39] Taken together, this means that Weber's interest in enchantment and disenchantment roughly coincided. Moreover, the timing is important because it broadly overlaps with Weber's visits to the Monte Verità commune. Hence, before we turn to the disenchantment of the world, we need to understand Monte Verità.

*

Max Weber spent two significant periods (1913 and 1914) with the Mountain of Truth (Monte Verità) community in Ascona, Switzerland. The Mountain of Truth was an early prototype for a hippie commune, full of nature people (*Naturmenschen*), and complete with nudity, free love, and vegetarianism. It also billed itself as a "nature cure." In contemporary terms, we might call it a holistic spa. It was organized around two charismatic figures, the radical psychoanalyst Otto Gross and the poet and nature prophet Gusto Gräser. According to one account, "Ascona itself was always full of people experimenting with everything between palm reading and tea-leaf reading to spells and séances and Ouija boards."[40] Moreover, Gräser was drawn to Asian religions (in particular, Taoism), and other members of the community were practicing theosophists who focused their attention on India. Thus, this group may have inspired Max Weber's own attitude toward Eastern religions. Weber spent two springs there looking for relaxation and an improvement in his health. From his letters, we know that Weber was not fully taken in by the community, but he also respected its idealistic spirit and became friends with various community members, including Countess Franziska zu Reventlow.[41]

Crucially for our purposes, in a letter dating April 4, 1913, Weber told his wife, Marianne, that he had just finished Reventlow's new novel, which he praised as "well-written."[42] What is important is not his literary taste, but that he had just read *Herrn Dames Aufzeichnungen* (Notes of Mr. Lady, 1913), which if you'll remember was an exposé of Ludwig Klages and the neo-pagan Munich Cosmic Circle (discussed in chapter 8). Strikingly, *Herrn Dames* often referred to the Kosmikers' belief in magic, even going so far as to give their philosophical account of enchantment; specifically, that when "one's essence is completely permeated by the primordial cosmic substance . . . then one is made just as powerful and those who are all-powerful can work magic (*zaubern*)"; it also recounted the Kosmikers' version of disenchantment—namely, that Protestant anti-paganism and "the light of reason" had extinguished the maternal "blood-light" (*Blutleuchte*) of magic.[43]

Weber recognized *Herrn Dames* a thinly veiled roman à clef depicting real people in the Schwabing district of Munich, some of whom he knew (such as Stefan George, discussed below).[44] This is significant because it would have suggested to the sociologist that some contemporary Germans continued to believe in magic, and yet saw it challenged by the rationalization of modernity. Indeed, Weber began writing about disenchantment at the end of that year, and this novelistic depiction of occult Munich was likely an influence.

Although it is unclear if Weber and Klages were acquainted by 1913, Weber began reading Klages's works sometime in that period as well. It is possible that Max came to know about Klages through his brother Alfred Weber, because in 1913 Alfred and Klages were both involved in the Free German Youth movement.[45] But Max and Klages had many friends in common.[46] Later Weber even had his handwriting analyzed by Klages, whose readings he thought were accurate.[47] Above all, they read each other's work. As noted in a previous chapter, the Neo-Pagan philosopher adopted Weber's "disenchantment of the world." But the conversation went both ways; Weber cited Klages on several occasions.[48] Weber observed, for example, that Klages's writings contained "very good remarks" on "the peculiar contraction and repression of natural life-impulses" brought about by rationalization.[49]

All told, Monte Verità seems to have left a strong impression on Weber. Returning to the community on April 9, 1914, Weber remarked in a letter to Marianne:

Now it is time to return 'home' [to Ascona], if one can refer so to this world full of enchantresses, charm, peril, and the yearning for happiness (*Glücks-begier*) . . . I must say: between this beautiful but in that sense "human" world based on *superficial* sensations, [Ascona] was a sort of *oasis* of purity.[50]

Here Weber is using "enchantresses" (*Zauberweiber*) to talk about Ascona in words that hint at the inversion of his famous "disenchantment" (*Entzau-berung*). Perhaps having been confronted with a community that had turned its back on the iron cage of modernity to take refuge in enchantment and mysticism, Weber was struck by it as in some ways a viable alternative. Moreover, it may have been this group Weber was discussing in the "Science as Vocation" lecture when he said: "It is, however, no humbug but rather something very sincere and genuine if some of the youth groups who during recent years have quietly grown together give their human community the interpretation of a religious, cosmic, or mystical relation, although occasionally perhaps such interpretation rests on misunderstanding of self."[51] To be fair, earlier in the same lecture, Weber criticized inauthentic religious eclecticism, but in these lines at least, he seems to be describing a positive, if somewhat naïve, model of utopian enchantment. At the very least, it shows that Weber was no stranger to his period's occult revival.

*

Weber's "disenchantment of the world" first appeared in print in the article "Ueber einige Kategorien der verstehenden Soziologie" (Some categories of interpretive sociology, 1913).[52] His initial tantalizing reference to disenchantment came as an example of the differences between psychology and sociology. Weber was in the process of arguing that actions can be rational for a given actor even if they are directed toward an aim that sociologists might not grant as rational. As he went on to note:

For instance, action that is oriented to magical notions is subjectively of an often much more instrumentally rational character than any non-magical "religious" conduct, since as the *disenchantment of the world* increases, religiosity is compelled increasingly to adopt subjectively, instrumentally irrational meanings (*Sinnbezogenheiten*) (for example, of a "conscientious" [*Gesinnungshaft*] or mystical kind).[53]

Restated, for Weber, *magic* is subjectively *instrumentally rational*. People cast spells for specific pragmatic purposes. In an increasingly disenchanted world, by contrast, Weber thinks that having foreclosed meaning in nature, religiously motivated actors often perform actions that are instrumentally irrational: in other words, actions that are directed against their seemingly rational interests, but instead invested with subjective meaning rooted in their specific conviction or mystical experiences.

To really understand Weber's conception of disenchantment, we also need to clarify what he meant by magic. He frequently referred to magic and enchantment in the context of his later writings on religion, but the closest he came to making an explicit definition is in a footnote in the section of *Die Wirtschaftsethik der Weltreligionen* (The economic ethics of the world religions) dealing with the religions of China. In the relevant section of the text, Weber remarks:

> A strict separation between what is "enchantment" (*Zauber*) and what is not is impossible in the world of pre-animististic and animistic ideas. Even plowing and other everyday achievement-oriented activities were "enchantment" in the sense of employing specific "forces" and later "spirits."[54]

It appears that enchantment or magic (the German *Zauber* could mean either) was initially rational. Indeed, Weber elsewhere associates magical powers with "world-mastery" or "world-domination" (*Weltbeherrschung*).[55] At the very least, early magic was not different from practical technologies except insofar as it was connected to the notion of spirits and pre-animistic occult forces.[56] That Weber saw a connection between (at least early) enchantment and technology is worth underscoring because multitudes of contemporary theorists think they are contravening Weber when they point to enchanting technology.[57] But Weber would not have been surprised by this, especially as this passage was not the only place where he theorized the coincidence of magic and technology.[58]

Significantly, Weber provides both his most systematic theorization of magic and even charts a whole trajectory of the history of enchantment in his incomplete final work, *Wirtschaft und Gesellschaft* (1922; *Economy and Society*). In brief, here Weber reiterated that magic was originally this-worldly instrumentally rational, focused on producing particular ends like starting fires and calling rain.[59] He cautioned his readers against anachronistically viewing the past from the standpoint of the modern view of nature and thereby assuming that we "can objectively distinguish in such behaviors those which are 'correct' from those which are 'incorrect,' and then designate the [false] attributions of causality as irrational, and the corresponding actions as 'magic' (*Zauberei*)."[60]

Weber thought that early magic was founded on neither irrationality, nor a belief in the ability to violate the laws of nature. Instead, as he elaborated, belief in magic was rooted in the sense that some objects and people possesses "extraordinary powers," often referred to as "'*mana*,' '*orenda*,' and the Iranian '*maga*' (which became '*magic*'), and which we will henceforth call 'charisma.'"[61] Crucially, magic and charisma are equivalent. Charisma, as Weber elaborated, can be an attribute of both people and objects, and is either claimed for one's self or bestowed, such as in an act of consecration.[62] Given that Weber is famous for importing a theory of charisma into sociology, it is striking that in this usage, it is primarily a synonym for magic.

The important thing about the reference to "mana" is that this allows Weber to describe magic as prior to any notion of spirits or gods.[63] Although Weber read James Frazer and was likely influenced by his notion of magic, this was not a Frazerian point about magic as a cultural practice before the appearance of religion.[64] Rather, Weber believed that religion and magic both initially existed in a pre-animistic phase and that an early process of abstraction causes people to believe "that there are certain beings concealed 'behind' the charismatically endowed natural objects, artifacts, animals, or persons, that give them their powers. This is belief in spirits. The 'spirit' is initially neither soul, nor demon, nor god, but something indeterminate, material yet invisible, impersonal and yet it is something thought to be possessed of volition."[65] According to Weber, this early idea of spirits then eventually tends to differentiate into separate notions of souls, gods, demons, and supernatural powers.[66] This is a key shift for Weber:

> Once the notion of a realm of souls, demons, and gods emerged, which is not tangible in the everyday sense, but regularly accessible only through symbols and meanings [seen] behind worldly existence . . . this reflected back on the meaning of the magical arts. . . . It was assumed that behind objects and events there was another more real, spiritual [realm] of which [ordinary life] was only a symptom or symbol [and then new types of professionals tried to influence or control this in symbolic ways]. . . . Thus a tidal wave of symbolic action buries primitive naturalism, with far-reaching consequences.[67]

To paraphrase, a crucial turning point in history is when humanity begins to produce a concept of a spiritual realm full of gods, demons, and dead souls.

This transforms the basic orientation toward the natural world, making it symbolic. The magical arts then come to occupy the position of interpretation (divination) and manipulation (spells) of this invisible, symbolic world. Later magicians and priests will professionalize partially according to whether they compel gods or worship them, although Weber noted that this differentiation is incomplete.[68] But the important thing is that humanity has come to read this world as symbolically significant by producing a contrasting other world.

Human cultures eventually then encounter a fork in the road. They can, as Weber elaborated elsewhere, cling to their notion of magic as he thinks happened in China and India. This preserves the culture's image of the world as a meaningful "enchanted garden" (*Zaubergarten*) but it comes at a cost.[69] In part this is because Weber thought that over time, magic/charisma gets invested in particular institutions (like the Brahmans or the Chinese emperor), which then exert a conservative function on the culture that delays its growth.

According to Weber, however, the Occident took a different route—namely disenchantment. The history of the West's rejection of magic is a story that Weber sketched many times, but never finished elaborating. One version occurs in a famous passage from the second edition of *The Protestant Ethic*: "That great historic process in the development of religions, the disenchantment of the world, which had begun with the old Hebrew prophets and, in conjunction with Hellenistic scientific thought, had repudiated all magical means to salvation as superstition and sin, came here to its logical conclusion. The genuine Puritan even rejected all signs of religious ceremony at the grave and buried his nearest and dearest without song or ritual in order that no superstition, no trust in the effects of magical and sacramental forces on salvation, should creep in."[70] Paraphrased, instead of producing an entrenched magical caste in the Occident, the Hebrew prophets' demonization of magic culminated in the Protestant—and especially Puritan—disenchantment of the world.

The claim that Protestants were against magic and superstitious rituals seems straightforward enough, but is worth remembering that Weber asserted elsewhere that Puritans and Jews did not doubt "the reality of magic," and repeatedly reminded his readers that "witches were also burned in New England."[71] Moreover, Protestants continued to believe in angels and demons.[72] So it is important to underscore what the "disenchantment of the world" is *not*. It is not the end of belief in magic. It is not the end of belief in some types of animating spirits. It is not a new pessimistic mood, nor is it the fragmentation of social cohesion. It is not the rise of instrumental reason, because magic is itself instrumental. It is not yet secularization insofar as disenchantment happens earlier and is first and foremost internal to religion. It is not the evolution of magic into religion, and religion in turn, into science à la Frazer, because Weber repeatedly reminds his readers that magic and religion often coincide.[73]

Many scholars, even sophisticated Weberians, mistake disenchantment for the various things I have dismissed above.[74] Having rejected these, the question becomes: What, then, is disenchantment? Keeping in mind Weber's multiplicities of rationality and his grand history of magic, I will now turn to Weber's more famous passages about disenchantment and give them a fresh look.

*

Weber's main clue in *The Protestant Ethic* is the reference to the repudiation of the "magical means to salvation." He continued the above by arguing, "There was not only no magical means of attaining the grace of God for those to whom God had decided to deny it, but no means whatever."[75] Succinctly put, it would seem that alongside the demonization of magic, what ultimately disenchanted the world was the Protestant conception of grace—that salvation is solely due to the sovereign grace of God (*sola gratia*). We might think especially of Calvinist notions of predestination, which suggest that salvation has nothing to do with the individual's "free" will, much less other rituals or symbolic performances. In this account, there is nothing a person can do to change God's mind. The oddity is that Weber reads irresistible grace as the epitome of disenchantment. But this was not his only word on disenchantment.

To return to "Science as Vocation" (*Wissenschaft als Beruf*, 1917) mentioned above, Weber's original topic was career opportunities for students who study the sciences; but by the end of his lecture he has strayed rather far from this theme. The key passage for our purposes is a moment in the talk when Weber began reflecting on the nature of scientific progress and what we have been calling intellectual or theoretical rationalization: "Let us first clarify what this intellectualist rationalization, created by science and by scientifically oriented technology, means practically. Does it mean that we, today, for instance, everyone sitting in this hall, have a greater knowledge of the conditions of life under which we exist than has an American Indian or a Hottentot? Hardly. . . . The savage knows incomparably more about his tools."[76]

Paraphrased, "savages" may not know much about the grand scheme of things, but an individual "savage" understands the functioning of all his or her culture's technologies and has mastered all that culture's knowledge. In a parallel passage in the 1913 "Kategorien" essay discussed above, Weber also contrasted savage and civilized knowledge, and argues that civilized people are no more subjectively "instrumentally rational" than savages.[77] By contrast, Western modernity is at the end of a long process of theoretical rationalization, meaning that it is impossible for a modern individual to master all our culture's knowledge and technology. Sociologists have long argued that one of the central features of modernization has been an increasing differentiation of labor. In both his speech and the "Kategorien" essay, Weber amplified this theme to describe modernization as a kind of hyper-specialization in which we each know proportionally less about the world around us.[78]

Crucially, "civilized people" have a different attitude toward ignorance than Weber's hypothetical "savage." Even when they lack knowledge, civilized people believe that they *could* know everything. As Weber put it in his lecture: "Unless he is a physicist, one who rides on the streetcar has no idea how the car happened to get into motion. And he does not need to know. He is satisfied that he may 'count' on the behavior of the streetcar, and he orients his conduct according to this expectation; but he knows nothing about what it takes to produce such a car so that it can move."[79] Modern people may be oblivious to even the most basic technology they interact with every day (e.g., how a computer monitor works), but they believe "that if one but wished one could learn it at any time."[80] The consequence of this presumption of knowledge is that in principle, "there are no mysterious (*geheimnisvollen*) unpredictable powers that come into play, but rather that one can, in principle, master all things by calculation. This means that the world is disenchanted."[81]

Weber's main argument about the ascent of theoretical rationality can be described dialectically. First, the more society knows, the less the individual knows; second, the less the modern individual knows, the more he or she thinks someone else knows. In this account we have banished occult forces not because the average American knows significantly more about the nature of, say, sunspots than people did five hundred years ago. But we are less likely to imagine that it is mysterious or magical and more likely to assume that there is a scientific explanation, even if we do not know what it is. Basically, moderns are less skeptical than primitive "savages," or perhaps we are more likely to assume that the world can be apprehended according to our subjective rationality.

A certain amount of the secondary literature promotes the idea that disenchantment means banishing the "mysterious" or a sense of wonder. But the parallel passage in the "Kategorien" essay makes no mention of mystery in reference to "savage" belief. Instead, Weber referred to the functionally unpredictable "powers that the savage wants to influence through his magician."[82] The main argument of the essay is also that it is not actual knowledge of the world that strips it of its hidden powers, but a subjective sense that the world is predictable or rational.

Taken to its fullest extension, intellectualization/theoretical rationalization produces a particular conundrum. Weber described this impasse in two key passages from different points of his corpus. In *Wirtschaft und Gesellschaft*, Weber argued: "[Theoretical rationality] conceives of the 'world' as a problem of 'meaning.' The more intellectualism suppresses the belief in magic and hence 'disenchants' the operations of the world—so that they lose their magical meaning and only 'are' and 'happen' but no longer signify anything—the *more urgently* the demand grows for the world and 'the orientation toward life' (*Lebensführung*) to appear ordered in a meaningful and significant way."[83] Theoretical rationalization is based in the need to make sense of the world, and it starts in religion, but having come to apprehend the world as rational, it has stripped the world of incalculable magic and thus meaning. This leads toward an impasse in which reason is unable to provide an orientation to life. As Weber argued in "Zwischenbetrachtung: Stufen und Richtungen der religiösen Weltablehnung" (Intermediate analysis: Levels and directions in the religious rejection of the world, 1916):

> Wherever rational, empirical knowledge has effected *the disenchantment of the world* and consequently transformed it into a causal mechanism, it comes into tension with the demands of the ethical postulate—that the world is divinely ordered, and so somehow an ethically and meaningfully oriented cosmos. For the empirical and completely mathematically oriented worldview rejects in principle any approach which asks for "meaning" from inner-worldly events. With every increase of empirical scientific rationalism, religion is increasingly pushed from the rational into the irrational realm.[84]

In effect, the advance of theoretical rationalization has become grounded in the assumption that the world is not directed by God, but is merely a causal mechanism. Moreover, Weber long argued against the idea that one could draw ethical value from a scientific or calculating enterprise. The result of the advancement of the Occidental search for meaning is a sense that ethical values are no longer located in the world, and the various areas of society are left to their own logics, leading toward a "polytheism" or fragmentation of value spheres. Although it might be tempting to see Weber's complaint as an example of a conflict between religion and science, it is worth remembering that the Puritans also disenchanted the world by taking the theology of grace to its fullest logical extension.

Strikingly, Weber did not think this direction of Occidental rationality was a foregone conclusion. In *Wirtschaft und Gesellschaft*, he suggested that Asian religions and Occidental religions parted ways because Asian thinkers "never abandoned the 'meaningfulness' of the empirical world." Instead they saw "karmic causality" as a "path toward illumination (*Erleuchtung*) and accordingly as a unity of 'knowledge' and [ethical] action." By contrast, this route was closed to monotheistic religions that encountered the "absolute paradox" of "an imperfect world created by a perfect God."[85] Accordingly, for this sort of religion, the intellectual attempt to find meaning in the world "led away from God, not toward him." However, Weber concluded this passage not by suggesting conversion to Buddhism, but by noting that the closest thing to this sort of orientation in the Occidental tradition is "philosophical" forms of "Occidental mysticism."[86]

*

We will turn to Weber's notion of mysticism in the next section, but before concluding I want to refer to another of Weber's criticisms of the hypertrophy of Western rationalization. If the disenchantment of the world is primarily a problem of theoretical rationality, Weber also spent a lot of time thinking about the negative consequences of the bureaucratization or overextension of formalized rationality.

Weber's famous condemnation of the "Iron Cage" (*stahlhartes Gehäuse*, literally "steel-hard shell") is often conflated with his discussion of the disenchantment of the world. One can see why these two concepts have been discussed together, especially given passages like this:

> No one knows who will live in this cage in the future, or whether at the end of this tremendous development entirely new prophets will arise, or there will be a great rebirth of old ideas and ideals, or, if neither, mechanized petrification, embellished with a sort of convulsive self-importance. For of the last stage of this cultural development, it might well be truly said: "Specialists without spirit, sensualists without heart; this nullity imagines that it has attained a level of civilization never before achieved."[87]

Scholars have spent a long time searching for the source of the reference in the conclusion to this passage.[88] Although Weber is often assumed to be quoting Goethe or Nietzsche, I have found an alternate and more plausible source in the writings of the economic historian Gustav von Schmoller, who is largely remembered today for being on the losing side of the famous *Methodenstreit*.[89] In *Grundriss der allgemeinen volkswirtschaftslehre* (Outline of general economics, 1900), Schmoller remarked,

> For some years, a great technocrat could characterize our haughty time not untruthfully by saying: "Sensualists without love and specialists without spirit, this nothingness imagines it stands on a height unequaled in the history of humanity." To which it is always possible to answer, all true human happiness lies in the balance between drives and ideals, between hopes and the practical possibility of satisfaction.[90]

To be sure, Weber reverses the expression, and there is a slight difference in wording.[91] Nevertheless, he made reference to this work in *Die Stadt* portion of *Wirtschaft und Gesellschaft*.[92] In the work as a whole, Schmoller argued for the capacity of the state to harmonize or balance these competing impulses. This quote from Schmoller suggests that Weber was also characterizing contemporary civilization in terms of an imbalance of drives and ideals, although Weber was significantly more pessimistic about the capabilities of the state.

Weber's iron cage would seem to reflect the suppression of irrational life impulses. As he discussed elsewhere in *The Protestant Ethic*: "The great historical significance of Western monasticism . . . [is that it] developed a systematic method of rational conduct with the purpose of overcoming the *status naturæ*, to free man from the power of irrational impulses and his dependence on the world and on nature. It attempted to subject man to the supremacy of a purposeful will, to bring his actions under constant self-control with a careful consideration of their ethical consequences."[93]

Weber described the Puritans channeling this repression of irrational impulses into their daily lives, which became a kind of asceticism in the world, expressed in constant toil and labor. He observed that "when asceticism was carried out of monastic cells into everyday life, and began to dominate worldly morality, it did its part in building the tremendous cosmos of the modern economic order."[94] If this sounds familiar, it is probably because Weber thought Klages was right: that modern society has alienated humanity from our basic life impulses. Moreover, the modern world focuses various forces of restraint into conflicting cultural norms and institutionalized in law and economic policy. This has resulted in constant, if often unexamined, value conflict between individual ethical orientations, norms that have been legally formalized, and the various competing demands of the capitalist economy.

*

In conclusion, it is worth reiterating that Weber described magic as based in the pre-animistic belief that some objects and people have special powers. Weberian disenchantment describes a world without ethical foundation, produced by the hypertrophy of theoretical rationality that has stripped everything in the world of its meaningful specialness. Again, it is worth emphasizing that this is a logic that emerges from within religion as a basic impulse to understand the world as meaningful. But in the hands of Occidental monotheisms, it runs into trouble. On the one side is a predestination that renders ethical action in the world irrelevant, and on the other is a scientific reduction of the world to causal mechanism that similarly undercuts the grounding for ethical action. In both cases, the world is no longer symbolic and nothing is truly special.

To put this in more systematic terms, Weber's disenchantment of the world, as a characterization of popular mentality, had four levels:

1. *Metaphysical realism* (the belief that the world is and does not represent)
2. *Ontological homogeneity* (the belief that there are no truly extramundane objects or people)
3. *Ethical predeterminism* (that God has already decided each individual's soteriological fate) or *value nihilism* (the excision of value from the world of fact)
4. *Epistemic overconfidence* (the belief that everything can be known by means of intellectualization/theoretical rationality)[95]

Weber also described a related conundrum: the iron cage of modernity. As mentioned above, this too had religious roots, representing the transformation of Puritan toil into capitalist labor. Nonetheless, the iron cage would not necessarily be shattered by a return of magic.[96] For instance, in his writings on China, Weber described Confucian governance as magical, but no less bureaucratic.[97]

I discuss what I think Weber imagined as a solution in the next section, but the majority of scholars do not think that Weber had much of a positive counterproject.[98] To be sure, a few old-fashioned Whig Weberians may think of him reveling in the triumph of rationalization, but it seems like quite a stretch to impose on a thinker whose characterization of modernity is so evocative of loss. Also, some scholars have read into Weber a cyclical return of re-enchantment, but there is scant evidence in his writings (discussed below). From the vantage of the Jena Romantics, the oddity of Weberian disenchantment is that it is an incomplete spiral. There are intimations of a return that Weber never completely articulated, leaving it to others to fill in the gaps. It is here that a turn toward Weber's unrecognized engagement with mysticism is in order.

WEBER THE MYSTIC AND THE RETURN FROM THE GOD ECLIPSE

> The unity of the primitive world image in which everything was concrete magic, has tended to split—on one side, into a rational cognition and rational mastery of nature; on the other, into "mystical" experiences. The ineffable content of such experiences is the only possible "otherworld" alongside the de-deified (*entgotteten*) mechanism of the world.
>
> MAX WEBER, *Die Wirtschaftsethik der Weltreligionen*, 1916

Scholars of religion are used to thinking of Max Weber as a secular sociologist with next to no personal faith. The quote that best exemplifies this aspect of Weber is taken from a letter Weber sent to Ferdinand Tönnies on February 19, 1909: "It is true that I am absolutely unmusical religiously and have no need or ability to erect any psychic edifices of a religious character within me. But a thorough self-examination has told me that I am neither antireligious *nor irreligious*."[99] Reading this quote, you might imagine Weber to be a man tone-deaf to religion, who nevertheless is not antireligious. This is the restrained and sensible Weber promoted by Talcott Parsons and a whole senior generation of sociologists. It is a portrait that has its roots in the biography written by Max's widow, Marianne Weber (1870–1954), *Max Weber: Ein Lebensbild* (1926), which has until recently been the single overriding source for Weber's life, and which quoted the letter above. While a number of intellectual and political biographies have been written since, Max Weber's personal life until recently had been largely unexplored.[100] This is primarily because Weber's archive has been closely guarded by the family trust, which only slowly allowed the publication of edited versions of Weber's works, lectures, and letters—a project that is still incomplete.

In this section, I aim to revise the old portrait of Max Weber. This is possible because we have now have to access sources outside of Marianne's biography: the reminiscences of his friends and family; a new biography Joachim Radkau's *Max Weber: Die Leidenschaft des Denkens* (Max Weber: The passion of thought), based on unprecedented access to Weber's archives; and more important, in 2012 the *Max Weber-Gesamtausgabe* finally finished publishing its edition of Weber's letters.[101] The Weber that appears in these sources was far from a value-free scientist-ascetic, and we can now recover his intense grappling with religious issues and even his flirtations with mysticism.

*

Returning to the oft-quoted letter addressing Weber's religious "unmusicality" will help us begin unraveling the classical portrayal. The very next sentence of his letter to Tönnies—omitted from Marianne's *Max Weber*—Weber added, "In this respect I see myself as a cripple, as a mutilated man whose inner destiny is to have to confess this [unmusicality] honestly."[102] Here he is expressing not a restrained neutrality toward all things religious, but an internal conflict. This is even clearer in the follow-up letter Weber wrote to Tönnies less than two weeks later (March 2, 1909):

> Numerous problems of cultural history an outsider cannot [fathom], no matter their amount of detailed knowledge, especially once you get to the problems of the historical meaning of mysticism. There, and only there, do I have the impression that . . . I must *experience* these psychological states to understand their consequences. I have to confess this even thought I myself am religiously "unmusical."[103]

It seems that what Weber meant by his unmusicality is that he has never had a mystical experience, but he also feels that this makes him spiritually "crippled" because he would like to have such an experience if only to understand the internal meaning of mysticism. Weber later wrote about mystical experiences and did so in detail.[104] Indeed, most of Weber's writings on mysticism postdate this letter. This has led Joachim Radkau to argue that Weber must have had a mystical experience himself.[105]

I address what Weber meant by "mysticism" below, but first I will examine evidence that he later saw himself as a mystic. Even Marianne reproduced a note in which Weber wrote to a young colleague, "To me the limit of 'confessing' is where things are involved that are 'sacred,'" they belong "within a circle of people who are personally very close to one another," and adding that "only a prophet or saint . . . is allowed to act differently."[106] Although Marianne located this quote alongside Max's rejection of any attempt to publically "awaken feelings of religious community," this suggests that he saw some things as sacred and believed that they needed to be kept inside the circle of close friends and family.

It is from these circles that we have the most evidence of Weber's mysticism. Max Weber's friend and colleague Karl Jaspers described Weber's series of emotional breakdowns had from 1897 to 1900 that ultimately let to his resignation from his teaching post. While many scholars suggest that this emotional crisis was triggered by the death of Weber's father, it was Jaspers's impression that Weber had undergone a profound spiritual crisis, following an illness during which he came to obsess on the existence of God.[107]

In later reminiscences, Weber's nephew Eduard Baumgarten described his uncle's religious life in terms of a grand sense of heroic destiny or fate (*Schicksal*).[108] Even more important, Baumgarten reported a conversation between Max and Marianne, which ran as follows:

[MAX]: Tell me, can you imagine yourself as a mystic?
[MARIANNE]: That is certainly the last thing I could imagine of myself. Can you imagine it of yourself, then?
[MAX]: It might be that I am one. . . . It is as if I could (and would) just as well withdraw myself entirely from everything.[109]

This dialogue is telling because throughout his work, Max Weber would describe mysticism in terms of a contemplative withdrawal from the world. But it is also far from conclusive.

In another set of reminiscences, first published in 1963, however, Weber's friend and colleague Paul Honigsheim recalled that Weber's personal religion was rooted in his ongoing conversation with God.[110] As befitting this proximity to the divine, Honigsheim thought that Weber considered himself to be a mystic and thus he "had a feel for mysticism" and was infuriated by what he saw as sham or inauthentic mysticism.[111] This is far from the unmusicality suggested by the original letter to Tönnies.

These scattered reminiscences are not conclusive evidence that Weber thought of himself as a mystic, but they suggest that he at least flirted with the idea. This is important because the frequent references to "mysticism" in Weber's published corpus are generally read as pejorative, but if he himself was even somewhat sympathetic to mysticism, they suggest instead (as I argue below) that he saw mysticism as a potential way out of disenchantment. Nor was his time in Ascona his only encounter with mystics firsthand, as the next pages will explore.

Weber in Occult Germany:
Stefan George

We are still very much under the spell of [Stefan George,] who conceives of his poetic profession as a prophet's office.

MARIANNE WEBER, *Max Weber: Ein Lebensbild*, 1926

A people is dead when its gods are dead.

STEFAN GEORGE, *"Der Krieg,"* 1917

We have already encountered the German poet, mystic, and prophet Stefan George (1868–1933) in chapter 8 as one of the Kosmikers. Indeed, he is today the most famous member of that group. George is remembered as an influential poet who had a role in the Conservative Revolutionary movement that sprang up in Germany in the wake of the First World War.[112] In his own day, George was a significant cultural force, developing a tight inner circle of followers who revered him as a master and even as a prophet. This George Circle was drawn from the German academic and artistic elite, including the historian Friedrich Wilhelm Wolters, the wealthy industrialist Robert Boehringer, and influential German-Jewish scholars and artists such as Friedrich Gundolf, Karl Wolfskehl, and Ernst Kantorowicz.[113] For a time, George was a member of Klages's Cosmic Circle, or perhaps more accurately, their circles merged for a while until struggles over vision and leadership ultimately caused them to separate.

The George Circle is relevant to our concerns because, as contemporary sociologist Wolf Lepenies has elaborated, it had an outsized influence on the early history of German sociology. For instance, Georg Simmel often described his own work as a sociological parallel to George's poetry.[114] Indeed, according to contemporaries, Simmel was sufficiently enthralled by the movement that he even adopted George's distinctive style of dress.[115] When Talcott Parsons was in Germany, he also studied sociology under a member of the George Circle.[116] Not to mention George's influence on less well-known social scientists (e.g.. Kurt Breysig and Edgar Salin).[117] Given that these were Max Weber's friends and colleagues, it is no surprise that Weber and George eventually came into contact.

One clue to the George Circle can be found in their references to their project as *"Geheimes Deutschland"* (Occult or Secret Germany).[118] For George and company, "Occult Germany" was a visionary and mystical political order, which lay hidden beneath the surface of mundane Germany.[119] Succinctly put, they were trying to blend artistic, political, and religious registers to imagine an alternate "German spirit" heavily tinged with a language of mystical communion and their version of neo-paganism. Although perhaps more artistic and less magical than the Munich Kosmikers, it is clear that the George Circle represented a similar nexus of enchantment.

An example of the group's project can be seen in George's eulogy for Hölderlin, in which he might just have easily been describing his vision of himself: "Those to whom the era of enlightenment had bequeathed a feeling for nature and a love of reason, called him a stranger on earth, forgetting that their much vaunted experience is vain and superfluous for one who has a covenant with the gods and with Destiny. . . . Not that his mystic and volcanic rhythms are intended as a model for the apprentice to poetry—more is at stake! . . . His unambiguous predictions which cannot be pried apart make him the pivot of Germany's immediate future and the prophet of a new god."[120] The themes in this passage—a suspicion of reason and embrace of destiny, mysticism, and a polytheistic sense of prophecy—were all central to George's project. It was a re-enchantment of the sort that might have appealed to Hölderlin and his fellows. Indeed, the idea that aestheticism could serve as a fortification against modernity was a common theme in the George Circle.[121]

In Marianne's biography, she discussed Weber's encounter with George in some detail. He had originally encountered George's poetry in the 1890s, but it had not left much of an impression on him. But later, after his nervous breakdown and ensuing depression, Marianne recounted that he "opened secret chambers of his soul that had previously been closed," which led to an appreciation of George's poetry.[122] In 1909, Weber met Gundolf, George's main disciple, and the two quickly became friends.[123] Weber became fascinated with the figure of George and avidly devoured his writings. From his side, Gundolf often described Max (and his brother Alfred) Weber as fellow travelers, writing to George in a letter: "Of all the professors, the two Webers seem to me to have felt most a sense of the deeper life."[124] Moreover, George's disciples praised Weber's *Protestant Ethic* for providing "evidence for the mechanizing effects of Protestantism," and suggested both movements had common cause in their opposition to "rationalism, Protestantism, and capitalism."[125]

But Weber was not without his criticisms of George's project and, according to Marianne, remarked in 1910:

> It is not easy to stop discussing a phenomenon that has aspects of real greatness like that of Stefan George. . . . And it seems to me that the only remaining positive goal is the striving for *self-deification (Selbstvergottung)*, for the immediate enjoyment of the divine in his own soul. The path to this is either

through ecstatic rapture or through contemplative mysticism. George and his school has, it seems to me, chosen the first path . . . but this path—and this is fatality—never leads to a mystical experience.[126]

Weber was admitting his fascination with George's "real greatness," even as he was not without his criticism. This passage is important for our purposes because Weber referred to a mystical experience of being filled with divinity, and then at the same time rejected "ecstatic rapture" as a route to it, suggesting that "contemplative mysticism" is a better path. Moreover, this was all before having encountered George in person.

According to Marianne, when Max Weber and Stefan George finally met later that year, Max found that his reservations were largely unwarranted, and while uninterested in becoming a follower, he found George to be a kindred spirit.[127] They met several more times over the following two years, and while they disagreed about many things—including the First World War—they seemed to have much in common.[128] Although Marianne noted that they lost touch with George, it seems that Weber kept up with George's poetry, and even years later he liked to recite it to guests.[129]

We also have another version of the encounter from George's disciple Friedrich Wolters. According to this account, George thought that Weber had a "great force" of character and praised his intelligence.[130] In the occultists' interpretation:

> The main oppositional forces, which Max Weber saw in effect in human history, were magic and knowledge. The realm of magic and charismatic enchantment (*Bezauberung*) achieved its aim through the means of illumination (*Erleuchtung*). . . . In contrast the realm of mental cognition achieved its aims through the means of [superficial] understanding (*Verstand*). . . . [But these two realms had become separated] because mankind had followed the path of logical disenchantment of the world (*Entzauberung der Welt*) through science and transformed [the world] into a causal mechanism.[131]

While they agreed with this sentiment, according to Wolters, the end result was that while the Weber was trapped, unable to reconcile these competing historical forces, his master George had found the way out. He was unable to lead Weber there because Weber had rejected George's charisma and ultimately was too much of a Protestant to understand George's paganism.[132]

But Weber may have been closer to this understanding than George and Wolters imagined. Indeed, it was in Weber's encounter with George that he first began to theorize charisma and its connection to magic and mysticism. Weber first wrote about "charisma" in a letter about George to his student Dora Jellinek.[133] Even in his published writings about charisma, Weber later made reference to George and his circle.[134] Moreover, there are hints that Weber had something in mind as a way to reconcile these contradictory impulses— namely, mysticism.

Even if Max Weber's personal religiosity is discounted, by attending to references to "mysticism," one can find another thread through Weber's work that connects a number of his major conceptual formations. Mysticism will turn out to be not an archaism for Weber, but one of the remaining possibilities for religion in the face of the disenchantment of modernity.

Mysticism against Mechanism

References to "mysticism" appear in Max Weber's earliest writings on religion. Mysticism is already present in the first edition of *The Protestant Ethic and the Spirit of Capitalism*, which was published initially as articles in 1904 and 1905. This text was influenced in part by a regular discussion group called the Eranos Circle, founded in Heidelberg in February 1904 by the Protestant theologian Gustav Adolf Deissmann. This group is not to be confused with the later Eranos Circle established in the 1930s at the Mountain of Truth in Ascona (frequented by C. G. Jung and Gershom Scholem), but it may be its distant ancestor.[135] The earlier group had also focused on the study of religious perennialism, including a positively valenced mysticism and Eastern religion, and among its regular participants were Ernst Troeltsch, Max Weber, and Weber's brother Alfred Weber.[136] Incidentally, Troeltsch was another scholar of religion who not only wrote on mysticism, but—as he confessed to his student Gertrud von Le Fort—was also himself a mystic in the model of Jakob Böhme.[137] Given that most of Weber's work prior to this discussion group was focused on economic history, it is no surprise that like Troeltsch and company, Weber came to understand mysticism as cross-cultural phenomenon based in a common human experience.[138]

The main problematic of *The Protestant Ethic* was an attempt to figure out how modern capitalism came to have its particular character or spirit. To do so, Weber traced the influence of the "religious forces" unleashed by the Protestant Reformation on particular "concrete aspects of capitalist culture," which were born in the Occident and later extended over the globe.[139] Importantly, the first edition lacked the discussion of "the disenchantment of the world," which was inserted later and has come to dominate subsequent readings of the work in terms of Protestant (and particularly Calvinist) rationalization. Compressing some of the nuance out of Weber's sophisticated argument, the main thrust of the first edition was that the character of modern capitalism emerged in two moments: with the birth of a notion of a calling or vocation, and its subsequent transformation by Calvinists into a kind of worldly asceticism. In brief, for the contemporary version of capitalism to take hold, people had to be convinced to dedicate their lives to a profession and to practice salvation by way of savings.

For our purposes, *The Protestant Ethic* is relevant because Weber read the early Protestant Reformation and the notion of the calling in terms of mysticism. As he put it in the text:

> The highest religious experience which the Lutheran faith strives to attain, especially as it developed in the course of the seventeenth century, is the *unio mystica* with the deity. As the name itself, which is unknown to the Reformed faith in this form, suggests, it is a feeling of actual absorption in the deity, that of a real entrance of the divine into the soul of the believer. It is qualitatively similar to the aim of the contemplation of the German mystics and is characterized by its passive search for the fulfillment of the yearning for rest in God.[140]

This passage gives us a sense of what Weber meant by "mysticism," or at least, mystical union: an experience of "the divine entering into the soul of the believer." While granting that the terminology of mystical union is unknown to the Lutheran confession, Weber nevertheless argued that by this period in Protestant history, it has become the highest experience of God possible. Moreover, as he argued elsewhere in the text, "mystical" experience is the pinnacle of religious experience.[141]

In a footnote to this passage in the first edition, Weber noted that "mystic contemplation and a rational attitude toward the calling are not in themselves mutually contradictory."[142] The compatibility between mysticism and rational attitudes is a theme Weber amplified in the second edition. We'll discuss that momentarily, but the point Weber subsequently elaborated is that the "calling" had its true origins in German mysticism. One of the typical criticisms of *The Protestant Ethic* is that Weber gives too much weight to Luther. But this is only on the surface level of the text, the argument at its most superficial reading. If we examine the asides and especially the footnotes, we find that the author of the calling was not Luther but a particular mystic of great personal interest to Weber, Johannes Tauler (1300–61).

To explain, "the calling" (*Beruf*) went from meaning "a task set by God" to being the standard name for one's profession or livelihood.[143] The term is therefore a key notion in Weber's works, occurring for instance in his famous vocation (*Beruf*) lectures. In *The Protestant Ethic*, Weber largely argued for the importance of Luther for popularizing the notion of a this-worldly calling. But as Weber put it in an important footnote: "The idea [of the calling] is found before Luther in Tauler, who holds the spiritual and the worldly *Ruf* (call) to be in principle of equal value."[144] This notion of worldly (as opposed to other-worldly or inner-worldly) mysticism is one that will come to be of particular interest to Weber, and here he is associating it with the mystic Tauler. The closest that Weber came to making this point in the body of the text is when he stated:

> In this Lutheran form the idea of a calling had to a considerable extent been anticipated by the German mystics. Especially in Tauler's equalization of the values of religious and worldly occupations, and the decline in valuation of the traditional forms of ascetic practices on account of the decisive significance of the ecstatic-contemplative absorption of the divine spirit by the soul. To a certain extent Lutheranism means a step backward from the mystics, in so far as Luther, and still more his Church, had, as compared with the mystics, partly undermined the psychological foundations for a rational ethics.[145]

Here Weber is describing Luther as a *step back* from the mystics' calling.[146] Weber was likely alluding to the concept of salvation by grace (discussed above), which he thought in some respect renders action in this world meaningless. What fits much better is Tauler's concept of "vocation," which encourages one to dedicate one's heart toward God and engage in a "poverty" of the soul, instead of a literal poverty of the flesh.[147] Nevertheless, Weber went to some length in the pages to follow to discuss how, having given birth to the notion of a calling, the mysticism (of Luther or Tauler) was effectively suppressed by a Calvinism that allowed for a practical, this-worldly religiosity to come to the fore. Although this argument is never made explicitly, we might see the whole narrative of *The Protestant Ethic* as charting the gradual domestication and eventual rationalization of the original spirit of mysticism.

It might appear that after providing the model of *unio mystica* as the calling, the mystic no longer has any place in the modern world and is fated to vanish like the magician or archaic prophet. But in Weber's later works, there are signs that mysticism began to emerge as both source and paradoxical counter weight to rationalization.

At the very least, as Hans Kippenberg has argued, when Weber returned to rewriting *The Protestant Ethic* with his concept of disenchantment in hand, he was led to reevaluate his understanding toward mysticism, shifting it from a mere "residual category" to a living possibility comparable to asceticism.[148] Indeed, the reading of Protestantism in mystical terms is further reinforced in the second edition, when Weber built on his previous observation to point out that the mystical and rational impulses are not fully opposed: "Now the history of philosophy shows that religious belief which is primarily mystical may very well be compatible with a pronounced sense of reality in the field of empirical fact. . . . Furthermore, mysticism may indirectly even further the interests of rational conduct."[149] Here we can see Weber working to suture magic and rationality; or in Wolters's conception, it might suggest that the realms of magic and knowledge intersect in the realm of mysticism. There are clues to the redemptive function of mysticism in other moments in Weber's writings.

In one of the most systematic reconstructions of Weber's concept of mysticism, the contemporary sociologist Volkhard Krech has demonstrated the importance of this concept in Weber's religious system.[150] Krech notes that mysticism functions in different ways in Weber's sociological typology and in his historical description of the development of religion.[151] In sociological sections of Weber's *Wirtschaft und Gesellschaft* (1922), the mystic is a contrasting type to the ascetic, but while the ascetic is inner-worldly or world-denying, the mystic is world-fleeing.[152] Mysticism is described as a kind of passive escapism, directed toward inner illumination (*Erleuchtung*).[153]

In the same text's account of religious history, however, Weber described the mystic as a cousin of the mystagogue (the leader of initiatory rites and ecstatic rituals). Both traditions, for Weber, are based in the idea of salvation as a union with the Godhead and hence are rooted in the individual intellectual need for redemption.[154] But while these are distinct figures with regard to their focus on contemplation and asceticism, for Weber the mystic can be possessed by the deity in such a way as to become the medium of revelation and in that sense take on the functions of a magician, mystagogue, or prophet.[155] Likewise, the mystic might seem to be a fulcrum figure capable of reviving a sense of connection to the divine and moving from passivity into action.[156] In sum, if self-deification is the ideal, then the mystagogue is the paramount type of mystic.

We can see evidence for this throughout Weber's corpus where disenchantment and mysticism are often juxtaposed; for example, in the passage from *Die Wirtschaftsethik der Weltreligionen* used as an epigraph: "The unity of the primitive world image in which everything was concrete magic, has tended to split—on one side, into a rational cognition and rational mastery of nature; on the other, into 'mystical' experiences. The ineffable content of such experiences is the only possible 'otherworld' alongside the de-deified (*entgotteten*) mechanism of the world."[157] Here it would seem the otherworld of mystical experience is the only site for values that have not been stripped from this world. In the famous lines of his Munich speech: "Precisely the ultimate and most sublime values have retreated from public life either into the transcendental realm of mystic life or into the brotherliness of direct and personal human relations."[158] Although it would take a whole monograph to finish elaborating the full structure of Weber's project, if one grants that some forms of mysticism are positive for Weber, one can see him working toward a set of oppositions: on one side, the alienation produced by bureaucracy, routinization, intellectual hyper-specialization; and on the other side, the potentially (but not necessarily) redemptive charisma, mysticism, and authentic prophecy. This Weber sounds more like Ludwig Klages than readers of either thinker would expect.

*

Weber argued that science did not produce values and that social scientists should steer toward value neutrality themselves. Building on Hume's famous *is–ought* distinction, Weber showed that the more we know of *is*, the less room there is for the *ought*. Put differently, greater knowledge of being means there is less room for us to locate ethics. It might seem therefore that there is no way to return value to a mechanized cosmos. It is clear that Weber believed that ethical ends cannot be determined on the basis of rationality. This might suggest a certain fatalism, as though he were looking at the end of history itself and imagining an inescapable unfolding of rationalization. But I think this is a mistaken reading.

I suggest instead that Weber sometimes imagined a way out of this impasse via a kind mystical experience that allows for a retrieval of values outside the frame of the purely rational. The route back from a world that has been de-deified might appear to be self-deification. But this is a seemingly lost path in the Occident, as Weber argued: "The redemptive method that was thus the path of self-deification and genuine mystical experience of the divine was foreclosed as blasphemous deification of the creaturely, and accordingly the final pantheistic consequences [of this genuine mysticism] were declared heterodox."[159] In effect, by way of self-deification or a nonordinary experience of oneness with the divine, it might appear that one could forge a new pantheistic prophecy. The world might be made meaningful and divine again. Weber was critical of those who went falsely in search of mystical experience, but he did seem to think that one might still find them. Furthermore, with mystical experience as the key, a leader could tap into charisma (think gift of charismata) and prophecy and in so doing escape the chains of bureaucracy and rationalization (at least before routinization set in).

Mysticism seems to be both the distant progenitor of capitalist modernity and perhaps one of its last remaining options. A person can still choose the contemplative life of transcendence pursued individually and on a mystical level. The mystic does not seem to be vanishing in modernity; if anything, it seems to be one of the positions suggested by the current age. We might imagine that for Weber, mysticism is the last route to access the transcendent God expelled by reason.

In my reading, this is not about cycles of disenchantment and re-enchantment. Weber never uses the term *re-enchantment*. He does remark in the "Science as Vocation" lecture that "only the bearing of man has been disenchanted" and that "we live as did the ancients when their world was not yet disenchanted of its gods and demons, only we live in a different sense. . . . As everybody sacrificed to the gods of his city, so do we still nowadays."[160] But in the parallel writings to this speech (such as the *Kategorien* essay that largely covers the same ground), these disenchanted gods are not mentioned. Indeed, the most straightforward interpretation of them is in the context of the First World War, unfolding at that moment. These gods are just the nation-states warring with each other, calling on us to sacrifice ourselves for nations instead of cities. So it might look as though the old unities and mysteries of primitive magic are gone for good. But if we read Weber as a Romantic in the mode of Schiller, what he was looking for was a higher-order synthesis, a return of enchantment or value in a higher key.[161] This would be nothing less than the birth of a new religion.[162]

CONCLUSION: DISENCHANTMENT DISENCHANTED

Max Weber knew that many of his contemporaries believed in magic. Even if he had never met Stefan George, read Reventlow's novel, or gone to Ascona, Weber would have had only to open a German newspaper to see evidence of popular belief in bibliomancy ("Zauberbibel und Wünschelrute," February 9, 1913), witches ("Die Hexe im Backofen," June 26, 1913), spiritualism and angels ("Die Engel von Mons," August 15, 1916).[163] It would have been hard for him to imagine that in Europe belief in magic had vanished completely.

Many scholars have argued that what Weber had in mind with "the disenchantment of the world" was a culture in which a sense of mystery and wonder had vanished. This interpretation is plausible insofar as Weber made one statement to that effect in his most oft-quoted lecture (even if it is not emphasized in those terms in the essay that parallels the lecture). This version of disenchantment might still allow for the claim that it emerges from the very logic of religious impulses and that banishing a sense of mystery is not the same thing as understanding. As an account of popular epistemology, this may be plausible but has obvious shortcomings.

This reading of Weber does not square well with what we know of European history. As far as we can reconstruct, medieval European peasants did not generally think of the world as mysterious. They understood their trades and tools, and insofar as they needed an explanation, they could turn to their priests for reassurance that the cosmos functioned according to God's plan and any seeming mystery was his will. Moreover, when we look toward extant European texts of magic, they often provide explanations for the way the world works and techniques for the control of the world. So it is rather hard to imagine "magic" in these sources as either irrational or steeped in mystery.[164]

One would also think that according to the model, as things became less comprehensible, they would become more magical. If Weberian magic stood for the unknown, the mysterious, the unpredictable, then we seem to have sidestepped disenchantment, since it would seem that the more complex our common theoretical knowledge gets, the more abstract and more disenchanted things get. Read another way, we might take it to mean that magic is really equivalent to skepticism (Agrippa would make a fine illustration). But if so, then we might have Hume, Derrida, or even Kant (see chapter 7) to blame for inadvertently providing philosophical justifications for regarding the world as fundamentally unknowable and therefore mysterious.

Again I want to underscore that this is not what Weber mainly meant by magic or disenchantment. Weber described magic as instrumentally rational and directed toward world mastery. The "magic garden" was not a state of complete harmony with nature, and recovering magic would not heal nature. Indeed, the whole line of critique that reads the disenchantment of the world as the domination of nature is left-Klages, not left-Weber (Adorno and company notwithstanding).

Weber's image of a disenchanted cultural sphere is one in which meaning has been pushed out of existence, rendering it no longer symbolic and ethical action meaningless. This was an impasse that could be arrived at by either denying the existence of God or by imagining a transcendent God who had preordained all things. It resulted in a state where mana/charisma/specialness no longer marked out specific individuals, rites, and objects with the same power. Crucially, disenchantment arose from a hypertrophy of theoretical rationality.

The basic need for a rationally meaningful cosmos had stripped the world of all irrationalities, and in so doing located ethics in a transcendent realm, which increasingly receded from sight. Nevertheless, the same basic needs remained.

Above I divided Weberian disenchantment into metaphysical realism, onto-logical homogeneity, ethical predeterminism/value nihilism, and epistemic overconfidence. There is counterevidence for these forms of disenchantment as well. Religious believers and philosophical skeptics often reject meta-physical realism. Moreover, charisma and even extramundane objects/people have far from vanished in contemporary Euro-American culture, where we have everything from fetishized celebrity artifacts to haunted houses. In the United States, epistemic overconfidence has withered in the face of right- and left-wing skepticism (against climate change and vaccines and so on). The popular faith in technology remains largely unchecked, but science is routinely attacked in the public sphere. I am more sympathetic to the issue of value nihil-ism, but it would be a mistake to think that it characterizes even most sectors of society. On a more sympathetic reading of Weber's model, one could argue that instead of a culture-wide "disenchantment of the world," the result has rather been a drive toward the disenchantment of the intellectual value sphere or specific disciplines. But there is more fundamental intervention I want to make in the standard interpretation of Weberian disenchantment.

Popular interpretations of Weber tend to assume that he was describing a world without magic. This reading is easy to dismiss both in terms of Weber's own understanding of the Puritan witch trials and knowledge of magical reviv-als. Indeed, I cannot emphasis this enough—the disenchantment of the world does not mean there is no magic. We understand Weber better if we read him as also theorizing the persistence of magic into modernity. What Weber envi-sioned can be further clarified on basic philological grounds. *Entzauberung* in German signals something that is in process. One of the most straightforward implications of this chapter would be to translate Weber's famous phrase not as "the disenchantment of the world" but instead as *"the disenchanting of the world."* "Disenchantment" suggests an accomplished state of affairs. But what Weber has in mind is not just a process, but also a program. All he's doing is identifying that this program is in place, not that it is completed. For there to be an active, ongoing disenchant*ing* of the world, magic has to be intact—somewhere, among some groups. There must therefore be pockets, entire regions, groups or classes where magic remains. If anything, disenchanting the world might seem destined to produce a "magic sphere" with a new host of professionals, subject to its own internal rationalization process.

Moreover, it is important to emphasize that for Weber to be right, the disenchanters do not have to be denying the existence of magic. They merely have to demonize it. The disenchanting of the world is in place once there are some elites who want to cut off magic as a path to salvation. In the first instance, disenchanting does not strip the earth of supernatural beings, so much as it depicts the world as demon haunted. This allows us also to see that "the disenchanting of the world" is not identical to the (putatively) anonymous process of rationalization. Yet, it is still alienating.

When Weber theorized rationalization, he argued that in the modern Occident, theoretical rationalization has if anything been further subsumed by the onset of formalized/institutionalized rationality, resulting in an iron cage. Weber spent time discussing the many forms of domination and violence enshrined in the modern state. To these we could add the ideas of Marx and a host of different condemnations of the contemporary capitalist world order. I mention this here because the iron cage and disenchantment are often entangled. Framed this way, however, it seems unlikely that re-enchantment (either a naïve revival of magic or even a recovery of ethics) would solve any of these issues. Leaving aside his Orientalist binary between a magical Asia and a magicless West, Weber himself seems to have both believed that Asia had not yet been disenchanted, and yet also been pessimistic about it.

Weber suggested that what the world needed was a new prophet. But he gave few clues as to where such could be found. Mysticism might be a potential way to bring God back into a godless world, mystical union as the path to re-deifying the cosmos. A charismatic magician could overturn the laws of bureaucracy and institute a new world-affirming ethical code, perhaps, but even this charisma would ultimately become routinized yet again. In my reading, Weber toyed with the idea of mysticism as a solution, but never fully committed to it, perhaps for good reason. Instead, Weber hinted at a messianic expectation or a longing for "genuine prophecy" in a prophetless age.

CONCLUSION

The Myth of Modernity

From Max Weber to the theorists of deconstruction, the link between modernity, rationalism, and western culture was not seen as simply contingent. It was seen as equally
constitutive of one or the other so that it is precisely this interweaving [of modernity,
rationalism, and western culture] that was seen as "the property of the West," the feature
that distinguished it from the rest of world.

ACHILLE MBEMBE, *De la postcolonie*, 2000

Every morning my grandmother used to rise at dawn, look out over the San-
gre de Cristo Mountains, and scatter ground cornmeal (*masa harina*) for the
spirits. To those outside the family, she was known as Felicitas Goodman, a
professor of anthropology and the author of several well-regarded scholarly
monographs on glossolalia, Mexican Pentecostal Christianity, and the anthropology of religion.[1] After her retirement, she went public with her belief in
spirits and ecstatic trances; scholars, scientists, and artists came from Europe,
Mexico, and the United States to participate in "shamanic" trance workshops
under her leadership. While my grandmother inspired me to become a scholar
of religion, I was always skeptical about the existence of the spirits. I was also
skeptical of a theme I often heard repeated in her community, that Western
modernity had lost its magic. That a notion of the loss of magic often went
hand in hand with belief in magic was an irony only amplified by the people I
have encountered since who expressed similar sentiments.

My grandmother's version of this formulation occurred in the first major
work to announce her spiritual experiences to the world, published in English
as *Where the Spirits Ride the Wind: Trance Journeys and Other Ecstatic Experiences* (1990).[2] In it, she gives an abbreviated spiritual biography—including
an account of her vision of the Virgin of Guadalupe that inspired her to attempt to contact the spirits—combined with an anthropological theory of ecstatic trance as a gateway to the alternate reality. At several points in the text,
she testifies to the existence of the spirits and provides concrete techniques by
means of which readers can enter into an ecstatic trance and experience the

alternate reality for themselves. Moreover, elsewhere she provides her own philosophy of magic, arguing that the alternate reality is

> an other-than-ordinary dimension of reality, in which the so-called laws of nature, discovered by Western science for ordinary reality, do not obtain. Especially the limits of time and space are invalid. The absence of these makes divination possible. Switching into the religious altered state also endows the subject with the ability to affect indeterminate systems, as well as a number of determinate ones, in a manner some Western observers have termed *magical*.[3]

My grandmother is hedging the language here because she was skeptical of the distinction between the categories religion and magic, but by and large she saw the alternate reality as the source of divination, spirits, and magical powers.

Tellingly, my grandmother concludes *Where the Spirits Ride the Wind* with a chapter titled "The Twilight of the Spirits," which attempted to explain why the spirits vanished and access to the alternate reality became no longer a commonplace. She examines the myths that she believes preserved signs of the originary loss, arguing, "In the Nordic myths we hear of Ragnarok, the doom of the gods, of their struggle against enemy forces, and of the eventual destruction of the earth. The Popol Vuh equally tells of murder committed against such men as Seven Makaw, a stand-in for the independent horticulturalists, by the new gods, who then create docile humans entirely of cornmeal, whom they even deprive of the gift of 'seeing.'"[4] Instead of leading her to interrogate the myth of modernity as rupture, she concludes that "agriculture ushered in the unbounded exploitation of our earth," which ultimately led to the twilight of the spirits, as the archaic bond between humanity and nature— and access to the alternate reality—had been largely foreclosed.[5] Fortunately, for the moment, "tribal" societies preserve these spiritual techniques that have been endangered by "the modern age."[6]

This text exhibits what should now be a familiar pattern. The moment of rupture is different inasmuch as it is in the transition from horticulture to agriculture—not the Protestant Reformation, or even the birth of monotheism. But we can see my grandmother pronouncing a myth of disenchantment that simultaneously explains the absence and presence of the spirits and magic. It also operates by postulating an opposition between modern and archaic, Europe and "tribal," which her neo-shamanic practices claim to bridge. I have introduced this familial example not to claim the heritage of the myth of disenchantment, but to reflect on the personal connections that were productive of my own interest in the subject. It is also telling that my grandmother came to this narrative not through occult research or magical texts but through the very human sciences I have been discussing here.[7]

In the introduction, I expressed three Foucauldian doubts about the myth of disenchantment or "modernity paradigm" that have been animating this work as a whole: the historical doubt (*is the disenchantment of the world truly an established historical pattern?*), the critical-historical doubt (*how, in the face of vibrant spiritualist and magical movements, did European societies come to think of themselves as disenchanted?*), and the politico-theoretical doubt (*have the workings of domination in Euro-American societies really belonged primarily to the mode of disenchantment?*). Here I will devote a section to addressing each of these doubts, and in so doing tie together some of the threads that have been woven throughout this book.

THE MYTHS OF (POST) MODERNITY

Scholars—modernizers and postmodernists alike—often contend that what most makes the modern world modern is that people no longer believe in magic and spirits. The age of myth is allegedly over, the gods have died, vibrant nature has been subjugated, and instrumental rationality and mechanistic materialism rule in their place. When pressed on the specifics, there is little consensus as to when this disenchantment set in, but scholars often admit that it only applies to a constrained geography (namely, Western Europe and North America). The primary aim of this work has been to push back against this narrative.

Disenchantment is a myth. The majority of people in the heartland of disenchantment believe in magic or spirits today, and it appears that they did so at the high point of modernity. Education does not directly result in disenchantment. Indeed, one might hazard the guess that education allows one to maintain more cognitive dissonance rather than less. Secularization and disenchantment are not correlated. Moreover, it is easy to show that, almost no matter how you define the terms, there are few figures in the history of the academic disciplines that cannot be shown to have had some relation or engagement with what their own epoch saw as magic or animating forces. This monograph has shown how different magic and spiritualist revivals entered the lives of modernity's main theorists, from Max Müller to Theodor Adorno to Rudolf Carnap. But it is not only theorists of disenchantment who were entangled with enchantment.

At this point we might expect counter-hegemonic disciplines to be engaged with the occult. For example, the influence of theosophy, witchcraft (Wicca), and neo-paganism on all three waves of the feminist movements has been well studied.[8] That artistic and literary movements often went together with magical rituals and spirit summoning should also be no surprise: the occult can be found from the Harlem Renaissance to the Surrealists, from Wassily Kandinsky to Victor Hugo to W. B. Yeats.[9]

What we might think of as the orthodox or establishment disciplines have been hardly less magically inclined. Spiritualism and theosophy have appealed to biologists like Alfred Russel Wallace and inventors like Thomas Edison. Nobel Prize–winning physicists from Marie Curie to Jean Baptiste Perrin to Brian Josephson have often been interested in parapsychology. Even computer scientists like Alan Turing believed in psychical powers. Moreover, despite the laments of the new materialists, panpsychism has been a persistent countercurrent in philosophical circles as well-known thinkers—including Spinoza, Leibniz, Goethe, Schopenhauer, Margaret Cavendish, Julien La Mettrie, Gustav Fechner, Ernst Mach, Henry David Thoreau, C. S. Peirce, William James, Josiah Royce, John Dewey, Henri Bergson, Samuel Alexander, Charles Strong, Pierre Teilhard de Chardin, Alfred North Whitehead, Charles Hartshorne, Albert Schweitzer, Arthur Koestler, and Gregory Bateson—all argued that the material universe should be thought of as thoroughly animated or possessed of mind and awareness. Mechanism has long had establishment enemies.[10] This list barely scratches the surface. When combined with survey after survey that suggests popular belief in the supernatural, miracles, witchcraft, spirits, and the mysterious (see chapter 1), it makes it hard to countenance the idea that disenchantment is the central feature of the history of the industrialized "West." As I interpret Max Weber, we live in a *disenchanting* world in which magic is embattled and intermittently contained within its own cultural sphere, but not a disenchanted one in which magic is gone. Restated, magic never truly vanished.

*

Disenchantment and enchantment were often brought together into a unity, such that their putative opposition fails to correspond. By way of illustration, I'd like to introduce another kind of figure—an ideal type, if you will: namely, the disenchanting magician. This manuscript has explored theorist of disenchantment obsessed with magic. But history also furnishes instances of the opposite case: magicians committed to what they thought of as disenchantment. For instance, the Jewish-American escape artist Harry Houdini (born Erik Weisz) was not only a stage magician, but he was also interested in the occult and spiritualist phenomena. Nevertheless, he dedicated almost twenty-five years of his life to exposing fraudulent spirit mediums. The famous magician therefore seemingly outdid nearly all his contemporaries in his efforts to dispel spirits from early twentieth-century America, even as he was busy dazzling the public with his own magical spectacles.[11] By way of another example, one might think of the French esotericist René Guénon, who attacked theosophy and spiritism in his writings while promoting his own "sacred science" and primordial Eastern wisdom. Magicians with incompatible visions aimed at both expunging one another's superstitions and recovering magic.

In addition to these magicians of disenchantment, one might think of the many bimodal concepts this book has explored, such as the paranormal, psychic powers, natural magic—concepts that are both enchanting and disenchanting. Indeed, as we have seen, the very terminology of disenchantment itself has been partially self-refuting, giving birth to numerous magical and spiritualist revivals. These examples make it hard to continence a straightforward opposition between enchantment and disenchantment.

*

Modernity is a myth. The term *modernity* is itself vague. There can be value in vagueness, but "modernity" rests on an extraordinarily elastic temporality that can be extended heterogeneously and in value-laden ways to different regions and periods. It also picks out different processes such as urbanization, industrialization, rationalization, globalization, capitalism, or various particular artistic, scientific, philosophical, or technological movements. To speak of "modernity" or "modernization" is always to select from within these and to surreptitiously bundle them together as symptoms of a larger master process. It often makes an actor out of the very thing that needs to be explained. Hence, modernity is not just vague; it is doing a lot of covert work, and its main feature is its capacity to signal a rupture or breach, which it marks as the expression of a single horizon of temporality. Moreover, when described in terms of the de-animation of the world, the end of superstition, the decay of myth, or even the dominance of instrumental reason, modernity signals a societal fissure that never occurred.

*

Postmodernity is a myth. This might seem to be a simple corollary to the earlier claims about modernity, but it is worth explaining in greater detail. Let me start with an example. In *Die Krisis der europäischen Kultur* (The crisis of European culture), the German philosopher Rudolf Pannwitz described what he saw as a calamity in European intellectual and cultural life, arguing that capitalism, shallow materialism, and conflicting nationalisms have produced an ethical vacuum. Strikingly, Pannwitz suggested that this collective zeitgeist has spawned a new type of person: "The postmodern man is an encrusted mollusk, a happy medium of decadent and barbarian swarming out from the natal whirlpool of the grand decadence of the radical revolution of European nihilism."[12] While the prose is rather florid, Pannwitz might seem to be describing our contemporary epoch, especially by connecting the postmodern with nihilism and a pervasive ethical disaster. It is not hard to find thinkers today who use similar terms to describe our current "postmodern crisis." But Pannwitz wrote this account in 1917, not 1987, much less 2017. The appearance of this text and even its term *postmodern* a century ago allows us to see that the postmodern condition is far from new. Nor was Pannwitz alone. Like the almost imperceptible tremors that anticipate a major earthquake, tantalizing references to the "postmodern" or "postmodernists" (Sp. *postmodernista*) began appearing more than a half century before the term would attain common currency.[13]

On a concrete level, what these examples show is that the term *postmodern* became lexically available shortly after 1901, when variants on the term *premodern* appeared and came into common usage in a number of European linguistic repertoires. No sooner had "modernity" become the quintessential periodization than it was possible to imagine its future eclipse. Postmodernism is often presented as a second rift after the rift that defined modernity. Postmodernism is often seen as a counterreaction to modernism, but the two movements largely coincided. Indeed, *postmodernism* and *modernism* would seem to have the same meaning insofar as they both aim to transcend the current moment, often by looking forward. Accordingly, both periodizations rest on the idea of a fundamental rupture from the past, which, while inflected differently, often rests on the very disenchantment narrative I have been working to dispel.

In sum, I have been arguing that in the hands of both proponents and critics, modernity is a philosopheme that comes with a rudimentary narrative structure attached. Every time something specific is termed "modern," that implies a story: "First there was *x*, and then everything changed." The word *modernity* always communicates myth, and it turns out that disenchantment is one of the stories we most like having told to us. Here I have been exploring our attraction to this particular tale and trying to put an end to it, along with all similar accounts of modernity.

THE MYTH OF DISENCHANTMENT
AS REGULATIVE IDEAL

By identifying modernity as myth, I join a small group of dissenters who have already come to call into question the term's utility. Postcolonialists and other social theorists have been working to fracture the reflexive linkage between Westernization and modernization, while historians of enchantment have demonstrated the importance of magic and spirits in American and European history. Taken together, this presents a puzzle: Europe appears not to have fit with central features of European modernization and indeed looks more like the rest of the world than the model would usually suggest. In this respect, Europe is not Europe.

In one of the most famous critiques of modernity, *Nous n'avons jamais été modernes* (1991; *We Have Never Been Modern*), Bruno Latour argues that the notion of modernity is predicated on the false claim that it is possible to separate fact from value, nature from culture. Therefore, modernity as a project historically aimed to maintain the difference between two distinct ontological zones—a nonhuman sphere of nature and a human sphere of culture—and then engaging in "purification" to get nature out of culture and culture out of nature. For Latour, this project was doomed to failure insofar as the moderns kept producing nature-culture hybrids even as they denied these hybrids are possible; hence his assertion that "we have never been modern." Although not incompatible with the argument I have been making here, the human sciences (including Latour's own sociology) were always an uncomfortable fit for this narrative precisely because they seem to be hybrids first and purifiers second, only inadvertently. They rest on the constant temptation to center the human-subject at the heart of nature while exploring the nature of the human. But perhaps this is a matter of emphasis.

My larger departure from Latour is that I argue that the human sciences have internalized the modern project not primarily in terms of a false nature-culture binary, but in the notion of "modernity" itself as the sign of a pure rupture or difference. In this way modernity has functioned as a master paradigm or episteme—what I have been calling a myth. In this project as a whole I have been largely working to disrupt this myth in genealogical terms, by tracing the layers of conceptual sedimentation that contributed to the most important subtype of the myth of modernity; namely, the myth of disenchantment. Put differently, instead of describing disenchantment itself, I have been chronicling the formation of the myth of disenchantment as a multifaceted regulative ideal.

First and foremost, I have provided an account of how this myth came into being. In brief, many of the figures we associate with the "scientific revolution" saw themselves as magicians, and the early enlightenment project was a quest for a divine science. Nevertheless, because of these attempts to de-demonize magic and enchant natural philosophy, "superstition" began shifting from being a Christian term (associated with misdirected worship or demonic covenants) to being a reference to beliefs in direct conflict with the newly forming image of a "philosophical," then "scientific" worldview. One of the first inflection points in the history of disenchantment as a regulative ideal turns out to be a shift in the oppositional structure of a religion-superstition binary to a science-superstition binary. It is no coincidence that the previous legacies of superstition—divination, magic, myth, and spirits—continued to be the foil of even scientific tracts that provided new rationales for old targets. Moreover, as the notion of a conflict between reason and faith, then science and religion began to take hold, the rejected terms remained as signs of where the categories intersected. This gave these terms a certain allure (as sites for the critique of modernity or scientific materialism, or ways to repair the science-religion divide), but it also made their suppression key to claims to scientific status.

In the process of early disciplinary formation, the human sciences all tended to assume modernity as a paradigm—that there was something distinctive and original in "modern" European thought and culture—even as they articulated different versions of this rupture within their respective fields. Moreover, they inherited a conception of archaic "superstition" formulated in the legacy of anti-paganism. This often led to the bias that a core feature of European modernity was to be found in the dismissal of magic, myth, irrationality, and spirits. There were inevitably vested interests—colonial, disciplinary, and occult—in maintaining this claim to uniqueness even as they interpreted it differently. European modernity was either a triumph or a tragedy. It either needed to recover magic or banish superstition completely. But European culture was not in fact as unique in this respect as these theorists believed. Modernity was a false paradigm. It was itself a myth.

*

The myth of disenchantment has two contradictory functions. On the one hand, it serves as a regime of truth, submerging the paradigm of modernity deeper into the core of the human sciences and producing various attempts (legal, pedagogical, colonial) to disabuse the other of superstitious thought. On the other hand, it is self-refuting, producing the very thing it describes as endangered, animating occult revivals, paranormal investigations, and new attempts to spiritualize the sciences. For this reason, it meets the needs of different constituencies, including those who want to banish magic and those who aspire to reinvigorate it.

Even within the sciences, disenchantment is repeatedly contravened as a regulative ideal. Physicists, anthropologists, and scholars of religion often try to reestablish spirits or magic in their respective disciplines, frequently as a way to heal the fissures between science and religion or humanity and nature. The anti-paganism or anti-superstition of the modern academy is only weakly or sporadically enforced, and while there have certainly been attempts to implement disenchantment, there have been equally frequent counterforces and revivals. For every psychoanalyst bemoaning magical thinking as madness, another embraces psychical powers or attempts to recoup the shaman as the ideal therapist. Alterity was not merely at the periphery, but rather the center.

As regulative ideal, the myth of modernity often collapsed into descriptive modernization or prescriptive modernism. Evidence for widespread belief in spirits has not historically been used to refute "modernity" as a paradigm, but instead has generally been taken to mean that modernity had not yet been completely actualized. In this respect, modernization theorists often grant Latour's idea that we have never been modern, to which they add the equivalent of Arthur Rimbaud's ironic imperative: "one *must* be absolutely modern" (*Il faut être absolument moderne*). This move presumes the existence of the modern rupture, but locates it elsewhere, giving vent to an aspirational desire. This notion was not simply a view from the colonies, but as Fredric Jameson has shown, it was also common in the metropole.[14] For instance, Germans looked to France for modernity, Parisians looked to London for the same, while the British were often looking to North America, which in turn often looked back to Europe. Modernity was everywhere and nowhere.

*

Enchantment is construed as a signifier of elsewhere or as an anachronism, a remainder of something lost. I mean this in several respects. Magic (Gr. *mageia*) has indicated foreignness since at least the fifth century BCE, when the term *magician* (*magos*) came into usage in Greek as a reference to a Persian ritualist or practitioner of a foreign mystery cult.[15] For more than a thousand years, spellbooks often claimed to be recovering the lost magical arts of Moses, King Solomon, Hermes Trismegistus, and even the biblical Adam.[16] Moreover, the gods, spirits, or fairies have been disappearing since at least Chaucer and arguably since Plutarch.[17] In this respect, magic is constantly vanishing, even as magicians have claimed to recover it. In sum, disenchantment is part of the trope of magic itself.

Closer to the chronology of our narrative, late eighteenth- and early nineteenth-century German philosophical circles gave birth to a set of modern laments involving the death of God, the de-divination of nature, the myth-of-the-end-of-myth, and the onset of nihilism. These philosophers often described these mythemes not in linear teleological terms, but as part of a spiral, whose final act has been generally overlooked. Nevertheless, one of the features of these mythemes—particularly after they took on canonical form—is that their genesis was projected backward and hung on various mythic epochs that soon came to be called the Enlightenment, the Renaissance, the scientific revolution, and the transition from mythos to logos in classical Greece.

Inheriting nineteenth-century myths alongside an influential occult revival, philosophers of the 1920s through the 1940s revived the question of "the Enlightenment" as a fight over the meaning of the Weimar Republic, the First World War, and then the horrors of fascism. The Vienna positivists celebrated enlightenment and disenchantment as ideological critique, even as they engaged in psychical research and identified positivism with magic. The Frankfurt School criticized the overextension of enlightenment and attacked the disenchantment of the world, even as they made it their business to expel or suppress occult movements. The struggle between "the Enlightenment" and "counter-Enlightenment" is mainly a twentieth-century myth, projected backward.

In the wake of the Second World War, understanding the seeds of fascism and totalitarianism became an international priority. The problem is that Nazism could be positioned on either side of "the Enlightenment" / "counter-Enlightenment" divide. Similarly, in the 1940s the idea of the "occult Nazi," or a sympathy between occultism and fascism appears as a theme, significantly in Lewis Spence, *Occult Causes of the Present War* (1940), which remobilized older anti-pagan rhetoric, and in the more philosophically sophisticated "Thesen gegen den Okkultismus" (Theses against occultism, 1951) by Theodor Adorno.[18] This idea that the occult was the cause of fascism only became more widespread in the ensuing decades.[19] I am not suggesting we in any way forgive Nazi atrocities, but the "occult Nazi" trope worked to render the Nazis more "other," and in some cases interrupted introspective endeavors to understand anti-Semitism within the Allied powers. It also provided a strong impetus for scholars to suppress their own occult beliefs lest they be branded fascist sympathizers. Given the Frankfurt School's place in this trajectory, it is tempting to read the repression of enchantment and the criticism of the disenchantment of the world as continuous.

Indeed, as a disciplinary rule, disenchantment is not much in evidence before the critique of disenchantment. Indisputably, people hid their hetero-dox beliefs earlier and lost jobs for attacking the established churches, and colonial officials often attacked "witchcraft" or stigmatized minority beliefs as "superstition"; but the repression of occult beliefs seems to have been incon-sistently applied in the nineteenth and early twentieth centuries. Our evidence for this is that as we have seen many earlier scholars who were largely open about their philosophy of magic, their practice of spiritualism, or their interest in theosophy and mysticism. The call to purge or hide occult beliefs appeared most strongly in the twentieth century, often in the context of the popular flourishing of those beliefs and often alongside a critique of modernization. Discipline founders were called on to either allay themselves with occult sci-ences or distinguish their project from pseudosciences, and as we saw with Sigmund Freud, this provided a concrete rationale to hide one's own occult beliefs. Nevertheless, they kept returning. In the 1960s and 1970s it seemed spirits, psychical powers, and even magic were back in the realm of the pos-sible in different human sciences, even if only marginally so.[20]

In the Anglophone academy, the 1980s and 1990s saw the ascendancy of bodies of theory that had been influential in the preceding decades in France and Germany. Competing philosophical movements were merged under the heading of poststructuralism, French theory, and postmodernism. Starting in the French and German departments, these modes of inquiry came to promi-nence in other fields, leading to an increase in cultural studies. In this context, "the Enlightenment" and "disenchantment" became increasingly important in the 1990s as anti-hegemonic theory became hegemonic, and a new set of occult revivals took place.

*

It might still seem that this debate is in the past. We have retired *the savage* and eliminated *superstition* from our disciplinary vocabularies, but as long as we hold to the contrasting terms, the occlusion remains. Let me give a concrete example. Anthropology has spent the last thirty years slowly purging itself of the notion of the primitive. But insofar as many anthropologists still hold to the notion of modernity, they have inherited half of an assumed binary while merely occluding the missing term. Moreover, it was this very notion of difference between modern and traditional societies that gave the early field its reason for being (and which were the roots of its differentiation from sociology and other sibling fields). In this sense, anthropology is haunted by an occluded primitive both presumed and bracketed out.

*

Let me approach this differently. We have long been taught to read the history of modern science as the mechanization of the world picture and to see it in terms of the history of physics. It has often been suggested that the very act of producing a systematic image of the world has led toward the evacuation of meaning. But a closer look at the history of physics shows this image not to cohere.

To sketch this trajectory in broadest strokes, even as Descartes liberated an autonomous realm for the thinking subject, his mechanism denied action at a distance and rejected the concept of the void. But this form of corpuscular mechanism was disrupted by Newton's emphases on occult forces like gravity, which produced action at a distance and also in some versions required constant divine or angelic intervention. Later natural philosophers worked to eliminate these, but as soon as Pierre-Simon Laplace and company purged the angels, the discovery of electricity as a seeming bridge between matter, mind, and nature reproduced a lively cosmos. Indeed, it was this research on electricity and magnetism, in both physics and biology, that gave a boost to mesmerists and spiritualists.

Then, when James Clerk Maxwell described electromagnetism mathematically, the rise of radioactivity and invisible rays cast us into the dawn of a vibratory atomic age. Again, pioneers of this science of the invisible like Edmund Fournier d'Albe argued that X-rays show not only the composition of the soul but also the reality of paranormal phenomena like ghosts. Just as quantum mechanics began to formalize the movement of fundamental particles, the Copenhagen interpretation marked out a limit on human knowledge and a position for subjectivity that we have still failed to overcome. Indeed, we can look to early proponents of the new physics like Wolfgang Pauli and J. Robert Oppenheimer for the turn to Oriental religion and mysticism that would later be popularized by New Age thinkers. Accordingly, we can repeatedly see in the realm of physics a dialectical alternation between disenchantment and enchantment.

*

Social theorists internalized an image of the scientific world picture quite independent of what physicists actually believed. Human sciences came into being modeled on this viewpoint even as they revived human primacy. A particular scientific world picture was often presented as a universal "Real" against which other myths were shattered. The Real is first and foremost an aesthetic realism, which serves to drain the universe of metaphor and constrain what is supposed to exist in the realm of possibility. The Real is presented as the neutral background against which human activity takes place.

There is plenty of preexisting critique of this realism (aesthetic and also ontological) and of reality-thought in general that laments the triumph of "reality"—that wishes to undo it, to smash the modern world picture in order to spring us loose from the discursive constrictions of the Real. To this I say, however: the Real was always multiple. The modern world picture never completed. The tyranny of reason or instrumental rationality never occurred. We are not stranded in the "desolate time of the world's night," forced to scan the horizon for glimmers of the messianic dawn. This is not necessary. It is wasted effort, because it assumes a type of authority that was never universal. It is like continuing to bemoan the tyranny of a positivism that has long been overthrown. We are already free. Once the nonreality of this authority is granted, there is an entire terrain of struggle that more or less evaporates.

AGAINST THE TIDE OF DISENCHANTMENT

I have been largely writing as a historian, albeit in the Foucauldian mode. But in the last few pages I want to gesture toward the political theory implied by my critique of the myth of disenchantment. In brief, I have been arguing that power in Euro-American societies has not belonged solely to the mode of disenchantment and that the critique of disenchantment appears to be part of the same power mechanism as the thing it criticizes.

It would be easier to be a partisan of either enchantment or enlightenment. To present the first as an emancipatory possibility, as so many have done, would be to describe enchantment as resistance "against the tide of modernity."[21] This would be to suggest that reawakening a sense of wonder, establishing universal ethics, or bringing back belief in magic or animate nature would be the route to overcoming the depersonalizing structures of modern domination. By contrast, to promote enlightenment would be to emphasize the importance of science or political liberalism, and focus politics on the stripping away of illusions. But neither being a magician or a disenchanter is necessarily redemptive. Power—both liberating and dominating, *potentia* and *potestas*—can be actualized by way of enchantment or disenchantment. Ideologies cloak themselves in both.

Take colonialism, for example. Scholars have shown that European colonists often spoke "the language of disenchantment" and aimed to eliminate indigenous "superstitions."[22] Witchcraft often served to mark the dividing line between so-called civilization and savagery. But European explorers and imperialists also presented themselves as gods, aiming to enslave indigenous peoples by convincing them of the reality of "white men's magic."[23] To further complicate the picture, there were figures like the British socialist Annie Besant, Olcott's successor as the leader of the Theosophical Society, who spent much of her later life promoting theosophy while championing the cause of Indian independence; or the British judge Sir John Woodroffe, who, when not serving as standing counsel to the colonial government of India, was publishing Tantric texts and hymns to the Goddess under the name Arthur Avalon.[24] Moreover, indigenous anticolonial movements have been both disenchanting (e.g., Maoists) and enchanting (e.g., Yihetuan "Boxers"). Therefore we can see magic as either domination or resistance, either colonial or postcolonial.

Part of the problem is that having granted the notion of modernity as a unity, the assumption often becomes that enchantment represents a single solution to diverse ills. But there is plenty of evidence that there have been bureaucracies fully committed to magic and ritual, that capitalism has the capacity to absorb all the magic of the world, that mythopoesis can be constant and no less alienating, and that technology and enchantment can be intertwined. Magic and secularism are not opposites. Even disenchantment and enchantment can be found together in the same text. We know all this because North America and Western Europe have not lost their magic.[25] One can find American presidents and their staff consulting with astrologers and psychics, the commercialization of esoteric traditions and books of magic, scholarship giving inadvertent birth to new occult movements, and even iPhone apps that let you consult the tarot.[26] Indeed, one could be drawn to New Age religion while building the atom bomb.

The Frankfurt School embodies the contradictions of the crusade against disenchantment. Critical theory's main message is often taken to be that enlightenment disenchantment has gone too far and transformed itself into the domination of nature and the dehumanization of humanity.[27] *Dialectic of Enlightenment* is one of the main contemporary touchstones for the critique of "the disenchantment of the world." But then we have a conundrum, as Adorno and company attempted to distance themselves from the German occult revival even as they drew inspiration from it, and in doing so they repeatedly condemned magic. In other words, Adorno and company are both a source of our unease with disenchantment and a source of disenchantment. Hence, they seem to have promoted the very thing they criticized.

The basic operating mode of critical theory is also one of unmasking myths. So it would look like a species of disenchantment, except that one of the main myths it wants to unmask is the enlightenment campaign to unmask myth. I do not want to fault Adorno and company for the very dialectical turns that make the movement so appealing to me, but merely to show the problems resulting from taking disenchantment and enlightenment to be in opposition.

From this vantage point, I too have been writing like a disenchanter. This project has been an attempt to undo *the myth that there is no myth*, which means that this project has also been demythologizing. I grant that this fact is interesting. As I have been arguing: thinking in terms of myth—and further, pursuing it, making a program of either re-enchantment or mythopoesis—is distorting. Thinking in terms of disenchantment—pursuing it, fetishizing the real, and aggressively demythologizing—is also distorting. What I think Adorno and company got right is that these two seeming opposites taken to the extreme ultimately converge.

Although this project has been rooted in its own kind of demythologizing, my allegiance is to neither side. Instead, I aim to repudiate the full extension of both. Indeed, my point is that the extreme of both modes transform into their opposite. By invoking the language of myth, it might seem that I have become a partisan of disenchantment, but my point is the reverse: that we can never fully escape myth. Criticism may imply demythologization, but we merely exchange one tale for another, albeit hopefully, a better one.[28] By challenging this narrative, I have been aiming to take up modernity and postmodernity together and exit both. This will not be an exodus into a mythless future. Contra Lyotard, I see no end to metanarratives. But I also see no reason to flee from them. Reason is historical. Thought is narrative.

NOTES

INTRODUCTION

1. Jules Courtier, *Rapport sur les séances d'Eusapia Palladino à L'Institut Général Psychologiquee en 1905, 1906, 1907 et 1908, Paris* (Mayenne: Institut Général Psychologique, 1908), 415. For more on Eusapia, see Christine Blondel, "Eusapia Palladino: La méthod expérimentale et la 'Diva des Savants,'" in *Des Savants face à L'occulte: 1870–1940*, ed. Bernadette Bensaude-Vincent and Christine Blondel (Paris: La Découverte, 2002), 143–71; and Carlos Alvarado, "Eusapia Palladino: An Autobiographical Essay," *Journal of Scientific Exploration* 25, no. 1 (2011): 77–101.

2. Courtier, *Rapport sur les séances*, 477.

3. For significant examples, see Max Horkheimer and Theodor Adorno, *Dialectic of Enlightenment* (Stanford, CA: Stanford University Press, 2002), 2; Zygmunt Bauman, *Intimations of Postmodernity* (London: Routledge, 1992), x–xi; Charles Taylor, *A Secular Age*, (Cambridge, MA: Harvard University Press, 2007), 25–27; and Marcel Gauchet, *The Disenchantment of the World* (Princeton, NJ: Princeton University Press, 1997).

4. Marie Curie, "*Fragments du journal tenu après la mort de Pierre* (Avril 1906–Avril 1907)," Pierre et Marie Curie: Papiers: V—DOCUMENTS A CARACTERE PRIVE, Bibliothèque nationale de France.

5. At various times there were other scientists, diplomats, and philosophers in attendance. Jules Courtier, the chief assistant at the Laboratory of Physiological Psychology at the Sorbonne, transcribed the proceedings in Courtier, *Rapport sur les séances*.

6. As Carlos Alvarado has noted, Eusapia first came to the attention of an Italian spiritualist, Giovanni Damiani, in about 1872, who wrote a letter about a clairvoyant called "Sapia Padalino" to the *Spiritual Magazine* in that year. Alvarado, "Eusapia Palladino," 81–82.

7. For the history of psychical research in France, see Nicole Edelman, *Voyantes, guérisseuses et visionnaires en France, 1785–1914* (Paris: A. Michel, 1995); Régine Plas, *Naissance d'une science humaine: La psychologie: Les psychologues et le "merveilleux psychique"* (Paris: La Découverte, 2000); John Monroe, *Laboratories of Faith: Mesmerism, Spiritism, and Occultism in Modern France* (Ithaca, NY: Cornell University Press, 2008); M. Brady Brower, *Unruly Spir-*

its: The Science of Psychic Phenomena in Modern France (Urbana: University of Illinois Press, 2010); and Sofie Lachapelle, *Investigating the Supernatural: From Spiritism and Occultism to Psychical Research and Metapsychics in France* (Baltimore: Johns Hopkins University Press, 2011).

8. For example, see Gérard Encausse (Papus), *Les rayons invisibles et les dernieres expériences d'Eusapia devant l'occultisme* (Tours: E. Arrault, 1896).

9. For a discussion, see Robert Grogin, *The Bergsonian Controversy in France, 1900–1914* (Calgary: University of Calgary Press, 1988); and George William Barnard, *Living Consciousness: The Metaphysical Vision of Henri Bergson* (Albany: State University of New York Press, 2012), esp. 249–56.

10. *Pierre Curie: Correspondances*, ed. Karin Blanc (Saint-Rémy-en-l'Eau: M. Hayot, 2009), 644 (emphasis in the original). I have consulted Susan Quinn, *Marie Curie: A Life* (New York: Simon & Schuster, 1995), 226, while preparing my own translation. For Pierre Curie's thoughts on these experiments, see *Pierre Curie: Correspondances*, esp. 575–79, 584, 635–36. See also Anna Hurwic, *Pierre Curie* (Paris: Flammarion, 1995), 247–50.

11. Letter to Countess Élisabeth Greffulhe, reproduced in *Pierre Curie: Correspondances*, 645.

12. Letter to Julian Ochorowicz, Marie Curie, *Korespondencja Polska Marii Skłodowskiej-Curie 1881–1934*, ed. Krystyna Kabzińska (Warsaw: Wydawnictwa IHN PAN, 1994), 54.

13. William James, "An Estimate of Palladino," *Cosmopolitan Magazine*, no. 48 (1910): 299 (emphasis in the original). Although at times James had his doubts about Eusapia, in a letter to Eleanor Sidgwick, he stated, "The proof seems overwhelming, and it has been an enormous relief to my mind to quit the balancing attitude which I have voluntarily maintained for 15 years, and come to a stable belief in the matter." *The Correspondence of William James*, 12 vols. (Charlottesville: University Press of Virginia, 1992–2004), 11:405–6. See also Andreas Sommer, "Psychical Research and the Origins of American Psychology," *History of the Human Sciences* 25, no. 2 (2012): 23–44.

14. As Latour puts it, "Haven't we shed enough tears over the disenchantment of the world? Haven't we frightened ourselves enough with the poor European who is thrust into a cold soulless cosmos, wandering on an inert planet in a world devoid of meaning?" Bruno Latour, *We Have Never Been Modern* (Cambridge, MA: Harvard University Press, 1993), 115.

15. Charles Taylor, "Western Secularity," in *Rethinking Secularism*, ed. Craig Calhoun, Mark Juergensmeyer, and Jonathan VanAntwerpen (New York: Oxford University Press, 2011), 38. See also Morris Berman, *The Reenchantment of the World* (Ithaca, NY: Cornell University Press, 1988), 2.

16. See *Encyclopedia of Religion*, ed. Lindsay Jones, Mircea Eliade, and Charles Adams (Detroit: Macmillan Reference, 2005), s.v. "Secularization," by Bryan Wilson; and José Casanova, *Public Religions in the Modern World* (Chicago: University of Chicago Press, 1994), 31.

17. See also Taylor, *A Secular Age*.

18. For examples of work both in and at the edge of new materialism, see: Stacy Alaimo, *Bodily Natures: Science, Environment, and the Material Self* (Bloomington: Indiana University Press, 2010); Karen Barad, *Meeting the Universe Halfway: Quantum Physics and the Entanglement of Matter and Meaning* (Durham, NC: Duke University Press, 2007); Jane Bennett, *Vibrant Matter: A Political Ecology of Things* (Durham, NC: Duke University Press, 2010);

William Connolly, *A World of Becoming* (Durham, NC: Duke University Press, 2010); Diana Coole and Samantha Frost, eds., *New Materialisms: Ontology, Agency, and Politics.* (Durham, NC: Duke University Press, 2010); Graham Harman, *The Quadruple Object* (Winchester: Zero Books, 2011); Eduardo Kohn, *How Forests Think toward an Anthropology beyond the Human* (Berkeley: University of California Press, 2013); Quentin Meillassoux, *Après la finitude: Essai sur la nécessité de la contingence* (Paris: Seuil, 2006); and Manuel Vásquez, *More Than Belief: A Materialist Theory of Religion* (New York: Oxford University Press, 2011). Although not normally included in this movement, for a similar critique—albeit with a different conclusion—see Gilbert Germain, *A Discourse on Disenchantment* (Albany: State University of New York Press, 1993).

19. See Barad, *Meeting the Universe Halfway*, for the first; for the second, see Jane Bennett, *The Enchantment of Modern Life: Attachments, Crossings, and Ethics* (Princeton, NJ: Princeton University Press, 2001). Bennett's work is especially interesting because she rejects the historical narrative of disenchantment, even as she calls for a revival of enchantment.

20. For example, see Edward Dolnick, *The Clockwork Universe: Isaac Newton, the Royal Society, and the Birth of the Modern World* (New York: HarperCollins, 2011).

21. By "world picture" (Ger. *Weltbild*), I mean to invoke a technical term, which I am taking from Dijksterhuis and Heidegger. See Eduard Jan Dijksterhuis, *De Mechanisering Van Het Wereldbeeld* (Amsterdam: J. M. Meulenhoff, 1950); and Martin Heidegger, "Die Zeit des Weltbildes" (1938), translated as "The Age of the World Picture" in Heidegger, *Off the Beaten Track*, trans. Julian Young and Kenneth Haynes (New York: Cambridge University Press, 2002).

22. Despite my debt to Lacan, I'd like to distance my use of "the Real" from his account of a kind of unattainable being in itself. Jacques Lacan, *Écrits* (New York: W. W. Norton, 2006).

23. For this claim, see Robert Richards, *The Tragic Sense of Life: Ernst Haeckel and the Struggle over Evolutionary Thought* (Chicago: University of Chicago Press, 2009), 344.

24. T. M. Luhrmann, *Persuasions of the Witch's Craft: Ritual Magic in Contemporary England* (Cambridge, MA: Harvard University Press, 1989), 8.

25. See, for example, Denise Buell, "The Afterlife Is Not Dead: Spiritualism, Postcolonial Theory, and Early Christian Studies," *Church History* 78, no. 4 (2009): 862-72.

26. I am mindful that by focusing so much attention on canonical figures, I risk structurally replicating Eurocentrism. But I think deconstructive work of this sort is needed especially as a complement to postcolonial and non-European-focused studies. Indeed, I intend this monograph to supplement research I am doing on the Japanese case.

27. Indeed, an analogous move could be done from the perspective of gender studies by showing that the central figures of the supposedly heteronormative patriarchy, from Descartes to Rousseau to Kant to Schopenhauer to Freud, were themselves practitioners of alternate sexualities that don't make it into the conventional narratives of the dominance of European modes of normativity.

28. For sociology as a component of secularization, see Guenther Roth and Wolfgang Schluchter, *Max Weber's Vision of History* (Berkeley: University of California Press, 1979), 144.

29. For three very different accounts of modernity as mythless, see Georges Bataille, *The Absence of Myth: Writings on Surrealism*, trans. Michael Richardson (London: Verso, 1994); Jean-Lucy Nancy, *La communauté désœuvrée*, 2nd ed. (Paris: Bourgois, 1999), esp. 157-58; and Sophia Heller, *The Absence of Myth* (Albany: State University of New York Press, 2006).

30. For an illuminating discussion of the term's discursive function, see Bruce Lincoln, *Theorizing Myth: Narrative, Ideology, and Scholarship* (Chicago: University of Chicago Press, 1999), ix.

31. This project is thus partially an exercise in what Hans Blumenberg calls "metaphorology." While I differ from Blumenberg in not distinguishing between myth and absolute metaphor, I agree with his rejection of the old opposition between mythos and logos. Hans Blumenberg, *Paradigms for a Metaphorology*, trans. Robert Savage (Ithaca, NY: Cornell University Press, 2010), 77. In calling these "myths," I aim to draw close to the early Greek meaning of μῦθος (*mythos*) as "story" or "narrative" while discarding the assumption that myths are necessarily archaic. See R. S. P. Beekes and Lucien van Beek, *Etymological Dictionary of Greek* (Leiden: Brill, 2010), 2:976.

32. Hans Robert Jauss, "Modernity and Literary Tradition," trans. Christian Thorne, *Critical Inquiry* 31, no. 2 (2005): 329–64.

33. Saurabh Dube, "Modernity and Its Enchantments: An Introduction," in *Enchantments of Modernity: Empire, Nation, Globalization*, ed. Saurabh Dube (New York: Routledge, 2009), 1–41.

34. Think of the equivalence of the words *modern* and *novel*.

35. Jauss, "Modernity and Literary Tradition."

36. This "myth of modernity" and its legitimation of colonization and violence are forcefully articulated in Enrique Dussel, *The Invention of the Americas: Eclipse of "the Other" and the Myth of Modernity*, trans. Michael Barber (New York: Continuum, 1995). This function of the discourse of modernity has been well explored by postcolonial theorists, but they have tended to overlook the ambivalence of modernity's major mythmakers.

37. Theodor Adorno, *Negative Dialektik* (Frankfurt: Suhrkamp, 1966); Erich Fromm, *Escape from Freedom* (New York: H. Holt, 1994); Max Horkheimer, *Eclipse of Reason* (New York: Continuum, 2004); Leo Löwenthal, "Das Dämonische," in *Gabe Herrn Rabbiner Dr. Nobel Zum 50. Geburtstag*, ed. Martin Buber (Frankfurt: J. Kauffmann, 1921), 50–62; Georg Lukács, *The Destruction of Reason* (Atlantic Highlands, NJ: Humanities Press, 1981); and Herbert Marcuse, *One-Dimensional Man: Studies in the Ideology of Advanced Industrial Society*, 2nd ed. (Boston: Beacon Press, 1991). See also Jürgen Habermas, *The Theory of Communicative Action*, 2 vols. (Boston: Beacon Press, 1984); and Habermas, *The Future of Human Nature* (Malden, MA: Polity, 2003).

38. As Lukács phrased it in his most polemical work: What was "Germany's path to Hitler in the sphere of philosophy"? Lukács, *Destruction of Reason*, 4.

39. Horkheimer and Adorno, *Dialectic of Enlightenment*, xiv.

40. Fromm, *Escape from Freedom*, 11–12.

41. Horkheimer, *Eclipse of Reason*, v.

42. Marcuse, *One-Dimensional Man*, xlii, 20.

43. Horkheimer and Adorno, *Dialectic of Enlightenment*, 82. I capitalize *Enlightenment* when it refers to a time period and use lowercase when it refers to a project.

44. Ibid., xviii.

45. Löwenthal, "Das Dämonische," 55.

46. Fromm, *Escape from Freedom*, 26.

47. Horkheimer, *Eclipse of Reason*, 15, 66–67.

48. Habermas, *Future of Human Nature*, 106.

49. Horkheimer and Adorno, *Dialectic of Enlightenment*, 2, 6.

50. Ibid., 9. Indeed, *Dialectic*'s original prospectus described the manuscript as exploring "the origins of the manifest crisis of modern culture in history and in the processes through which humankind established its rule over nature." Quoted in Rolf Wiggershaus, *The Frankfurt School: Its History, Theories, and Political Significance* (Cambridge, MA: MIT Press, 2007), 334.

51. I mean to extend to Adorno and company Paget Henry's critique of Habermas's reliance on rationality/myth binaries. Paget Henry, "Myth, Language, and Habermasian Rationality: Another Africana Contribution," in *Perspectives on Habermas*, ed. Lewis Hahn (Chicago: Open Court, 2000), 89–112.

52. Outside critical theory, claims about the contemporary "flight from reason" were central to James Webb, *The Occult Underground* (LaSalle, IL: Open Court, 1974).

53. Ulrich Beck, Anthony Giddens, and Scott Lash, *Reflexive Modernization: Politics, Tradition and Aesthetics in the Modern Social Order* (Oxford: Polity Press, 1994).

54. Pierre Bourdieu and Loïc J. D. Wacquant, *An Invitation to Reflexive Sociology* (Chicago: University of Chicago Press, 1992).

55. For example, Povinelli has noted how Australian anthropologists have been called in to adjudicate what counts as authentically indigenous and, in the process, by authorizing or de-authorizing different traditions, have transformed that culture. Elizabeth A. Povinelli, *The Cunning of Recognition* (Durham, NC: Duke University Press, 2002).

56. Christian Thorne, "Empires of Theory" (unpublished manuscript, 2015).

57. For a good example of this sort of work, see Robert A. Orsi, *Between Heaven and Earth: The Religious Worlds People Make and the Scholars Who Study Them* (Princeton, NJ: Princeton University Press, 2005).

58. For a critique of "egological" versions of reflexivity, see Bourdieu and Wacquant, *Invitation to Reflexive Sociology*, 40.

59. Carlos Castaneda's work is a prime example because his neo-shamanic revival seems to have been largely cobbled together out of books from the UCLA library.

60. John Hedley Brooke, *Science and Religion: Some Historical Perspectives* (New York: Cambridge University Press, 1991), 45–46.

61. Ronald Numbers, *Galileo Goes to Jail: And Other Myths about Science and Religion* (Cambridge, MA: Harvard University Press, 2009).

62. For a fuller survey of this argument, see Jason Ānanda Josephson, *The Invention of Religion in Japan* (Chicago: University of Chicago Press, 2012), 2–17.

63. For example, see Paul Feyerabend, *Against Method* (London: Verso, 2010); Sandra Harding, "Is Modern Science an Ethno-Science? Rethinking Epistemological Assumptions," in *Science and Technology in a Developing World*, ed. Terry Shinn, Jack Spaapen, and Venni Krishna (Dordrecht: Springer Netherlands, 1997), 37–64; and Thomas S. Kuhn, *The Structure of Scientific Revolutions* (Chicago: University of Chicago Press, 1970).

64. I also put these two critiques together in Josephson, *Invention of Religion in Japan*. Also signicant in this regard is Andrew Jewett, "Science and Religion in Postwar America,"

in *The Worlds of American Intellectual History*, eds. James T. Kloppenberg, Michael O'Brien, Joel Isaac, and Jennifer Ratner-Rosenhagen (New York: Oxford University Press, 2016), 237–56.

65. Peter Harrison, *The Territories of Science and Religion* (Chicago: University of Chicago Press, 2015), 108.

66. Ibid., 173, 187.

67. Serge Margel, *Superstition: L'anthropologie du religieux en terre de chrétienté* (Paris: Galilée, 2005); Michel de Certeau, "What We Do When We Believe," in *On Signs*, ed. Marshall Blonsky (Baltimore: John Hopkins University Press, 1985). See also H. Floris Cohen, *The Scientific Revolution* (Chicago: University of Chicago Press, 1994), 118.

68. Wouter Hanegraaff, *Esotericism and the Academy: Rejected Knowledge in Western Culture* (Cambridge: Cambridge University Press, 2012).

69. Even today, philosophers of science still debate the issue of the demarcation problem—namely, how to differentiate science from so-called pseudoscience or superstition. Interestingly, the paradigmatic case often seems to be astrology (which, it turns out, is harder to reject on philosophical grounds than one might at first suspect). See Massimo Pigliucci and Maarten Boudry, eds., *Philosophy of Pseudoscience: Reconsidering the Demarcation Problem* (Chicago: University of Chicago Press, 2013).

70. Michael Bergunder, " 'Religion' and 'Science' within a Global Religious History," *Aries* 16, no. 1 (2016): 86–141.

71. Jacques Derrida and Maurizio Ferraris, *A Taste for the Secret* (Malden: Blackwell, 2001), 5.

72. For a recent example, see Stephen Greenblatt, *The Swerve: How the World Became Modern* (New York: W. W. Norton, 2011). Note that his version of the myth of disenchantment occurs on p. 10.

73. Notably: Homi K. Bhabha, *The Location of Culture* (New York: Routledge, 1994); Gurminder Bhambra, *Rethinking Modernity: Postcolonialism and the Sociological Imagination* (New York: Palgrave, 2007); Dipesh Chakrabarty, *Provincializing Europe: Postcolonial Thought and Historical Difference* (Princeton, NJ: Princeton University Press, 2000), especially 28; Paul Gilroy, *The Black Atlantic: Modernity and Double Consciousness* (Cambridge, MA: Harvard University Press, 1993); Kwame Gyekye, *Tradition and Modernity: Philosophical Reflections on the African Experience* (New York: Oxford University Press, 2011); Achille Mbembe, *On the Postcolony* (Berkeley: University of California Press, 2001); V. Y. Mudimbe, *The Invention of Africa: Gnosis, Philosophy, and the Order of Knowledge* (Bloomington: Indiana University Press, 1988); and Edward Said, *Orientalism* (New York: Vintage Books, 1994). For more postcolonial critiques of disenchantment, see the following chapter.

74. Notably: Catherine L. Albanese, *A Republic of Mind and Spirit: A Cultural History of American Metaphysical Religion* (New Haven, CT: Yale University Press, 2007); Courtney Bender, *The New Metaphysicals: Spirituality and the American Religious Imagination* (Chicago: University of Chicago Press, 2010); Jeffrey Kripal, *Authors of the Impossible: The Paranormal and the Sacred* (Chicago: University of Chicago Press, 2010); Kripal, *Mutants and Mystics: Science Fiction, Superhero Comics, and the Paranormal* (Chicago: University of Chicago Press, 2011); Kripal, *Roads of Excess, Palaces of Wisdom: Eroticism and Reflexivity in the Study of Mysticism* (Chicago: University of Chicago Press, 2001); Joshua Landy and Michael Saler, eds., *The Re-enchantment of the World: Secular Magic in a Rational Age* (Stanford, CA: Stanford

University Press, 2009); John Lardas Modern, *Secularism in Antebellum America* (Chicago: University of Chicago Press, 2011); Alex Owen, *The Place of Enchantment: British Occultism and the Culture of the Modern* (Chicago: University of Chicago Press, 2004); Christopher Partridge, *The Re-enchantment of the West*, 2 vols. (New York: T & T Clark, 2004–06); Randall Styers, *Making Magic: Religion, Magic, and Science in the Modern World* (New York: Oxford University Press, 2004); Kocku von Stuckrad, *The Scientification of Religion* (Boston: De Gruyter, 2014); and Hent de Vries, "Media Res: Global Religion, Public Spheres, and the Task of Contemporary Comparative Religious Studies," in *Religion and Media*, ed. Hent de Vries and Samuel M. Weber (Stanford, CA: Stanford University Press, 2001), 3–42. Finally, of direct relevance is Egil Asprem, *The Problem of Disenchantment: Scientific Naturalism and Esoteric Discourse, 1900–1939* (Boston: Brill, 2014), which unfortunately only came to my attention during the in-press phase, and hence I do not have the space to fully engage with it in this manuscript.

75. Although my attention is on the discourse of the metropole rather than the colonial periphery, I see this project as an example of postcolonial theory and benefiting from the field's major insights. For an example of relevant work on the colonial periphery, see Robert Yelle, *The Language of Disenchantment: Protestant Literalism and Colonial Discourse in British India* (New York: Oxford University Press, 2013).

76. Michel Foucault, *Histoire de la sexualité, 1: La volonté de savoir* (Paris: Gallimard, 1976), 18–19.

CHAPTER ONE

1. For a history of this shrine, see Sarah Thal, *Rearranging the Landscape of the Gods* (Chicago: University of Chicago Press), 2005.

2. Jason Ānanda Josephson, "The Empowered World: Buddhist Medicine and the Potency of Prayer in Japan," in *Deus in Machina: Religion, Technology, and the Things in Between*, ed. Jeremy Stolow (New York: Fordham University Press, 2012), 117–41.

3. For more examples, see Ian Reader and George Tanabe, *Practically Religious Worldly Benefits and the Common Religion of Japan* (Honolulu: University of Hawaii Press, 1998). For anthropological accounts, see Honda Sōichirō, *Nihon Shintō Nyūmon* (Tokyo: Nihon Bungei-sha, 1985), esp. 20; and Ikuo Takeuchi, Utsunomiya Kyōko, and Arakawa Toshihiko, *Jujutsu Ishiki to Gendai Shakai* (Tokyo: Seikyūsha, 2010).

4. For the examples above, see: Adam Ashforth, *Witchcraft, Violence, and Democracy in South Africa* (Chicago: University of Chicago Press, 2005); Heike Behrend, *Alice und Die Geister: Krieg im Norden Ugandas* (München: Trickster Wissenschaft, 1993); Alexandra Boutros, "Virtual Vodou, Actual Practice: Transfiguring the Technological," in *Deus in Machina: Religion, Technology, and the Things in Between*, ed. Jeremy Stolow (New York: Fordham University Press, 2012), 239–59; Jean and John Comaroff, "Occult Economies and the Violence of Abstraction," *American Ethnologist* 26, no. 2 (1999): 279–303; Kirsten Endres, "Spirited Modernities: Mediumship and Ritual Performativity in Late Socialist Vietnam," in *Modernity and Re-enchantment: Religion in Post-revolutionary Vietnam*, ed. Philip Taylor (Lexington Books, 2007), 194–220; Peter Geschiere, *The Modernity of Witchcraft: Politics and the Occult in Postcolonial Africa* (Charlottesville: University of Virginia Press, 1997); David Hess, *Samba in the Night: Spiritism in Brazil* (New York: Columbia University Press, 1994); David Lan, *Guns*

and Rain: Guerillas and Spirit Mediums in Zimbabwe (Berkeley: University of California Press, 1987); Birgit Meyer, "Commodities and the Power of Prayer: Pentecostalist Attitudes towards Consumption in Contemporary Ghana," *Development and Change* 29 (1998): 751–76; Aihwa Ong, *Spirits of Resistance and Capitalist Discipline: Factory Women in Malaysia* (Albany: State University of New York Press, 1987); James Siegel, *Naming the Witch* (Stanford, CA: Stanford University Press, 2006); Tulasi Srinivas, *Winged Faith: Rethinking Globalization and Religious Pluralism through the Sathya Sai Movement* (New York: Columbia University, 2010); and John Thompson, "Santísima Muerte: On the Origin and Development of a Mexican Occult Image," *Journal of the Southwest* 40, no. 4 (1998): 405–36.

See also Nils Bubandt, *Democracy, Corruption and the Politics of Spirits in Contemporary Indonesia* (London: Routledge, 2014); Erwan Dianteill, *Des dieux et des signes: Initiation, écriture et divination dans les religions afro-cubaines* (Paris: Editions de l'École des hautes études, 2000); Kirsten Endres and Andrea Lauser, eds., *Engaging the Spirit World in Modern Southeast Asia* (New York: Berghahn Books, 2011); Paul Johnson, *Secrets, Gossip, and Gods: The Transformation of Brazilian Candomblé* (New York: Oxford University Press, 2002); Birgit Meyer and Peter Pels, eds., *Magic and Modernity: Interfaces of Revelation and Concealment* (Stanford, CA: Stanford University Press, 2003); Adam Mohr, *Enchanted Calvinism: Labor Migration, Afflicting Spirits, and Christian Therapy in the Presbyterian Church of Ghana* (Rochester, NY: University of Rochester Press, 2013); Henrietta Moore and Todd Sanders, eds., *Magical Interpretations, Material Realities: Modernity, Witchcraft and the Occult in Postcolonial Africa* (New York: Routledge, 2001); Todd Ramón Ochoa, *Society of the Dead: Quita Manaquita and Palo Praise in Cuba* (Berkeley: University of California Press, 2010); and Manuel Vásquez, *The Brazilian Popular Church and the Crisis of Modernity* (Cambridge: Cambridge University Press, 2008).

5. Denis Byrne, "The Fortress of Rationality: Archaeology and Thai Popular Religion," in *Cosmopolitan Archaeologies*, ed. L. Meskell (Durham, NC: Duke University Press, 2009), 73–74.

6. Flyers on the wall of Dobrá Tea in Northampton, MA, June 30, 2014. Bender discusses flyers at the Harvest Cooperative Supermarket in Cambridge, MA, in Courtney Bender, *The New Metaphysicals: Spirituality and the American Religious Imagination* (Chicago: University of Chicago Press, 2010), 21–22.

7. Catherine L. Albanese, *A Republic of Mind and Spirit: A Cultural History of American Metaphysical Religion* (New Haven: Yale University Press, 2007); and Bender, *New Metaphysicals*.

8. See Christopher Partridge, *The Re-enchantment of the West*, 2 vols. (New York: T & T Clark, 2004–06); Jeffrey Kripal, *Authors of the Impossible: The Paranormal and the Sacred* (Chicago: University of Chicago Press, 2010); and Kripal, *Mutants and Mystics: Science Fiction, Superhero Comics, and the Paranormal* (Chicago: University of Chicago Press, 2011). Kripal also uses "occulture" to signal the way that each culture "actualizes different potentials of human consciousness and energy" (*Authors of the Impossible*, 29).

9. Kripal, *Authors of the Impossible*, 6.

10. Karlyn Crowley, "New Age Feminism? Reading the Woman's 'New Age' Nonfiction Best Seller in the United States," in *Print Culture History in Modern America: Religion and the Culture of Print in Modern America*, ed. Charles Cohen and Paul Boyer (Madison: University of Wisconsin Press, 2009), 304–5. Topics taken from the top 20 in Amazon's "Best Sellers in

Books, accessed October 29, 2015, http://www.amazon.com/best-sellers-books-Amazon/zgbs/books/.

11. Examples of television programs include: *Most Haunted* (Living TV, UK), *Ghost Hunters* (Syfy Channel), *Celebrity Ghost Stories* (Biography, UK and USA), *Great British Ghosts* (UKTV), *Most Terrifying Places in America* (Travel), *Ghost Hunt* (TVNZ, New Zealand), and *Stalked by a Ghost* (Biography); even Animal Planet had its own show, *The Haunted* (in Norway: *Åndenes Makt* [The power of spirits] on TVNorge, with a Danish spinoff on TV3 Denmark); *Destination Truth* (Syfy) and *MonsterQuest* (History) hunt for cryptids like bigfoot and werewolves; while others like *Cursed* (Biography), *America's Psychic Challenge* (Lifetime), *Ancient Aliens* (History), *Britain's Psychic Challenge* (Channel 5, UK), *Psychic Detectives* (Court TV), and Битва экстрасенсов (Bitva ėkstrasensov, Battle of the Psychics [literally "those with extrasensory capabilities"], in Russia) focus on psychic powers. Not to mention the frequent testimonies to faith healing and other "miraculous gifts" on the Trinity Broadcasting Network and its Evangelical affiliates.

12. For psychic celebrities, think Derek Acorah, Theresa Caputo, John Edward, and James Van Praagh.

13. See Pew Forum on Religion and Public Life, "Many Americans Mix Multiple Faiths: Eastern, New Age Beliefs Widespread," Pew Research Center, December 2009, accessed September 27, 2014, http://www.pewforum.org/files/2009/12/multiplefaiths.pdf.

14. Combining "strongly agree" and "somewhat agree" in the above. YouGov Omnibus Research, "Tech and Skeptics," January 21, 2015. See also Jenny Hall, "I Believe In . . .", YouGov Omnibus Research, January 21, 2015, accessed October 17, 2015, https://today.yougov.com/news/2015/01/21/i-believe/.

15. The *paranormal* is the current preferred idiom for what used to be called "superstitions" insofar as it refers to putatively irrational beliefs. As the term *paranormal* is largely anachronistic to the material I'm considering, I'll be largely dropping it from the material I discuss in later chapters. Also to be clear, I am not taking as given the rationality or irrationality of any particular belief; rather, I am interested in the cultural characterization of certain beliefs as such.

16. They include in the paranormal: ESP, haunted houses, ghosts, telepathy, clairvoyance, astrology, communication with the dead, witches, reincarnation, and channeling.

17. This survey might sound like a quirky outlier, if not for an earlier Gallup survey from 2001 which similarly concluded that 76 percent of Americans believed in at least one paranormal category (and these numbers also showed a minor increase from Gallup surveys conducted in 1990). Frank Newport and Maura Strausberg, "Americans' Belief in Psychic and Paranormal Phenomena Is Up over Last Decade," Gallup News Service, June 8, 2001.

18. Baylor University, *The Baylor Religion Survey, Wave 1* (Waco, TX: Baylor Institute for Studies of Religion, 2005) and *The Baylor Religion Survey, Wave 2* (Waco, TX: Baylor Institute for Studies of Religion, 2007). The data is from 2005 unless marked. Combining "absolutely exist" and "probably exist" as well as "strongly agree" and "agree."

19. Michael Cuneo, *American Exorcism: Expelling Demons in the Land of Plenty* (New York: Doubleday, 2001), 270.

20. Christopher D. Bader, F. Carson Mencken, and Joseph O. O. Baker, *Paranormal America: Ghost Encounters, UFO Sightings, Bigfoot Hunts, and Other Curiosities in Religion and Culture* (New York: New York University Press, 2010), 184.

21. For a more recent account of contemporary "spiritual warfare," see Sean McCloud, *American Possessions: Fighting Demons in the Contemporary United States* (New York: Oxford University Press, 2015).

22. Bader, Mencken, and Baker, 194 (emphasis added).

23. It should be noted that Bader, Mencken, and Baker construe the category of the paranormal differently than the Gallup survey.

24. Bader, Mencken, and Baker, *Paranormal America*, 56–58, 69. For fieldwork with one African American spiritualist community, see LeRhonda S. Manigault-Bryant, *Talking to the Dead: Religion, Music, and Lived Memory among Gullah-Geechee Women* (Durham, NC: Duke University Press, 2014).

25. Bader, Mencken, and Baker, *Paranormal America*, 74–75.

26. Based on a 2006 survey of 439 college students. Robert Roy Britt, "Higher Education Fuels Stronger Belief in Ghosts," Live Science, accessed October 17, 2015, http://www.livescience.com/564-higher-education-fuels-stronger-belief-ghosts.html.

27. Loretta Orion, *Never Again the Burning Times: Paganism Revived* (Prospect Heights, IL: Waveland Press, 1995), 66–69; see also T. M. Luhrmann, *Persuasions of the Witch's Craft: Ritual Magic in Contemporary England* (Cambridge, MA: Harvard University Press, 1989), esp. 6–7, 99; and George Gmelch and Richard Felson, "Can a Lucky Charm Get You through Organic Chemistry?" *Psychology Today* (December 1980), 75–78.

28. Theodor Adorno, "Thesen gegen den Okkultismus," in Adorno, *Gesammelte Schriften* (Frankfurt: Suhrkamp, 2003) 4:273–280.

29. See, for example, Clyde Wilcox, Linzey Sharon, and Ted G. Jelen, "Reluctant Warriors: Premillennialism and Politics in the Moral Majority," *Journal for the Scientific Study of Religion* 30, no. 3 (1991): 245–58.

30. See Ann Braude, *Radical Spirits: Spiritualism and Women's Rights in Nineteenth-Century America* (Bloomington: Indiana University Press, 2001).

31. Achille Mbembe, *On the Postcolony* (Berkeley: University of California Press, 2001), 4.

32. Owen Davies, *America Bewitched: The Story of Witchcraft after Salem* (Oxford: Oxford University Press, 2013), 3, 203.

33. Ibid., 212, 225.

34. Ibid., 218.

35. See, for example, Antonia Blumberg, "Pat Robertson Blames 'Witchcraft in the Family' for Boy's Stomach Pains," *Huffington Post*, July 14, 2014, accessed October 17, 2015, http://www.huffingtonpost.com/2014/07/14/pat-robertson-witchcraft_n_5585736.html; and Richard Hartley-Parkinson, "Witches 'Are Putting Curses on Unborn Babies through Ultrasounds You Put on Facebook," *Metro UK*, February 18, 2015, accessed October 17, 2015, http://metro.co.uk/2015/02/18/witches-are-putting-curses-on-unborn-babies-through-ultrasounds-you-put-on-facebook-5068281/.

36. According to a Harris Poll survey of 2,250 adults conducted in November 2013, 26 percent believe in witches. Larry Shannon-Missal, "Americans' Belief in God, Miracles and Heaven Declines," Harris Poll, December 16, 2013.

37. See, for example, William E. Burns, *An Age of Wonders: Prodigies, Politics, and Providence in England, 1658–1727* (Manchester: Manchester University Press, 2002); and Stuart

Clark, *Thinking with Demons: The Idea of Witchcraft in Early Modern Europe* (New York: Oxford University Press, 1997). For an account of the persistence of belief in miracles, see Jane Shaw, *Miracles in Enlightenment England* (New Haven, CT: Yale University Press, 2006).

38. Combining "completely agree" with "mostly agree." Pew Forum on Religion and Public Life, "U.S. Religious Landscape Survey: Religious Affiliation: Diverse and Dynamic," Pew Research Center, February 2008, accessed September 7, 2016, http://www.pewforum.org/files /2013/05/report-religious-landscape-study-full.pdf.

39. As Hall famously characterized seventeenth-century New England; see David D. Hall, *Worlds of Wonder, Days of Judgment: Popular Religious Belief in Early New England* (Cambridge, MA: Harvard University Press, 1990).

40. The demographics least associated with paranormal belief are practicing Jews (62 percent still believe in at least one paranormal category) and Evangelical Christians (64 percent still believe). Bader, Mencken, and Baker, *Paranormal America*, 93.

41. Ibid., 201.

42. Frank Newport, "In U.S., Four in 10 Report Attending Church in Last Week." *Gallup News Service* (December 24 2013); while Gallup reports that 10–15 percent are regular churchgoers in the UK. Robert Manchin, "Religion in Europe: Trust Not Filling the Pews," Gallup News Service, September 21, 2004.

43. Frank Newport, "More Than 9 in 10 Americans Continue to Believe in God," Gallup News Service, June 3, 2011.

44. TNS Opinion and Social, "Biotechnology Report," *Eurobarometer* 73, no. 1 (2010): 204.

45. See Lyons, "Paranormal Beliefs Come (Super) Naturally to Some." Belief in "God" has been taken from TNS Opinion and Social, "Biotechnology Report," and Newport, "More Than 9 in 10 Americans Continue to Believe in God," and should be taken as a very rough approximation only.

46. Fiona Macrae, "We're More Likely to Believe in the Supernatural Than God?" *Daily Mail Online*, March 27, 2014, accessed October 18, 2015, http://www.dailymail.co.uk/news /article-2590349/God-Were-likely-believe-supernatural-Number-people-think-sixth-sense -higher-regularly-attend-church.html. The source is a One Poll survey of British adults with a sample size of 2,000.

47. For example, a recent 2015 survey of belief in Sweden by the polling firm Demoskop (sample size 1,113) showed belief (from high to moderate) in paranormal phenomena (*paranormala fenomen*) at 37 percent. Mikael Ingemyr, ed., "Vof-UndersöKningen 2015," *Föreningen Vetenskap och Folkbildning*, October 29, 2015. There is anecdotal evidence of a similar pattern in Norway; see Andrew Higgins, "Norway Has a New Passion: Ghost Hunting," *New York Times*, October 24, 2015, http://www.nytimes.com/2015/10/25/world/europe/for-many-norwegians -ghosts-fill-a-void.html.

48. Ina Schmied-Knittel, "Außergewöhnliche Erfahrungen: Repräsentative Studien und Aktuelle Befunde," *Zeitschrift für Anomalistik*, no. 8 (2008): 107. They also included "Déjà Vu" in their questionnaire. Moreover, in their analysis of this data, the German sociologists Schmied-Knittel and Schetsche also reject the idea of contemporary Germany as disenchanted, emphasizing their larger conclusion that "postmodern people" often have magical experiences. Ina Schmied-Knittel and Michael Schetsche, "Everyday Miracles: Results of a Representa-

tive Survey in Germany," *European Journal of Parapsychology* 20, no. 1 (2005): 3–4. See also Schmied-Knittel and Schetsche, "Psi-Report Deutschland: Eine Repräsentative Bevölkerungsumfrage Zu Außergewöhnlichen Erfahrungen," in *Alltägliche Wunder: Erfahrungen mit dem Übersinnlichen-wissenschaftliche Befunde*, ed. Eberhard Bauer and Michael Schetsche (Würzberg: Ergon, 2003).

49. Daniel Boy, "Les Français et les para-sciences: Vingt ans de mesures," *Revue française de sociologie* 31, no. 1 (2002): 35–45. For a classic ethnography of French witchcraft belief, see Jeanne Favret-Saada, *Les mots, la mort, les sorts* (Paris: Gallimard, 1977), translated as *Deadly Words: Witchcraft in the Bocage* (New York: Cambridge University Press, 1980).

50. Demyan Belyaev, "Opyt empiricheskogo issledovaniia geterodoksal'noi religioznosti v sovremennoi Rossii' Опыт эмпирического исследования гетеродоксальной религиозности в современной России," *Sotsiologicheskiie issledovaniia* 11 (2009), 88–98.

51. Birgit Menzel, "The Occult Revival in Russia Today and Its Impact on Literature," *Harriman Review* 16, no. 1 (2007), 1. For more scholarship on this subject, see Bernice Glatzer Rosenthal, ed., *The Occult in Russian and Soviet Culture* (Ithaca, NY: Cornell University Press, 1997).

52. Bobby Duffy, "Supreme Being(s), the Afterlife and Evolution," *Ipsos Global @dvisory*, April 25, 2011. The same study had God belief in the United States at 70 percent.

53. Gordon Gauchat, "Politicization of Science in the Public Sphere: A Study of Public Trust in the United States, 1974 to 2010," *American Sociological Review* 77, no. 2 (April 1, 2012): 167–87.

54. "The Spirit of Things Unseen: Belief in Post-Religious Britain," *Theos*, September 17, 2013, 7.

55. Although fairies are missing from most of these surveys, scholars have emphasized continuities between fairy lore and UFO abduction narratives. Jacques Vallée, *Passport to Magonia: From Folklore to Flying Saucers* (Chicago: Regnery, 1969); and Kripal, *Authors of the Impossible*. While no pollster focused directly on "ancient prophecy," in the 2005 Baylor survey, 28.2 percent reported having researched "the prophecies of Nostradamus." See Bader, Mencken, and Baker, *Paranormal America*, 107.

56. Scholars have also tracked various changes in the ontological status of spirits and magic in various law codes, which show how an attempt to eliminate the danger of witchcraft slowly evolved into an attempt to eliminate belief in witchcraft. See, for example, Edward Peters, *The Magician, the Witch, and the Law* (Philadelphia: University of Pennsylvania Press, 1978). But one should be careful about reading this history unidirectionally, and also be careful not to too quickly conflate laws and popular beliefs.

57. David Hufford, "Visionary Spiritual Experiences in an Enchanted World," *Anthropology and Humanism* 35, no. 2 (2010): 142–58.

58. Ernest Gellner, *Spectacles and Predicaments: Essays in Social Theory* (New York: Cambridge University Press, 1979), 61–64.

59. Theodor Adorno, *Minima Moralia: Reflections from Damaged Life*, trans. Edmund Jephcott (New York: Verso, 2005), 239.

60. George Ritzer, *Enchanting a Disenchanted World: Revolutionizing the Means of Consumption* (Thousand Oaks, CA: Pine Forge Press, 1999).

61. Geoffrey K. Nelson, *Cults, New Religions and Religious Creativity* (London: Routledge & Kegan Paul, 1987), 1–2.

62. Partridge, *Re-enchantment of the West*, vol. 1, esp. 38–70.

63. For further examples, see Robert Wuthnow, *After Heaven: Spirituality in America since the 1950s* (Berkeley: University of California Press, 1998), esp. 2; and David Lyon, *Jesus in Disneyland: Religion in Postmodern Times* (Cambridge: Polity Press, 2000), esp. 34. Although in very different terms, one might also think of Christof Schorsch, *Die New-Age-Bewegung: Utopie und Mythos der Neuen Zeit* (Gütersloh: Gütersloher Verlagshaus, 1988), esp. 154–55.

64. Robert Ellwood, *The Sixties Spiritual Awakening: American Religion Moving from Modern to Postmodern* (New Brunswick, NJ: Rutgers University Press, 1994); and Hugh McLeod, *The Religious Crisis of the 1960s* (Oxford: Oxford University Press, 2007).

65. Pauline Rosenau, *Post-Modernism and the Social Sciences: Insights, Inroads, and Intrusions* (Princeton, NJ: Princeton University Press, 1992), 148–49.

66. Zygmunt Bauman, *Postmodern Ethics* (Cambridge: Blackwell, 1993), 33. See also Bauman, *Intimations of Postmodernity* (New York: Routledge, 1992).

67. David Lyon, "A Bit of a Circus: Notes on Postmodernity and New Age," *Religion*, 23 (1993): 120. See also Christopher H. Partridge, "Truth, Authority and Epistemological Individualism in New Age Thought," in *Handbook of New Age*, ed. Daren Kemp and Lewis James (Boston: Brill, 2007), 231–54, which cites the same passage of Lyon.

68. Kripal, *Authors of the Impossible*, 16.

CHAPTER TWO

1. Alexandre Koyré, *From the Closed World to the Infinite Universe* (Baltimore: Johns Hopkins University Press, 1957).

2. Gilbert Germain, *A Discourse on Disenchantment* (Albany: State University of New York Press, 1993), 1–2; Manuel Vásquez, *More Than Belief: A Materialist Theory of Religion* (New York: Oxford University Press, 2011), esp. 39.

3. Dijksterhuis treats Newton as the culmination of the mechanization of the world picture. E. J. Dijksterhuis, *De Mechanisering Van Het Wereldbeeld* (Amsterdam: J. M. Meulenhoff, 1950). See also Edward Dolnick, *The Clockwork Universe: Isaac Newton, the Royal Society, and the Birth of the Modern World* (New York: HarperCollins, 2011).

4. Max Horkheimer and Theodor Adorno, *Dialectic of Enlightenment*, trans. Edmund Jephcott (Stanford, CA: Stanford University Press, 2002).

5. For example, Koyré gives all three roles in his grand narrative, *From the Closed World to the Infinite Universe*.

6. Despite the pioneering status of the Hermetic tradition, Yates often overstates its coherence. Frances Yates, *Giordano Bruno and the Hermetic Tradition* (Chicago: University of Chicago Press, 1964).

7. Koyré, *From the Closed World*, 39; Arthur Lovejoy, *The Great Chain of Being: A Study of the History of an Idea* (Cambridge, MA: Harvard University Press, 1936), 116.

8. Hegel claims it was Jacobi who brought Bruno to philosophy by comparing him to Spinoza; G. W. F. Hegel, *Vorlesungen über die Geschichte der Philosophie* (Leiden: A. H. Adriani,

1908), 777. Another key source for Bruno as a scientific martyr is Domenico Berti, *Vita di Giordano Bruno da Nola* (Florence: Paravia, 1868); and more recently, Michael White, *The Pope and the Heretic: A True Story of Giordano Bruno* (New York: William Morrow, 2003).

9. Giordano Bruno, *Cause, Principle and Unity: Essays on Magic* (Cambridge: Cambridge University Press, 1998).

10. For examples, see A. G. Molland, "Roger Bacon as Magician," *Traditio* 30 (1974): 445–60; and Molland, "Roger Bacon and the Hermetic Tradition in Medieval Science," *Vivarium* 31, no. 1 (1993): 140–60. Copernicus's connection to Hermeticism is controversial. The main evidence for Hermetic influence is Copernicus's phrase "*Trismegistus visibilem deum*" in *De revolutionibus orbium coelestium*. For Kepler, see Patrick Boner, *Kepler's Cosmological Synthesis: Astrology, Mechanism and the Soul* (Boston: Brill, 2013).

11. Specifically, Descartes read Agrippa, della Porta, and Ramon Lull. Desmond Clarke, *Descartes: A Biography* (New York: Cambridge University Press, 2006), esp. 53–58.

12. René Descartes, *Oeuvres De Descartes*, 12 vols. (Paris: Léopold Cerf, 1897–1910), 6:9. See also Clarke, *Descartes*, 41.

13. Lynn Thorndike, "The Attitude of Francis Bacon and Descartes towards Magic and Occult Science," in *Science, Medicine, and History*, ed. Ashworth Underwood (New York: Oxford University Press, 1953), 454.

14. Descartes called this science *mathesis universalis*; see esp. "Rules for the Direction of the Mind" in René Descartes, *The Philosophical Writings of Descartes*, 3 vols. (New York: Cambridge University Press, 1984), 1:18–19. For the divine nature of mathematics in Descartes, see Morris Kline, *Mathematics: The Loss of Certainty* (New York: Oxford University Press, 1980), 42–43.

15. See, for example, Betty Dobbs, *The Janus Faces of Genius: The Role of Alchemy in Newton's Thought* (Cambridge: Cambridge University Press, 1991).

16. Charles Webster, *From Paracelsus to Newton: Magic and the Making of Modern Science* (New York: Cambridge University Press, 1982), 68.

17. Isaac Newton, *Newton: Philosophical Writings*, ed. Janiak Andrew (New York: Cambridge University Press, 2004), 112, 116.

18. Richard Westfall, *Never at Rest: A Biography of Isaac Newton* (New York: Cambridge University Press, 1980); see esp. 319–20, 815–17.

19. Edward Davis, "Newton's Rejection of the 'Newtonian World View': The Role of Divine Will in Newton's Natural Philosophy," *Science and Christian Belief* 3, no. 2 (1991): 103–17; David Kubrin, "Newton and the Cyclical Cosmos: Providence and the Mechanical Philosophy," *Journal of the History of Ideas* 28, no. 3 (1967): 325–46; and Stephen D. Snobelen, "Cosmos and Apocalypse," *New Atlantis*, no. 44 (2015), 76–94.

20. John Maynard Keynes, "Newton, the Man," in *The Collected Writings of John Maynard Keynes*, ed. Society Royal Economic, 30 vols. (New York: Macmillan, 1971–89), 10:363–64.

21. For Boyle, see Lawrence Principe, *The Aspiring Adept: Robert Boyle and His Alchemical Quest* (Princeton, NJ: Princeton University Press, 1998). For Oppenheimer, see James Hijiya, "The Gita of J. Robert Oppenheimer," *Proceedings of the American Philosophical Society* 144, no. 2 (2000): 123–67; and Isidor Isaac Rabi, *Oppenheimer* (New York: Scribner, 1969), 7.

Other examples: for Alfred Russel Wallace, see Robert Richards, *Darwin and the Emergence of Evolutionary Theories of Mind and Behavior* (Chicago: University of Chicago Press,

1987), 176–84; for William James, see Deborah Blum, *Ghost Hunters: William James and the Search for Scientific Proof of Life after Death* (New York: Penguin Press, 2006); for Thomas Edison, see Neil Baldwin, *Edison: Inventing the Century* (Chicago: University of Chicago Press, 2001), esp. 95–96; for Arthur Stanley Eddington, see Matthew Stanley, *Practical Mystic: Religion, Science, and A. S. Eddington* (Chicago: University of Chicago Press, 2007); for Wolfgang Pauli, see Suzanne Gieser, *The Innermost Kernel: Depth Psychology and Quantum Physics* (New York: Springer, 2005). See also Mark Morrisson, *Modern Alchemy: Occultism and the Emergence of Atomic Theory* (New York: Oxford University Press, 2007).

22. Harding summarizes: "One phenomenon feminist historians have focused on is the rape and torture metaphors in the writings of Sir Francis Bacon." Sandra Harding, *The Science Question in Feminism* (Ithaca, NY: Cornell University Press, 1986), 113; see also 115–16. For an early example, see Ludwig Feuerbach, "Geschichte der neuern Philosophie von Bacon von Verulam bis Benedict Spinoza" (originally published 1833), reproduced in Ludwig Feuerbach, *Sämmtliche Werke* (Leipzig: Wigand, 1846–90), vol. 4, esp. 66. See also Fritjof Capra, *The Turning Point: Science, Society, and the Rising Culture* (New York: Simon and Schuster, 1982), 56; Carolyn Merchant, *The Death of Nature: Women, Ecology, and the Scientific Revolution* (New York: Harper, 1993), 33; and Norman Wirzba, *The Paradise of God: Renewing Religion in an Ecological Age* (New York: Oxford University Press, 2007), 67–68, 81. Bacon plays an important role in Robert Yelle, *The Language of Disenchantment: Protestant Literalism and Colonial Discourse in British India* (New York: Oxford University Press, 2013), esp. 74, 88–91. But in Yelle it is Bacon's attempt to formulate a universal language, rather than to dominate nature, that is at stake.

23. Ernst Cassirer, *The Platonic Renaissance in England* (Austin: University of Texas Press, 1953), 48. See also Peter Pesic, "Proteus Unbound: Francis Bacon's Successors and the Defense of Experiment," *Studies in Philology* 98, no. 4 (2001): 428–56; and Carolyn Merchant, " 'The Violence of Impediments': Francis Bacon and the Origins of Experimentation," *Isis* 99, no. 4 (2008): 731–60.

24. Horkheimer and Adorno, *Dialectic of Enlightenment*, 2 (emphasis added).

25. For Foucault's "knowledge-power" (Foucault sometimes reversed the terms as "power-knowledge" French *pouvoir-savoir*), see Michel Foucault, *Histoire de la sexualité, 1: La volonté de savoir* (Paris: Gallimard, 1976), esp. 93, 130–31. For examples of Bacon and Foucault together, see Béatrice Han, *Foucault's Critical Project: Between the Transcendental and the Historical* (Stanford, CA: Stanford University Press, 2002), 112; and José María Rodríguez García, "Scientia Potestas Est—Knowledge Is Power," *Neohelicon* 28, no. 1 (2001): 109–21.

26. William Leiss, *The Domination of Nature* (Buffalo, NY: McGill-Queen's University Press, 1994), esp. 71; Merchant, *Death of Nature*, esp.164–65. See also David Hawkin, "The Disenchantment of Nature and Christianity's 'Burden of Guilt,'" *Laval Théologique et Philosophique* 55, no. 1 (1999): 65–71; Susanne Scholz, "The Mirror and the Womb: Conceptions of the Mind in Bacon's Discourse of the Natural Sciences," in *Feminism and the Enlightenment*, vol. 1 of *Feminism*, ed. Mary Evans (New York: Routledge, 2001), 173–80; Pierre Hadot, *The Veil of Isis* (Cambridge, MA: Belknap Press of Harvard University Press, 2006), 93.

27. See Paolo Rossi, *Francesco Bacone: Dalla magia alla scienza* (Bari: Laterza, 1957); Charles Webster, *The Great Instauration: Science, Medicine and Reform, 1626–1660* (New York: Holmes & Meier, 1976); John Henry, *Knowledge Is Power: How Magic, the Government*

and an Apocalyptic Vision Inspired Francis Bacon to Create Modern Science (Lanham, MD: Icon Books, 2003); Stephen McKnight, *The Religious Foundations of Francis Bacon's Thought* (Columbia: University of Missouri Press, 2006); and Peter Harrison, *The Fall of Man and the Foundations of Science* (New York: Cambridge University Press, 2007). Also, after the early drafts of this chapter and independently using the phrase "the Science of Magic," I came across a dissertation by Sophie Weeks, "Francis Bacon's Science of Magic" (University of Leeds, 2007), to which I find myself largely in agreement. Points of accord will be noted below.

28. Rossi, *Francesco Bacone*. For astrology, see also Webster, *From Paracelsus to Newton*, 31.

29. I am agreeing here with Weeks, "Bacon's Science of Magic."

30. Bacon, *De augmentis*. Reproduced in *The Works of Francis Bacon*, ed. James Spedding, Robert Ellis, and Douglas Heath, 14 vols. (London: Longmans, 1857–74), 1:456–57. My translation.

31. Latin in *Works of Francis Bacon*, 1:573, translated in ibid., 4:366–67. See also 3:351.

32. Latin in *Works of Francis Bacon*, 1:573, I amended the translation appearing in 4: 366. See also Weeks, "Bacon's Science of Magic," 2.

33. To be sure, in *Novum Organum* (1620), Bacon does remark, "*Scientia & Potentia humana in idem oincident, quia ignoratio causæ destituit effectum.*" In English, "Human knowledge and human power come to the same thing, for ignorance of cause puts the effect beyond reach." Francis Bacon, *The Instauratio Magna, Part 2: "Novum Organum" and Associated Texts*, ed. Graham Rees (Oxford: Clarendon, 2004), 64–65. But again, this is not the same as saying "knowledge is power," and when scholars want that phrase they usually (incorrectly) cite Bacon's meditations.

34. Reproduced in Francis Bacon, *A Harmony of the Essays*, ed. Edward Arber (London: Constable, 1871), 128.

35. Steven Matthews, "Francis Bacon and the Divine Hierarchy of Nature," in *The Invention of Discovery, 1500–1700*, ed. James Fleming (Burlington, VT: Ashgate, 2011), 42.

36. Francis Bacon, *Sacred Meditations* (1598), reproduced in Bacon, *Harmony of the Essays*, 129.

37. Bacon, *The Instauratio Magna, Part 2*, 19. See also *Works of Francis Bacon*, 4:493–504.

38. See Peter Harrison, "The Book of Nature and Early Modern Science," in *The Book of Nature in Early Modern and Modern History*, ed. Klaas van Berkel and Arjo Vanderjagt (Dudley, MA: Peeters, 2006).

39. Serge Margel, *Superstition: L'anthropologie du religieux en terre de chrétienté* (Paris: Galilée, 2005).

40. Thomas Aquinas, *Summa Theologica* (Westminster: Christian Classics, 1981), 3:1585.

41. Pedro Ciruelo, *Reprouación de las supersticiones y hechizerias* (Valencia: Ediciones Albatros, 1978), 39, translated in Stuart Clark, *Thinking with Demons: The Idea of Witchcraft in Early Modern Europe* (New York: Oxford University Press, 1997), 478.

42. Both the Latin *superstitio* and the German *Aberglaube* were used. See, for example, Martin Luther, *D. Martin Luthers Werke: Kritische Gesammtausgabe* (Graz: Akademische Druck- und Verlagsanstalt, 1964), 6:539.

43. Ibid., 54:195–299. It is worth noting that Luther started not as a schismatic but a reformer within the institution of the church, and it was only in later works such as this that his critique of the pope as Antichrist took shape.

44. Translated in Euan Cameron, *Enchanted Europe: Superstition, Reason, and Religion, 1250-1750* (New York: Oxford University Press, 2010), 166.

45. Ibid., 169.

46. See ibid., which is a fuller study of the concept of superstition in the period from 1250-1750.

47. Ulinka Rublack, *Reformation Europe* (New York: Cambridge University Press, 2005), 10-11.

48. See, for example, *Works of Francis Bacon*, 3:251.

49. Ibid., 6:416.

50. Ibid., 3:245

51. Ibid., 4:53-64.

52. Ibid., 4:432.

53. Ibid., 4:56.

54. Ibid., 4:88.

55. Ibid., 4:87-89.

56. Ibid., 6:416.

57. Ibid., 4:172-73 (emphasis added).

58. Think: Sylva sylvarum (1627).

59. See Merchant, "Violence of Impediments."

60. See Alan Soble, "In Defense of Bacon," in *A House Built on Sand*, ed. Noretta Koertge (New York: Oxford University Press, 2000), 195-254. Perhaps Bacon's most damning phrase is from *Temporis Partus Masculus*, which states, "I am come in very truth leading to you Nature with all her children to bind her to your service and make her your slave." Cited and translated in Benjamin Farrington, "Temporis Partus Masculus: An Untranslated Writing of Francis Bacon," *Centaurus* 1, no. 3 (1951): 197.

61. Robert Darnton, *The Great Cat Massacre and Other Episodes in French Cultural History* (New York: Basic Books, 1984), 194; Denis Diderot, 'Prospectus de l'*Encyclopédie*," (1750) reprinted in *Encyclopédie; ou, Dictionnaire raisonné des sciences, des arts et des métiers*, ed. Denis Diderot and Jean le Rond d'Alembert, 28 vols. (1751-72), 5:635, in ARTFL Encyclopédie Project, accessed January 7, 2011, http://encyclopedie.uchicago.edu. Hereafter, *Encyclopédie* references will be cited by their volume and page number. Different variations of the Corberon quote above appear in Antoine Faivre, "Un familier des sociétés ésotériques au dix-huitième siècle: Bourrée de Corberon," *Revue des sciences humaines*, no. 126 (1967): 268; and Auguste Viatte, *Les sources occultes du Romantisme: Illuminisme—théosophie, 1770-1820* (Paris: Champion, 1965), 1:247-48. I've followed Faivre. See also *Encyclopedia of the Enlightenment*, ed. Michel Delon (Chicago: Fitzroy Dearborn, 2001), s.v. "Alchemy," by Didier Kahn, 1:50-55.

62. Darnton, *Great Cat Massacre*, 191-209.

63. Ibid., 211.

64. For example, Denis Diderot, *De la suffisance de la religion naturelle* (1770). Diderot moved from deism to atheism to pantheism (and perhaps back).

65. The *Système Figuré* did have a separate heading for a "Pneumatology of Knowledge of the Spirit" that was closer to this other meaning. In his chart Bacon also had a place for the "magical," as a subheading under "Natural Prudence."

66. To be sure, they lived after a legal shift in the status of witches, discussed below.

67. Wolfgang Behringer, *Witchcraft Persecutions in Bavaria* (Cambridge: Cambridge University Press, 2002), 353.

68. Henri Beaune, *Les sorciers de Lyon: Épisode judiciaire du XVIIIe siècle* (Dijon: Rabutot, 1868), 30–67. Admittedly, Guillaudot and company were executed under the charge of sacrilege, but the issue was his possession of magical books. While this is often regarded as the last of its kind in France, other executions of murder by poisoning in the years that followed were often directed at witches, and it would take more research to uncover when physical poisoning and magical poisoning became fully differentiated.

69. Bernard Traimond, *Le pouvoir de la maladie: Magie et politique dans les Landes de Gascogne, 1750–1826* (Bordeaux: Université de Bordeaux, 1988).

70. See Diderot and d'Alembert, *Encyclopédie*, 9:853.

71. Cassirer argues that "the gravest obstacle" to the Enlightenment conception of truth was "those divergences from truth which do not arise from a mere insufficiency of knowledge but from a perverted direction of knowledge." Ernst Cassirer, *The Philosophy of the Enlightenment* (Princeton, NJ: Princeton University Press, 1951), 160–61.

72. Voltaire cited in Cameron, *Enchanted Europe*, 308.

73. One might also think of Bernard Le Bouyer de Fontenelle, *Histoire des oracles* (1687).

74. Immanuel Kant, *Kritik Der Urteilskraft*, ed. Klemme Heiner and Giordanetti Piero (Hamburg: F. Meiner, 2006), 175.

75. *Encyclopédie*, 15:669–70. I've translated *traits invincibles* as "irresistible bonds," but an even more literal translation would be "invincible lines" or "traits."

76. See Jean-Baptiste Thiers, *Traité des superstitions*, 1679.

77. For the *philosophes*, this was an asymmetrical disenchantment insofar as they committed themselves to a theology that denied the reality of an active agent of evil and hence aimed primarily to define the diabolical out of existence. See Nadia Minerva, *Il Diavolo: Eclissi e metamorfosi nel Secolo dei Lumi* (Ravenna: Longo, 1990). This is a thread that goes back significantly to Balthasar Bekker's *De betoverde weereld*. See, for example, *"Incubes"* in *Collection complette des oeuvres de M. de Voltaire* (Genève, Cramer, 1768–77), 23:500–502.

78. *Des oeuvres de Voltaire*, 28:429.

79. Wouter Hanegraaff, *Esotericism and the Academy: Rejected Knowledge in Western Culture* (Cambridge: Cambridge University Press, 2012), 163 (emphasis in the original).

80. *Encyclopédie*, 16:253–61. Fabre has shown that much of Diderot's entry is basically translated from Johann Jakob Brucker. See Jean Fabre, "Diderot et les Théosophes," *Cahiers de l'Association internationale des études francaises* 13 (1961): 203–22.

81. *Encyclopédie*, 16:253.

82. Paracelsus, *Paracelsus: Essential Theoretical Writings* (Leiden: Brill, 2008).

83. See, for example, Paracelsus, *Liber de nymphis, sylphis, pygmaeis et salamandris et de caeteris spiritibus* (1566). The seeming contradiction of his commitment to medicine, magic, and Christian faith is addressed in Andrew Weeks, *Paracelsus: Speculative Theory and the Crisis of the Early Reformation* (Albany: State University of New York Press, 1997); and Charles Webster, *Paracelsus: Medicine, Magic and Mission at the End of Time* (New Haven, CT: Yale University Press, 2008).

84. Webster, *From Paracelsus to Newton*, 4.

85. Later the main representative for theosophy and Böhme's thought in France was Louis

Claude de Saint-Martin (1743–1803), discussed in greater detail in David Allen Harvey, *Beyond Enlightenment: Occultism and Politics in Modern France* (DeKalb: Northern Illinois University Press, 2005). Voltaire and other *philosophes* would ultimately attack Saint-Martin and his work (ibid., 18).

86. Ariel Hessayon, "Boehme's Life and Times," in *An Introduction to Jacob Boehme: Four Centuries of Thought and Reception*, ed. Hessayon (New York: Taylor & Francis, 2013), 14; Andrew Weeks, *Boehme: An Intellectual Biography of the Seventeenth-Century Philosopher and Mystic* (Albany: State University of New York Press, 1992).

87. Weeks, *Boehme: An Intellectual Biography*, 151.

88. Cyril O'Regan, *Gnostic Apocalypse Jacob Boehme's Haunted Narrative* (Albany: State University of New York Press, 2002), 3.

89. Antoine Faivre, *L'ésotérisme*, 4th ed. (Paris: Presses Universitaires de France, 2007); Joscelyn Godwin, *The Theosophical Enlightenment* (Albany: State University of New York Press, 1994).

90. *Encyclopédie*, 16:253–54.

91. Ibid., 16:253.

92. Ibid., 16:254–55. See also Fabre, "Diderot et les Théosophes."

93. *Encyclopédie*, 1:57.

94. For example, Diderot makes reference to Gerolamo Cardano and Martín del Río. Ibid., 4:1070–71.

95. Ibid., 3:410.

96. Ibid., 9:852–54.

97. The discussion of divine magic is consistent with a similar tension in the entry on "miracles"; see ibid., 10:560–62.

98. See Jon Ruthven, On the Cessation of the Charismata: The Protestant Polemic on Post-biblical Miracles (Sheffield: Sheffield Academic Press, 1997); and D. P. Walker, "The Cessation of Miracles," in *Hermeticism and the Renaissance: Intellectual History and the Occult in Early Modern Europe*, ed. Ingrid Merkel and Allen Debus (Washington, DC: Folger Books, 1988), 111–24.

99. *Encyclopédie*, 9:853–54.

100. See Thomas Aquinas, *Compendium Theologiae* (ca. 1273); see also Robert Bartlett, *The Natural and the Supernatural in the Middle Ages* (New York: Cambridge University Press, 2008).

101. For instance, in 1682, after the "Affair of the Poisons" (*L'affaire des poisons*), the government of Louis XIV issued an edict that effectively defined the issue of witchcraft in terms of pretended magic. But it did not deny the existence of magic; indeed, it left the execution of witches for diabolical pacts in place (which continued to be enforced). See Brian Levack, "The Decline and End of Witchcraft Prosecutions," in *The Oxford Handbook of Witchcraft in Early Modern Europe and Colonial America*, ed. Levack (Oxford: Oxford University Press, 2013), 433.

102. See Clark, *Thinking with Demons*, 1997.

103. The Witchcraft Act of 1735 was replaced in 1951 with the Fraudulent Mediums Act, directed at those who make money by fraudulently claiming to be a psychic or spiritualist medium. Interestingly, the main champion of the 1951 act was Labour MP Thomas Brooks, himself an ardent spiritualist, who was aiming to protect genuine mediums from frauds. This later

act was only replaced in 2008 with an EU consumer protection regulation focusing on unfair marketing practices.

104. *Encyclopédie*, 9:852. A description with plenty of precedents, including Francis Bacon.

105. See ibid., 3:420; see also the original *Système Figuré*, which lists *"magie naturalle"* as a subbranch of chemistry.

106. James Van Horn Melton, *The Rise of the Public in Enlightenment Europe* (Cambridge: Cambridge University Press, 2008), 88.

107. Owen Davies, *Grimoires: A History of Magic Books* (Oxford: Oxford University Press, 2009), 98–100.

108. Albertus Parvus Lucius (pseud.), *Secrets merveilleux de la Magie naturelle et càbalistique du Petit Albert* (Lyton: N.p., 1752), 10, 61.

109. Hanegraaff, Esotericism and the Academy, 177. See also Graziella Federici-Vescovini, *Le Moyen Âge magique: La magie entre religion et science du XIIIe au XIVe siècle* (Paris: J. Vrin, 2011).

110. As Kant argued in his critique of Emmanuel Swedenborg's mystical visions, if even a few spirit tales were true, it would call the whole basis of natural philosophy into question. Immanuel Kant, *Träume eines Geistersehers, erläutert durch Träume der Metaphysik* (Königsberg: Kanter, 1766). This is discussed in greater detail in chapter 5.

111. For example, Descartes suggested *esprits animaux* ("animal spirits") as a way to explain the interface between mind and body. René Descartes, *Les passions de l'âme* (Paris: N.p., 1728), 51f.

112. Many encyclopedists were Freemasons; see Frank Kafker and Serena Kafker, *The Encyclopedists as Individuals: A Biographical Dictionary of the Authors of the Encyclopèdie* (Oxford: Voltaire Foundation, 1988); and Margaret Jacob, *Living the Enlightenment: Freemasonry and Politics in Eighteenth-Century Europe* (New York: Oxford University Press, 1991). Regarding alchemists: Jean-Jacques Rousseau's interest in alchemy can be seen in his *Institutions chimiques*. The adventurer and alchemist Giacomo Casanova knew d'Alembert (at least, according to Casanova's memoirs). Paul-Jacques Malouin was likely an alchemist; see his entry on "Alchimie," *Encyclopédie*, 1:248–49. For others, see Kafker and Kafker, *Encyclopedists as Individuals*, 400–401. For one magician, see ibid., 289.

113. Michael Buckley, *At the Origins of Modern Atheism* (New Haven, CT: Yale University Press, 1987), 249.

114. Diderot notes that his chemistry teacher Guillaume François Rouelle believed in alchemy and taught it as part of his course. Denis Diderot, *Oeuvres complètes de Diderot*, ed. Jules Assézat (Paris: Garnier frères, 1875–77) 6:409.

115. See Jean Ehrard, "Matérialisme et naturalisme: Les sources occultistes de la pensée de Diderot," *Cahiers de l'Association internationale des études francaises* (1961): 189–201; and Jacques Proust, "Diderot et la physiognomonie," *Cahiers de l'Association internationale des études francaises* (1961): 317–29. I think the jury is out on Diderot's Paracelsianism, but see Ehrard's "Matérialisme et naturalism."

116. Jean-Paul Jouary, *Diderot et la matière vivante* (Paris: Messidor/Editions sociales, 1992).

117. See Buckley, *Origins of Modern Atheism*, 249–50.

118. Some conservative Catholics were suspicious that the *philosophes* were covertly Protestant. See Darrin McMahon, *Enemies of the Enlightenment: The French Counter-Enlightenment*

and the Making of Modernity (New York: Oxford University Press, 2002); Graeme Garrard, *Counter-Enlightenments: From the Eighteenth Century to the Present* (New York: Routledge, 2006).

119. Augustin Barruel, *Mémoires pour servir à l'histoire du jacobinisme*, 1798. See Garrard, *Counter-Enlightenments*, esp. 8, 43–48.

120. Paul Kléber Monod, *Solomon's Secret Arts: The Occult in the Age of Enlightenment* (New Haven, CT: Yale University Press, 2013), 263.

121. To be fair, the messiness of the Enlightenment in general has been a central feature of recent Enlightenment studies; for example, Dorinda Outram, *The Enlightenment* (New York: Cambridge University Press, 1995).

122. A key text was the English translation of Ernst Cassirer's *Die Philosophie der Aufklärung* (1932) into *The Philosophy of the Enlightenment* (1951), although there were scattered usages of the phrase in English earlier. Garrard, *Counter-Enlightenments*, 6.

123. Even today the French scholarship does not use the term *l'Éclaircissement* (lit. "the Enlightenment") to talk about any period at all, and the revival of the *Siècle des Lumières* (age of lights) as an analogue to the Enlightenment similarly took off in the 1950s. Garrard, *Counter-Enlightenments*, 6.

124. A key milestone in this debate was, again, Cassirer's *Die Philosophie der Aufklärung*.

125. Not that anachronism is a cardinal sin, but it should be used self-consciously.

126. Foucault's famous "*Qu'est-ce que les lumières?*" is less about an era than an attitude, and when Foucault touches on periodization, he uses "modernity."

127. Robert Sinnerbrink, *Understanding Hegelianism* (Stocksfield: Acumen, 2007), 89.

128. Steven Shapin, *The Scientific Revolution* (Chicago: University of Chicago Press, 1996), 2. See also Bernard Cohen, *Revolution in Science* (Cambridge, MA: Harvard University Press, 1985), 396–403.

129. Sydney Ross, "Scientist: The Story of a Word," *Annals of Science* 18, no. 2 (1962): 66–67.

130. Ibid., 69–70. Also, the term *scientist* was coined by William Whewell in 1834 in a review article bemoaning the fragmentation of the sciences.

131. Johann Christoph Adelung, *Grammatisch-kritisches Wörterbuch der hochdeutschen Mundart* (Vienna: Pichler, 1808), 4:1582–83, translated in Frederick Gregory, "Hans Christian Ørsted's Spiritual Interpretation of Natural Science," in *Hans Christian Ørsted and the Romantic Legacy in Science*, ed. Robert Michael Brain, R. S. Cohen, and Ole Knudsen (Dordrecht: Springer, 2007), 403–4.

132. See Bas van Bommel, *Classical Humanism and the Challenge of Modernity: Debates on Classical Education in 19th-Century Germany* (Berlin: De Gruyter, 2015), 80–107.

133. To be clear, biblical philology often was undertaken by Protestant scholars who had explicitly theological aims in mind. It was particularly in the nineteenth century that historical criticism was deployed by thinkers like David Strauß in ways that were interpreted as antireligious and thus contributing to the sense that scientific philology and Christian revelation might be in opposition.

134. Peter Harrison, *The Territories of Science and Religion* (Chicago: University of Chicago Press, 2015), 119.

135. See Hanegraaff, *Esotericism and the Academy*, for a version of this argument.

136. The occultists and magicians often understood themselves to be Christians. See, for example, Jean Pierre Laurant, *L'ésotérisme Chrétien en France au XIXe siècle* (Lausanne: L'Age d'Homme, 1992).

CHAPTER THREE

1. David Krell, *The Tragic Absolute: German Idealism and the Languishing of God* (Bloomington: Indiana University Press, 2005), 19.

2. See ibid., 16–17; Ernst Behler, *Philosophy of German Idealism* (New York: Continuum, 1987), xvi–xvii; and Christoph Jamme and Helmut Schneider, eds., *Mythologie der Vernunft: Hegels "Ältestes Systemprogramm des deutschen Idealismus"* (Frankfurt: Suhrkamp, 1984).

3. An early popular source was Antoine Banier, *La mythologie et les fables expliquées par l'histoire*, 3rd ed. (1738–40). See also Jean Seznec, *The Survival of the Pagan Gods* (New York: Pantheon Books, 1953); and Burton Feldman and Robert Richardson, *The Rise of Modern Mythology, 1680–1860* (Bloomington: Indiana University Press), 1972.

4. For the formulation "longing for myth," see George S. Williamson, *The Longing for Myth in Germany: Religion and Aesthetic Culture from Romanticism to Nietzsche* (Chicago: University of Chicago Press, 2004), 3. See also George Mosse, *The Nationalization of the Masses: Political Symbolism and Mass Movements in Germany* (New York: Fertig, 1975), 6; Philippe Lacoue-Labarthe, *Heidegger: La politique du poème* (Paris: Galilée, 2002); and Dieter Sturma, "Politics and the New Mythology: The Turn to Late Romanticism," in *The Cambridge Companion to German Idealism*, ed. Karl Ameriks (New York: Cambridge, 2000), 219–38.

5. The call for the construction of a modern mythology was significantly foreshadowed in a 1767 fragment from Herder. *Johann Gottfried Herder: Selected Early Works, 1764–1767* (University Park: Pennsylvania State, 1992), 228–29. Friedrich Schlegel's discussion of "new mythology" is the most famous, but his brother August Wilhelm also occasionally made similar gestures. See Ralph W. Ewton, *The Literary Theories of August Wilhelm Schlegel* (The Hague: Mouton, 1972), 31–38.

6. Friedrich Schelling, *System des transzendentalen Idealismus* (Tübingen: Cottaschen Buchhandlung, 1800), 477–78. While preparing my own, I consulted the translation in F. W. J. Schelling, *System of Transcendental Idealism (1800)*, trans. Peter Heath, (Charlottesville: University Press of Virginia, 1978), 232–33. See also Friedrich Schlegel, "Rede über die Mythologie" (1800), in *Kritische Friedrich-Schlegel-Ausgabe*, ed. Ernst Behler (Munich: Schöningh, 1967), 2:284–351.

7. See Wolfgang Müller-Funk. *The Architecture of Modern Culture: Towards a Narrative Cultural Theory* (Berlin: De Gruyter, 2012), 75; see also Williamson, *Longing for Myth in Germany*.

8. As Christian Thorne has observed, the sheer repetitiveness of Europe's story of its own turn to rationality implies "less the triumphant emergence of reason than an embarrassing intellectual fitfulness, less a scholarly awakening than a philosophical narcolepsy, so that we must imagine Europe dozing off, repeatedly, only to jog itself freshly awake after each new nodding." Christian Thorne, *The Dialectic of Counter-Enlightenment*. (Cambridge, MA: Harvard University Press, 2009), 4.

9. Friedrich Nietzsche, *The Gay Science* (New York: Cambridge University Press, 2001), 199.

10. Ibid., 120.

11. See, for example, Peter Fritzsche, ed., *Nietzsche and the Death of God: Selected Writings* (Boston: Bedford, 2007); and Roy Jackson, *Nietzsche and Islam* (London: Routledge, 2007), 17.

12. Johann von Rist, *Dichtung von Johann Rist* (Leipzig: Brockhaus, 1885), 215. For this hymn as the possible origin of Nietzsche's phrase, see Eric von der Luft, "Sources of Nietzsche's 'God Is Dead' and Its Meaning for Heidegger," *Journal of the History of Ideas* 45, no. 2 (1984): 263–76. See also Eugen Biser, "Die Proklamation von Gottes Tod," *Das Hochland* 56 (1963): 137–52.

13. Jean Paul, *Siebenkäs, Flegeljahre*, ed. Norbert Miller and Wilhelm Schmidt-Biggemann (Frankfurt: Zweitausendeins, 1996, 273). I have amended the translation appearing in Jean Paul, *Flower, Fruit and Thorn Pieces*, trans. Edward Henry Noel (Leipzig: Bernhard Tauchnitz, 1871), 281–82.

14. G. W. F. Hegel, *Werke* (Frankfurt: Suhrkamp, 1969–71; hereafter cited as GHW), 17:291. I consulted the translation in Carlos João Correia, "Schelling and the Death of God," in Nietzsche, *German Idealism and Its Critics*, ed. Katia Hay (Boston: De Gruyter, 2015), 157.

15. GHW, 2:432 (emphasis added). Hegel uses almost the same phrase in the *Phänomenologie*.

16. Deland Anderson, "The Death of God and Hegel's System of Philosophy," *Sophia* 35, no. 1 (1996): 36–37.

17. For another reference to the end of myth, see G. W. F. Hegel, *Lectures on the Philosophy of History* (London: Bell, 1894), 2:20. For Herder's anticipation of this theme, see note 5 above.

18. Alexander Altmann, "Lessing und Jacobi: Das Gespräch über den Spinozismus," *Lessing Yearbook*, no. 3 (1971): 25–70; Frederick Beiser, *The Fate of Reason: German Philosophy from Kant to Fichte* (Cambridge, MA: Harvard University Press, 1987); and Eckart Förster, *The Twenty-Five Years of Philosophy: A Systematic Reconstruction* (Cambridge, MA: Harvard University Press, 2012), esp. 75–99.

19. Friedrich Heinrich Jacobi, *Werke* (Leipzig: Fleischer, 1819). 3:55. I have consulted the translation in Förster, *Twenty-Five Years of Philosophy*, 76.

20. Assmann argues that in their use of *"Hen kai pan,"* Jacobi and Lessing—both Freemasons—were gesturing at what they saw as Egyptian mysteries about the unity of God and cosmos. Jan Assmann, " '*Hen kai pan': Ralph Cudworth und die Rehabilitierung der hermetischen Tradition*," in *Aufklärung und Esoterik*, ed. Monika Neugebauer-Wölk (Hamburg: Felix Meiner, 1999), 38–52. YASUKATA Toshimasa, however, has argued that this expression may have come from Jacobi and that Lessing may have actually written *"hen ego kai panta"*(I am one and all) YASUKATA Toshimasa, *Resshingu to doitsu keimō: Resshingu shūkyō tetsugaku no kenkyū* (Tokyo: Sōbunsha, 1998).

21. Jacobi, *Werke*, 3:55.

22. Beiser, *Fate of Reason*, 44.

23. Jonathan Israel, *Radical Enlightenment: Philosophy and the Making of Modernity, 1650–1750* (New York: Oxford University Press, 2001).

24. Abraham Anderson, *The Treatise of the Three Impostors and the Problem of Enlightenment* (Lanham: Rowman & Littlefield, 1997).

25. Johann Georg Wachter, *Spinozismus im Jüdenthumb; oder, Die von dem heutigen Jüdenthumb und dessen Geheimen Kabbala Vergötterte Welt* (Spinoza in Judaism; or, Contemporary Judaism and its secret Kabbalistic deification of the world, 1699); Daniel Schwartz, *The First Modern Jew: Spinoza and the History of an Image* (Princeton, NJ: Princeton University Press, 2012), esp. 30.

26. Pierre Bayle, *Dictionnaire historique et critique*, 5th ed. (Amsterdam: P. Brunel, 1740), 4:254.

27. Ibid.

28. Lucien Febvre, *The Problem of Unbelief in the Sixteenth Century* (Cambridge, MA: Harvard University Press, 1982), 132–35; Alan Kors, *Atheism in France, 1650-1729* (Princeton, NJ: Princeton University Press, 1990), 10–11.

29. See also Michael Buckley, *At the Origins of Modern Atheism* (New Haven, CT: Yale University Press, 1987), 10.

30. Kors, *Atheism in France*, 39.

31. Buckley, *Origins of Modern Atheism*, 355.

32. Beiser, *Fate of Reason*, 46.

33. Horst Stuke, "Aufklärung," *Geschichtliche Grundbegriffe* 1 (1972): 243–342, esp. 246.

34. James Schmidt, *What Is Enlightenment? Eighteenth-Century Answers and Twentieth-Century Questions* (Berkeley: University of California, 1996), 2.

35. Stuke, "Aufklärung," 246, 267.

36. Schmidt, *What Is Enlightenment?*, 2.

37. Beiser, *Fate of Reason*; Hermann Timm, *Gott und die Freiheit: Studien zur Religionsphilosophie der Goethezeit* (Frankfurt: Vittorio Klostermann, 1974), 22–23.

38. Beiser, *Fate of Reason*, 83.

39. Jacobi translated in ibid., 84.

40. Ibid., 81. In roughly the same period, Jacob Obereit also used the term *nihilism* in *Der Wiederkommende Lebensgesit der verzweifelten Metaphysik* (1787). Scholars debate whether Jacobi or Obereit were the first to use it in this sense. For more on Obereit, see Timm, *Gott und die Freiheit*, 348–59. For more on Jacobi and nihilism, see Theobald Süß, "Der Nihilismus Bei F. H. Jacobi," *Theologische Literaturzeitung* 4, no. 76 (1951): 193–200.

41. For example, see Jacobi's "Concerning the Doctrine of Spinoza," in Friedrich Heinrich Jacobi, *The Main Philosophical Writings and the Novel "Allwill"* (Buffalo, NY: McGill-Queen's University Press, 1995), esp. 205.

42. Jacobi, "Concerning the Doctrine of Spinoza," 519.

43. See also Jacobi's "David Hume on Faith" (1815), in Jacobi, *Main Philosophical Writings*, esp. 583.

44. Kant became popular because it was thought he could resolve the pantheism dispute. Beiser, *Fate of Reason*, 45.

45. Johann Gottfried Herder, *God: Some Conversations* (Indianapolis: Bobbs-Merrill, 1963).

46. See Assmann, *"Hen kai pan,"*; Beiser, *Fate of Reason*, 44.

47. For Hegel, Schelling, and Hölderlin, see Terry Pinkard, *Hegel: A Biography* (New York: Cambridge University Press, 2000), 31–33. For Schlegel, see Elizabeth Millán-Zaibert, *Frie-*

drich Schlegel and the Emergence of Romantic Philosophy (Albany: State University of New York Press, 2007), 54–62. For Jean Paul and Jacobi, see Josef Müller, "Jean Paul und Jacobi," *Zeitschrift für Philosophie und philosophische Kritik*, no. 140 (1910): 108–10.

48. Timm, *Gott und die Freiheit*, 22–23.

49. See, for example, Klaus-Peter Schroeder, *Das alte Reich und seine Städte: Untergang und Neubeginn, die Mediatisierung der oberdeutschen Reichsstädte im Gefolge des Reichsdeputationshauptschlusses, 1802/03* (Munich: Beck, 1991).

50. Matthew Levinger, *Enlightened Nationalism: The Transformation of Prussian Political Culture, 1806–1848* (Oxford: Oxford University Press, 2002), 131.

51. See Joachim Whaley, *Germany and the Holy Roman Empire* (Oxford: Oxford University Press, 2012), 2:580, 623–24.

52. Heinrich Heine, *Samtliche Schriften* (Munich: C. Hanser, 1968), 3:473–74; Bruno Bauer, *The Trumpet of the Last Judgement against Hegel the Atheist and Antichrist* (Lewiston, NY: Mellen Press, 1989), 97, 122.

53. Max Stirner, *Der Einzige und sein Eigentum* (Berlin: Dreigliederungsverlag, 2002), 81. I slightly amended the translation in Stirner, *The Ego and Its Own*. trans. Steven Byington (New York: Cambridge University Press, 1995), 138. For Stirner's influence on Nietzsche, see Thomas Brobjer, "Philologia: A Possible Solution to the Stirner-Nietzsche Question," *Journal of Nietzsche Studies* 25 (2003), 109–44.

54. Martin Heidegger, *Gesamtausgabe* (Frankfurt: Vittorio Klostermann, 1976–2011), 5:248.

55. In some respects, the seeds of the idea of secularization can be found in Hegel.

56. Ian Hunter, "Secularization: The Birth of a Modern Combat Concept," *Modern Intellectual History* 12 (2015): 1–32, esp. 30. For Rothe's theosophy, see Richard Rothe, *Stille Stunden* (1872).

57. Novalis, *Hymns to the Night and Spiritual Songs*, trans. George MacDonald (London: Temple Lodge, 1992), 46.

58. Novalis, *The Birth of Novalis: Friedrich Von Hardenberg's Journal of 1797, with Selected Letters and Documents* (Albany: State University of New York, 2007).

59. 1800: "When poetry's enchanting shroud." For the German text, I have used Friedrich Schiller, *Sämtliche Werke*, 2nd ed. (Munich: Hanser, 2006), 1:163–73.

60. 1800: "Never aware of the spirit that guides her / Never glorified (*Sel'ger*) through my saintliness (*seligkeit*)."

61. This line occurs only in the first edition.

62. Representative works include: Eliza Butler, *The Tyranny of Greece over Germany* (New York: Cambridge University Press, 1935); Henry Hatfield, *Aesthetic Paganism in German Literature* (Cambridge, MA: Harvard University Press, 1964); Suzanne Marchand, *Down from Olympus: Archaeology and Philhellenism in Germany, 1750–1970* (Princeton, NJ: Princeton University Press, 1996); Walther Rehm, *Griechentum und Goethezeit: Geschichte eines Glaubens* (Bern: Francke, 1952); Ludwig Uhlig, ed., *Griechenland Als Ideal: Winckelmann Und Seine Rezeption in Deutschland* (Tübingen: Narr, 1988); and Damian Valdez, *German Philhellenism* (New York: Palgrave Macmillan, 2014).

63. Hatfield, *Aesthetic Paganism*, 21, 74.

64. Johann Joachim Winckelmann, *Kleine Schriften und Briefe* (Weimar: H. Böhlaus Nachfolger, 1960), 31.

65. See chapter 5.

66. Think: Hölderlin, *Hyperion; oder, Der Eremit in Griechenland* (1797–99).

67. Schiller, *Sämtliche Werke*, 5:709–10.

68. Friedrich Schiller, "Some Thoughts on the First Human Society Following the Guiding Thread of the Mosaic Documents," *Fidelio* 5, no. 3 (1996): 74–81. See also Walter Grossmann, "Schiller's Philosophy of History in His Jena Lectures of 1789–90," *PMLA* 69, no. 1 (1954): 156–72.

69. The expression "dark abyss of time" is from Buffon and then Paolo Rossi, *The Dark Abyss of Time* (Chicago: University of Chicago Press, 1984). For shifts in the sense of temporality, see Edward Thompson, "Time, Work-Discipline, and Industrial Capitalism," *Past and Present* (1967): 56–97; and Reinhart Koselleck, *Vergangene Zukunft: Zur Semantik geschichtlicher Zeiten* (Frankfurt: Suhrkamp, 2006). See also Karl Löwith, *Meaning in History: The Theological Implications of the Philosophy of History* (Chicago: University of Chicago Press, 1949).

70. Think of Kant, *Idee zu einer allgemeinen Geschichte in weltbürgerlicher Absicht.*

71. "Die vier Weltalter" described four ages: the golden age of the gods, the age of pastoral culture, the age of labor and heroes, and then finally the rise of Christianity, but it explicitly anticipated entering a fifth (post-Christian) age. Schiller, *Sämtliche Werke*, 1:417–19.

72. To be clear, Schiller occasionally suggests the Greeks were exceptional compared to other primitive peoples.

73. Schiller, *Sämtliche Werke*, 5:707–8.

74. Ibid., 5:728.

75. Ibid., 1:418.

76. See Benno Zuiddam, "Plutarch and God-Eclipse in Christian Theology," *Ploutarchos*, no. 6 (2009): 83–100.

77. For biblical precedents, think Luke 4:41 and Mark 3:11–15.

78. While preparing my own, I consulted the translation in Novalis, *Philosophical Writings*, trans. Margaret Mahony Stoljar (Albany: State University of New York Press, 1997), 148.

79. One of the first attacks on Schiller for being anti-Christian was Friedrich Leopold Graf zu Stolberg, "Gedanken über Herrn Schillers Gedicht: Die Götter Griechenlandes," *Deutsches Museum* 8 (1788): 97–105.

80. See W. H. Carruth, "The Religion of Friedrich Schiller" *PMLA* 19, no. 4 (1904): 496–582; and Jeffrey High, "Friedrich Schiller, Secular Virtue, and the 'The Gods of Ancient Greece,'" in *Enlightenment and Secularism*, ed. Christopher Nadon, (Lanham, MD: Lexington Books, 2013), 315–24.

81. Schiller, *Sämtliche Werke*, 5:344–58. For the background on Schiller's theosophy, Riedel emphasizes Friedrich Christoph Oetinger and Jakob Hermann Obereit. Wolfgang Riedel, *Die Anthropologie des jungen Schiller* (Würzburg: Königshausen und Neuman, 1985). Schiller was likely also influenced by his teacher Jakob Friedrich Abel, author of *Philosophische Untersuchungen über die Verbindung der Menschen mit höheren Geistern* (1791).

82. See Ernst Benz, *Les sources mystiques de la philosophie romantique allemande* (Paris: Vrin, 1968). Franz von Baader's role in this process will be discussed in chapter 7.

83. When Böhme was largely forgotten in Germany, he retained followers in England. Wouter Hanegraaff, *Swedenborg, Oetinger, Kant: Three Perspectives on the Secrets of Heaven* (West Chester, PA: Swedenborg Foundation, 2007), 67. See also Martin Weyer-Menkhoff, *The*

Pietist Theologians: An Introduction to Theology in the Seventeenth and Eighteenth Centuries (Malden, MA: Blackwell, 2005).

84. Glenn Magee, *Hegel and the Hermetic Tradition* (Ithaca, NY: Cornell University Press, 2001); and Stefan Andriopoulos, "Occult Conspiracies: Spirits and Secret Societies in Schiller's 'Ghost Seer,'" *New German Critique*, no. 103 (2008): 65–81. As Mayer has argued, this recovery was messy insofar as many philosophers referred to Böhme without having really read him. Paola Mayer, *Jena Romanticism and Its Appropriation of Jakob Böhme* (Montreal: McGill-Queen's University Press, 1999), 80, 216.

85. For Schlegel's juxtaposition of Spinoza and Böhme, see Jochen Schulte-Sasse, *Theory as Practice: A Critical Anthology of Early German Romantic Writings* (Minneapolis: University of Minnesota Press, 1997), 190.

86. Schiller, *Sämtliche Werke*, 5:352. I follow most Schiller scholarship in reading Julius as Schiller's proxy.

87. Ibid., 5:344.

88. The language of hieroglyphics occurs again in "Die Sendung Moses" (1789), but here as the symbols of an Egyptian secret or Hermetic monotheism hidden behind the apparent polytheism of the pharaohs. Ibid., 4:789–95. Interestingly, Schiller reads early Judaism in terms of Freemasonry.

89. Friedrich Schiller and Christian Gottfried Körner, *Schillers Briefwechsel mit Körner* (Leipzig: Veit, 1892), 1: 396–97.

90. Hatfield, *Aesthetic Paganism*, 121.

91. Ibid.

92. Friedrich Schiller, *On the Aesthetic Education of Man: In a Series of Letters* (New York: Ungar, 1965); Frederick Beiser, *Schiller as Philosopher: A Re-examination* (New York: Clarendon Press, 2005), 3–4.

93. Beiser, *Schiller as Philosopher*; Steven Martinson, *Harmonious Tensions: The Writings of Friedrich Schiller* (Newark: University of Delaware Press, 1996).

94. The pendulum likely refers to Huygens's famous planetary pendulum. For the damnation of Newton in German philosophical circles, see Thomas Ahnert, "Newtonianism in Early Enlightenment Germany, C. 1720 to 1750," *Studies in History and Philosophy of Science Part A* 35, no. 3 (2004): 471–91; and Frederick Burwick, *The Damnation of Newton: Goethe's Color Theory and Romantic Perception* (Berlin: De Gruyter, 1986).

95. Schiller also attacked the medical materialisms of La Mettrie and Helvétius; see Roland Krebs, "Le jeune Schiller face au matérialisme français," *Revue germanique internationale*, no. 22 (2004): 25–42.

96. Friedrich Schiller, *Nachlese zu Schillers Werken nebst Variantensammlung* (Stuttgart: Cotta, 1840), 1:274.

97. See Hans-Dietrich Dahnke, "Die Debatte um die Götter Griechenlandes," in *Debatten und Kontroversen: Literarische Auseinandersetzungen in Deutschland am Ende des 18: Jahrhunderts*, ed. Hans-Dietrich Dahnke and Bernd Leistner (Berlin: Aufbau-Verlag, 1989), 193–269.

98. Novalis is discussed above; Hölderlin, Hegel below. Heine wrote an homage titled "Die Götter Griechenlands" (1827). For Feurbach, see *Das Wesen der Religion* (1846). For Dittnar, see *Zur Charakterisirung der nordischen Mythologie im Verhältniss zu andern Naturreligionen* (Eine Skizze, 1848). Oehlenschläger's *Hakon Jarl* (1808–09) dramatizes this in theatrical form,

but it can also be found in *Nordiske Digte* (1807). For Procter, see (under the pseudonym Barry Cornwall) *The Flood of Thessaly* (1823). Elizabeth Barrett Browning's response was critical: "The Dead Pan" (1844).

99. GHW, 1:231.

100. In *Vorlesungen über die Ästhetik*, Hegel praises "The Gods of Greece" in terms of its imagery, rhythm, and pathos. GHW, 14:113–15.

101. GHW, 1:197, translated in G. W. F. Hegel, *Early Theological Writings* (Chicago: University of Chicago Press, 1961), 146.

102. Michael Forster, *Hegel's Idea of a Phenomenology of Spirit* (Chicago: University of Chicago Press, 1998). Forster also notes that Schiller's "Gods of Greece" was an inspiration for the project of Hegel's phenomenology. Ibid., 23.

103. GHW, 12:242, translated in G. W. F. Hegel, *Lectures on the Philosophy of History* (New York: Prometheus, 1991), 215.

104. GHW, 12:243; Hegel, *Philosophy of History*, 215.

105. GHW, 12:244; Hegel, *Philosophy of History*, 216. Compare Hegel's *"Natur ist entgöttert"* with Schiller's *"Die entgötterte Natur."*

106. Schiller, *Sämtliche Werke*, 4:768.

107. M. H. Abrams, *Natural Supernaturalism: Tradition and Revolution in Romantic Literature* (New York: Norton, 1971).

108. I'm broadly sympathetic to Lovejoy's critique of *Romanticism* as a meaningless term, but less interested in his attempt to recoup it as a periodization. See Arthur Lovejoy, "The Meaning of Romanticism for the Historian of Ideas," *Journal of the History of Ideas* 2, no. 3 (1941): 257–78.

109. Friedrich Hölderlin, *Sämtliche Werke* (Berlin: Propyläen, 1922), 3:236 (emphasis added). I consulted the translation in Abrams, *Natural Supernaturalism*, 237 while preparing my own.

110. Schiller, *Sämtliche Werke*, 5:645–51.

111. Schelling translated in Abrams, *Natural Supernaturalism*, 182.

112. Adam Oehlenschläger, *Oehlenschlägers digterværker og prosaiske skrifter* (Copenhagen: A. F. Host, 1851–54), 25:147–48.

113. Olivier Schefer, "L'idéalisme magique de Novalis," *Critique* 673–74, no. 6–7 (2003): 514–27.

114. Novalis, *Die Werke Friedrich von Hardenbergs: Historische-kritische Ausgabe* (Stuttgart: Kohlhammer Verlag, 1960–2006), 2:761, 3:297, 2:547; see also 2:546, esp. "Magie ist = Kunst, die Sinnenwelt willkührlich zu gebrauchen." See also Novalis, *Notes for a Romantic Encyclopaedia* (Albany: State University of New York Press, 2007), xxiv.

115. Hölderlin, *Sämtliche Werke*, 1:310.

116. For the reference to Schiller, see Jacob Burckhardt, *Griechische Kulturgeschichte* (Berlin: Spemann, 1898–1902), 2:384. For Jacobi, Burckhardt, *Geschichte des Revolutionszeitalters* (Munich: Beck, 2009), 69, 962. For Herder, Burckhardt, *Reflections on History* (London: Allen & Unwin, 1943), 67. Burckhardt mentions Hegel repeatedly, if critically, and Burckhardt was likely influenced by Hegel's staging of history in terms of a series of ruptures. Burckhardt attended Schelling's lectures, see Burckhardt, *Briefe*, ed. Max Burckhardt (Wiesbaden: Insel-Verlag, 1952), 1:202–3.

117. Burckhardt, *Griechische Kulturgeschichte*, 4:270.

118. Jules Michelet, *La Sorcière: The Witch of the Middle Ages*, trans. Lionel Trotter (London: Simpkin, 1863), 19–21. Michelet frequently refers to Schiller. Jules Michelet, *Précis de l'histoire modern* (Paris: Colas, 1827), 130–38.

119. Notably, Georg Conrad Horst, *Dämonomagie, oder Geschichte des Glaubens an Zauberei und dämonische Wunder (*Frankfurt: Wilmans, 1818); and Wilhelm Gottlieb Soldan, *Geschichte der Hexenprozesse* (Stuttgart: Cotta, 1843).

120. Jules Michelet, *Histoire de France* (Paris: Librairie Internationale, 1871–76), vol. 7, *La Renaissance*.

121. Jacob Burckhardt, *The Civilization of the Renaissance in Italy* (New York: Penguin Books, 1990), 98.

122. John Hinde, *Jacob Burckhardt and the Crisis of Modernity* (Ithaca, NY: McGill-Queen's University Press, 2000), 222. See also Jacob Burckhardt, *Judgements on History and Historians* (New York: Routledge, 2007), 84; and Lionel Gossman, *Basel in the Age of Burckhardt* (Chicago: University of Chicago Press, 2000).

123. Burckhardt, *Civilization of the Renaissance*, 187–88.

124. Howard argues that Burckhardt's thesis in turn was a partial secularization of his notion of the biblical Fall. Thomas Howard, *Religion and the Rise of Historicism: W. M. L. De Wette, Jacob Burckhardt, and the Theological Origins of Nineteenth-Century Historical Consciousness* (New York: Cambridge University Press, 2000).

125. Wilhelm Windelband, *Die Geschichte der neueren Philosophie: In ihrem Zusammenhange mit der allgemeinen Cultur und den besonderen Wissenschaften dargestellt* (Leipzig: Breitkopf und Härtel, 1878), vol. 1. Tellingly, the title of that volume was "Von der Renaissance bis Kant," and Windelband cites Burckhardt within, although he was also gesturing toward Kant's famous reference to the "Zeitalter der Aufklärung." For Windelband as the originator of the Enlightenment periodization, see Stuke, "Aufklärung," 340–41.

126. Wilhelm Nestle, *Vom Mythos zum Logos: die Selbstentfaltung des griechischen Denkens von Homer bis auf die Sophistik und Sokrates* (Stuttgart: Kröner, 1942). Nestle discusses Burckhardt in his earlier *Euripides, der dichter der griechischen aufklärung* (Stuttgart: Kohlhammer, 1901). Heidegger makes frequent references to Burckhardt; for example, Martin Heidegger, *The Essence of Truth on Plato's Cave Allegory and Theaetetus* (New York: Continuum, 2002), 46.

127. For Koyré's reading of Burckhardt, see Alexandre Koyré, *Místicos, espirituales y alquimistas del siglo XVI alemán* (Madrid: Akal, 1981), 53.

128. Weber cites Burckhardt repeatedly, and the Weber archive contains Burckhardt, *Griechische Kulturgeschichte*, annotated in Weber's hand. See Max Weber Archive, Mü Ordner 2 + 3, Bayerischen Akademie der Wissenschaften.

CHAPTER FOUR

1. Talal Asad, *Genealogies of Religion: Discipline and Reasons of Power in Christianity and Islam* (Baltimore: Johns Hopkins University Press, 1993); Jonathan Z. Smith, *Imagining Religion: From Babylon to Jonestown* (Chicago: University of Chicago Press, 1982).

2. Michel Despland, *L'émergence des sciences de la religion* (Paris: L'Harmattan, 1999); Daniel Dubuisson, *L'Occident et la religion: Mythes, science et idéologie* (Brussels: Complexe, 1998);

Tomoko Masuzawa, *The Invention of World Religions* (Chicago: University of Chicago Press, 2005); Arie Molendijk, *The Emergence of the Science of Religion in the Netherlands* (Leiden: Brill, 2005); Eric Sharpe, *Comparative Religion: A History* (New York: Scribner's, 1975).

3. Peter Harrison, *"Religion" and the Religions in the English Enlightenment* (New York: Cambridge University Press, 1990); Lynn Hunt, Margaret Jacob, and Wijnand Mijnhardt, *The Book That Changed Europe* (Cambridge, MA: Harvard University Press, 2010).

4. Philippe Borgeaud, *L'histoire des religions* (Gollion: Infolio, 2013); and Guy Stroumsa, *A New Science: The Discovery of Religion in the Age of Reason* (Cambridge, MA: Harvard University Press, 2010).

5. Fitzgerald's account of religious studies as liberal ecumenical theology straddles these positions: Timothy Fitzgerald, *The Ideology of Religious Studies* (New York: Oxford University Press, 2000).

6. Hans Thomas Hakl, *Eranos: An Alternative Intellectual History of the Twentieth Century* (Ithaca, NY: McGill-Queen's University Press, 2013); Jeffrey Kripal, *Roads of Excess, Palaces of Wisdom: Eroticism and Reflexivity in the Study of Mysticism* (Chicago: University of Chicago Press, 2001); Steven Wasserstrom, *Religion after Religion: Gershom Scholem, Mircea Eliade, and Henry Corbin at Eranos* (Princeton, NJ: Princeton University Press, 1999). Similarly, Styers has demonstrated the importance of "magic" as a contrasting object in the formation of religion as a scholarly category, while Kippenberg has noted that the field guarded cultural resources that would have otherwise been marginalized by Enlightenment rationalism. Randall Styers, *Making Magic: Religion, Magic, and Science in the Modern World* (New York: Oxford University Press, 2004); Hans Kippenberg, *Die Entdeckung der Religionsgeschichte* (München: Verlag C. H. Beck, 1997).

7. Georg Simmel, *Gesamtausgabe* (Frankfurt: Suhrkamp, 1989), 17:274–75. Translated by Mark Ritter and David Frisby in Georg Simmel, *Simmel on Culture* (Thousand Oaks, CA: Sage Press, 2000), 288–89 (emphasis added).

8. In the Anglophone world, the key works that promoted the notion of a conflict between religion and science were Andrew Dickson White, "The Battle-Fields of Science" (1869), and John William Draper, *History of the Conflict between Religion and Science* (1874). In German, the notion of a conflict occurred a few decades earlier, with the "materialism controversy" (*Materialismusstreit*) kicking off in 1854 with the publication of Rudolph Wagner, *Menschen-schöpfung und Seelensubstanz* (The creation of man and the substance of the soul, 1854) and the response by Carl Vogt, *Köhlerglaube und Wissenschaft* (Blind faith and science, 1855). For more about the materialism controversy, see Frederick Beiser, *After Hegel: German philosophy, 1840–1900* (Princeton, NJ: Princeton University Press, 2014), 53–96. See also Michael Bergunder, "'Religion' and 'Science' within a Global Religious History," *Aries* 16, no. 1 (2016): 88–89.

9. As Larsen has shown, the idea that the Victorians actually lost faith was largely a myth, but one that emerged in the period itself. Timothy Larsen, *Crisis of Doubt: Honest Faith in Nineteenth-Century England* (Oxford: Oxford University Press, 2008).

10. Simmel, *Simmel on Culture*, 289.

11. There are many "hauntologies" of the nineteenth century, but see especially: Ann Braude, *Radical Spirits: Spiritualism and Women's Rights in Nineteenth-Century America* (Boston: Beacon Press, 1989); John Kucich, *Ghostly Communion: Cross-cultural Spiritualism in Nineteenth-Century American Literature* (Hanover, NH: University Press of New England,

2004); Alex Owen, *The Place of Enchantment: British Occultism and the Culture of the Modern* (Chicago: University of Chicago Press, 2004); John Lardas Modern, *Secularism in Antebellum America* (Chicago: University of Chicago Press, 2011); and Ann Taves, *Fits, Trances, and Visions: Experiencing Religion and Explaining Experience from Wesley to James* (Princeton, NJ: Princeton University Press, 1999). The number of adherents comes from Geoffrey Nelson, *Spiritualism and Society* (New York: Routledge, 1969), 259, but estimates vary. Nelson also argues that the peak of spiritualism in Great Britain was not 1870 but 1954. Ibid., 269.

12. For example, the Shakers widely reported encounters with spirits from 1841 to 1845.

13. Jean Claude Schmitt, *Les revenants: Les vivants et les morts dans la société médiévale* (Paris: Gallimard, 1994).

14. Before 1875, the term *theosophy* was generally associated with Böhme. See Jean-Pierre Laurant, *L'ésotérisme chrétien en France au XIXe siècle* (Lausanne: L'Age d'Homme, 1992), 55.

15. This claim is made explicit in H. P. Blavatsky, *Isis Unveiled*, 2 vols. (New York: Bouton, 1892), 1:x–xi.

16. For debates on the relationship between spiritualism and scientific accounts of causation, see Alfred Russel Wallace, *On Miracles and Modern Spiritualism* (London: James Burns, 1875).

17. See, for example, Allan Kardec, *Le livre des esprits* (Montréal: Presses Sélect, 1979).

18. Rudolf Otto, *Das Heilige: Über das Irrationale in der Idee des Göttlichen und sein Verhältnis zum Rationalen* (München: Beck, 2004), 31; Bronislaw Malinowski, *Magic, Science and Religion, and Other Essays* (Garden City: Doubleday, 1954), 50. For a discussion of Marcel Mauss, Durkheim, and his followers' relationship to spiritualism, see Ivan Strenski, "Durkheim, Judaism, and the Afterlife," in *Reappraising Durkheim for the Study and Teaching of Religion Today*, ed. Thomas A. Idinopulos and Brian Wilson (Leiden: Brill, 2002), 111–43.

19. Edward B. Tylor, *Primitive Culture*, 2 vols. (London: Murray, 1891), 1:424–25.

20. In parallel, many American spiritualists appropriated the Quakers into their lineage. Bret Carroll, *Spiritualism in Antebellum America* (Bloomington: Indiana University Press, 1997).

21. I follow Segal, not Kippenberg, in interpreting Tylor's concept of "survival" as a negative term. Robert Segal, "Tylor: A Test Case of Kippenberg's Thesis," in *Religion im kulturellen Diskurs: Festschrift für Hans G. Kippenberg*, ed. Brigitte Luchesi and Kocku von Stuckrad (Berlin: de Gruyter, 2004), 17–31.

22. Tylor, *Primitive Culture*, 2:253.

23. Ibid., 1:101.

24. Ibid., 101.

25. Ibid., 106–7, 122.

26. Ibid., 106.

27. Ibid., 121.

28. Ibid., 111–112.

29. Ibid., 116–131.

30. Ibid., 122.

31. Ibid., 125–28.

32. See especially ibid., 141.

33. Robert Segal, "Tylor's Anthropomorphic Theory of Religion," *Religion* 25 (1995): 23–30.

34. Tylor, *Primitive Culture*, 1:129.

35. For example, see ibid., 424–26.

36. Tylor's account is reproduced in George Stocking Jr., "Animism in Theory and Practice: E. B. Tylor's Unpublished 'Notes on 'Spiritualism,'" *Man* 6 (1971): 88–104.

37. Andrew Lang, "Protest of a Psycho-Folklorist," *Folklore* 6, no. 3 (1895): 241.

38. Andrew Lang, *The Making of Religion* (New York: Longmans, 1909); this is discussed in greater detail in the next chapter.

39. For a discussion of the French occultism and politics more broadly, see David Allen Harvey, *Beyond Enlightenment: Occultism and Politics in Modern France* (DeKalb: Northern Illinois University Press, 2005).

40. For the twists and turns of Éliphas Lévi's biography, see Paul Chacornac, *Éliphas Lévi, rénovateur de l'occultisme en France (1810–1875)*, (Paris: Chacornac frères, 1926); and Christopher McIntosh, *Eliphas Lévi and the French Occult Revival* (London: Rider, 1972).

41. For how Lévi's project initially emerged in neo-Catholic and socialist contexts, see Julian Strube, "Socialist Religion and the Emergence of Occultism: A Genealogical Approach to Socialism and Secularization in 19th-Century France," *Religion* 46, no. 3 (2016): 359–388.

42. Éliphas Lévi (as Abbé Constant), *La Bible de la liberté* (Paris: Le Gallois, 1841), 17–19, 93.

43. Chacornac, *Éliphas Lévi*, 59–60.

44. For Lévi's use of *théosophie*, see Éliphas Lévi, *Histoire de la magie* (Paris: G. Baillière, 1860), 142. For a discussion of Lévi's contribution to esoteric terminology, see Antoine Faivre, *Access to Western Esotericism* (Albany: State University of New York Press, 1994), 34. I have consulted both French editions and English translations of Lévi's more famous works. For convenience, references in what follows will be to the English translation when possible and to the French only when my translation substantially differs.

45. See Éliphas Lévi, *The History of Magic* (London: Rider, 1922), 3;, and Lévi, *Transcendental Magic* (New York: William Rider & Son, 1923), 3, 4, 23.

46. Lévi, *History of Magic*, 158.

47. Lévi, *History of Magic*, 159 (emphasis added). Lévi follows Cornelius Agrippa in recovering folk rituals as forms of lost magic. See Heinrich Cornelius Agrippa, *De occulta philosophia libri tres* (New York: Brill, 1992), esp. 409. Agrippa's *De occulta philosophia* was also one of Tylor's main sources for theorizing magic in *Primitive Culture*.

48. See also Éliphas Lévi, *Le grand arcane; ou, L'occultisme dévoilé* (Paris: Chamuel, 1898).

49. Levi, *History of Magic*, 2.

50. See, for example, Lévi, *Transcendental Magic*, 3, 4, 23.

51. See also Éliphas Lévi, *The Key of the Mysteries*, trans. Aleister Crowley (London: Rider, 1969), 37. For the background to Lévi's famous image of the Sabbatic goat, see Youri Volokhine, "Pan en Egypte et le bouc de Mendès," in *Dans le laboratoire de l'historien des religions: Mélanges offerts à Philippe Borgeaud*, ed. Francesca Prescendi and Youri Volokhine (Geneva: Labor, 2011), 627–50.

52. For Lévi's complex and often contradictory ideas of Luficer and the devil and for his position in the history of "Romantic Satanism" more broadly, see Ruben van Luijk, *Children of Lucifer: The Origins of Modern Religious Satanism* (New York: Oxford University Press, 2016), esp.127–144.

53. Indeed, Helena Blavatsky would be dogged by charges that she had in some sense pla-

giarized Éliphas Lévi, or at the very least adopted his project wholesale. See Jeffrey D. Lavoie, *The Theosophical Society: The History of a Spiritualist Movement* (Boca Raton, FL: Brown-Walker Press, 2012), esp. 256–58.

54. Éliphas Lévi, *Dogme et rituel de la haute magie*, 2 vols. (Paris: G. Baillère, 1861), 1:99. For Lévi's interlocators, see Joscelyn Godwin, *The Theosophical Enlightenment* (Albany: State University of New York Press, 1994), 28–40.

55. Lévi, *Transcendental Magic*, 180, 267.

56. Ronald Decker, Thierry Depaulis, and Michael Dummett, *A Wicked Pack of Cards: The Origins of the Occult Tarot* (New York: St. Martin's, 1996).

57. The other important figure in this regard is Jean-Baptiste Alliette, known as Etteilla.

58. Lévi, *Transcendental Magic*, 43.

59. Ibid., 95–96. He also describes the tarot as simultaneously Hermetic, Kabbalistic, magical, and theosophical (ibid., 278). For Lévi's position in the history of Kabbalah, see Wouter J. Hanegraaff, "The Beginnings of Occultist Kabbalah: Adolphe Franck and Eliphas Lévi," in *Kabbalah and Modernity: Interpretations, Transformations, Adaptations*, ed. Boaz Huss, (Boston: Brill, 2010), 107–128.

60. Lévi, *Transcendental Magic*, 42, 349, 373.

61. Lévi, *Key of the Mysteries*, 14.

62. Éliphas Lévi, *La clef des grands mystères suivant Hénoch, Abraham, Hermès Trismégiste et Salomon* (Paris: Félix Alcan, 1897), i.

63. Friedrich Max Müller, *Natural Religion: The Gifford Lectures Delivered before the University of Glasgow in 1888* (New York: Longmans, Green, 1898), 57–58; Herbert Spencer, *Ecclesiastical Institutions* (New York: D. Appleton, 1886), 827f.

64. Lévi, *Key of the Mysteries*, 9.

65. Ibid., 66.

66. Ibid., 9, 16. In this term "absurd," Lévi evokes a kind of Kierkegaardian fideism.

67. Ibid., 16.

68. Ibid., 9.

69. Ibid., 24.

70. Lévi, *Le grand arcane*, 94.

71. Jane Bennett, *Vibrant Matter: A Political Ecology of Things* (Durham, NC: Duke University Press, 2010). Lévi's magnetic vitalism was clearly drawing on Franz Mesmer's "animal magnetism."

72. See especially Éliphas Lévi, *La science des esprits* (Paris: G. Baillière, 1865), 181, 266; and Lévi, *Dogme et rituel de la haute magie*, 1:167, 171–175, 205, 236.

73. Lévi, *Transcendental Magic*, 62.

74. For example, see Lévi, *Dogme et rituel de la haute magie*, 1:182.

75. Ibid.

76. Lévi, *La science des esprits*, 52, 161–62.

77. At the very least, one might argue that religious studies initially suggested a point of overlap between Protestant triumphalists and esotericists.

78. For examples, see Masuzawa, *Invention of World Religions*, 207; and Bruce Lincoln, *Theorizing Myth* (Chicago: University of Chicago Press, 1999), 67.

79. Müller attacked materialism explicitly in an attempt to revalorize a lost subjectivity as an explanatory mechanism and postulated instead a complementarity between a subjective spirit and objective matter. Friedrich Max Müller, *Three Introductory Lectures on the Science of Thought* (Chicago: Open Court, 1888).

80. See Friedrich Max Müller, *Chips from a German Workshop*, 5 vols. (New York: C. Scribner's Sons, 1869–81), 3:74–99.

81. The title makes sense if one notes that Müller was using "psychological" the way our contemporaries might use "spiritual." See Friedrich Max Müller, *Theosophy; or, Psychological Religion: The Gifford Lectures Delivered before the University of Glasgow in 1892* (New York: Longmans, 1893; hereafter cited as *MMT*), esp. xvi.

82. For Müller as a Lutheran, see G. Beckerlegge, "Professor Friedrich Max Müller and the Missionary Cause," in *Religion in Victorian Britain: Culture and Empire*, ed. John Wolffe (Manchester: Manchester University Press, 1997), esp. 189.

83. Thomas McCormack, "Friedrich Max Müller, 1823–1900," *Open Court* 535 (1900): 743.

84. MMT, viii–ix. In particular, he describes his lectures on the "Logos," "Alexandrian Christianity," "Dionysius the Areopagite," and "Christian Theosophy" as the most important.

85. For religious studies as text-based philology, see ibid., esp. 27–28.

86. Ibid., 23 (emphasis added).

87. Müller, however, argued for a deist reading of miracle as rooted in a rational sense of wonder. Ibid., 25.

88. Friedrich Max Müller, *Lectures on the Science of Religion* (New York: Scribner, 1872), 11.

89. Friedrich Max Müller, *Selected Essays on Language, Mythology and Religion* (New York: Longmans, 1881), 1:23.

90. In some respects Müller's program is less a classical version of *prisca theologia* and more closely evokes a later New Age verison of *philosophia perennis*.

91. Müller, MMT, 24.

92. Friedrich Max Müller, *Physical Religion* (New York: Longmans, 1891), 5–7.

93. MMT, 89.

94. Ibid.

95. Ibid. Where we today use the word *culture*, Müller tends to use the term *nation*, but we might imagine *nation* as standing in for the German *volk*.

96. Ibid., 90.

97. Ibid., 93.

98. Ibid., 91 (italics in the original).

99. Ibid. Müller alternates "theosophy" and "Psychological Religion" as synonyms. For the sake of consistency in what follows, I will use "theosophy" except in direct quotes.

100. Ibid., 93.

101. As Müller states, "It should be known once for all that one may call oneself a theosophist, without being suspected of believing in spirit-rappings [*sic*], table-turnings, or any other occult sciences and black arts." Ibid., xvi.

102. Ibid., 95, 311.

103. Ibid., 474.

104. Müller had previously described the Veda as both "natural revelation" and the epitome of "Physical Religion." Ibid., 8, 95.

105. Ibid., 95. Contemporary scholars generally refer to Vedas in plural, but Müller instead preferred the singular Veda.

106. Ibid., 112.

107. Ibid., 142–43.

108. Ibid., 91.

109. Ibid., 423, 526.

110. Ibid., 72–86. It is interesting that Müller makes the case for common Aryan origins, given that a shared historical basis would have seemed unnecessary. He also discounts the "Semitic" history of Christianity.

111. Ibid., 446–7.

112. Ibid., 423.

113. Ibid., 447.

114. Ibid., 380–81, 422–23.

115. Ibid., 381.

116. Ibid., 384.

117. Ibid., 385.

118. Gottfried Leibniz, *Nouveaux essais sur l'entendement humain*, ed. Jacques Brunschwig (Paris: Flammarion, 1990); John Locke, *An Essay Concerning Human Understanding*, ed. P. H. Nidditch (New York: Oxford University Press, 1979), 402.

119. MMT, 388.

120. Ibid., 382.

121. Ibid., 388. See also Elizabeth Knoll, "The Science of Language and the Evolution of Mind: Max Müller's Quarrel with Darwinism," *Journal of the History of the Behavioral Sciences* 22 (1986): 3–22.

122. MMT, 388.

123. Ibid., 521.

124. Ibid., 417.

125. Ibid., 538.

126. Ibid.

127. Ibid., 541–42.

128. Some scholars have noticed the uncanny parallels between the Theosophical Society and religious studies; for example, David Chidester, *Empire of Religion: Imperialism and Comparative Religion* (Chicago: University of Chicago Press, 2014); and Kocku von Stuckrad, *The Scientification of Religion* (Boston: De Gruyter, 2014).

129. See Steven Sutcliffe, "The Origins of New Age Religion between the Two World Wars," in *Handbook of New Age*, ed. Daren Kemp and Lewis James (Boston: Brill, 2007), 61. Corrected membership figures are from Gregory Tillett, "Charles Webster Leadbeater 1854–1934: A Biographical Study" (PhD diss., University of Sydney, 1986), 944.

130. Olav Hammer, "Theosophical Elements in New Age Religion," in *Handbook of the Theosophical Current*, ed. Olav Hammer and Mikael Rothstein (Boston: Brill, 2013), 237–59; Suzanne Newcombe, "Magic and Yoga: The Role of Subcultures in Transcultural Exchange," in *Yoga Traveling: Bodily Practice in Transcultural Perspective*, ed. Beatrix Hauser (New York: Springer, 2013), 57–79; and Stephen Prothero, *The White Buddhist: The Asian Odyssey of Henry Steel Olcott* (Bloomington: Indiana University Press, 1996).

131. Wouter Hanegraaff, *New Age Religion and Western Culture: Esotericism in the Mirror of Secular Thought* (Albany: State University of New York, 1998), 95.

132. William Emmette Coleman, "Appendix C: The Sources of Madame Blavatsky's Writings," in *A Modern Priestess of Isis*, by Vesvelod Sergteevich Solovyoff [Всеволод Соловьёв, Vsevolod Solov'ev] (New York: Arno Press, 1976).

133. Boris De Zirkoff, "Helena Petrovna Blavatsky: General Outline of Her Life Prior to Her Public Work," in *H. P. Blavatsky: Collected Writings*, ed. Boris De Zirkoff (Wheaton, IL: Theosophical Press, 1950), xxv–lii.

134. Joscelyn Godwin, "Blavatsky and the First Generation of Theosophy," in *Handbook of the Theosophical Current*, ed. Olav Hammer and Mikael Rothstein (Boston: Brill, 2013), 20–21.

135. De Zirkoff, *Blavatsky: Collected Writings*, 1:141.

136. Ibid.

137. Lévi, Transcendental Magic, 3–5.

138. Blavatsky, *Isis Unveiled*, 1:ix.

139. De Zirkoff, *Blavatsky: Collected Writings*, 1:142; see also 1:116; and Christopher Partridge, "Lost Horizon: H. P. Blavatsky and Theosophical Orientalism," in *Handbook of the Theosophical Current*, ed. Olav Hammer and Mikael Rothstein (Boston: Brill, 2013), 309–34.

140. Blavatsky, *Isis Unveiled*, 2:635–36.

141. Blavatsky also expressed occasional anti-Semitism. For a contemporary critique of the "magical negro" trope, see Matthew Hughey, "Cinethetic Racism: White Redemption and Black Stereotypes in 'Magical Negro' Films," *Social Problems* 56, no. 3 (2009): 543–77.

142. Blavatsky, *Isis Unveiled*, 1:25.

143. Ibid., 1:5.

144. Ibid., 1:38 (emphasis added).

145. Ibid., 2:639.

146. Christopher Hutton and John Joseph, "Back to Blavatsky: The Impact of Theosophy on Modern Linguistics," *Language & Communication*, no. 18 (1998): 184.

147. Ibid., 184–86; Helena Petrovna Blavatsky, *The Secret Doctrine: The Synthesis of Science, Religion, and Philosophy*, 2 vol. (London: Theosophical Press, 1888), 2:198–200, 661–62.

148. Théodore Flournoy, Des Indes à la planète Mars: Étude sur un cas de somnambulisme avec glossolalia (Paris: F. Alcan, 1900).

149. An exception is Hutton and Joseph, "Back to Blavatsky."

150. Benjamin Lee Whorf, *Language, Thought, and Reality: Selected Writings*, ed. John Carroll (Cambridge, MA: MIT Press, 1956), 249, 252, 269.

151. Émile Burnouf, "Le Bouddhisme en Occident," *Revue des Deux Mondes*, July 1888, 840–72. We've understandably excised Burnouf because of his racism.

152. Donald Lopez, *Prisoners of Shangri-La: Tibetan Buddhism and the West* (Chicago: University of Chicago Press, 1998), 49–54.

153. Ibid., 52; Adele Algeo, "Beatrice Lane Suzuki and Theosophy in Japan," *Theosophical History* 11, no. 3–16 (2005); and ʏᴏsʜɪɴᴀɢᴀ Shin'ichi, "Suzuki Daisetsu and Swedenborg: A Historical Background," in *Modern Buddhism in Japan*, ed. ʜᴀʏᴀsʜɪ Makoto, ōᴛᴀɴɪ Eiichi and Paul Swanson, (Nagoya: Nanzan, 2014), 112–43.

154. Other notable scholars who were members of the Theosophical Society include Edward Conze, Alexandra David-Néel, and G. R. S. Mead.

155. For example, for the history of Theosophy in Japan, see YOSHINAGA Shin'ichi, "Kindai Nihon ni okeru Shinchigaku shisō no rekishi," *Shūkyō Kenkyū* 84, no. 2 (2010): 375–96.

156. The crisis was caused by Krishnamurti refusing the mantel of World Teacher in 1929.

157. Regarding the term *subtle body*, see Geoffrey Samuel and Jay Johnston, eds., *Religion and the Subtle Body in Asia and the West* (New York: Routledge, 2013), 2.

158. Denis Diderot and Jean le Rond d'Alembert, eds., *Encyclopédie; ou, Dictionnaire raisonné des sciences, des arts et des métiers*, 28 vols. (1751–72), 14:78, in ARTFL Encyclopédie Project, accessed January 7, 2011, http://encyclopedie.uchicago.edu.

159. For examples, see Jason Ānanda Josephson, *The Invention of Religion in Japan* (Chicago: University of Chicago Press, 2012), 8–11.

160. My friend Sarah Hammerschlag taught a course with this title.

161. For more on "academic gnosticism," see Kripal, *Roads of Excess*, 1–15; and Kripal, *The Serpent's Gift: Gnostic Reflections on the Study of Religion* (University of Chicago Press, 2007). Jeffrey Kripal has also recently laid out an esoteric genealogy for the comparative study of religion—in a textbook, no less—via the Hermetic revival of the Renaissance, Müller, theosophy, spiritualism, transcendentalism, and, above all, the American counterculture and the paranormal. See Kripal, *Comparing Religions: Coming to Terms* (Wiley-Blackwell, 2014).

162. I will argue for an option that is neither re-Christianization, re-universalization, nor the balkanization of increasing particularism. For this, see Jason Ā. Josephson-Storm, "Absolute Disruption: The Future of Theory after Postmodernism," work in progress.

163. For example, see Carroll, *Spiritualism in Antebellum America*.

164. See *The Life and Letters of the Right Honourable Friedrich Max Müller* (New York: Longmans, 1902), 1:306, 315.

165. The Oxford Bodleian Library holds a set of letters that Bulwer-Lytton and Müller exchanged during the years 1885–90. Bulwer-Lytton also dedicated *The Coming Race* to Müller. Edward Bulwer-Lytton, *The Coming Race* (Middletown, VT: Wesleyan University Press, 2005), xxvi. Bulwer-Lytton's association with Lévi is recounted in several places, including Waite's introduction to Lévi, *Transcendental Magic*.

166. See Blavatsky, *Isis Unveiled*, 2:246–48.

167. *Life and Letters of Müller*, 2:313.

168. For a different interpretation of Olcott's encounter with Müller, see Donald Lopez, *Buddhism and Science: A Guide for the Perplexed* (Chicago: University of Chicago Press, 2008), 155–59.

169. Henry Olcott, *Old Diary Leaves* (Adyar: Theosophical Publishing, 1904), 3:164–65.

170. Ibid., 4:57–58.

171. P. D. Ouspensky, *Tertium Organum* (New York: Vintage Books, 1970), 271–72.

172. For one survey of this theoretical terrain, see José Casanova, *Public Religions in the Modern World* (Chicago: University of Chicago Press, 1994), 11–39. For the Enlightenment as the beginning of radical disenchantment, see Keith Thomas, *Religion and the Decline of Magic* (New York: Scribner, 1971); and Michel Vovelle, *Piété baroque et déchristianisation en Provence au XVIIIe siècle* (Paris: Plon, 1973).

173. For this in early Christian studies, see Denise Buell, "The Afterlife Is Not Dead: Spiritualism, Postcolonial Theory, and Early Christian Studies," *Church History* 78 (2009): 862–72.

CHAPTER FIVE

1. Reproduced in Angela Bourke, "Reading a Woman's Death: Colonial Text and Oral Tradition in Nineteenth-Century Ireland," *Feminist Studies* 21, no. 3 (1995): 553–86.

2. Ibid. See also Angela Bourke, *The Burning of Bridget Cleary* (New York: Viking, 2000); and Joan Hoff and Marian Yeates, *The Cooper's Wife Is Missing: The Trials of Bridget Cleary* (New York: Basic Books, 2000).

3. See esp. Hoff and Yeates, *The Cooper's Wife Is Missing*.

4. Bourke, *Burning of Bridget Cleqry*, esp. 164.

5. Richard Dorson, *The British Folklorists: A History* (Chicago: University of Chicago Press, 1968). See also Anonymous, "The Witch-Burning at Clonmel," *Folklore* 6, no. 4 (1895): 373–384; and Leland Duncan, "Fairy Beliefs and Other Folklore Notes from County Leitrim," *Folklore* 7, no. 2 (1896): 161–83.

6. John Morley, *The Struggle for National Education* (London: Chapman and Hall, 1873), 63.

7. Cited in Alex Owen, *The Place of Enchantment: British Occultism and the Culture of the Modern* (Chicago: University of Chicago Press, 2004), 17.

8. For this list, see Frank Turner, *Contesting Cultural Authority: Essays in Victorian Intellectual Life* (New York: Cambridge University Press, 1993), 192–93; supplemented by David Bebbington, *Victorian Religious Revivals* (New York: Oxford University Press, 2012); David Blackbourn, *Marpingen: Apparitions of the Virgin Mary in Bismarckian Germany* (New York: Knopf, 1994); and Marie Vernet, *La Vierge à Pellevoisin* (Paris: Téqui, 1979).

9. See Stephen Sharot, "Magic, Religion, Science, and Secularization," in *Religion, Science, and Magic*, ed. Jacob Neusner, Ernest Frerichs, and Paul Flesher (New York: Oxford University Press, 1989), 261–84.

10. See Ivan Strenski, *Understanding Theories of Religion* (Walden: Wiley Blackwell, 2015), 66, 71. See also Robert Ackerman, "Anthropology and the Classics," in *A New History of Anthropology*, ed. Henrika Kuklick (Malden: Blackwell, 2008), 149; and Daniel Pals, *Eight Theories of Religion* (New York: Oxford University Press, 2006), 32.

11. Pals, *Eight Theories of Religion*.

12. For example, see Gilbert Germain, *A Discourse on Disenchantment* (Albany: State University of New York Press, 1993).

13. Henrika Kuklick, *The Savage Within: The Social History of British Anthropology* (New York: Cambridge University Press, 1991), 26.

14. Talal Asad, ed., *Anthropology & the Colonial Encounter* (New York: Humanities Press, 1973), esp. 16–17. See also Eric R. Wolf, *Europe and the People without History* (Berkeley: University of California Press, 1997); Adam Kuper, *The Reinvention of Primitive Society* (New York: Routledge, 2005); and George Stocking, *Victorian Anthropology* (New York: Free Press, 1987).

15. German *Volkskunde* has received some critical attention; for example, Hannjost Lixfeld, *Folklore and Fascism: The Reich Institute for German Volkskunde* (Bloomington: Indiana University Press, 1994).

16. Andrew Lang, *Custom and Myth* (London: Longmans Green, 1884), 11. See also Alan Dundes, *Interpreting Folklore* (Bloomington: Indiana University Press, 1980), 3.

17. Marjorie Morgan, *National Identities and Travel in Victorian Britain* (New York: Palgrave, 2001).

18. Richard Dorson, *Peasant Customs and Savage Myths* (Chicago: University of Chicago Press, 1968).

19. Alan O'Day, *Irish Home Rule, 1867–1921* (New York: St. Martin's Press, 1998).

20. They debated whether to understand these systems as evidence for evolutionism or diffusionism. See Dorson, *Peasant Customs and Savage Myths*, esp. 265.

21. For example, Lewis Henry Morgan, *Ancient Society* (London: Macmillan, 1877). Morgan does recognize some cultural "survivals."

22. James Augustus St. John, *The Education of the People* (London: Chapman and Hall, 1859), 32.

23. James Farrer, *Primitive Manners and Customs* (New York: H. Holt, 1879), 279.

24. Ronald Hutton, *Blood and Mistletoe: The History of the Druids in Britain* (New Haven, CT: Yale University Press, 2009), 339–41.

25. See, for example, Dorson, *Peasant Customs and Savage Myths*, 63.

26. Farrer, *Primitive Manners and Customs*, 280.

27. James Frazer, *The Golden Bough: A Study in Comparative Religion*, 1st ed. (London: Macmillan, 1890), 1:viii–ix. Hereafter *The Golden Bough* will be abbreviated *GB* and followed by edition, volume, and page numbers.

28. One significant passage describes a historical progression including different ages of superstition, with one marked by the distinction between religion and magic. *GB*, 1E 1:32.

29. Robert Ackerman, *J. G. Frazer: His Life and Work* (New York: Cambridge University Press, 1987), 81–82.

30. *GB* 1E, 1:348; Ackerman, *Frazer: Life and Work*, 110.

31. Here Frazer would be agreeing with Hegel, who had argued in *Vorlesungen über die Philosophie der Religion* that "magic" (*Zauberei*) was the first form of religion. G. W. F. Hegel, *Werke* (Frankfurt: Suhrkamp, 1969–71), 16:278.

32. For example, see *GB* 1E, 1:174–75.

33. We can see behind this charge a whole history of Protestant anti-Catholicism. One can also hear echoes of David Strauß, *Das Leben Jesu, kritisch bearbeitet* (1835).

34. *GB* 1E, 2:370.

35. Ibid., 2:371.

36. James Frazer, *Selected Letters of Sir J. G. Frazer*, ed. Robert Ackerman (New York: Oxford University Press, 2005), 63.

37. Ibid., 137–38.

38. It is telling that Frazer did not make a distinction between religion and magic in an earlier letter to Baldwin Spencer (September 15, 1898). While it could mean that Frazer developed his signature schema sometime between September and November, it is more likely that Frazer came to idea earlier but cautiously refrained from expressing it. Ibid., 126.

39. Ackerman, *Frazer: Life and Work*, 110; Peter Baker, "The Mild Anthropologist and the Mission of Primitive Man" (PhD diss., University of Cambridge, 1980); and Robert Fraser, *The Making of "The Golden Bough"* (New York: St. Martin's Press, 1990), 120–21.

40. Jevons insisted on a basic division in the primitive psyche between *magic*, which refers to a world that humans can control and which they identify as natural; and *religion*, which refers

to a world that that humans cannot control and which they identify as supernatural. But he also explicitly rejected the view that "all religion has been developed out of magic." Frank Jevons, *An Introduction to the History of Religion* (New York: Macmillan, 1896), 24–25.

41. Hermann Oldenberg, *Die Religion des Veda* (Berlin: W. Hertz, 1894), 58–59; see also 476–79.

42. Frazer Collection 20:1, Trinity College, University of Cambridge.

43. Pausanias, *Pausanias's Description of Greece*, trans. James Frazer (London: Macmillan, 1913), 5:264.

44. *GB* 2E, 1:xvi.

45. Another likely influence was William Edward Hartpole Lecky, *History of the Rise and Influence of the Spirit of Rationalism in Europe* (1882), cited in *GB* 3E, 11:42.

46. For influential early works of this sort, see John Aubrey, *Remaines of Gentilisme and Judaisme* (1687–1689); John Brand, *Observations on Popular Antiquities* (1813); Thomas Crofton Croker, *Fairy Legends and Traditions of the South of Ireland* (1825–28); and Madame d'Aulnoy, *Les Contes des Fées* (1698, translated into English as *Fairy Tales*, 1699).

47. According to the *OED*, the first meaning of *fairy* is "enchantment, magic," and its first usage in this sense in English dates from about 1330. For example, the "Fayrie knight" of *Gerileon of Englande* (1592) was a magical human knight, not a fairy. See also Noel Williams, "The Semantics of the Word Fairy," in *The Good People*, ed. Peter Narváez (Lexington: University Press of Kentucky, 1997), 457–78.

48. For the idea of the winged fairy, see Nicola Bown, *Fairies in Nineteenth-Century Art and Literature* (New York: Cambridge University Press, 2001), 45–47.

49. William Wilde, *Irish Popular Superstitions* (Dublin: McGlashan, 1852), 120–21.

50. Classification according to the Aarne-Thompson motif-index.

51. Quotation from Carole Silver, *Strange and Secret Peoples: Fairies and Victorian Consciousness* (New York: Oxford University Press, 2000), 192. See also Linda-May Ballard, "Fairies and the Supernatural on Reachrai," in *The Good People*, ed. Peter Narváez (Lexington: University Press of Kentucky, 1997), 47–93; and Barbara Rieti, *Strange Terrain: The Fairy World in Newfoundland* (St. John's: Memorial University of Newfoundland, 1991), 1–14.

52. Hugh Miller, *The Old Red Sandstone* (Boston: Gould and Lincoln, 1851), 260.

53. Geoffrey Chaucer, *The Riverside Chaucer*, ed. Larry Benson (Oxford: Oxford University Press, 1988), 116.

54. Marjorie Johnson, *Seeing Fairies: From the Lost Archives of the Fairy Investigation Society* (San Antonio: Anomalist Books, 2014); Rieti, *Strange Terrain*.

55. See: Bulwer-Lytton, "Complaint of the Last Faun" (1834); Brontë, *Shirley* (1849); Graves, *Fairies and Fusiliers* (1918); Kipling, *Puck of Pook's Hill* (1906); and Yeats, *Fairy and Folk Tales of the Irish* (1888).

56. John Aubrey, *Three Prose Works: Miscellanies, Remaines of Gentilisme and Judaisme, Observations* (Carbondale: Southern Illinois University, 1972), 290.

57. For example, ibid., 204.

58. Robert Cromek, *Remains of Nithsdale and Galloway Song* (London: Alexander Gardner, 1880), 248.

59. Ibid., 248. Also cited in Lizanne Henderson and Edward Cowan, *Scottish Fairy Belief: A History* (East Linton: Tuckwell Press, 2001), 28.

60. See Andrew Cheviot, *Proverbs, Proverbial Expressions, and Popular Rhymes of Scotland* (Detroit: Gale, 1969), 398; Henderson and Cowan, *Scottish Fairy Belief*, 87–88; and W. Jenkyn Thomas, *The Welsh Fairy Book* (Mineola: Dover, 2001), 12–17.

61. Henderson and Cowan, *Scottish Fairy Belief*, 28. See also John Selden, *Table Talk* (Edinburgh: Fairbairn, 1819): "There never was a merry world since the fairies left dancing, and the parson left conjuring" (124).

62. Richard Corbet, *The Poems of Richard Corbet* (London: Longman, 1807), 215.

63. Discussed in chapter 2, but see especially D. P. Walker, "The Cessation of Miracles," in *Hermeticism and the Renaissance: Intellectual History and the Occult in Early Modern Europe*, ed. Ingrid Merkel and Allen Debus (Washington, DC: Folger Books, 1988).

64. See Silver, *Strange and Secret Peoples*, 193, 198.

65. Lady Archibald Campbell, "The Men of Peace: Faerie Scotland," *Occult Review*, January 1909, 25–39.

66. See *GB* 2E, 1:74–75, 3E, 10: 323–24. Also in James Frazer, *Psyche's Task* (London: Macmillan, 1913), 166.

67. James Frazer, *The Gorgon's Head, and Other Literary Pieces* (London: Macmillan, 1927).

68. Frazer's library contained at least the following accounts of fairy farewell: Aubrey, *Remains of Gentilism*; Campbell, *Superstitions of the Highlands*; Chaucer, *The Canterbury Tales*; Hartland, *The Science of Fairy Tales*; Johnson, *A Journey to the Western Islands of Scotland* (partial version). Frazer Collection 20:1, Trinity College, University of Cambridge.

69. "The Trows in Shetland," *Scotsman*, January 19, 1893, Frazer Collection 21:1, Trinity College, University of Cambridge.

70. *GB* 2E, 1:xvi, 3:459.

71. See Pals, *Eight Theories of Religion*, 11; John Vickery, *The Literary Impact of the Golden Bough* (Princeton, NJ: Princeton University Press, 1976), 13.; and Ackerman, *Frazer: Life and Work* , 304.

72. Auguste Comte, *Opuscules de philosophie sociale, 1819–1828* (Paris: E. Leroux, 1883), 100.

73. A detailed discussion appears in an article I am currently preparing for publication, with the working title "Faith in Society: August Comte, Henri de Saint-Simon, and Sociology as Politics and Post-Religion."

74. *GB* 2E, 1:63.

75. Ibid., 1:73.

76. See, for example, Herbert Spencer, *The Principles of Sociology* (New York: D. Appleton, 1900), vol. 1.

77. Andrew Lang, *The Making of Religion* (London: Longmans, 1898). This debate is discussed in Randall Styers, *Making Magic: Religion, Magic, and Science in the Modern World* (New York: Oxford University Press, 2004), 81–84.

78. Richard Broome, *Aboriginal Australians: A History since 1788* (Crows Nest: Allen & Unwin, 2010), 100–121.

79. Probably the most important of these accounts was Baldwin Spencer and Francis James Gillen, *The Native Tribes of Central Australia* (1899).

80. Contemporary scholars have noted that European colonists often claimed to have discovered such indigenous peoples. See David Chidester, *Savage Systems: Colonialism and Com-*

parative Religion in Southern Africa (Charlottesville: University Press of Virginia, 1996); and J. Z. Smith, "Religion, Religions, Religious," in *Critical Terms for Religious Studies*, ed. Mark Taylor (Chicago: University of Chicago Press, 1998), 269–84.

81. George Angas, *Savage Life and Scenes in Australia and New Zealand* (London: Smith, Elder, 1847), 1:88, cited in *GB* 3E, 12:5.

82. See especially *GB* 2E, 1:72–73.

83. Even the *Encyclopedia Britannica* of 1875 repeated the claim that Aboriginal people had "no religion." Cited in Richard Broome, *Aboriginal Victorians: A History since 1800* (Crows Nest: Allen & Unwin, 2005), 101.

84. See Patrick Dove, *The Science of Politics* (London: Johnstone, 1850), 1:128.

85. *GB* 2E, 1:71.

86. Ibid., 74.

87. Ibid., 63.

88. Ibid., 61 (emphasis added).

89. See ibid., 63–64; see also 45.

90. Quoted in ibid., 66.

91. Ibid., 66.

92. Ibid., 61.

93. Ibid., 63.

94. Kurt Vonnegut, *Cat's Cradle* (New York: Dial Press Edition, 2010), 218.

95. *GB* 2E, 1:61–62.

96. Edward B. Tylor, *Primitive Culture*, 2 vols. (London: Murray, 1891), 1:121–22.

97. *GB* 2E, 1:62.

98. Ibid., 9–12.

99. Ibid., 28–34 (header). Expanded into "magical telepathy," *GB* 3E, 1:119–34.

100. *GB* 3E, 3:459.

101. *GB* 2E, 1:130. This also appears in *GB* 1E, 1:32.

102. *GB* 2E, 1:74–75.

103. See James Frazer, *The Worship of Nature* (New York: Macmillan, 1926), 10–11.

104. *GB* 2E, 3:460.

105. Ackerman, *Frazer: Life and Work*, 25–26.

106. Frazer, *Gorgon's Head*, 316.

107. *GB* 2E, 3:459.

108. Frazer, *Worship of Nature*, 1.

109. Ibid., 2–3.

110. Ibid.

111. Ibid., 3.

112. Ibid., 9.

113. Ibid., 10.

114. Ibid., 10.

115. Ibid.

116. Ibid., 8.

117. Ibid., 8.

118. Ibid., 4

119. Ibid., 4.

120. C. E. Montague, *Disenchantment* (London: Chatto & Windus, 1922), 278.

121. As will be shown in chapter 10, Weber came to disenchantment in 1913.

122. "Three Forms of Thought," *New York Times*, November 29, 1897.

123. Roger Luckhurst, *The Invention of Telepathy* (New York: Oxford University Press, 2007), 160–67.

124. George R. R. Martin, *A Clash of Kings* (New York: Bantam Books, 1999), 442.

CHAPTER SIX

1. Aleister Crowley, "Liber 73:The Urn: The Diary of a Magus" (unpublished manuscript, ed. Hymenaeus Beta [William Breeze], n.d.), accessed July 7, 2013, http://www.rahoorkhuit.net /library/libers/pdf/lib_0073.pdf. The strange book and the dying lion occurred in a dream that Crowley had on February 15, which he reflected on in July 12, 1916. Ibid., 23, 33.

2. Ibid., 33–34. The sobriquet came from Crowley's condemnation in an editorial, "The Wickedest Man in the World," *John Bull*, March 24, 1923.

3. Richard Kaczynski, *Perdurabo: The Life of Aleister Crowley*, 2nd ed. (Berkeley, CA: North Atlantic Books, 2010), 277–78.

4. Jean Fuller. *The Magical Dilemma of Victor Neuburg*. London: W. H. Allen, 1965, 223–224.

5. Crowley, "The Urn," 23.

6. Ibid., 33.

7. Ibid., 35.

8. Aleister Crowley, *The Confessions of Aleister Crowley: An Autohagiography* (London: Arkana, 1989), 808–9. Note the reference to "Dying God," which Crowley drew from Frazer.

9. Michel Foucault, *Histoire de la folie à l'âge classique* (Paris: Gallimard, 1972), 296–315; and Mark Micale, "On the 'Disappearance' of Hysteria: A Study in the Clinical Deconstruction of a Diagnosis," *Isis* 84 (1993): 496–526.

10. Karl Popper, *The Poverty of Historicism* (New York: Basic Books, 1957), 13–16, quotation on 13. See also Robert Merton, *Social Theory and Social Structure*, 3rd ed. (New York: Free Press, 1968), 475–79.

11. I generally avoid the formulation "Western esotericism." The expression is useful insofar as it evokes European appropriations of South and East Asian thought, but the excessive emphasis on "Western" presents an Orientalized East-West binary and ignores esotericism's global impact.

12. *Perdurabo* was written by a follower of Crowley's new religion, but it is a solid scholarly biography. Marco Pasi's *Aleister Crowley e la tentazione della politica* (Milan: FranoAngeli, 1999) was updated, translated, and reissued as Marco Pasi, *Aleister Crowley and the Temptation of Politics* (Durham, NC: Acumen, 2014).

13. The biographical summary that follows is primarily based on Kaczynski, *Perdurabo*, and a skeptical reading of Crowley's *Confessions*, supplemented with John Symonds, *The Great Beast: The Life and Magick of Aleister Crowley* (London: Mayflower Books, 1973), 237–39.

14. Kaczynski, *Perdurabo*, 4, 14.

15. Ibid., 16.

16. See, for example, Aleister Crowley, *The Law Is for All: The Authorized Popular Commentary to the Book of the Law-Liber AL vel Legis* (Tempe, AZ: New Falcon Publications, 1996), 99; and Aleister Crowley, *Crowley on Christ*, ed. Francis King (London: Daniel, 1974), 157.

17. Kaczynski, *Perdurabo*, 31–32. Crowley left Trinity without graduating in 1897.

18. For Crowley's admiration for Shelley see Kaczynski, *Perdurabo*, 33–34.

19. Even before Crowley met members of the order in person, he had read their work. See Aleister Crowley, *Magick: Liber ABA* (San Francisco: Weiser Books, 1997), xxxi.

20. Ellic Howe, *The Magicians of the Golden Dawn: A Documentary History of a Magical Order 1887–1923* (London: Routledge, 1972).

21. Crowley, *Confessions*, 393. See also Kaczynski, *Perdurabo*, 123–29.

22. Crowley, *Confessions*, 393.

23. Ibid., 394.

24. Aleister Crowley, *The Equinox of the Gods* (New York: New Falcon, 1991), 117–18.

25. Many of the themes that would define *The Book of the Law* appear in Crowley's earlier diaries and writings. For example, in a June 1903, diary entry, he already stated "My Gods were those of Egypt, interpreted on lines closely akin to those of Greece." Crowley, *Magick: Liber ABA*, xxxv.

26. See Crowley, *Law Is for All*.

27. Kaczynski, *Perdurabo*, 127–29.

28. Crowley, *Magick: Liber ABA*, 63.

29. Kaczynski, *Perdurabo*, 151.

30. Pasi sees Crowley's life as divided into two different phases: an individualistic mystical phase and a later prophetic mission. Marco Pasi, *Crowley and the Temptation of Politics*, 25.

31. Kaczynski, *Perdurabo*, 205–8, 231–34, 472–81.

32. Ibid., 548.

33. Ibid., 344.

34. See Ronald Hutton, "Crowley and Wicca," in *Aleister Crowley and Western Esotericism*, ed. Henrik Bogdan and Martin Starr (New York: Oxford University Press, 2012), 285–306.

35. See also in Bodgen and Starr, *Aleister Crowley and Western Esotericism*: Hugh Urban, "The Occult Roots of Scientology? L. Ron Hubbard, Aleister Crowley, and the Origins of a Controversial New Religion," 335–68; and Asbjørn Dyrendal, "Satan and the Beast: The Influence of Aleister Crowley on Modern Satanism," 369–94.

36. See Hugh Urban, *Magia Sexualis: Sex, Magic, and Liberation in Modern Western Esotericism* (Berkeley: University of California Press, 2008), esp. 109–39.

37. Crowley appears on the cover of the Beatles' *Sgt. Pepper's Lonely Hearts Club Band* (1967), and he is mentioned or quoted in numerous songs, including: David Bowie's "Quicksand" (1971), Raul Seixas's "Sociedade Alternativa" (1974), Ozzy Osborne's "Mr. Crowley" (1980_, Marilyn Manson's "Diary of a Dope Fiend" (1995), and the Klaxons' "Magick" (2006).

38. The full title of the spell text is "Liber LXX - Σταυρος Βατραχου, the Ceremonies proper to obtaining a familiar spirit of a Mercurial nature as described in the Apocalypse of St. John the Divine from a frog or toad." Reproduced in Symonds, *Great Beast*, 237–39.

39. Ibid., 238.

40. Crowley, *Confessions*, 808.

41. Aleister Crowley, "The Temple of Solomon the King (Continued)," *Equinox* 1, no. 7 (1912): 362. See also Crowley, *Confessions*, 360; Crowley, *Golden Twigs*, ed. Martin Starr (Chicago: Teitan Press, 1988), viii; and Kaczynski, *Perdurabo*, 119.

42. *The Works of Aleister Crowley*, 3 vols. (Foyers, Scotland: Society for the Propagation of Religious Truth, 1905–07), 2:130–39.

43. Crowley, *Confessions*, 360.

44. *Works of Crowley*, 2:133–34.

45. Aleister Crowley, "A∴A∴ Curriculum," *Equinox* 3, no. 1 (1919): 13–20; and Crowley, *Confessions*, 190.

46. *Works of Crowley*, 2:233.

47. Aleister Crowley, "The Attainment of Happiness: A Restatement of the Purpose of Mystical Teachings," *Vanity Fair* (November 1916): 55, 134.

48. Ibid.

49. Crowley, *Confessions*, 244.

50. See, for example, Aleister Crowley, "Liber Astarté vel Berylli (Liber 175)," *Equinox* 1, no. 7 (1912): 23–32.

51. Later Crowley refined his terminology, arguing: "Magick is getting into communication with individuals who exist on an higher plane than ours. Mysticism is the raising of oneself to their level." Crowley, *Magick: Liber ABA*, xxiii.

52. Aleister Crowley, *Liber 777 and Other Qabalistic Writings*, ed. Israel Regardie (York Beach: Weiser, 1986), ix.

53. Ibid., 3–14.

54. Crowley refers to his debt to Blavatsky in ibid., x.

55. "The only man worthy of our notice is Frazer of the Golden Bough." Ibid.

56. Crowley, *Confessions*, 513.

57. For all of these but Nietzsche, see Henrik Bogdan, "Envisioning the Birth of a New Aeon," in *Aleister Crowley and Western Esotericism*, ed. Henrik Bogdan and Martin Starr (New York: Oxford University Press, 2012), 89–106.

58. The Plymouth Brethren preached that the world would go through seven ages before the Rapture and Christ's return. See Bogdan, "Envisioning a New Aeon," 99–100.

59. Crowley may have discovered Bachofen through his reading of Frazer.

60. Aleister Crowley, "Liber Legis [the Old Commentary]," *Equinox* 1, no. 7 (1912): 400. Cited in Bogdan, "Envisioning a New Aeon," 90.

61. Aleister Crowley, *Magick without Tears* (Las Vegas: Falcon Press, 1989), 303.

62. Crowley, "Liber Legis," 303; Crowley, *Confessions*, 370.

63. Crowley, *Magick: Liber ABA*, 163.

64. Crowley, "Liber Legis," 400.

65. Especially vol. 4, *The Dying God*, and vols. 5–6, *Adonis, Attis, Osiris*.

66. Quoted in Bogdan, "Envisioning a New Aeon," 92.

67. Crowley is likely gesturing here toward Müller's theory of solar mythology. Müller's theory is rooted in his philological reconstruction of the names of various deities, which he suggested proved their origins in various early Aryan words originating in the context of the diurnal motion of sun and moon. For instance, he claimed that Daphne originally meant the

dawn and Apollo meant the sun. So the myth in which Apollo pursued Daphne was originally a metaphopr for the sun following the dawn. Müller and company's ability to read anything as a solar myth was quickly satirized. Already in 1870 the Anglo-Irish clergyman Richard Littledale had joked that "the story of Max Müller" must itself be a solar myth, as Müller's name could be reconstructed as a (very tennous) reference to the sun and his own relocation from Germany to England was cleary a metaphor for the East-West solar movement. So Müller himself must be nothing more than a myth. See Michael Carroll, "Some Third Thoughts on Max Müller and Solar Mythology," *Archives Européennes de Sociologie* 26, no. 2 (1985): 262–90.

68. Crowley also wanted magick also to reject "charlatanism" and "obscurantism" and embrace carefully recorded magical experiments.

69. Crowley, *Magick: Liber ABA*, 135; Egil Asprem, "Magic Naturalized? Negotiating Science and Occult Experience in Aleister Crowley's Scientific Illuminism," *Aries* 8, no. 2 (2008): 150.

70. Crowley, *Magick: Liber ABA*, 123.

71. Crowley, *Magick without Tears*, 218–19.

72. James Frazer, *The Golden Bough: A Study in Comparative Religion*, 3rd ed. (London: Macmillan, 1906), 1:218–19, cited in Crowley, *Magick: Liber ABA*, 124 (emphasis in the original).

73. Frazer, *Golden Bough*, 1:52–53.

74. For Crowley, the magician does not beg spirits; she compels them. Crowley, *Magick: Liber ABA*, 216.

75. Wouter Hanegraaff, "How Magic Survived the Disenchantment of the World," *Religion*, no. 33 (2003): 361.

76. Crowley, *Magick: Liber ABA*, 215.

77. Aleister Crowley, *Moonchild* (New York: Weiser, 1970), 42. Although the work is fiction, it also relies on Crowley's system of magic.

78. Crowley, *Magick: Liber ABA*, 216–17.

79. Ibid., 224.

80. Crowley and Frazer were not in complete agreement about magic. One significant difference was in that while they shared an antipathy toward spiritualism, Crowley argued that communication with spirits and other supernatural beings was a crucial component of the magician's repertoire.

81. This was a continuation of the schema Crowley had worked in *Liber 777*.

82. Richard Kaczynski, "The Crowley-Harris Thoth Tarot: Collaboration and Innovation," in *Tarot in Culture*, ed. Emily E. Auger (Clifford, ON: Valleyhome Books, 2014), 147, 164.

83. Brian Vickers, introduction to *Occult and Scientific Mentalities in the Renaissance*, ed. Vickers (New York: Cambridge University Press, 1984), 17. Cited in Hanegraaff, "How Magic Survived," 359.

84. Hanegraaff, "How Magic Survived," 377.

85. Ibid., 370–71.

86. Egil Asprem, "Magic Naturalized? Negotiating Science and Occult Experience in Aleister Crowley's Scientific Illuminism," *Aries* 8, no. 2 (2008): 139–65.

87. Aleister Crowley, *The and Other Essays* (Tempe, AZ: New Falcon, 1998), 19, 15.

88. Ibid.

89. Ibid., 20.

90. Ibid., 19.

91. Aleister Crowley, *The Scrutinies of Simon Iff* (Chicago: Teitan Press, 1987), 27.

92. Crowley, 20.

93. Ibid., 20–21.

94. Ibid., 37.

95. Aleister Crowley, editorial, *Equinox* 1, no. 1 (1909): 1–6.

96. Aleister Crowley, "Liber Exercitiorum," *Equinox* 1, no. 1 (1909): 25–36.

97. E.g., Crowley, *Confessions*, 224.

98. Crowley, *Magick: Liber ABA*, 126. As Crowley put it elsewhere: "Magick is the science and art of causing change to occur in conformity with the Will. In other words, it is Science, Pure and Applied. This thesis has been worked out at great length by Dr. Sir J. G. Frazer." Aleister Crowley, *The Book of Thoth* (New York: Weiser, 1969), 40.

99. Crowley, *Magick: Liber ABA*, 126.

100. Ibid., 128 (*"Science . . . comprehension,"* emphasis in the original; *"For instance . . . expressions,"* emphasis added).

101. Ibid., 194.

102. Ibid., 129.

103. Aleister Crowley, "The Worst Man in the World Tells the Astounding Story of His Life," *Sunday Dispatch*, June 18, 1933.

104. Crowley, *Magick without Tears*, 64.

105. Asprem, "Magic Naturalized?", 149–50

106. See Crowley, *Magick: Liber ABA*, 215.

107. Kaczynski, *Perdurabo*, 547.

108. Crowley, *Golden Twigs*.

109. I have been unable to confirm Ackerman's assertion that Jessie Weston was a member of the Order of the Golden Dawn. See Robert Ackerman, *The Myth and Ritual School: J. G. Frazer and the Cambridge Ritualists* (New York: Garland, 1991), 219. Regardless, Weston claimed to know initiates of lost Grail rites, stating: "No inconsiderable part of the information at my disposal depended upon personal testimony, the testimony of those who knew of the continued existence of such a ritual and had actually been initiated into its mysteries." Jessie Weston, *From Ritual to Romance* (New York: Doubleday, 1957), 4–5. Margaret Alice Murray (*The Witch-Cult in Western Europe*, 1921) argued that witches were practitioners of a pagan religion that had been transmitted from pre-Christian times. This was more than an academic interest, and Murray was not above casting the occasional spell herself. Gerald Gardner, one of the founders of modern Wicca, not only borrowed from Crowley, but also followed his lead in turning toward *The Golden Bough* as a source of pagan rites and spells. For Murray and Gardner, see Ronald Hutton, *The Triumph of the Moon: A History of Modern Pagan Witchcraft* (New York: Oxford University Press, 1999), 200–201, 205–40. For Crowley's influence on modern Wicca, see Leo Ruickbie, *Witchcraft out of the Shadows: A Complete History* (London: Robert Hale, 2004), esp. 104–5.

110. Israel Regardie, *The Golden Dawn: A Complete Course in Ceremonial Magic*. (St. Paul, MN: Llewellyn Publications), 1989.

CHAPTER SEVEN

1. For the recension history of *Die Traumdeutung*, see Lydia Marinelli and Andreas Mayer, *Dreaming By the Book: Freud's the Interpretation of Dreams and the History of the Psychoanalytic Movement* (New York: Other Press, 2003).

2. Sigmund Freud, *Die Traumdeutung*, 4th ed. (Leipzig: Franz Deuticke, 1914), 48n2.

3. Carl du Prel, *Die Philosophie der Mystik* (Leipzig: Günther, 1885), 306. Quoted in Freud, *Die Traumdeutung*, 474n1.

4. Freud, *Die Traumdeutung*, 474n1.

5. Freud had first used *Unbewußte* in his coauthored monograph *Studien über Hysterie* (1895) but had not yet begun to theorize it significantly. The term *Unbewußte* had a long history prior to both du Prel and Freud. It was coined with a slightly different spelling (*Unbewußtseyn*) by Ernst Platner in 1776. See Elke Völmicke, *Das Unbewußte im Deutschen Idealismus* (Würzburg: Königshausen & Neumann, 2005), 11–12.

6. Freud could also have found a very similar idea in Hartmann, *Philosophie des Unbewussten* (1869).

7. Freud, *Die Traumdeutung*, 416–17n1. For the influence of Hartmann on Freud, see Marcel Zentner, "Nineteenth-Century Precursors of Freud," in *The Freud Encyclopedia* (New York: Routledge, 2002), 370–83; and Yvon Brès, "Home, Carus, Hartmann-histoire de l'inconscient," *Revue Philosophique de la France et de l'Étranger* 2, no. 194 (2004): 225–30, esp 228.

8. Corinna Treitel, *A Science for the Soul: Occultism and the Genesis of the German Modern* (Baltimore: Johns Hopkins University Press, 2004), 40.

9. Frazer may be an exception, as he either had no occult interests or was able to hide them so well that they have been lost.

10. Freud attacked the concept of degeneration. Sigmund Freud, *Drei Abhandlungen zur Sexualtheorie* (Leipzig: F. Deuticke, 1905).

11. Daniel Pick, *Faces of Degeneration: A European Disorder* (New York: Cambridge University Press, 1989); and Sander Gilman, *Difference and Pathology* (Ithaca, NY: Cornell University Press, 1985).

12. Max Nordau, *Entartung* (Berlin: Duncker, 1892), translated in Max Nordau, *Degeneration* (New York: Appleton, 1895), 537; see also 209.

13. Nordau, *Degeneration*, 22.

14. Ibid., 45. I modified very slightly the translation in Nordeau, *Entartung*, 1:86.

15. Nordau, *Degeneration*, 214.

16. Ibid., 215–16.

17. Ibid., 217.

18. See Treitel, *Science for the Soul*; and Moritz Bassler and Hildegard Châtellier, *Mystique, mysticisme et modernité en Allemagne autour de 1900* (Strasbourg: Presses Universitaires de Strasbourg, 1998); Nicholas Goodrick-Clarke, *The Occult Roots of Nazism* (New York: New York University Press, 1992); Hans-Jürgen Glowka, *Deutsche Okkultgruppen, 1875–1937* (Munich: Arbeitsgemeinschaft für Religions- und Weltanschauungsfragen, 1981); Arthur Magida, *The Nazi Séance* (New York: Palgrave, 2011); Andreas Sommer, "Normalizing the Supernomal: The Formation of the Gesselschaft Für Psychologische Furshung," *Journal of the History of the Behavioral Sciences* 49, no. 1 (2013): 18–44; Klaus Vondung, *Magie und Manipulation: Ideologischer*

Kult und politische Religion des Nationalsozialismus (Göttingen: Vandenhoeck, 1971); Barbara Wolf-Braun, *Medizin, Okkultismus und Parapsychologie im 19. und frühen 20. Jahrhundert* (Wetzlar: GWAB-Verlag, 2009); and Heather Wolffram, *The Stepchildren of Science: Psychical Research and Parapsychology in Germany, c. 1870–1939* (New York: Rodopi, 2009).

19. Immanuel Kant, *Theoretical Philosophy, 1755–1770* (Cambridge: Cambridge University Press, 2002), 336 (italics in the original).

20. Wouter Hanegraaff, *Swedenborg, Oetinger, Kant* (West Chester: Swedenborg Foundation, 2007); Gregory Johnson, introduction to *Kant on Swedenborg: Dreams of a Spirit-Seer and Other Writings*, by Immanuel Kant (West Chester: Swedenborg Foundation, 2002); and Alison Laywine, *Kant's Early Metaphysics and the Origins of the Critical Philosophy* (Atascadero, CA: Ridgeview, 1993).

21. For example, René Descartes, *Les Passions de l'Ame* (Paris: N.p., 1728), 51–52.

22. Kant, *Kant on Swedenborg*, 309

23. Immanuel Kant, *Critique of Pure Reason* (Indianapolis: Hackett, 1996), 303.

24. Nietzsche argued, "God became the 'thing-in-itself.'" Friedrich Nietzsche, *The Anti-Christ, Ecce Homo, Twilight of the Idols, and Other Writings* (Cambridge: Cambridge University Press, 2005), 18.

25. Descartes's idea of "passions" somewhat complicates this picture insofar as they parallel what would later be regarded as emotions or unconscious drives.

26. Immanuel Kant, *Anthropology from a Pragmatic Point of View* (Cambridge: Cambridge University Press, 2006), 23–26.

27. Ibid., 24.

28. Ludger Lütkehaus, *Dieses wahre innere Afrika: Texte zur Entdeckung des Unbewussten vor Freud* (Frankfurt: Fischer Taschenbuch Verlag, 1989), 20–22. As Lütkenhaus observes, European thinkers produced parallel imagery of a racialized black Africa alongside a dark unconscious.

29. For resonances between Kant and gothic literature, see Marshall Brown, *The Gothic Text* (Stanford, CA: Stanford University Press, 2005).

30. G.W.F. Hegel, *Werke*, ed. Eva Moldenhauer and Karl Markus Michel, 20 vols. (Frankfurt: Suhrkamp, 1971), 8:178–79, translated in Hegel, *The Logic of Hegel* (Oxford: Clarendon Press, 1874), 131.

31. Ibid. Thanks are due to Christian Thorne for this observation.

32. For Hegel's reading in mysticism, see Glenn Magee, *Hegel and the Hermetic Tradition* (Ithaca, NY: Cornell University Press, 2001).

33. Arthur Schopenhauer, *On the Fourfold Root of the Principle of Sufficient Reason and Other Writings* (New York: Cambridge University Press, 2012), 411.

34. Ibid., 415.

35. Ibid., 412.

36. Ibid., 416.

37. Ibid., 413.

38. Karl Ludwig August Friedrich Maximilian Alfred, Freiherr von Prel is usually referred to as Baron Carl du Prel. For a more extensive discussion of du Prel and his work, see Tomas Kaiser, "Zwischen Philosophie und Spiritismus: Quellen zum Leben und Werk des Carl du Prel" (PhD diss., Lüneburg University, 2006).

39. See Treitel, *Science for the Soul*, 42.

40. Andrew Weeks, *German Mysticism from Hildegard of Bingen to Ludwig Wittgenstein* (Albany: State University of New York Press, 1993), which despite its title is a wonderful and nuanced work.

41. Bernard McGinn, *The Mystical Thought of Meister Eckhart: The Man from Whom God Hid Nothing* (New York: Crossroad Pub, 2001), 1–2; Ernst Benz, *Les sources mystiques de la philosophie romantique allemande* (Paris: Vrin, 1968), 1; Roland Pietsch, "Franz von Baader's Criticism of Modern Rationalism," *Sophia Perennis* 2, no. 2 (2010): 15–29.

42. For the two semantic fields and the debate, see Volkhard Krech, "Mystik," in *Max Webers "Religionssystematik"* (Tübingen: Mohr Siebeck, 2001), 242–44. See also William James, *Varieties of Religious Experience* (New York: Routledge, 2002), esp. 330.

43. Carl du Prel, *Die Philosophie der Mystik* (Leipzig: Günther, 1885), 1:119. I have largely followed the translation in du Prel, *Philosophy of Mysticism*, trans. C. C. Massey. (London: George Redway, 1889), 1:142.

44. Du Prel, *Philosophy of Mysticism*, 1:78.

45. For debates about du Prel's portrayal of Kant, see Robert Hoar, "Ein unaufgeklärtes Moment in der Kantian Philosophie," *Philosophische Monastshefte* 29 (1893): 278–91.

46. Karl Joel, *Der Ursprung der Naturphilosophie aus dem Geiste der Mystik* (Jena: Diederichs, 1906). Pfleiderer argued that the religious philosophy of Plato has demonstrated "higher unity of the mystery religions and philosophical thought." Otto Pfleiderer, *Religion und Religionen* (Munich: Lehmanus Verlag, 1911), 2:170.

47. For du Prel's occult readership, see Arthur Waite, *Studies in Mysticism and Certain Aspects of the Secret Tradition* (London: Hodder, 1906); and Carl Kiesewetter, *Geschichte des neueren Occultismus: Geheimwissenschaftliche Systeme von Agrippa von Nettesheim bis zu Karl du Prel* (Leipzig: Friedrich, 1891).

48. For examples, see Richard Noll, *The Jung Cult: Origins of a Charismatic Movement* (Princeton, NJ: Princeton University Press, 1994); and John Kerr, *A Most Dangerous Method: The Story of Jung, Freud, and Sabina Spielrein* (New York: Knopf, 1993).

49. The work was dictated by Jung to Aniela Jaffé. Deirdre Bair, *Jung: A Biography* (Boston: Little, Brown, 2003), esp. 626.

50. C. G. Jung, *Erinnerungen, Träume, Gedanken von C. G. Jung* (Zürich: Rascher, 1962), esp. 155, 159.

51. C. G. Jung *Memories, Dreams, Reflections* (New York: Pantheon Books, 1989), 150–51.

52. Jung, *Erinnerungen, Träume, Gedanken*, 160.

53. See C. G. Jung, *The Gnostic Jung*, ed. Robert Segal (Princeton, NJ: Princeton University Press, 1992).

54. Peter Gay, *A Godless Jew: Freud, Atheism, and the Making of Psychoanalysis* (London: Yale University Press, 1987), 30–31.

55. Jean-Luc Nancy, *Adoration: The Deconstruction of Christianity II* (New York: Fordham University Press, 2013), 95, 100–101; see also 49. To be clear, Nancy argues that Freud is also skeptical toward science.

56. Harold Bloom, *Ruin the Sacred Truths* (Cambridge, MA: Harvard University Press, 1989), esp. 150, 161.

57. Paul Ricoeur, *Freud and Philosophy: An Essay on Interpretation* (New Haven, CT: Yale

University Press, 1986), 32–33. Broadly put, Ricoeur sees Freud as capable of purifying religion. For an attempt to recover a theological Freud, see Eric Santner, *On the Psychotheology of Everyday Life: Reflections on Freud and Rosenzweig* (Chicago: University of Chicago Press, 2001).

58. Sigmund Freud, *Psychopathology of Everyday Life* (New York: Macmillan, 1914), 309 (italics in the original).

59. Ibid., 310.

60. For example, Freud, "Zwangshandlungen und Religionsübungen" (Obsessive actions and religious practices, 1907).

61. Sigmund Freud, *Totem and Taboo: Some Points of Agreement between the Mental Lives of Savages and Neurotics* (New York: Routledge, 2001), 91.

62. Ibid., 99.

63. Ibid., 94.

64. Ibid., 102.

65. Ibid., 90–91.

66. Ibid., 105.

67. See also ibid., 97. For Haeckel's famous biogenetic law, see Ernst Haeckel, *Generelle Morphologie der Organismen* (Berlin: G. Reimer, 1866), 2:7.

68. Sigmund Freud, *The Future of an Illusion* (New York: Norton, 1975), 30. See also Mary Kay O'Neil and Salman Akhtar, *On Freud's* The Future of an Illusion (London: International Psychoanalytical Association), 2009.

69. Freud, *Future of an Illusion*, 43.

70. Ibid., 51.

71. For Rolland's theory of mysticism and the longer back-and-forth that followed, see William Parsons, *The Enigma of the Oceanic Feeling* (New York: Oxford University Press, 1999).

72. Sigmund Freud, *Civilization and Its Discontents* (New York: Norton, 1962), 19.

73. Sigmund Freud, *New Introductory Lectures on Psycho-Analysis and Other Works* (London: Hogarth, 1964), 42. As discussed below, in the next pages, Freud turned around and advocated occult investigations.

74. Freud referred to "our predecessors in psycho-analysis, the Catholic fathers" in a 1909 letter to Oskar Pfister; see *Psychoanalysis and Faith: The Letters of Freud and Pfister* (New York: Basic Books, 1964), 21. For psychoanalysis as exorcism, see Luisa de Urtubey, *Freud et le diable* (Paris: Presses universitaires de France, 1983); and H. C. Erik Midelfort, "Charcot, Freud, and the Demons," in *Werewolves, Witches, and Wandering Spirits*, ed. Kathryn A. Edwards (Kirksville, MO: Truman State University Press, 2002), 199–215. For another account of the intertwined relationship between psychology and spiritualism, see Janet Oppenheim, *The Other World: Spiritualism and Psychical Research in England, 1850–1914* (New York: Cambridge University Press).

75. Sigmund Freud and C. G. Jung, *Briefwechsel* (Frankfurt: Fischer, 1974), 241–42. I have slightly amended the translation from Sigmund Freud and C. G. Jung, *The Freud-Jung Letters* (Princeton, NJ: Princeton University Press, 1974), 218; see also 215–16.

76. Freud and Jung, *Briefwechsel*, 243; Freud and Jung, *Letters*, 220. This was likely a gesture toward *gematria* in particular.

77. Ernest Jones, *The Life and Work of Sigmund Freud* (New York: Basic Books, 1953–57), 3:382.

78. Ibid., 3:381 (emphasis added).

79. Thomas Rabeyron and Renaud Evrard, "Perspectives historiques et contemporaines sur l'occulte dans la correspondance Freud-Ferenczi," *Recherches en psychanalyse* 13, no. 1 (2012): 97–111.

80. Ibid., 99–102.

81. F. X. Charet, *Spiritualism and the Foundations of C. G. Jung's Psychology* (Albany: State University of New York Press, 1993), 199.

82. Ibid.; Paul Roazen, *Freud and His Followers* (New York: Knopf, 1974), 233.

83. Jones, *Sigmund Freud*, 3: 397.

84. Freud and Jung, *Letters*, 429 (emphasis added). Freud also warned Jung to be cautious.

85. Sigmund Freud and Sándor Ferenczi, *The Correspondence of Sigmund Freud and Sándor Ferenczi* (Cambridge, MA: Belknap Press of Harvard University Press, 1993–2000), 1:274.

86. Jones, *Sigmund Freud*, 3: 393.

87. Sigmund Freud and Karl Abraham, *The Complete Correspondence of Sigmund Freud and Karl Abraham, 1907–1925* (New York: Karnac, 2002), 550.

88. E. James Lieberman and Robert Kramer, *The Letters of Sigmund Freud & Otto Rank* (Baltimore: Johns Hopkins University Press, 2012), 136–42.

89. Sigmund Freud, *Letters of Sigmund Freud* (New York: Basic Books, 1960), 334.

90. Translated in Sigmund Freud, *The Interpretation of Dreams* (New York: Basic Books 2010), 617–19.

91. Freud's *"Das Unheimliche"* (*The Uncanny*, 1919) also touched on his own uncanny experiences. It is also worth noting that in this text, Freud lists animistic belief in magic, a world of spirits, and "the ominipotence of thought" as paradigmatic of the uncanny. Sigmund Freud, *The Uncanny*, trans. David McLintock (New York: Penguin Books, 2003), 144, 147.

92. Phyllis Grosskurth, "The Idyll in the Harz Mountains: Freud's Secret Committee," in *Freud and the History of Psychoanalysis*, ed. Toby Gelfand and John Kerr (Hillsdale, NJ: Analytic Press, 1992), 347.

93. Jones, *Sigmund Freud*, 3:392.

94. Sigmund Freud, *Beyond the Pleasure Principle, Group Psychology and Other Works* (London: Hogarth Press, 1975), 193.

95. Sigmund Freud, *Psychopathology of Everyday Life* (New York: Norton, 1990), 334.

96. Sigmund Freud, "Some Additional Notes on Dream-Interpretation as a Whole," in *The Ego and the Id and Other Works* (London: Hogarth, 1975), 135–36.

97. Jones, *Sigmund Freud*, 3:394.

98. Ibid.

99. Ibid., 3:394–395.

100. Freud, *Letters*, 334. Not to mislead, Freud was describing his own scientific prejudices against spirits in particular.

101. Freud, *Beyond the Pleasure Principle*, 178.

102. Freud, *New Introductory Lectures on Psycho-Analysis*, 33.

103. Freud, *Beyond the Pleasure Principle*, 178 (emphasis added).

104. Jones, *Sigmund Freud*, 3:395.

105. Ibid., 395–96 (emphasis added).

106. Freud referred to thought transference as a fact in a letter to Weiss in 1935; see Edoardo

Weiss, *Sigmund Freud as a Consultant: Recollections of a Pioneer in Psychoanalysis* (New York: Intercontinental Medical Book Corp., 1970), 69.

107. Freud, *New Introductory Lectures on Psycho-Analysis*, 54–55.

108. Ibid.

109. Freud, *Totem and Taboo*, 34.

110. See ibid., 35.

111. Ibid., 34–35.

112. Ibid., 71.

113. Ibid., 71–73.

114. Ibid., 107.

115. Ibid., 23–24.

116. Freud 1974, 218. See also Jones, *Sigmund Freud*, 3:390.

117. Jones, *Sigmund Freud*, 3:301, 391.

118. Jones recounted that under certain instances of intense stress, Freud engaged in symbolic gestures to ward off misfortune, and Freud was bothered by his own clairvoyant dreams. See ibid., 3:382, 389.

119. Freud, *Totem and Taboo*, 103.

120. By way of exceptions, see Roger Luckhurst, *The Invention of Telepathy* (New York: Oxford University Press, 2007). Derrida also carried on Freud's telepathy.

121. For example, see Frank Sulloway, *Freud, Biologist of the Mind: Beyond the Psychoanalytic Legend* (New York: Basic Books, 1979).

122. For example, George Devereux, *Psychoanalysis and the Occult* (New York: International Universities Press, 1970).

123. D. J. Bem, "Feeling the Future: Experimental Evidence for Anomalous Retroactive Influences on Cognition and Affect," *Journal of Personality and Social Psychology* 100 (2011): 407–25.

124. Ludwig Binswanger, *Sigmund Freud: Reminiscences of a Friendship* (New York: Grune & Stratton, 1957), 8.

125. Maurice Blanchot, "La fin de la philosophie," *Nouvelle Revue Française*, 81 (1959): 286–98; Leszek Kołakowski, *Metaphysical Horror* (New York: Blackwell, 1988), 7.

126. Theodor Adorno, *Kants Kritik der reinen Vernunft* (Frankfurt: Suhrkamp, 1995), 168. While preparing my own translation, I consulted Theodor Adorno, *Kant's Critique of Pure Reason* (Stanford, CA: Stanford University Press, 2001), 110–11.

CHAPTER EIGHT

1. See Roderich Huch, *Alfred Schuler, Ludwig Klages und Stefan George: Erinnerungen an Kreise und Krisen der Jahrhundertwende in München-Schwabing* (Amsterdam: Castrum-Peregrini, 1973); Franz Wegener, *Alfred Schuler, der letzte deutsche Katharer: Gnosis, Nationalsozialismus und mystische Blutleuchte* (Gladbeck: KFVR, 2003); and Friedrich Wolters, *Stefan George und Die Blätter für die Kunst* (Berlin: Bondi, 1930), 240–73. For psychical research, see Albert von Schrenck-Notzing, *Physikalische Phänomene des Mediumismus* (Munich: Reinhardt, 1920), 104–9; and Schrenck-Notzing, *Experimente der Fernbewegung (Telekinese)* (Stuttgart: Union Deutsche Verlagsgesellschaft, 1924), 190–93. For their connection to other

370 Notes to Pages 210–213

occult thinkers, see: Wegener, *Alfred Schuler*, 31–32; George L. Mosse, "The Mystical Origins of National Socialism," *Journal of the History of Ideas* 22, no. 1 (1961): 81–96; Robert Norton, *Secret Germany: Stefan George and His Circle* (Ithaca, NY: Cornell University Press, 2002), 115–16; and Alfred Schuler, *Cosmogonische Augen* (Paderborn: Igel, 1997), 21, 35–36. The Kosmikers were especially influenced by Papus (Gérard Encausse), Joséphin Péladan, and Éliphas Lévi, even as they disparaged Helena Blavatsky and theosophy.

2. Ludwig Klages, *Rhythmen und Runen* (Leipzig: Barth, 1944), 332. For their attempt to magically heal Nietzsche, see Huch, *Alfred Schuler, Ludwig Klages und Stefan George*, 29–30.

3. Wolters, *Stefan George*, 241–43.

4. Elke-Vera Kotowski and Gert Mattenklott, eds., *"O dürft ich Stimme sein, das Volk zu rütteln!": Leben und Werk von Karl Wolfskehl, 1869–1948* (Hildesheim: Olms, 2007).

5. For Derleth's relation to the Eranos Circle, see Hans Thomas Hakl, *Eranos: An Alternative Intellectual History of the Twentieth Century* (Ithaca, NY: McGill-Queen's University Press, 2013), 17–25.

6. Norton, *Secret Germany*, 305–10.

7. Wegener, *Alfred Schuler*, 9. See also Alfred Schuler, *Alfred Schuler: Fragmente und Vorträge aus dem Nachlass*, ed. Ludwig Klages (Leipzig: Barth, 1940), 159–60.

8. Franziska zu Reventlow, *Herrn Dames Aufzeichnungen* (Munich: Langen, 1913), 68–69, 138; Theodor Lessing, *Einmal und nie wieder: Lebenserinnerungen* (Gütersloh: Bertelsmann, 1969) , 325; and Norton, *Secret Germany*, 152.

9. Schuler, *Fragmente und Vorträge*, 159–268.

10. Ibid., 159–160.

11. Ibid., 33, 95, 160. See also Schuler, *Cosmogonische Augen*, 41.

12. Klages, *Rhythmen und Runen*, 270.

13. See Reventlow, *Herrn Dames Aufzeichnungen*, 74–75.

14. See, for example, Norton, *Secret Germany*, 119–20; and Schuler, *Fragmente und Vorträge*, 152.

15. Schuler's symbol for this queer paganism was the *Hakenkreuz*, or swastika; and he seems to have been partially responsible for introducing this terrible sign into German life. But for Schuler, the swastika represented not the hypermasculinity of the Third Reich, but a phallic homosexuality.

16. Reventlow, *Herrn Dames Aufzeichnungen*, 142–43.

17. Ibid., 71.

18. For a contemporary political account of "thing-power," see Jane Bennett, *Vibrant Matter: A Political Ecology of Things* (Durham, NC: Duke University Press, 2010).

19. Klages quoted in Hans Eggert Schröder, *Ludwig Klages: Die Geschichte seines Lebens* (Bonn: Bouvier, 1966), 1:22. The biography here is largely summarized from Reinhard Falter, *Ludwig Klages: Lebensphilosophie als Zivilisationskritik* (Munich: Telesma-Verlag, 2003), 14–28.

20. Klages quoted in Schröder, *Ludwig Klages*, 1:89.

21. Alfred Rosenberg, *Gestalt und Leben* (Halle: M. Niemeyer, 1938); and Rosenberg, *Der mythus des 20. Jahrhunderts* (Munich: Hoheneichen-verlag, 1943), 137. See also Falter, *Ludwig Klages*, 107. Klages's own anti-Semitism will be discussed below.

22. Klages, *Rhythmen und Runen*, 312.

23. For examples of where these claims appear in Klages's work, see Ludwig Klages, *Sämtliche Werke*, ed. Ernst Frauchiger, 12 vols. (Bonn: H. Bouvier, 1964-92). There are many examples, but see 1:109, 3:648, 4:212, 6:539.

24. Ibid., 1:122, 757-58, 814.

25. Ibid., 3:614.

26. *"Herrschaft über die Natur,"* passim; see, for example, ibid., 3:4, 393.

27. Ibid., 3:614-15.

28. Ibid., 3:475-82, 614-15.

29. Ibid., 4:575-77.

30. "Logocentric" *(logozentrischen)*; see, for example, ibid., 3:720.

31. Ibid., 2:907, 4:494.

32. Ibid., 5:221-22.

33. Ibid., 3:353-498.

34. Ibid., 6:254.

35. See ibid., 1:80, 542.

36. Ibid., 3:614-26.

37. Ibid., 3:67, 390.

38. See ibid., vols. 7 and 8; and 3:614-36.

39. The *Institut für Sozialforschung* was first established in 1923, but Horkeimer took over only in 1930.

40. Benjamin is discussed below. For other examples, see: Theodor Adorno, *Negative Dialektik* (Frankfurt: Suhrkamp, 1966), 111; and Max Horkheimer and Theodor Adorno, *Dialectic of Enlightenment*, trans. Edmund Jephcott (Stanford, CA: Stanford University Press, 2002), 42, 194, 260, 263; Ernst Cassirer, *The Philosophy of Symbolic Forms* (New Haven, CT: Yale University Press, 1996), 4:23-41; Jürgen Habermas, *Wahrheit und Rechtfertigung* (Frankfurt: Suhrkamp, 1999), 178; Martin Heidegger, *Überlegungen XII-XV (Schwarze Hefte 1939-1941)* (Frankfurt: Klostermann, 2014), 21; Karl Löwith, *Nietzsches Philosophie der Ewigen Wiederkehr des Gleichen* (Hamburg: Meiner Verlag, 1986), 199; and Georg Lukács, *The Destruction of Reason* (Atlantic Highlands, NJ: Humanities Press, 1981), 522-39.

41. Giorgio Agamben. *Opus Dei: An Archaeology of Duty* (Stanford, CA: Stanford University Press, 2013), 40; Georges Bataille, *Oeuvres Complètes*, ed. Michel Foucault (Paris: Gallimard, 1970-88), 1:458; Michel Foucault, *Dits et écrits I, 1954-1969* (Paris: Gallimard, 1994), 133; Félix Guattari, *Lines of Flight: For Another World of Possibilities* (New York: Bloomsbury, 2016), 217-18; Jacques Lacan, *De la psychose paranoïaque dans ses rapports avec la personnalité* (Paris: Éditions du Seuil, 1975), 44, 48, 50, 315; Paul de Man, *The Post-romantic Predicament* (Edinburgh: Edinburgh University Press, 2012), 169.

42. Historians of German intellectual history will want to know that Klages's first significant philosophical work, *Mensch und Erde* (discussed below) also preceeded Oswald Spengler's famous *Der Untergang des Abendlandes* (1918; *The Decline of the West*). Moreover, Spengler was clearly well read in Klages's writings, as Spengler refers to multiple works. See, for example, Oswald Spengler, *Urfragen: Fragmente aus dem Nachlass*, ed. Anton Mirko Koktanek. (Munich: Beck, 1965), 7-8, 29, 48, 73, 174, 190-93, 204-8.

43. Important scholarly treatments in German include: Michael Großheim, *Ludwig Klages und die Phänomenologie* (Berlin: Akademie-Verlag, 1994); and Hans Kunz, *Martin Heideg-*

ger und Ludwig Klages: Daseinsanalytik und Metaphysik (Munich: Kindler, 1976). Since the initial draft of this chapter in late 2012, the first significant English monograph on Klages has appeared: Nitzan Lebovic, *The Philosophy of Life and Death: Ludwig Klages and the Rise of a Nazi Biopolitics* (New York: Palgrave Macmillan, 2013). Also Joseph Pryce has now translated some of Klages's shorter works into English; see Ludwig Klages, *The Biocentric Worldview: Selected Essays and Poems of Ludwig Klages*, trans. Joseph Pryce (London: Arktos, 2013); and Klages, *Cosmogonic Reflections: Selected Aphorisms from Ludwig Klages*, trans. Pryce (London: Arktos, 2015); where we overlap, I have retrospectively compared my translations to his and occasionally fixed them where appropriate.

44. Reventlow, *Herrn Dames Aufzeichnungen*, 61, 75.

45. Schuler, *Cosmogonische Augen*, 114, 220. Schuler described disenchantment in terms of a loss of blood-light.

46. See, for example, ibid., 113–14, 120.

47. For example, KSW, 1:451, 3:479–82, 580.

48. *Mensch und Erde* is one of Klages's few major works translated into English, and I've consulted Pryce's translation while preparing my own.

49. KSW, 3:614.

50. Ibid., 614–15.

51. Ibid., esp. 619–23.

52. Ibid., 621. See also Klages, *Biocentric Worldview*, 34.

53. First quote: Klages, *Biocentric Worldview*, 32; KSW, 3:618. Second: Klages, *Biocentric Worldview*, 42; KSW 3:628.

54. Klages, *Biocentric Worldview*, 42; KSW, 3:628.

55. Klages, *Biocentric Worldview*, 32; KSW, 3:619.

56. KSW, 3:615–22.

57. Ibid., 627.

58. Ibid., 626–27. See also Klages, *Biocentric Worldview*, 39–40.

59. Klages's anticapitalism might be a surprise for readers who are tempted to see any critique of capitalism as Marxist.

60. KSW, 3:627; Klages, *Biocentric Worldview*, 41.

61. KSW, 2:815.

62. Ibid., 1:673.

63. For example, Walter Sokel, *The Writer in Extremis: Expressionism in Twentieth-Century German Literature* (Stanford, CA: Stanford University Press, 1959), 95.

64. KSW, 2:1119–20.

65. Ibid., 2:1116–42.

66. Ibid., 1:7.

67. Ibid., 2:1330–1400.

68. For Klages, *Geist* is iconoclastic and therefore against the gods. It is the monotheist attitude in the action of the philosopher. Klages, *Rhythmen und Runen*, 306.

69. Cited in KSW, 6:xvii. As you might expect, Klages sees Heraclitus as being derailed by his conception of logos. Ibid., xviii. An obvious likely inspiration for Klages's ontology is Nietzsche. See, for example, Friedrich Nietzsche, *Writings from the Late Notebooks*, ed. Rüdiger

Bittner (New York: Cambridge University Press, 2005), esp. 26; and Jean Granier, "La pensée nietzschéene du chaos," *Revue de Métaphysique et du Morale* 76, no. 2 (1971): 132–39.

70. T. M. Luhrmann, *Persuasions of the Witch's Craft: Ritual Magic in Contemporary England* (Cambridge, MA: Harvard University Press, 1989), 118.

71. Following Klages, *Cosmogonic Reflections*, 102. KSW, 2:1367.

72. KSW, 3:479.

73. Ibid., 6:652.

74. *Reification* entered common English use as translation for the German *Verdinglichung*, which also means literally "transforming something into a thing." Also, compare to the ontology in Engel's *Dialektik der Natur* (1883).

75. As Klages put it in *GWS* : "We have counted, weighed, and measured that which could be counted, weighed, and measured. We have quantified the world in width, height, and depth . . . We have by means of these things obtained the famous 'dominion over nature.'" KSW, 1:2. See alongside 4:699.

76. Horkheimer and Adorno, *Dialectic of Enlightenment*, 260n6.

77. Ibid., 194. Klages is discussed alongside Nietzsche, Gauguin, and Stefan George.

78. Ibid.

79. See Theodor Adorno, *Minima Moralia: Reflections from Damaged Life*, trans. Edmund Jephcott (New York: Verso, 2005), 239.

80. For an account of the influence of Klages and *Lebensphilosophie* on Adorno, see Axel Honneth, "L'esprit et son objet: Parentés anthropologiques entre la dialectique de la raison et la critique de la civilisation dans la philosophie de la vie," in *Weimar; ou, L'explosion de la modernité*, ed. Gérard Raulet (Paris: Anthropos, 1984), 97–112.

81. *Logozentrischen* first appears in sections of Klages's *Nachlaß*, dating from 1900. Klages, *Rhythmen und Runen*, 304–5. For *anthropozentrische*, see ibid., 256. The expanded term *logocentrism (Logozenstrismus)* first appears in writings about Klages in the 1930s; see, for example, Martin Ninck, "Zur Philosophie von Ludwig Klages," *Kant Sudien* 36, no. 1–2 (1931): 148–57.

82. See, for example, Jacques Derrida, *De la grammatologie* (Paris: Édtions de Minuit, 1967), 11. For an attempt to draw the connection between Klages and Derrida, see Jean Pierre Faye, *La raison narrative* (Paris: Éditions Balland, 1990), esp. 192–93.

83. KSW, 3:720. See also Klages, *Biocentric Worldview*, 56–57.

84. KSW, 1:571.

85. Ibid., 4:575–77.

86. *Biozentrismus*, or more commonly, *biozentrische*.

87. KSW, 6:203, 312.

88. Ibid., 1:768

89. Ibid., 3:623, 628; Klages, *Biocentric Worldview*, 36, 42.

90. KSW, 3:482 (emphasis added). The term rendered "difference" above is more literally "distance," but the dialectic between proximity and distance is Klages's way of addressing difference.

91. Ibid., 363–64.

92. Ibid., 355–56.

93. See ibid., 390–441, esp. 397.

94. Moreover, Klages argued: "The solution of the so-called riddle of the world is the ecstatic internalizing of the mystery of the world." Ibid., 410.

95. Ibid., 393.

96. Ibid., 398.

97. Ibid., 398–99. Think also of Goethe's *Vorbeirauschenden Freude.*

98. Ibid., 398.

99. Ibid., 399–400.

100. Klages, *Rhythmen und Runen,* 261; Klages, *Cosmogonic Reflections,* 73.

101. KSW 3: 628–29; Klages, *Biocentric Worldview,* 42.

102. Reventlow, *Herrn Dames Aufzeichnungen,* 61, 71.

103. For example, Klages, *Rhythmen und Runen,* 289, 330. Note that the emphasis on "life" was crucial to Nazi biopolitics.

104. For how the Nazis co-opted Klages and his openness to their efforts, see Lebovic, *Philosophy of Life and Death: Klages and Nazi Biopolitics,* 162–64.

105. See Lisa Fittko, "The Story of Old Benjamin," in *The Arcades Project,* ed. Rolf Tiedemann (Cambridge, MA: Harvard University Press, 1999), 946–54.

106. Michael Löwy, *Walter Benjamin: Aviso de incendio: Una lectura de las tesis "Sobre el concepto de historia"* (Buenos Aires: Fondo de Cultura Económica, 2003), 41.

107. Terry Eagleton, *Walter Benjamin; or, Towards a Revolutionary Criticism* (London: Verso Editions, 1981), 81. See also Jürgen Habermas, "Consciousness-Raising or Redemptive Criticism: The Contemporaneity of Walter Benjamin," *New German Critique,* no. 17 (1979): 30–59; and John Fekete, "Benjamin's Ambivalence," *Telos,* no. 35 (1978): 192–98.

108. See, for example, Stéphane Mosès, *L'ange de l'histoire: Rosenzweig, Benjamin, Scholem* (Paris: Seuil, 1992).

109. For instance, these terms all occur frequently in the occult journal *Zentralblatt für Okkultismus: Monatsschrift zur Erforschung der gesamten Geheimwissenschaften* (1907–33).

110. For example: Theodor Adorno, *Prismen: Kulturkritik und Gesellschaft* (Berlin: Suhrkamp Verlag, 1955), esp. 238–39; and James McBride, "Marooned in the Realm of the Profane: Walter Benjamin's Synthesis of Kabbalah and Communism," *Journal of the American Academy of Religion* 57, no. 2 (1989): 241–66.

111. See, for example, Bram Mertens, *Dark Images, Secret Hints: Benjamin, Scholem, Molitor and the Jewish Tradition* (New York: P. Lang, 2007).

112. Gershom Scholem, *Walter Benjamin: The Story of a Friendship* (New York: Schocken, 1981), 38. See also Howard Eiland and Michael Jennings, *Walter Benjamin: A Critical Life* (Cambridge, MA: Belknap Press of Harvard University Press, 2014), 93–94; and Mertens, *Dark Images, Secret Hints.* For Pulver and his connection to esotericism, see Hakl, *Eranos,* 123.

113. Franz Joseph Molitor, *Philosophie der Geschichte oder über die Tradition,* 4 vols (Frankfurt/Munster: Hermann/Theissing, 1827–53).

114. See Walter Benjamin, *Briefe,* ed. Gershom Scholem and Theodor Adorno (Frankfurt: Suhrkamp, 1966), 1:112. See also Werner Fuld, "Walter Benjamins Beziehung zu Ludwig Klages," *Akzente,* no. 28 (1981): 274–87; Eiland and Jennings, *Benjamin: A Critical Life,* 63, 80–81; and Scholem, *Benjamin: Story of a Friendship,* 19.

115. Benjamin, *Briefe,* 1:515. Benjamin did mention his doubts about the work, but this is compatible with his sense that Klages was being picked up by unsavory elements. Hence Ben-

jamin's reference to the proto-Fascists who "carry volumes of Klages in their packs." *Walter Benjamin: Selected Writings* (Cambridge, MA: Belknap Press of Harvard University Press, 2004–06), vol. 2, part 1, 321.

116. See Walter Benjamin, *Gesammelte Schriften*, ed. Rolf Tiedemann and Hermann Schweppenhäuser (Frankfurt: Suhrkamp, 1972–89).

117. See Theodor W. Adorno and Walter Benjamin, *The Complete Correspondence, 1928–1940*, ed. Henri Lonitz (Cambridge, MA: Harvard University Press, 1999), 182–83.

118. Ibid., 61.

119. Lorenz Jäger, *Adorno: A Political Biography* (New Haven, CT: Yale University Press, 2004), 199.

120. For examples, see Habermas, "Consciousness-Raising or Redemptive Criticism"; and Kathleen Kerr-Koch, *Romancing Fascism: Modernity and Allegory in Benjamin, de Man, Shelley* (New York: Bloomsbury, 2013), 47–50; and for a nuanced treatment, see Lebovic, *Philosophy of Life and Death*.

121. Georg Stauth and Bryan S. Turner, "Ludwig Klages (1872–1956) and the Origins of Critical Theory," *Theory, Culture & Society* 9 (1992): 45–63.

122. In reference to Stauth and Turner, Stirk argues, "There have been attempts to claim that Adorno and Horkheimer were influenced by Klages . . . [but] the argument never gets beyond analogies." Peter Stirk, *Critical Theory, Politics and Society* (London: Continuum, 2005), 199.

123. Eiland and Jennings, *Benjamin: A Critical Life*, 80–81.

124. Benjamin, *Gesammelte Schriften*, 4:366.

125. Benjamin, *Briefe*, 1:516–17.

126. Eiland and Jennings, *Benjamin: A Critical Life*, 3, 71, 101–2; Benjamin, *Briefe*, 1:15.

127. Steven Wasserstrom, *Religion after Religion: Gershom Scholem, Mircea Eliade, and Henry Corbin at Eranos* (Princeton, NJ: Princeton University Press, 1999).

128. See, for example, Gershom Scholem, *Major Trends in Jewish Mysticism* (New York: Schocken Books, 1961), 2.

129. Benjamin, *Briefe*, 1:282, 637. See Gary Smith, "Die Zauberjuden: Walter Benjamin, Gershom Scholem, and Other German-Jewish Esoterics between the World Wars," *Journal of Jewish Thought and Philosophy* 4, no. 2 (1995): 227–43; Jacob Taubes, *From Cult to Culture* (Stanford, CA: Stanford University Press, 2010), 235–47; and Manfred Voigts, *Oskar Goldberg: Der Mythische Experimentalwissenschaftler* (Berlin: Agora-Verlag, 1992).

130. Oskar Goldberg, *Die Wirklichkeit der Hebräer* (Berlin: David, 1925), esp. 15–18.

131. Benjamin, *Briefe*, 1:253.

132. See Esther Ehrman, "Erich Unger's 'The Natural Order of Miracles,'" parts 1 and 2, *Journal of Jewish Thought and Philosophy* 11, no. 2 (2002): 135–89; and Margarete Kohlenbach, "Religion, Experience, Politics: On Erich Unger and Walter Benjamin," in *The Early Frankfurt School and Religion*, ed. Kohlenbach and Raymond Geuss (London: Palgrave, 2005), 64–84.

133. Eiland and Jennings, *Benjamin: A Critical Life*, 81, 124.

134. Gershom Scholem, *On Jews and Judaism in Crisis* (New York: Schocken, 1976), 275.

135. Erich Gutkind, *Siderische Geburt: Seraphische Wanderung vom Tode der Welt zur Taufe der Tat*. PDF edition digitized and edited by Peter Godzik, March 2013, http://www.pkgodzik .de/fileadmin/user_upload/Gutkind/Erich_Gutkind__Siderische_Geburt.pdf, 58–59.

136. Ibid., 3.

137. Ibid., 32–33.

138. Ibid., 33.

139. Mitrinović writing under the pseudonym M. M. Cosmoi, "World Affairs," *New Age* 29, no. 8 (June 23, 1921): 87–88; and "World Affairs," *New Age* 29, no. 12 (July 21, 1921): 135–36.

140. Shulamith Behr, "Wassily Kandinsky and Dimitrije Mitrinovic," *Oxford Art Journal* 15, no. 1 (January 1, 1992): 81–88; and Andrew Rigby, *Initiation and Initiative: An Exploration of the Life and Ideas of Dimitrije Mitrinović* (New York: Columbia University Press, 1984).

141. Erich Gutkind, *The Body of God* (New York: Horizon Press, 1969), 15.

142. See Susan Buck-Morss, *The Origin of Negative Dialectics: Theodor W. Adorno, Walter Benjamin and the Frankfurt Institute* (New York: Free Press, 1977), 90–95.

143. Sean Carney, *Brecht and Critical Theory: Dialectics and Contemporary Aesthetics* (London; New York: Routledge, 2005), 50–51.

144. See Benjamin, *Gesammelte Schriften*, 2:206.

145. Ibid., 204.

146. Ibid., 209.

147. Esther Leslie, *Walter Benjamin: Critical Lives* (London: Reaktion Books, 2007), 89, 91, 160.

148. Benjamin, *Gesammelte Schriften*, 6:192–94. Admittedly, he suggested that excluding "magical" energy would be necessary to legitimate this new form of astrology.

149. Walter Benjamin, *On Hashish* (Cambridge, MA: Belknap Press of Harvard Univeristy Press, 2006), 58.

150. Julian Roberts, *Walter Benjamin* (London: Macmillan Press, 1982), 178.

151. Schuler, *Fragmente und Vorträge*, 167.

152. See Benjamin, *Gesammelte Schriften*, 4:366–67; Karl Wolfskehl, *Gesammelte Werke* (Hamburg: Claassen, 1960), 2:419–22.

153. *Benjamin: Selected Writings*, 3:18–19.

154. See also Benjamin, *Gesammelte Schriften*, 3:44.

155. Klages was drawing on Goethe's *Urbild*, but nevertheless, for Benjamin, Klages was the key figure in reinterpreting the term.

156. See Max Pensky, "Geheimmittel: Advertising and Dialectical Images in Benjamin's Arcades Project," in *Walter Benjamin and* The Arcades Project, ed. Beatrice Hanssen (New York: Continuum, 2006), 113–31.

157. Walter Benjamin, *The Arcades Project* (Cambridge, MA: Belknap Press, 1999), 473.

158. Adorno and Benjamin, *Complete Correspondence*, 61.

159. *Benjamin: Selected Writings*, 1:427.

160. Eiland and Jennings, *Benjamin: A Critical Life*, 163, 696.

161. For all their interest in esotericism, Scholem and Benjamin shared a rejection of the neo-paganism of the Klages circle. See Benjamin, *Briefe*, 1:409–10.

162. *Benjamin: Selected Writings*, 1:486 (emphasis added).

163. Ibid., 486.

164. Ibid., 487.

165. Ibid.

166. Walter Benjamin, *The Correspondence of Walter Benjamin, 1910–1940*, ed. Gershom

Scholem and Theodor Adorno (Chicago: University of Chicago Press, 1994), 84 (emphasis added).

167. Benjamin, *Gesammelte Schriften*, 1:125. See alongside Anson Rabinbach, "Critique and Commentary/Alchemy and Chemistry: Some Remarks on Walter Benjamin and This Issue," *New German Critique*, no. 17 (1979): 3–14.

168. Benjamin, *Gesammelte Schriften*, 1:126. Benjamin is playing with *Scheitern* (failures) and *Scheit* (piece of wood).

169. *Benjamin: Selected Writings*, 2:216.

170. The Kosmikers often saw themselves as above the vulgar occult milieu of their day. So while they often praised specific spiritualists and occults, they often distanced themselves from the Theosophists and other popular forms of esotericism that they saw as merely commercial charlatanism.

171. For an alternate reading of Benjamin as primarily a disenchanter, see Richard Wolin, *Walter Benjamin: An Aesthetic of Redemption* (Berkeley: University of California Press, 1994), esp. xliii.

172. See, for examples, *Benjamin: Selected Writings*, 2:184, 804, and 4:154–55.

173. Letter to Patrick Waldberg, translated in Georges Bataille, *Encyclopaedia Acephalica: Comprising the Critical Dictionary & Related Texts*, ed. Robert Lebel and Isabelle Waldberg (London: Atlas Press, 1995), 14.

174. Georges Bataille, *Œuvres Complètes*, ed. Michel Foucault (Paris: Gallimard, 1970–88), 2:278.

175. Ibid., 2:273.

176. Bataille, *Encyclopaedia Acephalica*, 15–16.

177. See, for example, Georges Bataille, *Visions of Excess: Selected Writings, 1927–1939*, ed. Allan Stoekl (Minneapolis: University of Minnesota Press, 1985), 199.

178. Stuart Kendall, *Georges Bataille: Critical Lives* (London: Reaktion, 2007), 8.

179. References to mysticism, magic, and occult themes occur throughout Bataille's published work; see especially Georges Bataille, *L'Apprenti Sorcier du cercle communiste démocratique à Acéphale: Textes, lettres et documents, 1932–1939* (Paris: Editions de la Différence, 1999). For scholarly commentary, see Peter Connor, *Georges Bataille and the Mysticism of Sin* (Baltimore: Johns Hopkins University Press, 2000); Amy Hollywood, *Sensible Ecstasy: Mysticism, Sexual Difference, and the Demands of History* (Chicago: University of Chicago Press, 2002); and Andrew Hussey, *The Inner Scar: The Mysticism of Georges Bataille* (Atlanta: Rodopi, 2000), esp. 2.

180. For a structural comparison of both thinkers, see Thomas Rolf, "Das Subjekt auf dem Siedepunkt: Zur Phänomenologie der Ekstase bei Ludwig Klages und Georges Bataille," in *Georges Bataille: Vorreden zur Überschreitung*, ed. Andreas Hetzel and Peter Wiechens (Würzburg: Königshausen & Neumann, 1999), 113–31.

181. Bataille, *Œuvres Complètes*, 1:458. Bataille was referring to Ernest Baron de Seillière, *De la déesse nature à la déesse vie* (Paris: F. Alcan, 1931), 133.

182. Théodore Flournoy, *Des Indes à la planète Mars: Étude sur un cas de somnambulisme avec glossolalia* (Paris: F. Alcan, 1900).

183. Deleuze wrote an introduction to *Mathesis; or, Studies on the Anarchy and Hierarchy*

of Knowledge, by Johann Malfatti de Montereggio; to give a sense of the work, the first chapter is titled "Mathesis as Hieroglyph or Symbolism of the Triple Life of the Universe; or, The Mystical Organon of the Ancient Indians." See Christian Kerslake, "The Somnambulist and the Hermaphrodite," in *Culture Machine* 9, no.1 (2007).

184. Giorgio Agamben, *The Signature of All Things* (Cambridge, MA: Zone Books, 2009).

185. Peter Sloterdijk, *Philosophical Temperaments: From Plato to Foucault* (New York: Columbia University Press, 2013), ix.

186. Roy Bhaskar, *From East to West: Odyssey of a Soul* (New York: Routledge, 2000).

187. See Luce Irigaray, *Between East and West: From Singularity to Community* (New Delhi: New Age Books, 2005); and Hollywood, *Sensible Ecstacy*.

188. I have in mind *"La pharmacie de Platon"* (Plato's pharmacy) in Jacques Derrida, *La dissémination* (Paris: Editions du Seuil, 1972). For Derrida and telepathy, see Nicholas Royle, *Telepathy and Literature* (Cambridge: Blackwell, 1991), 1–15.

189. For example, Theodor Adorno, *Gesammelte Schriften* (Frankfurt: Suhrkamp, 2003), 1:196, 341, 4:273–80, 5:60, 6:113, 7: 132, 219, 10:217, 11:220, 20:216–17.

CHAPTER NINE

1. Friedrich Stadler, *Der Wiener Kreis Ursprung, Entwicklung und Wirkung des Logischen Empirismus im Kontext* (Vienna: Springer, 2015), 615–45.

2. For scholarship on Moritz Schlick, see *Stationen: Dem Philosophen und Physiker Moritz Schlick zum 125. Geburtstag*, ed. Friedrich Stadler and Fynn Ole Engler (New York: Springer, 2009). The Vienna Circle was also referred to as "logical empiricism," but in what follows I generally use "logical positivism" because the main subject of the chapter is the antipositivist criticisms that polemically entangles Comte's sociology, Ernst Mach's empiriocriticism, the Vienna Circle, and a so-called positivist attitude.

3. Nelböck's thesis was "Die Bedeutung der Logik im Empirismus und Positivismus," 1930.

4. Stadler, *Der Wiener Kreis Ursprung*, 633.

5. Joey Sprague and Diane Kobrynowicz, "A Feminist Epistemology," in *Handbook of the Sociology of Gender*, ed. Janet Chafetz (New York: Springer, 1999), 25–43; for "faith in reason," Jürgen Habermas, "The Analytical Theory of Science and Dialectics," in *The Positivist Dispute in German Sociology*, by Theodor W. Adorno et al. (London: Heinemann, 1976), 147.

6. The role of positivism as a contemporary philosophical scapegoat has not escaped notice. See Michael Friedman, *Reconsidering Logical Positivism* (New York: Cambridge University Press, 1999), xiii; and Michael LeMahieu, *Fictions of Fact and Value: The Erasure of Logical Positivism in American Literature* (New York: Oxford University Press, 2013), 15.

7. For examples, Helen Malson, *The Thin Woman: Feminism, Post-Structuralism, and the Social Psychology of Anorexia Nervosa* (New York: Routledge, 1998), 45–36; NOZAKI Yoshiko, *Struggles over Difference: Curriculum, Texts, and Pedagogy in the Asia-Pacific* (Albany: State University of New York Press, 2005), 222–23; and Elisabeth Schüssler Fiorenza, *Democratizing Biblical Studies* (Louisville, KY: Westminster Press, 2009), 68.

8. In order: E. Sreedharan, *A Textbook of Historiography* (New Delhi: Orient Longman, 2004), 194; Patrick O'Sullivan, *Economic Methodology and Freedom to Choose* (New York: Rout-

ledge, 2012), 20; Kwame Anthony Appiah, *Cosmopolitanism: Ethics in a World of Strangers* (New York: Norton, 2006), 17–22; and *Encyclopedia of Rhetoric and Composition* (New York: Garland, 1996), s.v. "Logical Positivism," by Arabella Lyon, 406–7.

9. Ernst Cassirer's neo-Kantianism is sometimes described as the path not taken. See Michael Friedman, *A Parting of the Ways: Carnap, Cassirer, and Heidegger* (Chicago: Open Court, 2000); and, to a lesser extent, Peter Gordon, *Continental Divide: Heidegger, Cassirer, Davos* (Cambridge, MA: Harvard University Press, 2010).

10. Jean-François Lyotard, *The Inhuman: Reflections on Time* (Stanford, CA: Stanford University Press, 1991), 71.

11. Charles Jencks, *What Is Post-modernism?* (New York: St. Martin's Press, 1986), 6; omitted from later editions. See also Michael LeMahieu, *Fictions of Fact and Value: The Erasure of Logical Positivism in American Literature, 1945–1975* (New York: Oxford University Press, 2013), 195.

12. Ben Agger, "Critical Theory, Poststructuralism, Postmodernism: Their Sociological Relevance," *Annual Review of Sociology* 17 (1991): 105–31; Richard Kearney, introduction to *Continental Philosophy in the 20th Century*, ed. Kearney (New York: Routledge, 2003), 2; and Dominick LaCapra, "Criticism Today," in *Jean François Lyotard: Critical Evaluations in Cultural Theory*, vol. 2, ed. Victor E. Taylor and Gregg Lambert (New York: Routledge, 2006), 279.

13. Glock suggests that there is a "common consent" that the positivists were "the most influential philosophical school of the last one hundred years." Hans-Johann Glock, *What Is Analytic Philosophy?* (New York: Cambridge University Press, 2008), 68.

14. Robert Scharff, *Comte after Positivism* (Cambridge: Cambridge University Press, 1995), 1.

15. Hans-Joachim Dahms, *Positivismusstreit: Die Auseinandersetzungen der Frankfurter Schule mit dem logischen Positivismus, dem amerikanischen Pragmatismus und dem kritischen Rationalismus* (Frankfurt: Suhrkamp, 1994).

16. Max Horkheimer, *Gesammelte Schriften* (Frankfurt: Fischer, 1988) 9:399–400.

17. Ibid., 3:25–27.

18. Ibid., 4:155.

19. See also ibid., 4:162–216.

20. For example, Theodor Adorno, *Minima Moralia: Reflections from Damaged Life*, trans. Edmund Jephcott (New York: Verso, 2005), 70.

21. Theodor Adorno, *Critical Models: Interventions and Catchwords* (New York: Columbia University Press, 2005), 8.

22. Theodor W. Adorno et al., *The Positivist Dispute in German Sociology* (London: Heinemann, 1976), 55–56.

23. LeMahieu, *Fictions of Fact and Value*, 24–37.

24. Theodor Adorno, *Hegel: Three Studies* (Cambridge: MIT Press, 1999), 101; and LeMahieu, *Fictions of Fact and Value*, 33.

25. Theodor Adorno, *Negative Dialectics* (New York: Continuum, 2007), 9; LeMahieu, *Fictions of Fact and Value*, 33.

26. Adorno, *Negative Dialectics*, e.g., 86–87, 99, 112–13, 403.

27. Max Horkheimer, *Eclipse of Reason* (New York: Continuum, 2004), 4.

28. Ibid., 15, 66–67.

29. Ibid., 41. (emphasis added).

30. Max Horkheimer, "The End of Reason," *Studies in Philosophy and Social Science* 9 (1941): 379

31. Horkheimer, *Eclipse of Reason*, 51.

32. Max Horkheimer and Theodor Adorno, *Dialectic of Enlightenment*, trans. Edmund Jephcott (Stanford, CA: Stanford University Press, 2002), 11.

33. Ibid., 19.

34. Ibid., 4–5.

35. Ibid., 13.

36. Martin Heidegger, *Gesamtausgabe* (Frankfurt: Vittorio Klostermann, 1976–2011), 40:228 (emphasis in the original). I have only slightly modified the translation from Friedman, *Parting of the Ways*, 22.

37. They were assisted by Schlick's students Friedrich Waismann and Herbert Feigl.

38. Herbert Feigl, *Inquiries and Provocations: Selected Writings, 1929–1974* (Hingham: Kluwer 1981), 70.

39. Ibid., 57.

40. *The Philosophy of Rudolf Carnap* (Chicago: Open Court, 1963), 57. See also Thomas Uebel, "Carnap, the Left Vienna Circle, and Neopositivist Antimetaphysics," in *Carnap Brought Home*, ed. Steve Awodey and Carsten Klein (Chicago: Open Court, 2004), 247–78.

41. For the manifesto, see Otto Neurath, *Empiricism and Sociology* (Boston: Reidel, 1973), 301, 303. See also George Reisch, "Planning Science: Otto Neurath and the International Encyclopedia of Unified Science," *British Journal for the History of Science* 27, no. 2 (1994): 153–75; and Philipp Frank, *Modern Science and Its Philosophy* (Cambridge, MA: Harvard University Press, 1949), 17–18, 72–78.

42. See Frank, *Modern Science*, 77; Neurath, *Empiricism and Sociology*, 315.

43. Otto Neurath, *Philosophical Papers, 1913–1946* (Boston: Kluwer Boston, 1983), 92. For the evolving boat metaphor, see Nancy Cartwright, Jordi Cat, Lola Fleck, and Thomas Uebel, *Otto Neurath: Philosophy between Science and Politics* (New York: Cambridge University Press, 1996), 89–166.

44. Cartwright et al., *Otto Neurath*, 188.

45. Rudolf Carnap, "Überwindung der Metaphysik durch logische Analyse der Sprache," *Erkenntnis* 2, no. 1 (1931): 219–41, translated in Carnap, "The Elimination of Metaphysics through Logical Analysis of Language," in *Logical Empiricism at Its Peak*, ed. Sahotra Sarkar (New York: Garland, 1996), 60–81.

46. Carnap, "Elimination of Metaphysics," 68.

47. It is easy to spot problems with this theory; for example, "all crows are black" would be meaningless because one could never empirically examine all crows.

48. Carnap, "Elimination of Metaphysics," 78.

49. Ibid.

50. Carnap was hinting at a specific aesthetic philosophy and even art. As I argue in a post on my blog, there are some historical grounds for thinking of an elective affinity between logical positivism and magical realism. See Jason Ā. Josephson-Storm, "Positivism and Magical Realism," *Absolute Disruption: Theory after Postmodernism* (blog), {1/17/2017}, https://absolute-disruption.com/2017/1/17/positivism-and-magical-realism/.

51. Carnap, "Elimination of Metaphysics," 80.

52. Neurath, *Empiricism and Sociology*, 327; Feigl, *Inquiries and Provocations*, 372.

53. Reproduced in Stadler, *Der Wiener Kreis Ursprung*, 153. See also Peter Galison. "Aufbau/Bauhaus: Logical Positivism and Architectural Modernism," *Critical Inquiry* 16, no. 4 (1990): 709-52.

54. Later continued as the *Neue Metaphysische Rundschau*. Nicholas Goodrick-Clarke, *The Occult Roots of Nazism* (New York: New York University Press, 1992), 25-26; and Corinna Treitel, *A Science for the Soul: Occultism and the Genesis of the German Modern* (Baltimore: Johns Hopkins University Press, 2004), 175.

55. Neurath, *Empiricism and Sociology*, 301; Rudolf Carnap, *The Logical Structure of the World; and Pseudoproblems in Philosophy* (Chicago: Open Court, 2003), xvii.

56. Robert Ammerman, *Classics of Analytic Philosophy* (Indianapolis: Hackett, 1990), 8-9.

57. Carnap, "Überwindung der Metaphysik," 65-66.

58. *Philosophy of Rudolf Carnap*, 10. See also Uebel, "Carnap, the Vienna Circle, and Antimetaphysics."

59. Rudolph Carnap Papers, 025-75-10, Special Collections, University of Pittsburgh Library.

60. *Philosophy of Rudolf Carnap*, 33-34.

61. Neurath, *Empiricism and Sociology*, xiii.

62. Allan Mitchell, *Revolution in Bavaria, 1918-1919* (Princeton, NJ: Princeton University Press, 1965).

63. Cartwright et al., *Otto Neurath*, 21. For more on Neurath's directorship at the German War Economy Museum, see Nader Vossoughian, "The War Economy and the War Museum: Otto Neurath and the Museum of War Economy in Leipzig, c. 1918," in *Otto Neurath's Economics in Context*, ed. Elisabeth Nemeth, Stefan W. Schmitz and Thomas E. Uebel (Dordrecht: Springer Netherlands, 2007), 131-39.

64. Goodrick-Clarke, *Occult Roots of Nazism*, 148.

65. Cartwright et al., *Otto Neurath*, 47.

66. Neurath, *Empiricism and Sociology*, 17.

67. Cartwright et al., *Otto Neurath*, 60.

68. Neurath, *Empiricism and Sociology*, 252.

69. Ibid., esp. 278.

70. Ibid., 297.

71. Neurath, *Philosophical Papers*, 240.

72. Neurath, *Empiricism and Sociology*, 305.

73. Ibid., 292.

74. Ibid., 292.

75. Ibid., 269-70.

76. Ibid., 295.

77. Ibid., 356.

78. Hans Hahn, *Empiricism, Logic, and Mathematics* (Boston: Kluwer Boston, 1980), 19.

79. Ibid., 5.

80. Neurath, *Philosophical Papers*, 237.

81. Ibid., 242.

82. Dahms, *Positivismusstreit*, 69–181.

83. Neurath, *Philosophical Papers*, 242.

84. *Wiener Kreis: Texte sur Wissenschaftlichen Weltauffassung*, ed. Michael Stöltzner and Thomas Uebel (Hamburg: Meiner, 2006), 26 (emphasis added). I've largely followed the translation in Neurath, *Empiricism and Sociology*, 317.

85. Carnap in Greg Frost-Arnold, *Carnap, Tarski, and Quine at Harvard: Conversations on Logic, Mathematics, and Science* (Chicago: Open Court, 2013), 142, 194: "*Magik ist kognitiv . . . Ein Tier kann Magie haben, aber keine Metaphysik!*"

86. Von Mises praised modern atomic physics for recovering "the questions of ancient alchemists" and embracing positions reminiscent of Pythagoreans and Kabbalists. Richard von Mises, *Naturwissenschaft und Technik der Gegenwart* (Leipzig: Teubner, 1922), 16.

87. Otto Neurath, "Wege der wissenschaftlichen Weltauffassung," *Erkenntnis* 1 (1930): 107. I have largely followed the translation in Neurath, *Philosophical Papers*, 33. See also Otto Neurath, "Magie und Technik," *Erkenntnis* 2 (1931): 82–84.

88. Neurath, "Wissenschaftlichen Weltauffassung," 108. I have largely followed the translation in Neurath, *Philosophical Papers*, 33.

89. Ibid.

90. Otto Neurath. *Empirische Soziologie*. Vienna: Springer, 1931, 6. I have only slightly amended the translation appearing in Neurath, *Empiricism and Sociology*, 321.

91. Neurath, *Philosophical Papers*, 33–34 (emphasis added).

92. Ibid., 35.

93. Ibid., 34.

94. Ibid., 34–36.

95. Ibid., 36.

96. Neurath argued that modern psychology has discovered the truth of a range of ideas previously worked out in the magical domain. Ibid.

97. Ibid., 34–35.

98. Neurath, *Empiricism and Sociology*, 322.

99. Neurath, *Philosophical Papers*, 35–37.

100. Ibid., 35.

101. Neurath, *Empiricism and Sociology*, 322.

102. Neurath, *Philosophical Papers*, 39.

103. Ibid.

104. Neurath, *Empiricism and Sociology*, 329 (emphasis added).

105. Eleonora Zugun's name is also sometimes written "Eleonore," and occasionally her family name is given with an umlaut as Zügun. See "Fata care are în ea pe diavolul," *Unirea Poporului*, January 30, 1927, 5; Peter Mulacz, "Historical Profiles in Poltergeist Research," in *From Shaman to Scientist*, ed. James Houran (Lanham: Scarecrow Press, 2004), 127–90; Harry Price, *Leaves from a Psychist's Case-Book* (London: Gollancz, 1933), 227–49; Hans Rosenbusch, "Aus der Zugun-Literatur," *Zeitschrift für kritischen Okkultismus* 3, no. 1 (1927): 45–55; and Zoë Countess Wassilko-Serecki, "The Early History and Phenomena of Eleonore Zügun," *British Journal of Psychical Research* 1, no. 5 (1927): 134.

106. Wassilko-Serecki, "Eleonore Zügun ," 134.

107. Kubi Klein, "Das verhexte Dorf," reprinted in *Revalobund Monatschrift* 1, no. 5 (1925): 129–40.

108. Hans Hahn, Richard Hoffmann, Hans Thirring, Karl Wolf, Alfred Winterstein, and Michael Dumba, "Die Phänomene der Eleonore Zugun: Wiener Gelehrte für Gräfin Zoe Wassilko," *Zeitschrift für Parapsychologie 3* (1927): 189.

109. Steven Beller, *Vienna and the Jews, 1867–1938* (New York: Cambridge University Press, 1989), 15–16.

110. Hans Hahn, *Gesammelte Abhandlungen* (Vienna: Springer, 1995).

111. For Hahn's intellectual impact, see ibid., 1:16.

112. One exception was the short-lived Viennese Wissenschaftlicher Verein für Okkultismus (Scientific Society for Occultism).

113. Anita Gregory, *The Strange Case of Rudi Schneider* (Metuchen: Scarecrow Press, 1985), 10.

114. Schrenck-Notzing published this research as *Experimente der Fernbewegung (Telekinese) im Psychologischen Institut der Münchener Universität und im Laboratorium des Verfassers*, 1924.

115. Thomas Mann, *Okkulte Erlebnisse* (Berlin: Alf Häger Verlag, 1924).

116. Harry Price, Stefan Meyer, and Karl Przibram, *Rudi Schneider: The Vienna Experiments of Professors Meyer and Przibram* (London: National Laboratory of Psychical Research, 1933).

117. Karl Menger, *Reminiscences of the Vienna Circle and the Mathematical Colloquium* (Boston: Kluwer, 1994), 15.

118. While these investigations gradually became less important for Wagner-Jauregg and Schlick, for Thirring and Hahn they became something of an obsession.

119. Menger in Hahn, *Empiricism, Logic, and Mathematics*, xv–xvi.

120. See Mulacz, "Historical Profiles in Poltergeist Research."

121. University of Vienna Archive, B35–1461/3.

122. Zoë Countess Wassilko-Serecki, "Observations on Eleonore Zugun: 1," *Journal of the American Society for Psychical Research* 20, no. 9 (1926): 513–523.

123. Zoë Countess Wassilko-Serecki, "Observations on Eleonore Zugun: 2," *Journal of the American Society for Psychical Research* 20, no. 10 (1926): 599.

124. Wassilko, "Eleonore Zugun 2," 600–601.

125. Although not credited on YouTube, the film was probably made by the Emelka-Kultur-Gesellschaft in Munich in 1927. "Eleonore Zugun," YouTube video, 9:55, posted by "cienciaspsiquicas," Decmber 5, 2013, accessed June 5, 2014, http://youtu.be/MIiB5ck20s8.

126. Wassilko, "Eleonore Zugun 2," 595; Hahn, et al., "Die Phänomene der Eleonore Zugun.

127. Menger in Hahn, *Empiricism, Logic, and Mathematics*, xvii (emphasis in the original).

128. Ibid., xvi.

129. Menger, *Reminiscences of the Vienna Circle*, 15–16.

130. Ibid.

131. Feigl, *Inquiries and Provocations*, 303.

132. Ibid., 314.

133. *William James on Psychical Research* (Clifton, NJ: Kelley, 1973), 41. The psychic medium Leonora Piper was James's white crow.

134. Richard von Mises, *Probability, Statistics and Truth* (New York: Macmillan, 1957), 74. For his other paranormal research, see Richard von Mises, *Kleines Lehrbuch des Positivismus* (The Hague: Stockum, 1939), 216–19; and von Mises, *Selected Papers of Richard von Mises* (Providence: American Mathematical Society, 1964), 2:527, 530–36, 544–45.

135. Von Mises, *Selected Papers*, 2:536.

136. Hao Wang, *Reflections on Kurt Gödel* (Cambridge, MA: MIT Press, 1995), 18; and John Dawson, *Logical Dilemmas: The Life and Work of Kurt Gödel* (Wellesley, MA: Peters, 1997), 30.

137. Georg Kreisel, "Kurt Gödel, 28 April 1906–14 January 1978," *Biographical Memoirs of Fellows of the Royal Society* 26 (1980): 148–224, esp. 155, 218.

138. Dawson, *Logical Dilemmas: Life of Gödel*, 153; see also 165.

139. Robert Tragesser and Mark van Atten, "Mysticism and Mathematics: Brouwer, Gödel, and the Common Core Thesis," in *Essays on Gödel's Reception of Leibniz, Husserl, and Brouwer*, ed. Mark van Atten, (Springer, 2015) 180.

140. Dawson, *Logical Dilemmas*, 30.

141. Ibid.

142. Ibid.

143. A. W. Carus, *Carnap and Twentieth-Century Thought* (New York: Cambridge University Press, 2007), 50.

144. Gary Stark, *Entrepreneurs of Ideology* (Chapel Hill: University of North Carolina Press, 1981), 103–6. For more on Diederichs, see George Mosse, *The Crisis of German Ideology* (New York: Grosset, 1964), 52–63.

145. Carus, *Carnap and Twentieth-Century Thought*, 55.

146. Cited in ibid., 55–56.

147. Cited in ibid., 56.

148. Rudolph Carnap Papers, 025–72–05, Special Collections, University of Pittsburgh Library.

149. Carnap, *Philosophy*, 23.

150. Heinrich Neider, Rudolf Haller, and Heiner Rutte, "Gespräch mit Heinrich Neider: Persönliche Erinnerungen an den Wiener Kreis," *Conceptus*, no. 28–30 (1977): 23.

151. Carnap, *Philosophy*, 25.

152. Ibid., 26.

153. Ray Monk, *Ludwig Wittgenstein: The Duty of Genius* (New York: Free Press, 1990), 182–83.

154. Bertrand Russell, "Obituary: Ludwig Wittgenstein," *Mind* 60, no. 239 (1951): 297–98.

155. Ludwig Wittgenstein, *Tractatus Logico-Philosophicus* (New York: Routledge, 2001), 89.

156. The relevant thinkers of Jewish descent included, in the Frankfurt School: Theodor Adorno, Walter Benjamin, Erich Fromm, Max Horkheimer, Leo Löwenthal, Herbert Marcuse, and Friedrich Pollock; and in the Vienna Circle: Herbert Feigl, Philipp Frank, Hans Hahn, Olga Hahn, Felix Kaufmann, Richard von Mises, Otto Neurath, Friedrich Waismann, and Edgar Zilsel. Many of these thinkers were the children of Jewish converts or had only one Jewish parent.

157. Ralf Dahrendorf, "Remarks on the Discussion," in *The Positivist Dispute in German Sociology*, by Theodor Adorno et al. (London: Heinemann, 1976), 125.

158. Cited in David Frisby, introduction to the English translation of Adorno et al., *The Positivist Dispute in German Sociology*, ix.

159. For the Vienna Circle's writings on ethics, see *Ethics and the Will: Essays*, ed. Brian McGuinness and Joachim Schulte (Boston: Kluwer, 1994).

160. "Remarks on Frazer's *Golden Bough*," trans. John Beversluis, in Ludwig Wittgenstein, *Philosophical Occasions, 1912-1951*, ed. James Klagge and Alfred Nordmann (Indianapolis: Hacket, 1993), 116. Next to these words, Wittgenstein wrote *S* for *schlecht* (bad).

CHAPTER TEN

1. Francis King, ed., *The Secret Rituals of the O.T.O.* (London: Daniel, 1973), 7.

2. Ellic Howe, "Theodor Reuss: Irregular Freemasonry in Germany, 1900-23," *Ars Quatuor Coronati* 91 (1978): 28-46. For more on Reuß's sex magic, see Hugh Urban, *Magia Sexualis: Sex, Magic, and Liberation in Modern Western Esotericism* (Berkeley: University of California Press, 2008), 96-108; for his influence on the Eranos Circle of Ascona, see Hans Thomas Hakl, *Eranos: An Alternative Intellectual History of the Twentieth Century* (Ithaca, NY: McGill-Queen's University Press, 2013), 37.

3. See Peter König, *Der Grosse Theodor-Reuss-Reader* (Munich: Arbeitsgemeinschaft für Religions- und Weltanschauungsfragen, 1997), 245.

4. Max Weber, "Science as Vocation" (*Wissenschaft als Beruf*), originally a speech delivered at Munich University, translated in H. H. Gerth and C. Wright Mills, *From Max Weber: Essays in Sociology* (New York: Oxford University Press, 1946), 194, 155 (emphasis added).

5. Talcott Parsons, "Max Weber, 1864-1964," *American Sociological Review* (1965): 171-75; and Stephen Kalberg, *Max Weber's Comparative-Historical Sociology* (Cambridge: Polity, 1994).

6. Wolfgang Mommsen, *Max Weber und die deutsche Politik* (Tübingen: Mohr, 1959); and Raymond Aron, "Max Weber and Power Politics," in *Max Weber and Sociology Today*, ed. Otto Stammer, trans. Kathleen Morris (New York: Harper, 1971), 83-100.

7. Anthony Giddens, *Capitalism and Modern Social Theory: An Analysis of the Writings of Marx, Durkheim and Max Weber* (Cambridge: Cambridge University Press, 1971); John Love, *Antiquity and Capitalism: Max Weber and the Sociological Foundations of Roman Civilization* (New York: Routledge, 1991); and Karl Löwith, *Max Weber and Karl Marx* (New York: Routledge, 1993).

8. Kieran Allen, *Max Weber: A Critical Introduction* (Ann Arbor, MI: Pluto Press, 2004); and Andrew Zimmerman, "Decolonizing Weber," *Postcolonial Studies* 9, no. 1 (2006): 53-79.

9. Lawrence Scaff, *Fleeing the Iron Cage: Culture, Politics, and Modernity in the Thought of Max Weber* (Berkeley: University of California Press, 1989); Árpád Szakolczai, *Max Weber and Michel Foucault: Parallel Life-Works* (New York: Routledge, 1998); Nicholas Gane, *Max Weber and Postmodern Theory: Rationalization versus Re-enchantment* (New York: Palgrave, 2002); and Andrew Koch, *Romance and Reason: Ontological and Social Sources of Alienation in the Writings of Max Weber* (Lanham, MD: Lexington Books, 2006).

10. Paul Honigsheim, "Max Weber: His Religious and Ethical Background and Development," in *The Unknown Max Weber*, ed. Alan Sica (New Brunswick, NJ: Transaction, 2003);

and Anthony Carroll, *Protestant Modernity: Weber, Secularisation, and Protestantism* (Scranton, PA: University of Scranton Press, 2007).

11. Wolfgang Schluchter, "Die Paradoxie der Rationalisierung" *Zeitschrift für Soziologie* 5, no. 3 (1976): 256–84; Schluchter, *The Rise of Western Rationalism: Max Weber's Developmental History* (Berkeley: University of California Press, 1981); Ann Swidler, "The Concept of Rationality in the Work of Max Weber," *Sociological Inquiry* 43, no. 1 (1973): 35–42. Hennis argues that the central theme in Weber is not rationalization as such, but the rationalization of "*Lebensführung.*" Wilhelm Hennis, *Max Weber: Essays in Reconstruction* (London: Allen & Unwin, 1988).

12. Richard Jenkins, "Disenchantment, Enchantment and Re-enchantment: Max Weber at the Millennium," *Max Weber Studies* 1 (2000): 11.

13. For example, Weber quotes Schiller's *Der Geisterseher* in his own *Max Weber Gesamtausgabe*, I/10, 279 (see note 14).

14. *Max Weber Gesamtausgabe* (Tübingen: Mohr Siebeck, 1984–2012; hereafter cited as *MWG*.), abteilung I: band 19, 103–4. The *MWG* is divided into sections (indicated by roman numeral) and bands (sometime subdivided into volumes). In what follows, the first number refers to the section, then band (then volume if appropriate), then page (e.g., *MWG*, I/22-2, 75).

15. Jakob Friedrich Fries, *Die Geschichte der Philosophie dargestellt nach den Fortschritten ihrer wissenschaftlichen Entwickelung* (Halle: Waisenhauses, 1837), 1:307.

16. A second suggestive "*Entzauberung der Welt*" occurs in Edmund Pfleiderer, *Gottfried Wilhelm Leibniz als Patriot, Staatsmann und Sildungsträger* (Leipzig: Fues, 1870), 479. But there is no direct connection to Weber.

17. Friedrich Tenbruck, "The Problem of Thematic Unity in the Works of Max Weber," *British Journal of Sociology* 31, no. 3 (1980): 321. A close read of even Weber's most quoted sentence on disenchantment (cited above) suggests that intellectualization and rationalization are related to be not identical to disenchantment.

18. Weber, *Protestant Ethic*, 140n9.

19. For example: Roger Brubaker described sixteen meanings of the rational. Hennis suggested that for Weber, rationalization could mean anything. Schluchter partitioned Weber's rationalism (*Rationalismus*) into three forms: (1) scientific-technical, (2) metaphysical-ethical, and (3) practical. Walter Wallace argued that behind the apparent disorder there was a single meaning of rationality—namely, "*consciously rule-bound comparison and choice among alternative means to a given end.*" See Rogers Brubaker, *The Limits of Rationality* (London: Allen & Unwin, 1984), 2; Wilhelm Hennis, "Max Weber's Central Question," *Economy and Society* 12, no. 2 (1983): 157; Wolfgang Schluchter, "Die Paradoxie der Rationalisierung: Zum Verhältnis von Ethik und Welt bei Max Weber," *Zeitschrift für Soziologie* 3, no. 5 (1976): 256–84; and Walter Wallace, "Rationality, Human Nature, and Society in Weber's Theory," *Theory and Society* 19, no. 2 (1990): 206 (italics in the original).

20. Stephen Kalberg, "Max Weber's Types of Rationality: Cornerstones for the Analysis of Rationalization Processes in History," *American Journal of Sociology* 85, no. 5 (1980): 1145–79. I disagree with Kalberg's conflation of substantive and value rationality and other points that will be noted. A similar scheme was also put forth by Levine, who adds a distinction between subjective and objective rationality I find somewhat persuasive, but not as relevant to the issues

of this chapter. Donald Levine, "Rationality and Freedom: Weber and Beyond." *Sociological Inquiry* 51, no. 1 (1981): 5–25.

21. Kalberg, "Max Weber's Types."

22. *MWG*, I/23: 176, translated in Max Weber, *Economy and Society* (Berkeley: University of California Press, 1978), 26.

23. Ibid. Kalberg collapses value and substantive rationality. But I think Weber's substantive (*materiale*) rationalization is closer to his formalized rationality, not his value rationality.

24. Max Weber, *Gesammelte Aufsätze zur Religionssoziologie* (Tübingen: Mohr, 1922), 1:266.

25. *MWG*, I/22–2, 272.

26. Ibid.

27. Weber, *Economy and Society*, 37, 107–8, 226, 818.

28. Kalberg lumps substantive and value rationality together; I see it as an institutionalized evolution of value rationality.

29. *MWG*, I/23, 251.

30. Weber called this "traditional" irrationality, but as his definition makes clear, he was referring to a kind of habitus. Weber, *Economy and Society*, 25; *MWG*, I/23, 175.

31. Weber, *Economy and Society*, 25. *MWG*, I/23, 175.

32. *MWG*, I/19, 484–514.

33. Weber, *Protestant Ethic*, xxxviii–xxxix.

34. This is especially clear in Weber's writings about music, which discuss the advent of musical scales and the standardization of musical notation as examples of rationalization. Max Weber, *The Rational and Social Foundations of Music* (Carbondale: Southern Illinois University Press, 1969).

35. Weber, *Protestant Ethic*, xxxviii.

36. Peter Ghosh, *Max Weber and the Protestant Ethic: Twin Histories* (Oxford: Oxford University Press, 2014), 259, 264.

37. Kalberg, "Max Weber's Types," 1152. The closest Weber came to this sentiment is in the lectures that make up "General Economic History," where he described prophecy as releasing the world from magic.

38. Stefan Breuer, "Magie, Zauber, Entzauberung," in *Max Webers "Religionssystematik"* (Tübingen: Mohr Siebeck, 2001), 119–30.

39. Weber remarked that the section of the text including the reference to disenchantment was originally written earlier. Schluchter argued that this means that disenchantment was something that Weber had in place for some time. Wolfgang Schluchter, *Rationalism, Religion, and Domination: A Weberian Perspective* (Berkeley: University of California Press, 1989), 417, 523n34. But it seems more plausible to me that Weber inserted the reference to disenchantment in the essay in 1913, just as Weber inserted the references to disenchantment into the later edition of *The Protestant Ethic*. See also Schluchter, *Die Entzauberung der Welt: Sechs Studien zu Max Weber* (Tübingen: Mohr Siebeck, 2009), esp. 1–17.

40. Martin Green, *Mountain of Truth: The Counterculture Begins, Ascona, 1900–1920* (Hanover, NH: University Press of New England, 1986), 176.

41. Most important, Else and Frieda von Richthofen. *MWG*, II/8, 147–203, 571–72, 575–611.

42. Ibid., 8, 181.

43. For disenchantment, see Franziska zu Reventlow, *Herrn Dames Aufzeichnungen* (Munich: Langen, 1913), 61–75.

44. *MWG*, II/8, 181.

45. Martin Green, *The Von Richthofen Sisters* (New York: Basic Books, 1974), 235.

46. Common acquaintances of Max Weber and Ludwig Klages included Else Jaffe, Reventlow, and the ex-fellow Kosmikers Stefan George and Karl Wolfskehl. See *MWG*, II/8, 660.

47. Green, *Von Richthofen Sisters*, 352.

48. E.g., Weber, *Protestant Ethic*, 130n10.

49. Weber, *Religionssoziologie*, 1:530.

50. *MWG*, II/8, 605. *Glücksbegier* is hard to render in English (literally "desire for happiness" or fortune; but it also evokes *Glücksbringer*, meaning "lucky charm" or "talisman").

51. Weber, "Science as Vocation." 155

52. Johannes Winckelmann, "Die Herkunft von Max Webers Entzauberungs-Konzeption." *Kölner Zeitschrift für Soziologie und Sozialpsychologie* 32, no. 1 (1980): 12–53.

53. Max Weber, *Gesammelte Aufsätze zur Wissenschaftslehre* (Tübingen: Mohr, 1922), 409 (emphasis added).

54. *MWG*, I/19, 175.

55. Ibid., 483–484.

56. I agree with Stefan Breuer that *Magie* and *Zauberei* are functionally synonymous in Weber's writings. Breuer, "Magie, Zauber, Entzauberung."

57. For a fascinating theorization of magic and technology, see Richard Stivers, *Technology as Magic: The Triumph of the Irrational* (New York: Continuum, 1999). To be fair, Weber did occasionally portray magic and technology as opposed. In a late lecture, Weber remarked: "Prophecies have released the world from magic and in so doing created the basis for [Occidental] modern science and technology, and capitalism." Max Weber, *General Economic History* (New York: Collier Books, 1961), 205

58. See *MWG*, I/19, 403–7. It should be noted that Weber especially associated the coincidence of magic and science/technology with China, and sometimes suggested that it held Asia back from the same kind of rationalization that unfolded in the West.

59. *MWG*, I/22-2, 121–22.

60. Ibid., 122.

61. Ibid.

62. Ibid., 122–23.

63. This is also likely a reference to Robert Ranulph Marett's conception of pre-animism.

64. For Weber's reading of Frazer, see *MWG*, I/22-2, 46–50, and esp. 132.

65. Ibid., 123–24.

66. Ibid., 125–26.

67. Ibid., 128–29.

68. Ibid., 157–58.

69. Ibid., I/19, 407.

70. I have restored "the disenchantment of the world" but otherwise reproduced Parsons's translation. Max Weber, *The Protestant Ethic and the Spirit of Capitalism*, trans. Talcott Parsons (New York: Routledge, 1992), 61.

71. For example, *MWG*, I/19, 349, 450.

72. Weber, *Protestant Ethic*, 57.

73. For example, Weber argued that Jesus was "above all a magician." *MWG*, I/22-2, 441.

74. For an appraisal of the Weberian orthodox of disenchantment and its obvious flaws, see Jenkins, "Disenchantment, Enchantment and Re-enchantment."

75. Weber, *Protestant Ethic*, 61.

76. Weber, "Science as Vocation," 139.

77. Weber, *Wissenschaftslehre*, 449.

78. Weber, "Science as Vocation," 139; Weber, *Wissenschaftslehre*, 448-449.

79. Weber, "Science as Vocation," 139.

80. Ibid. In the *Kategorien* essay, Weber described this idea as what gives the civilized world its "rational tone" (*rationale Note*). Weber, *Wissenschaftslehre*, 449.

81. *MWG*, I/17, 87. I have slightly amended the translation from Weber, "Science as Vocation," 139.

82. Literally "functionally irrational" in Weber, but I read it with the same meaning as the "Science as Vocation" lecture; namely, focused on unpredictability. Weber, *Wissenschaftslehre*, 449.

83. *MWG*, I/22-2, 273 (emphasis added).

84. Ibid., I/19, 512 (emphasis added).

85. Ibid., I/22-2, 334-36.

86. Ibid.

87. Weber, *Protestant Ethic*, 124.

88. Stephen Kalberg translator's note in Max Weber, *The Protestant Ethic and the Spirit of Capitalism* (Chicago: Fitzroy Dearborn, 2001), 246n132.

89. It is not uncommon to find scholars attributing the quotation to either Nietzsche or Goethe. For example, see Marcel Hoogenboom and Ringo Ossewaarde, "From Iron Cage to Pigeon House: The Birth of Reflexive Authority," *Organization Studies* 26, no. 4 (2005): 601; Anthony Giddens, *In Defence of Sociology: Essays, Interpretations, and Rejoinders* (Cambridge: Polity Press, 1996), 22.

90. Gustav von Schmoller, *Grundriss der allgemeinen volkswirtschaftslehre* (Leipzig, Duncker & Humblot, 1900), 1:225.

91. It is possible Schmoller's technocrat reflects some more distant source, but this seems to be the proximate origin of Weber's argument.

92. *MWG*, I/22-5, 71.

93. Weber, *Protestant Ethic*, 72.

94. Ibid., 123.

95. For a different way to parse Weber's notion of disenchantment, see Egil Asprem, *The Problem of Disenchantment: Scientific Naturalism and Esoteric Discourse, 1900-1939* (Boston: Brill, 2014), 32.

96. Disenchantment and the iron cage do share an opposition to charisma. Weber often suggests that magicians are charismatic figures and that charisma has a tendency to overturn bureaucracy, at least until it is routinized.

97. Weber, *Religionssoziologie*, 1:311.

98. See, for example, Koch, *Romance and Reason*.

99. Marianne Weber, *Max Weber: A Biography* (New York: Wiley, 1975), 324.

390 Notes to Pages 287-291

100. The main exception is Mommsen, *Max Weber und die deutsche Politik*.

101. Joachim Radkau, *Max Weber: Die Leidenschaft des Denkens* (München: Hanser, 2005), translated (and somewhat abridged) as Joachim Radkau, *Max Weber: A Biography* (Malden, MA: Polity, 2011).

102. *MWG*, II/6, 65; Radkau, *Max Weber: Die Leidenschaft*, 807.

103. *MWG*, II/6, 70 (emphasis added).

104. See ibid., I/22-2, 323-24.

105. Radkau, *Max Weber: Die Leidenschaft*, 808.

106. Marianne Weber, *Max Weber*, 599; Radkau, *Max Weber: Die Leidenschaft*, 806.

107. For the death of Max Weber's father as a psychological trigger, see Arthur Mitzman, *The Iron Cage: An Historical Interpretation of Max Weber* (New York: Knopf, 1970), 148-163. For Jasper's interpretation, see Radkau, *Max Weber: Die Leidenschaft*, 312.

108. Eduard Baumgarten, *Max Weber: Werk und Person* (Tübingen: Mohr, 1964), 658-59.

109. Ibid., 677;. Radkau, *Max Weber: Die Leidenschaft*, 812.

110. Paul Honigsheim, "Erinnerungen an Max Weber," in *Max Weber zum Gedächtnis: Materialien und Dokumente zur Bewertung von Werk und Persönlichkeit*, ed. René König and Johannes Winckelmann (Cologne: Westdeutscher Verlag, 1963), 270.

111. Radkau, *Max Weber: Die Leidenschaft*, 813; Honigsheim, "Erinnerungen an Max Weber," 268.

112. Robert Edward Norton, *Secret Germany: Stefan George and His Circle* (Ithaca, NY: Cornell University Press, 2002).

113. Although George was openly homosexual and had a number of Jewish disciplines, his fans also included the Nazi propaganda minister Joseph Goebbels (who named a literary prize after him) and Claus von Stauffenberg, the German Wehrmacht officer who tried to assassinate Hitler and who, rumor has it, referred to George's "occult Germany" when he was shot before the firing squad. Thomas Karlauf, "Stauffenberg: The Search for a Motive," in *A Poet's Reich: Politics and Culture in the George Circle*, ed. Melissa S. Lane and Martin A. Ruehl (Rochester, NY: Camden House, 2010), 327.

114. Wolf Lepenies, *Between Literature and Science: The Rise of Sociology* (New York: Cambridge University Press, 1988), 280-81. See also Michael Landmann, "Georg Simmel und Stefan George," in *Georg Simmel und Die Moderne*, ed. Heinz-Jürgen Dahme and Otthein Rammstedt (Frankfurt: Suhrkamp, 1984), 147-73.

115. David Frisby, *Georg Simmel* (New York: Routledge, 2002), 23.

116. Parsons studied under Edgar Salin. Lepenies, *Between Literature and Science*, 286.

117. Ibid., 258, 265.

118. Stefan George, *Das Neue Reich* (Berlin: Georg Bondi, 1928).

119. Norton, *Secret Germany*; and Bernd Johannsen, *Reich des Geistes, Stefan George und das Geheime Deutschland* (Munich: Verlag Dr. Hut, 2008), 1.

120. *The Works of Stefan George* (Chapel Hill: University of North Carolina Press, 1974), 427.

121. Friedrich Gundolf, *George* (Berlin: Georg Bondi, 1920), 1.

122. Marianne Weber, *Max Weber*, 455.

123. Joshua Derman, *Max Weber in Politics and Social Thought: From Charisma to Canonization* (New York: Cambridge University Press, 2012), 53.

124. Lepenies, *Between Literature and Science*, 292.

125. Marianne Weber, *Max Weber*, 461 (Marianne's paraphrase).

126. Ibid., 457–59; Marianne Weber, *Max Weber: Ein Lebensbild* (Tübingen: Mohr, 1984), 465–67.

127. Marianne Weber, *Max Weber*, 460–462.

128. Norton, *Secret Germany*, 478.

129. Marianne Weber, *Max Weber*, 595.

130. Wolters, *Stefan George*, 471.

131. Ibid., 474.

132. Ibid., 477.

133. Thomas Karlauf, *Stefan George: Die Entdeckung des Charisma* (Munich: Blessing, 2007), 412. See also Thomas Kroll, "Max Webers Idealtypus der charismatischen Herrschaft und die zeitgenössische Charisma-Debatte," in *Max Webers Herrschaftssoziologie: Studien zu Entstehung und Wirkung*, ed. Edith Hanke and Wolfgang Mommsen (Tübingen: Mohr Siebeck, 2001), 47–72.

134. *MWG*, I/23, 497. He also likely had in mind notions of apostolic charismata.

135. For the Swiss Eranos Circle, see Hakl, *Eranos*; Steven Wasserstrom, *Religion after Religion: Gershom Scholem, Mircea Eliade, and Henry Corbin at Eranos* (Princeton, NJ: Princeton University Press, 1999); and *Pioniere, Poeten, Professoren: Eranos und Monte Verità in der Zivilisationsgeschichte des 20. Jahrhunderts*, ed. Elisabetta Barone, Matthias Ridel, and Alexandra Tischel (Würzburg: Königshausen, 2004). It is likely that Rudolf Otto was inspired by the then-defunct Heidelberg group when he suggested the name Eranos to Olga Fröbe-Kapteyn.

136. Radkau, *Max Weber: Die Leidenschaft*, 455–58.

137. Gertrud von le Fort, *Hälfte des Lebens: Erinnerungen* (Munich: Ehrenwirth, 1965), 89.

138. Weber had been thinking about Protestantism and capitalism since 1898. We can also see the influence of William James, whom Weber read.

139. Weber, *Protestant Ethic*, 49.

140. Ibid., 67.

141. Ibid., 193n66.

142. Ibid., 189n49.

143. Ibid., 39.

144. Ibid., 165n8.

145. Ibid., 45. I omitted the phrase *"wie bei Besprechung der mittelalterlichen religiösen Ethik,"* which appears only in the second edition.

146. Ibid., 40. Weber expressed less confidence about this claim in an early note; see 159n3.

147. Johannes Tauler, *The Inner Way: Being Thirty-Six Sermons for Festivals* (Memphis: General Books, 2010).

148. Hans Kippenberg, *Die Entdeckung der Religionsgeschichte* (München: Verlag C. H. Beck, 1997), 237.

149. Weber, *Protestant Ethic*, 67–68.

150. Volkhard Krech, "Mystik," in *Max Webers "Religionssystematik"*, ed. Hans Kippenberg and Martin Riesebrodt (Tübingen: Mohr Siebeck, 2001), 241–62. Krech has observed that there was a lively debate among Weber's contemporaries in about 1900 concerning the meaning

of mysticism and its universality as a category, with Weber's colleagues Simmel and Troelsch weighing on the issue.

151. Ibid., 252.

152. Ibid., 258.

153. Ibid., 261.

154. Ibid., 254–56.

155. Ibid., 255.

156. Krech largely argues—not without good reason—that the mystic, for Weber, is a typological and basically negative category.

157. *MWG*, I/19, 103

158. Weber, "Science as Vocation," 155.

159. *MWG*, II/22–2, 333.

160. Weber, "Science as Vocation," 148; see also 149: "Many old gods ascend from their graves; they are disenchanted and hence take the form of impersonal forces."

161. Indeed, in a particularly tantalizing passage in the *Zwischenbetrachtung*, Weber does speak for the power of the aesthetic in terms that would have appealed to Schiller, and he suggests that art is capable of carrying "magical effects" (*magischer Wirkungen*) and thus might be able to function as a source of this-wordly meaning and perhaps even salvation. *MWG* I/19, 499–501.

162. Weber cautioned against attempts to intellectually form new religions without "new and genuine prophecy" ("Science as Vocation," 155). But this implies that a genuine prophecy might exist.

163. These newspaper reports come from the *Berliner Volkszeitung, Berliner Tageblatt,* and *Neue Hamburger Zeitung.* And there are many more examples just from that three-year period.

164. See Robert Bartlett, *The Natural and the Supernatural in the Middle Age* (New York: Cambridge University Press, 2008); Gregory Dawes, "The Rationality of Renaissance Magic," *Parergon* 30, no. 2 (2013): 33–58; and Carlo Ginzburg, *The Cheese and the Worms: The Cosmos of a Sixteenth-Century Miller* (Baltimore: Johns Hopkins University Press, 1980).

CONCLUSION

1. Felicitas Goodman's representative works include: *Speaking in Tongues: A Cross-cultural Study of Glossolalia* (1972), *The Exorcism of Anneliese Michel* (1980), *Ekstase, Besessenheit, Dämonen: Die geheimnisvolle Seite der Religion* (1991); and *Maya Apocalypse: Seventeen Years with the Women of a Yucatan Village* (2001).

2. Published first as Felicitas Goodman, *Wo die Geister auf den Winden reiten* (Freiburg im Breisgau: Bauer, 1989).

3. Felicitas Goodman's reply in Michael Winkelman, "Magic: A Theoretical Reassessment and Comments and Replies," *Current Anthropology* 23, no. 1 (1982): 47 (emphasis added).

4. Felicitas Goodman, *Where the Spirits Ride the Wind: Trance Journeys and Other Ecstatic Experiences* (Bloomington: Indiana University Press, 1990), 219–20.

5. Ibid., 223.

6. Ibid.

7. My grandmother had no interest in Western esotericism, but read many of the theorists discussed in this volume, including James Frazer, E. B. Tylor, Sigmund Freud, and Max Weber.

8. Cynthia Eller, *Living in the Lap of the Goddess: The Feminist Spirituality Movement in America* (New York: Crossroad, 1993); Wendy Griffin, "The Embodied Goddess: Feminist Witchcraft and Female Divinity," *Sociology of Religion* 56, no. 1 (1995): 35–48; Chris Klassen, ed., *Feminist Spirituality: The Next Generation* (Lanham, MD: Lexington Books, 2009).

9. Jon Woodson, *To Make a New Race: Gurdjieff, Toomer, and the Harlem Renaissance.* (Jackson: University Press of Mississippi, 1999; Nadia Choucha, *Surrealism and the Occult: Shamanism, Magic, Alchemy, and the Birth of the Artistic Movement* (Rochester, NY: Destiny Books, 2009).

10. For this list of panpsychists, see David Skrbina, *Panpsychism in the West*, (Cambridge, MA: MIT Press, 2005). Not to say that all these thinkers were part of the establishment when they wrote, but rather that many have been (retroactively) canonized.

11. For another take on the history of "secular magic," see Simon During, *Modern Enchantments: The Cultural Power of Secular Magic* (Cambridge, MA: Harvard University Press, 2004).

12. Rudolf Pannwitz, *Die Krisis der europäischen Kultur* (Nuremberg: Hans Carl, 1917), 64.

13. It is often claimed that John Watkins Chapman was the first to use the expression *postmodern* in 1870. For this claim, scholars usually cite Steven Best and Douglas Kellner, *Postmodern Theory: Critical Interrogations* (New York: Guilford Press, 1991), 5. But Best and Kellner's source for this is Higgins, which only identifies the painter as "Chapman" and places the date as around 1880. Dick Higgins, *A Dialectic of Centuries* (New York: Printed Editions, 1978), 7. So barring further evidence, I think this attribution is likely specious. One of the first examples I've verified is: J. M. Thompson, "Post-Modernism," *Hibbert Journal* 12, no. 4 (1914): 733–45. In the Spanish-speaking world, there are provocative appearances of *postmodernista* in the Uruguayan poetry scene by at least as early as 1931. Carlos Reyles, *Historia sintética de la literatura uruguaya* (Montevideo: A. Vila, 1931), 2:1.

14. Fredric Jameson, *A Singular Modernity: Essay on the Ontology of the Present* (London: Verso, 2002), 211.

15. Fritz Graf, *Magic in the Ancient World* (Cambridge, MA: Harvard University Press, 1997), 20. See also Richard Kieckhefer, *Magic in the Middle Ages* (New York: Cambridge University Press, 1989), 10–12, although variations of the term *magic* really came into vogue in Roman usage.

16. For examples, see Owen Davies, *Grimoires: A History of Magic Books* (Oxford: Oxford University Press, 2009), esp. 6–43.

17. See chapters 3 and 5.

18. To be clear, I'm not debating to what extent the occult was or was not an influence on Nazism, but rather the emergence of "occult Nazis" as a trope that was later used to discredit occultism.

19. See Monica Black and Eric Kurlander, eds., *Revisiting the "Nazi Occult"* (Rochester, NY: Camden House, 2015).

20. In anthropology, for instance, debates about psychical research returned to the fore. Margaret Mead was a believer in psi powers and a member of the American Society for Psychical Research. In print she asserted that scientists and occultists should work together to

provide "new insight into the powers attributed to seers and clairvoyants, to those who have the power to 'see' auras, to communicate with plants, to dream or visualize events outside the bounds of time." Reprinted in Margaret Mead and Rhoda Mètraux, *Aspects of the Present* (New York: Morrow, 1980), 52–53.

21. Michael Löwy and Robert Sayre, *Romanticism against the Tide of Modernity* (Durham, NC: Duke University Press, 2001).

22. Robert Yelle, *The Language of Disenchantment: Protestant Literalism and Colonial Discourse in British India* (New York: Oxford University Press, 2013); David Chidester, *Savage Systems: Colonialism and Comparative Religion in Southern Africa* (Charlottesville: University Press of Virginia, 1996).

23. Gananath Obeyesekere, *The Apotheosis of Captain Cook: European Mythmaking in the Pacific* (Princeton, NJ: Princeton University Press, 1992); Vincent Wimbush, *White Men's Magic: Scripturalization as Slavery* (New York: Oxford University Press, 2012).

24. Hugh Urban, *Tantra: Sex, Secrecy Politics, and Power in the Study of Religions* (Berkeley: University of California Press, 2003), 134–64.

25. Indeed, the attack on disenchantment might seem misdirected insofar as magic is not gone, just repressed.

26. For example: Ronald and Nancy Reagan's well-known connection to astrologers (esp. Joan Quigley), Woodrow Wilson's consultation of the "prophet" Edgar Cayce, and Abraham and Mary Lincoln's spiritualist séances; Richard Nixon is also reported to have consulted the psychic Jeane Dixon. This list is far from exhaustive.

27. Martin Jay, *The Dialectical Imagination: A History of the Frankfurt School and the Institute of Social Research, 1923–1950* (London: Heinemann, 1973).

28. Theodor Adorno, *The Positivist Dispute in German Sociology* (London: Heinemann, 1976), 121.

INDEX

267, 280, 290, 305, 384n156; Jewishness, 197, 202, 205; and paranormal belief, 327n40. *See also* anti-Semitism; Judaism

Joel, Karl, 191

Jones, Ernest, 197–203, 205

Jones, George Cecil, 153

Josephson, Brian, 305

Judaism: Benjamin and, 226–30; Cosmic Circle and, 210; de-divination and, 85–86; folklore studies and, 129; Freud and, 193; Hegel and, 85–86; mysticism and, 228; Spinoza and, 70; Weber and, 280. *See also* anti-Semitism; Kabbalah

Jung, Carl, 104, 179, 191–93, 196–99, 293

Kabbalah, 42, 43, 81–82, 104, 163, 227, 228, 230

Kafka, Franz, 270

Kalberg, Stephan, 272, 275

Kandinsky, Wassily, 230, 305

Kant, Immanuel, 20, 73, 74, 171, 184, 207–8, 247; Adorno and, 208; du Prel and, 189–91; enlightenment and, 53, 72; Freud and, 189, 208; ghosts/spirits and, 185; magic and, 185; on the phenomenal/noumenal, 186, 190, 206; Schopenhauer and, 188–89; skepticism and, 299; Swedenborg and, 185, 191; unconscious mind and, 186

Kantorowicz, Ernst, 290

Keightley, Thomas, 130

Kepler, Johannes, 42

Keynes, John Maynard, 43

Kipling, Rudyard, 138

Kippenberg, Hans, 295

Klages, Ludwig, 20, 209–25, 260; Adorno and, 215, 220, 228, 233, 238, 239; animism and, 219; anti-Semitism and, 225; Bataille and, 237, 238; Benjamin and, 20, 209, 215, 227–28, 230–34, 236, 238, 239; Cosmic Circle and, 210–11, 212–13, 276, 290; cosmic eros/rush and, 221–24; disenchantment and, 216, 220; esotericism and, 212; *Geist* and, 217–20; Horkheimer and, 215,

220; magical philosophy and, 209, 213–15; Schiller and, 77, 216; Schuler and, 212; science and, 216; Weber and, 216, 276, 285, 297, 299

Koestler, Arthur, 305

Kohn, Eduardo, 5

Körner, Christian Gottfried, 82

Kosmikers. *See* Cosmic Circle

Koyré, Alexandre, 42, 59, 92

Krech, Volkhard, 296

Kreisel, Georg, 264

Kripal, Jeffrey, 23–24, 37, 122, 322n74, 324nn8–9, 328n55, 329n68, 346n6, 353n161

Kristeva, Julia, 237

Lacan, Jacques, 206, 215, 238

Landauer, Gustav, 230

Lang, Andrew, 98, 101, 128–29, 135, 141, 151

language: philosophy of, 105, 112–13. *See also* linguistics

Laplace, Pierre-Simon, 313

Lash, Scott, 11

Latin America, 23. *See also names of specific countries*

Latour, Bruno, 3, 6, 41, 308, 310

LaVey, Anton, 159

Le Fort, Gertrud von, 293

Leibniz, Gottfried Wilhelm, 43, 81, 112, 305

Leiss, William, 45

LeMahieu, Michael, 243

Lepenies, Wolf, 290

Lessing, Gotthold, 69–70, 72, 73

Lessing, Theodor, 225

Lévi, Éliphas, 19, 101–11, 113–16, 120, 122–23, 152; Crowley and, 161–62, 168–69, 172; Scholem and, 229

Lévi-Strauss, Claude, 176

Lévy-Bruhl, Lucien, 255

libertinism, 58, 158

Liebstökl, Hans, 236

linguistics, 116, 118–19. *See also* language: philosophy of

Popper, Karl, 155, 267

positivism, 20–21, 65, 86, 254–55, 258, 263–64, 266, 267–68, 311, 314; critique of, 240–45; dispute, 267; logical, 20, 207, 240–43, 246–49, 251, 253, 254, 268; politics and, 250. *See also* Vienna Circle; *and under* Adorno, Theodor; Frazer, James George; Freud, Sigmund; Horkheimer, Max

postcolonialism, 16–17, 79, 307, 315

postmodernism, 35, 36, 44, 59, 66, 91, 209, 226, 306–7, 312, 316

poststructuralism, 5, 176, 209, 213, 215, 221–22, 225, 238, 242, 312

precognition, 24, 263, 265. *See also* psychic ability

Price, Harry, 261

primitive (concept of), 17, 79–80, 83, 84, 94, 98–101, 104, 128, 129, 181, 203–5, 207, 214, 216, 255, 312; in folklore studies, 132–33, 141–43, 147. *See also* savage (concept of)

Procter, Bryan, 85

projection: astral, 20; psychological, 158, 193, 203–5, 207

prophecy, 22, 33, 42, 43, 109, 155, 184, 256, 291, 297–98, 301

Protestantism, 4, 14, 29, 47–48, 58, 61, 67–68, 129, 139, 257–58; anti-paganism and, 276; religious studies and, 95, 107; Weber on, 270–71, 280, 291, 296. *See also* cessation of miracles; Protestant Reformation

Protestant Reformation, 13, 48, 65, 92, 137, 293–94, 303. *See also* Protestantism; secularization

Przibram, Karl, 261

pseudoscience, 15, 145, 201, 312, 322n69. *See also* demarcation problem

psychic ability, 24, 29. *See also* precognition; telekinesis; telepathy

psychical research, 2, 16, 19, 151, 159, 183, 190, 200–201, 309; in Austria, 260–63; by Carnap, 265–66; by James, 264; by logical positivists, 268, 311

psychics, 1, 24, 26–27, 29, 56, 119, 189, 198

psychoanalysis, 20, 96, 179, 180, 181–82, 184, 191, 193, 194, 196, 199, 200–202, 206

Ptolemy, 54

Pulver, Max, 227

Puritanism, 49, 270–71, 280, 283, 285, 286, 300. *See also* Protestantism

Putnam, Hilary, 242

queer theory, 12

Quine, W. V. O., 242

Rabelais, François, 158

racialism, 117, 129, 184

racism. *See* anti-Semitism

Radkau, Joachim, 287, 288

Rang, Florens Christian, 230

Rank, Otto, 179, 199

rationalism, 6, 8, 11, 61, 73, 81, 94–95, 123, 189, 216, 291, 306. *See also* irrationality; rationality

rationality, 5, 8, 9, 65, 66, 91, 92, 95, 99, 154, 215, 221, 298, 386nn19–20; formalized or institutionalized, 273–74, 284, 301; instrumental, 4, 18, 47, 214, 239, 244–45, 272–73, 275, 277–78, 280, 282, 304, 306, 314; technological, 9; theoretical or intellectual, 272–73, 281–84, 286, 299, 301. *See also* irrationality; rationalism

realism: aesthetic, 313–14; agential, 5

reason, instrumental. *See* rationality: instrumental

re-enchantment, 87, 93, 106, 150, 172, 175, 176, 183, 236, 239, 270, 286, 291, 298, 301, 316. *See also* disenchantment; enchantment

Regardie, Israel, 159, 175, 176

regulative ideal, 3, 16, 308–10

reification, 219–20, 222, 238

reincarnation, 25–26

religion: as category, 12–14, 60, 99, 121, 124; comparative, 94–95, 104, 105, 107, 109, 119, 154; Crowley and, 160–63, 166, 169,